OUR CHANGING WORLD

SELECTED AND EDITED BY

SYLVIA F. ANDERSON   MARTHA J. NIX

University of Washington

AND

ANNE E. WINDHUSEN

OUR
CHANGING
WORLD

HARPER & BROTHERS PUBLISHERS

NEW YORK AND LONDON

CONTENTS

v

CONTENTS

CONTENTS

To our colleagues who have given invaluable aid, and to the authors and the publishers who have granted permission to reprint their selections, we make grateful acknowledgment.

TO THE INSTRUCTOR

HOW OFTEN HAVE WE ALL WISHED THAT THE CONTAGION OF ENTHUSIASM FOR WRITING MIGHT IN TRUTH BECOME "A LITTLE madness in the blood" of all the apathetic or rebellious freshmen "taking Comp." And how rarely have we dealt with their boredom beyond a rebuke, spoken or implied. We have too frequently been content to place the blame upon them, forgetting that we have chosen their books, made their assignments, and directed their classroom hours without regard for their interests.

Given an essay that touches upon their experiences, illuminates their bewilderment before some puzzling phenomenon, or sets their minds speculating on something vital in their own world, they lose their apathy and rebellion and speak and write with vigorous interest. To capture this interest and make of writing a living, eager experience of communicating to others the ideas and thoughts that animate the writer is the instructor's responsibility.

In recognition of this responsibility we have compiled a collection of expository writings and outlined the study procedures. This book endeavors to meet the wide and various interests and activities of college students, to present the world as they see it, or might see it if their curiosities were awakened, and to help them find the satisfaction which self-expression means. Consequently, we have had two objectives before us: selecting pertinent and stimulating subject matter, and relating this material to the expression of ideas in writing. These objectives demand a choice of articles which are both interesting and well written, and of study suggestions which emphasize the form of composition. The selections chosen, we believe, fulfill these demands.

To present a correlated pattern we have arranged them in five sections. Each instructor is urged to assign the selections in the order which best serves his purposes, for, while we think each section in its entirety gives a more complex picture of the particular aspect of living with which it deals than any single selection can give, we intend no compulsion in this arrangement. There is, however, good reason for assigning Part Five early in the course, for it is directly concerned with the development of skill in reading and writing, and supplements the study of rhetoric and technique.

The five sections follow a natural sequence in presenting a survey of man in the physical universe and his part in the cultural history of mankind; particular aspects of his domination of nature and investigation of its secrets; a consideration of immediate issues in the modern world; the arts as an enrichment of everyday living; and the specialized province of reading and writing as it concerns the student of composition. In Part One the selections introduce the student to the general nature of the universe in which he lives and the rôle played by man. These essays should serve to awaken the student's curiosity about the physical world, and, by holding up to him the mirror of biology, psychology, and anthropology, give him a glimpse of his own powers and possibilities as a human being. They should likewise give him some background for an understanding of the natural and social sciences and help him to overcome any handicap in reading which results from an unfamiliarity with general scientific terms. Part Two narrows the range of his attention to man's efforts to subdue and use his environment, and to solve some of the riddles of earth that he may make living less hazardous and more satisfying. The essays in this section show the student ways by which man conquers the unknown in the study and in the laboratory, as well as in the field and in the mechanical world. Part Three centers around the immediate scene and the complexities of today. Here the student is asked to look critically at his own world and its divergent currents that he may reflect upon the larger implications of the headlines he reads and the conversations he hears and takes part in. Since the bulk of his reading and interests is concerned with his own present, these selections are likely to suggest subjects about which he will wish to write. Part Four places the emphasis upon the creative spirit of man and its relationship to his skills. The student should realize that a scientific age nourishes the arts as well as the sciences, and that the arts should be an integral part of his everyday life if it is to be as fruitful and enjoyable as he can make it. Part Five is a workshop for the student of composition, in which his attention is directed to the problems of reading and writing that he may learn to read comprehendingly and to write effectively. Since to write effectively he must have words, these selections are designed both to make him want to build a vocabulary and to suggest the means for doing it.

This insistence upon the student's need for words and more words, and an understanding of their meanings, has led us to include a section, "Vocabulary Building," as part of the exercises entitled "Laying the Groundwork," for we believe that the study of unfamiliar words and the use of the dictionary should be a necessary preliminary to the student's reading and study. In addition to the vocabulary drill, the exercise material provides other questions and suggestions which have a twofold purpose. Some, entitled "Preparation for Reading," are intended to rouse the student's curiosity about the subject matter of the selection he is to read, and to increase the thoughtfulness of his reading. While he can find an answer to these questions, either explicit or implied, in the text of the essay, the purpose of each is primarily to set him thinking about the subject before he begins reading. Other specific questions on information, opinions, and ideas expressed in the essay are given under the title, "Appraising the Results." These are to be considered as guides to an understanding of the content and purpose of the particular selection.

The foreword, "To the Student," presents those basic exercises and instructions which apply to all reading and to an understanding and analysis of all the selections in the book. We have given the student homely advice about how to study, and have emphasized the steps by which he can learn to read and to study more effectively. There are also concrete directions for analyzing the selections in the book as models of expository writing. These include specific questions on the analysis of the thought content of the whole selection and of its rhetorical form, of the paragraph as a unit, and of words as tools for expression. Most of these questions apply to each essay, and we have therefore not felt it necessary to repeat them in the individual exercises; but the student should refer to these questions in connection with every essay.

You can use this book, with or without a rhetoric, for either experimental or conventional teaching. It offers a variety of models for the study of types of exposition and methods of development: examples and illustrations; specific detail; comparison, contrast, and analogy; and reasons and cause and effect. The selections, for the most part, lend themselves well to the intensive study of outlining, paragraph analysis, and transitions. So essential do we consider outlining as an aid to clear thinking and consequently to good writing that we have provided an analytical sentence outline of one of the selections.

In our selecting and editing and in our study exercises we have been insistent upon the fact that clear thinking is fundamental to writing and reading—that training in coherent, logical, honest thinking precedes all training in writing as it does all talking, since it is the origin of good writing and sound speech. No instructor of composition can ignore this relationship and the charge it lays on him to train his students to think before they write.

We have tried to include many kinds of writing on many subjects, not only for the pleasure and profit of the student but also for your enjoyment and success in using the book. As Thomas Love Peacock said: "Tastes depend on the fashion. There is always a fashionable taste: a taste for driving the mail—a taste for acting *Hamlet*—a taste for philosophical lectures—a taste for the marvelous—a taste for the simple—a taste for French dances and Italian singers and German whiskers and tragedies—a taste for enjoying the country in November and wintering in London till the end of the dog days—a taste for making shoes—a taste for picturesque tours—a taste for taste itself, or for essays on taste; but no gentleman would be so rash as to have a taste of his own, or his last winter's taste, or a taste, my love, but the fashionable taste." Whatever your taste in composition, it should be possible for you to follow it in as flexible a book as this.

TO THE STUDENT

"WHY, OF COURSE!" YOU PROBABLY WILL PROTEST INDIG-nantly. "I am in college, and I wouldn't be here if I couldn't read."

And yet, as Mr. Embree points out in his article, "Can College Graduates Read?" (p. 479), the evidence is accumulating that some of you cannot read, and that many more of you do not, even if you can. If he is right (and there seems to be sufficient evidence to support him), the charge is serious, for it is difficult indeed for any student to get an education in college without the ability to read with comprehension.

Stop to consider some of the difficulties you have had in your courses: the low grades you made in tests even though you had spent long hours poring over your books; the baffled despair at your inability to wrest from the printed page the meaning you knew must be buried there; the surprising blankness of your mind when you were questioned in class about a chapter you believed you really had understood, for you had "read it three times"; the appalling difference between what you thought a writer had said and what the instructor proved he actually said. All these difficulties are evidence that you were not reading efficiently.

Consider, too, how extensively study involves reading—not recreational reading, such as a thrilling yarn of detectives and gangsters, or a romantic tale of two brave men and a glamour girl, or a blow-by-blow account of the latest prize fight as seen by an atavistic reporter from the safety of his ringside seat, but serious reading for information. Much of the reading you do in college will not be easy; it will, nevertheless, be interesting, informative, stimulating if you have acquired the ability to read intelligently. And most assuredly the opposite is also true: you will find such reading difficult, dull, and perhaps even incomprehensible if you do not master the technique of ferreting out the meaning of what you read, and of relating to your own thinking and actions the facts presented and the opinions expressed by the writer.

The simple procedure which follows should help you to discover the origin and nature of your difficulties, and, if followed strenuously, should bring you dividends, not only in your composition courses, but also in your other studies and in the genuine pleasure that the adventure of reading can give you once you have mastered technique. You will, of course, not find your troubles vanishing magically; you will need practice, but the returns will almost immediately be evident to you.

READING SUGGESTIONS

I. THE APPROACH

1. Have the best possible conditions for concentration on your reading. If you can, study in a quiet room, where your attention will not be diverted by such distractions as the conversation of family or friends, or a radio, or traffic. A closed door will usually be respected by would-be intruders, particularly if you firmly refuse to be led astray should someone fail to take the hint and walk in to chat. Learn to say "No" to such intruders.

2. See that lighting and ventilation are satisfactory. The light should be sufficiently strong for clear vision, but it should not shine into your eyes, either directly or from the side. Place your lamp in such a position that disturbing shadows are not thrown across the page. Watch ventilation, for a smoke-filled room will mean inflamed and tired eyes; and a stuffy, hot room will soon bring drowsiness and dullness.

3. Study at a table of the proper height for writing and for a book rest. Keep this table exclusively as a work table *devoted to study*. On it have necessary equipment easily available: pens, ink, pencils, paper, *and a dictionary*—not

a ninety-eight-cent drugstore edition, but a standard collegiate edition (some 1,000 pages in length). An unabridged
dictionary is, of course, even better, but it should be conveniently near you, not downstairs in the library.

4. Provide yourself with a study chair—a straight-backed
chair of the proper height is best. Do not allow yourself to
be too comfortable; if you sink back luxuriously into an
overstuffed chair or sprawl on a davenport, you will not be
able to give active attention to your work.

5. Make sure that your eyes don't need attention. A persistent feeling of strain probably means that you have some
defect of vision, the correction of which may be the key to
solving your reading troubles.

6. Exclude disturbing ideas from your mind while you
are reading. It will not help you to worry about whether
you will have time to prepare all your work, or whether
you will be able to convince the judge next day that you
were going only thirty an hour, or whether you will be able
to explain that n.s.f. check to your father, or whether the
snow will be right for skiing next week-end.

7. Allow yourself sufficient time to read your assignment
carefully. Since reading speed varies among individuals, you
will have to determine for yourself how much time you
should allow. Remember also that it will vary according to
the kind of reading: recreational or informational, simple
or difficult.

8. Settle down to work without delay. Stop finding other
things to do. If you waste time debating whether to put off
your work until later, or complaining about the length of
assignments, you will merely make matters worse. Postpone
those "important" telephone calls, or limit them to thirty
seconds. In short, stop dawdling.

II. THE ACTUAL READING

1. Before you begin to read the selection assigned, spend
a few minutes surveying the subject in order to get a feeling
of "being at home" with it. Consider the title: What does
it suggest to you? For example, the title, "Highway to the
Moon," obviously cannot be taken literally, for not even

the most ambitious engineer has contemplated a project of such magnitude. What, then, is the title supposed to suggest? Probably this highway is some intellectual thoroughfare down which the adventurous and courageous may travel.

2. Then turn to the study suggestions at the end of the selection. The first division, "Preparation for Reading," is intended to introduce you to the subject matter of the selection and thus to put you into a receptive frame of mind. Speculate about these questions. Quite probably you will not be able to answer them completely or in detail, but try to piece together those well-nigh forgotten bits of information which you can recall. You may profitably discuss these questions with a fellow student; do not, however, forget that you are about to begin to work, not to have a bull session.

3. Proceed, next, to the section, "Vocabulary Building." You doubtless do not need to be reminded that you suffer from word trouble. Probably, also, you have already discovered that there is no shortcut to accumulating an adequate supply of words of whose meanings you are sure. These suggestions outline practical work which, if followed consistently, will bring many words into your active writing and speaking vocabulary, and many more into your reading vocabulary.

This section includes a list of words which you should look up if you have any doubt about their meanings. Sometimes the list is divided into two groups: first, words you should look up before you begin to read, for as a rule they have limited definitions and therefore their meanings do not depend upon the context to any great extent; second, words which you should check as you read, for their meanings are best determined in their context. For each word find one word or phrase which can be substituted for it with no change in meaning. In addition to these lists of words, special vocabulary studies are usually included. These are concerned with derivations, synonyms, and references to allusions in the text. If there are other words you do not know, look them up also.

These words, with their meanings and pronunciations,

should be recorded in a systematic fashion so that you can review them easily. Arrange them in a column on the page so that, while you are reviewing them, you can cover the definitions with a sheet of paper. Remember that clarity, precision, and exactness of diction are more important than the mere number of words; hence, if there are a great many unfamiliar words, you may prefer to center most of your attention on some fifteen or twenty of them, although never to the complete exclusion of the others. In order to get new words firmly fixed in your mind, use them in sentences. It is also helpful to use them in conversation and in writing when possible.

4. Approach your reading with a desire to find out what the writer has to say and how he relates his ideas to your interests and opinions. Sometimes you will agree with him; sometimes you will disagree. Sometimes he will give you new information; sometimes he will merely present familiar material in a new manner or with new implications. You must read, then, with two objects in mind: to understand what is said, and to compare the facts, opinions, theories, experiences, and conclusions of the writer with your own. The best procedure is to write down these points as you read, especially those which you find yourself emphatically accepting or rejecting. This can be used as a basis for the final evaluation which you should make after you have finished reading.

5. Keep in the foreground of your thinking the necessity for discovering the one controlling idea which the writer wishes to drive home by the combined force of the plan he adopts, the facts and illustrations he selects, the line of logic he follows, and the manner of expression he uses. This one point (often called the thesis) is not always easy to isolate. You may be helped by remembering that usually it is given either at the beginning or at the end, that occasionally it is given piecemeal, that frequently it is repeated, and that once in a while it is implied, not expressed.

6. Read attentively, with the aim of comprehending every sentence and every paragraph. As soon as you notice that your mind is wandering, *stop*. Recall what you have been

reading, and when you have found the point in the text where your attention wavered, pick up the thread and continue your reading. If you have the hit-and-miss habit of skimming, you can correct it best by actually forcing yourself to read thoughtfully, with concentration, until you have established a new reading habit.

7. If the thought of a sentence or paragraph which you have read *with attention* is not clear, try to find out where the trouble lies. Is the meaning of a word not clear? Is the structure of the sentence or paragraph difficult? Have you missed some important transition? Have you overlooked some relationship of ideas? These are only some of the possible difficulties. Often you may have to tackle the passage again, in a new way if possible. For example, you may outline a complicated paragraph, analyze or rephrase a troublesome sentence, or trace the line of logic step by step.

Make notes, for class discussion, of passages which baffle you in spite of all your efforts. Try to determine whether the obscurity comes from some word or phrase which the writer, as often happens, has used carelessly. (Read "The Tyranny of Words," by Stuart Chase, p. 517.) Frequently you will find it possible to isolate the exact word, phrase, or sentence causing the obscurity.

8. As you read, make brief, meaningful marginal notes. Ordinarily one note summarizing clearly the main idea of the paragraph will be sufficient. Additional subpoints may be necessary for a long paragraph. You will also find it useful to mark cues which the author gives you by means of transitional words and phrases, summaries, forecasts, or indicated divisions of thought.

9. From time to time stop for a few minutes to think over what you have read. Mentally run over the main points that have been established and attempt to relate them to each other and to the main purpose (thesis).

10. When you have finished reading, write a clear one-sentence statement of the main idea of the entire selection.

11. Finally, make your appraisal of the content. Actually, if you have been reading intelligently, you have been constantly appraising by comparing the facts, experiences, the-

ories, and conclusions presented by the writer with your own. Now, however, you should bring all these points together and determine the extent to which you are willing to alter your views as a result of the information you have obtained from your reading. Of course, you should never be willing to accept uncritically the ideas of an author, nor should you blindly and stubbornly reject them because they run counter to what you believe. The conclusions of a writer must stand or fall because of the strength or weakness of the evidence and logic supporting them, and not because of his reputation, position, or age, or because of your preferences or prejudices. (Read "On Various Kinds of Thinking," by James Harvey Robinson, p. 489.) In short, as a critic, you should remember that your criticism must be honest, fair, intelligent, and constructive.

BASIC EXERCISES

As students of composition you are reading these examples of expository writing not only for their content, but also for their rhetorical form, and therefore you should analyze the way in which the authors express their ideas and opinions. In studying the form of each selection, you should determine the plan each author has used, and consider the effectiveness of this plan, the choice of words, and the devices employed for gaining interest. From such an analysis you should learn certain basic principles of writing so that you can employ similar methods in the exposition of your own ideas. The following exercises summarize basic principles of composition to guide you in your study.

I. THE ANALYSIS OF THE WHOLE SELECTION

1. What is the thesis? Is it stated or implied? If it is stated, where is it found? Is it repeated in the essay?
2. What are the main divisions of thought?
3. Point out the transitions that show where one main division ends and another begins. Do any refocus the reader's attention upon the thesis?
4. Is the general plan inductive or deductive; that is, does it proceed from the general to the particular, or from the particular to the general?
5. Why is the plan suited to the subject material and to the purpose of the author?

6. Account for the selection of details in relation to the author's purpose.
7. What is the purpose of the beginning: for example, to interest the reader, to bridge the gap between what he already knows and what the author has to say, or to suggest or state the thesis?
8. What is the purpose of the ending: for example, to summarize, to state or restate the thesis, to suggest the application of the thesis, or to challenge the reader to action?
9. How has the author indicated the relative value of his ideas: by proportion? by position? by calling them to the reader's attention with special phrasing?

II. THE ANALYSIS OF PARAGRAPHS

1. Show that each paragraph is a unit in itself within the selection and yet is related to a larger plan and so marks an advance in the argument of the whole.
2. Is a topic sentence expressed in each paragraph? If not, summarize the idea of the paragraph in a sentence of your own. Do the topic sentences express the subject by announcing it at the beginning or by summarizing it at the end?
3. Determine the basis of the division into paragraphs: for instance, a change in scene or time, or a change from one section of the subject to another.
4. What is the average length of paragraphs? In what way do the subject and the treatment influence the length of each paragraph? How do you account for the short paragraphs? Could any be combined?
5. What is the order of the material within the paragraphs: for example, general to specific (deductive), specific to general (inductive), time or place, familiar to the unfamiliar, or least to the most important?
6. What methods are used to develop the paragraphs: specific details, examples or illustrations, comparison or contrast or analogy, definition, division or classification, description, or narration?
7. How are the paragraphs linked to each other: by words, by phrases, by sentences, or by ideas? How are the sentences within the paragraph linked to each other?
8. If certain details in a paragraph are more important than others, how are they emphasized?

III. THE ANALYSIS OF EXPRESSION

1. What effect has the author's choice of words upon the general style of the essay; that is, is the diction familiar, colloquial, common, scientific, learned, literary, or ornate?
2. Do you like the author's choice of words? Give reasons for your answer.
3. Note the diction: is it concrete or abstract, specific or general, connotative or denotative, figurative or literal?
4. How much variety is there in sentence length? To what extent does this contribute to the effectiveness of the expression?
5. Observe any characteristic sentence form: for example, parallel, balanced, loose, or periodic.
6. How do the choice of words and the form of the sentences affect the rhythm of the expression?

PART ONE

Time, Space, and Man

The Long View

HIGHWAY TO THE MOON[1]

John Hodgdon Bradley, Jr.

MAN, STANDING AT THE VERGE OF A VAST AND UNCHARTED
FUTURE, TURNS TO THE PAST FOR HELP. PERSPECTIVE SHOULD
yield a pattern and a prophecy. And if there is any hope for
the casuals who drift along the highways of time, it should be
visible somewhere in the scene. But the past is a desert grave-
yard and man does not readily discern the hope he seeks. Dead
bones and dead ambitions stretch cold and chill and countless
over the ground. Futility, like a foul bird, hovers in the air.

The future has ever been the suckling of the past, and
creatures have ever inherited the framework of their fate
from their parents. Self-conscious man, viewing the dismal
panorama, sees in himself the same inadequacy that bore
upon those who went before, the inadequacy of race as well
as individual to grapple the grim legions of decay. The repeated cycles of growth and dissipation of vital energy, the
cruel prodigality of reproduction, the unyielding grip of custom, the downward drag of retrogressive forces are the poi-
soned gifts of the past to the present, of beast to man.

Yet nature, lover of paradox, allows the delicate flower of
rational hope to bloom, not where earth is warm and life
throbs passionately, but where failure and death have laid
low the land. For out of the discouragement of the past, intelligence has somehow emerged. Rising in ages too distant
to be seen with clearness, it has broken a trail to the present, a
trail that has grown not only longer, but also straighter and
wider. To-day it is a well marked road that has never been
known to lead a traveler into disaster. No one can say where

[1] Reprinted from *Parade of the Living* by John H. Bradley, Jr.; copyright,
1930, by Coward-McCann, Inc. By permission of the author and of the publisher.

it will ultimately go, but man, the hopeful animal, believes that at its end things as they are will have become as they ought to be. For man the highway of intelligence leads to the moon.

Although we still print hearts on valentines, we no longer believe this worthy organ the source of affections. Nor do liver and spleen, except in the clichés of language, continue to breed human emotions. Since the time of Vesalius, those qualities that form the personality of man—instinct, reason, memory, imagination, emotion—were known to be children of the nervous system. Through four hundred years a mountain of evidence has accumulated to show that all the qualities we esteem in man, the qualities that make life tolerable, are functions of the nervous system. The poetry of a soul breathed into man by God has become the science of an evolving cerebral cortex. Fortunately in this case the facts do not destroy the poetry. They do not alter the quality of the human soul. By giving it a material base and a history, they add to it the glory of a growing triumph through the past and the promise of improvement in the future.

Long before a brain found lodging in the head of any animal, nerves threaded the flesh of simple creatures and guided them on their way. Long before true nervous tissues became the wires of communication between animals and their world, muscles received stimulation directly from the environment. And long before this, before the cells in the animal body were multiplied, simple protozoans must have held in their tiny bodies the essence of nervous activity.

No animal could ever have lived without some means of distinguishing good from bad in the outside world, and some ability to regulate his movements accordingly. Perhaps in the beginning all life resembled the modern one-celled *Paramecium* whose microscopic droplet of living jelly can move toward food and away from danger. Without the slightest observable trace of nerve tissue, this creature can vary his reactions to meet exigencies imposed by a fickle environment. Every day of his life *Paramecium* exercises a crude sort of choice, and by so doing, suggests the probable foundations upon which the perception of higher creatures was erected.

Sponges, lowest of living many-celled animals, epitomize the next stage in the evolution of a nervous system. Although in death a few are devoted to the pores of the human body, in life they are only concerned with the pores of their own bodies. Opening and closing these pores and thus controlling the food-freighted currents of water, has filled the life of every sponge since the Algonkian era. The control of each pore is lodged in simple muscle cells that receive stimulation directly from the outside world and are nowise nervously connected with the muscles that control the flow of water through neighboring pores. Because sponges have never grown beyond this primitive adjustment to surroundings, they have remained the most sluggish among the multicellular animals, one of the best examples of stagnation in nature. But there is compensation for everything. If a fish is foolish enough to bite off the top of a sponge, the fish undoubtedly suffers indigestion, but the sponge proceeds as placidly as before, insensate to both insult and injury.

Nature, always tiring of simplicity, early built into the bodies of corals and their kin the rudiments of a true nervous system. Touch any part of the sac-like body of a coral polyp and the animal will quickly contract. A network of simple nerve fibers evenly distributed just beneath the surface carries outside stimulation to the inner muscles of the body. Corals, like sponges, can undergo with equanimity the loss of a considerable portion of anatomy. Every part of the body is independent of every other part because each part possesses a neuromuscular mechanism adequate to its needs.

Very early in the history of life a variety of animals grew tired of watchful waiting and began to grope impatiently for food. They poked their brainless heads into a world full of bumps. It was not sufficient that they possess a simple nervous system diffused impartially throughout their bodies. That part which took the lead into the unknown needed something more. Perhaps it was from this need that the first organ resembling a brain was born.

Molluscs, worms, and arthropods grew small bunches of nerve cells in the fore parts of their bodies, from which chains of simpler nerve tissue dragged aft. By this means, sensations received through the skin were carried to the various muscles of the body. Because head and mouth were most frequently in contact with the world, these parts became sensitized above the rest of the body. An eternity of time and an infinity of change lie between these creatures and man, yet the first worm that crawled over the mud of a pre-Cambrian shore carried with him the prophecy of human personality.

Man, always appreciative of his own good qualities, likes to think of his brain as a unique gift from heaven. It is, to be sure, the only organ in the human body not easily excelled by similar organs in a host of other mammals. Although it is the most intricate structure in the entire animal kingdom, it is none the less the offspring of brains that saw service for millions of years in the heads of humble creatures. Man's brain is no more original than most of the thoughts that spring from it.

The crude models of a central nervous system preserved in the fossils of some of the earliest backboneless animals were built to a pattern that nature has never since forsaken. Just as the first automobile contained rudiments of the modern limousine, so the first nervous systems suggested the last. In the early fishes the brain and spinal cord of man were clearly foreshadowed. A fossil ostracoderm from Silurian rocks of Germany preserves the oldest record of a true brain. As in man, the brain of this primitive fish was an enlargement at the front end of the spinal cord, terminating in a tube whose purpose was to register the sensations of smell. Just behind and corresponding to the human cerebrum was an enlargement of the ostracoderm brain. Behind this was the still larger heart-shaped mid-brain, connecting as does the similar structure in man with the organs of sight and possibly of hearing. The hind-brain was club-shaped, expanded in front, but lacked the high differentiation of the human cerebellum.

From that day to this, brains have remained ever the same under a gaining complication in the details of structure. The fossil brain of one of the ancestors of the sturgeon was cracked out of a nodule from a lower Carboniferous rock in central Kentucky. It proved that fishes had gained keen vision and sharp hearing since the days of the ostracoderms, qualities no doubt essential in a fish, since without them the ostracoderms had died. The ability to reason had obviously not yet appeared, nor indeed did it ever become an outstanding charm among wearers of the fin and scale.

The fossil record of the lower four-footed land animals is unsatisfactory because the brains of these creatures are imbedded in fat, and the form is nearly always destroyed by death. Enough reptilian brains have been preserved, however, to prove the gradual perfection of this organ. On land the sense of smell is a vital necessity. The oldest specimen of a reptilian brain was found in Permian rocks, and it showed a decided increase in the size and complexity of the olfactory lobes over those of fishes. On land locomotion is more difficult than in water. Early Mesozoic reptiles exhibited a marked growth in the cerebellum, the portion of the brain concerned with the coördination of bodily movements.

The earliest mammalian brains were reptilian in character. They were small and the cerebellum was larger than the cerebrum. Soon, however, when competition made intelligence both respectable and valuable, the cerebrum (organ of thought) became fully as prominent as the cerebellum. After the Eocene epoch the mammalian brain increased in size and complexity. Convolutions increased, the cerebrum outdid the cerebellum. Almost without exception, those mammals who survived to the present had larger and more complicated brains than the average of their companions, whereas those who failed had smaller and simpler brains. Mentality had at last become the wielder of destiny.

Thus flying rapidly up the ages we arrive at the brain of man. It is the perfection of all that was good in its predecessors. It is not likely that earth will ever see a better brain. If improvement is to bless the lot of man, it will come not through a gain in the size and complexity of his brain, but through an extension of its use.

Intelligence, that rarest distillation of the perfected brain, is a will-o'-the-wisp that eludes the barriers of definition. No scientist is wise enough to explain how it is made, nor certain when it first appeared. The successive stages in the evolution of the brain are crystallized in the heads of living animals from fish to man, and it is to them we must turn for some suggestion as to the history of the brain's functions.

It becomes clear at once that the business of most brains is not to manufacture intelligence. That quick adjustment to new conditions characteristic of human mentality is rarely displayed by any other animal. Yet because we like to think in terms of ourselves and because we are congenitally senti-mental, we see human intelligence in all sorts of innocent creatures.

A man catches a fly in a room dark except for a narrow rectangle of light allowed to enter through a partly opened window. The insect beats and buzzes against the walls of his prison, and when the hand is undoubled sails to the open window and escapes. Judging from printed interpretations of a multitude of similar incidents the average man would say that the fly realized his danger, and when the opportunity came, quickly and willfully chose the only correct avenue of escape.

Unfortunately this proof of intelligence in flies suffers if a flame is made the only bright spot in the room. For the poor fly is so built that he must go toward the light whether it frees him or fries him. Like the behavior of the fly, that of almost all other animals is largely if not entirely outside the range of voluntary control, regardless of the fact that many animal reactions are beneficial.

Our sentimentality is magnanimous. We often see in ani-mals not only the intellect of man but also his feelings. Every year the bookstalls display a crop of literature dealing with the human side of birds, beasts, and even flowers. The books of the Nimrods are noteworthy. Human choice and emotion are attributed to animals who in most cases merely follow blindly the frozen paths of age-old instinct. The myth of the bravery of big game has grown from a double root: the habit of seeing everything in our own image, and the human desire to conquer in fair fight. It is not sporting to murder a cow in a pasture; so the hunter who murders an antlered cow of the woods builds a myth which not only enables him to pull the trigger but even to boast of it afterwards. Although the charge of a wounded animal may be only the misguided instinctive attempt of a weak-visioned creature to escape, the hunter invariably dresses the action in terms of human virtue or vice.

Controlled laboratory experiments in nearly all cases lead to the conclusion that animal behavior falls in one of the three great groups of reactions known as tropisms, reflexes, and instincts. Such reactions occur repeatedly and cannot be altered by the individual even in the face of certain death. An earthworm rises to the surface of the ground after a rain and replenishes the liquors of his body so that he may continue to burrow along the dark path of his destiny. For millions of years earthworms have risen to the rain. This behavior is probably only an accidental variation that survived because it was useful.

Once acquired, however, such behavior is a steel bar that will not bend. For some time birds have made use of this custom of earthworms to solve the problem of breakfast. The earthworms have persisted in their habits, not from a spirit of bravado, but simply because they are powerless to alter them. Nature will not alter them unless they are harmful on a large scale, and then only through the extermination of the worms as well as the habits.

The capacity for true thought is scarcely more conspicuous in animals with nervous endowments far greater than those of earthworms. If fishes possess intelligence, they must possess it in high degree to be able to hide all signs of it from the prying eye of the investigator. Amphibians are not much more satisfactory, although with superhuman patience a frog can be proved to possess a very slight ability to learn from experience. Reptiles and birds, although richer in the range of their activities, are not distinguished for wit or moral strength. Only in the mammals can positive proof of memory, inference, and other marks of mentality be obtained. Yet even in this high society there are many disappointments. The guinea pig, pet of the experimenter, is as dull as a fish. The chimpanzee, on the other hand, is uncomfortably bright.

Despite the meager display of mentality in most animals, there is a definite correlation between the excellence of their brains and the variety and complexity of their behavior. A turtle leads a richer life than a herring, and a herring comes nearer to freedom than a worm. Although true intelligence flowers only in the brains of a few higher mammals and man, it is clearly akin to the more complex instincts. Both have grown with the growth of the brain. The roots of human mentality lie deep in the clay of past ages even though its branches stretch toward the sky.

We do not have to pry far into ourselves for the marks of our heritage. Libations of blood so recently poured at the feet of our brute instincts have not yet dried on the battle-fields of Europe. And even in times of comparative peace—ignorance, prejudice, fear, custom, whimsy, and sentimentality guide the actions of men.

It is disconcerting to realize how much of the behavior of man is of purely instinctive origin, behavior which though always flowing from the nervous system, and often compli-cated, is no more intelligent than the performance of an adding machine. I cough, breathe, and digest food just as unconsciously and unwillfully as any animal. Like an animal I respond to the urge to protect myself and to reproduce. In countless ways I am controlled by the herd with which I run. A sheep starves if he strays from the pack, and I am ridiculed if I wear a straw hat in January.

But the slow bulging and wrinkling of the cerebrum did more than imbed the blind instincts of the past. It nursed the seeds of a richer future. There are weeds in the soil where mentality grows, but the gardener who knows them can keep them in check even if he fails to exterminate them. The hope of man lies in the fact that he has been appointed gardener to his own destiny. The spade and trowel of intelli-gence have been in his hands for more than twenty thousand years. Although he has used them with little knowledge of what he hoped to accomplish, language has somehow grown in his garden and from it the fruits of art and science. Only now is man beginning to know how to direct his tools to a conscious purpose. He has begun to learn how to control some of the forces in the environment, and it is not presumptuous to hope that he may learn to control more effectively the instinctive emotional forces within himself.

Even though man may never hope for better tools than he now has, he may hope for more knowledge of how to use them. There may never come a finer Michelangelo, Dante, Darwin, or Christ, but there is plenty of room for a wider dissemination of their powers, for a richer mental and emotional life in each individual.

Man has traveled a long distance without consciously directing his footsteps. Nature has done fairly well by him. She has imposed many handicaps but she has given him, alone among her swarming brood, an intelligence to counterbalance. He has not yet begun to climb the heights of mental and spiritual development. If he does not reach the moon it will be his own fault.

LAYING THE GROUNDWORK

Preparation for Reading

1. What were some prehistoric animals and plants whose fossil remains have helped scientists to reconstruct a partial picture of early geologic ages?
2. How does the research of the scientist who reconstructs these early ages resemble detective work?
3. Can you advance a theory to explain why the mammoth perished? The dinosaur?
4. Nature has so equipped insects and animals physically that they can perform actions impossible for man to equal; for example, a fly can walk upside down on a ceiling; a snake can shed its entire skin. Give other examples.

Vocabulary Building

1. Find the definitions and pronunciations of the following geologic names, and then compare your notes with the chart given by Sears in "The Pageant of Life," pp. 17-18: *Algonkian, Pre-Cambrian, Carboniferous, Permian, Mesozoic, Eocene.*
2. Look up the following scientific terms before you begin to read, and record their meanings and pronunciations: *protozoans, polyp, molluscs, cerebellum, olfactory, tropisms, amphibians.*

3. Find when each of the following men lived, and the activity of each: *Vesalius, Dante, Michelangelo, Darwin*.
4. Who was Nimrod? What is the meaning of this word as used today?
5. Check the meanings of the following words in their context, and note pronunciations: *verge, perspective, panorama, prodigality, paradox, cliché, exigencies, epitomize, insensate, rudiments, equanimity, intricate, congenitally, magnanimous, libation, presumptuous*.

APPRAISING THE RESULTS

1. What ground does Bradley find in the records of the past for taking a gloomy view of the prospects of man on earth? What ground for hope in the same records?
2. Show how the complexity of the nervous system increases from its form in the one-celled organism to its form in man.
3. Trace the development of the structure of the brain from its earliest form in prehistoric fishes to the form now found in man.
4. What evidence does Bradley give that animal behavior falls largely under the reactions known as tropisms, reflexes, and instincts?
5. Explain the statement: "The hope of man lies in the fact that he has been appointed gardener to his own destiny."
6. What evidence do we find that we have not used our intelligence as well as we might to promote the welfare of our species? What kind of world could we hope to build if we gave intelligence full play?
7. Suggest changes in our educational system which would make it more effective in promoting intelligent action.
8. Criticize the statement: "You can't change human nature."
9. To what extent is the material of this selection factual? Does theory enter? unsubstantiated opinion? controversy?

SELECTING THE THEME SUBJECT

1. Develop fully your answer to one of the foregoing questions.
2. Organize your observations of the habits of some kind of plant or insect or animal life; for example, dandelions, mushrooms, fleas, ants, spiders, toads, snakes, bats, robins, rats, coyotes, squirrels.

3. Tell what the study of biology, or some other science, has done to give you a better understanding of yourself and your world.
4. Explain what evolution means to you.
5. Describe the struggle for survival as you have observed it in animal or plant life.
6. Write a paper classifying some group of related plants or animals; for example, fish, vegetables, trees, insects.

THE PAGEANT OF LIFE[1]

Paul B. Sears

THE PUZZLE OF THE EARTH'S HISTORY REMINDS ONE OF THOSE
CLEVERLY BUILT ORIENTAL BOXES WHICH OPEN WITH SUCH SUR-
prising ease when the secret spring is touched. Land-forms
and their constituent rocks, seemingly a scrambled confusion,
became orderly and legible by the magic of a very simple idea
—that of uniformity. As soon as the geologist began to assume
that mesas and valleys, sandstones and shales, had been formed
in the past by the same processes that now operate to produce them, the very earth about him became luminous and
vocal with its story. And today the pious literalist who would
have all of us believe that Genesis is a notebook instead of a
magnificent poem must concede that geology is at least a
workable subject; the oil wells which build his churches and
pay his taxes are stubborn realities. Even the boys on the
street know how such wells are located, or at any rate have a
wholesome respect for the craft of the "rock-hound."

Yet this uniformitarianism, which started as an assumption
and has earned its right to be called a great natural law, does
not imply by any means that the earth and its inhabitants have
always been what they are today. The operation of forces,
and the behavior of matter in nature may be changeless, but
there is no sameness or monotony in their visible expression.
Each morning's sun, almost literally, looks upon a new earth.

It did not take the geologist long to realize that the pattern
of land and sea had gone through an amazing series of transformations. Old ocean bottom can be found in many places
some thousands of feet above the present sea level, while the

[1] From *This Is Our World*, by Paul B. Sears, copyright 1937, University of
Oklahoma Press, Norman. Reproduced by kind permission of the publishers.

substantial real estate of other days is now the playground for fishes. The geologist knows better than anyone how passing a thing is the immediate landscape.

Moreover his associate, the student of fossil plants and animals, reminds us that the living part of the environment has moved along with the course of time. It is a very different thing to be alive in a world of trees, grasses, and warm-blooded mammals than it would be to find ourselves in the midst of great forests of ferns, peopled and ruled by reptiles. Life has changed with the changing of the landscape and the shifting of the continents.

So much for landscape and life. Climate remains; what of it? So far as any particular spot is concerned, the rocks themselves bespeak constant change of climate. Today a dry, sparse, and scrubby forest may cover shallow seams of coal which could only have been formed in some dark and ancient swamp in a region of high rainfall. Or oyster shells may crop to the surface in the Wyoming hills and form little spots of desiccated alkaline desert where once the air was muggy above the brackish covers of ocean. Certainly the climate of any particular spot must change with its distance from the sea and its position on a changing continent.

This is not, however, the whole story. The red-beds which stretch like a pink girdle across our southern states carry the record of great continental deserts. At other times coal was formed over large areas of the earth by the piling up of luxuriant vegetation that was the antithesis of desert conditions. And masses of earth and rock, hundreds of miles from their point of origin, once piously called "diluvium" and attributed to the Noachian disaster, are now known to have been scraped along by continental ice caps of inconceivable bigness as compared with the shrunken polar snow fields of today. There is plenty of reason to know, in other words, that at various times the climate of our planet as a whole was shifted in one direction or another. And even during periods of relative stability, such as the past ten thousand years, we have discovered that climate has gone through marked changes, less revolutionary of course, but sufficient to make a difference in the boundaries of forests and plains, and in the fortunes of bison and men, horses, camels, and pine trees.

Science will not rest, of course, while these intriguing problems of the past afford a single clue whose meaning remains unsolved. This putting together a story after it has happened is really glorified detective work, hazardous and delicate, carried on by indirection and inference. It is not a task for those who seek pontifical authority or who dread the havoc which new evidence can wreak upon beloved theories.

Nor, let us remember, is it a mere selfish indulgence of idle curiosity. Society has a stake in the search. Concerning the present there is much which we shall not know without a more complete knowledge of the past. The disastrous drought of the 1930's reminds us of the need for a better understanding of the rhythm of climate. The time-table of the earth and its changes may not interest everybody, but it certainly concerns us all. The problem of human culture, its origins, movements, and characteristics is coming increasingly to be a problem of environmental change. There is an archaeology of environment no less than of flints, pottery, and bones.

The drainage ditches and dumps from a modern city may be unsavory places, but if the city were to disappear, they might constitute its only record, and a useful one it would be to the trained eye. Similarly the beds of sediment washed from ancient continents are today our chief source of information about them. The character and disposition of these sediments tell us much about the former land surface and the conditions under which its population lived. Slow sedate streams flowing through broad valleys carpeted with rich soil and abundant life bring to the ocean very different materials from those scoured down by the infrequent, ungovernable washouts of a dry, inhospitable land. But mainly we depend for our knowledge of past conditions upon the remnants of life itself. We can reconstruct the course of life from the fossil remains of such organisms as have been suitably preserved.

Even with a fairly satisfactory knowledge of fossil remains, there are of course dangers in deducing too much about the conditions under which their original possessors lived. Who, knowing where the elephant thrives today, would guess that exploration would yield the frozen carcasses of his close kin in the barren arctic wastes of Siberia? And even the professional botanist gets a jolt from Professor Seward's photograph of tree ferns which are growing today near the margin of a glacier in the southern hemisphere. Yet interrupted, dim, and deceptive as our glimpses of past life may be, they tell us much. Very briefly, then, let us examine some of the higher spots in the record.

Before we can discuss a few of the great problems of adjustment between life and its environment which have been encountered along the way, it is well to see something of the order in which living things developed, and the kinds which dominated the earth at different stages in the past. Hit-and-run tourists that we are, we shall have to use a guide. Here it is, the time-table used by geologists, in a very much simplified form. And if, in the succeeding pages of this chapter, we become lost, we can turn back to it.

A Simple Table of Geological Time

Here the whole of geological time is divided into five great eras; these in turn are divided into periods. Memoranda of the fossil record are added here and there as guides.

Era	Period
CENOZOIC	
Quaternary	
Recent	Modern Man (30,000 years)
Pleistocene or Glacial	Early Man
Tertiary	
Pliocene	
Miocene	Three-toed horse ... pre-human anthropoid
Oligocene	Specialized mammals
Eocene	Primitive mammals, vegetarian and carnivorous
MESOZOIC	
Cretaceous	End of the great reptiles ... modern vegetation ... primitive birds and small early mammals
Jurassic	Reptiles rule the earth
Triassic	Origin of the flowering plants

Era	*Period*
PALEOZOIC	
Permian	Conifers replace the ferns . . . primitive reptiles
Carboniferous	Ferns clothe the earth . . . insects, amphibians, very early reptiles
Devonian	Great forests of ferns and primitive conifers . . . first land vertebrates . . . rich invertebrate fauna . . . many fish
Silurian	Early simple land-plants . . . primitive fish
Ordovician	Great reefs of simple seaweeds
Cambrian	Invertebrates only . . . marine forms (Perhaps a billion years ago)
PROTEROZOIC	
ARCHAEOZOIC	Pre-Cambrian . . . Simple marine plants and invertebrates . . . scanty remains

This table tells us some interesting and significant things at a glance. We see that human history is a trifling fragment of geological time. Life of some sort has been present upon the earth for a period of almost inconceivable length. Speaking bluntly, it has existed long enough for almost anything to have happened.

And we can see that much has happened. The actual beginnings of life itself are lost; but there is plenty of evidence of a steady advance from the greatest simplicity to an amazing complexity. The earliest remains are those of soft-bodied plants and animals. Firm skeletons and the organization thereby made possible were a matter of gradual achievement, of repeated, not always successful, trial.

The record is full of great groups that rose to power and abundance, only to recede and disappear in the face of their own followers, like successive chords in some titanic modulation.

The table tells us also of the earlier enrichment of life within the sea and its prolonged struggle thereafter to move upon the land and become adjusted to all manner of conditions there. And since the sea is far more constant than the land, the striking changes of the latter part of geological time largely concern the life on land.

We also see in this simple outline of events that animals in the past, as now, have been dependent upon plants for subsistence. Each great wave of animal development is preceded by an appearance of the appropriate and necessary plant life. Land flora came before land fauna. The flowering plants arose ahead of the mammals. And it is pretty clear from the table, too, that the passing of time has tightened the fabric of interdependence among living things. The half-million kinds of insects now in existence are involved with each other and the rest of the living world beyond any power of separation or retreat.

As for man, most recent and most specialized of all organisms, and in his own conceit most powerful, he is the spoiled darling of the whole system. Because he can utilize and apparently control all other organisms, he is likely to forget that he is the beneficiary of a prolonged and delicately balanced development. Thus far in his history he has done more to destroy than to perpetuate that balance. And the deep undertones of the scientific record reënforce the somber words of prophecy, "Let him that standeth take heed lest he fall."

With these very general facts about the past of life, let us retrace our steps examining certain phases of the scene in greater detail. As we do so, let us bear in mind that the record of the fossils is sketchy and imperfect. What proportion of our worthy citizens have access to the august portraits of the eight great-grandparents; indeed, how many know the names of these dignitaries? An expert on heraldry states that not more than a handful of families in England can trace an authentic lineage a thousand years, and even among the lines of these exalted few there is no doubt plenty of shadow and mystery. The ancestral record of living organisms goes back some hundreds of millions of years. Only by the luckiest coincidence is an individual preserved and later revealed to the eyes of science. The remarkable thing is not that there are vast gaps in the story, but that it hangs together as well as it does.

So far as beginnings are concerned the record is tantalizing. How did life first begin? What was the first vertebrate, the first flowering plant? There is little comfort for those who seek an answer to such questions. We seldom find fossils of anything but groups which have been long and well established and whose individuals died in great numbers under circumstances favoring their preservation.

Calendars however, whether scientific or ecclesiastical, must have a point of beginning, and so the calendar of fossil time begins its great primary era, the Paleozoic, with the Cambrian. But it must not be thought that the Cambrian is therefore the time when life began. Far from it. The Cambrian is merely the period whose rocks are marked by the first abundance of fossils. And while these fossils consist of invertebrate animals and seaweeds, they are all well enough developed and far from being really primitive. Some Cambrian trilobites might deceive a nearsighted gourmet into thinking them shrimp or crayfish. Marine plants abounded, and the seas of Cambrian time were swarming with animals having special organs of locomotion, digestion, sense-perception, and nervous systems to coördinate them all.

Looking backward from this zero hour we find only scattering fossils. Some structures indeed resemble the tufted or massive seaweeds of today, but we are not too sure that these are really fossils and not ancient fairy gardens like those Jack Frost makes with ice crystals. If simplicity is any guide to the earliest life, we can draw up specifications; we know the viruses today which have no visible organized form but which can increase their own substance, that substance being protein-like. We also know bacteria which can manufacture their own food without the aid of sunlight or the green pigment in leaves. That is as far as we can go. We do not even know whether such archaic life came into being in shallow seas or, as Professor Chamberlain suggests, somewhere on land. But living substance today requires the salts found in sea water, and certainly the sea has been, if not the womb, at least the cradle of early life.

Before the middle of the primary era, a balance was established within the ocean which has persisted without great disturbance until the present. The hungry life of ocean is fed by sunlight. Since this light diminishes rapidly with depth, the surface is a welter of floating life known as plankton.

Myriads of microscopic plants convert minerals, water, and carbon dioxide into food, upon which countless invertebrates feed. Upon these in turn the larger forms, predominantly the vertebrate fish, are fed. This plankton is the great pasture of the sea, and its débris, constantly settling to the bottom, supports animals at greater depths, meanwhile helping to supply the sediments which in time become rock.

If the plankton is like pasture, there is anchored life in shallow waters which might be likened to forests. Great reefs of lime-secreting algae and other seaweeds have, since early geological time, afforded shelter and food to animal life.

Since its establishment this pattern has become enriched and altered in detail, of course. Primitive fishes have been replaced by more specialized types, while mammals and flowering plants originating on the land have sent representatives such as the whale, the seal, and the ribbon grass back into the ocean. Trilobites have been replaced by modern crustaceans. The life of ocean today has flowered into an amazing richness of form, yet on the whole remains at a restrained level of organization. Both animals and plants show a great development of microscopic, small and moderate sized organisms, highly interdependent and affording means of support to those most primitive, as well as most ancient, of known vertebrates—the fish.

Endless modifications of structure and function are involved in the ancient and intricate pattern of ocean life. Bottom feeders tend to be horizontally flattened, sluggish, often armored on the back. Rapid swimmers, notably the fish, are beautifully and effectively streamlined. "Tail like a mackerel, head like a cod," is still a boat builder's formula. Sedentary forms, such as molluscs, sponges, and corals, are actively moving during their juvenile period and thus migrate and spread. Floating plants growing submerged may have special pigments which help absorb the scanty sunlight that filters down to them.

But the great primary era, or Paleozoic, which witnessed the conquest of the ocean by life, also saw another great adventure set going. This was the invasion of the land, where conditions are not as constant as within the sea, and where hazard is present at every step. Early Paleozoic fossils of the Ordovician and particularly the Silurian include bizarre plants whose fitness for land becomes more pronounced with the passing of time. Certainly these were not far removed from the soft-bodied seaweeds. But behind a veil we have not yet penetrated there were developing races of mighty, if primitive, trees. Without known precursors we see these forests burgeon forth in the mid-Paleozoic or Devonian where their trunks, sometimes five feet in diameter, are abundantly preserved. And peopling these forests were the first insects, land molluscs, and those first land vertebrates, the amphibians. The problem of a bulky, permanent land vegetation was on the road toward a solution. But as yet there was no evidence of an animal population commensurate with the organic material being produced.

As the Paleozoic moved past its zenith of the Devonian, there occurred the dazzling afterglow of the coal measures, or Carboniferous time. We have little means of knowing what was taking place on the high ground of the continental interiors, but in coastal swamps and on low ground there were amazing forests of ferns and other weird trees without true flowers. Accumulating more rapidly than they could be decayed, their remains furnish many of our present coal beds. Among dank recesses the insects and amphibians continued to thrive, while from the latter a higher form of vertebrate animal, the primitive reptiles, emerged. These reptiles laid their eggs upon land instead of in the water, and were land animals from the moment of hatching instead of spending a period of juvenile probation in the water as did the amphibia. The emergence of the higher animals was now complete. Henceforth individual species might return to the water to live, but the group as a whole had been graduated onto land.

When the Carboniferous period was succeeded by the time of cold and deserts—the Permian, which ended the Paleozoic —it became evident that the mighty ferns and their kin had not solved the problem of surviving the hardships of living upon land. Their great, delicate-tipped fronds, their unprotected growing points, their complicated, uncertain method of reproduction, and their limited facilities for thickening and branching became a liability. They disappeared, practically speaking. But alongside of them the ancestors of the modern "evergreens" and other cone-bearing seed plants weathered through, for they were better protected at every stage of life history.

Thus the secondary or Mesozoic era was ushered into a world landscaped, so far as we know, by cone-bearing trees and peopled by the vigorous, youthful group of reptiles. Gradually during this era the climate of the earth again became genial as it had been in the Devonian and Carboniferous, so that the Mesozoic era ended with another luxuriant outburst of life—the Cretaceous.

Meanwhile the reptiles had multiplied until they possessed the earth and to an extent its waters and the air above it. Powerful, sometimes swift, and in many ways efficient, they nevertheless bore the seed of their own destruction. Their body temperature was not effectively regulated, so that cold rendered them sluggish. They generally laid their eggs in the ground and gave the young rather scanty attention. Equally important, their central nervous system was poorly developed, inadequate to control the vast mechanical system of their bodies.

Throughout the Mesozoic, the plant world had become enriched by the development of flowering plants, including many kinds which still persist about as they were then—the oaks, hickories, magnolias, sassafras, to name but a few. And these flowering plants were perfectly suited to nourish and shelter, not only the growing hordes of insects but the warm-blooded birds and primitive mammals which put in their appearance at the end of the Mesozoic, that is, in Cretaceous time.

These small pioneer mammals were literally in at the death of the great reptile groups. It is often suggested that along with their greater intelligence and more continuous activity, they may have possessed a penchant for sucking reptile eggs, as well as an ability to hide out from the ubiquitous monsters who laid them. Thus plausibly may we think of

David and Goliath or Gulliver and the Lilliputians foreshadowed in the unsmiling humor of the ancient cosmos.

At any rate the Tertiary division of geologic time began
in a world of flowering plants and primitive mammals, with
the earth cleared of its saurian dragons. And as time proceeded this period witnessed the prolonged and classic history
of the horse and the more obscure birth of other modern
mammals. Undoubtedly the development of great continental
grasslands or steppes was a potent factor in these events, but
unhappily for us much of that side of the story is lost. We
do not know when or how the grasses, so admirably suited to
dry climates and to grazing, had their origins. We have to
work by inference, based upon the teeth and other anatomical
features of such fossils as we have found. Among other animals of the late Tertiary was the precursor of man.

As the Tertiary was finally replaced by the Quaternary in
which we of the present live, the earth had approximately its
present geographical pattern, substantially, although by no
means all of its present vegetation and animal life. For the
Quaternary has been a period of great climatic stress. Not
once, but repeatedly have the great polar ice caps so thickened
that their enormous weight caused them to spread in a grinding, viscous flow until they reached deep into what are at
present temperate climates. Seemingly enough water was im-
pounded in the frozen masses each time to lower the sea level
considerably. And each advance of the ice caused, we know,
profound shifting of the plant and animal life in its pathway.
In Europe this resulted in impoverishing the rich Tertiary
life, for mountains cut off retreat to the south; but in North
America the avenue of escape toward the south was open
and with each recession of the ice, the displaced communities
came back close behind its melting edge.

Between advances have been interglacial epochs resembling the present, and of which the present may well be but
one. Obviously such profound oscillations of climate have
played a large part in producing the present pattern and
composition of life upon the earth. Surface changes produced
by the ice often created barriers, isolating groups and favoring minor evolutionary developments. And the youthful

topography, usually rich in minerals, provided a variety of habitats suitable to a wide range of organisms.

Man was on the scene not later than the third interglacial epoch. Aided by his superior intelligence, such as it is, and by the marvelous inventive genius which his hand has made possible, he survived—to begin his slow battle for dominion of the earth in postglacial time. Fitting at first into living communities of plants and animals without essentially altering their balance, he has emerged into dominance. So complete is his control that in most parts of the earth today he is surrounded by communities which have been profoundly modified by his own interference. For the first time in its geological history, earth is overrun and ruled, not by a group of organisms, but by a single species. Will this species avoid the fate of the mighty groups which preceded it?

LAYING THE GROUNDWORK

Preparation for Reading

1. What is the work of the geologist?
2. In round numbers estimate the probable age of the earth; the length of time life has existed on it.
3. How do we know that some mountain peaks were once under water? that the surface of the earth is still unstable?
4. What do you know about the forms of animal and vegetable life which existed in early geologic ages?

Vocabulary Building

1. Before reading "The Pageant of Life," find the meanings and pronunciations of the following words: *mesas, shales, brackish, diluvium, archaeology, anthropoid, carnivorous, conifers, invertebrates, amphibians, fauna, trilobites, virus, plankton, algae, crustaceans, Cenozoic, Mesozoic, Paleozoic, Proterozoic, Archaeozoic.*
2. From what common root are the following terms derived: *carnivorous, carnage, carnal, carnation, carnival?*
3. Check the meaning of each of the following words in its context and note the pronunciation: *constituent, luminous, sparse, desiccated, antithesis, pontifical, havoc, unsavory, sediment, authentic, intricate, sedentary, zenith, penchant, ubiquitous.*

APPRAISING THE RESULTS

1. In what sense is it true that there is uniformity in the operation of forces and the behavior of matter in the processes of nature?
2. What evidence is there that the pattern (a) of land and sea, (b) of living things, and (c) of climate has gone through a series of transformations in the course of the earth's history?
3. Check these statements "true" or "false." Defend your choice. (a) Human history is a fragment of geologic time. ——— (b) Life has developed from simplicity to complexity. ——— (c) Each great wave of animal development is preceded by the appearance of appropriate plant life. ——— (d) Life forms in the sea today are more constant than land forms. ——— (e) Reptile life flourished during the Mesozoic period.
4. Summarize the main steps in the development of living forms.
5. Explain how all life in the sea depends upon plankton. Could the same case be made for the dependence of all land life on plants? (Cross reference: Carson, "Undersea," p. 154.)
6. Discuss the question with which the selection ends: "Will this species avoid the fate of the mighty groups which preceded it?"
7. Is this selection largely opinion or facts? What sources did Sears probably use to obtain the facts he uses?

SELECTING THE THEME SUBJECT

1. Explain the geologic history of some district which you know. Become an amateur detective and write from first-hand observation.
2. Account for the climate of your own section of the country.
3. Explain some special phase of weather, for example, tornadoes.
4. Develop one of the following topics: Beach Life at Low Tide; Vegetation of Arctic Regions; Changes in Vegetation as One Ascends a Mountain; How Desert Plants Have Adapted Themselves to Their Environment; The Cause of Dust Storms.
5. Explain the work of the Government Weather Bureau.
6. Explain how insects affect the welfare of mankind.
7. Write a logical defense of, or an attack on, government control of natural resources, for example, control of oil.

THE EVOLUTION OF THE PHYSICAL WORLD[1]

Arthur Stanley Eddington

LOOKING BACK THROUGH THE LONG PAST WE PICTURE THE BE-
GINNING OF THE WORLD—A PRIMEVAL CHAOS WHICH TIME HAS
fashioned into the universe that we know. Its vastness appals
the mind; space boundless though not infinite, according to
the strange doctrine of science. The world was without form
and almost void. But at the earliest stage we can contemplate
the void is sparsely broken by tiny electric particles, the germs
of the things that are to be; positive and negative they wander
aimlessly in solitude, rarely coming near enough to seek or
shun one another. They range everywhere so that all space
is filled, and yet so empty that in comparison the most highly
exhausted vacuum on earth is a jostling throng. In the beginning was vastness, solitude and the deepest night. Darkness
was upon the face of the deep, for as yet there was no light.

The years rolled by, million after million. Slight aggregations occurring casually in one place and another drew to
themselves more and more particles. They warred for sovereignty, won and lost their spoil, until the matter was collected round centers of condensation leaving vast empty spaces
from which it had ebbed away. Thus gravitation slowly parted
the primeval chaos. These first divisions were not the stars
but what we should call "island universes" each ultimately to
be a system of some thousands of millions of stars. From our
own island universe we can discern the other islands as
spiral nebulæ lying one beyond another as far as the telescope
can fathom. The nearest of them is such that light takes
900,000 years to cross the gulf between us. They acquired

[1] From *Science and the Unseen World*, by Arthur Stanley Eddington. By
permission of The Macmillan Company, publishers.

rotation (we do not yet understand how) which bulged them into flattened form and made them wreathe themselves in spirals. Their forms, diverse yet with underlying regularity, make a fascinating spectacle for telescopic study.

As it had divided the original chaos, so gravitation subdivided the island universes. First the star clusters, then the stars themselves were separated. And with the stars came light, born of the fiercer turmoil which ensued when the electrical particles were drawn from their solitude into dense throngs. A star is not just a lump of matter casually thrown together in the general confusion; it is of nicely graded size. There is relatively not much more diversity in the masses of new-born stars than in the masses of new-born babies. Aggregations rather greater than our Sun have a strong tendency to subdivide, but when the mass is reduced a little the danger quickly passes and the impulse to subdivision is satisfied. Here it would seem the work of creation might cease. Having carved chaos into stars, the first evolutionary impulse has reached its goal. For many billions of years the stars may continue to shed their light and heat through the world, feeding on their own matter which disappears bit by bit into ætherial waves.

Not infrequently a star, spinning too fast or strained by the radiant heat imprisoned within it, may divide into two nearly equal stars, which remain yoked together as a double star; apart from this no regular plan of further development is known. For what might be called the second day of creation we turn from the general rule to the exceptions. Amid so many myriads there will be a few which by some rare accident have a fate unlike the rest. In the vast expanse of the heavens the traffic is so thin that a star may reasonably count on travelling for the whole of its long life without serious risk of collision. The risk is negligible for any individual star; but ten thousand million stars in our own system and more in the systems beyond afford a wide playground for chance. If the risk is one in a hundred millions some unlucky victims are doomed to play the rôle of "one." This rare accident must have happened to our Sun—an accident to the Sun, but to us the cause of our being here. A star journeying through space casually overtook the Sun, not indeed colliding with it, but approaching so close as to raise a great tidal wave. By this disturbance jets of matter spurted out of the Sun; being carried round by their angular momentum they did not fall back again but condensed into small globes—the planets.

By this and similar events there appeared here and there in the universe something outside Nature's regular plan, namely a lump of matter small enough and dense enough to be cool. A temperature of ten million degrees or more prevails through the greater part of the interior of a star; it cannot be otherwise so long as matter remains heaped in immense masses. Thus the design of the first stage of evolution seems to have been that matter should ordinarily be endowed with intense heat. Cool matter appears as an afterthought. It is unlikely that the Sun is the only one of the starry host to possess a system of planets, but it is believed that such development is very rare. In these exceptional formations Nature has tried the experiment of finding what strange effects may ensue if matter is released from its usual temperature of millions of degrees and permitted to be cool.

Out of the electric charges dispersed in the primitive chaos ninety-two different kinds of matter—ninety-two chemical elements—have been built. This building is also a work of evolution, but little or nothing is known as to its history. In the matter which we handle daily we find the original bricks fitted together and cannot but infer that somewhere and somewhen a process of matter-building has occurred. At high temperature this diversity of matter remains as it were latent; little of consequence results from it. But in the cool experimental stations of the universe the differences assert themselves. At root the diversity of the ninety-two elements reflects the diversity of the integers from one to ninety-two; because the chemical characteristics of element No. 11 (sodium) arise from the fact that it has the power at low temperatures of gathering round it eleven negative electric particles; those of No. 12 (magnesium) from its power of gathering twelve particles; and so on.

It is tempting to linger over the development out of this

fundamental beginning of the wonders studied in chemistry and physics, but we must hurry on. The provision of certain cool planetary globes was the second impulse of evolution, and it has exhausted itself in the formation of inorganic rocks and ores and other materials. We must look to a new exception or abnormality if anything further is to be achieved. We can scarcely call it an accident that among the integers there should happen to be the number 6; but I do not know how otherwise to express the fact that organic life would not have begun if Nature's arithmetic had overlooked the number 6. The general plan of ninety-two elements, each embodying in its structural pattern one of the first ninety-two numbers, contemplates a material world of considerable but limited diversity; but the element carbon, embodying the number 6, and because of the peculiarity of the number 6, rebels against limits. The carbon atoms love to string themselves in long chains such as those which give toughness to a soap-film. Whilst other atoms organise themselves in twos and threes or it may be in tens, carbon atoms organise themselves in hundreds and thousands. From this potentiality of carbon to form more and more elaborate structure a third impulse of evolution arises.

I cannot profess to say whether anything more than this prolific structure-building power of carbon is involved in the beginning of life. The story of evolution here passes into the domain of the biological sciences for which I cannot speak, and I am not ready to take sides in the controversy between the Mechanists and the Vitalists. So far as the earth is concerned the history of development of living forms extending over nearly a thousand million years is recorded (though with many breaks) in fossil remains. Looking back over the geological record it would seem that Nature made nearly every possible mistake before she reached her greatest achievement Man—or perhaps some would say her worst mistake of all. At one time she put her trust in armaments and gigantic size. Frozen in the rock is the evidence of her failures to provide a form fitted to endure and dominate—failures which we are only too ready to imitate. At last she tried a being of no great size, almost defenceless, defective in at least one of the more important sense-organs; one gift she bestowed to save him from threatened extinction—a certain stirring, a restlessness, in the organ called the brain.

And so we come to Man.

LAYING THE GROUNDWORK

Preparation for Reading

1. How would you account for the origin of the earth?
2. Why does not the moon, as it circles the earth, fly off into space or crash into the earth?
3. The sun is about 93 million miles from the earth. Light travels at approximately 186,300 miles a second. How long does it take light to reach the earth?
4. A light year is the distance light travels in a year. In miles, what is this distance?

Vocabulary Building

1. Look up the definition of vitalism. Then formulate a definition of *Vitalists* and *Mechanists*. (See paragraph 8.)
2. What is the meaning of the root of the word *primeval* and of the prefix? Explain the use of the same prefix in the following words: *prima donna, primary, primitive, prince, primate.*
3. Check the meanings of these words in the context and their pronunciations: *void, sovereignty, nebulæ, aggregation, ætherial, dispersed, diversity, inorganic, integers, prolific.*

APPRAISING THE RESULTS

1. What was the character of the void before "island universes" began to form?
2. What part did gravitation play in the formation of "island universes"? in the formation of stars?
3. According to Eddington, what seems to have been the first impulse of creation? the second? the third?
4. In what way can our earth be said to be an exception to Nature's plan?
5. Why has the element carbon a key position in the development of life forms on the earth?
6. What reception was given the discoveries and teachings of early astronomers, for example, Galileo? Have we entirely overcome

this aversion to changing our views? Give evidence to support your conclusion.

SELECTING THE THEME SUBJECT

1. Explain the difference between astronomy and astrology.
2. Discuss the superstitions commonly associated with astronomical bodies, for example, the belief that "blood on the moon" means war.
3. Trace the use of stars and sun and moon in poetry and sentimental songs.
4. Explain how a microscope or a telescope works. Compare the two.
5. Explain how a navigator uses the sun and stars and planets.
6. Read Genesis, Chapter i. Then compare the account of creation given there with the account given by Eddington.

Man and the Social Group

NEW CONCEPTIONS OF MAN AND HIS WAYS[1]

James Harvey Robinson

NOT ONLY HAVE THE SCIENTISTS IN THE LAST HUNDRED YEARS TAUGHT US THAT MAN IS PHYSICALLY DESCENDED FROM EARLIER forms of organic life. They have also made it clear that our mind has its animal origins as well, without a knowledge of which we cannot intelligently understand human ways of thinking. Anthropologists and students of cultural history have explored that long period of human development prior to any written records—more than ninety-nine per cent of all human existence on our planet. They have described the long and tedious journey along man's "rough road" from abject savagery to twentieth century civilization. All these studies have opened up a whole new panorama, not only to historians but to students of the social sciences and public affairs in general. The material brought forth is invaluable for understanding human behavior in all ages. It enables us to know what it means to behave like human beings, and why we do so behave.

For what, then, are we indebted to scientific discoveries of the last seventy-five years—discoveries made by biologists, anthropologists, and comparative psychologists? What are the main facts about mankind unknown and unrecognized by practically all writers on human nature and conduct seventy-five years ago which are generally accepted by scientific investigators today? Little can be said here about anyone of them, but in the aggregate they form an imposing mass of new knowledge upon the basis of which it may be possible, as time goes on, to reform humanity by abolishing many long-

[1] From *The Human Comedy*, by James Harvey Robinson. Reprinted by permission of Harper & Brothers, publishers.

33

standing fears, disorders, and disgraceful practices and by raising mankind to a higher plane of insight and contentment.

The older writers about man had little interest usually in
his history. They knew almost nothing about his career in
Europe before the Greeks. In Christian countries it was supposed that the first man and woman were created with fully
developed speech and a fine degree of intelligence about four
thousand years before Christ. During the past seventy-five
years it has become clearer and clearer that men have been
living on the earth for perhaps a million years, running about
on their hind legs, and with a unique bodily equipment which
has enabled them very gradually indeed to amass the knowledge and arts of which they are now possessed. Some of the
earlier skulls would indicate that there were once human
races which did not have as good brains as those which developed later. Originally men lived like wild animals, without
fire and clothes or much in the way of speech. But they differed sharply from all other creatures in their power to make
discoveries which could be imitated by the young or adopted
by one tribe from another.

In bodily form and physical functions man resembles very
closely apes and monkeys. Like them he begins his physical
existence as a tiny egg, and his organs suggest for a short
time in his mother's womb peculiarities of a fish. He retains
through life muscles to wag a tail or move his ears. Most of
those who reject man's animal genealogy have never taken
the trouble to see how they looked when they were an embryo
six weeks old. We never get over being an animal and some
of the worst mistakes of the past have been due to the failure
to recognize ourselves as animals. Those familiar with the
incredible powers of animals and plants big and little feel no
shame in freely accepting their share in the stupendous
miracle and mystery of *life*.

There is a variety of evidence to indicate that men lived as
savage hunters during ninety-nine per cent of the time they
have been wandering upon the earth—so slow was their
progress in the beginning. They had learned during this
period to make a fire and probably to clothe themselves in

pelts, and to talk better and better. They certainly greatly improved the shape and increased the variety of their flint tools and weapons. Only some twelve thousand years ago were spinning and weaving, pottery, crops, and domesticated animals added to man's heritage. He became a farmer and shepherd as well as a hunter and fisher. He had no easy way of gaining his daily food, however; he knew nothing of reading or writing, of cities and fine buildings. As yet he was more ignorant than the lowest savage to be found on earth today— and yet he had bread, fire, and clothes.

About the time that, according to the ideas of a hundred years ago, the first man and woman were created, the people of the Nile Valley were rapidly outrunning all that humanity had previously accomplished. They had begun to write and read, to construct stone tombs and before long to gather in towns, rear magnificent temples, employ copper instead of flint, and work gold and precious stones into designs difficult for our best artificers to imitate today. They wrapped their dead in linen sheets of wondrous fineness and dreamed strange dreams of the life to come. This is, of course, recent history. The Egyptians and still more obviously the Greeks, with their noble sculpture, based on the statues of the Egyptians, their temples, vases, dramas, and bold philosophizing—all are very close to us when we consider the long dark period in which for hundreds of thousands of years savage man was making the discoveries upon which all civilization has ever since depended. The rest of the story was fairly well known to the older guides of man, except for our own Age of Surprises, which has upset so many settled calculations of the past. Or it would be better to say should and will upset them. For it is too soon for many people to perceive the great revisions of belief that this tremendous extension of man's history and his so very recent discoveries demand. We are not used to the notion that, could we trace our ancestry back, we should find it soon merging into that of illiterate savages and finally into that of wild animals. This assumption can, however, become the most clarifying, even the most cheering and comforting of any suggestion that has ever been made about man's origin and fate. It serves to wipe out a vast number of puzzles which have hitherto harassed those who sought to solve the riddles of human conduct and feeling. It greatly simplifies our attitude toward ourselves and others. While it sets up new problems it eliminates old ones. It should beget at once patience and toleration, and at the same time hope and emulation. It should fill us with wide-eyed wonder at the tragic struggle of mankind against ignorance and incapacity rather than with peevish despair over his failures. Let us now look at some of the strange new ideas that have come with the discovery that men were once wild animals and that what we call civilization in its more elaborate developments is a very recent thing in human history.

II

Not only is the whole human race derived originally from wild animals, but each boy and girl enters the world as a wild animal. Nothing in the way of civilization is inborn, as are the form and workings of our bodies. Everything that goes to make up civilization must be acquired anew in infancy and childhood, by each and all of us. Had we been born in a tribe of Australian aborigines we would have learned to talk and act as they do. We should have known nothing of reading and writing, and would have believed all the things told us and could not have helped it. If with the same capacities that we now exercise in making terms with the complexities which surround us today we had been born in China in the time of Confucius, or in Rome in the days of Augustus, we should have acted and believed as did those around us. Accordingly, we have little personal responsibility in regard to our ideas of right and wrong, of the proper and improper, because we had nothing to do with them. They were imposed upon us. The same is true of our religious convictions and conceptions of duties and obligations. Rarely do we come later to doubt in any comprehensive fashion what we are taught in childhood. Early beliefs seem self-evident and in the case of many people they are not seriously modified throughout life. We find ourselves often left with no other defense than that father or mother taught me thus and so and it seems a wretched form of treason even to listen to a questioner. Moral leaders like Dwight L. Moody, Anthony Comstock, William Jennings Bryan, Frances Willard, Clarence True Wilson, John S. Sumner, to cite a few conspicuous instances, never altered their childish notions about how to live and what to believe. They either left unread or cast aside all works that would have given them truer and more critical information about the Bible. Their strenuous careers were devoted to urging others to accept the ideas which they themselves happened to have been taught before they were twelve years old; and to making everyone stop doing the things which they had been told as children were naughty. All of them made a wide appeal because they found plenty of sympathizers, in the same plight as they.

The human offspring is at the start a sadly helpless and utterly dependent thing. It can get its food from the first, in the manner of a dog or calf, but months elapse before it can walk or talk. It fumbles with its blocks and toys and gradually learns to manage them, cultivating thereby a sense of shape, hardness, weight, and balance. Blocks will not roll, but balls will. The child's parents begin to tell him the things which they themselves learned as children. He is defenseless against the prejudices of his elders whether they be Hopi Indians or live on Park Avenue. A very charming book appeared a few years ago, called *The Mirror of Witches*, which shows how the people of New England brought up their children to attribute their pains and discomforts to bad persons who made "poppets," and by sticking pins in them afflicted those they disliked. The most learned clergymen and judges of the time had been taught the same ideas when children and continued to hold them their lives long. It seems rarely to occur to us that had we lived in Salem in 1692 we should inevitably have clung tenaciously to beliefs that seem to us now baseless and cruel. But we are still in the same plight. We have all been taught and continue to believe many things that would not bear reinspection. It has been my particular and conscious effort to revise my childish impressions, and now I find myself farther away from myself at twelve than at twelve I was removed from the famous Boston witchmonger, Cotton Mather. I could write out a long list of items which I have

rejected or come to accept since I was in the high school. And
yet in moods of depression I readily perceive all sorts of
childish fears and scruples cropping up. I never really got over
trying not to offend my mother, whom I never disobeyed, although I did plenty of things which she had not happened
to forbid but of which I suspected she would have disap-
proved. These personal reminiscences are introduced merely
to set the reader wondering about himself. My case must be
a common one, although rather exaggerated, by a perhaps unusual tendency to miscellaneous speculation and questioning.
It is hard, however, to believe that if I were now twelve
with the particular outfit of impressions and beliefs I at
present have, I could possibly alter them in so thoroughgoing
a fashion were I to live amidst the influences of the coming
fifty years. Is this merely another instance of the childish impression of finality or a plausible conjecture that during the
next fifty years mankind will be mainly engaged in growing
up to what has been discovered during the past half century?
This process will involve, no doubt, much increase of knowledge and many rectifications of the beliefs of those who have
taken the most pains in reaching them. At least the discovery
of man's animal origin, of the methods by which civilization
has been built up, including the ready impressionability of
childhood and the permanence of beliefs acquired when we
were inferiors and dependents will not be surrendered but
expanded and utilized to make education something far more
efficient than it could be when the mistakes of the past played
so great a part in its conception and methods.

III

Mind is considered man's chief glory and the instrument
which has enabled him to accomplish all the wonders of
civilization. He can reason as no other animal and so has
devised many religions and arts and institutions, built up
imposing systems of philosophy and theology, acquired knowledge of the world and its inhabitants and sought out many
inventions to feed, clothe, protect, adorn, and amuse himself
in ways unknown to his savage ancestors. Great and essential
is the mind! But how different are the conceptions of it which

are now being brought forward from those of the past. There is even a rumor that some investigators deny its existence altogether. This seems at first sight perfectly preposterous. Without a mind how is our rational conduct to be explained? There must surely be something in us that plans, wills, decides, that makes inferences from the past and conjectures in regard to the future, that is our constant guide in all we do. Only one who has lost his mind could be so absurd as to deny its existence. Have not the philosophers written long treatises on the mind? John Stuart Mill defines it as that "mysterious something which feels and thinks." And I suppose that this would appeal to most people as a good short statement.

The recent emphasis given to the study of animal behavior, coupled with the new assumption that men themselves were not long ago (from a geological standpoint) leading lives not so very different from the creatures nearest them in form and capacity must surely alter for us the opinions of our forefathers who had none of this new information. Again, the development of infants and children, who seem to show little signs of "mind" when they are born, suggests a new theory of thinking which makes it possible to dispense, as some believe, with that "mysterious something" which has hitherto been "mind" or "reason." It is very difficult to state this change of attitude in any short and clear way, but some little notion may be given of the trend of the more critical thinking of today.

Our thinking depends upon words, as will later be explained. Now it has always been possible to use words that did not correspond to things or experiences and to make sentences that sounded as if they meant something, yet did not. One of the signs of the times is that scientifically-minded people are becoming much more careful about the terms they use. Mephistopheles reminds the student in *Faust* that he will not get far in philosophy and theology if he does not learn to employ words that have no very clear significance; that it is far easier to use a word than to find a meaning for it. Francis Bacon complained that the medieval philosophers used a great many words, especially "essence" which was just a word not a thing. Modern critics are pointing out that almost all former philosophers dealt with many "concepts" which were purely imaginary. Plato, for example, refers to "The Good," "The True," and "The Beautiful." He seems to imply that they existed somewhere or in some way independently of things, acts, and thoughts which we find ourselves pronouncing "good," "true," and "beautiful." There was long and heated contention over this phase of the matter during the Middle Ages. Now various writers are beginning to wonder whether there is anything in the processes which each of us observes within us of thinking, remembering, imagining, reasoning, deciding, which makes it necessary to assume that there is a single agent or "mysterious something" that dwells within our bodies and performs all these difficult tasks, whether we call it mind, intelligence, will, or reason. We may say that our digestion is good or bad, but if we have any knowledge of physiology we mean no more than that a very intricate series of chemical processes and muscular actions takes place either smoothly or distressingly. We do not believe that there is a commander-in-chief looking on and giving directions or misdirections. Once men thought heat and cold were *entities* and that they might be mixed in different proportions, for this is what "temperature" originally meant. Now we know that the molecules merely change the rapidity of their movement and chemists have discovered the point where all molecular motion ceases and nothing can ever be colder than that. So heat and cold are not *things*, but just processes.

These illustrations will show why in recent attempts at clear thinking there is a tendency to beware of such words as the mind, reason, the will, and even consciousness and especially the recklessly-employed expression "the unconscious." All these look like imaginary agents rather than observable processes. We cannot do more than take note of how we and others behave; how we ourselves think and feel and how others tell us they think and feel. This is all the data available. And in trying to understand human behavior in this comprehensive sense it does not help, but heavily hampers, the investigator to try to bring in the mind, reason, or the will. He is afraid that if he does so he will drop into the old easy habit of substituting mere words for actual happenings.

Formerly it was customary to make the sharpest possible distinction between mind and body. And all sorts of efforts were made to bridge the gulf between them or explain how the mind, being immaterial and without substance, could direct and control the action of arms and legs, which are heavy material things. No one ever reached any satisfactory solution of this puzzle. It seemed easy to explain how, if a stone were thrown into a lake, it would make a splash, because matter could work upon matter. But how could the mind which was not made of matter cause your hand to reach for a stone and heave it into the water? It is one of the most astonishing results of recent thought that this hoary old question is getting answered, partly by dropping out old assumptions on which the philosophers worked, partly by new knowledge. It must be remembered that Christian teachers have almost always had a contempt for the body which perishes and a sublime conception of the importance of the soul which they believed to be eternal, destined to survive forever either in a state of ineffable bliss or indescribable torture. In dealing with the mind and with reason the philosophers always had this conception of the soul in the background. They also felt the body to be its transitory instrument. It was made of matter, and matter to them was dead, contemptible stuff in which the soul was imprisoned. The ascetics systematically maltreated their bodies as vile enemies ever dragging them into temptations. The flesh was a millstone hanging on the neck of the spirit. While philosophers were rarely ascetics, they could not but be deeply influenced by the religious doctrines which they accepted. They thought of matter as inert and they knew very little indeed of the vast stream of life which had been flowing down the ages and out of which man finally emerged.

No present-day chemist or physicist would think of matter as inert and impotent stuff. They know that it is filled with indescribable activity. It is on the go every instant, never by any possibility at rest. It keeps constantly rearranging itself into new designs each with its peculiar properties. The

chemists have learned to make substances which never existed before. They become creators who, owing to the still
unexhausted potentialities of atomic and molecular combinations, can make any number of lovely dyes and perfumes out
of black, malodorous coal tar.

As regards the human body, if one will but find out how
it is made and how it acts, it fills one with a veneration akin
to religious awe. The old ignorant talk about the body
indulged in by those who pride themselves on their spiritu-
ality seems downright blasphemy. There are at least fifteen
thousand different species of animals whose bodies consist of
one cell only, so small that you can rarely see much of their
form and ways without magnifying them from three hundred
to five hundred times their size. If they are the size of a fine
needle point, say a hundredth of an inch across, they can
with the microscope be made to appear as big as a mouse or
a rabbit. They all make a living by hunting or trapping, they
can evade danger, learn something by experience, have signs
of memory, adjust themselves to novel circumstances and
propagate their kind in many different ways according to
their nature. It would be well if some clergymen would
magnify the Lord by magnifying a stentor or lacrymaria. But
it is cheaper and easier to dismiss biologists as "materialists"
than to be God's playfellow. From the very first all living
things exhibit a certain awareness of surrounding objects; act
purposively in protecting themselves, in getting a livelihood
and in reproducing. The very little creatures of which we
have been speaking have no eyes, ears, or noses. They can
feel in their blindness and they have something corresponding to taste, for they will eject things which disturb them.
Yet we hardly think of them as having a mind or reason.
It is in their nature to behave as if they did. All that has
been recalled above it will be noted is the statement of facts
which anyone can observe who will take the trouble. They
are not quoted from some revered authority, nor are they
assumptions. They seem to be just plain facts. I have seen
this much myself.

Man's body has a history reaching back to one-celled
creatures. Each generation had to get enough to eat and

protect itself long enough to produce a succeeding generation. When man took on his present bodily form he had to
do the same things in order that you and I should be here
to consider how we came about. He had the foundation of
astounding viability or keep-going-ness before he exhibited
any evidence of what we call mind. Like a dog he could dodge
a falling tree without knowing anything as yet of the laws
of gravitation. He could climb a hill with no notion of
musculature. He could eat a banana without being able to
classify it botanically. He was so made, however, that he
could handle things more dexterously than any other animal
and so could judge of their weight, softness and hardness,
warmth and cold, form and texture, rigidity and pliability.
Apes' hands are not so well made for manipulation as man's,
and hoofs, paws, and claws are poor instruments for finding
out much. Man, too, had a better brain than any other
creature. He could make more use of what he found out.
This is an obscure matter indeed! The main point is to show
how it is possible to conceive of man starting with the ways
of an animal and gradually learning to make distinctions,
inferences, gain clearer memories, imagine more vividly,
imitate more consciously, and finally experiment and plan.
This means nothing less than that he was very gradually
getting a "mind," superior to that of any of his predecessors
and with promise of indefinite increase. Mental processes
are, in short, the chief elements in civilization and increase
along with man's other arts. They are not a "mysterious
something" implanted in every human being, but a slowly
developed awareness of things and the capacity to make more
and more discoveries and see how they can be used to better
human conditions. The current information and its application prevailing in any group of people is handed on ready
made to every child. *There can be indefinitely more "mind"
accumulated as time goes on, now that we have the trick.*
Never was the "mind" in general so good as it now is; it has
been vastly improved during the past fifty years, and there
seems nothing to prevent it from being vastly better fifty
years hence. Evidently the mind and body are not separate
things. The body antedated the human mind by hundreds

of millions of years and we may expect a great increase of wisdom when we get over the older notions of the mind being an independent entity aspiring to go its way regardless of the shrewd old organism which has proved its ability to manage living so long before the mind came into action. Man's new acquisition "mind," while it has enabled him to generate and develop civilization, has not the well-tried inerrancy of bodily processes and has consequently led to many sad mistakes.

IV

One of the most fundamental characteristics of mankind is his talking. Only very lately, however, has language begun to be understood and its origin is by no means so mysterious as it formerly seemed. Older writers were prone to define speech as a method of conveying ideas. They also set off words sharply from acts. It would appear, however, on more careful inspection that words and sentences are rarely and exceptionally employed primarily to impart ideas; and that they were in the beginning and have continued to be overt acts. They are part of human conduct, beginning with noises and cries such as many creatures beside man are accustomed to use without any apparent expression of an idea. And man's bark like the dog's can often be worse than his bite. A scornful taunt consisting of mere words may produce a bruise more painful and lasting than a kick. To be told to "get out" is as effective as having the door slammed in your face. A letter made of just words may function quite as poignantly as actual caresses or a spanking. Business is largely transacted by written promises. By just talking, clergymen, teachers, politicians, lawyers, and editors can make a living—for their words are as marketable as would be the apples they might grow or the shoes and stockings they might make. A recent writer has pointed out that among savages silence is an unfriendly act. When human beings meet they are expected to make noises of some kind, and the fewer ideas conveyed the better. Of course words are employed too to convey ideas and information, but very commonly they are gestures made with the vocal organs rather than the hands or shoulders. If we will but observe our own words and those we listen to or find written in books, newspapers, or on stock certificates, we can hardly fail to agree that words are acts intimately associated with all our other actions.

The sounds made by various birds and quadrupeds have been found to be practically associated with getting food, defending themselves, and the process of mating and rearing the young. Man can now make so many kinds of noises that there is every reason to guess that he was a great chatterer from the first. His exceptional powers of observation, experimentation, and his intricate brain cortex enabled him to discover new ways of using his vocal organs as he learned new ways of using his hands. As he made discriminations and distinctions he could reinforce his discoveries by making a peculiar sound, which led in time to the familiar process of creating names which could be used when the various objects or situations could not be pointed to or described by gesture. He began to be able to tell about things and each name accepted by the tribe served to set off some particular thing more clearly than hitherto from the gross mass of vague impressions. A name sharpened each object and act and thereby made thinking clearer. For example, when one learns the terms for the various parts of an automobile he is sure to understand their intercorrelation and functioning far better than he could possibly do if he just looked at it as a whole. So man's progress has come with making distinctions and salting them down with names, and this helped him to get more understanding and also to raise his untutored children to the degree of understanding prevailing in the tribe.

The infant, starting as a speechless little animal, first learns that vague noises bring relief when he is hungry or suffering from a loose safety pin. Before long, however, he shows a passion for naming things, accepting sometimes those suggested by his elders, sometimes preferring his own. Dr. Watson has often called attention to the fact that what we call thinking is just talking to ourselves. While there may be some reservations to be made, I believe that anyone who will watch himself will find that this is essentially true. Between each sentence as I am writing at this moment I find myself talking a little to myself, about what Wundt, Jesperson, Mrs. De Laguna, and John Watson have said about talking, and am asking various questions as to how much better we might get along with ourselves in controlling strings of disagreeable memories and apprehensions if we did but ask ourselves "why am I carrying on such a fool and fruitless conversation with myself? I should be infinitely bored if I had to listen to anyone else making such idiotic remarks."

I have learned to talk to myself in terms of the discoveries, or suggestions and guesses, if you will, sketched out above. It seems as if they were much nearer the actual happenings in the history of mankind than those taught me when I was a boy. Many old problems disappear, lifted off as was Christian's pack. New perplexities take their place, but they are real rather than imaginary. This chapter is not a formal argument for the new ways of viewing ourselves, but a scant statement of the notion of man's nature and origin which I suspect will gradually prevail. We are in a way satiated with the mechanical miracles of the last seventy-five years and have come to expect new ones of the same sort. We have now to recognize that a scientific study of our own nature in the light of the past and present may open up a second period of miracles which will make us far less ashamed of man's doings than we find ourselves today.

LAYING THE GROUNDWORK

Preparation for Reading

1. Does your concept of civilization depend upon the kind of group into which you were born? Justify your answer.
2. How do you suppose speech originated? How does a child learn to attach meanings to words?
3. Are children born with a sense of right or wrong? If not, how do they acquire their views of right and wrong?

Vocabulary Building

1. Before reading the selection, find the meanings and pronunciations of the following words: *unique, genealogy, reminiscences, entities, ascetics, stentor, lacrymaria, viability, pliability.*

2. Explain the use of the Greek combining forms *anthropo, bio, psycho,* and *logy,* and of the suffix *ist* in the following words: *anthropologist, biologist, psychologist.*
3. What are the meanings of the following literary references: Mephistopheles, in *Faust,* and Christian's pack?
4. Explain the use of the Greek combining form *philo* in these words: *philosophy, philanthropy, philharmonic, philology, philately.*
5. What is the meaning of the prefix *mal* in *malodorous*? Give other words with the same prefix.
6. As you read, check the meaning of each of the following words in the context and its pronunciation: *panorama, aggregate, incredible, stupendous, artificers, emulation, tenaciously, plausible, rectifications, preposterous, intricate, ineffable, inert, impotent, propagate, overt, poignantly, cortex, satiated.*

APPRAISING THE RESULTS

1. What is the value of knowing the long course of human history in understanding human behavior?
2. Why does Robinson say that the child enters the world "a wild animal"?
3. What are some beliefs generally accepted today about the nature of man which would not have been accepted by many, if any, 150 years ago?
4. Why do we welcome a change in our material life (such as a change from candle to kerosene, to gas, to electricity), but question a change in political, economic, or social life?
5. Does tolerance mean that one should accept all beliefs and practices as equally good?
6. As man looks at the long struggle through which the race has passed, why should he be hopeful rather than despondent?

SELECTING THE THEME SUBJECT

1. Select one of the subjects suggested by the questions and develop your opinions about it. Try to find out what *facts* you have for your belief, or whether you are prejudiced.
2. Describe in detail some psychological experiment of which you have heard or in which you have taken part.
3. Present the question of racial or national prejudice as you have observed it in school, in the community, in social rela-

tions, in economic or political activities; i.e., Negro, Japanese, Mexican, Jew.

4. Write a process theme showing: How We Learn; How We Remember; How to Train a Puppy; How to Improve One's Study Habits; How National Prejudices Are Played Upon in Spreading Propaganda.

5. What are some of the beliefs which you have held in the past and which you now reject? What are some of the beliefs you are now wondering about? Organize your replies in a paper.

THE DIFFUSION OF CULTURAL TRAITS[1]

Franz Boas

THE STUDY OF THE TYPES OF CULTURES FOUND THE WORLD OVER GIVES THE IMPRESSION OF AN ENORMOUS DIVERSITY OF FORMS. The differences are so great that we may be inclined to think that every one of these cultures developed quite independently and that the peculiar genius of the people has found expression in the forms under which they live. This impression is strengthened by the fact that the people themselves differ in appearance. The African Negro, the Australian, the Siberian native, the people of the Pacific Islands, each have their own peculiar bodily build and their own peculiar culture.

Added to this is the observation that the people constituting every one of these societies consider themselves as independent units, specifically distinct from all their neighbors. This finds its strongest expression in the fact that many primitive people designate themselves as human beings, while all their neighbors are designated by specific names in the same way as animals are designated by names. Thus the Eskimos call themselves human beings, the Indians whom they know in some regions only by hearsay are considered as dog-like animals, and the white people with whom they came into contact in later times are considered as descended from dogs. The specific differences are keenly felt, while the similarities are neglected.

The objective study of cultures and of types of man shows that notwithstanding all these apparently fundamental differences cultural strains have passed from one people to the

[1] From *Social Research*, September, 1937. By permission of the author and of the publisher.

other, that no culture can be assumed to be self-developed and no type to be pure, unmixed with foreign strains.

This can be most easily shown by a study of the distribution of languages. The migrations of primitive people in early times covered whole continents. A few examples will suffice. A certain American language is spoken in the vast area extending from the Yukon to Hudson Bay; south of this area live people speaking entirely different languages, but dialects of the same language which is spoken in the north reappear locally in Oregon and California and in the vast territory north and south of the Rio Grande. This can be understood only on the assumption that at one time these people migrated over this immense area. In southern Brazil the Carib language is spoken. It reappears locally north of the Amazon River and on the West Indian Islands. The Bantu languages spoken in Africa cover the whole district from south of the Sahara, southward almost to the extreme southern end of Africa. The language of the Malay, which is spoken in southeastern Asia, found its way eastward to all the islands of the Pacific Ocean and is also spoken by the inhabitants of part of Madagascar.

These inferences based on similarities of languages can also be proved by historical migrations. The great Arab migration, which started in Arabia and at the time of its greatest extent covered the whole of north Africa and part of Spain, and which also influenced all the languages of the Near East, occurred after Mohammed's time. We know that the so-called Aryans invaded India at a very early time. The Greeks migrated from the north into what later became Greece. The Celts of western Europe migrated eastward as far as Asia Minor. The Teutonic migrations destroyed the Roman Empire, and later on the great Turkish migrations swept over a large part of eastern Europe as well as over a large part of Siberia. Thus we actually see mankind on the move since the very earliest times. The whole settlement of America occurred within a comparatively short period. Evidently the American aborigines lived on the continent not earlier than the beginning of the last warm period before the last ice age, coming presumably over the land bridge which is now Bering

Sea, and spreading from there as far as the extreme southern part of South America.

It is not only language that was carried by migrations all over the world; it is also easy to show that inventions and ideas were carried from one area to another, partly by migration, partly by cultural contact. One of the most striking examples is found in the distribution of folk tales. The European folk tale of the couple that escaped a pursuing monster by throwing backwards a number of objects which were transformed into obstacles is well known all over Europe. A comb thrown down becomes an impenetrable thicket, a whetstone an insurmountable mountain, a small amount of oil becomes an extensive lake, all of which detain the pursuer. This complicated story containing all the elements mentioned is found not only all over Europe but all over the Asiatic continent and also in northwestern America reaching as far as California, and eastward even in Greenland and Nova Scotia. In more recent times we find that the most isolated tribes of South America tell tales which were carried by Negro slaves to the coast of Brazil.

Equally striking are certain similarities in political organization characteristic of the Old World but entirely absent in America and other outlying regions. The whole political organization of Africa shows a high development of administration through kings and their ministers in charge of war, judicial procedure and so on—analogous to the ancient organization of European states. Judicial procedure by means of courts taking evidence, administering the oath and finally ascertaining the truth by ordeal is found in a vast part of the Old World, while it is entirely foreign to people that had never been in contact with the Old World.

Perhaps still more convincing is the distribution of agriculture. Wheat and barley are two characteristic plants on which early agriculture is based all over the temperate zone of the Old World, while rice is characteristic of another extended area. The home of the wild plants from which wheat and barley are derived must be looked for somewhere in western Asia, from where they spread from tribe to tribe. In the same way early American agriculture is based on the use of Indian corn which was developed from a native plant of the western highlands of Mexico, from where it spread southward as far as the Argentine republic and northward to the Great Lakes.

Thus a detailed study of cultural traits proves beyond cavil that there is not a single people in the primitive world that has developed its culture independently.

Much of the diffusion must have been accompanied by actual intermingling of tribes. The people speaking the language of the Yukon River, to whom we referred before and who live now on the Rio Grande, differ in type from the people of the north but are similar in appearance to their neighbors who speak an unrelated language. This would not have happened if they had not intermingled with them at the same time that they adopted many important traits of their culture. In South Africa the intermingling of types is perhaps not equally clear but another striking feature of mutual influence may be seen in a linguistic change. The Bushmen of southern Africa have a peculiarity of speech which does not occur in any other part of the world. They produce sounds not by breathing out but by sucking in. This habit, which is considered an ancient African trait, is found in weak traits on the Gold Coast in equatorial West Africa, but only one of the Bantu tribes, who are neighbors of the Bushmen, have adopted the habit of producing strong sounds by sucking in, as the Bushmen do.

If we want to understand the way in which these fundamental modifications of cultures occur we have to remember that the conditions of contact among primitive tribes are very different from what has occurred in more modern times. Most primitive tribes are small; sometimes the whole number of individuals may not be more than a few hundred. Wars between neighboring groups are common and almost everywhere it is customary for the men to be killed, while the women are taken along as captives. These become the mothers of the following generation, so that it may happen that a large number of children grow up bilinguals, with the cultural habits of the mothers having a far-reaching influence upon the behavior of the children.

The study of distribution of cultural traits brings out one very characteristic feature: the details of the culture may be similar among different tribes but the general structure will retain fundamental differences. To give an example, one of the most important ceremonials of our North American Indians is the Sun Dance, an elaborate ceremonial the details of which are widespread over our western plains. The meaning of the ceremonial is quite different in the different areas and it is fitted into the fundamental religious ideas of each tribe. We can perhaps best understand these differences when we consider our own culture. All over Europe, and wherever the white race has gone, the fundamental traits are the same; inventions, religion, fundamental traits of state organization are alike. And nevertheless there are decided national patterns which allow us to differentiate between the cultural life of different areas as well as of different times.

It is interesting to follow the processes of acculturation. Evidently in many cases it is due to war. We have already mentioned the importance of the introduction of foreign women. In many cases conquest leads to the establishment of stratified societies of a class of masters to whom the native population becomes subject. This has been the case in the history of Europe as well as in the history of Africa. In Africa we see that pastoral people conquered agricultural communities and became the nobility to whom the natives became subjects. Such conquests led to economic adjustments, and in many traits the conquerors adopted the customs of the old population while these in turn adopted the traits of the invaders. It must not be assumed that every stratified society originated in this manner, because sometimes internal conditions, family privileges and so on have led to similar results. In other cases economic and social advantages favored the adoption of foreign customs. This was obviously the case in the spread of agriculture both in the Old World and in America. In a similar way new religious ideas which strengthen the emotional energy of the people and awaken them from indifferent attitudes have had a powerful influence in modifying cultural life.

One of the many remarkable changes of culture due to an

introduction of foreign invention is the change all over North America which occurred with the introduction of the horse. After the introduction of the horse the pursuit of the buffalo became easier and some of the tribes which had been hunting the buffalo on foot were now able to roam over a wider area and gave up agriculture almost entirely, becoming more or less nomadic hunters. Notwithstanding the readiness with which foreign cultural traits are adopted we may also observe in many cases a strong resistance to changes of life. This occurs particularly when new ideas cannot be fitted into the general cultural habits of the people. As an instance may be mentioned the difficulty of adjusting native tribes to the fundamental idea of capitalism. Very rarely do we find among primitive people that wealth can be used to produce more wealth by utilizing the power it may give over other members of the community. Wealth is of value only in so far as it enables the owner to improve his social standing by liberality, or by making a show with his property. In this lies one of the reasons which make it so difficult to assimilate the American Indians, to whom the idea of capital as producing wealth is entirely foreign.

In modern society the conditions favorable to cultural contact are ever so much greater than those existing in primitive society. First of all, the numbers of individuals constituting each unit are infinitely larger than those occurring in primitive society, and within each group diffusion occurs with the greatest rapidity. Our schools, the commercial exploitation of inventions, are of such a character that new ideas and new objects are distributed with incredible rapidity. Most of these extend beyond national boundaries because international trade and international communication make it impossible for any idea to be confined to a single nation. On the other hand general, structural attitudes find much greater resistance than in the small tribes because the inertia of the enormous masses of the population is much greater than that of a small tribal group. It is less difficult to introduce a new idea into the well established structure of a small group than to break down the habits of thought of millions.

We are too much inclined to consider the development of

civilization in Europe as an achievement of Europe alone, and to assume that Europe has always been the giver, not the recipient of new ideas. We are likely to forget that in antiquity the exchange of inventions and ideas extended from China all over the continent to Europe, and that the indirect contact between the Far East and Europe contributed much to the development of European civilization. We are likely to forget the immense service that Arab scientists did to Europe in reëstablishing contact with Greek thought. Later on, when contact with the Far East was interrupted by the Turkish invasion of eastern Europe and the development of the Mongolian empire, the need for contact with the east led to maritime discoveries, and the discovery of America brought inventions to Europe which modified life in many parts of the Old World. I need only mention the introduction of Indian corn, which in an incredibly short time found its way to all parts of the Old World that were adapted to its cultivation, or the use of tobacco, which has reached all parts of the inhabitable world.

Peculiar types of cultural assimilation developed with colonization. Greek colonies sprang up on all the shores of the Mediterranean and hand in hand with them went a strong influence of Greek culture upon the surrounding people. Still more effective was Roman colonization, which not only carried the habits of Roman life into outlying provinces but led to Latin becoming the language of these countries, so that the languages of what is now Spain, of France, of what is now Roumania disappeared and provincial Latin took their place. During the Middle Ages a similar process occurred in central Europe when German colonists reoccupied the former habitat of German tribes which had been filled by Slavic groups. The process that occurred there may still be observed in Mexico, where Spaniards are still colonizing in Indian territory and where we see the Indian languages gradually giving way to Spanish. There is little doubt that the process of assimilation which occurred in Greek and Roman colonization and later on in Germany was of the same type. In Mexico we see the Spaniards settling in small towns. A hybrid population develops with fair rapidity and the town as a trade center attracts the Indians. Intercourse is first by means of poorly developed Spanish which is gradually adopted by a large part of the native population. Gradually the influence of the town increases in importance, with the final result that the native language disappears and the natives and the Spaniards form a single community. According to the character of the migrating population there would of course be differences in the resultant social structure. When the colonists are poor and uneducated the native population and the colonists may merge into a single community. When the colonists are supported by a central power they may become the masters of the territory and a stratified society results.

It is interesting to compare with this the conditions of immigration into countries which are already more or less settled. We may observe this in our own country as well as in South America, Australia, or South Africa. The immigrants who arrive are drawn from many different countries and form always a minority in a larger and economically stronger group, so that their only hope of success in the new country is based on a gradual assimilation. It is not only economic stress, however, which brings about the assimilation of the new colonists to the new environment but also the strong social influence of the majority among whom they live. An interesting example of this kind was observed about thirty years ago in a New York school in a part of the city which had been inhabited by an Irish population then being replaced by Italians. The school had been for some time Irish, with a sprinkling of Italian children. The Italian children had learned an Irish pronunciation of English, and even when they increased to about ninety per cent of all the children they all spoke English with an Irish accent. By the pressure of the majority all immigrants become assimilated, no matter what nationality they belong to, and their own influence is comparatively slight.

It is of considerable practical interest for us to understand what happens in the process of assimilation, how far old habits are stable and how far they are influenced by their new environment. A number of studies made on American immigrants throw light on this question. It has repeatedly been shown that the physical development of children of immigrants differs from that of their parents. During the last century the stature of Americans and also of Europeans has increased noticeably, but the immigrants who came here during the last seventy years have always belonged to the same economic level and their stature has remained quite stable. Their children, however, follow the general increase which is found in the American population. Furthermore, the form of the body of immigrants' children undergoes certain changes, and though the cause is still obscure the result is that in bodily form they differ from their parents. This does not mean that they tend to approach a general American type, but merely that the new environment and new mode of life influence the bodily build.

The changes in their behavior are much more noticeable. It is not only that they adopt American tastes and language, a process which results from contact between children of many nationalities in school, but their motor habits also change from foreign types to what we might call an American type. The Italians and the Jews accompany speech with characteristic gestures. The Italian describes what he has to say with a wide sweep of motions, while the Jew follows his line of thought with short, rather jerky movements. The assimilated Italians and Jews substitute for these movements the descriptive and emphatic motions which are characteristic of American habits, or when they belong to more sophisticated classes tend to suppress all gestures. Statistics also show that the immigrant becomes adjusted very quickly to American social habits. This becomes particularly striking in criminal statistics. On the whole, crimes against property among the immigrants from Europe are comparatively rare, while they are exceedingly common in our American city population. But the distribution of crime in the second generation, that is, among the descendants of immigrants, is quite similar to that found in the American population of native parentage.

All this is merely an expression of the fact that when an individual is exposed to a new environment his descent is almost irrelevant when compared to the stress to which he is exposed in his new mode of life.

A review of all the data which have been summarized here altogether too briefly shows that the assumption that any culture is autonomous, uninfluenced from outside sources, or that each type of man produces a culture which is an expression of the biological make-up of the race to which he belongs, is quite untenable. We see everywhere types of culture which develop historically under the impact of multifarious influences that come from neighboring people or those living far away.

LAYING THE GROUNDWORK

Preparation for Reading

1. Define culture. Then read the definitions in the dictionary.
2. What attitude do most people take when comparing the relative merits of their customs with those of other peoples?
3. In the sixteenth century the English language was not spoken to any great extent outside of the British Isles. Where is it spoken today, and how do you account for its spread?
4. What are some of the agencies which spread inventions, ideas, and customs from one part of the world to another?

Vocabulary Building

1. Before you read, find the derivations, the meanings, and the pronunciations of these words: *aborigines, analogous, linguistics, nomadic, exploitation, inertia, autonomous, (un)tenable, multifarious.*
2. Find the common derivation of *sophisticated, sophomore,* and *sophistry.* Compare their meanings.
3. What does the word *provincialism* mean when used in connection with language? Relate this meaning to the meaning of *provincial.*
4. Explain the meaning of these words and phrases as they are used in the selection: *proved beyond cavil; acculturation; a stratified society.*

APPRAISING THE RESULTS

1. This selection exemplifies one way of presenting a thesis which the writer knows runs counter to common opinion. Number the paragraphs to facilitate your analysis, and then find the answers to the following questions: (a) What is the function of paragraphs 1 and 2? of paragraphs 3, 9, and 21? (b) What evidence is presented in each paragraph from 4 to 8, inclusive, to support the statement made in paragraph 3? (c) How do paragraphs 10, 11, 12, and 13 each help to establish the claim that cultures diffuse? (d) In paragraphs 14 and 15, what forces making for the acceptance of change, and what forces making for rejecting change, are cited? (e) What common misconception is corrected in paragraph 16? What is the thought relation between the two sentences in the final paragraph?

2. Note how much of the development depends upon examples.

3. How does a knowledge of cultural traits of other peoples, and of the cultural debt which each people owes to other peoples, make one more tolerant in his racial and national attitudes?

SELECTING THE THEME SUBJECT

1. Analyze your feelings toward foreigners. Try to discover whether you are expressing an emotional attitude or a rational judgment.

2. The spread of cultures has meant at times the spread of evils, such as diseases and insect pests. Write a paper explaining how one of these evils spread, and what steps have been taken to combat it.

3. Write a paper explaining the way in which American styles are influenced by a current interest in a particular foreign country.

4. Explain why we are slow in making some desirable social, economic, or political change. For example, show why we have not yet adopted the Child Labor Amendment.

5. Describe the cultural pattern of some national or racial group in your community.

RACE OR PLACE?[1]

Malcolm H. Bissell

"THE NORDICS HAVE TRULY BEEN A GREAT RACE." WITH THIS STATEMENT FEW WILL DISAGREE. WHEN, HOWEVER, IT IS claimed that the Nordics have been the greatest race of all time, and that all the most advanced civilizations have been due solely to this super-race of blond giants, it is time to restrain our imaginations.

Such extravagant statements, especially when made in the name of science, stand as an ever-needed warning of the tendency of human emotions to run away with reason and common-sense. We believe them, not because of any convincing array of scientific evidence, but because we want to believe them—that is, if we fancy we are Nordics ourselves. Having once convinced ourselves of the innate superiority of our own race (or religion, or country, or party), we can easily find "evidence" to support our conviction. The process is known as "rationalizing," and is one of the most universal of all human traits; even scientists are prone to fall victims to it unless they are constantly on guard against it. It is all the more insidious and dangerous because it is largely unconscious.

There is nothing new in the gospel of Nordic superiority. It is, in fact, only a 19th Century phase of the age-old doctrine of the divine right of certain groups or classes of men to be masters and exploiters of others. Daniel Defoe, the author of *Robinson Crusoe*, felt called upon to ridicule the racial arrogance of his own people in 1701, and many of the greatest scholars of all nations have repeatedly exposed the

[1] From *The Scientific American*, December, 1933. Reprinted by permission of the author and of the publisher.

flimsiness of the claims of the ultra-dogmatic race exalters. Yet so powerful is the force of human emotions and passions, and so frail the voice of calm reason, that the doctrine of racial divine right constantly reasserts itself, and ever and again becomes an incentive and a justification for intolerance, hatred, and oppression. To-day we are once more witnessing the demonstration of this fact.

The Nordic doctrine is an offshoot of Aryanism (indeed the terms "Nordic" and "Aryan" are often used interchangeably by the popular expounders of race supremacy), the chief exponent of which was Count Joseph Arthur de Gobineau, a French aristocrat who died in 1882. Gobineau claimed that one race alone, the Aryans, has been the creator and sustainer of all that is good and great in civilization. The idea of an Aryan race was based on the discoveries of similarities in the languages of the Indo-European group, which led to the theory that all these languages were derived from a common stem, the Aryan language. This, it should be emphasized, is a thoroughly scientific theory, based on indisputable evidence. But Gobineau and his disciples assumed that the existence of an Aryan language implies also the existence of an Aryan race.

Having created this mythical race, they attributed to it all virtue and excellence, and saw in it the source of every great civilization of antiquity and of modern times. The Nordics were represented as descendants of the original Aryans who settled in northern Europe, and from whom in turn came the Teutonic and Anglo-Saxon peoples. But, in spite of all efforts, no one has ever been able to produce the slightest bit of real evidence that any such race as the Aryans ever existed. There is no necessary relation between language and race, and the very use of the term "Aryan" in a racial sense—as the Germans are using it to-day—has no justification whatever.

As to the Nordics, their origin is not only unknown, but—though this is a point discreetly avoided by the glorifiers of the "yellow haired giants"—it is by no means certain that they represent a pure racial strain.

Whatever their origin, the Nordics have certainly been a

vigorous people, and infusions of their blood have undoubtedly contributed much to the progress of central and southern Europe. The same, however, can be said of various other races. The fusion of two or more different stocks, provided they are vigorous and of good quality, usually produces offspring of marked ability and vitality, which very often is superior to any of its progenitors. The Nordic need therefore make no apologies even if he is the descendant of Asiatic, negroid, and Mediterranean peoples. He in turn has contributed many elements of strength to other peoples, and there is no ground whatever for the assertion that the mixture has always been a eugenic catastrophe. The contrary is far more likely to be true, and we are quite justified in saying that the fusion, rather than the Nordic, has been the important factor.

In the present state of our knowledge it is impossible to make a valid claim of inherent superiority for any racial group whatever. We do not know whether such inherent differences exist between races, because we have not yet been able to devise any way of measuring them. Much has been made of certain so-called "intelligence tests," but it has been repeatedly shown that these do not measure intelligence apart from cultural and environmental factors.

Nevertheless, the legend of Nordic superiority persists. We are told that the glory of Greece was due solely to the invasion of Nordic tribes, that Rome was great and powerful so long—and only so long—as she kept her Nordic blood pure, that the rise of Spain is to be attributed to the blood of Nordic Visigoths and her decline to its dilution, that the Renaissance was a purely Nordic phenomenon, and so on.

Leaving aside for the moment other considerations, let us examine the fundamental element in all these claims. To what extent is the statement justified that "the Greeks, Romans, and a few others were at the time of their greatness true Nordics"? It is obviously not an easy matter to determine the racial composition of peoples who lived in long past centuries. Of one thing alone we may be fairly certain—that with the countless wars, migrations, and invasions of prehistoric and early historic times, it is very unlikely that many peoples of unmixed blood existed in Europe during the Greek and Roman era. Statements regarding the pure Nordic composition of such peoples as the Sabines, the Etruscans, and even the Greeks and Romans themselves rest mostly on the "will to believe" of the race dogmatists and are certainly not supported by such anthropological evidence as is available. The Spartans, for example, who have been hailed as typical Nordics, are classed as Alpines by Dixon. The Etruscans, again, are blithely asserted to have been pure Nordics; but of these very people Hertz, the author of *Race and Civilization*, says: "Only one fact seems established beyond all doubt, namely, that they were *not* Indo-Germans nor Nordics."

There is little or no real evidence that either the Greeks or the Romans were pure Nordics, or even dominantly Nordic, at any time. If some Greek gods are represented as blond, this is not true of the majority, and certainly not of the major deities. Zeus and Hera, the greatest of all, are referred to as dark-haired in the Iliad, and Poseidon is called "black-curled" in both the Iliad and the Odyssey. The fact that the Greeks found something strange in the blondness of the Scythians, Gauls, and Teutons indicates that Nordic features were not common among them.

But it is not necessary to resort to elaborate researches to show the absurdity of most of the claims of the Nordic enthusiasts. They damn themselves by their own contradictions. The Renaissance, for example, which is hailed by German race dogmatists as the result of a Teutonic (Nordic) invigoration of decadent Italy, is denounced by Gobineau, the high priest of Teutonism, as the triumph of anti-Teutonic forces. Scores of similar contradictions from the writing of the Nordic glorifiers might be quoted.

While it would be foolish to deny the significance of race in the evolution of nations and civilizations, it is extremely difficult to separate the racial factor from others that are equally or more important. But it is characteristic of the race dogmatists to ignore completely all these other factors. To attribute the greatness of Spain solely to an infusion of Nordic blood, and her decline to the submergence of the

Nordic element by other races, without considering the enormously significant historical and geographic factors involved, is, to say the least, highly unscientific. And, if the Nordics are the exclusive bringers of civilization and progress, how can we account for the fact that for centuries during the Middle Ages the Moorish civilization in Spain—which can hardly be attributed to Nordic influences—was by far the most advanced and enlightened in all Europe?

It is comparatively easy to reduce the extravagant claims of the Nordic fanatics to absurdity, but it is far less easy to find a definite and satisfactory explanation for the rise and decline of civilizations and nations. The problem is highly complex and perhaps will always defy solution. One fact in particular, which seems to have been strangely overlooked by the Nordic boosters, should serve to make us cautious in accepting fantastic claims as to the all-powerful effect of race. For many centuries northern Europe has been inhabited by a population overwhelmingly Nordic. Yet until the last few hundred years it has been the most backward part of the continent. No civilization ever originated there; nor have the Nordics ever developed any civilization of their own. Were these blond giants incapable of creating one?

At any rate, civilization began in more southerly climes inhabited by other races. India, Mesopotamia, Egypt, Crete, the eastern Mediterranean—these were the earliest centers. As history progressed, the focus of power and culture shifted from the eastern Mediterranean or Aegean region to the central and western Mediterranean, and then to the countries bordering the North Sea and the Atlantic. Not until this stage was reached did the Nordic peoples of northern Europe come to play a conspicuous part in world history. If race is the one and all-powerful factor in civilization, why did these superior Nordics remain untutored barbarians while less gifted races were inventing the alphabet, building empires and carrying on far-flung trade? Or, if it was merely the timid stay-at-homes who remained in the northern homeland, why did these same dregs of the "Great Race" suddenly rise to world power and leadership? Our Nordic boosters cannot have their cake and eat it too. The racial composition of the British Isles has changed very little since the 12th Century. At the beginning of the 16th Century Britain was a small and relatively insignificant island kingdom; 200 years later she was a great world power. How can we possibly explain this change in terms of race?

These examples show clearly how important geographic and historical factors may be in determining the destiny of nations. The mere fact that the British Isles were on the outer edge of the world, remote from the main currents of trade and culture, prevented them from attaining major importance in world affairs, *so long as western civilization focused on the Mediterranean Sea.* But, with the discovery of America and the beginning of the Atlantic era, these islands were suddenly thrust to the center of the stage, as it were; their location on the eastern edge of the ocean, facing the New World, gave them advantages they had not previously possessed, and the rise of Britain to leadership followed speedily. Italy, which had previously held the strategic position in Europe by reason of her location in the center of the Mediterranean and her control of the overland trade with the East, now found herself shoved off to one side. The discovery of the sea route to India, which took place at about the same time, still further decreased the significance of the Mediterranean. The commercial importance of the Italian cities, and consequently their wealth and power and prestige, rapidly declined. Clearly we cannot attribute this decline solely to racial factors!

New discoveries and inventions brought still other geographic elements into play. The steam engine and the industrial era which it inaugurated caused profound political as well as social and economic changes. During the last 200 years world dominance has been written more and more in terms of horsepower. And horsepower means primarily coal and iron. To ignore these two foundation stones of industrial supremacy and speak only of Nordic blood is to take leave of common-sense. To what extent the British Empire and the position of the United States in world affairs have been built on coal resources is perhaps not possible to state, but we may be certain that had there been no vast stores of underground

fuel buried in the rocks of Britain and America, the history of the last two centuries must have been very different.

The life story of civilization, like that of the individual, is made up of the interplay of hereditary and environmental factors. The geographer is profoundly impressed with the importance of the environmental elements. We have mentioned only a few of these; there remain many others, the effects of which are equally striking. Whether or not these environmental factors are of greater importance than all others in determining what men do, is a moot question. But there is no doubt that they favor or handicap him to a very great degree, and to some extent at least, set limits beyond which he cannot go. Civilization is a rare product, developed only a few times and at a few places on earth. In every case it has necessarily been an adaptation to the environment that gave it birth. We cannot, therefore, fairly compare the accomplishments of different peoples or different civilizations without at the same time comparing their opportunities. Least of all can we categorically deny the *ability* of a people to achieve, because under a given set of conditions they failed to accomplish what other peoples have accomplished under different conditions. The Mayas of Central America and Yucatan built a great civilization. To class them as an inferior race, whose capacity for progress was definitely limited, because they did not equal the achievement of the Greeks, is unwarranted. The Mayas labored under two very severe handicaps; they had no beasts of burden and no iron. What would the Greeks have done without horses or cattle or iron? They inherited all these from other peoples. The environment of the Mayas provided no such advantages, and yet in some respects they surpassed the Greeks!

Such comparisons are of course of no value. They tell us nothing of relative capacities. We do not know the causes of the decline of the Maya civilization and we have no right to assign it arbitrarily to limitations of race. Competent students find many other possibilities; Huntington, for example, thinks it was largely due to climatic changes. Indeed this same author finds that climate has everywhere been a far more potent factor than race in the evolution of civilization, and it must be admitted that the evidence he adduces in support of this claim is much more convincing than that of the Nordic boosters.

Thus, perhaps, it is not race but *place* that counts most. Relief, climate, soils, plants and animals and minerals, all play their part in the working out of human history. We can hardly regard it as pure coincidence that the region bordering the North Sea and the western North Atlantic, which contains seven tenths of the world's coal and nine tenths of its iron, and includes the areas of most stimulating climate, also has dominated world history for the past 200 years. We do not doubt the importance of race; but nature has more than one way of loading the dice!

LAYING THE GROUNDWORK

Preparation for Reading

1. Check the following terms plus or minus according to whether you have a strong feeling of liking or dislike: Scotch ——, Chinese ——, Jews ——, Japanese ——, Irish ——, French ——, Turks ——, Mexicans ——, English ——, Czechs ——, Swedes ——, Russians ——, Spanish ——, Germans ——, Italians ——, Norwegians ——, Slovaks ——, Americans ——, Hindus —— Dutch ——, Indians ——. Try to account for your feeling.

2. Does the possession of a common language necessarily mean a common race? Illustrate your answer by reference to the United States.

Vocabulary Building

1. Before reading the selection, identify the following: *Daniel Defoe, Sabines, Etruscans, Iliad, Odyssey.*

2. Check also the meanings and pronunciations of these words: *insidious, exploiters, progenitors, eugenic, anthropologist, dogmatists, prestige, categorically.*

3. What is the derivation of the word *Renaissance*? Why is this term applied to the cultural upsurge of the fourteenth to sixteenth centuries?

4. Show how the following groups of words are related in derivation and meaning: *innate, natal,* and *nature; load the dice* and *the die is cast; fanatic* and *fan* (baseball); *inaugurate* and

a Roman *augur*; *moot* question and *moot* court; *gospel* and *gossip*.

APPRAISING THE RESULTS

1. This selection is an interesting example of logic. Careful study of the procedure it exemplifies should teach you something of the method of presenting a controversial subject in a logical way. Note that the development is concerned with two questions: is the doctrine of Nordic superiority tenable; and if it is not, is there any other theory which can be advanced to explain the development of civilizations?

2. Analyze the selection. The following steps may be used as a guide: (a) Why is the distinction drawn between *great* and *greatest* in the first paragraph? (b) Why does the author remind the reader, in the second paragraph, of the insidious danger of rationalizing? (c) What is the purpose of the third paragraph? (d) Trace the line of argument by which Bissell refutes the claims of Nordic superiority, and if you find any weak links in the chain, indicate the nature of the weakness. (e) Then trace the line of argument used to establish a substitute theory.

3. Defend or attack each of the following statements on the basis of the knowledge you have gained through reading the selection: (a) Immigrants from northern Europe are superior to those from southern Europe. (b) The white race is inherently superior to the black race. (c) Actual achievement is a true index of *ability* to achieve. (d) That Americans are a superior people is proved by the fact that the United States is the greatest country in the world. (e) That men have greater creative powers than women is shown by the larger number of men who have been famous artists and writers. (f) A variety of races have contributed to the cultural advance of the United States. (g) There is no evidence that dangerous and fallacious racial and national hatreds exist in the world today.

SELECTING THE THEME SUBJECT

Write a paper developing one of the subjects listed above.

PART TWO

The Conquest of Earth

Using and Abusing the Land

LAND OF PLENTY[1]
Rexford Guy Tugwell

THE CLASSICAL EMPIRES SEEM TO HAVE VIOLATED THE AXIOM THAT ACTIVITIES OTHER THAN AGRICULTURE CANNOT BE DEVELoped until there is a surplus of food. Farming then had advanced so little over its earliest primitive methods that adequate sustenance could be insured only by systems of exaction. The rural population, impoverished and often enslaved, frequently revolted; and even in periods of comparative quiet, there existed no such stable peasantry as later nations had. Only in the last few centuries have workers in the fields and vineyards gradually become free; and only in present years have they attained any considerable economic dignity.

In this, the people of primitive times were probably better off than were those in what we like to call the "civilizations" of Egypt or Greece. For primitive people can hardly have suffered more than did the early slaves; or, for that matter, than the medieval serfs, or even the peasants of the seventeenth century. Anthropologists used to be fond of correlating types of culture, such as "patriarchal," "matriarchal," and the like, with contemporary systems of land cultivation. Later writers are more sceptical of these grand generalizations; but there is an obvious connection between a nomadic, or even a pastoral, agriculture and the development of such a patriarchy as existed among the Hebrew tribes, just as there is a similar show of reason for matriarchy among the settled, village-living Indians of the southwestern United States. And an impoverished and servile food-producing class

[1] From *Current History*, February, 1938. Reprinted by permission of the author and of the publisher.

71

goes far to explain the ultimate weaknesses of Greece and Rome.

Even if caution seems advisable in generalizing, there are certain other obvious influences of the food supply on primitive customs and tabus as well as on later more civilized social behavior: flesh, fish, milk, eggs, fowl, and many other kinds of food have been forbidden among some peoples; and where groups have survived, their dietary laws have also persisted along with other ceremonial observances. That certain natives in the French Congo abhor milk, that Tuaregs reject fish and eggs, that Tasmanians will eat no flesh—these customs have had no continuing importance. But the Hebrew rejection of pork, the Mohammedan avoidance of spirits, and the Roman Catholic rejection of flesh on days of abstinence are instances which reveal the connection between primitive cultural development and the food supply as well as the persistence of customs relating to the diet. Farmers are conservative folk when it comes to changes in technique or in kinds of crops; but the peculiarly slow evolution of agriculture owes something, also, to the conservatism of consumers.

As the peoples around the Mediterranean gathered themselves, in successive eras, into powerful states whose literary and artistic remains we regard as so precious, there lay at their basis changes in food production which at once made them possible and furnished their greatest dangers. In Egypt the annually renewed Nile soils were so rich that the single crop grown there in classical times—wheat—could not exhaust them; and production was great enough so that part of it could be extorted from the peasants for the support of city artisans and a leisure class. Yet, in spite of an elaborate system of royal granaries, famines were frequent in years when the floods failed. Ultimately, however, they went some distance toward the prevention of famine.

The evolution of Hellenic culture was accompanied by remarkable dietary changes. Meat was the chief food in the archaic period when pastures were plenty, towns small, and population not too crowded. Homer's heroes were great meat-eaters; their descendants ate cereals and fish instead of meat. A Greek humorist could have made a good deal of the accompanying change in attitude. For flesh, which was once despised, came into repute as it grew so scarce as to be available only to the rich.

The Greek pastures were overworked, probably, and, in consequence, eroded. What was more serious was the limited amount of arable land which caused the city states, as population grew, to look for their grain abroad. The insuring of supplies and fair prices for them came to be a considerable governmental problem. There was a gradual evolution from the encouragement of free trade and the suppression of monopoly to the actual taking over of the supply-function—a practice which some modern nations may have to repeat if they continue the pursuit of self-sufficiency. Athens, for instance, turned from the close supervision of free merchants to sending out procurers, provided with funds, into distant corn markets. No city, from the third century on, kept to the old system; all had official importers. At Samos the food supply was bought with a fund provided by extraordinary taxation. In Sicily there were three bodies of officials: buyers, receivers, and wardens. These last were the state's distributing agents. Under the Greco-Egyptian monarchy, there was the still further development possible in a country which produced its own grain: the state organized the storage and sale of produce; it provided the means of transport; and, by managing the export monopoly, it kept prices at a profitable level for farmers.

The Romans had a better agrarian policy. Small peasant proprietorships were their ideal; and, under their administration, these began to spread throughout the Mediterranean basin. They also discovered rotation, an idea which did not advance far in Roman times, but lay dormant in such faraway places as Flanders and Britain for a thousand years before its logic was finally worked out and fallows were abandoned in favor of roots and legumes. The great difficulty in later Roman times was the exhaustion of the capital's own immediate hinterland and consequent dependence on imported supplies. Characteristically the great grain regions closest at hand were conquered and enslaved. The conflict with

Carthage was a grain war for the mastery of Sicily. And the extent to which Rome came to depend on Egypt is indicated by Tacitus: "Whoever made himself master of Alexandria, with the strongholds which by sea and land were the keys to the whole province, might with a small force, make head against the power of Rome, and blocking up the plentiful corn country, reduce all Italy to a famine." Literally, this was true.

FEUDAL DEFICIENCIES

The barbarians who swept down on Rome had only the crudest notions of husbandry; their victory brought with it a decline in the rural arts which the succeeding ten centuries scarcely sufficed to make good. For the Roman system of peasant proprietorships, which was, of course, mostly an ideal, but which, with excellent administration, was spreading slowly, broke down everywhere, and what followed was something less good: feudalism, a local coalescing which had more to do with physical protection than with an adequate supply of food.

The feudal ideal was self-sufficiency—such sufficiency as there was. The manorial organization has been described too often to need repetition. But it may be recalled, particularly, that open-fields were the rule from Southern England to Alsace. The cultivated lands were divided usually into two, rarely into three, parts. Some cereal, usually wheat, rye or barley, was planted in these fields alternately; in the odd year they lay idle. The list of crops grown was very short: the three cereals together with peas and beans and a few green vegetables, to be eaten in their season.

Medieval towns were small. Only a few were so large as to draw supplies from more than a day's mule-ride away. They fitted nicely behind their walls, and outside there were, instead of suburbs, artisans' gardens. The diet was necessarily scanty for town or country dweller, especially in winter when only dried or salted foods were available.

Meals were eaten at most twice a day until Elizabeth's time; and it would not be far wrong to guess that most common wooden bowls were filled with puddings and stews to be eaten with bread and beer. But there were, as has been noted, differences in agricultural practice here and there which, when the Renaissance swept out of the South and East of Europe into the North and West, were to communicate themselves gradually and to have startling cumulative results. The difference it made to the English that, in the seventeenth century, turnips, clovers, and cabbages found their way first into gardens and then into the fields, is measured, perhaps, by what we call the industrial revolution which the agricultural revolution made possible. For by the middle of the eighteenth century the enclosures, the new arable techniques, and the abandonment of fallows had transformed rural England. And, besides, the potato had now made its way from Indian culture in the Andes to Spain, to Germany and to England. And within fifty years the sugar-beet was to make a further transformation of the diet possible. Taken together, the new variety of crops and their increased yields began to banish the famines which until then had frequently decimated populations—though this victory was not to be complete until the age of steam; Malthus, in the nineteenth century, still counted them an important population factor.

FOOD AND THE INDUSTRIAL REVOLUTION

When England was merry its people were known as beef-eaters; but that was only after the turnip and the clover had crossed the channel. For not till then could animal husbandry really become important. The great lack, in medieval times, was a succulent winter food for both men and animals. The great scourges, the scurvies, and the fevers which periodically decimated the populations of Europe were only partly caused by insanitation; another cause was malnutrition. But, given cabbage for kraut, the Germans could live through the winter and multiply; and given fresh meat, milk, and turnips, the English could revolutionize their industry, build cities, and establish a world-wide empire.

The greatest food gift to the world was perhaps wheat; but one could easily argue for the potato; and still a better case could be made for maize. Both these last had to wait for America's discovery. But from the first settlements Americans had maize, and the potato came to North America in the Pilgrims' cargoes. The new world had all of Europe's experience to draw on; but she also had new land—and maize. Nevertheless, any further transformation in farming methods was impossible until the age of chemistry and machines, of quick communication, and of the revelation of the hidden hungers which starve men with full bellies. It is out of these basic conditions that the new agricultural revolution is developing.

Clapham, writing just after the Great War, observed that the nineteenth was a century of accelerating change. He was writing of France but the reasons he gave are applicable everywhere: the accumulating effect of the revolutions which removed customary and legal hindrances to change; the increased vitality of a race lifted out of misery; and improvements in communication. The tempo of change has accelerated now, until there are far fewer places where a medieval peasant would feel at home. Indeed, the insistent theme of rural philosophers that farming is less a business than a way of life, begins to have a homesick undertone. For the self-sufficiency and isolation of the rural community have everywhere been weakened if not destroyed. The farm is becoming an adjunct of the factory, merely one source of raw materials; and the organization of agriculture has, for the first time in history, to be regarded not as a great given principle of society but as something which is instrumental to more important social aims, and therefore subject to scrutiny. The rural arts are no longer sacred, except to backward-looking politicians. The farms are required to produce what we want; we no longer merely take what they prefer to give us. In the Western world, city populations are now greater than rural ones, and city standards are, in consequence, supplanting the older traditional ones of country life. This urban dominance is rapidly working out its political consequences. Farmers get less and less support for the protection of their privilege to be inefficient just because they have a traditional way of life. They are required to adjust themselves to the going prevalence of science and machines;

and great, of course, is the anguish, and many are the crises which accompany this reversal.

Self-sufficiency Is Costly

The modern problem of the food supply has to be stated in terms which are wholly irrelevant to locality. Self-sufficiency, even though it serves as an ideal for certain nations, is suspected even there because of its sheer cost. It is clung to tenaciously, and protected with the apparatus of diplomacy and tariffs; it is also backed by the full technical resource of science and industry. But measured in diet and levels of living it is still costly. The discovery that an urban and sedentary people ought to consume less meat, alcohol, and wheat took no account of dictators' wishes—nor of farmers' either, for that matter. The increased uses of dairy products, tropical fruits, beverage-berries, and oils, the expanded consumption of sugar and preserved or fresh vegetables were determined by adjustments among the masses of consumers, who were gradually enlightened concerning their own needs. But the new diet is one which cannot be supplied in any one region; the whole world must coöperate to supply every individual's daily needs if he is to be kept in that health and vigor which we seem to have determined to create and preserve even if human activity comes to no further end. The irreducible necessity involved in this purpose is access to the world's food resources; quick and unhindered transport to local markets; and an ability among consumers to share in the diet thus provided. This is an undertaking of such magnitude as to make it seem not at all strange if a long time should be required to approximate it. It denies so many old privileges, reduces so many customs and rights to absurdity, and conflicts with so many faiths—religious, political, and economic—that no one should be surprised at determined opposition in many places, accompanied by national upsets, even wars, before even a good measure of the achievement is accomplished. Yet no one, even those who throw up the barriers, and provide the occasions of conflict, is so hardy as to set himself in theoretical opposition to the general purpose.

Farmers Caught in "the Scissors"

Throughout the era of industrialism and political democracy, governments have been faced insistently with the problem of reconciling the interests of the rural population with those of city people. Until the nineteenth century in Britain and the twentieth century in the United States, France, and Germany, the farmers still outnumbered all other classes. They consequently had a political strength which is gradually being lost today. Indeed, in no country now, with a few exceptions such as Denmark, and temporarily the United States, because of the peculiar organization of our Senate, are farmers apt to prevail in the numerous crises of this long struggle. The economist's new measuring tools have made clearer how acute these differences are, and how weak the farmers have become. The problem, in market terms, is defined as "the scissors," which means the relative power of farmers in the exchange of their produce for the goods of others, and the serious decline, over a long period, of their purchasing power. In the attempt to satisfy both groups of claimants on the national income, most governments have been forced, in recent years, to some measure of relief. In the United States various surplus-control measures have been vigorously pushed on the theory that price disadvantages arose from over-supply. Opponents have argued as vigorously that what is needed is lower costs so that farmers may prosper even with lower prices. In other countries similar proposals have been met with more or less the same answer.

The Great War precipitated the more modern phase of this struggle by interrupting trade, depopulating the farms, and setting up clamorous demands for cheap food. Controls were set up everywhere of which a good type was the United States Food Administration, which fixed minimum farm prices, set up maximum differentials in marketing, and enforced transport preferences. Farmers prospered moderately and expanded their production; but at the end of the War, with the world's enhanced productive capacity again flooding its markets, and with a period of deflation setting in, agriculture entered a serious and prolonged period of depression.

It was made worse by the cumulative results of increased productive efficiency, most of which was fostered by governments and universities. Various sciences of plant and animal breeding, pathology, chemistry, and the like had increased production in various ways; perhaps as important as any was the new technique of dry-farming. There are numerous areas in the world, most of them in the lee of rain-catching mountains such as the Caucasus and the Rockies, which had been agriculturally worthless, or nearly so, because of semi-aridity. At present all these regions are producing food—at a terrific expense of wasted soil, it is true, but nevertheless producing it. The consequence of expanded areas and increased yields for the time, at least, has been great surpluses of staple foods—and that too when vast numbers of consumers are turning away from the old staples and adopting the reduced diets suitable to sedentary life. Agricultural production, for instance, in the United States, was 14 per cent greater in the period 1922-26 than in the period 1917-27—an increase 50 per cent more rapid than that of population—and this on a declining area of crop land, with fewer farmers, and with grain consumption diminished by the substitution of tractors for horses. The same phenomenon, sometimes to a greater, and sometimes to a less, degree has been evident in other regions, but especially, of course, in Russia, in Africa, and in South America.

The Conquest of Hunger

There is something both magnificent and tragic in this campaign against man's most ancient and pressing enemy—hunger. The conquest is not yet consolidated, of course, but the techniques of the agricultural arts and of quick transport already run faster than the multiplication of mouths to be fed. What remains to be done is the most difficult task of all and will consequently be the last achievement in the general evolution toward universal plenty. We have not yet learned how to make new food supplies available to all. No country, not even the United States, can assume the ultimate pride of having abolished starvation. What remains to be done lies in the field of social management. The Greeks and

Romans had the world to themselves—they could draw for food on vast areas of primitive farming without much organized resistance. Today the exploitation of backward areas is a matter of bargaining and compromise among many claimants. Because of dietary and technical changes, self-sufficiency, however, is just as impossible now as it was then. Markets not only for salt, spices, and luxury goods, but for many bulky staples, are international. Governments are necessarily faced with increasingly complex problems of adjustment; their nationals have not only to sell but also to buy. It is no wonder that almost first among the problems of statesmanship are these which have to do with this commerce: how shall tariffs be adjusted? how shall credits be arranged? how far can nationals be protected in selling, buying or collecting debts? No less a problem of statesmanship is involved in internal policy-making: Shall farmers be protected from price-competition? How far ought governments to go in specific encouragement of special cultures? Ought production or marketing to be controlled? Shall more or less vigorous standards of quality be set and enforced? All these and many more are persistently pressing.

Modern problems are in a way different from and in a way similar to those which always existed. Populations are denser and more urban; diets are more varied and depend on further sources; customs of producing, of distributing, even of consuming have changed radically. Nearly every country in the Western world has for the moment solved the crude problem of the food supply: no fear is felt in times of peace that there may be famine. But nationalist aims have been allowed to shape policy so that diets have been inadequate; and standards of living have been kept down by an apportionment of income which has kept whole classes in poverty. In the United States a really good diet would require a doubling, as well as a rearranging of crop production, a situation which is as true of other countries. But these are difficulties with the social system rather than with ways of producing. If we run short of food it will be because consumers are unable to buy what the farmer has to sell, not because our land, our people, or our distributive mechanisms have failed us.

DIET AND CIVILIZATION

We may expect, once present objectives are shaped into administrative mechanisms, that interest will shift to dietary control. It will look to an enlarged use of animal and dairy products, a decrease in the consumption of cereals, and a more varied supply of green fruits and vegetables. It will also set up warnings against over-processed food materials which attract the eye and the taste but undermine the health through a shortage of natural minerals, organic chemical compounds, vitamins, and bacteria. Out of nutrition laboratories there will come the determining facts for future policy.

Before the word "vitamin" was invented the economist Patten was accustomed to speak of "nutrins." He had always been interested in the sequence which ran from secure food supplies to better nutrition and from there on to what he called the "creative economy." It seemed to him an understandable development. He borrowed from psychologists and physicians; but he generalized as an economist, showing how the pulse of better blood fed nerve and gland and how the perfectly grown and nourished body-structure set the conditions for harmonious adjustment to the world—and for changing it as well. What civilization might become if it were shaped by a well-fed generation he did not attempt to predict; but it was clear to him that it would be strange to us—and inevitably better.

An adequate supply of nutrins does not involve merely full stomachs; it means stomachs filled with stuffs which yield good blood. Much of our action is internally determined. We do not always react in stereotyped ways to exterior stimuli; many times we actually act rather than react. The sum of these actions and reactions we call institutions and our institutions are us—not any one of us but all of us. Thus society runs its life-lines back to its supply of food and requires of its farmers, its organizing services, its government policy, the guardianship of its nutrins. This is the first duty of statesmanship in industry and government. And if the terms have changed and raised the tests of sufficiency, there is still the fundamental duty to the race which all of us must face. We seem to forget it in many of the exigencies of profit-making or of struggles for place. And we have neglected to set the proper safeguards of public policy about it. But those are perhaps only the lags between knowledge and accomplishment with which we are familiar in many fields. Our policy will catch up and require conformance.

LAYING THE GROUNDWORK

Preparation for Reading

1. "Land of Plenty" is a study of social history in terms of food—the supply and the kinds of food and the methods of production. The author traces the evolution of agricultural practices from primitive communal society, through "classic" civilizations with their institution of slavery, through feudalism with its serfdom, through the Industrial Revolution, down to our scientific, mechanized age. The basic problem of the past centuries was the production of sufficient food to maintain not only a rural producing class but also an urban working class and a small group of professional people, artists, and idlers. Abundance can now be produced; however, the distribution of this abundance to all and the improvement of the dietary standards are problems which society must still solve. Keep this analysis in mind as you study the selection.

2. Here are a few of the many questions about agricultural practices and the food supply which remain unanswered: Why are more and more farmers getting poorer and poorer at the same time that they are producing more and more with greater efficiency? Why must carloads of oranges be dumped while thousands of babies die for lack of vitamins? Why is the price of eggs fifteen cents on the farm and two or three times that price in the city? List other problems.

Vocabulary Building

1. Look up these words: *axiom, tabus, extorted, artisans, archaic, coalescing, manorial, cumulative, decimated, succulent, sedentary, pathology, deflation, lee, exploitation, stereotyped, exigencies.*

2. Find a meaning pertinent to agriculture: *granaries, rotation, dormant, legumes, husbandry, arable, fallows, enclosures.*

APPRAISING THE RESULTS

1. Explain the axiom: "Activities other than agriculture [building, trading] cannot be developed until there is a surplus of foods."
2. The kind of organizational structure of a group seems to be correlated with the food supply and agricultural practices. Hence, explain why a pastoral or nomadic system is correlated with a patriarchy, a village system with a matriarchy, an unstable government with a servile producing class.
3. The food supply has influenced food customs. What are some of these customs, and how do they slow up change in agriculture?
4. How did Egypt manage to get the surplus of foods necessary before she could build her "civilization"? How did Greece manage? Rome? What part did government play in each?
5. What was the manorial system of production? What foods were available in the medieval town?
6. During the Agricultural Revolution enclosures were substituted for open fields, new farming techniques were adopted, and new crops introduced. Explain the importance of each of these changes. Why was it necessary for the Agricultural Revolution to *precede* the Industrial Revolution?
7. Find the statement: "Any further transformation [after the changes of the Agricultural Revolution] in farming methods was impossible until the age of chemistry and machines, of quick communication, and of the revelation of these basic hidden hungers which starve men with full bellies." Note the relation of this sentence to the paragraphs which follow it. Is the statement sound?
8. Answer these questions about the conflict between agrarian and urban interests: Why have farmers by and large lost political control? How were agrarian problems aggravated by the Great War? by efficiency and science? by dry-farming?
9. To what extent have we made a conquest of hunger? What still remains to be done?
10. Why cannot governments today solve the food problem by exploiting backward peoples? by becoming self-sufficient?

11. What is the relationship between a healthful diet and progress toward a better civilization?
12. According to the author, what is the first duty of industry and statesmanship? Do you think they are fulfilling this duty?

SELECTING THE THEME SUBJECT

Titles for themes: Life of Women on the Farm; Food, Health, and the Poor; Dietary Diseases; The Wolf at the Farmer's Door; Underconsumption or Overproduction?; The Relation of Distribution Costs to High Prices; Is the Farmer Slow to Change?; Farmers' Cooperatives.

IS THE UNITED STATES A PERMANENT COUNTRY?[1]

Morris Llewellyn Cooke

"THE EARTHWORM POPULATION OF ILLINOIS IS FALLING AT A TRAGIC RATE!"

This was a distinguished engineer's way of saying that soil erosion prompted by man's careless methods of land use is undermining the very foundation of America's existence. The assertion was made in 1927 before a congressional committee considering appropriations for flood control on the Mississippi River, and it is even truer today than it was then. Any fisherman knows that worms are not found in sand or in soils either desiccated or devoid of humus.

Those occasions when water piles up in the main stems of our large rivers—the Ohio, the Missouri, or the Connecticut, for instance—so that they overflow their banks, are dramatic. The blow strikes suddenly with a minimum of warning. The railroads are paralyzed, homes are devastated, and sometimes lives are lost. The structure of normal living is temporarily shattered. On the other hand, there is nothing spectacular about soil losses—nothing to make headlines. Rather they represent a steady drain which, beginning in the early days of our country, has been greatly accelerated since the turn of the century through easily identified causes. Effectually meeting this threat will require an effort quite out of scale with any the Republic has heretofore been called on to make.

Unless there is a marked change in our present agricultural methods, we have, as a virile nation, perhaps less than 100 years to go. The United States is not a permanent country

[1] From *Forum*, April, 1938. Reprinted by permission of the author and of the editors.

unless we make it so. It is not permanent in the sense that England and Ireland and Holland are permanent. Why the difference? England has a sod agriculture affording the maximum of protection for her soils, with fairly constant and always gentle rains. In this country we have developed a plowed —and in the case of corn, cotton, and tobacco a cultivated— agriculture, exposing our soils over wide areas to the destructive battering of normally heavy downpours.

When white men first reached these shores the forests covered fully twice their present area, and, except for a small area of desert and waste land, the balance of what is now the continental United States had a protective cover of grass. The dominant type of agriculture first practiced—and this naturally on the more level areas—did no great harm. The products of each farm were consumed on that farm, except for a minimum of localized barter. A large part of each farm was retained in grass; there was a plentiful use of animal manure on the plowed fields; and both rotation and diversification of crops were practiced. The ominous exception was the tobacco culture of the South.

But the struggle for cash crops has progressively changed all this. Single-crop farming—cotton and tobacco in the South and wheat and corn in the West—has removed the tree and grass cover over increasingly large areas and in some sections has led to the use of artificial fertilizers in place of animal manure. Our fast spreading system of farm tenancy affords little incentive for the farmers to care for the soil. To exhaust one farm and move on to the next has been the custom. Increase in the population and the movement of that population westward have led to the utilization of less fertile, more sloping, and therefore more erosible areas. The drainage of swamplands on a wide scale has not only brought poor land into agricultural use but also has frequently ruined adjacent land by lowering the levels of subsurface waters.

One of America's great teachers—Shaler of Harvard—once said of our civilization:

It is now a question whether human culture, which rests upon the use of the soil, can devise and enforce ways of dealing with the earth which will preserve this source of life so that it may support the men of the ages to come. If this cannot be done we must look forward to the time—remote it may be, yet clearly discernible—when our kind, having wasted its great inheritance, will fade from the earth because of the ruin it has accomplished.

Congressman Maury Maverick in his *A Maverick American* quotes a warning issued in 1818 in South Carolina:

This system [of agricultural practices], if it may be so called, of perpetual exhaustion, has impoverished our lands to an alarming degree, and if pursued for half a century more, would make this interesting portion of the state a perfect desert . . . and ruined from future recovery by deep washed gullies, etc.

On a recent visit the Congressman found the prediction completely fulfilled. He quotes an ancestor as saying, "The best citizen is the one who fills in the most gullies."

MAN-MADE FLOODS

Water in increasing proportions runs off the land instead of sinking into the soil. The faster it runs off, the more damage it does, first in eroding the land and later in overflowing the banks of streams and filling costly reservoirs with the products of erosion. This increase, both in the amount and in the rapidity with which rain and melting snow run off the land, is primarily responsible for the increase in the vehemence of floods and for low water in our streams. Most streams are fed by springs which go dry progressively as the subsurface water levels fall. There has been no change in the weather sufficient to account for the growing extremes in both high and low water.

We are facilitating floods through several types of man-made channels. As a small boy I knew the main road from Gettysburg to Harrisburg in Pennsylvania. During winter and spring there were times when it lay ankle and knee deep in mud and water. That same road has well-maintained ditches, on either side, not only draining the roadbed but quickly carrying water falling on the roadway and the adjacent fields to nearby streams. We have today 3,000,000 miles of public roads with well-maintained ditches on either side—6,000,000 miles of drainage trenches standing ready to hurry the raindrop to the sea. Most of these ditches are less than 50 years old.

There are also millions of newly made gullies in every State in the Union—some of them more than 100 feet deep—feeding down to the roadside ditches directly into the streams. Into most gullies lead many smaller gullies. One can easily identify 1,000 gullies on a photograph in my possession of a completely eroded farm in the Piedmont of Alabama. Gullying is a cancerous growth that feeds on itself. Even the depressions between crop rows that run up and down hillside slopes provide gutters down which rainfall rushes into the nearest stream.

Thus natural waterways, from the smallest streams to the largest rivers, are called on to take care of an enormously increased volume of water speeding from millions of acres of unabsorptive, erosion-exposed subsoil and from hundreds of millions of new tributaries developed as the result of improper land use and the changes man has made in the natural environment. Obviously we are asking our rivers to carry, over occasional short periods, more water than they were created to carry. Rain and water from melting snow, which should be sinking *into* the ground, is rushing *over* it, contributing to erosion and floods, dust storms and disease and poverty.

An especially sinister factor in this situation is that after the topsoil goes—and it takes several hundred years for nature to make *one inch* of topsoil—the unstable subsoil begins to erode and go downstream. Before long you find this unfertile material—water-assorted sand and "raw" clay—blanketing our fertile valley lands. In the recent report of the Great Plains Committee is shown a photograph of a 16-foot-thick section taken in Coon Valley, Wisconsin. The lower 10 feet are obviously of fertile silt, 10,000 years in being deposited. But the upper 5 feet are just as obviously sandy material deposited in the last 60 years—or since eroding forms of agriculture have been established in the area draining into it.

PRODIGAL AMERICA

Almost up to the beginning of the present administration, the term *conservation* was considered all but synonymous with reforestation. The event which first gave national currency to the term—the governors' conference called by President Theodore Roosevelt and held at the White House in December, 1907—was largely a forestry show, because of the dramatic presentation by Forester Gifford Pinchot and of the further conviction of the then head of the Bureau of Soils of the Department of Agriculture, as follows:

The soil is the one indestructible, immutable asset that the nation possesses. It is the one resource that can not be exhausted; that can not be used up. As a national asset the soil is safe as a means of feeding mankind for untold ages to come.

But, by the time Franklin D. Roosevelt came to the presidency, the evidence that all was not well with the lands of the United States was too striking to be ignored further. The average yield per acre of our principal grain crops had been declining, notwithstanding improved cultural techniques, advances in crop improvement and animal breeding, and the use of fertilizers and lime. Year by year the acreage of abandoned farms was increasing, as evidenced by the fact that 29 States east of the Mississippi River and 3 States west of it showed marked decreases in farm acreage between 1920 and 1930. Again erosion in its various stages was nearly everywhere visible; and gullying, especially in certain sections of the South and West, had caused complete abandonment and ruin of farms. Further, practically all our streams were carrying an obviously increased load of silt. Three million tons of soil, according to reliable estimates, are stripped by water erosion alone from the fields and pastures of the country every year—the soil equivalent of 1,500,000 acres, or enough to load a train that would encircle the globe 18 times at the equator.

When the Soil Conservation Service was organized in 1933, 100,000,000 acres of agricultural lands had been essentially ruined, in so far as further immediate cultivation is concerned; 100,000,000 more acres had lost most or all of their productive topsoil; and the process of wastage had begun actively on still another 100,000,000 acres. Most of this land could have been saved, had we not developed early in our American life the habit of thinking of our agricultural domain as limitless and inexhaustible or had we not fallen into the extravagant habit of clearing a farm, using it until its vitals had been washed away, and then turning to the once bountiful and seemingly inexhaustible store of virgin land for another farm.

Attention is beginning to be diverted from the soil-erosion situation through the promotion of two important and apparently tenable theses. We are told, in language that lures, first, that a full regimen of synthetic foods—largely chemically derived—is at hand; second, that such foods as are grown will have their roots in pans of water electrically heated and chemically treated. This latter is called "tray" agriculture.

Only a rash person would deny the possibility of radical future changes in methods of growing foodstuffs and in the diet of man and beast. But, if authoritative estimates of the rate at which soil and water erosion are progressing are even measurably accurate, we have less than a generation in which to get these matters under control. Irrespective of what may be accomplished in the laboratory in such a brief period in the way of devising better methods of forcing plant growth, it is hardly possible that such developments will in the near future appreciably affect the grand total of agricultural production. It is frequently possible to affect radically and in a very short time some narrow sector of human activity. But our millions of farmers are individualistic and rooted in old ways. They change slowly.

New and sound ideas as to the utility of synthetic foods are to be expected. But, in view of the many thousands of years during which the digestive systems of man and beast have developed, we can expect only negligible changes in diet in the decades during which the nation is to conquer soil erosion or be conquered by it. Unfortunately the promises of developments in these two fields do tend to create a psychology which diverts us from our urgent task.

We must now face the fact that as a nation we are in the same position as an individual who has been told by the doctor that he has tuberculosis or cancer. We are well along in an earth disease that, unless checked, will be our undoing as certainly as neglected cancer or tuberculosis is the undoing of an individual. Neither individuals nor nations snap out of deadly diseases. But, when the doctor's advice is taken early enough and seriously enough, nations as well as individuals can expect reasonable recovery.

A PRACTICAL PROGRAM

The Soil Conservation Service early in its drive adopted the co-ordinated or complete land-treatment plan as its method for controlling erosion and conserving more of the water that falls on the land. Since then, the Service has successfully followed the plan throughout the country in a program which now involves more than 500 conservation project areas in 43 States. These projects comprise approximately 18,000,000 acres of privately owned land and 38,000,000 acres of public land and have enlisted the enthusiastic support of 50,000 co-operating farmers. Probably more than 150 different methods of land treatment and gully control are being employed to fit local conditions of soil, topography, climate, and type of agriculture. Among the more outstanding practices are contour cultivation; terracing; strip cropping; rotations; retirement of critically erosible areas to the permanent protection of grass, trees, or shrubs; improvement of farm woodlands; pasture and range improvement; control of gullies; conservation of water in small ponds and reservoirs; water diversion and spreading; and rehabilitation of wild life. Co-operating with this national program, 70,000 members of the Civilian Conservation Corps engaged on soil and water conservation, working on more than 4,000,000 acres located in 38 States, during the last fiscal year planted 112,000,000 trees, collected 2,110,000 pounds of tree seed, and built 2,302,805 check dams and 7,000 miles of fences.

The Department of Agriculture, under the invalidated Agricultural Adjustment Authority Act, sought to divert lands producing surplus crops to hay and pasture. Under the

substitute legislation, the Department makes grants to farmers who plant soil-conserving crops and follow other water-
and soil-conserving practices. Twenty-two States have already
enacted legislation, recommended by the Department, designed to promote conservation. President Roosevelt's plan
for dividing the country into seven conservation districts
means regional planning for regional problems, wherein upstream engineering, covering the whole field of soil and water
conservation, will be co-ordinated with downstream activities.

Although more has been done during the last three years
to curb accelerated runoff and erosion than in all our previous history, damage and wastage through the dual process are
still spreading faster than control measures are being applied.
Even so, on the basis of what has been accomplished, I am
convinced that it is possible to get under way a proper land-
use program which within 15 or 20 years could be applied to
all land urgently needing treatment and that the job could
be completed about as effectively as man can hope to complete it within 30 or 40 years. The cost, necessary and wholly
worth-while as it is, will be tremendous. But could it be otherwise? Remember that in salvaging the situation we will be paying the bills for a profligacy running back 200 years and more.

In any crisis the first requisite of ultimate victory is a
sensing of the difficulties. Here we have to admit that science
does not yet know how adequately to safeguard all types of
land used for agricultural purposes. We are learning and
learning fast, but old techniques must be improved, and
new ones are still to be worked out. If the ravages of our
soils and the lessening of our water reserves are to be arrested,
a vast peacetime army will have to be recruited, and this
personnel is yet to be educated and trained. Most difficult
of all, millions of landowners and land operators must be
convinced that the right to possess and to use land carries
with it the obligation to safeguard it, as was provided in the
Napoleonic code.

Our attack along these lines must be immediate and energetic, for really serious illness can be successfully attacked
only in the early stages. In other words, unless we have this
gangrenous growth of soil erosion well in hand within the

next 20 to 25 years, efforts made subsequently will have to be heavily discounted, because our certain penalty will be the rise of a whole new series of physical, economic, and social problems that will stand effectually in the path of American progress.

PEACETIME SACRIFICE

Before it is too late to matter much, the American people must learn the great difference between financial accounting and social accounting. To date, the worth-whileness of practically all our peacetime activities has been judged by the one all-compelling standard of the market place, i.e., whether they pay tangibly in dollars and cents. Such judgments are reached by the techniques of financial accounting, as contrasted with a social accounting which operates on a long-time point of view and has in mind the interest of all of us rather than of a single individual or of a restricted group.

A Texan recently inherited a farm property from his father, who had paid $1 an acre for it at a time when it was capable of producing a bale of cotton to the acre. Notwithstanding the fact that it had deteriorated so that it produced only one eighth of a bale to the acre, it was recently sold for $150 an acre. This transaction appears splendid from the standpoint of financial accounting but not so good when judged by the long-time interests of a free people. If there is one lesson which the depression has taught, it is that what may be good for the individual may be disastrous for society as a whole; conversely, what is good for society will prove in the end to be good for the individual.

It may be sound constitutionally to allow John Doe and Richard Roe to ruin their farms, through failing to practice soil-conserving measures, on the ground that they have title in fee simple. But, if enough people are allowed to act on this theory for just a few more decades, we will not have enough farms to feed us.

Confronted by such a problem as that of conserving the waters and soils of our country, one wonders whether the democracies of the world are calling for enough sacrifices in the pursuit of peacetime activities, as the dictatorships are undoubtedly doing. May it not be that the standards of the market place are insidiously shortening and narrowing our point of view? Democracies give a good account of themselves in war—why not in peace? Why, if it is of good repute to die that one's country may live in security and freedom, should it not be of at least equal repute to live for the same purpose and to sacrifice in so doing? If we are to save our basic resources of soil and water, we individually must sow more than we shall ever reap in our own lifetime!

Only so can we follow Vachel Lindsay's lead in saying:

> Come, let us see that all men
> Have land to catch the rain,
> Have grass to snare the spheres of dew,
> And fields spread for the grain.

Only so can the American dream be fulfilled.

LAYING THE GROUNDWORK

Preparation for Reading

1. What great national catastrophes, like floods or dust storms, has America experienced? What were their causes?
2. How have engineers tried to combat and prevent their recurrence?
3. What has reforestation to do with conservation of soil?

Vocabulary Building

1. Look up these words before you read: *erosion, desiccated, humus, silt, topography, invalidated, rotation, decades, barter.*
2. Identify: *Agricultural Adjustment Act, Piedmont, Vachel Lindsay, Civilian Conservation Corps.*
3. Explain what is meant by *strip cropping, contour cultivation, title in fee simple, virgin land, sod agriculture.*
4. As you read look up these words: *devoid, devastated, accelerated, virile, diversification, ominous, incentive, discernible, perpetual, vehemence, facilitating, sinister, immutable, tenable, profligacy, requisite, gangrenous, tangibly, insidiously, salvaging, deteriorated.*
5. Study the root of the word *radical* and note our common use of this word.

APPRAISING THE RESULTS

1. Explain the title. What countries are called permanent? Why?
2. Tell how our agricultural practices have resulted in depletion of the land.
3. What are the causes and effects of man-made floods?
4. Why does the author call one section "Prodigal America"? What does the expression mean?
5. What practical program for conservation have we begun? Where?
6. Note the development of paragraphs: topic sentences, use of examples, statistics, quotations. Which of these methods are important for evidence? Which for interest? Find a paragraph developed by contrast.
7. Note the general organization: (a) the situation is described; (b) the causes are examined; (c) a program is presented. Explain why the essay is divided into five sections.
8. With the basic plan of the selection in mind, write a sentence outline of it.

SELECTING THE THEME SUBJECT

1. Select some local or national problem and write about it, keeping in mind the need: (a) to describe the situation, (b) to examine the causes, (c) to present a program.
2. In a theme discuss the topographical features of your neighborhood.
3. Discuss some picturesque aspects of pioneer farming or describe its hardships.
4. Theme subjects: T.V.A.; Commercial Fertilizers as Aids in Conservation; The Importance of County Fairs; The Work of the 4-H Clubs; "Tray" Agriculture as a Substitute for Soil Conservation.
5. In a paper show the significance of the Mississippi River in American history or life.

Technique in a Machine World

THE DESERT SHALL BLOSSOM AS THE ROSE[1]

J. D. Ross

OUT IN THE FAR WEST, IN THE STATE OF WASHINGTON, A GIANT STRUCTURE, COULEE DAM, IS NEARING COMPLETION. THIS GREAT-est of dams is the key structure in the far-flung Columbia Basin project, which with forty years of labor and a round billion dollars' expenditure is to create a blooming garden empire from a desert of sage brush, and incidentally to de-velop some ten million horsepower in hydroelectric power plants. Mightiest power stream on the American continent, the Columbia is second only to the Mississippi in volume of flow. Unlike the slow-moving Father of Waters, however, the Columbia River rushes through a canyon 750 miles in length under the great impelling force of a 1300-foot fall from Canada to the ocean. Ten giant dams will still this great tor-rent to a chain of lakes, and at each dam a power house will take its toll of the river's energy before permitting the flow to enter the lake below. Bonneville Dam, farthest downstream of the ten and forty miles east of Portland, Oregon, already stands completed, with two of its ultimate ten electric gen-erators in service. Coulee Dam, to be finished in 1941, is by far the largest of the ten, and most important because it will form a reservoir 151 miles long, whose great capacity released in the dry season will double the output of each of the ten power plants below; and because at Coulee it is possible to divert the water for the vast irrigation project.

During the last glacial period, a few millennia ago, the ice cap moving southward blocked the channel of the prehistoric Columbia at a point eighty miles west of what is now Spokane, Washington, where the river makes a giant bend from south-

[1] Used by permission of the author.

west to northwest. As the ice barrier rose, the river, with ten times its present flow, spilled over the south rim of the canyon and soon cut a new channel six hundred feet deep, two to five miles wide, and forty miles long, to the great precipice where the three-mile-wide stream dropped four hundred feet in a cataract two and a half times as high as Niagara, with a volume of fifty Niagaras. When the ice cap melted and let the river back to its original bed, it left the new channel, its thundering waterfall dry and still. The canyon is now Grand Coulee, the precipice the famous Dry Falls. From the deep pool that still lies below the precipice the canyon extends another twelve miles south to Soap Lake, where the river seems to have spread out over an area extending many miles, before finding its way back to its channel near the present Priest Rapids.

It is this area, extending roughly eighty miles south from Soap Lake and sixty miles wide, that is now to be reclaimed by irrigation. The plan evolved by the United States Bureau of Reclamation and the Army Engineers after years of study and investigation follows the lead of Nature herself. Coulee Dam will again block the canyon at the great bend of the Columbia. It will not be high enough to spill the river into Grand Coulee; that would take a structure more than a mile long and a thousand feet high. Nor do we need the entire flow of the stream. Ten per cent of it is ample to water the million and a quarter acres of the project. So the engineers balance the cost of dams of various heights and giant electric pumps to lift water over the canyon rim, to arrive at the best economic combination to achieve the desired result. Grand Coulee itself, blocked at each end by comparatively small dams, is used as an equalizing reservoir to receive the water from the pumps and release it to the two great canals that will carry it by gravity to the valley below.

About thirty-five years ago the lands to be watered from Grand Coulee were homesteaded to settlers who were encouraged to try dry farming by a few years of abnormal rainfall that brought partial crops. These homesteads have been abandoned for many years. Only a few forward-looking men realized the great possibilities and worked through the years to find a way to bring water to the land. A plan to build a canal from the Pend Oreille, a distance of one hundred thirty miles, was abandoned because of the cost. Pumping from the near-by Columbia with the 500-foot lift was too expensive at existing power rates. The plan proposed, and now pursued, is economically sound because the returns from the sale of power will pay the cost of the dam, but there still remained the task of financing. Private capital built one of the smaller dams with its power plant at Rock Island, and power filings were made on one or two others. The greater project was obviously out of reach of private capital. Only the Federal Government could provide the means and subordinate immediate profit to the ultimate good; and the Government seemed definitely not interested in so vast a project so far from the populous East. Private utility interests, especially, were alarmed at the development of so much power and its possible effect on utility stocks and bonds. It remained for President Roosevelt, looking ahead to the finished project and its great benefits to the whole country, to take the decisive step toward its realization. In the fall of 1933, he authorized the beginning of Bonneville and Coulee Dams as Public Works Projects.

The Bureau of Reclamation of the United States Department of the Interior had already prepared the first plans for Coulee Dam, and work began immediately. The first four years saw the site cleared to bed-rock and the foundation of the dam carried above high water, leaving only a routine job of placing concrete, unhindered by flood or earth slide, to complete the dam. Rising 550 feet from bed-rock, 4300 feet long and 500 feet thick at the base, the dam is by far the largest block of masonry ever built. Only Boulder Dam is higher, rising 740 feet in its narrow canyon, but Boulder contains less than half the volume. The Great Pyramid, for sixty centuries man's greatest structure, contains less than a third of the eleven and a quarter million cubic yards of masonry in the finished Coulee Dam. Engineers call this a gravity dam, meaning that it will be able by sheer weight to withstand the millions of tons of water pressure. Such a dam must rest on solid rock, and the existence of a granite ledge under the stream bed determined its final location. Roughly 100 feet below the river bed, the floor of granite was scored with three canyons 100 feet deeper still. All loose material— boulders, gravel, and silt—was removed, as well as the weathered surface of the solid rock itself, before the concrete foundations were poured. Altogether twenty million cubic yards of material were excavated, of which one million were granite from the bed-rock. Before such a cavern could be dug it was necessary to divert the river and make sure that its uneasy flood waters could not find their way in to pour vast quantities of silt and boulders into the unfinished excavation beneath its bed.

Twice the work at Coulee was seriously endangered: once by an immense earth slide, once by a leak that threatened to demolish the coffer-dam. River diversion was first accomplished by driving 17,000 tons of interlocking steel piling to make a steel barrier 100 feet high extending from the west bank out to the center of the stream and back to the same bank in a half-mile bow that enclosed the west half of the dam site. After that portion was excavated the west half of the dam was carried up well above river level, with temporary channels left to carry the river through that part of the dam while the whole operation was repeated on the east side of the dam. When the west excavation was almost complete, a mass of millions of tons of earth, poised directly over the deepest part, broke over the barrier placed to hold it and moved inexorably toward the pit. While giant shovels rushed to take the weight from the top of the moving mass, a refrigeration plant capable of freezing eighty tons of ice per day was set up near-by and pipes to carry freezing brine were driven into the slide, which was frozen to a depth of 25 feet over an area of 4500 square feet, to make a frozen earth dam that successfully held the slide for eight months until the concrete was carried above the danger line. Still more dramatic was the sudden rush of water under a section of the east coffer-dam, in a flood that threatened to fill the excavation and in a few hours to set the job back a year. By throwing thousands of yards of gravel into a fill on the river side of the leak while driving a sheet pile wall inside the dam and forcing a mixture of sawdust, sand, cement and Bentonite, a mineral that expands like cooking rice when wetted, into the gravel at the leak, the flow was stopped with minutes to spare, and another construction record was set at Coulee, for never before was a breaking coffer-dam repaired from the inside.

Other world records were set by the great conveyor system of rubber belts that carried 48,000 yards of material per day from the pit to the dump a mile away, and by the concrete mixers and placing equipment able to pour 18,000 cubic yards of concrete per day. Along with speed new standards of quality were achieved in the work. Foundation grouting was carried to depths of 300 feet by drilling into the rock and forcing cement into the seams at high pressure. Supplementing miles of sample rock cores taken out of the foundation by diamond drills, a giant core drill pierced a hole large enough to permit a man to descend through the foundation strata and make direct inspection of the quality and placement of the rock. The average strength of more than three thousand test cylinders made of the mass concrete for the dam was 5545 pounds per square inch after 28 days' time to set, nearly double the strength that used to be required for such material.

Spillways 1650 feet long with capacity to carry a million cubic feet of water per second are provided in the center section of the dam. This is twice the flow ever recorded, although it is estimated that the flood of 1894 may have reached 725,000 cubic feet per second. This dam is built to stand as long as the eternal hills into which it keys.

Twin power plants, one on each side of the channel just below the dam, will each contain a row of nine giant turbogenerators rated at 150,000 horsepower per unit—the largest ever built. Of the total 2,700,000 horsepower installed capacity 1,120,000 horsepower is so-called "firm" power: that is, power available 100 per cent of the time, or the amount that can be generated at extreme low water supplemented by draft from the storage reservoir. The remainder is secondary or seasonal power.

On the west bank of the river just upstream from the dam and approximately 250 feet in elevation above the river bed, is to be the largest pumping plant in the world, with twelve pumping units, each rated at 19,200 cubic feet of water per second, and driven by a 62,500-horsepower motor. Each of these pumps will deliver water into a 10-foot diameter discharge pipe leading over the south canyon wall to a great canal that will carry the water into the balancing reservoir in the Grand Coulee. The total lift will be 280 feet and the pumps will operate entirely on secondary or seasonal power, since the flow of the Columbia, fed by melting snow and ice, is always high during the summer irrigation period. This balancing reservoir is to be formed by closing off the upper 23 miles of Grand Coulee with a dam at each end approximately 70 feet high, to form a basin of 27,000 acres, with a useful capacity of 339,000 acre feet, which means sufficient water to cover 339,000 acres one foot in depth. From the lower end of the balancing reservoir a main canal will be carried 11 miles south to a point near the top of the dry falls, where it will branch into an east and west canal, the former of which will be 156 miles long, and the latter 101 miles long. These canals will follow the contours down each side of the valley and almost completely surround the area to be irrigated. This area comprises a total of 1,200,000 acres, including approximately 200,000 acres to be reclaimed by pumping from the main canals to elevations not exceeding 100 feet.

The new garden spot will extend south from Soap Lake to the junction of the Snake River with the Columbia, and eastward from the east bank of the Columbia approximately sixty miles. The soil here is volcanic ash, exceedingly fertile when watered. The climate is moderate with a long growing season, highly favorable for the raising of wheat, alfalfa, apples, peaches, grapes and nuts, and for dairy products. The completion of the project will make room for 40,000 families, giving each an average of 30 acres. Counting the prosperous towns and cities created by the new wealth, and allowing four per family, the population of this part of central Washington will reach close to half a million people. Already refugees from the Dust Bowl, many of whom are competent farmers, are anxiously awaiting the opening of the new lands. The experience of the Yakima, Ellensburg, and Wenatchee valleys just west of the Columbia proves what can be done when water is available. Crop failures in these valleys are unknown, and their fruits have a worldwide reputation.

A special Act of Congress prohibits speculation in Grand Coulee lands. The settler will pay from $5 to $10 per acre, plus his share of the cost of the irrigation investment alone, with an annual charge for his share of the cost of maintenance and operation of the irrigation works. A 40-acre farm completely equipped will cost approximately $10,000, most of which will be spread over long-time payments, so that a real farmer will have no difficulty in paying for his home out of its earnings.

The two giant power plants will produce eight and one-third billion kilowatt-hours of "firm" electric energy annually, with four and a quarter billion kilowatt-hours of "secondary" or seasonal power in addition. The three northwestern states, Washington, Oregon and Idaho, now use four billion kilowatt-hours per year. What is to be done with the vast new supply? How can it be distributed? What of Bonneville power, and the eight other power plants between Coulee and Bonneville? The answer is found in the history of the electric industry. Beginning in 1887 the use of electricity in America doubled, on the average, every four years and eight months, for forty-two years; it grew tenfold each sixteen years. The depression came, and later the recession, but the 1937 use is one-third greater than in the "boom" year, 1929, and 11 percent ahead of 1936. Even when we include the depression years we find a rise from 151 million to 121 *billion* kilowatt-hours annually in the fifty years ending with 1937. This is a growth rate of 14.2 percent per year—a tenfold increase in less than eighteen years. The average home in this country uses 793 kilowatt-hours annually, at an average rate of 4.39 cents per kilowatt-hour. One district of 150 homes in Seattle, Broadmoor, used 7332 kilowatt-hours per home in 1937, paying an average rate of 1.44 cents per kilowatt-hour. There appears no limit to the use of current when rates are within reach of the income. We can only guess what electricity will be used for ten or twenty years from now. Twenty years ago the home radio was unknown, the refrigerator and electric range nearly so. Only in the past two years have we begun to realize that our lamps are pitifully weak and must be brightened tenfold if our eyes are to function at their best. Industrial uses of current, vast as they are, promise still greater increase. Electricity is simply energy in its most usable form. For electro-chemical processes there is no substitute form. For industrial heating the accurate control and elimination of waste widens that field of use for electricity every year, despite a higher cost per heat unit for current than for oil or other fuel under prevailing rates. Electric power is the corner stone in the foundation of national defense, because power is necessary to make all water materials. This is much more true today than it was during 1917 and 1918, when the freight cars needed to haul coal to the steam plants caused a national car shortage. If we can be sure of anything in the world today, it is that the use for electricity will continue to grow. We shall see a million horsepower where now is a hundred thousand. Whether it comes in eighteen years, or war speeds it to sixteen years or less, we shall see the tenfold increase.

Where will this power come from? Our oil reserves are woefully small for such a strain. Our coal seems almost inexhaustible, but the mines are getting deeper and the best grades are scarce. The United States Geological Survey estimates the total amount of water power that can be developed in the entire country at 84 million horsepower, or 71 million more than we now use. The natural increase in demand would exhaust that amount in less than ten years. The undeveloped water power is in the West and South, and the industrial East must continue to build coal-burning plants as long as the present limitation of three hundred miles for electric transmission obtains.

That limitation may be removed, however, before many months, and we may be able to send Coulee power to New York City with no more loss than we now meet in any transmission line. The solution is simple, though it may sound technical to the layman. It is to use high-tension *direct cur-*

rent instead of the alternating current now universally used for long-distance transmission. Two wires at 700,000 volts pressure to earth would deliver the two million electrical horsepower now used in New York City from the Columbia River plants with only a 10 percent loss in transmission. There is no scientific reason why this cannot soon be done. Direct-current transmission waits only the development of a high-voltage rectifying tube. With tubes already made we can transmit from Coulee to the eastern Idaho phosphate beds, 650 miles, and the distance might be raised to 1000 miles with existing facilities. With such a transmission system no part of the nation would be out of reach of power plants in another part. There will be no regional power shortages— only a national shortage. As the daily peak of demand follows the sun across the country, power will flow first to the east, then to the west. A saving of 20 to 30 percent in total capacity of generators will result, for the peak of demand is three and a half hours later in San Francisco than in New York.

The value of such a system in the national defense is incalculable. It will permit war industry to be set up at any point of advantage. The lines themselves will form "carriers" for communication, more reliable in emergency than radio or telephone. The great steamplants may be placed at the point where fuel is cheapest. No water-power site will lack a market because of distance from the load center, for the whole nation will be within reach. In such a picture there is little place for worry over the ultimate use of power from Grand Coulee.

Meanwhile other provision must be made for immediate distribution of the power. The Bonneville Administrator has already surveyed a 270-mile high-voltage line of the conventional alternating-current type to connect Coulee to Bonneville and form the backbone of the future system into which all ten Columbia River plants will deliver. The same conductors can carry direct current when that is made available. These great plants are developed for the benefit of the consumer, and the Bonneville Act provides that preference must be given public agencies over private power companies in the allotment of the power. Twenty-five of the thirty-nine Washington counties have organized themselves as Public Utility Districts, with authority to buy or generate their own power and distribute it to their citizens. With the cities of Seattle and Tacoma, which operate their own public plants, the Public Districts represent the great majority of the state's 1,600,-000 people. The transmission lines from Bonneville, for which the conductors, towers and poles are already purchased and are being delivered, will reach those districts nearest that plant. The line to Coulee will ensure an integrated Columbia River development, to be connected with the municipal plants of the Northwest, including the million horsepower Skagit plants of the City of Seattle, to make a public super-power system covering the entire district. A uniform rate for firm power at wholesale anywhere on the Bonneville transmission lines has been set at $17.50 per kilowatt per year—two mills per kilowatt-hour based on continuous all-year use of the power. At the Bonneville plant, without transmission, the rate is $14.50, and a rate of $11.00 per kilowatt-year on the lines, or $9.50 per kilowatt-year at the plant, is made for secondary or seasonal power. The "objective" retail rate for the home, recommended for adoption by cities and power districts using Bonneville power, is

First 50 kw.-hr. per month................	2½¢ per kw.-hr.
Next 150 kw.-hr. per month................	2 ¢ per kw.-hr.
Next 100 kw.-hr. per month................	1 ¢ per kw.-hr.
Next 1700 kw.-hr. per month................	½¢ per kw.-hr.
Excess above 2000 kw.-hr. per month........	¾¢ per kw.-hr.
Minimum monthly bill....................	50 ¢ per meter

This rate is less than half the usual residence rate in this country. Experience proves that such a rate will permit the consumer to double and triple his use, for with each rate reduction new uses become possible.

The first use for Columbia River power is to supply the immediate increase of demand in the Northwest. No surplus capacity exists. A dry season would bring a serious shortage, for the Federal plants and the Skagit plants of Seattle constitute the only new capacity in the district since the depression.

The new lower rate will permit distribution to farms now without electricity, and a much wider use on farms already served. Experience in the Broadmoor district in Seattle, borne out by that in Winnipeg and the Ontario cities, would indicate that all the power could be used in the home. The development of industry is of fundamental importance to the Northwest. Its raw materials should be processed before they are shipped. Raw materials shipped from the Orient— silk, tung oil—should be transformed to the finished article before they are sent east. The district is rich in minerals— zinc, lead, copper and manganese, all requiring electric power in their preparation for use. The world's greatest deposit of phosphate rock, a necessary fertilizer for our land if it is to continue to support our population, lies in eastern Idaho. Electric power is the only other necessary ingredient for making a balanced fertilizer. Most of the manufactured articles, of steel, metal, glass, textiles and even wood, are shipped to the Northwest from the East. Branch factories using Columbia power would save transportation expense and profitably supply the local demand.

Critics miss the real meaning of these great public projects. It is not a question of their cost, for the power will pay the interest and retire the debt. The real question is: What wealth and convenience will appear in the farms and orchards and at the end of the power line? The farmer will pay for his land. The customer pays for his current, and puts every kilowatt-hour to use for a purpose to his benefit. In the building of a prosperous empire in the desert the whole nation benefits. Just as critics questioned the justification for building Panama, only to see the canal become a necessity, just as the "white elephant," Boulder Dam, has become the foundation for the prosperity of southern California, so criticism of the Columbia River project is already turning to enthusiastic approval as the realization of its meaning is seen. We stand on the threshold of a new age—the Age of Superpower. In a world bending its energies toward destruction, the nation that can and will build a Coulee and a Bonneville holds the hope of the future of our civilization.

LAYING THE GROUNDWORK

Preparation for Reading

1. What part does electricity play in industry, communication, transportation, heating, and the conservation of labor?
2. What are some of the major developments of electric power in this country? in other lands?
3. What conditions are necessary to the successful development of irrigation projects? Name some irrigation projects in this country and enumerate the major crops which are produced in the irrigated areas.
4. How did each of the following aid in the development of electricity: Franklin, Faraday, Morse, Ohm, Volta, Hertz, Edison, Marconi, Bell?

Vocabulary Building

This selection contains few difficult words or allusions. Look up any which you do not know.

APPRAISING THE RESULTS

1. Locate Coulee Dam and describe the geologic conditions which made it possible. What two main purposes will the dam serve?
2. Why did the construction of Coulee Dam have to wait for government financing? When and by whom was it finally authorized?
3. Compare the magnitude of this dam with that of other gigantic structures. What were the problems which had to be solved in its construction?
4. When the dam is completed, how much power will be available, and how will it be used? How will the general availability of this power over a wide area tend to promote greater consumption and thus make for lower rates?
5. When the Columbia projects are completed, what part will they play in supplying power, locally and nationally?
6. Describe the proposed irrigation plans.
7. What arguments have been advanced against the advisability and the practicability of the dam? Are these arguments sound? Give reasons for your answer.

SELECTING THE THEME SUBJECT

1. Write a paper presenting the arguments for or against public ownership and control of power.
2. Describe a power or irrigation project with which you are familiar.
3. Titles for themes: National Defense and Power; Electrical Power and the Housewife; The Industrial Uses of Electricity; Electric Street Cars or Gasoline Buses?; Heating and Refrigeration by Electricity; The Problem of Long-distance Power Transmission; Electric Gadgets in the Home; Early Experiments in Electricity; Power Developments in the Soviet Union, in Holland, and in the Scandinavian Countries; Modern Communication by Means of Electricity; Better Lighting for the Home; The Use of Electricity in Medical Practice; Public Safety and Electricity; Electric Power and the Farmer; Uses of the Radio and the Wireless Telegraph in Protecting Lives at Sea or in the Air; A Comparison of Power Rates in Different Sections or Cities in the United States.

WHEN YOU DRIVE FAST[1]

Curtis Billings

IN THE WHOLE REALM OF AUTOMOBILE SAFETY—ABOUT WHICH
NOT TOO MUCH IS KNOWN—THERE IS NOTHING SO CONFUSED AND
confusing as the relation of speed to accidents. Most people
will agree (because they feel it in their bones) that as speeds go
up accidents become more severe, but few motorists realize
how great is the effect of an increased rate of travel on an
accident involving a car; and almost nobody understands
why it is that accidents are *more likely* to occur at high speed.

In fact many would be quick to dispute this latter point.
They themselves have driven cars or have ridden in cars
traveling up to 80 or 90 miles an hour without an accident,
without, indeed, any particular feeling of discomfort or
danger. It is not easy for them to see why such rates in themselves are hazardous, and it is difficult to demonstrate that
they are. The physical laws involved are complicated and
explanations of them must be somewhat technical; but with
speeds ever increasing and the death rates from automobile
accidents leaping higher correspondingly, it would seem vital
for the American motorist to understand the forces he must
deal with when he pushes his accelerator down.

Physicists in their laboratories sometimes roll marbles
down inclined planes to demonstrate the tremendous increase
in the energy of a moving body as its speed goes up. In this
way they show beyond dispute that as the speed of a moving
object is doubled, its energy (or destructive force) increases
four times; as its speed is tripled, its energy increases nine
times; and as its speed is quadrupled, its ability to destroy

---

[1] From *Harper's Magazine*, July, 1936. Reprinted by permission of the author and of the publishers.

itself and whatever it strikes is increased sixteen times. In
other words, the energy of a moving body increases as the
square of its speed.

That this bit of theoretical knowledge, which teachers
spout so glibly, has a direct bearing on motor vehicle accidents can be shown from the records. E. Raymond Cato, chief
of the California Highway Patrol, recently said that in his
State a fatality seldom occurs to passengers of cars going less
than 20 miles an hour, that, on the other hand, the majority
of slain motorists were riding in automobiles traveling in
excess of 45. Michigan records show that if you are going to
have an accident there your chances of killing someone are
five times as great if you are traveling over 50 miles an hour
as they are at a rate under 20. Numerous States and cities
have reduced automobile deaths promptly by lowering
average driving speeds; and, obversely, they have experienced
sharp and sudden increases in fatalities when they relaxed
their control of speed.

It is, however, one thing to adduce data to prove that accidents grow worse as speeds go up; it is quite another to show
how and why accidents are *more likely* to occur at high speed.
The latter is the more difficult task, but the lesson to be
learned is even more valuable to the driver.

R. A. Moyer, associate professor of highway engineering at
Iowa State College, made a four-year research of the action of
automobiles on highways, paying particular attention to the
effects of variations in speed. His study illuminates this whole
problem. He distinguishes three important types of accidents
which seldom occur at low speeds and shows why they occur
at high speeds. In all three accidents the driver loses control
of his car: in the first case he loses control because of speed
and surface roughness; in the second case because of speed
plus unwise or inadequate braking; in the third case because
of speed at curves. The accident in any of the cases may be
one in which the car collides with another machine or strikes
a tree or bridge head or runs off the road and turns over, or
does any of the hundred and one things that cars do when
they are out of control. Inasmuch as the speeds are high,
the accidents are usually frightfully severe.

II

Surface roughness is a greater factor than one would ordinarily suppose. Who has not driven over a rutted dirt road pitted with hub-deep holes? Nothing happened and the car was in no particular danger of turning over or bouncing into the ditch. But one was driving at a very low rate of speed, probably in second or low gear. At high speed it would be impossible to drive on such a road. One of the smoothest surfaces in the world, that at Daytona Beach, Florida, was too rough to meet the requirements of the world's fastest driver, Sir Malcolm Campbell. For it was a surface roughness quite imperceptible to the eye that caused Sir Malcolm to leave Daytona and go to the perfectly level salt flats of Utah, there to make his world record of more than 300 miles an hour. A waviness in the beach bed at Daytona measuring only two inches to the hundred feet was sufficient at the rates Sir Malcolm traveled to send his six-ton racing car soaring through the air.

The only contact between a car and the highway is through the tires. As one drives along a level road the tires make a uniform contact with the surface. But as waves or other aberrations appear the contact varies. In the instant after leaving the crest of a bump, however small, the tires *tend* to leave the pavement and this reduces the area of the tire that is pressing against the road. As the speed of the car goes up this tendency increases until the tire actually does leave the surface.

A car need not be traveling at an extremely high rate to "take off." Forty-five miles an hour is sufficient if the rise on the surface measures only four inches in forty feet. The take-off amounts to a veritable flight if the speed is 70 or 80 miles an hour when the car shoots over such a bump. While rises of this height are common enough on old pavements and on unpaved surfaces, they are rather rare, fortunately, on new pavements. They are especially numerous of course in localities where the subgrade is poor, as near bridges and culverts, and where frost has caused the pavement to heave and settle.

The weight of the car has nothing to do with the tendency to take off: one is as likely to do it in a Cadillac as in a Ford. Speed and the steepness of the rise or bump are the only factors.

On curves it is easy to see why this sudden reduction of the friction between the tire and the roadway may cause the driver to lose control of his machine. The thing that keeps a speeding car on a curve (when centrifugal force is always trying to impel it off in a straight line) is the sidethrust friction between the tires and the road. This friction must continue or the car will go into a skid. If on a perfectly dry pavement there is a bump on the surface which momentary inattention or a defect in vision induces the driver to overlook, the all-important friction will be reduced and in that instant centrifugal force will get its chance at the car. By cool, quick work the driver may avert a crash, but if he cannot, the car may slide off the curve and land bottom-side up along the fence line—as many do.

The same thing can occur on the straightaway. Even here one occasionally turns and sometimes sharply, as when one passes a vehicle and cuts back into line before an oncoming machine gets too close. In such a maneuver the same forces are brought into play as on a curve. When one is traveling straight ahead, a bump over which the wheels of only one side of the car pass may throw the vehicle sideways with such force that control is lost. Or, indeed, when the whole car takes off evenly, a strong cross wind catching it in midair can wrench control away from the driver.

Professor Moyer says that surface roughness on the speedway at Indianapolis (which looked so smooth to the spectators) probably was the outstanding circumstance in the series of accidents which took the lives of 27 drivers and mechanics there. "The variations in the surfaces of many miles of our main highways are so great that 70 or 80 miles an hour are impossible with safety," he declares.

III

Of all driving operations the one which causes the most skidding is the improper use of brakes or the use of improper brakes at high speed. When a car skids it is out of control. If one is skillful and the highway is wide and if other cars are not nearby, one can sometimes manipulate the car out of the skid and back into control; but too often the driver does not know how to do this or cannot act fast enough to regain command of his vehicle.

Tests show that if there is 40 per cent more braking power on one side of the car than on the other, an attempt at a sudden stop at the rate of 40 miles an hour can and usually will pull the machine out of its lane of traffic and into the adjacent lane. If the greater power is on the left side, this means swerving the car suddenly into the lane of oncoming traffic; if it is on the right side, it means forcing the car onto the shoulder of the highway or perhaps into a bridge head, guard rail, or ditch. Automobiles have been observed to skid end for end on dry pavements when all the braking force was delivered on one wheel.

But are brakes as faulty as this common enough to warrant special notice? In conducting his researches Professor Moyer tested the brakes of 2,134 cars taken at random. Of these 31 per cent had brakes which had at least 40 per cent more braking power on one side than on the other. The brakes on fully half of the cars in use were found to be inadequate. One can appreciate how much more hazardous such brakes are as speeds increase beyond the forty-mile-an-hour mark. The swerving can be so violent that control of the vehicle is utterly lost. And such swerving always occurs in dangerous situations —situations which called for the emergency stop.

So much for the dangers involved in the use of improper brakes. Now let us consider the *improper use* of brakes and how this causes and accentuates skids. At the outset I might say that at low speed on ordinary pavements there is scarcely such a thing as the improper use of brakes: braking can be improper only at speeds which are too high for conditions.

First it is necessary to explain how brakes act. When a motorist decides to stop he must depend largely upon the friction which can be developed at two points on his car. The first of these is between the brake bands and the drums, the second between the tires and the road. It may seem odd, but the actual stopping of the car is brought about at the weaker of the two points, *i.e.,* the one with the less friction, because it is at this point where the slippage occurs which takes up the car's energy. Thus when traveling on a dry abrasive surface the coefficient of friction or gripping power of the tires on the road surface is generally greater than that developed by the brakes. Under these conditions the slippage at the brakes will provide the friction necessary to stop the car. If the brakes exert a stronger drag on the car than that provided by the tires and the road, they will lock the wheels, causing the tires to slide, thus bringing the car to a stop. There are numerous conditions which affect the gripping power of the tires on the highway. First, no two types of road surfaces exert the same power. Loose dirt or mud or ice or snow may cover the surface and reduce drastically the available friction. Second, tires are important. Even though variations between them are not so great as between road surfaces, new tires with good treads have a higher coefficient of friction on ordinary pavements than old ones which have been worn smooth. The third and most important condition is the speed at which the car is traveling; for on paved roads the all-important friction between tire and surface decreases as the speed increases so that when one needs the most friction one has the least. At very high speeds on wet surfaces even comparatively weak brakes will have more friction than can be developed between the tire and the road, and applying them will lock the wheels and throw the car inevitably into a skid.

We all know that when a machine begins to skid on ice the most dangerous thing for the driver to do is to put on the brakes. Doing so will only make the skid worse because the driver loses what benefit he had from the turning of the wheels. The same thing is true at high speeds on perfectly dry pavements. When, under these conditions, a car begins to skid or when it becomes so unmanageable that it is difficult to steer it and you think it is going to skid, jamming on the brakes may lock one or more wheels at once, sending the car into a skid from which it is impossible to save it.

It would be well to point out to the reader at this point that there is a very great difference between skidding at low speeds and at high. If you are driving on ice at a necessarily low rate and your car begins to skid you can frequently turn the front wheels in the same direction in which the rear wheels are sliding and resume control. But if you are traveling at a high rate on a curve and strike an unlooked-for patch of ice, mud, or even water, or, if at this rate on a dry pavement you apply the brakes, the car will go into a skid *within your reaction time* or, in other words, quicker than you can think. The instruction to turn the wheels with the skid is of no use whatever. The car has skidded off the road and perhaps turned over so quickly that you simply do not know what happened. It can occur in a tiny fraction of a second, and the average person requires at least three-quarters of a second to react to such a situation. By the time he is able to react he is wrecked. One must remember then that the proper control of a car on a slippery pavement or on a curve at high speed is not a braking problem, but a problem of steering combined with the skillful use of the throttle.

Professor Moyer says that motor-car manufacturers have a problem in developing brakes which are adequate for the high driving speeds of to-day. What is urgently needed, he says, is a braking system in which the wheels cannot be locked, a system which will deliver maximum braking resistance at each wheel for each type of road surface, and which will provide stopping forces equally balanced right and left for both front and rear wheels.

IV

We have seen that high speeds make accidents more likely to occur on highways of even moderate roughness and that emergency stops by the use of brakes are ever so much more hazardous at high speeds than at low. Now why is a driver apt to lose control of his car on curves while traveling at a high rate of speed, and what can he do about it?

A car on a curve is, as we have seen, the object of attention of two opposing forces and the outcome of their tug-of-war is of utmost importance to the passengers. These forces are centrifugal force on the one hand and sidethrust friction between the tires and the road on the other, aided by the pull of gravity if the curve is banked. Although few drivers realize it, when taking a curve at a high rate the wheels are always out of line with the direction of travel and so the car really slips or slides round the curve at an angle. This is true of any car which takes a curve at a rate higher than that for which it was banked, but it is especially evident in a racing car taking a curve at maximum speed. This "slip angle" may be so large that the rear end of the car is several feet farther out on the curve than the front end. The greater the speed the greater the slip angle must be, because the friction required to hold the car on the road increases as the square of the speed. Thus at 40 miles an hour the amount of friction needed to hold a car on a curve is not twice but four times the amount needed at 20 miles an hour. Increasing the slip angle will provide the friction up to a certain point, but above that point the car will go into a skid or turn over or otherwise pass out of the control of the driver. The slippage at 80 miles an hour even on a comparatively gentle highway curve is so great that the most skillful driver will have difficulty in steering.

Accidents on curves are usually the result of entering the curve too fast. This is true both on racing courses and on public highways. It is the prime error and the motorist all too frequently makes it. He is lured on by a fast, quiet automobile, a highway that looks smooth and wide, and utter ignorance of the forces that go to work on his vehicle when he attempts to turn. I shall not go into a discussion of radial acceleration but shall merely point out with all the emphasis that I can give to words that a fast driver must slow down on entering a curve unless he is content to risk his life and the life of everybody riding with him at every twist of the highway.

Despite the fact that the outcome of an automobile race depends largely on the speed with which the drivers can take the turns and despite the fact that racing drivers are extremely expert daredevils, they all slow down to enter a curve. The braking action in slowing down throws the rear end of the car out on the curve to provide the wide slip angle they need. Slowing down also enables a driver to turn his steering wheel from its position on the straightaway, or tangent, to the new angle required by the curve.

Almost every driver has had the harrowing experience of attempting to take a curve so fast that he found it impossible to make the necessary adjustment in his steering angle. He turned the wheel either too far or not far enough and wove unsteadily back and forth across the highway with the car almost out of control. While this may rightfully be termed reckless driving, Professor Moyer says that the fault does not lie entirely with the driver. If highway engineers were to design *transition* curves such as are universally used by the railroads, much of the danger of driving on curves would be removed. Instead of consisting of an arc of a circle connecting two tangents or straightaways, which requires the driver to make a sudden large adjustment in his steering angle, the transition curve is made up of arcs of gradually increasing curvature as one approaches the center of the curve. Thus as the driver enters the curve it is necessary for him to turn the steering wheel only slightly. As he continues on the curve he gradually keeps on turning the wheel until he reaches the circular arc itself. He has come to this circular arc very gradually and leaves it by the same gentle gradations.

This improvement would give a driver on a curve two or three times the margin of safety that he now has. In other words, if a curve is such that a racing driver can barely drive round it safely at 60 miles an hour, and the average motorist cannot manage it safely above 40—and there are many such curves—building transitions into the curve would enable the motorist to take it at 60 as safely as he now can at 40. The device would not impel faster driving or even encourage it; it would simply spare the lives of a lot of people who unwittingly attempt to enter curves too fast.

Banking a curve so that gravity will be utilized to offset centrifugal force is a great help to motorists, but they must remember that curves are not banked for high rates of speed and that gravity remains constant for all speeds while centrifugal force increases as the square of the speed. Just because a curve is banked the motorist must not attempt to maintain any rate he chooses—if he wants to live.

The danger of encountering snow, ice, or mud on a curve (or water on some types of pavements) is so apparent that it scarcely needs mention. A driver is entirely dependent on the frictional resistance of the tires on the road, and if this resistance is reduced suddenly his car will go into a skid.

It is seen then that accidents on curves are far more likely to occur at high speed. For the driver who wants to be safe on our present highway curves there is one thing to do: reduce speed, particularly when entering the curve.

v

This discussion of the dangers of fast driving would be incomplete without mention of one other aspect of it: how high speed affects the accelerating power of an automobile and why one must allow a far greater distance for passing a car going 60 miles an hour than one going 30, even though one's machine is capable of such a high rate as 90. Accidents resulting from the exercise of poor judgment in passing cars when a third car is approaching from the opposite direction are particularly serious because they occur at high rates and frequently take the form of head-on collisions.

Professor Moyer says that a 1934 Ford V-8 or a car of like accelerating ability requires 600 feet to pass a car which is traveling 30 miles an hour. (This assumes that the overtaking car is following the other at a safe distance before starting to pass and that it will not cut back into line until a safe clear distance between it and the passed car is available.) More than twice this distance, or 1,350 feet, is required to pass a car traveling at 60 miles an hour. To pass one going 80 miles an hour, 1,875 feet are needed. The reason for this great increase in necessary distance is that the ability of an automobile to accelerate decreases as its speed goes up. It is far easier for your car to accelerate from 30 to 40 miles an hour than from 60 to 70 miles an hour because in the former instance it has more reserve power.

If an automobile is approaching from the opposite direction as you decide to pass another machine on the road, how much clear distance must you have between your car and the one which is approaching? If it is coming at 40 miles an hour and you are trailing a car traveling at 30, the required clear distance is 1,050 feet. But if you are trailing a car traveling at 60 and the approaching automobile is coming at the same rate, to pass safely you will need no less than 2,300 feet, or almost half a mile. Since it is impossible to judge speeds accurately, a safe rule to follow is this: do not attempt to pass a car which is moving at 40 miles an hour or more unless there is a clear distance between your car and an approaching car of one-half to three-quarters of a mile. When in the slightest doubt wait until the approaching car has gone by. Other rules which grow out of this discussion are as follows:

1. Drive slowly over rough surfaces. At high rates of speed beware of even small bumps and rises on the pavement.

2. Keep your brakes equalized and never apply them if the car begins to zigzag on a curve or to skid.

3. Slow down *before* entering a curve.

4. Remember, the higher the speed the worse the accident. Fatal accidents are most common at speeds above 45 miles an hour.

It is a question whether the American motoring public taken as a whole will ever learn how to handle an automobile safely at speeds above 50 miles an hour. Can the thirty million drivers in the country be capable of the precision of control that such rates demand? Surely they cannot be unless they comprehend the physical laws that they are up against when they sit behind the wheel—laws which are inviolable, which no traffic judge, however lenient, can set aside.

LAYING THE GROUNDWORK

Preparation for Reading
1. What do you think is the chief cause of automobile accidents?
2. Are pedestrians or drivers more to blame for accidents?
3. Do you drive too fast in your own opinion? your family's? a court's, if you should have an accident?
4. Should manufacturers make cars capable of doing 90 to 100 miles an hour when the speed limit is 25-30 miles in town, and 45-50 in the country? Of what value is the additional speed to the ordinary driver?

Vocabulary Building

1. Look up these words: *accelerator, physicists, demonstrate, tremendous, quadrupled, veritable, theoretical, glibly, adduce, data, aberrations, culverts, centrifugal, abrasive, drastically, coefficient, radial, tangent, transition curves, gradations.*
2. Is it easier for you to remember technical than abstract words? Explain the reasons for your answer.

APPRAISING THE RESULTS

1. What is the central theme of this essay? Where is it stated? Why are the section divisions indicated?
2. What law of physics is involved in this problem of speed? Where is it discussed in the selection?
3. What is the relation between speed and fatal accidents?
4. Explain the factors which make speed dangerous. What research has been done on this point?
5. Why do cars skid? How must car manufacturers improve brakes?
6. Explain how speed affects the accelerating power of an automobile. How is the principle involved in accidents?
7. Are there other causes of accidents Mr. Billings does not mention? What is the basis of his selection of causes?

SELECTING THE THEME SUBJECT

1. Compile a chart of automobile accident figures for your own community and from it develop a theme on home driving conditions.
2. Interview the traffic officers of your community and write a paper summarizing their reports.
3. Defend or attack the statement: "We are driving a 20th Century machine along 19th Century horse and buggy roads."
4. Make a study of different parking plans in various places to decide if there is more or less progress here than in the plans for highways. Report your findings and conclusions.
5. Discuss: (a) traffic congestion on city streets, (b) good manners for drivers, (c) the automobile and technological unemployment, (d) the farm and the automobile.

CATCHING UP WITH THE INVENTORS[1]
Arthur Train, Jr.

HAVE YOU AN "ELECTRIC PIG" IN YOUR KITCHEN TO GRIND UP THE GARBAGE? DO YOU EAT STRAWBERRIES OUT OF SEASON grown in a chemical solution? Is your house guarded by an "electric eye"? Has your radio a facsimile printing attachment? Are your clocks electrically timed? Does your car have a continuous gear ratio? Do you receive your milk in a paper container? Do you use the kind of film in your camera that makes it possible to take difficult indoor pictures with an ordinary lens? Have you seen any stereoscopic or three-dimensional movies? Have you air-conditioning in your home? How many prefabricated houses are there in your neighborhood? How many "modern" houses? How often do you take the *Normandie* or the *Queen Mary* or Diesel electric streamlined trains or sleeper planes? Do you pick up the telephone at your elbow and call Hobart, Tasmania? If not, why not?

All these things are possible. The mere enumeration of them gives the characteristic atmosphere of the times in which we live. But if these things are characteristic of to-day, a majority of us are living twenty or thirty years in the past. For the introduction of technological developments is unfortunately not limited by time alone; it is limited by a number of other factors. The most important of these in the battle of survival is cost. Then there is the constitutional inability of most persons to grasp the implications of something that differs from what they have been accustomed to; it is hard to put new wine into old bottles. Then there is

[1] From *Harper's Magazine*, March, 1938. Reprinted by permission of the author and of the publishers.

organized labor which disputes the right of the machine to take jobs away on the one hand, and on the other, capital, which has invested in expensive tools and hesitates to see them rendered obsolete. All of these impediments can be reduced to one main underlying difficulty, which is that the course of technological progress, instead of being steady, is highly irregular.

According to a careful survey made a few years ago of a typical American locality, half the families whose total incomes are under $2,000 a year have radios, while all the families with incomes of $10,000 and over have them. Half the families in the under $2,000 group own cars, but at $5,000 and beyond they all do. Only 14 families per thousand under $5,000 a year own a high-priced car, and only 114 above $5,000 own two cars. Only 55 families per thousand in the under $2,000 a year group own automatic refrigerators and at $10,000 and over there are still only 302. One hundred and seventy-one of these own refrigerators costing over $300. In the under $2,000 group there are 24 families who occasionally visit Europe; there are 140 in the $10,000 and over group. The Department of Commerce Survey on the consumer use of selected goods and services by income classes in the main substantiates these findings, except that in the cities that were investigated more people in the higher-income brackets had refrigerators.

As for air-conditioning, it will have to become considerably cheaper before more than a few thousand families in the United States can afford to have it in their homes. A facsimile recorder, if anyone wanted it, would cost about $100; but of course there would have to be a service to supply the necessary copy. At the present time two newspaper stations are supplying such a service to 100 sets. A television receiving set in its present stage of development would cost in the neighborhood of $300. There are few private individuals in the country who could afford the luxury of a television transmitting set, which to-day costs around $300,000.

On the other hand, in 1922 a superheterodyne receiving set with only four tubes, and still battery operated, cost as much as $350. The merest $20 set to-day is far superior to it in tone and selectivity. Until recently the cost of the family automobile went down as steadily as its quality increased. From a luxury it has become a necessity, and the same is rapidly becoming true of the electric refrigerator.

On this basis, it may be fair to assume that the far more complicated television receiving apparatus might drop in the next 30 or 40 years to from one-half to one-quarter of its present price, and without auditory or visual perspective or color, might well cost around $50. Manufacturers, basing their estimates on the progress of television in England, expect to sell about 20,000 sets the first year. Thus it will probably be a long time before every home has a television receiving set, and two-way point-to-point television for individuals belongs to the more distant rather than to the immediate future.

Moreover, it is not the actual cost of a new appliance that determines its adoption, but, unless it provides an entirely new service, its comparative cost—it has to be nearly as cheap as the next best thing in its line. Cost of course did not stop thousands of persons from buying expensive Leicas and those nice little movie cameras, and we also know that there is no way of telling when a process which now seems expensive may suddenly become cheap. Nevertheless, how many persons would buy a facsimile recorder for $100 when the current to run it alone would cost as much as the newspaper you can buy on the corner? How many persons who already had a television set would pay an additional $100 for visual and auditory perspective and another $100 for color provided no way were discovered to lessen the cost of these additional effects?

II

In the Report on Technological Trends and National Policy of the National Resources Committee, S. C. Gilfillan, formerly Curator of Social Sciences at the Museum of Science and Industry in Chicago, implies that in the past scientific writers have demonstrated their ability to predict the technological aspects of the future with a considerable degree of accuracy. We all know of course that, in addition to studying the art of flying, Leonardo da Vinci toyed with the idea of tanks and submarines, but gave them up as too pernicious. As a prophet Jules Verne did well. In *Looking Backward*, written in 1888, Edward Bellamy painted a fair picture of many technological developments of to-day. Even the old Hippodrome shows of our childhood were not as fantastic as they evidently were intended to be. But the report goes on to point out that of 65 predictions made in an article in the *Scientific American* in 1920, 78 per cent have been or will be proved right and 22 per cent wrong. Of 25 predictions made by Steinmetz in an article twenty-one years ago, 76 per cent have been or will shortly be realized, 24 per cent are doubtful, and there are no real errors. Unless there were also many other science writers whose predictions have been overlooked or forgotten because they were wrong, this would seem to imply that the prediction of future technological developments might be put on a scientific basis.

Well, it is a great temptation to try one's hand at this sort of thing because it almost always makes good reading. The less conscientious writers almost inevitably succumb to the temptation to make such copy salable by sensationalizing it, so that the Sunday supplements are full of lurid descriptions of death rays, rocket planes, germ warfare, trips to the moon, the conquest of death, the production of human beings in the laboratory, and so on. These descriptions are all right as far as they go, except that the last line is always omitted, and that line is, "and then Johnny woke up." No one has yet attempted the far more difficult and less ingratiating task of picturing what the world will be like fifty years from now, taking into account the factors which impede technological progress and to which I have already summarily referred, such as (in addition to the comparative cost of the appliances themselves) the psychological resistance of the public to innovation, the danger of increased unemployment, the relation of wages to the cost of living, investment in obsolete plants, and the suppression of patents. To paint such a picture with anywhere near the accuracy of, shall we say, the luckier ones among the earlier prophets, one would have to have a notion of the form of government and kind of economic system we are likely to have. Lacking this foreknowledge, the best one can do is attempt to describe the kind of future world the technologists *could* make for us, and then enumerate and analyze the obstructing factors.

The relationship between scientists, engineers, and the ultimate consumer may be graphically expressed by three concentric circles. The innermost circle or core represents the scientists who, generally speaking, are working at pure theory. It is here that you will find men exploring the possibilities of the cathode ray, the breakup of the atom, and the immortality of flesh tissues, and making other inquiries which may not affect our environment for the next century or more. The next circle represents the men who translate the theories that have a contemporary application into living things of steel and magnesium and resin and concrete. Finally, the outermost circle represents us humble mortals who may or may not buy and use what the engineers have built for us, according to our psychological limitations. In the past it has generally taken about thirty-three years for an invention to travel from the inner core to the outer rim, although to-day the gap is decreasing. To paint a sensational picture of the future you need only dip your brush into the cosmic pigments with which the men of the innermost circle are working; to paint an exciting one you need only describe the materials in the hands of the engineers; but the true picture, considerably less dramatic, concerns itself with the everyday things with which common men and women surround themselves.

The temptation is all the greater to overlook the effect of the various resistances in painting a picture of the future, because it is undeniable that to-day we are in the midst of sensational developments whose implications are ignored by the average man. We are impressed by the great winged birds that span the oceans, but when we look at the caps on bottles of beer or the glass in our car windows it does not occur to us that a silent revolution is taking place. Recent developments in organic chemistry, metallurgy, and electronics are not only as startling as those of transportation and communication, but in many instances have made the latter possible.

Since this is a game that anyone can play, one guess being as good as another, let's see what we can do with it. If we confine ourselves to inventions that are either born or in the laboratory stage, we shall not fall into the error of producing apocalyptic visions after the manner of the Sunday supplements. Moreover, we can check our statements against those of the National Resources Committee's report which was compiled in good faith by a group of experts.

It is unfortunately impossible within the confines of one article to make a study of probable future trends in the various technological fields. About all one can do is to uncover a little peephole and look through it for an instant. If we are so rash as to say what we see, half the scientists in the country will rise up to tell us that there is absolutely no reason why the picture should not be entirely different, although there may be comfort in the fact that by the time anybody is actually in a position to prove us wrong we shall probably be either dead or senile.

III

Our hero, then, John Doe, born in the year of grace 1938, was in bed and asleep at the time our story begins in 1988. (No synthetic substitute for sleep had then been discovered.) Progress in biology, biochemistry, food technology, and related sciences was responsible for the fact that he was considerably heavier and taller than his forefathers, and also that, although half a century old, he was neither too fat nor too thin, and like Uncle Ned had "plenty of wool on the top of his head, the place where the wool ought to be."

The sounds of the city were filtered at the intake-ducts of the air-conditioning apparatus, and such few persistent discords and jangles as did penetrate into the room were deflected toward the ceiling by the walls which slanted gently upward, like the glass windows of radio broadcasting control rooms, where they were absorbed by special insulation. The entering air passed through a dust filter and was freed from other germs by ultra-violet rays. Research into the effects of ionization, barometric pressure, condensation nuclei, and the existence of a metastable state of oxygen had made it possible to supply Mr. Doe's room with air as invigorating as that of the seashore or the mountains. Its chemical composition was nicely calculated to give him a maximum of refreshment at night, while during the day its temperature, humidity, and degree of ionization were automatically varied from time to time in order to avoid the soporific effect of monotony. Incidentally, synthetic air, long considered fantastic, was well on the way toward becoming a reality.

Presently, as the radio-controlled clock proclaimed in a soothing voice that it was time to get up (for its direct reading dial showed the hour of seven), the air became sensibly warmer. Heating was provided by the simple process of running the refrigerator mechanism in reverse, although some architects recommended heating coils in the walls or radiant wires in the ceiling.

Although it was dark and rainy outside, the room was gradually flooded with a diffused light. The quantity required was measured out with nice accuracy by the ever-watchful photocell, and on sunny days when clouds passed over the sun, the light in the room would remain constant. This light was provided by a type of gaseous discharge lamp, perhaps employing carbon dioxide, infinitely more efficient than the old-fashioned incandescent filament bulbs, and containing as good a proportion of infra-red and ultra-violet rays as that of the brightest summer sun, which were automatically turned on at intervals.

Meanwhile—the first item in a pre-selected program from different stations—the television screen faded in on an energetic man in a football sweater who beckoned to Mr. Doe to arise and begin his setting-up exercises. In apartment houses these television images were usually "piped" along a coaxial cable (an invention which the public of the '30s had failed to realize was as revolutionary as the telephone itself); but for private homes and for general purposes the old-fashioned system of coaxial cable and linked radio stations had been superseded by the "Yale lock" style of multiple wave-lengths using various permutations and combinations to give broader wave-band availability of an unlimited number of channels.

The bathroom into which Mr. Doe stepped for his matutinal shower was a prefabricated affair made like an automobile, all the various appliances such as tub, shower, basin, and toilet forming one integrated unit, with special metallic walls for the outer casing. Three identical bathrooms were grouped with it to form a square in the center of the house, so that a minimum of plumbing was required. The old-fashioned system of using thousands of gallons of water to dilute and remove waste, thereby sacrificing its valuable chemical properties, had long ago been superseded by chemical disposal of sewage. The development of new detergents also made it possible to "wash" without water if anyone so desired.

While Doe was slipping into a pair of shorts and a light, three-quarter length rayon fabric smock, which, after all, is all that anyone would need in an air-conditioned home, he haphazardly pushed in various buttons controlling the automatic tuning of his television set so that he might see with his own eyes what was going on in the different parts of the world. He was a man who liked to spend money on gadgets, and the morning paper had been printed out for him by the facsimile recorder while he slept. It was his habit to leave it on just as people in the old days left the radio on, and from the reams of stuff it printed out he would pick what he wanted and throw the rest away. Most of the time, however, he preferred to hear the news rather than read it.

The vegetables and fruit that graced the Doe table out of season had never known the rich soil of a truck garden. Some—possibly the more expensive ones—had been grown in a vegetable factory in the heart of the community center, in a heated tray containing various salts. Others had come in black iron, plastic-coated cans, flash-heated to preserve the natural flavor of the contents, while others, at the other end of the scale, reached his kitchen in a frozen state. Mr. Doe habitually reflected with satisfaction that he never had any trouble getting whatever he wanted whenever he wanted it, and that the real significance of chemically produced crops and other mechanical aids to agriculture was that they permitted an efficient control of the food supply.

His house was situated at a considerable distance from the city, in an "integrated" neighborhood which had been carefully planned by a city planning board. The houses were grouped about a park, and in addition to the school and library there was a central air-conditioning plant and a community center with a television transmission set, an auditorium whose television receiving set boasted color and three-dimensional sound and sight, a trailer camp, all kinds of recreational facilities, the vegetable factory, the poultry factory, and the plant where garbage was converted into fertilizer.

The house itself was somewhat smaller and had smaller rooms than one would have expected of a man with Mr. Doe's means. The large custom-built house had long ago gone the way of the large custom-built automobile. It was a long, low, flat-roofed building made up of a cluster of prefabricated units whose irregular arrangement prevented it from looking monotonous. Unlike the houses of the early part of the century and all preceding eras, whose aim was to give an impression of volume, the whole building was so translucent, neutral, and fragile-looking, so broken into planes by terraces and porches, that it gave the impression of being no more than a part of the out-of-doors which had been etched into the frame with a few strokes of a sharp pointed pencil.

In the construction of the house the use of wood, bricks, and plaster had practically been superseded by panels of beryllium and magnesium alloys; low-grade silicas, or glass-like materials; sheet materials such as asbestos cement, and occasionally plastic which had been developed to a point where its resistance to atmosphere was known. A considerable use was made of moving partitions which made it possible to enclose a small space when privacy was required, and still provide a large space when it was not. The insulation, of "mineral fluff," was of course built into the prefabricated panels.

In the various rooms many of the pieces of furniture were made of plastic molded as a unit, while others were made of magnesium alloy. In place of cushions, spongelike synthetic upholstery was used. Some of the most beautiful hangings were of translucent glass fabric.

Outside of a few first editions and beautifully bound volumes with handsome illustrations, Mr. Doe's library contained few books. It consisted chiefly of little drawers filled with thousands of tiny reels of film a few millimeters in width. On his table was a reading machine about the size of a portable typewriter, which projected the tiny photographed pages onto a small screen. Each of these tiny films also carried a sound track, and at his own discretion he could play them on a talking book. Wherever he went Mr. Doe carried a camera hardly bigger than a watch and also a tiny sound-recording device, so that anything he saw or heard during the day he could conveniently remember by mechanical means. The day had not arrived (predicted by Sarnoff back in 1936) when each individual would have his own wave-length and by means of a pocket radio could communicate with anybody anywhere. In Doe's office the principle of mechanical aids to memory was developed to a high state of efficiency. All of his records were "remembered," selected, and analyzed on photoelectric tabulating machines with far greater efficiency than the human brain could achieve and in much less time.

An inventory of the various objects and materials used in Mr. Doe's house would show that the strawboard and fiberboard that lined the walls, the insulating material between them and the outer wall, sometimes the outer wall itself, the synthetic textiles which comprised the clothing of much of the family, and the waterproof materials which protected them if they ever went out in the rain, and all small knick-knacks from ash trays to bottle caps, were made of various types of thermo-plastic resin derived from such inexpensive raw materials as soy bean, bagasse, sugar cane, straw, wood pulp, sorghum, linseed, flaxseed, cottonseed hulls, oat hulls, nut shells, Jerusalem artichokes, fruit pits, and skim milk.

We have seen how in Mr. Doe's house the electric eye, or photoelectric tube, coupled with the thyratron tube which enables it to act on what it sees, automatically measured the amount of illumination necessary to replace the waning light of day. It also performed the functions of a whole corps of servants. It opened the garage door as you drove up, opened the door between the kitchen and the dining room when someone advanced with a tray, opened the door of the refrigerator, and opened and closed windows. But its duties did not end with the fall of day. All night long it was on guard as night watchman, ready to give warning by ringing bells, turning on floodlights, photographing the intruder, paralyzing him with tear gas, and sending for the police.

The roof of the house, as in all houses at that time, was used as a landing field for the family's collection of steep-flight airplanes of assorted sizes, the top storey being used as a garage. Doe didn't bother to use his car very often, and in general it was relegated to trips to the community center and to use by the children, playing the role of the station wagon of the late '30s. Its two-cycle motor, smaller, lighter, and more efficient than the old fashioned four-cycle one, could easily drive it along at an average speed of seventy miles an hour on the highly efficient fuels of those days. Such speeds, however, seemed like crawling to Mr. Doe and his friends, who used small steep-flight planes for short hops and giant stratosphere planes for distance flying.

IV

This, then, is an attempt to describe a part—a fragment—of what we might reasonably expect the engineers to give us, although, in all honesty, it should be pointed out that it *might* be entirely different. Ideally, however, the engineers could probably make available, to most of us, most of the things I have described here, plus a number of essentials which are not novel enough to figure in the description. The productivity of existing plants, especially if some way could be found to replace the obsolete ones, is more than enough to care for our needs, and also, although this is more delicate, at prices that we could afford, as is in the main borne out by the report of the Brookings Institution and the report of the National Survey of Potential Product Capacity.

Most people find it hard to believe what they hear about the country's potential productivity. The reason for this is that such statements usually presuppose ideal conditions, just as did the picture of Mr. Doe's environment. Let us now take that picture and turn it into reality.

We gave Mr. Doe a prefabricated house, that is to say, made of prefabricated units. But many architects think that the one thing they can be reasonably sure a man of his means would not want would be a prefabricated house. A man of means is likely to want a house that demonstrates his financial ability to build himself something that expresses his own taste and his own individuality. As good taste becomes more widespread, such persons will be more and more likely to build houses that harmonize with the locality and with the landscape of their own particular acres.

We gave Mr. Doe a modern house, which would presumably be furnished in the modern style; but what happened to the original French expression of the "modern" style in furniture when it came over from Paris fifteen years ago? At first it was taken up by persons of taste and means, but when the department stores got hold of it and spread it among the crowd, the people of taste and means dropped it like a hot penny and went rushing headlong into a Victorian revival. Perhaps they were disturbed by the enthusiastic adoption of the "modern" style by hotels, bars, and restaurants.

The prefabricated house is more suited to persons with low incomes. But prefabricated houses are already on the market and the working man has not got them. This is partly because they are still too expensive. There is actually no prefabricated house quoted to-day that could not be built more cheaply in the usual way under favorable conditions. And to anticipate a future difficulty rather than a present one, there is a possibility of obstruction on the part of local and regional real-estate interests and plasterers' and wood-

workers' organizations. It is a fact that to-day in some localities union painters will not handle a spray gun and that the
union specifies the maximum width of brush a man may use
on a particular job.

It is all very well to speak of a plastic chair, or even of a
plastic room, molded as a unit; but there is no use on earth
for a plastic chair unless it is cheaper and more durable than
any other kind. Chairs can be made more cheaply of plastic
to-day than of wood or steel tubing, but the die is very expensive and it would be necessary for manufacturers to order
large quantities of the same type of chair. Of course new
synthetic combinations are continually being discovered,
plastics are becoming cheaper, and continuous instead of
intermittent production is already possible. If the time ever
comes when tables and chairs can be sold at really low prices,
plastic furniture will be in considerable demand.

When we come to the moot question of television we
get what is perhaps the best example of how little the public
is able to grasp the problems of technology and how far they
may sometimes get ahead even of the scientists. The people
who are demanding television have no conception of the
difficulties involved which translate themselves into terms of
cost.

In order to see a picture in black and white, without visual
or auditory perspective, just as you see it in the movies to-day,
it is only necessary to transmit one picture along one channel
of certain band width. This, however, is a difficult enough
feat in itself, inasmuch as each picture must consist of no
less than 200,000 separate elements of light and shade, and
30 pictures are transmitted a second, making in all 6,000,000
picture elements a second.

Now if you want to transmit auditory perspective you
need a second sound-pickup apparatus. If you want to transmit color you have to "trip" or switch in a relay to actuate
a red screen alternating with a blue screen, but still on one
channel, for every one you sent without it. And for this a
"video" channel, twice as wide, would be necessary. Again,
if you want visual perspective or stereoscopic effect, you
might have to multiply the band width by three to accommo-

date the three additional channels. In all, you might have
to be equipped to transmit three pictures in the time it now
takes to transmit one, unless of course someone finds a simpli-
fying principle of which we are unaware at present. Engineers
are now working on the substitution of color elements for
some of the elements which give the outline; but for the
time being, if you were to try to get all these on the same
channel, it would require the transmission of 18,000,000
elements a second. Moreover, in the present usable radio
spectrum there is no place to accommodate the band widths
which this kind of thing would demand. And we haven't yet
enough practical experience in the use of such waves. Enough
has been said to show that a television set cannot be im-
provised out of an old cigar box and a couple of coils of
wire. There are some engineers who argue that the problem
is so complex that even the desirability of solving it is open
to question.

Taking television as an example, it can be argued that
to-day we are gadget-conscious, like a child with new toys
or a materially ambitious man who has for the first time
acquired enough money to surround himself with the things
he wants. But it is quite possible that before very long man
will be bored with his new toys and will begin to work in
the direction of originality, individuality, taste, and imagination. An interesting example is the imported "Bauhaus" idea
being applied at Harvard and in Chicago, which represents
an attempt at a synthesis of technology, artisanship, and
æsthetics in design. The Bauhaus produced the first welded
tubular chair in the modern style and some of the first modern houses. It represents a mile post along the road to in-
tegration.

V

We have seen that the life of an invention, as such, used
to average about thirty-three years from the time it was conceived in the mind of the inventor until the time when, having overcome the successive difficulties in its path, it finally
achieved commercial adoption. The lag between invention
and application is as old as history. Queen Elizabeth con-

sidered the use of carriages effeminate. In America in the last century it was thought that the sight of trains rushing across the country under their own power would drive people mad, and in Germany it was contended that at fifteen miles an hour blood would spurt from the passengers' noses, mouths, and ears. Napoleon called gas lighting *"une grande folie."* Faraday was contemptuously referred to as "the frogs' dancing master." The steamboat was known as "Fulton's Folly." The first automobile was required by law to be preceded by a man carrying a red flag by day and a red lantern by night. When the typewriter was introduced it was thought that women would break down under the strain of a six months' training course. Historical examples are plentiful enough to suggest that in the past all new ideas were at one time considered impractical.

Throughout history, workers have fought bitterly and sometimes with violence their displacement by the machine. To-day the worker is less vociferous, and it is generally agreed that new machines create new jobs, both for their own construction and repair, as in the case of dial telephones, but also through the creation of new wants, as in the case of the automobile and the radio. And we are becoming cautious— for example, although the Rust cotton-picker is being tried out in Russia, where there is no unemployment, we still hesitate to use it.

Now a great many people argue that the strongest resistance of all comes from invested capital, which naturally does not like to see plants rendered obsolete and profitable operations turned into losing ones. C. F. Kettering pointed out that the research worker was a man employed to keep people dissatisfied with what they have. And one banker described research as an activity which only served to make banking hazardous. There is little that illuminating gas can do, for instance, that electricity cannot, yet the utilities are too heavily committed to make the change. The newspapers are reluctant to take up radio activities which may make their plants unnecessary. A still better example is the development of what are called "grandeur" movies, using a film and a screen both much larger than at present, and giving greater clarity of detail; this has been held up by the difficulty of re-equipping all the theaters.

On the other hand, so much good work has come and is coming out of the research laboratories of the great corporations that it would be unfair to fail to credit private initiative with its share in the onward march of technical progress. Certainly the chemical industry cannot be charged with failing to look ahead and act upon its prognostications. Perhaps the most that can be said is that bankers and executives have a tendency to think in terms of equipment and to be over-reluctant to make changes. The engineer, who is the best qualified to perceive the advent of what may later necessitate fundamental changes of policy, is not often enough called into consultation.

With industrial enterprises everywhere at the mercy of the irregularity of technological progress, which shoots out in various directions at different rates of speed, only to curl up here and deflate there, like some subaqueous plant in a speeded-up motion picture, the credit structure is subjected to undue strain. Bankers are understandably afraid of waking up overnight and finding themselves hanging onto the coattails of a hitherto respectable business which through no fault of its own finds itself headed for the rocks.

Perhaps it would be possible to remove the resistance to technological progress by insuring organizations against obsolescence just as individuals are insured against old age, disease, and death. This might be done by a government agency operating along the principles of Social Security, for otherwise the insurance companies would find themselves in the position of betting against progress.

But could even a dictator with a galaxy of intelligences at his disposal shorten the process of psychological re-orientation, physiological re-education, physical re-equipment, and economic adjustment in such a way as to enable a people to enjoy the fruits of its own creative ability and enterprise? Would a democratic government be willing to go to the trouble and expense of reviving the ancient and hitherto dubious calling of soothsayer or prophet, and making it respectable? Could the art of prophecy, at least as far as technological evolution is concerned, be made as scientific as long-range weather-forecasting promises to become?

Critics of the Report on Technological Trends say that if this Report is an example of what happens when a commission attempts to unravel the intricate skein of our continuing development, it disproves its own case, and that the self-perpetuation of any such group would be undesirable. Needless to say, much of this criticism comes from experts who were not invited to be on the Commission. You can solve almost any problem in the world provided you choose the right man to cope with it, but somebody has to be able to select the man.

If there is any one prediction that can be safely ventured upon, it is that we shall increasingly be obliged to turn to the scientist and to his way of thinking. Our future is in the hands of the technologists. But to-day we still hold them back and delay the fulfillment of their prophecies.

LAYING THE GROUNDWORK

Preparation for Reading

1. Judging by the past, what reception do you suppose will be given by the public to those new inventions which threaten to force a change in daily routine? Give examples from history to illustrate your answer.
2. What are some inventions which are now ready for widespread adoption, but which have not yet been adopted?
3. How do the following factors enter into the speed of adoption of a new invention: the costs to the consumer, the scrapping of existing plants, patent monopolies, and labor displacement?

Vocabulary Building

1. Look up these words: *facsimile, stereoscopic, ingratiating, cathode, resin, metallurgy, electronics, servile, synthetic, biochemistry, ionization, metastable, soporific, coaxial, permutations, matutinal, detergents, translucent, etched, æsthetics, vociferous, prognostications, subaqueous, galaxy.*
2. Who was Faraday? Bellamy? What is the Bauhaus?
3. Explain the meaning of these phrases as they occur in the text:

an electric eye; a prefabricated house; apocalyptic visions; an integrated neighborhood.

APPRAISING THE RESULTS

1. What is the purpose of the series of questions in the first paragraph? What is the relation of the last sentence in the paragraph to paragraph 2?
2. What special factors working against change are listed in paragraph 2? What main underlying difficulty is pointed out?
3. What is the relation of the widespread adoption of an invention to income levels? to relative costs of the inventions?
4. Have scientific writers had any degree of success in prophesying technological change? What is wrong with Sunday supplement prophecies? What two checks does Train apply to his prophecy?
5. List inventions which have become commonplace for John Doe. What is the unifying principle of each paragraph in Section III?
6. Could we with our present productive capacity produce the things which are given in the ideal picture of John Doe's world?
7. What are some of the factors (given in Section IV) which will probably alter the speed and kind of innovations which are suggested in the ideal picture?
8. What conclusion does Train reach in Section V as to the feasibility and value of prophesying technological change? Who should be the prophets?

SELECTING THE THEME SUBJECT

1. Explain some mechanism, for example, an electric eye, an oil burner, a glider.
2. Develop one of these titles: Streamlining in Industry; The Present Use of Plastics; Design in Automobiles; Synthetic Foods; Chemistry and Fabrics.

The Insatiable Curiosity of Man

THE EVOLUTION OF EYES[1]
Thomas Hall Shastid

AGES AGO, WHEN EARTH HAD COOLED AND LIFE HAD BEGUN TO
APPEAR IN ITS TEPID WATERS, ONE OF THE FIRST THINGS DEVEL-
oped was eyes. Even the ameba, the lowliest of all known animals, of which countless trillions exist today precisely as they
were when life originated on this planet, may be said to possess eyes. Or rather, the ameba's body is all eye—every portion of the ameba can perceive light. But while in the process
of evolution some eyes, like this generalized light-sense of
the ameba, have stood quite still, others, like the literally
superhuman eyes of birds, have moved forward incredible
distances.

When we come to the insects we find that they have two
kinds of eyes: simple and compound. If one looks at a common house-fly one can see that its head consists almost entirely of two large, dark-brown lobes, the compound eyes,
each made up of more than 4000 eye-units. From each compound eye a mosaic picture—of more than 4000 minute pic-
ture-fragments—is conveyed to the fly's central nervous system. The fly also has three single eyes, situated, in the form
of a triangle with its sharpest point downward, in the space
above and between the two compound eyes.

The compound eyes of the fly are used for distance, i.e.,
three to four yards, and the single eyes for near vision, from
one to two inches. Some insects have only compound eyes,
some only single, but most of them have both. None of these

[1] From *The American Scholar*, Autumn, 1933. As condensed in *The Reader's Digest*, December, 1933. Reprinted by permission of the author and *The American Scholar* and *The Reader's Digest*.

insect eyes have any movement—the eyes are set on the fly's head as solid as so many jewels in a watch.

Leaving the insects, we find that the fishes are the first of the great backboned class of animals. In fishes, Nature produced the first true focusing arrangements and muscles with which to move eyes in their sockets. But fish are color-blind. Tell this to a fisherman with his brightly colored flies and he will laugh derisively, but it is a demonstrable fact. Fish can distinguish between different colors, but do not see them as colors—only as various shades of gray, precisely as a color blind person would. Fish have also a very restricted visual field, seeing scarcely anything below the level of the head.

The reptilia added little to eyes. In general snakes have very poor sight. Most of them see only objects in motion and are nearly deaf too, so that their knowledge of the world reaches them largely by way of the little forked tongue, probably the most wonderful tactile organ in existence. This feels myriads of vibrations in the atmosphere which, to our coarse sense of touch, are non-existent.

Birds' eyes are the most remarkable of all earthly eyes, being often both telescopic and microscopic. In birds the visual acuteness is almost incredible, in some instances 100 times as great as that in men. A bit of grain that human eyes can barely see at a distance of one yard, a bird can see distinctly at a distance of 100 yards. This remarkable sight is almost a necessity because the sense of smell in birds is exceedingly poor. Even vultures, contrary to popular superstition, do not smell their food even though it be carrion, but see it.

Mammals may be classified as non-primates and primates, the primates including monkeys, apes, and men. In nearly all the non-primates the eyes are not set out on the front of the face but at the side of the head. Scarcely any of the non-primates have any overlapping of the visual fields of the two eyes and those which do have some overlapping have no true stereoscopic vision—vision with depth and relief to it. Hares and rabbits actually have the fields overlapping behind their heads (behind, because these animals are not hunters, but hunted), yet they have no stereoscopic vision.

A very great difference exists among mammals in the shape of the pupil when in contracted condition. The domestic cat has a narrow vertical pupil, which it needs for the purpose of hunting its prey up and down trees. (This is not true of all the cat family; lions and all the larger *felidae* have round pupils.) The horse has pupils which are wide horizontally in order that the animal, when grazing, can see sidewise, both to right and to left, over a wide expanse of ground. A horse's eyes, also, are placed prominently up and out on the corners of its head so that it can aim a kick at a wolf—the horse's natural enemy—without turning the head.

All eyes that shine in the dark do so by virtue of a concave reflector behind the retina. The purpose is to enable the animal to see better in the dark. The little light that is stirring in the outer world enters the pupil, passes through the transparent retina which utilizes this light for vision, and on to the reflector, which sends it back to the same object from which it came. Here it is joined to the fresh, original light from the object, and the same process is repeated. Thus the carnivora and some other animals, whose vision is very much poorer than ours by day, see much better at night. And that is why primitive man lived in great terror of the dark. He was eater by day, eaten at night.

All the primates have strong focusing muscles. In all the monkeys and apes the eyes, just as in men, can both be converged on the same point, and stereoscopic vision thus obtained—but not very long maintained. Only in man, of all the mammals, does there seem to be a continuous binocular and stereoscopic vision. Even in the human child, however, the eyes do not as a rule move in perfect unison with each other till about three months after birth, because stereoscopic vision, in the history of life, is an extremely recent appearance. This explains the ready loss-of-binocularity (cross eyes) in many persons as the result of eye-strain.

Whenever our eyes are in motion they are stone blind, excepting only when they move without changing the point at which they look. Anyone can easily convince himself of the truth of this statement. Let him stand before a mirror and look at the image of one of his eyes. Let him look first at the right side of that eye, then at the left side of the same eye, and then back again. Never, so long as he lives, will he see his eye in motion. The reason is that, just so soon as an eye begins to move, it is blind. We are never conscious of the blind interval, partly because the picture which is last seen before the eye begins moving persists in the sight-center of the brain and thus laps a little over the interval during which the retina is blind. But the chief fact is that the retina, by means of its motion blindness, gets minute intervals of rest with very great frequency all through our waking hours. In this way, too, the blurry and therefore useless pictures which we should receive if the eyes saw while in motion are avoided.

One peculiar thing about man's eyes, dominancy and serviency, is not found in the eyes of animals. In all mammals the eyes are *two* little cameras, each producing a tiny picture, but in the brain of man only one composite or stereoscopic picture is seen. The unique feature about the vision of a man is that the two eyes do not contribute equally to the formation of this single picture. In a right-handed person the right eye contributes practically all of the picture, in a left-handed person the left eye. In other words the right eye is almost invariably the window the brain looks through, with the left eye merely adding a little accessory information. When the right eye is closed, the left eye promptly extends its visual fields to the normal limits of the right. To test whether or not you have dominancy or serviency in your eyes, look at a tiny spot in the wall at a distance of a few feet. Next, while still looking at the spot, take a finger-ring and hold it where you will be looking through it. Then close your left eye, and see if you still see the spot through the ring. If you are right-handed, you will. Next close your right eye and look at the spot with your left and you will see it outside the ring. If you are left-handed, the result will be reversed.

Dominancy and serviency in eyes, like right-handedness and left-handedness, have come into the world very late. In no animal, so far as I have been able to learn, is there any such thing as handedness or eye-dominancy. This peculiar state of affairs is producing a condition which will eventually result in consequences of vast importance. As one result, I be-

lieve that in the course of countless ages man's two eyes will
come closer and closer together, the bridge of the nose will
diminish and sink, and finally at the spot where the bridge of
the nose now appears there will stand one large, cyclopean
eye. This single, central eye will regain stereoscopic vision
just as many birds have stereoscopic vision in each eye now.
Although the field of view will then be narrower than now,
the eye will probably be both microscopic and telescopic;
and, finally, most important of all, it will probably be able to
perceive as light many forms of energy which now produce
in human eyes no sort or kind of perception.

LAYING THE GROUNDWORK

Preparation for Reading

1. Why can animals see in the dark better than man? Do they see
better by day? For what purpose do the pupils contract?
2. Why do we say "the camera eye," "the focus of attention,"
"blind as a bat," "a bird's-eye view," "a blind spot"?

Vocabulary Building

1. Look up the derivations, meanings, and pronunciations of:
*tepid, ameba, incredible, derisively, tactile, stereoscopic, car-
nivora, binocular, accessory, cyclopean.*
2. Distinguish between the *primates* and the *non-primates.*
3. What is the difference between the words *reptiles* and *reptilia?*
feline and *felidae?*

APPRAISING THE RESULTS

1. Why does Shastid call the eyes of birds superhuman? What
does he say of the eyes of insects, fishes, reptilia, mammals?
2. Explain why we are not conscious of the "blind interval"
Shastid says we have when our eyes are in motion. What is
the relationship between this characteristic and the way we
see moving pictures?
3. Explain dominancy and serviency and their relation to the
right and left eyes, and the right and left hands. How can
you determine which of your eyes is dominant?
4. What forecast does Shastid make about the future development of eyes? On what does he base his prediction?

5. Compare this excerpt with the original. Explain its condensation.
6. Analyze the plan of this selection. Trace its development.

SELECTING THE THEME SUBJECT

1. Write a paper describing the structure of the eye or the ear.
2. Make a study of the history of eyeglasses. Acknowledge your sources of information in footnotes.
3. Explain how a camera works or how to make a photographic dark room.
4. Discuss the technique of color photography, or the process of developing and printing negatives.
5. Additional theme topics: The Kodak Fiend; The Candid Camera Craze; Eye Appeal in Advertising; The Aesthetic Eye; The Unseeing Eye.

WHERE LIFE BEGINS: THE NATURE OF THE VIRUS[1]
George W. Gray

THE VIRUS HAS BEEN KNOWN FOR MORE THAN 40 YEARS. IT HAS LONG BEEN A CANDIDATE FOR RECOGNITION AS THE MOST ELE-mentary living thing, and Duggar's suggestion[2] offers presumptive argument for such rating. But first let us review what is known of the virus. Recent research can help us, for within the last two years an exciting discovery has been made. Wendell M. Stanley is the discoverer.

Dr. Stanley is an organic chemist. A graduate of Earlham College, he spent postgraduate years at the University of Illinois working on leprosidal compounds, then studied in Germany on a fellowship from the National Research Council, and in 1931 joined the staff of the Rockefeller Institute for Medical Research in New York. In 1932 the Institute opened additional laboratories near Princeton, and Stanley went there with definite designs on the virus.

The nature of the virus is one of the key problems of pathology. Such destructive diseases as infantile paralysis, influenza, parrot fever, rabies, "St. Louis" encephalitis or sleeping sickness, yellow fever, and certain types of tumorous growths are propagated by these invisible carriers; therefore virus investigation is a major project for medical research. Pathologists and other biologists have specialized on biological aspects, and have turned up many important facts about the physiological effects of the virus and its response to various agents. Stanley the chemist was asked to specialize on

---

[1] From *The Advancing Front of Science*, by George W. Gray. Copyright, 1937, by Whittlesey House: McGraw-Hill Book Company, Inc. Reprinted by permission of the author and of the publisher.

[2] Dr. E. M. Duggar of the University of Wisconsin speculated that a lone gene might be a destructive agent. (Editors' note.)

chemical aspects—to find out, if he could, what a virus is in terms of molecules, and what the molecules are in terms of atoms: how large, how massive, how composed, how reactive.

He chose for his inquiry the oldest known virus, that which causes the tobacco mosaic disease. This is a pestilence dreaded by tobacco growers, for if one plant in a field contracts the disease, the infection usually spreads through the entire acreage, stunting the plants, puckering their foliage, and causing the leaves to assume the mottled appearance of a mosaic. Back in 1857, when mosaic disease was first recognized, it was confused with a plant pock affliction, and not until 1892 did the botanists realize that the two diseases are different. This discovery was made by the Russian investigator Iwanowski, and he startled the bacteriologists of his day by announcing that the juice of infected tobacco-mosaic plants remained infectious after it had passed through a Chamberland filter.

Now a Chamberland filter is a porcelain affair with pores so fine that if a pint of distilled water is placed in the filter, many days will elapse before the liquid percolates through, unless strong suction is applied. There was no known bacterium that could get through such minute holes. And yet, the agent which communicated the tobacco mosaic disease readily passed. Other experimenters confirmed Iwanowski's findings, and six years later the first filtrable carriers of an animal contagion were discovered in the foot-and-mouth disease. Since then scores of afflictions affecting plants, animals, and man have been identified as virus infections. Of all the viruses, tobacco mosaic virus is conspicuous in its possession of properties which enable it to be worked with easily. Furthermore, it has long been regarded as typical and representative.

On the acres near Princeton, Stanley grew thousands of tobacco plants, infected them with the disease, later ground up the dwarfed, puckering, mottle-leafed plants, pressed them to a pulp, and collected the juices. Somewhere in the gallons was the virus. You could not see it, you could not accumulate it in a filter, you could not culture it in agar or in any of the soups used to grow bacteria. You knew it was there only by its destructive effect. For if you took a drop of the juice and touched it to a healthy plant, within a few days the leaves showed the unmistakable signs of mosaic. The virus was there. But how to get at it chemically?

The known ingredients of protoplasm may be grouped in five classes of substance: metal salts, carbohydrates, lipoids or fatty compounds, [extractives], and proteins—these last the most complex of all. There are certain enzymes which break up proteins. Protein splitters, or protein digesters, they are called. Pepsin, for example, does precisely that in the stomach, and will do the same in a test tube. What would it do to the virus?

Stanley put some of the infectious tobacco juice in a test tube, poured in pepsin, kept the mixture at the temperature and in the other conditions favorable for pepsin digestion, and at the end of the experiment tested the solution for infection. It had none. Rubbed on the leaves of healthy tobacco plants it showed no power to transmit the disease. Obviously the pepsin had destroyed the infectious principle in the juice. But pepsin digests only proteins—it has no effect on lipoids, hydrocarbons, carbohydrates, and salts. From this it seemed reasonable to conclude that the virus material is protein.

There are chemicals which precipitate proteins. These were tried on the virulent tobacco juice. Immediately certain substances dropped down as solid precipitates, and it was found that thereafter the juice had no power to infect. But when some of the precipitate was added to neutral liquid, the solution immediately became infectious. This plainly said that the disease carrier resided in the protein precipitate, and Stanley now began a campaign to trace the carrier down to its source.

He dissolved the precipitate in a neutral liquid, and added an ammonium compound which has the faculty of edging protein out of solution without changing the protein. A cluster of crystals began to form at the bottom of the test tube—somewhat as sugar crystals form in syrup. But these might not be a single pure stuff, so Stanley sought to refine them. He removed the crystals, dissolved them in a much larger volume of neutral liquid, and with the help again of the ammonium compound brought this more dilute solution to crystallization. His next step repeated the process, but with still greater proportion of the liquid. In this way, by increasing the dilution each time, the chemist carried his material through ten successive fractionations and recrystallizations. One would assume that by now the substance was pure, that all extraneous materials had been separated out, also that all living matter had been eliminated—for we know no plant or animal, no bacterium, no protoplasm, that can undergo crystallization and remain the same. So the experiment seemed ripe for a supreme test.

Stanley took a pinch of the product of that tenth recrystallization, dissolved it in a neutral fluid more than 100 million times its bulk, rubbed a drop of the solution on the leaves of a healthy tobacco plant, and awaited the result. The test was conclusive. Within the usual time the plant showed all signs of an acute outbreak of the mosaic disease. Surely in the crystals we have the virus. And since, by all rules of chemistry, the crystals have been refined to the pure state and may be accepted as an uncontaminated single substance, it seems reasonable to believe that *the crystals are the virus.*

I have watched them through the microscope: a mass of white needlelike structures bristling in every direction. It is not supposed that each needle is a virus. Just as each crystal of sugar is made of numerous molecules of sugar, so it is presumed that each of these crystalline spikes is a cluster of millions of molecules of the protein, and that *each molecule is a single virus.*

Stanley's chemical analysis shows that the virus molecule is composed of carbon, hydrogen, nitrogen, and oxygen. Unlike many other physiologically active proteins, it contains no sulphur and no phosphorus. Just how many atoms of each element are present, and the arrangement of the atoms in molecular architecture, are details still in process of investigation. But the evidence indicates that the molecules are enormous.

Ingenious physical measurements of the molecules were recently made by The Svedberg, at the University of Upsala, and by Ralph W. G. Wyckoff, at the Rockefeller Institute, using centrifuges of the ultra type. The apparatus is a whirling machine capable of doing better than 100,000 revolutions per minute. Dr. Svedberg's apparatus is made of steel, and is driven by a stream of oil pumped at high pressure. Dr. Wyckoff's apparatus is made of an aluminum alloy, and its turbine is driven by compressed air. In both machines, the rotating part is housed in a chamber made of 3-inch armor-plate steel—a safeguard to protect the operator in case of explosion. If a dime is placed in the ultracentrifuge, and the apparatus is rotated at a certain velocity, the centrifugal force is so great that the dime presses out with an effect equal to the weight of half a ton. The purpose, however, is not to perform trick stunts with dimes, but to separate mixtures of molecules, using a principle long familiar in the dairyman's cream separator. In the ultracentrifuge this principle is harnessed to the utmost degree of control. Under the accelerated fling of centrifugal force generated by the rotating mechanism, molecules in solution are separated, each is thrown out with a speed proportional to its mass, and by timing the period required for its separation the molecular weight and size of any constituent may be determined. Dr. Stanley sent Professor Svedberg samples of his crystals, and at the same time supplied specimens to his colleague Dr. Wyckoff, and to the test of this indirect weighing and measuring machine the substance was subjected.

The results are in remarkable agreement. Both Svedberg and Wyckoff independently reported that the weight of Stanley's crystalline protein is approximately 17,000,000 (in terms of hydrogen's atomic weight of 1). The largest molecule known up to this time was that of the animal protein called hemocyanin (which is the pigment of earthworm blood), with a molecular weight of about 5,000,000. Thus Stanley's find is more than three times heavier. In size it appears to be egg-shaped with a diameter of about 35 millimicrons. The corresponding dimension of the hemocyanin is 24 millimicrons. And a millimicron is 1/25,400,000 inch.

The tobacco mosaic protein thus provides the chemists, the molecular architects, the microcosmic adventurers, with a perfectly enormous molecule for their exploration: a structure many times more massive and complex than anything heretofore analyzed. It must consist of hundreds of thousands of atoms, possibly of millions.

It provides the biologists with an indubitable specimen of the invisible stuff that is responsible for so many human ills, and if we can learn in intimate detail the ways of the tobacco mosaic virus we may get some important flashes of information on the ways of the virus of the common cold and other hidden enemies of mankind. Many points of correspondence have recently been found, properties in which the plant virus shows characteristics similar to the animal virus. Thus, it is known that the common cold affects many species of animals. Similarly, the tobacco mosaic virus affects tomato, phlox, and spinach plants, as well as tobacco. H. S. Loring, one of Stanley's coworkers, recently extracted a crystalline substance from the juices of diseased tomato plants, and the substance was found to be a protein identical with that extracted from the juices of the diseased tobacco plants. The protein has also been isolated from mosaic-diseased spinach and phlox plants.

Another point of similarity between the tobacco mosaic virus and the virus of animal diseases lies in this: that both may be inactivated and rendered harmless. Thus Pasteur found that by drying the spinal cords of dogs which had died of hydrophobia, he obtained a material which was harmless; and yet it seemed to contain the principle of the hydrophobia carrier, for a person inoculated with the material gained a certain immunity to the disease. Stanley has found that by treating his crystalline protein with hydrogen peroxide, or formaldehyde, or other chemicals, or by exposing it to ultraviolet light, he causes its virulence to vanish. When the virus is rubbed on the leaves of healthy plants, no ill effects follow. And yet the crystals appear to be the same as those of the virulent untreated protein. When they are analyzed by x-ray bombardment they show the same diffraction pattern, when weighed they show the same molecular weight, and, most important of all, when injected into animals they produce an antiserum which when mixed with solutions of active virulent virus is able to neutralize or render inactive such solutions. There are slight chemical differences, however, and it is Dr. Stanley's idea that the effect of the treatment is to alter certain active groups of the huge molecule—to switch certain towers or ells of its architecture, as it were—but to leave the structure as a whole unchanged. These experiments with inactivation of the tobacco mosaic protein seem to promise results that will be helpful to the human pathologist searching the frontiers of immunization.

Additional support for the idea that the tobacco mosaic protein is a virus was obtained early in 1937 by Stanley and Wyckoff. They found that, instead of depending on chemical means to isolate the virus, they could accomplish the result mechanically with the ultracentrifuge. By whirling a solution of juices from the diseased plants, repeating the process with the heavy precipitate thereby obtained, and doing this over and over again, they found it practicable to separate the activating substance from the mixture. In this way Stanley and Wyckoff isolated the molecule of another plant virus, the infectious ring-spot disease. By the same method they isolated the activating agent of still other vegetable diseases, potato mosaic, severe etch, cucumber mosaic, finding that the concentrations of these viruses in the host differed widely. Most important of all is their demonstration that the activating substance of each of these highly contagious plant diseases is a heavy protein molecule similar in general to the first found, the tobacco mosaic protein of Stanley's pioneering chemical experiments.

But man, whose virus diseases are of *animal* nature, wants to know of the virus that affects animals. Has any research progress been made in that direction? Yes, an interesting beginning, just announced. There is a highly contagious animal disease known as "infectious papillomatosis" which affects rabbits. It causes warty masses to grow on the ears and other parts of its victims, and has been attributed to a filtrable virus carrier. This disease was first described by R. E. Shope; and recently Wyckoff and J. W. Beard obtained some of the warty tissue from Dr. Shope, ground it up, made a solution of it, and subjected this solution to the new technique of the ultracentrifuge. In this way they isolated a heavy protein which when tested on healthy rabbits immediately communicated the disease. But rabbits frequently develop warts which are not infectious, and so as a further test the investigators obtained some of this noninfectious warty tissue, and subjected it to the same treatment. They were unable to obtain from this solution any heavy protein, though repeated trials were made. Apparently the giant molecules flung out of the solution of the infectious tissue are a virus which is not present in other warts. And by weight and measurement the wart virus proves to be a tremendous molecular structure weighing something more than 20,000,000 and measuring about 40 millimicrons in diameter. Thus the first animal virus to be isolated is a larger, more massive, and presumably a more complex molecule than that of the first discovered plant virus, the carrier of tobacco mosaic. But all our evidence points to many similarities among these various disease-carrying substances, and very many lines of research are now being pushed with the tobacco mosaic protein on the idea that it is not only a virus but a representative species of the whole virus family, both plant and animal.

Is it alive? Stanley reminds you that it can be crystallized, a property that we think of as purely inanimate and wholly chemical. He points to the additional fact that it has not been cultured in a test tube. This would seem to say that it is not a bacterium. A few bacteria placed in a nutrient soup will rapidly multiply into uncounted millions, but the crystalline protein shows no growth behavior in a glass vessel, no metabolism, no reproduction.

And yet, observe what happens when it comes in contact with the inner tissue of a tobacco plant or other vegetable host. Instantly the molecules begin to multiply. An almost imperceptible particle of a crystal will infect a plant, and in a few days the disease will spread through a field, producing an amount of virus millions of times that of the original. It exhibits a fecund ability to propagate itself, to extend its occupancy of space and time at the expense of its environment. Is not this a characteristic of living things?

Perhaps the virus is a molecule of double personality, alive and yet not alive—animated by its environment when that environment is specific to its nature, but passive in any other environment. The discovery of this substance and the elucidation of its properties is one of the most important biological advances of our century. In 1936, when Dr. Stanley presented his comprehensive paper reporting the research to the American Association for the Advancement of Science, the Association esteemed the report the most important on its agenda and awarded Stanley its $1,000 prize.

LAYING THE GROUNDWORK

Preparation for Reading

1. What is thought to be the cause of the common cold, influenza, and infantile paralysis?
2. Why must a scientist work with the utmost precision in his laboratory technique?

Vocabulary Building

You will probably need to look up some of these words: *presumptive, organic* (chemistry), *pathology, propagated, percolates, ingredients, protoplasm, precipitate, extraneous, ingenious, centrifuges, velocity, indubitable, inoculated, virulence, defraction, immunization, elucidation.*

APPRAISING THE RESULTS

1. What is a virus? What is the importance of the Chamberland filter to the laboratory worker?
2. Explain the process of isolating and weighing the virus molecule.
3. Why is the discovery of the virus important?
4. This essay is a definition. Trace the method of development. Compare Gray's method with Gunther's in the latter's "What Is a Racket," p. 262.

SELECTING THE THEME SUBJECT

1. Write a theme defining one of these terms: virus; atomic structure; pseudo-science; poetic instinct; jazz; democracy; conditioned response; bourgeoisie; slang; fascism.
2. Write a theme on one of the following topics: How to Prevent Colds; The Prevention of Infantile Paralysis; The Importance of Pasteur to Modern Medicine.
3. Explain a laboratory experiment in which you have participated, or a scientific discovery of which you know. Make your account concrete, yet intelligible to the layman.

UNDERSEA[1]

Rachel L. Carson

WHO HAS KNOWN THE OCEAN? NEITHER YOU NOR I, WITH OUR
EARTH-BOUND SENSES, KNOW THE FOAM AND SURGE OF THE TIDE
that beats over the crab hiding under the seaweed of his tide-
pool home; or the lilt of the long, slow swells of mid-ocean,
where shoals of wandering fish prey and are preyed upon, and
the dolphin breaks the waves to breathe the upper atmosphere. Nor can we know the vicissitudes of life on the ocean
floor, where the sunlight, filtering through a hundred feet of
water, makes but a fleeting, bluish twilight, in which dwell
sponge and mollusk and starfish and coral, where swarms of
diminutive fish twinkle through the dusk like a silver rain
of meteors, and eels lie in wait among the rocks. Even less is
it given to man to descend those six incomprehensible miles
into the recesses of the abyss, where reign utter silence and
unvarying cold and eternal night.

To sense this world of waters known to the creatures of
the sea we must shed our human perceptions of length and
breadth and time and place, and enter vicariously into a universe of all-pervading water. For to the sea's children nothing
is so important as the fluidity of their world. It is water that
they breathe; water that brings them food; water through
which they see, by filtered sunshine from which first the red
rays, then the greens, and finally the purples have been
strained; water through which they sense vibrations equivalent to sound. And indeed it is nothing more or less than sea
water, in all its varying conditions of temperature, saltiness,
and pressure, that forms the invisible barriers that confine

[1] From *The Atlantic Monthly*, September, 1937. Reprinted by permission of
the author and of the publisher.

each marine type within a special zone of life—one to the shore line, another to some submarine chasm on the far slopes of the continental shelf, and yet another, perhaps, to an imperceptibly defined stratum at mid-depths of ocean.

There are comparatively few living things whose shifting pattern of life embraces both land and sea. Such are the creatures of the tide pools among the rocks and of the mud flats sloping away from dune and beach grass to the water's edge. Between low water and the flotsam and jetsam of the high-tide mark, land and sea wage a never-ending conflict for possession.

As on land the coming of night brings a change over the face of field and forest, sending some wild things into the safe retreat of their burrows and bringing others forth to prowl and forage, so at ebb tide the creatures of the waters largely disappear from sight, and in their place come marauders from the land to search the tide pools and to probe the sands for the silent, waiting fauna of the shore.

Twice between succeeding dawns, as the waters abandon pursuit of the beckoning moon and fall back, foot by foot, periwinkle and starfish and crab are cast upon the mercy of the sands. Every heap of brine-drenched seaweed, every pool forgotten by the retreating sea in recess of sand or rock, offers sanctuary from sun and biting sand.

In the tide pools, seas in miniature, sponges of the simpler kinds encrust the rocks, each hungrily drawing in through its myriad mouths the nutriment-laden water. Starfishes and sea anemones are common dwellers in such rock-girt pools. Shell-less cousins of the snail, the naked sea slugs are spots of brilliant rose and bronze, spreading arborescent gills to the waters, while the tube worms, architects of the tide pools, fashion their conical dwellings of sand grains, cemented one against another in glistening mosaic.

On the sands the clams burrow down in search of coolness and moisture, and oysters close their all-excluding shells and wait for the return of the water. Crabs crowd into damp rock caverns, where periwinkles cling to the walls. Colonies of gnome-like shrimps find refuge under dripping strands of brown, leathery weed heaped on the beach.

Hard upon the retreating sea press invaders from the land. Shore birds patter along the beach by day, and legions of the ghost crab shuffle across the damp sands by night. Chief, perhaps, among the plunderers is man, probing the soft mud flats and dipping his nets into the shallow waters.

At last comes a tentative ripple, then another, and finally the full, surging sweep of the incoming tide. The folk of the pools awake—clams stir in the mud. Barnacles open their shells and begin a rhythmic sifting of the waters. One by one, brilliant-hued flowers blossom in the shallow water as tube worms extend cautious tentacles.

The ocean is a place of paradoxes. It is the home of the great white shark, two-thousand-pound killer of the seas, and of the hundred-foot blue whale, the largest animal that ever lived. It is also the home of living things so small that your two hands might scoop up as many of them as there are stars in the Milky Way. And it is because of the flowering of astronomical numbers of these diminutive plants, known as diatoms, that the surface waters of the ocean are in reality boundless pastures. Every marine animal, from the smallest to the sharks and whales, is ultimately dependent for its food upon these miscroscopic entities of the vegetable life of the ocean. Within their fragile walls, the sea performs a vital alchemy that utilizes the sterile chemical elements dissolved in the water and welds them with the torch of sunlight into the stuff of life. Only through this little-understood synthesis of proteins, fats, and carbohydrates by myriad plant "producers" is the mineral wealth of the sea made available to the animal "consumers" that browse as they float with the currents. Drifting endlessly, midway between the sea of air above and the depths of the abyss below, these strange creatures and the marine inflorescence that sustains them are called "plankton"—the wanderers.

Many of the fishes, as well as the bottom-dwelling mollusks and worms and starfish, begin life as temporary members of this roving company, for the ocean cradles their young in its surface waters. The sea is not a solicitous foster mother. The delicate eggs and fragile larvæ are buffeted by storms raging across the open ocean and preyed upon by diminutive monsters, the hungry glass-worms and comb jellies of the plankton.

These ocean pastures are also the domain of vast shoals of adult fishes: herring, anchovy, menhaden, and mackerel, feeding upon the animals of the plankton and in their turn preyed upon; for here the dogfish hunt in packs, and the ravenous bluefish, like roving buccaneers, take their booty where they find it.

Dropping downward a scant hundred feet to the white sand beneath, an undersea traveler would discover a land where the noonday sun is swathed in twilight blues and purples, and where the blackness of midnight is eerily aglow with the cold phosphorescence of living things. Dwelling among the crepuscular shadows of the ocean floor are creatures whose terrestrial counterparts are drab and commonplace, but which are themselves invested with delicate beauty by the sea. Crystal cones form the shells of pteropods or winged snails that drift downward from the surface to these dim regions by day; and the translucent spires of lovely *Ianthina* are tinged with Tyrian purple.

Other creatures of the sea's bottom may be fantastic rather than beautiful. Spine-studded urchins, like rotund hedgehogs of the sea, tumble over the sands, where mollusks lie with slightly opened shells, busily straining the water for débris. Life flows on monotonously for these passive sifters of the currents, who move little or not at all from year to year. Among the rock ledges, eels and cunners forage greedily, while the lobster feels his way with nimble wariness through the perpetual twilight.

Farther out on the continental shelf, the ocean floor is scarred with deep ravines, perhaps the valleys of drowned rivers, and dotted with undersea plateaus. Hosts of fish graze on these submerged islands, which are richly carpeted with sluggish or sessile forms of life. Chief among the ground fish are haddock, cods, flounders and their mightier relative, the halibut. From these and shallower waters man, the predator, exacts a yearly tribute of nearly thirty billion pounds of fish.

If the underwater traveler might continue to explore the ocean floor, he would traverse miles of level prairie lands;

he would ascend the sloping sides of hills; and he would skirt deep and ragged crevasses yawning suddenly at his feet. Through the gathering darkness, he would come at last to the edge of the continental shelf. The ceiling of the ocean would lie a hundred fathoms above him, and his feet would rest upon the brink of a slope that drops precipitously another mile, and then descends more gently into an inky void that is the abyss.

What human mind can visualize conditions in the uttermost depths of the ocean? Increasing with every foot of depth, enormous pressures reach, three thousand fathoms down, the inconceivable magnitude of three tons to every square inch of surface. In these silent deeps a glacial cold prevails, a bleak iciness which never varies, summer or winter, years melting into centuries, and centuries into ages of geologic time. There, too, darkness reigns—the blackness of primeval night in which the ocean came into being, unbroken, through æons of succeeding time, by the gray light of dawn.

It is easy to understand why early students of the ocean believed these regions were devoid of life, but strange creatures have now been dredged from the depths to bear mute and fragmentary testimony concerning life in the abyss.

The "monsters" of the deep sea are small, voracious fishes with gaping, tooth-studded jaws, some with sensitive feelers serving the function of eyes, others bearing luminous torches or lures to search out or entice their living prey. Through the night of the abyss, the flickering lights of these foragers move to and fro. Many of the sessile bottom dwellers glow with a strange radiance suffusing the entire body, while other swimming creatures may have tiny, glittering lights picked out in rows and patterns. The deep-sea prawn and the abyssal cuttlefish eject a luminous cloud, and under cover of this pillar of fire escape from their enemies.

Monotones of red and brown and lustreless black are the prevailing colors in the deep sea, allowing the wearers to reflect the minimum of the phosphorescent gleams, and to blend into the safe obscurity of the surrounding gloom.

On the muddy bottom of the abyss, treacherous oozes threaten to engulf small scavengers as they busily sift the dé-

bris for food. Crabs and prawns pick their way over the yield-
ing mud on stilt-like legs; sea spiders creep over sponges
raised on delicate stalks above the slime.

Because the last vestige of plant life was left behind in the
shallow zone penetrated by the rays of the sun, the inhabitants of these depths contrast strangely with the self-supporting assemblage of the surface waters. Preying one upon another, the abyssal creatures are ultimately dependent upon
the slow rain of dead plants and animals from above. Every
living thing of the ocean, plant and animal alike, returns to
the water at the end of its own life span the materials that
had been temporarily assembled to form its body. So there
descends into the depths a gentle, never-ending rain of the
disintegrating particles of what once were living creatures of
the sunlit surface waters, or of those twilight regions beneath.

Here in the sea mingle elements which, in their long and
amazing history, have lent life and strength and beauty to a
bewildering variety of living creatures. Ions of calcium, now
free in the water, were borrowed years ago from the sea to
form part of the protective armor of a mollusk, returned to
the main reservoir when their temporary owner had ceased
to have need of them, and later incorporated into the delicate statuary of a coral reef. Here are atoms of silica, once imprisoned in a layer of flint in subterranean darkness; later,
within the fragile shell of a diatom, tossed by waves and
warmed by the sun; and again entering into the exquisite
structure of a radiolarian shell, that miracle of ephemeral
beauty that might be the work of a fairy glass-blower with a
snowflake as his pattern.

Except for precipitous slopes and regions swept bare by
submarine currents, the ocean floor is covered with primeval
oozes in which there have been accumulating for æons de-
posits of varied origin; earth-born materials freighted sea-
ward by rivers or worn from the shores of continents by the
ceaseless grinding of waves; volcanic dust transported long
distances by wind, floating lightly on the surface and eventually sinking into the depths to mingle with the products of
no less mighty eruptions of submarine volcanoes; spherules
of iron and nickel from interstellar space; and substances of

organic origin—the silicious skeletons of Radiolaria and the frustules of diatoms, the limey remains of algæ and corals, and the shells of minute Foraminifera and delicate pelagic snails.

While the bottoms near the shore are covered with detritus from the land, the remains of the floating and swimming creatures of the sea prevail in the deep waters of the open ocean. Beneath tropical seas, in depths of 1,000 to 1,500 fathoms, calcareous oozes cover nearly a third of the ocean floor; while the colder waters of the temperate and polar regions release to the underlying bottom the silicious remains of diatoms and Radiolaria. In the red clay that carpets the great deeps at 3,000 fathoms or more, such delicate skeletons are extremely rare. Among the few organic remains not dissolved before they reach these cold and silent depths are the ear bones of whales and the teeth of sharks.

Thus we see the parts of the plan fall into place: the water receiving from earth and air the simple materials, storing them up until the gathering energy of the spring sun wakens the sleeping plants to a burst of dynamic activity, hungry swarms of planktonic animals growing and multiplying upon the abundant plants, and themselves falling prey to the shoals of fish; all, in the end, to be redissolved into their component substances when the inexorable laws of the sea demand it. Individual elements are lost to view, only to reappear again and again in different incarnations in a kind of material immortality. Kindred forces to those which, in some period inconceivably remote, gave birth to that primeval bit of protoplasm tossing on the ancient seas continue their mighty and incomprehensible work. Against this cosmic background the life span of a particular plant or animal appears, not as a drama complete in itself, but only as a brief interlude in a panorama of endless change.

LAYING THE GROUNDWORK

Preparation for Reading

1. For those who know the seashore, and all the varied forms which make up its pattern of life, "Undersea" needs no intro-

duction. For those who have never walked the hard-packed ocean sands, it will serve as a vicarious experience.

2. Miss Carson is a scientist; here she is a creative writer as well. Read this selection to appreciate her description of the sensuous beauty of the sea. Read it aloud.

3. Why has the sea always been important in literature?

Vocabulary Building

Look up these words: *vicissitudes, abyss, fauna, vicariously, marauders, sanctuary, arborescent, paradoxes, diatoms, buffeted, phosphorescence, crepuscular, sessile, fathoms, voracious, foragers, detritus, dynamic, ephemeral.*

APPRAISING THE RESULTS

1. How does sea water form barriers which confine types of marine life to zones?

2. What effect have the tides upon sea and beach life?

3. Explain how the ocean can be said to have *pastures, prairie lands, ravines,* and *an abyss.* What forms inhabit these different areas?

4. How does Miss Carson explain the life span of a particular animal or plant as "a brief interlude in a panorama of endless change"?

5. What kind of readers did the writer have in mind? Had she had scientists in mind, what variation in approach, facts, vocabulary, and style would she probably have made?

6. Study the rhythm and beauty of the prose. Isolate structural characteristics which help to create this effect, such as inversion, alliteration, figurative language, accented syllables.

7. This selection is rich in color suggestion. List the colors named and the words strongly suggestive of color.

8. Make a list of descriptive verbs from the essay.

9. List hyphenated words which remind you of "rosy-fingered" dawn, "gray-eyed" Athene, and similar double adjectives Homer used.

SELECTING THE THEME SUBJECT

1. Select some phase of science, or industry, or everyday life. Explain it in an imaginative manner without sacrificing accuracy.

2. These titles may suggest others to you: Sunday in the Park; Creatures of the Air (aviators); The Woods at Night; Riding the Brakebeams; Blast Furnace; Dynamo; Among the Snow Peaks; The Jungle.
3. Describe some aspect of sea life: the beach at low tide, the lure of the sea, how a diver works, colors in shells or sea plants, the dunes, recovering sunken treasures, deep-sea fishing.
4. Explain the submarine, or the bathysphere, or water analysis.

NATURAL HISTORY FOR EVERYBODY[1]
Donald Culross Peattie

> At every season and in every climate Nature lies at your back
> door ready to make you a happier and better citizen—IF you
> know what to look for.

TWELVE YEARS AGO, WITHOUT A JOB AND WITH A WIFE AND
LITTLE GIRL TO SUPPORT, I WALKED INTO A NEWSPAPER OFFICE
and asked to be allowed to write a nature column. The editor, in a welter of next Sunday's pictures of gangsters in the
morgue and dimpling society buds, told me wearily but
kindly that I might try. But he'd have to kill it if, as he supposed, the response was nil.

The day came when I had to have a secretary to battle with
that response. I don't attribute this to any popularity of
mine, but to the popularity of nature, in which my friendly
editor did not believe. The column was only a daily jotting of
the things I saw that everybody might see. But when the readers began to help me write it, they showed me more than I
could show them. They showed me that nature belongs to
everyone. That nobody hungers for it like the city dweller.
That the young, believed so hedonistic, only need a little
help to turn their interests into this widest and healthiest
field. That the mature and the older are not too old to want
to learn, and find in nature pleasures of which neither years
nor adversity can deprive them. That there is a vast army of
intelligent reporters abroad in the land who could assist
natural science.

There is nothing that any of us can do to help a chemist
or a physicist, but when biologists want to make a bird census,

[1] Reprinted by permission of *Natural History* and of *Readers Digest*.

or study migration, or predict the next wild rodent plague, or save a forest from the saw mill, they need all the help they can get from amateurs. Many of the greatest naturalists, living and in our past, were themselves amateurs. The amateur spirit—that is, doing a thing for the love of it—is pure gold and doesn't differ from the credo of the professional naturalist, except that the latter, poor devil, gets a very low salary for performing a great many routine duties. But amateurs, holding down their jobs, whether in the office or the nursery and kitchen, keep their appointments with nature like a lover.

Remember Fabre teaching school, Audubon tending store, Alexander Wilson at his loom; their time afield was precious so they made the most of it. Audubon at last earned the right to give all his days to his great passion for birds; Fabre never got free, but left an immortal name. Men and women today, busy at their professions, are in like fashion serving this mistress who rewards devotion with a deep satisfaction. A Chicago doctor, who has only a small back yard in one of the crowded parts of the city, has become one of the foremost names in the work of bird-banding; to him, at his metropolitan station, have come bob-white and saw-whet owl, Wilson's thrush and Montana junco—ninety kinds in some five years, with a total of many hundreds of individuals. Every one of these he banded, and he found that year after year certain birds would return. Birds banded by other workers, in Canada, in South America, come to his harmless trap, and so he has assisted in mapping the mysterious skyroads of the birds.

A New York business man, with only his Sundays in which to get away, has made a specialty of that fascinating bird, the osprey; instead of trying to know a little about everything, he decided to know everything about this one thing, so that he now ranks as an authority. A dean in Harvard law school made botany his avocation; a judge on the Massachusetts bench found that his collection of flowers from all over the world was eagerly consulted by scientists, and bit by bit he began himself to publish short notes and then longer articles.

For knowledge begins in curiosity. Curiosity begins in childhood, and does not always die even if long denied. The owner of a Pennsylvania coal mine, who had always wanted to be a naturalist, stood resolutely by his business for 30 years; the day after he finally closed his desk he started out in the field to study the fungi. He became after he was 60 one of the authorities in mycology consulted by professionals. A doctor with an interest in reptilian life practices a dozen years in one place, and when he has learned all that there is to know about snakes and toads in that region, moves on and hangs his shingle in fresh fields; he too has a reputation. A Chicago lawyer breaks away for a week of nightlife in the back woods of Louisiana where he consorts with that nocturnal prowler, the black wolf; the Academy of Sciences publishes his findings. A Manhattan advertising man has just had a brilliant success with his book of insect photography, in that unknown jungle which is the vacant lot next to yours.

These successful amateurs each won a name. But a big reputation is not the ideal; it is an incidental award. The fame of scientific achievement comes slowly and it is not widespread. Scientists are properly suspicious of people eager to get themselves talked about. Even for amateurs science is a kind of a religion. It requires conscience and humility, and like religion it can utilize the humblest efforts. The smallest thing well done contributes its mite to the treasury of knowledge. It is not too much to add that a love and a research of nature can mean in any life a happiness comparable with that which religion brings. If you want to find divinity in nature, you will undoubtedly perceive it there. Or if it satisfies you more to discover simply beauty or order, you will find that nature is the embodiment, and very nearly the sum total, of these things. And if it is enough for you just to find out something you did not know before, there will be no end to your fun.

For you don't have to make great discoveries or comb the world for the rare. It is enough if you enjoy yourself in the adventure of learning what is at any rate new to you. And there is no telling what you may turn up that will be new to everybody. A boy of ten who had read the greatest authority on ants in his age discovered, by watching in his own garden "the mankind of insects," things that were not in his book. He determined from that moment to become the historian of the ants, and while also engaged in reforming the treatment of the insane and in dealing kindly with human sex problems, he made himself the greatest formicologist of his time—Auguste Forel.

So that even the most famous naturalists necessarily began in the most complete and bottomless ignorance. Many of them were entirely self-taught. And luckily in the natural sciences anybody can be his own master. College instruction is faster than self-instruction, and it eliminates trial and error hazard, but nothing sticks like the facts you found out for yourself.

In those twelve years of writing a nature column in the newspapers, my most appealing letters came from people who wanted to know how to learn. They hadn't had formal training or they wouldn't have been writing to me. Some were young and hunting vocations and avocations; some were older, and had at last the time to do what they wanted. Most challenging of all were those who were in the full swing of life. They heard the beguiling whistles of the birds; they glimpsed from the commuter's train window the fields filling up with wild flowers; they saw the wheeling of the unknown constellations over their suburban roofs. And they saw that human life is short; the years rush down the stream and do not return; and all about is a greater life, zestful, enchanting and deeply significant. They asked to know; they brought their minds, like thirsty cups, inquiring for the fountain.

It springs for everyone, and it is found in all places. On the flat tarred gravel roofs of the city, unknown to the sleepers below, nest the night-hawks. To the puddles in an excavation for an office building in Washington, D. C., in 1928 came flocks of knots and sanderlings, ruddy turnstones and black-bellied plovers. The whole mystery of life is in the inky cloud of frogs' eggs in a ditch, and the riddle of instinct is there for anyone to read in the pavement ants.

My correspondents wanted to know what to look for, and how to understand what they saw. Almost none of them had much money to spend upon technical equipment, but fortunately there is no other kind of education or hobby that requires so little outlay. They hadn't much time, but they could teach themselves much in those quarter hours that we so often devote to futile worries or to reading the parts of the paper that we don't care about.

I disagree with the logical-sounding maxim that you should study nature not books. You should study them both; a good book will unriddle nature faster than the beginner could hope to do it. He needs beginner's books, but he will not stay with them long. As a rule, he does not have to buy the books he needs; they are in the public library, and the librarian should be asked to help. Most librarians are highly trained and unappreciated friends who are eager to make their institution useful. Probably you will soon find that some books are so good that you have to own them, but it is a mistake to let a bookstore hurry you into buying. With any kind of nature book you are justified in demanding to take the book home to examine. It is better to buy a book that looks just a little hard, because you will soon have caught up with it, than to invest in one that has little to tell you.

The pocket guide is a fine thing for beginning field work. Its disadvantage is that it is usually so general that it doesn't tell enough about the region in which you live. Your librarian knows that your state museum or natural history survey or nearest college has published local manuals and studies that are twice as interesting and handy as anything a bookstore carries. These are either free or sell at a nominal price.

It is astonishing how every community has in it at least one person who knows a great deal about the natural sciences. The high-school teachers of biology are often splendidly trained these days; colleges, however small, may be employing Ph.D.'s of big universities, men who carry on the inspiration of the greatest teachers. State parks, and the state and Federal foresters, can often help you to just what you need to know. It is a wonderful and inspiring thing to see how everyone in this free-masonry is willing, often eager, to share his knowledge. For it is the mark of a member of it to keep nothing for himself and to get everyone interested in his own field. Even two enthusiasts make a learned society. The way to find the other fellow is to ask the librarian who it is that is always keeping out the books you yourself are wanting.

If you live in the country, adventure begins at your back gate. Urbanites have great museums, free lectures, expeditions to join, guided by the informed. Suburbanites sometimes think they enjoy neither advantage, but in their sphere flourish the Audubon societies, and the Wild Flower Preservation societies. Or if there are none of these things in your town, why not start some? My hint for organization would be, no dues, no parliamentary rigmarole, and plenty of meetings afield. If you prefer to be a chapter of a national organization, editors, teachers, librarians know how to get you started.

But if instead of organizing, you want to start right out to be a naturalist on your own, and you wonder how to equip yourself, remember what John Muir said when asked how he prepared for an expedition. "I put a loaf of bread and a pound of tea in an old sack," said he, "and jump over the back fence."

Some people think of nature as something you can collect. Alas for the butterflies, birds' eggs, ferns and orchids! A collection as something to be studied or as a record can be precious to you; it is often the small boy's way of getting interested, and—except perhaps in the case of birds' eggs or the rarer wild flowers—should not be discouraged. But what is called the collecting mania is not related to science, or particularly to the enjoyment of nature; the possessive craving and the urge to have something that nobody else has, break the first rules of honest science. If you are going to make a collection, remember that its future use to you or anyone else will depend on labeling every specimen with the date and place, and doing your work in standard style, whether it is making an herbarium of plants or mounting bird skins. A visit to the men at the nearest college or museum will show you what you have to do.

Many beginners sweat needlessly after the rare. Rarity is just a comparative term. And in the natural sciences it doesn't mean much. As a rule, a very rare flower is merely an exceptional or unsuccessful species. Common objects have the widest and the deepest significance, and there is never any end to what one can learn about them. Instead of the rare, go after what is new to you; you get the same or a greater thrill.

There are collections you can make that museums themselves may envy. Herbaria, for instance, are overflowing with specimens of flowers; they are weak on fruits and seeds. A correlated collection is well worth while; for instance, the fruits and seeds that the local birds eat. Can you handle water colors? Paintings of the local fungi are the best way of collecting them, since they preserve so badly.

Do you keep a "punctual almanac of the birds' first coming back"? Such records, well kept, are valuable to science. Still more valuable will your nature diary be if it records the little known autumn migrations, or the departure dates. Science is interested in taking censuses—actual counts of individual numbers. The Audubon Society now has amateur observers all over the country taking a census of birds during Christmas week, and another of nestings in June. It is on the look-out for a sudden rise or falling off in the population of rabbits, field mice, squirrels, chipmunks, tree rats. These fluctuations give other animals, including man with his daily bread, serious trouble. So that when you find a dead animal in the woods or fields, it is worth noting it down, and you should try to discover what caused its death. When there are no visible clues, the case is most interesting of all, for it usually means that starvation or disease has claimed another victim.

One could go on multiplying the useful and exciting things that the amateur, working locally, could accomplish. Nothing, for instance, has even been said about the rapid rise in importance of animal motion pictures and what the camera fan could do in this field. That doesn't mean provoking unnatural combats between wild beasts, but shots of bird and quadruped and reptile living their own private lives. By running these through slowly, scientists have discovered the answers to questions that the unaided eye could not settle.

But not picture-taking, not note-taking, not collecting nor studying books will take the place of mind and heart stored with living experience. The richest men are those who have always lived well. Those who have traveled most widely are those who have really seen what lies about them. When we stand under the stars we can admire a remote and frosty beauty; we see a few hundred points of light scattered in the eternal constellations. But the lens of the telescope brings the nearer bodies of heaven leaping toward us. It shows us in deep and awesome perspective thousands of stars that had been buried in limitless night. So knowledge, even a little knowledge, whether achieved through theory or practical experience, puts a new dimension into every scene. We can behold it as something more than a beautiful picture. It is peopled with friends, whom we call by name, and exciting strangers. All is fresh, all is of moment. And in this newly revealed world a man may walk, happy in the mastery that is his at the price of some curiosity, even a little effort.

LAYING THE GROUNDWORK

Preparation for Reading

1. What do you understand by the term "natural history"?
2. How does the study of natural history increase your understanding of the world in which you live and your enjoyment of it?

Vocabulary Building

1. Look up these words: *hedonistic, rodent, avocation, reptiles, mycology, formicologist.*
2. Identify: Fabre, Audubon, Alexander Wilson, Academy of Sciences, Maxim, John Muir.

APPRAISING THE RESULTS

1. State the thesis of the selection.
2. Examine the last five "sentences" of paragraph two. What would have been a more conventional punctuation? Why did the author use fragments?
3. Explain the relation of the amateur to the professional naturalist. What do you know of the work of some of the great

naturalists: Fabre, Audubon, Agassiz, Maeterlinck, Burroughs, Muir?

4. What personal pleasure can the study of natural history give one? What practical needs are served by the researches of natural scientists? How can one learn to be a natural scientist?

5. What is the right, and what the wrong, way to make a collection?

6. Discuss the following statements: (a) "There is a vast army of intelligent reporters abroad in the land who could assist natural science." (b) "The whole mystery of life is in the inky cloud of frogs' eggs in a ditch, and the riddle of instinct is there for anyone to read in the pavement ants." (c) "Even two enthusiasts make a learned society." (d) "If you live in the country, adventure begins at your back gate." (e) John Muir's statement of his equipment and procedure as a natural historian: "I put a loaf of bread and a pound of tea in an old sack, and jump over the back fence."

SELECTING THE THEME SUBJECT

1. Write a paper analyzing your experience in some phase of natural science.

2. Describe a walking tour which amateur naturalists would enjoy in your locality, and explain their interest.

3. Titles for themes: Hunting with a Kodak; The Collecting Mania; Life in Ponds and Ditches; Communistic Ants (or Bees); Why Birds Migrate; Bird Life in My Back Yard; The Pleasures of Fishing; On Being an Amateur Botanist; My Garden; The Practical Value of the Research of Natural Historians; How Plants Disperse Their Seeds; Habits of the Coyote (or some other wild animal); My Collection of Butterflies.

PART THREE

Building a Better World

Education for a Changing Age

THE SCHOOL IN A PROGRESSIVE AND INDUSTRIAL DEMOCRACY[1]

Edward H. Reisner

THE UNDERTAKING WHICH HAS BEEN ASSIGNED ME IS TO DE-
SCRIBE THE JOB OF THE SCHOOL IN PRODUCING PERSONS FIT TO
live in a progressive industrial and democratic society. What
I shall say in fulfillment of this assignment represents my
own point of view and possibly no one of you will entirely
endorse it. However, my purpose is to place before you for
your thoughtful consideration a clear statement of at least
one way of answering the question implied in the topic.

A considerable part of such answer must lie in the interpretation which is made of the words, "a progressive industrial and democratic society"—not all the answer, to be
sure, because there is a factor of individual physical and
mental endowment which cannot be left out of such an
issue. However, with your permission, I shall pay almost
exclusive attention to the social aspects of the problem in
this connection.

Let us be frank to say that the "progressive industrial and
democratic society" about which we are thinking is the
United States on Armistice Day, 1937. Perhaps these words
do not accurately apply in all particulars. Certainly this
country is highly industrialized. Its political forms are those
commonly called by the name of democracy. And it can
hardly be denied that it is changing, if not *progressing*. But
by what right and to what extent is the United States worthy

[1] "The Job of the School in a Progressive Industrial and Democratic Society."
From *Teachers College Record*, April, 1938. Reprinted by permission of the
author and of the publishers.

to be described as "a progressive industrial and democratic society"? What is our country really like as a society?

DIVERGENT IDEAS OF OUR SOCIETY

The answers to this question are various and even contradictory among themselves. One answer which is often heard is something like this: Admitting that not everything is perfect, this is the best country on God's footstool. We have the highest standard of living among the working classes to be found anywhere. We have exceptional opportunity for the person of ability and character to get ahead and rise in the social-economic scale. Our institutions guarantee free and full participation of all citizens in decisions regarding public administration and policy. Every man may speak his mind on public questions. We have freedom of press, religion, and assembly. No dictators tell us what we shall think, what we shall do, and when we shall be happy. We have a system of public education which gives every boy and every girl the chance to make the most of his abilities. Taking it all in all, this is a pretty good country and we like it. Let those who don't like it go somewhere else—to Russia, to Utopia, or go jump in the ocean. At any rate, let them quit raising hell about American life and institutions.

Such an estimate of our country is one that we have all heard. And who, during the past few years, has not seen the United States painted in colors very dark indeed, something like the following: Our economic system has broken down with ten million workers out of jobs and five million youth between sixteen and twenty-four years of age who have never had a job at all. A handful of people among us have a sinful surplus of wealth and wield enormous social power while a large part of the people are living in houses unfit for human habitation, subsisting on an inadequate diet, going without sufficient clothing, denied dental and medical care enjoying no security whatever against loss of employment illness, total disability, and old age, a constant prey to anxiety for themselves and their children.

As for our boasted political freedom, it is said that this i badly moth-eaten. There is no political party which represent the underprivileged classes, but rather political control is exercised by the "haves" for their own advantage and without consideration of the depressed poor. Public administration is frequently in alliance with the forces of crime. Several million Negro citizens have no votes at all and newspapers owned by the wealthy create the political opinion of all the rest. The air is free to those who have money to buy radio time, except in the case of a communist who proposes to face the "mike" at Terre Haute, Indiana, and other cities of the West and South. Even the schools, they would say, are free in the upper grades only to the children of the moderately well to do. The educational opportunity which American children enjoy is largely a matter of geography, as there are many states, and many communities in almost all states, where the inadequacy of the schools is a national disgrace. And within those schools the teachers are so thoroughly cowed by a conservative public, acting through super-conservative boards of education, that they cannot lead the pupils to a thoughtful consideration of the realities of the American social scene, but must drill them in the catechism of American greatness and prepare them to grab their own handful of American prosperity.

A view of American life made up so exclusively of its deficiencies is likely to create a steady mood of pessimism regarding the possibilities of making anything better, or even good, come out of it and to suggest the alternative of radical change of fundamental political and economic institutions. A fresh, new start is thought of as desirable and embraced as possible.

Perhaps most of us here today reject both these views of the American scene as inadequate. We cannot accept the easy optimism of the first or the thoroughgoing pessimism of the second. We do not see the historical present as the embodiment of perfection, nor do we see the possibility of moving in the direction of a better society except as we utilize the adjustments which have already been achieved. Too great satisfaction with what we are and have would stay any effort to rise above the inadequacies of our contemporary situation, while complete disillusionment and an altogether negative appraisal of what has been achieved would dislodge the fulcrum upon which the leverage of social progress is to be exerted.

A realistic view of American society today must take account both of historical factors and of certain profoundly significant elements of current social change. The historical factors are the foundations of contemporary conservatism. They are present in powerful degree and must be taken into account. On the other hand, there are forces operating in our society which are insistently compelling departures from old social attitudes and traditional institutional arrangements. Any system of education which can fit persons to live in the United States during the next generation must take account of both the conservative elements and those which are working for change.

THE LAND OF OPPORTUNITY

The older, and until recently, the dominant pattern of our social existence was agrarian, individualistic, and exploitative. From the beginning of colonial history until almost the close of the nineteenth century cheap or free land to the West beckoned to the unsuccessful and ambitious in the East. The period was also one of steady and spectacular increase in population and rise in land value, which almost automatically accrued to the advantage of those first in possession. During that entire time, the colonies and later the United States were the land of opportunity for the depressed classes of Europe, who thronged to our shores in successive waves and became units of our society and participants in the bounties of our natural resources and of a favorable social trend.

There are other areas of the world which have responded in like way to the population-surge and to the exploitation by men and women from older parts of Europe, but certainly the American scene in this respect is one of the most remarkable that can be viewed in human history. Poor Irish came from their poverty-stricken holdings in the Emerald Isle to work for a generation with pick and shovel and then through their sons and later descendants capture important influence in municipal politics and in the economic and social life of their communities. Germans from the peasant and artisan classes expanded under the free institutions of the United States into substantial landowners, took advantage of free education for their children and saw them entering the professions and holding high places in commerce and manufacture. Poor Jewish immigrants who had lived beyond the pale in Russian, Polish, or Hungarian ghettos saw their children filling the colleges and going on to attain a social standing and importance guaranteed by their ability and stimulated by their long-obstructed ambition. Poor miners and laborers from the Slavic parts of Europe entered the mines and the steel mills of the United States and now their sons are playing on the football teams of our colleges and universities.

Each wave of immigration seemed to be shoved upward in the American scale of living by the one succeeding it. Under the generous political institutions and the favorable economic circumstances of American life, it seemed as if the shackles which had bound human beings in their European environment were broken and all their resources of ability and character and determination were allowed to develop. It is true that in this social scene there were individuals who were going down in the scale as well as those who were going up, but the dominant movement was upward and the general conviction held that if a person did not get ahead, it was his own fault. A society triumphantly surging forward to higher levels of economic security and power was indifferent to the stragglers who fell by the way and those unfit for the march who never started. When Governor Smith recounts the story of his rise from the Fulton Fish-market to the governorship of New York State and to the top of the Empire State Building, he is giving only one conspicuous version of a theme which might be recounted millions of times for different individuals. So many citizens of the United States today have personally participated in this bountiful quality of American life that they resent any implication that times have changed and that the horn of plenty is now less full. They seem to think that their favorable position and their economic security are due entirely to their own effort. They neglect the factor of environment which has made it possible for their personal qualities to win such high economic rewards.

But the stubborn fact remains that the conditions *have changed*. All the free land which is worth taking up for agricultural projects has been assigned. Our wealth is coming more and more to depend upon our elaborative industry. The flood of immigration has been stopped by a legislative ban, and there is no longer coming to this country an annual increment of population ready to be exploited in the hope of having its turn next. We are faced with the problem of conserving resources rather than squandering the heritage of a bountiful nature. Our problem has become one of conservation instead of exploitation. The United States faces the dramatic alternative of developing into a society like the older European societies where scarcity of land and restricted opportunity for social progress resulted in an agrarian peasant class and an industrial proletariat, or of going ahead to discover ways in which science and improved forms of social management and a new sense of community will make it possible to maintain the factor of individual opportunity or at least provide social significance for all individuals within the common national bond.

New Demands of an Industrial Society

A second historical development which is powerfully present in American society today is the progressive urbanization and industrialization which have been going forward with rapid acceleration since the days of the war between the states. The development of the factory system of production was accompanied not only here but almost wherever it has appeared with a tremendous amount of exploitation of workers and with complete disregard of social responsibility. The same rugged individualism which captured for personal use hundreds of thousands of acres of rich farm land, gold and iron mines, virgin forests and water-power sites was applied to the exploitation of the men, women, and children who worked in factories and whose labor was the foundation of the profits and wealth of the managers and owners of the plant.

During the historical development of our industrial system, and to an extent at the present, the capitalist-owner and manager of a factory, or a mine, regarded labor in exactly the same spirit as the farmer looked upon his hundred acres and called it his own. The sad fact was slowly learned that these two types of ownership and control were not alike and what was possible in a farming society became impossible and destructive in an industrial society. The struggle toward this realization is one of the major trends in the history of the last one hundred and fifty years, not only in the United States but wherever the industrial system has developed. Other countries had learned this lesson before our own, for here agrarian independence and individualism have been so strong and other factors of individual opportunity have been operating with such power, that we have been painfully slow in accepting the verdict that an industrial society has needs, problems, and rules which are not those of a nation of farmers.

Among these new insights into the nature and demands of an industrial society is the recognition of human labor, not as a lot of obstreperous and inferior "hands" who are to be used up in the interest of greater profits, but as the necessary human complement in the industrial enterprise, deserving to be fostered and rewarded and treated as individuals in their own right. Among the important battlefields in this long struggle were those which concerned the recognition of the right of labor to organize and to fight for what it considered to be its rights, the restriction of hours of labor— first of women and children and latterly of all workers—to a reasonable time, the elimination of child labor, the development of safety and health conditions in industrial plants, and the passing of compensation measures for workmen injured in the pursuit of their labor.

At present the industrial societies of the world are pressing forward to a new conception of the responsibility of society to the human beings who carry on the work of the mills and factories and mines. They are providing for the relief of unemployed workers. They are instituting schemes of socialized medical care and hospitalization. They are providing old-age pensions for those who have reached the time when they can no longer hold their own in the industrial system. They are concerning themselves to provide for the millions of productive workers, homes that are comfortable and attractive. They are surrounding those homes with opportunities for recreation for old and young. They are redoubling their efforts to provide public educational opportunity for the gifted children of the laboring class to improve their individual gifts and add them to the store of technical, artistic, scientific, and managerial skill and ability which are necessary to the development of a greater and happier industrial society.

Let me express again the opinion which is shared by many who have greater right than I to express it, that the United States, a developing industrial nation, is lagging far behind other industrial nations of the world in many aspects of this enlarged program which society must and will undertake for its workers.

DEMOCRATIC SOCIAL CONTROL

A third factor in the present social scene which has historical roots is that of democratic social control. Into their fundamental laws the people of the United States wrote their determination to be free from the abuses of personal liberty which had been a commonplace under eighteenth century European governments. They demanded freedom of speech, of assembly, of press, and of conscience. By the assertion of the right of habeas corpus they eliminated the possibility of imprisonment for political ends exercised by a dictatorial government.

Over and above providing this basis of representative government as the method of public control and guaranteeing the rights of individuals against dictatorial repression, democracy in the United States has meant a certain equality among the citizens. Differences of religious belief and practice have not been allowed to serve as handicaps against full participation in political life. Differences in birth, education, and wealth are levelled at the polls.

The practical deficiencies of the democratic system which developed in the United States were numerous and in some cases ugly. Politics tended to become a career followed for its own purposes and rewards and without reference to the public welfare. Generally speaking, the best and most able people were too busy making money or being respectable to take part in politics besides casting their votes long after the real chance of affecting the choice of men or issues had been taken away. There has also been a bad condition of venality in American politics. Vote-buying has traditionally been a feature of political campaigns and the purchase of legislators and officials by the forces of organized business and vice has been a commonplace. We have also had a long history of inefficient, inexpert service in administrative offices, which have been filled as a reward for party effort.

It would be too much to say that all these weaknesses of our democratic system are simply historical in character, for some of them are still in existence today. However, there are many forces which have been working valiantly during the last seventy-five years for the improvement of these unsatisfactory conditions and much improvement has occurred. The extension of civil service has reduced the factor of inefficient administration. The development of a new social conscience has greatly lessened the amount of political corruption. We seem gradually to be learning how to run a democratic state.

Whatever the deficiencies of democracy as a going political system which we have to acknowledge, I should like to say that even in its present immature, imperfect form, democracy—exactly democracy as practiced in the United States—is one of the most precious things that have evolved in the long course of human history. We are essentially, in spite of certain exceptions which are plain to the eye—we are essentially a free people. We are not controlled by any dictator either of the communist or the fascist variety. Public policy among us grows out of the full and free examination of issues placed before an electorate who register their preferences at the polls, and in a spirit of good sportsmanship we have learned to accept the decision of the majority. Let me say again, in cold blood and with full realization that it sounds a bit enthusiastic—an election day in the United States, with all its limitations, is one of the supremely fine spiritual products of a million years of human evolution.

To turn briefly to a fourth historical development within our country, individualism has always been running a race with the "sense of community" and for a long time has seemed to be far out in front. The dominant social note over long periods has seemed to be that individuals may get ahead rather than that individuals may get ahead together in the common enterprise of a search for welfare and happiness for all. At the present time there is strong evidence of a demand for a new sense of interdependence among all the parts of our society. We seem earnestly to be taking up the project of developing a co-operative community. We are demanding more and more that the simple neighborliness which characterized our more primitive social development shall be enlarged and strengthened so as to bring together in the spirit of good neighborliness the entire great nation which we have become.

Can we agree among ourselves, ladies and gentlemen, that "a progressive industrial and democratic society" is one which is seeking in increasingly generous ways to provide the working millions of our population with the material basis of the good life; a society which is aware of the debt which it owes to everyone who does productive work and is willing to invest such work with its true social and spiritual significance; a society which is becoming conscious of all its forces of wealth and intellect and character and striving to bind them together into an interdependent co-operative community in which the welfare of each becomes, in practical and effective ways, the interest of all?

THE JOB OF THE SCHOOL

If we are in agreement that the community which has just been suggested in its major outline is what the United States is, or what the United States may come to be, one of the major aspects of the job of the school in preparing citizens to live in such a community becomes clear. In the first place the school should impress upon the minds of all future citizens a realization of the precious heritage which is theirs. The school should give them a healthy respect for and a critical understanding of the actualities, historical and present, of American life and institutions. It should give them a sense of the more immediate possibilities of social development, which the new social conscience is demanding and working toward. And, finally, the school should provide its pupils, who are going to be the voting citizens of tomorrow, with a conception of the greater, richer, happier community which some day will come into existence, and to the coming of which they are enlisted to make their contribution.

About this part of the job of the school I would have no uncertainty, no fumbling, no sense of problem. It represents a frame of values which I would build into the lives of pupils so as to make it an active, vital part of them. Call it indoctrination if you will, but if I could cause to arise in the heart of every boy and girl of school age in this country today the spirit of love for their country and a determination to make it a better, happier place for human beings to live in, I would accept the responsibility and do it.

When it comes to ways and means of bringing about this ideal, the spirit of instruction must follow a different mode. Here we must have information for the facing and solving of problems—a recognition of practical difficulties which must be surmounted before ideal ends can be accomplished. The instruction as to ways and means must be realistic, concrete, critical. Let us have no indoctrination regarding the tariff, or the agricultural administration act, or the management of unemployment relief, or the makeup and functions of the Supreme Court. If this quality of instruction is demanded for the proper preparation of future citizens for their duty, it is absolutely essential that the right to think, the right to examine issues on their merits, the right to examine alternative systems of economic and political control, should be a part of the atmosphere of every American school. The only live issues in the social studies are controversial issues and they must be brought into the schools and attacked as problems, the solution of which depends upon an unbiased and uncontrolled examination of facts. Freedom of inquiry, freedom of examination, freedom of decision, are of the essence of our political system as a whole. We can do no less than guarantee a similar atmosphere of intellectual freedom within the institution which is preparing boys and girls for the more mature exercise of the same social process.

Finally, it is the part of the school in a progressive industrial society to assist in the reinvestment of labor of all kinds and degrees with the spiritual quality which it should possess. No job in the whole category of human labor need be low and menial if it is done by a real person. The common arts of the household take on a new and higher quality when carried on with the aid of science and intelligence and when their high human significance is understood and acknowledged. It is the job of the school to lift the farmer from the category of "hayseed" and "rube," share-cropper and "poor white" and place his work on that level to which scientific practice raised it. It is the job of the school through training in skills and the development of attitudes, to lift the term mechanic out of its present implied connotation as of one who does a rather inferior kind of work to which is attached dubious social esteem and make of it the symbol of an honorable and important agency for the maintenance, the success, and the progress of an industrial society.

The American school is and has been a great institution, and has contributed powerfully to the development of American society. But the American school has emphasized more the giving of opportunity to the individual than the inculcation of a sense of social responsibility. Historically it seems to have been carried on more with reference to the idea of giving pupils their chance to get ahead than with the idea of impressing upon them their duty to the community. The American school may well continue and extend this factor of individual opportunity, but it will not be doing its whole job until, much more adequately than it does now, it impresses upon our youth an ideal of a greater and better

American community and enlists them wholeheartedly in the fight to bring that community into existence.

LAYING THE GROUNDWORK

Preparation for Reading

1. What does the phrase "progressive industrial and democratic society" mean to you?
2. What are the social sciences? Why are they taught?
3. What do you expect to gain from your college education?
4. What part should the schools play in preparing young people to take their places in adult society as workers, thinkers, leaders, voters?
5. Who should go to college? What should be done for those without money?

Vocabulary Building

1. Compare the meanings of these words: *industrial* and *agrarian;* *conservatism, liberalism,* and *radicalism; urban* and *rural; indoctrination* and *inculcation; proletariat* and *bourgeoisie.*
2. Identify: *Utopia, ghettos, Slavic.*
3. Explain the terms *fulcrum* and *leverage* as they are used in the last sentence in paragraph 8.
4. Look up these words: *increment, cowed, catechism, artisan, divergent, obstreperous, complement, venality.*

APPRAISING THE RESULTS

1. What limitations does the author make in the three introductory paragraphs?
2. Summarize the two extreme contrasting points of view of the nature of our society.
3. Why does the author believe that neither of these views is adequate? What point of view does he take? Of the three points of view, which would you accept?
4. Show how the first section, "Divergent Ideas in Our Society," is developed by contrast.
5. What are the four historical and social developments the author traces?
6. What four concepts should the school give its pupils? Why does the author call them "a frame of values"?

7. Why must the means for achieving this ideal be "realistic, concrete, critical"?
8. How is educational opportunity a matter of geography? What sections of the country have the poor school systems? Why?
9. Do you agree with Mr. Reisner's opinions and suggestions? If not, explain why you differ.
10. Should the schools give more vocational training? How would this practical training affect apprenticeships and industry?
11. What experimental changes are going on in the schools today?

SELECTING THE THEME SUBJECT

1. Compare your school with that of your grandfather: aims, subjects studied, age and background of students, size of school, classroom methods, sports.
2. Write a paper on the tradition of "The Little Red School House."
3. Discuss the faults you find with the education you have received. Be concrete and specific in your charges.
4. Defend or attack the right of the schools to teach controversial subjects, such as evolution, political doctrines, sex education.
5. Write a paper explaining "academic freedom" as it affects both the teacher and the student.
6. Additional theme subjects: Adult Education; N.Y.A.; Vocational Training; Training for Citizenship; Subsidizing Athletes and Scholars; A Comparison of Rural and City Schools.

WHAT IS A LIBERAL EDUCATION?[1]

Max Savelle

WE ARE TODAY IN THE MIDST OF A NATIONWIDE DISCUSSION OF THE OBJECTIVES OF EDUCATION. FROM THE HIGH SCHOOL SENIOR who is picking out a college to enter next fall to the university president who is trying to make his university fulfill its obligations to society, men are asking, everywhere, what are the objectives of education? What is education really for?

In the course of this discussion, some four ways of education have been suggested. Certain educators have said that the chief objective of education is to prepare a man to make a living by rendering some high-class professional service to society. In this way, they say, the needs of both society and the individual are most perfectly supplied, and there is little need for anything more. A second group say that there is more; that the university, over and beyond professional or vocational training, must be prepared to supply the broader educational needs, in so far as possible, of every individual who enters its gates. Beginning with the interests and the knowledge the student has when he arrives at the university, they would allow him to follow his own interest or caprice toward a more general education; but they would not require him specifically to study any particular thing.

Another group of educators, led by one of our best-known university presidents, takes the position that the core of higher education is to be found in a discipline calculated to "train the mind." They do not mean that the student's mind is to be trained for any particular thing, but, rather,

[1] A radio talk given on the Stanford University Hour, March 21, 1938. Used by special permission of the author and of the National Broadcasting Company, Inc.

189

that by this discipline he will be prepared to tackle most of the intellectual problems that may present themselves to him in the course of his life. Certainly, there is much to be said for this idea. But there is a fourth group of educators who maintain that the core of every civilized man's intellectual preparation for life should be what is called a *liberal education*. It is a surprise and a shock to these men to find that extremely little conscious effort is being made in the universities of this democracy to achieve the greatest possible refinement and enrichment of the cultural and emotional life of the student, or to promote in him the exercise of genuine intellectual tolerance, or to formulate in him the habit of receptivity to intelligent change. It is surprising and shocking, at a moment when we are coming to realize more poignantly than ever how precious our intellectual liberty really is, to find that these elements in a liberal culture are left almost entirely to chance or to the individual caprice of the student.

Yet it seems to me that these are precisely the qualities of mind that a liberal education ought to cultivate. The word "liberal" means "free"; but it also carries with it the thought of *bestowing freedom* upon the man who enjoys it. And a liberal education is called that because it *is* the sort of education that is calculated most effectively to free the minds of men. It should free the student from ignorance and deepen his intellectual and emotional comprehension of life and its problems; it should give him the intellectual basis for a free and intelligent choice of his way of life; it should free him from intolerance and reaction; and it should free and inspire him to cultivate that intangible and delicate thing that we call the human spirit. It must, of course, be free; but its greatest value lies in its quality of bestowing intellectual freedom upon the student who subjects himself to it.

Now, to be specific, of what does this sort of education consist?

To begin with, it should be remembered that human progress has been the result of two things: the instinct of human beings to adapt themselves to their environment at any given time and place, and the use men have made of what their fathers have taught them. The first, the instinct for adaptation, does not change; but it can be educated, I believe, and that is why the education that is dedicated to training the mind is so important. But it is in the realm of the second, that is, the understanding and use of what our fathers have taught us, that a truly liberal education must do its work.

Obviously, the core of such an education is man's cultural heritage. That means history. Not the history of names and dates, to be sure, but the history of social forms, of economic practices and institutions, of political institutions and thought, of religion, of philosophy and science, of literature, and of art. Nor is it the history of these things only as they took place prior to the year 1900, or even 1914. It is the history of these things as they have evolved, and as they have constantly changed, from the earliest time to the inevitable changes that are taking place about us at this present moment. It seems to me that only by some such study as this can any man really get an idea of what civilization has been or what it is. This, then, the historical study of our cultural heritage, should be, I think, the core of our university curriculum.

But that is not all. Language is the most essential tool of the human mind; and the greatest thoughts and the most sublime emotions of our ancestors have been expressed that way. Therefore, I should think that the study of literature and language should be included in the essential curriculum of a liberal education. Not only should it be included because every educated man should know how to use his own language and that of other peoples, but also because the study of literature and languages makes it possible for the student to share the most profound intellectual and emotional experiences the race has ever had.

There is a third essential ingredient in a liberal education. One of the most serious responsibilities of the university is to help the student to feel *at home* in the universe in which he lives. And that means it must teach him science; for science is the great unifying principle of the modern age, just as religion was the great unifying principle of the Medieval Civilization in Europe. Every educated man should know the elementary facts of the physical and biological sciences; but, most of all, he should comprehend the ultimate atomic unity of all the material universe, and that he is an integral part of that unity. Only thus, it seems to me, can he come to feel reasonably at home in a universe that otherwise might seem unfriendly and inexplicable; but once he achieves this feeling of at-home-ness, his life almost inevitably should be freer and more rational.

In my curriculum for a liberal education, then, you see these three groups of studies: the cultural heritage, languages and literatures, and science. It seems to me that this curriculum, properly taught, should have certain distinctly liberalizing effects upon the minds of the students who take it.

First, it should give the student the intellectual basis for a free and intelligent choice of his way of life. The man who had never heard of any sort of career besides sheep-herding would not be able to choose anything else, simply because of his ignorance. He might have the talents of the greatest engineer in the world, but if he had never heard of the sort of thing that engineers do, or the sort of training they get, he certainly would never be a great engineer; and not only he, but society also, might be the loser. How is a man to choose a career freely if he doesn't know of the many sorts of careers that are open to him? How is he intelligently to choose his political philosophy, or his religion, or his social attitudes, if he doesn't know what there is to choose from? The sort of education I have in mind would present to him a complete picture of human civilization and the various things he might be expected to do as his part in it. His choice of a career, therefore, would no longer be the result of chance. He would be freed of the limitations of his ignorance, and he would be free to choose his way of life from among all possible ways, upon the basis of intelligence and genuine interest.

There is a second and much greater effect in the direction of freedom that this sort of education may be calculated to have upon the student. If a man comes to learn, by the study of history, that there have been many different political forms adopted and used over great periods of time by many millions of men, he will realize that all the forms must have had their value for the time and place in which they were used. When he comes to realize that there are millions of men in the world today who gladly accept forms of government other than that of American democracy, he must also realize that there must be something about those other forms that makes them attractive or satisfactory to the people who have adopted them. He almost inevitably must come, it seems to me, to the position of true tolerance that recognizes that other ways and other manners, though they may not appeal to us, may be just as good as our own for those who use them.

Or, when a man comes to realize that the forms of social organization have changed, from the tribe to the city, from the city to the empire, from the empire back to the medieval manor, and from the manor to the nation, then he realizes that no one form may probably be expected to remain forever without change. Institutions and ideas are constantly changing. They have always been changing, and they always will. What effects would the realization of this fact have upon our student? It seems to me that it should teach him that no institution, no matter how old, is eternal; that he must be prepared for change, for change will surely come; and that it is absolutely imperative for him, as an educated man, to open his mind to all proposals that give promise of better things for the future, in order that he may make sure that the better, and not the worse of the new things shall be adopted.

The second great effect of this liberalizing education, then, is the cultivation of tolerance, and the freeing of the human mind from any sort of fanatical attachment to old and antiquated ideas or institutions that have outlived their usefulness.

But there is a third freeing effect of the liberal education. This sort of education should deepen and enrich the lives of men. It should bring to them the enjoyment of good literature, and provide for them the opportunity and the incentive to read the great books of the race that they will never have time to read after they get out of college. It should introduce them to the emotional and intellectual experiences of the greatest minds and souls who have lived before us. Most of all, it should inspire the student to try his own wings in the flights of imagination or investigation that must take place if the cultural heritage of our children is to be greater than that which was handed down to us.

A great deal depends, of course, upon the teacher. Our universities are full of men who have so lost themselves in the exploration of their own little corners of scientific or pseudo-scientific knowledge that they have completely lost sight of the fact that the chief aim of education is the cultivation of the human spirit. A great deal of the inspirational value of a liberal education comes from the student's contact with great teachers like William James, Henry Adams, James Harvey Robinson, and David Starr Jordan; and the university and its education can be no more liberal or more inspiring than its teachers. Yet, aside from this, it seems to me that the university should build its curriculum with a *conscious purpose of cultivating this elusive, finest quality of the human mind* without which all our boasted civilization must be utterly without meaning. The point, indeed, of all my speech is that many of our universities have overlooked these intangible things that are the finest flower of our civilization, and that it is high time to make a conscious, positive effort to cultivate in our graduates these so-called liberal virtues.

Such, then, is my conception of a liberal education—an education that frees the mind of ignorance and gives it the intellectual basis for free and intelligent choice of a way of life; that frees men from intolerance and reaction, and consciously cultivates the virtues of genuine tolerance and a receptivity toward intelligent change; that frees the minds of men from the inhibitions of ignorance and superstition and fear, and encourages them to continue forever the processes of the human spirit that have resulted in what we call creative progress. Such an education is absolutely indispensable for the successful operation of a democracy. It is an education that is and must be free; but it is an education that comes to a man, bringing with it real intellectual freedom.

LAYING THE GROUNDWORK

Preparation for Reading

1. What is the chief purpose of education?
2. How do you define "a liberal education"?
3. Why do most universities no longer demand Latin or Greek as an entrance requirement? Why are modern languages usually required?

Vocabulary Building

1. Look up these words: *poignantly, heritage, ingredient, inexplicable, incentive, receptivity.*
2. What is the common derivation of *caper* and *caprice*?
3. What are the different meanings of the word *discipline*? How is it related in derivation to *disciple*? How is it used in this essay?

APPRAISING THE RESULTS

1. What is the thesis? Where is it found?
2. What is the function of the first paragraph? of the fifth? of the tenth?
3. What is the main idea of each of the major divisions?
4. In the first and third divisions, how does the author emphasize the idea which he considers most important?
5. Make a study of the transitions that link the paragraphs.
6. Outline the selection.
7. What studies does the author say will make the student feel "at home in the universe in which he lives"?
8. Why should education make the student realize that change is inevitable?
9. Explain how Savelle's ideal of a liberal education develops a spirit of tolerance.

SELECTING THE THEME SUBJECT

1. Write a theme developing the idea that a liberal education "is indispensable for the successful operation of a democracy."
2. Attack or defend the idea that "the chief objective of education is to prepare a man to make a living."

3. Explain your conception of the chief function of education and how the school should fulfill it.
4. Develop one of these titles: Desirable Qualities in Teachers; The College in Fact and Fiction; The Value of Skepticism; The Cloistered Life; College Is Changing Me; The Value of the Educated Man to the Community; College Subjects not in the Catalogue.

A LONG TRAIN OF ABUSES[1]

H. A. Overstreet

OUR FOREFATHERS HAD ONE ADVANTAGE OVER US—THEY KNEW, OR THOUGHT THEY KNEW, THEIR ENEMY. HAVING NO DOUBTS, they could go ahead and do what the situation required. We, of this century, are in a more difficult position. We know well enough that, in spite of the brilliant successes of our technological age, there is evil about, but for the life of us we cannot say: "Behold the villain." To be sure, there are those who believe they can detect the enemy. They name it capitalism, or excessive wealth, or monopoly, or high finance; or, if the shoe pinches on the other foot, they name it communism, or socialism, or radicalism, or trade unionism, or denial of free enterprise. They may even do as one contemporary nation does and name it the Jew. Most of us, however, have not the good fortune—or the ill—to be thus certain; and being without certainty, we feel unable to gird up our loins and do battle for the Lord.

For us, therefore, there will have to be a preliminary time of getting our minds clarified; and the best way in which we can do this is to pass in review the long "train of abuses," to use the phrase of the Declaration of Independence, that has marred and still mars the course of our energetic but very much bewildered American civilization.

THE DECLINE OF THE FARMER

The first of these is the abuse of that member of our nation whom we have celebrated in story and lauded in song. That the man of the soil is indispensable to our life-enterprise,

[1] Reprinted from *A Declaration of Interdependence*, copyright, 1937, by W. W. Norton & Company, Inc., by special permission of the publishers.

that he is the sturdy root-hold of our activities, has been a commonplace of our thinking. We have believed in his type of life, have been confident of the virtues he has developed by his contact with growing things. When Thomas Jefferson thought of democracy, he thought of the democracy of rural folk. In our less urbanized moments we like to say that character comes out of the soil.

But the man of the soil has been pushed more and more out of the American picture. Why this is so is difficult to say. Industry, thrift, integrity, dogged courage in the face of nature's perversenesses—all of these have continued to characterize the farmer. But instead of making him richer as the country has grown in wealth, they have made him poorer. As he has learned to produce, he has found the fruits of his production mysteriously going elsewhere. Cities have been built, great fortunes made, a whole civilization has advanced in material prosperity, but the farmer has been loaded with increasing debt until farms and foreclosures have come to be almost synonymous terms, and the "rural slum" has become a growing blot on the landscape.

This leaves us with a paradox: we have lauded personal industry—hard, honest work—as a basic human virtue; but the course of our more recent history shows that, for the farmer, hard, honest work of itself does not pay. Apparently we have built into our system of life something that mysteriously contradicts our own belief about life: our best virtue has managed somehow to become the worst kind of business. Where we used to say: "Go west, young man," advising thereby an extension of rural triumphs, we have been saying, in effect, "Leave the farm, young man."

Somewhere within the system that has otherwise so brilliantly developed there lurks an enemy. If a civilization is indeed to be built upon sturdy virtues, this enemy will have to be discovered. For a democracy that increasingly destroys its farm-folk is headed toward failure. If honest work cannot be made to pay, something that is neither work nor honest will inevitably take its place. One of the chief problems of our contemporary democracy, therefore, is the recapturing of rural opportunity for making both a livelihood and a life.

THE PLIGHT OF THE ARTISAN

The second member of our civilization in whom we have placed our trust is the artisan. We have been proud of the fact that we have not been a civilization resting upon the backs of slaves. We have believed in the value of the man with the tools and have regarded him as co-equal with the farmer in the building of a genuine society.

Whitman sang of him:

I hear America singing, the varied carols I hear,
Those of mechanics, each one singing his, as it should be, blithe and strong,
The carpenter singing his as he measures his plank or beam,
The mason singing his as he makes ready for work, or leaves off work.. . . .

If Whitman were alive today, he would probably himself sing a muted song—or an indignant one. His independent artisan is too often either out on the picket line protesting against being exploited, or working in a factory, submissive to the rule of take-it-or-leave-it. Even if he is employed with a fair degree of steadiness, he has fallen from his earlier estate. He has ceased to be the purposer and planner of his work. The tools—of the steel-worker, the auto mechanic, the factory hand—are not his own, and what he makes with the tools is beyond his saying or gainsaying. He has been moved from the purposing to the processing end. Others decide and plan; he follows orders. He is the passive worker who makes what he is told to make and has to let it go at that.

As a consequence, he is fairly helpless in the ordering of his economic life. A system, so complicated that it is beyond his understanding or control, holds him in its grip. He has been called a cog in a machine. If the machine moves, he moves. If it stops, he is unable to start it. In a country blessed with vast wealth, actual and potential, the worker is all too frequently underpaid and insecure. He has to fight for what he gets, and in many cases he is not even permitted to fight. To be sure, there are aristocrats among the workers who have been able to force recognition of their claims, but they are in so small a minority that they are the exception which makes the rule vivid by contrast. The average worker is subject to exploitation by the powerful and to racketeering by his fellows. He is not singing a very happy song.

Again, something mysteriously frustrating has entered the system of our life. Because of it, we have not been able to build a civilization of workers justly treated, happily productive, and genuinely honored. On the contrary, for some bewildering reason, the democratic integrities of our life have got out of hand, and we witness a working population made more or less confusedly aware that there is something profoundly at fault in the setup of our economic scheme.

THE BUSINESS MAN

Meanwhile, having become a business civilization, we have lauded the business man. We have known him as the driving force of our life. We have witnessed, through his energy and resourcefulness, the rapid transformation of a primitive land into an advanced material culture. Hence we have put our trust in him, so much so that the term, "a business administration," came, for a time, to mean the best in intelligent efficiency.

But something curiously defeating has happened to the average business man. In the earlier years of the nation he was master of his enterprise. He could see it through from beginning to end. He could know its ramifications, control its processes. Sound business sense was not an empty term. It could apply in thousands of cases, because there were thousands of business enterprises in which an intelligent mind could grasp all the details and direct all the processes.

Within a few decades a curious change has occurred. Any sizable business is now so widely ramifying, is subject to so many scarcely discernible influences—tariffs, currency fluctuations, new inventions, style changes, political manipulations, financial thimble-rigging, legal restrictions and interpretations—that the average business man is almost as helpless in the situation as the worker. He does largely what an uncontrollable system of forces requires him to do. If, in the unpredictable ups and downs of economic life, he comes through successfully, he takes a deep breath and keeps thankfully on; if he does not come through, he goes more or less resignedly into bankruptcy and tries to start over again, with yet another handicap added in the way of a damaged business reputation.

Meanwhile, somewhere in the picture, are the dim tracings of powers that, octopus-like, stretch over the land. The average business man knows that they are there and that they have hold of him; but he knows it so confusedly, that, as likely as not, through his activities and expressed opinions, he places himself the more firmly within their grasp. In his economic Rome he does what his ruling Romans mysteriously bid him do. His "sound business sense" has come to be a sense of knowing how to conform to a system that compels him.

Nevertheless, being human and proud, he rationalizes the situation otherwise. He still sees himself, romantically, as the driving force of the nation. If it is pointed out to him that he, too, is the victim of a system in which anti-social powers are variously in control, he is as likely as not to fly into a rage and deny the imputation as disloyal. Business, he will assert, particularly American business, is fundamentally sound. He becomes emotionally self-defensive. He organizes to promote plausibility rather than to tackle the problems that a new social and economic order has brought into being. Through his chambers of commerce he stoutly defends the economic order that defeats him. In his luncheon clubs he puts on a semblance of liberality and social-mindedness. But all the while he is the victim of his own threefold lack of power: (1) to comprehend an economic situation far more intricate than his forefathers ever encountered; (2) to detect and combat sinister forces that have gained control—of him as well as of the rest of us; and (3) to set about organizing business in terms of the widespread interdependence of modern life. And the sad part of it is that although he himself is a victim, he continues stoutly to insist that the system which victimizes him is worthy of our veneration and of our loyal defense.

CHILDREN

It has been a tradition among us to care about what happens to our children. The establishment of public schools and their increasing development has been one, but only one, evidence of the belief that a democracy for adults does not function properly unless there be genuine opportunity for the young. During the past few decades, however, a number of things have happened that have gone far to nullify this concern for fullness of opportunity. Here, again, it is difficult to say precisely wherein the evil has lain. But even a superficial survey of the life-conditions of young people makes it evident that, deeply as we may have cared for our children, our caring has been made largely ineffective by influences that seem to have been beyond our control.

One of the gravest symptoms of our social failure is the prevalence of crime among the youth of the land. When we investigate, we note a close correlation between crime and environment. It is not in the well-built quarters of our cities or of our countrysides, we discover, that crime reaches its high levels, but in those blighted regions, both urban and rural, where housing has deteriorated, sanitary conditions are at a premium, and the opportunities for wholesome recreation are lacking. It may be said of many thousands of children throughout the land that, so far as achieving the sturdy social virtues is concerned, they are handicapped, if not beaten, at the outset.

During the recent decades we built up our cities without giving any particular thought to the social consequences of environments. We permitted economic eagerness to erect factories and skyscrapers, to create high speculative land- and housing-values, to crowd families into quarters too small for decent living. In rural areas we permitted various forms of tenantry to flourish under conditions of the most abject poverty. Without quite realizing what we were doing, we subordinated our democratic interest in human beings to our economic interest in successful ledger balances. The result has been that for equality of environmental opportunity we have substituted a pattern of suburb and slum, of residential area and blighted region, of owners' mansions and tenants' shacks. We have built inequality into the essential living conditions of our existence, and countless numbers of children have been the victims.

Again, as our technological age has advanced in energy and productiveness, we have not hesitated to reach out for our children and to place them, for our financial gain, in shops, factories, and mines. If ever there was a denial of the basic spirit of democracy, it is found in the deliberate and widespread refusal to give to the children of the poor those opportunities for a childhood of quiet growth that have been given to the children of the more happily circumstanced.

However, the subordination of the human to the economic has resulted in a still more widespread injury, because in this case it affects the rich as well as the poor. Ostensibly the interest of adults is to prepare a world fit for the habitation of their children. But we are increasingly realizing that the economic world is not one in which the finest qualities of human beings can freely develop. Honesty, straightforwardness, generosity, helpfulness—these seem to have hard going in an economic system based on fiercely competitive self-interest. All too often we discover that our children, grown to adolescence or maturity, must adopt the current methods of deviousness and dishonesty if they are to get ahead in the world.

Somehow all of the above circumstances show the presence of an evil in the system of our life. It is difficult to describe, more difficult to combat, but it is there. And so, rich and powerful as we are, we are still unable to make a homeland that is just to its children and greatly fit for them to inhabit.

THE PROFESSIONS

Of all occupations, the professions have held a position of peculiar honor. This has been true because the professions are enterprises in which the primary interest is not money-getting. A physician, irrespective of payment, is supposed to give of his time and skill when the situation requires it; a lawyer to be at times, without compensation, a defender of the poverty-stricken or of public interests; a minister is supposed to be ready on all occasions to comfort and guide those in distress, moreover he is supposed to be less interested in his salary than in opportunities for extending spiritual welfare; a teacher is supposed to be concerned primarily with the intellectual and cultural growth of his students. Hitherto we have not expected such motivation on the part of business men and workers. For reasons that we need not here analyze, we have taken it for granted that interest in earnings must, with these, be primary.

In the professions, therefore, we have a type of motivation that is of profound promise for the future. While, even in them, self-interest naturally is present, another interest begins to play an important part. The professions, in other words, are anticipatory of the time when all occupations will be carried on with a primary concern for human well-being.

Since this is so, it is of peculiar moment to note what has been happening to these avowedly pro-social enterprises.

THE PHYSICIAN

We may take first the case of the physician. Increasingly, as the science and art of medicine have improved, he is expected to subject himself to a long and expensive training. It might be supposed that, having given the best energies of his young life to equipping himself for human service, he would be permitted to use his powers to the best social advantage. As a matter of fact, no sooner does he emerge from his interneship than he finds himself in the position of having to compete for patronage. He may enter the profession with high ideals, but in far too many cases he finds that the way of the doctor must be the way of the astute business man. He finds a profession in which there are various practices not unlike those of interlocking directorates. Fee-splitting, the exaggeration of ailments to correspond to bank accounts —these things are not unknown and are not publicly talked about, but every physician knows they exist to the hurt of the social objectives of the profession.

One admits these things in sorrow and in full recognition of the fact that most physicians will not bring themselves to obviously anti-social practices. The sorrow is the greater as one notes that the honest physicians all too frequently suffer for their medical integrity and are regarded by their less conscientious colleagues with ironic pity.

We can plainly see that the spirit of acquisitiveness which we take for granted as acceptable in the economic area becomes intolerable when it is the spirit of medical life. Nevertheless, as our economic system has grown in intensity and power, this spirit has not been absent from the medical profession.

To be sure, the profession has to carry its own share of blame. The training of physicians has become so highly specialized that the average graduate of a medical school is in almost total ignorance of the social implications of his profession. He is still trained as if his work were to be performed in a social vacuum. The result has been that at a time when medical men should be keenly alive to the social opportunities and obligations of their work, and equally alive to sinister forces that negate their best contributions, they are in such ignorance of social matters that as frequently as not they support the very system that makes victims of themselves.

Fundamentally, however, the evil would seem to lie in the contradictory nature of our social expectations. To have one type of motive rule in one part of society and another in another part handicaps those who have the better motive. Thus to ask a physician to forego making what he can out of his medical skill while the business man is permitted to make all that he possibly can out of his special skill is like asking one youngster in a game of football to be a good sport and play fair while another is permitted to do unsportsmanlike damage to his opponents. We have asked for a high motivation in the medical man, but we have done nothing whatever to guarantee him even a modest livelihood if he takes us at our word and places human service above monetary gain.

The advance of medicine has been one of the brilliant triumphs of our recent decades. So great has it been that many of the diseases that now afflict numbers of people need no longer be suffered. Nevertheless they still strike down the young and the old for the simple reason that a profession which should be highly socialized is still geared to the motive of individualized competition.

THE LAWYER

The lawyer, supposedly, is an agent of justice. But of the lawyer it has not inaptly been said that "he begins with ideals and ends with deals." It is almost inevitable that it should be so. As in the case of medicine, the modern world has made no provision for a profession of the law free from the pressure of economic competition. The lawyer must live, and in order to do so he must have clients. The average individual almost never has need for a lawyer's services. Hence the lawyer has been compelled to devote himself to service in the region in which fees are sufficiently large and frequent to make a livelihood possible. In the main, he has become the expert assister of economic enterprises in their effort to gain as much as possible for themselves and still remain ostensibly within the law. Becoming a corporation lawyer has been the most acceptable way of reaching a desirable level of economic assurance.

Thus while many an astute physician has learned the art of making himself indispensable to the well-to-do, the astute lawyer has learned this art in relation to the more aggressively acquisitive. In so far as the social system compels him to enter the economic scramble, it has reaped its harvest of a legal profession cast in the mold not of social justice but of devious and ofttimes anti-social practices. It has, in short, forced the legal profession to adopt the ethics and outlook of the very economic powers against which legal protection is often most needed.

The profession is itself not without its share of blame. For here, too, as in the case of the physician, the training of lawyers has been so specialized as to take little account of the social implications of the law and the social opportunities of the lawyer. The result has been a profession which is all too often a bulwark of privilege and a hindrance to social advance.

THE MINISTER

We have looked to the minister as the spiritual leader of the community. Quite apart from creedal distinctions, we have meant by spiritual leadership the wisdom and courage to liberate life. We have looked to the minister as to one who could know the truth that would set us free. He has not always known it. All too frequently he has been a purveyor of enslaving dogmas. But the pattern of the preacher has been that of the liberator. We have looked upon him not as a partisan of special, material interests but as a defender of those enduring truths that belong to all life and that should liberate all life.

But the man of the church has not escaped the evils of the contemporary world. He, too, has had to live; he, too, has been tempted to possess those appurtenances of life that make for freedom from worry and for cultivation of the human refinements. In more or less subtle ways he has taken the line of least resistance. He has found it easier to depend upon his wealthy pew-holders than upon more humble folk. And as he has looked down from his pulpit upon his supporters, he has not found it easy to say the things that he might say about various forms of injustice in an acquisitive society. He has all too frequently taken the easy way of rationalizing religion as a concern with other-worldly matters and has turned a carefully negligent mind away from those cruelties of man to man which might rouse a prophet to indignant protest.

To be sure, he has been bolstered in this by the fact that even the exploited of his congregation have all too frequently regarded church as a place where they could find a super-earthly relief from the pressing problems of the workaday world. They, no more than the privileged, have wished to be wrenched out of that peace by an insistent call to an effort that they are too depleted to make.

The man of the church has lent himself to these two influences and has, in large measure, become the spokesman of a kind of peace so far removed that it has had practically no effect in a world crying for the peace of social understanding.

THE TEACHER

Where the minister has been honored as the spiritual leader, the teacher has been honored as the intellectual leader in the community. Such leadership has carried with it the obligation to seek the truth wherever it is to be found.

In the early days of our democracy, the truth-finding of the teacher was a relatively simple matter. It had to do with the elementary tools of life—reading, writing, arithmetic, geography, history, and such science as then existed. So far as the finding and transmission of factual truths is concerned, the teacher has not notably failed. Education has been our pride to such an extent that we have lavished expenditures upon schools and colleges, and we have been glad to accord to teachers an almost perfect freedom of instruction. We have done more. While the financial rewards of teaching have, on the average, been slight, we have saved teachers from the competition for economic advantage that has been the lot of the physician, lawyer, and minister. In our public systems of education we have at least set the pattern for such freedom from money-getting as has made it possible for the teacher to devote himself single-mindedly to the interests of his pupils.

Nevertheless, forces in the modern world have invaded the teaching profession in a way insidiously destructive of the services which the teaching profession ought to render. In the tool subjects the teacher has been free. In subjects having to do with social, political, and economic relationships, the teacher has been subtly bound by the conventions and opinions of dominant minorities within his society. He has not been free to seek and transmit truths that profoundly concern the day-by-day relationships within his community. He has had either to ignore injustices and maladjustments or to suffer the consequences of teaching what powerful interests have found it to their advantage not to have taught. Thus, as economic forces have increasingly controlled our modern life, the teacher has more and more become their instrument, or their victim, or both.

The result is that with few exceptions the schools and colleges are intellectual guides only in so far as intellectual guidance is not in conflict with the privileged interests that now dominate our community life. In short, in spite of our lip-worship of the teacher as an intellectual leader, he has been reduced to the position of an intellectual adherent of the powers that are in command.

It is not pleasant for teachers to contemplate this, and it is therefore not surprising at the present time that there are stirrings that indicate an unwillingness to be the mere yes-men of a system that looks suspiciously like one that ought to be renovated. But the grip of the dominating powers can be incredibly great, and the teacher in the end may be defeated. Whether genuine democracy in education will prevail would seem to depend upon whether we shall be willing to take seriously the admonition to seek the truth that it may set us free.

DEMOCRACY BECOMES OLIGARCHY

One of our gravest disappointments has been democratic government. It seemed an easy thing for our founding fathers to conceive of a government ruled by the people, even though it is true that in the beginning many of them wished to limit "the people" to the holders of property. The democratic principle of self-rule seemed not an impossible one. To select a worthy neighbor and ask him to lend an honest, disinterested mind to matters that affected the community appeared wholly reasonable. The confidence that the founding fathers had in the principle of self-rule has been transmitted to their offspring, and we, the offspring, are still of a mind to believe that the government of ourselves by our selected neighbors is not only possible but the best of all forms yet conceived.

Nevertheless we have our moments of doubt. In theory we believe in representative government. When, however, we see it in practice, we wonder how long we can successfully continue under its ineptitude and corruption. The term "politician" has become with us largely a term of distrust, even of contempt.

When we ask ourselves why this is so, the obvious answer —although it may not be the sole one—is that politics has become the tool of business—as well as a business in itself. There is a sufficient reason for this. A society in which the most powerful drive is that of self-interest has found it impossible, by the mere ceremony of electing them, to transform its self-interested neighbors into public-spirited servants of the commonwealth. Given self-interest as the most approved motivation, elected officials have gone the easy way of feathering their own nests. Politics, in short, has become, in large measure, public business turned to private advantage. This has been the more in evidence as corporate interests have found it to their benefit to establish friendly working relations with the elected representatives of the people.

Thus our democratic principle of representative government has been subtly transformed into the oligarchic one of government by ruling cliques, and the term "sovereign people" serves chiefly as the verbal reminder of the kind of government we once aimed to establish.

A New Instrument of Power

Each age develops its peculiar instruments of power-over-others; for in every age there are those who are eager to gain and hold privileges that others do not possess. When, in our American charter of liberties, we emphasized the right of individual initiative and freedom of opportunity, we announced our opposition to the then-prevailing instrument of power, namely, noble birth. To be born into the family of a duke or lord was to be presented at birth with a charter of privileges that the child of the commoner could not possibly possess. Ours was, indeed, a fundamental revolution in so far as it made this particular instrument of power thereafter inoperative.

But it would be a naïve individual who would suppose that the task was completed and that equality of opportunity was from then on an accomplished fact. Every age, as we have said, develops its own instruments of power-over-others, and ours has been no exception. In every age, too, the current instrument gets itself invested with a certain prestige. The dukes and lords managed to be thought of as more than usually valuable types of human beings. The commoner was led to regard them with respect if not with reverence. The king was in the tradition of divinity and could do no wrong.

When we turn a realistic eye upon our age, we note a new instrument of power-over-others which, in true historic fashion, has managed to invest itself with a prestige that puts it beyond the pale of average criticism. The new instrumentality is that of "high finance." From the time when the banker first took the monies that his customers had placed in his charge and issued certificates of credit beyond what he had in hand, to the present day of the great investment bankers, an instrumentality for the control of life was being shaped which today is more powerful than any we have known in the entire history of man.

Credit, as we know, is the life blood of a people, and they who control credit control life. It was for this reason that our founding fathers attempted to safeguard the nation by placing the issuance of currency wholly in the control of Congress. To permit currency to be in private control, issuable or withdrawable at the will of private individuals, would have been to deliver the nation into the hands of private interests. For to issue credit is to grant the power of economic life. To withdraw credit is to injure or kill that life. Hence our founding fathers placed this power within the control of a public body, which ostensibly would use it for the public good.

Since those days, however, many things have happened, not the least of which has been the subtle shaping of an instrument through which the manifest will of the framers of the Constitution has been largely nullified. This instrument is the bank loan. The bank loan is privately created credit. It can be issued, within limits, at the will of bankers, and likewise withdrawn at their will. Today such credit constitutes roughly 80 per cent of the currency of the land. Where, then, the framers of the Constitution laid down the rule that Congress alone shall have the power to issue currency, a situation quietly developed to the point at which private bankers had the power to issue four-fifths of the currency of the country.

In other words, a public function became a private privilege. The rulership of the nation's life departed from the publicly-elected representatives to self-elected financiers. Government slipped through the fingers of the people and lodged in a new type of relatively irresponsible dukes and lords, with a financial king more or less dimly discernible.

THE WAY IT WAS DONE

How the masters of credit-financing gradually, through processes of interlocking directorates, achieved their complete overlordship of finance, industry, insurance, communication, and transportation is a long story—too long to be told here. The interested reader can get it most vividly in Louis ([the late] Justice) Brandeis' *Other People's Money*. In that book he declares:

"The dominant element in our financial oligarchy is the investment banker. Associated banks, trust companies and life insurance companies are his tools. Controlled railroads, public service and industrial corporations are his subjects. Though properly but middlemen, these bankers bestride as masters America's business world, so that practically no large enterprise can be undertaken successfully without their participation or approval."[2]

It is well to ponder these words: "practically no large enterprise can be undertaken successfully without their participation or approval." They are an ironic commentary upon the statement so often made by the defenders of the economic *status quo* that the present system is one which encourages the utmost freedom of initiative. "These bankers bestride as masters America's business world."

"The key to their power," Brandeis continues, "is combination." In the first place, there was the legal consolidation of banks and trust companies; then there were affiliations brought about by stockholdings, voting trusts, and interlocking directorates in banking institutions which were not legally connected; and finally, there were the gentlemen's agreements, joint transactions, and "banking ethics," which

[2] Louis D. Brandeis, *Other People's Money*, p. 4 (Frederick A. Stokes Co.).

unofficially eliminated competition among the investment bankers.

In the second place, the organization of railroads into huge systems, the large consolidations of public service corporations, and the creation of industrial trusts directly played into the hands of the associated New York bankers, for these businesses were so vast that no local, independent bank could supply the necessary funds.

These factors alone, however, "could not have produced the Money Trust . . . another and more potent factor of combination was added." It is this third factor that is most astounding.

Investment bankers were dealers in stocks, bonds, and notes. As such, they performed one necessary function in our kind of society. In order that they should possess the public's confidence, they had to be able, with complete objectivity, to estimate the soundness of what they sold. Hence they could not themselves, properly, have an interest in the investments. They had to be middlemen pure and simple.

But not so. Through the purchases of voting stock they became the directing power in the very enterprises—railroads, public service and industrial corporations—that were the *issuers* of the securities they sold.

But more than this. They purchased voting stock in the great enterprises, like life insurance companies and other corporate reservoirs of the people's savings, that were the *buyers* of securities. So they made for themselves a ready market for the securities which they themselves issued.

And finally, they became the governing power in banks and trust companies. These were the depositories of the savings of the people. As holders of these savings they were able to make loans to (their own) corporations; these in turn could issue securities that the investment bankers could readily sell to their own corporations as well as buy at figures acceptable to themselves and sell at conveniently higher prices to their own depositors and the public.

"Thus four distinct functions, each essential to business, and each exercised, originally, by a distinct set of men became united in the investment banker. It is to this union of business functions that the existence of the Money Trust is mainly due."

And Brandeis concludes his analysis with this ominous observation:

"The development of our financial oligarchy followed, in this respect, lines with which the history of political despotism has familiarized us: usurpation, proceeding by gradual encroachment rather than by violent acts; subtle and often long-concealed concentration of distinct functions, which are beneficent when separately administered, and dangerous only when combined in the same persons. It was by such processes as these that Caesar Augustus became master of Rome."

Here, then, in democratic America, were a usurpation of powers and a despotism so subtly concealed that most Americans have been only vaguely aware that it existed.

Words have a curious power to betray us. Democracy is still regarded as essentially a matter of political rights. But at a time when the control of credit is the control of the major life-enterprises, the word democracy must be broadened into its new implications. There can be no genuine, full-bodied democracy unless it penetrates to all the corners of our economic life, making freedom of economic initiative a reality and not an empty verbalism.

AND SO . . .

As we review the foregoing, we realize that the nation "conceived in liberty and dedicated to the proposition that all men are created equal" is not the nation as we now know it. Something has happened to divert us either from a course we meant to take or from one we ought to have taken.

It is difficult to know precisely what this something is. It is quite possible that the unintended revolution brought many things to pass for which we were both individually and socially unprepared. In any event, the nation that we have come to love is not the nation that we can unreservedly admire. We are doing many things that the genuine spirit of democracy should not permit, and we are doubtless leaving undone many another that should be done. We are not, indeed, as yet prepared to say that "there is no health in us," but we probably would agree that the health of our democracy is only "so-so."

LAYING THE GROUNDWORK

Preparation for Reading

1. Read the Declaration of Independence. Copy the sentence in which the phrase, a "train of abuses," occurs. Who was abused, by whom, and for what? To what development in our national life since 1775 does the author call attention by substituting "Interdependence" for "Independence" in the title of the book from which this chapter is taken?

2. How would you define democracy? Is the franchise sufficient guarantee of equality? Is economic power equally distributed? Is political equality a fact or an ideal? Is there any relation between one's economic power and the amount of liberty one can exercise? Are the opportunities for a successful "pursuit of happiness" the same for all our people?

3. Which of the following do you consider in harmony with American ideals of democracy: old age pensions, slums, equal rights for women, prohibition, lynching, child labor, safety legislation in industry, the eight-hour working day, free high school education, labor unions, compulsory saluting of the flag in school, medical aid for all, stock market speculation, government power development, rule by vigilantes, racial discrimination?

Vocabulary Building

1. How many of these words are in your active vocabulary: *integrity, perverseness, paradox, exploitation, racketeering, frustrated, ramifications, decade, plausibility, sinister, veneration, nullify, deteriorated, ostensibly, deviousness, astute, acquisitiveness, ethics, dogmas, insidiously, ineptitude, naïve, usurpation?*

2. Explain the following words and phrases in their context: *thimble-rigging, blighted areas, interlocking directorates, fee-splitting, anti-social practices, lip-worship, yes-men, founding fathers, beyond the pale, financial oligarchy, status quo.*

APPRAISING THE RESULTS

1. Analyze the selection in respect to the following points: the thesis and its relation to the title; the purpose of the two in-

troductory paragraphs; the purpose of the final section; and the basic plan of development.

2. Do you think the subheadings contribute to interest and clarity? Could they have been omitted without jeopardizing the organizational structure and the coherence of the selection?

3. Show how the short paragraphs could have been combined into longer ones. Why do you think the author used these short units?

4. What is the plight of the farmer? of the artisan? of the various other groups? Is the author always fair and accurate?

5. What instrument of power does the author see as a threat to our democracy? How does this power exercise its control?

6. With what ideas do you agree? disagree? Analyze your reactions.

SELECTING THE THEME SUBJECT

1. Elaborate on the plight of any one of the groups discussed in the selection. Base your paper on first-hand experience.

2. Explain how the farmer is affected by one of the following: tariffs, credit monopoly, wages of urban workers, the high cost of distribution, absentee ownership of farms, changes in diet of consumers.

3. Explain one of the following: a brokerage, a picket line, a bloc.

4. Develop one of these titles: The Corner Grocer; The Chain Store and the Consumer; Law and Social Changes; The Ethics of the Market Place; Some Misconceptions About Racketeering; The Living Church; Jury Duty and Citizenship; The Exploited Child.

COTTON TENANCY[1]

Charles S. Johnson, Edwin R. Embree, and W. W. Alexander

COTTON HAS BEEN THE MOST IMPORTANT AMERICAN COMMER-
CIAL CROP. IT IS LINKED HISTORICALLY WITH MANY OF OUR
characteristic institutions: the plantation system, the rise and
collapse of slavery, and, to an amazing degree, with the culture of the entire South. For more than a century, this
greatest of economic assets has been also our greatest social
humiliation. The Kingdom of Cotton, reared first upon the
backs of black slaves, is supported today by an ever-increasing
horde of white and black tenants and share-croppers whose
lives are hopelessly broken by the system. Although adding
a billion dollars annually to the wealth of the world, the
cotton farmers themselves are the most impoverished and
backward of any large group of producers in America.

The cotton tenants live at the level of mere subsistence.
But they are not the only sufferers under the evil despotism
of King Cotton. The devotion to a single crop has left the
whole region of the Old South dependent upon the fluctuations of one commodity, at the mercy of the success of a
single plant. Continuous tilling of one crop has worn out
soil over wide areas which previously were rich and fertile.
Devotion to a commercial harvest has left an abundant farm
region destitute of food crops, and its people living on a
shockingly meager and ill-balanced diet.

The past five years of economic depression have accentuated the problems and aggravated the evils of American cotton culture. Changes in world markets and the development of substitute materials now threaten the life of the industry. The growth of cotton in the Southwest, and the prospect of increasing use of machinery in tilling and picking, make it certain that the ancient order of cotton culture in the Old South is doomed. Sweeping changes in southern farming must come swiftly if millions of former plantation workers are not to be completely wrecked—if the region itself is not to suffer violent ruin.

The Cotton Belt

The cotton belt as determined by soil, climate, and rainfall, lies between 25° and 37° north latitude. Cotton culture now occupies a belt 300 miles north and south, stretching 1,600 miles from the Carolinas to western Texas. In this area 125 million acres are devoted to this single crop—nearly as great an amount of land as is given to all other crops together in this huge region.

Until the Civil War cotton was produced chiefly under the plantation system with slave labor. Free or white workers had no place on the old plantations. The presence or absence of cotton culture largely determined the racial distribution of the population in American settlements during the period from the middle of the 18th to the middle of the 19th century. Negro slavery and cotton grew up together in the Old South, beginning in the Carolinas, which were most typical of cotton culture and the plantation order a century or more ago. But this one crop system, essentially exploitative of the soil, always found it easier to move westward to newer land than to preserve or restore the old farms. Thus the cotton area, carrying slavery and the plantation with it, moved steadily to Georgia and Alabama, then on to Tennessee, Mississippi, and Louisiana. More recently, with the former slaves simply transformed into almost equally dependent tenants, and with ever-increasing numbers of white laborers drawn into the meshes of tenancy, the cotton area has moved on westward to Texas, Arkansas, Oklahoma, and finally to southern California. Expansion westward proceeded very gradually until after 1910, when, at the time of the World War, came a tremendous expansion of the Southwest.

The belt is marked by dense farm populations. While the South, as a whole, is the most thickly populated rural area in America, the cotton belt is the most densely peopled region in the South. Negroes, remaining from slavery times, contribute large numbers to the older sections, forming over forty per cent of the total inhabitants of South Carolina, Georgia, and Alabama, and slightly more than half the population of Mississippi. But Negroes no longer make up the bulk of cotton tenants. White workers, in an increasing flood, have been drawn into the cotton fields, until today they outnumber the blacks more than five to three.

TENANCY

In the ten chief cotton states over sixty per cent of those engaged in the production of this crop are tenants. The computations of Rupert B. Vance place the number of tenant families in the cotton belt at 1,790,783. Of these, 1,091,944 are white, and 698,839 are colored. The family units of white tenants are larger than the colored, due in part to the earlier break-up of Negro families and the high infant death rate. The total number of individuals in these tenant families runs to approximately five and a half million whites and slightly over three million Negroes.

Tenancy for decades has been steadily increasing. The number of farms operated by tenants in the South was high enough in 1880, when 36.2 per cent were run by tenants. By 1920 the percentage of tenancy had reached 49.6, and in 1930 it was 55.5. These figures are for the South as a whole. In the cotton belt the percentage of tenancy is still higher. Out of every hundred cotton farms, over sixty are operated by tenants.

Up to the Civil War cotton laborers universally were Negro slaves. It is one of the strange facts of the history of the slave period that white non-slaveholding families, in spite of their numbers and their destitution, were given no place in the expanding cotton culture, save where they were able to hang on to the fringes of the industry as overseers or as small independent farmers. After Emancipation, however, white families began to compete with Negroes for the new kind of slavery involved in tenancy. The white tenants have increased steadily, filling the new openings in the expanding industry, and taking places left vacant by Negroes who migrated from the plantations to northern and southern cities. In the decade from 1920 to 1930, white tenants in the cotton states increased by 200,000 families—approximately a million persons. During the same decade Negro tenants decreased by 2,000 families as a result of mass movements to cities. Since 1914, this Negro migration to the North alone has exceeded a million and a half persons. Increasingly, therefore, the problems of the rural South in general, and of cotton tenancy in particular, are those of native white families much more than of Negroes.

WHAT IS A TENANT?

A farm tenant, in the widest meaning of the term, is any person who hires the farm which he operates, paying for the use of the land either by a share of the crop which he raises or by cash rental or both. Now the renting of land is not in itself a bad thing; it is customary in other parts of America and to a limited extent in Europe. It is a simple means of getting access to land by persons who have not capital enough to purchase farms. Normally it is regarded as a step on the road to independent ownership. The evil is not in renting land but in the traditions and practices which have grown up about it in the South.

Tenants may be divided into three main classes: (a) renters who hire land for a fixed rental to be paid either in cash or its equivalent in crop values; (b) share tenants, who furnish their own farm equipment and work animals and obtain use of land by agreeing to pay a fixed per cent of the cash crop which they raise; (c) share-croppers who have to have furnished to them not only the land but also farm tools and animals, fertilizer, and often even the food they consume, and who in return pay a larger per cent of the crop.

In considering cotton tenancy, the first group may be almost ignored. Those who have definite agreements with landlords as to exact rental prices are few in number and their status is so independent as to remove them from the system of subservient tenancy. The share tenants and share-croppers are the two great subdivisions of the dependent workers in the cotton belt. The difference between these two classes is simply one of degree. The share tenants, since they supply much of their own equipment, are able to rent the land on fairly good terms, usually on the basis of paying to the owner not more than one-fourth or one-third of the crop raised. The share-croppers, on the other hand, having almost nothing to offer but their labor, must pay as rent a higher share of the product, usually one-half of the crop. In addition, of course, both tenants and croppers must pay out of their share of the crop for all that is supplied to them in the way of seed, fertilizer, and food supplies. "Tenancy," as used in the present report and as commonly applied in the South, is a general term covering both the share tenants and the share-croppers, but not the renters. As a matter of fact, over one-third of all tenants in the South, and over half of the Negro tenants are croppers, that is, in the lowest category of poverty and dependence.

The risk of the tenant increases, of course, in proportion to what he is able to contribute to the contract. There is almost no financial risk assumed by the share-cropper who furnishes only his labor (and that of his family), who receives his equipment and supplies and even his food, from the owner. The share tenant, who supplies his own tools and work animals, assumes more risk, and in return expects a larger share of the earnings. The renter of course assumes much greater risk. In turn the landlord's potential profits increase as he assumes more and more of the risk. Therein lies a danger to the tenant. It is to the advantage of the owner to encourage the most dependent form of share-cropping as a source of largest profits. And he wishes to hold in greatest dependence just those workers who are most efficient. A shiftless and inefficient cropper is of little value to the owner and is expelled, unless, in a serious labor shortage, absence of any worker is even more costly than the presence of an incompetent one. The industrious and thrifty tenant is sought by the landlord. The very qualities which might normally lead a tenant to attain the position of renter, and eventually of owner, are just the ones which make him a permanent asset as a cropper. Landlords, thus, are most concerned with maintaining the system that furnishes them labor and that keeps this labor under their control, that is, in the tenancy class. The means by which landowners do this are: first, the credit system; and second, the established social customs of the plantation order.

As a part of the age-old custom in the South, the landlord keeps the books and handles the sale of all the crops. The owner returns to the cropper only what is left over of his share of the profits after deductions for all items which the landlord has advanced to him during the year: seed, fertilizer, working equipment, and food supplies, plus interest on all this indebtedness, plus a theoretical "cost of supervision." The landlord often supplies the food—"pantry supplies" or "furnish"—and other current necessities through his own store or commissary. Fancy prices at the commissary, exorbitant interest, and careless or manipulated accounts, make it easy for the owner to keep his tenants constantly in debt.

The plight of the tenant at annual settlement time is so common that a whole folklore about it has grown up in the South.

A tenant offering five bales of cotton was told, after some owl-eyed figuring, that this cotton exactly balanced his debt. Delighted at the prospect of a profit this year, the tenant reported that he had one more bale which he hadn't yet brought in. "Shucks," shouted the boss, "why didn't you tell me before? Now I'll have to figure the account all over again to make it come out even."

Of course every story of this kind, and such stories are innumerable, can be matched by tales of unreliability and shiftlessness on the part of the tenant. The case against the system cannot be rested on any personal indictment of landlords any more than it can be vindicated by stories of the improvidence of tenants. The fact is that landlords generally act as they find it necessary to act under the system; tenants do likewise. The development of bad economic and social habits of whatever kind on the part of both landlords and tenants is direct evidence of a faulty system.

Even more than the credit system, the traditions of the region hold the tenant in thrall. The plantation system developed during slavery. It continues on the old master and slave pattern. For many years, even after Emancipation, black tenants were the rule in the cotton fields and the determination to "keep the Negro in his place" was, if any-thing, stronger after the Civil War than before. Although white families now form the great majority of the cotton tenants, the old "boss and black" attitude still pervades the whole system. Because of his economic condition, and be-cause of his race, color, and previous condition of servitude, the rural Negro is helpless before the white master. Every kind of exploitation and abuse is permitted because of the old caste prejudice. The poor white connives in this abuse of the Negro; in fact, he is the most violent protagonist of it. This fixed custom of exploitation of the Negro has carried over to the white tenant and cropper. Yet it has been impos-sible to bring about any change, even to get the poor white workers to take a stand, since any movement for reform is immediately confused with the race issue. Because of their insistence upon the degrading of three million Negro tenants, five and a half million white workers continue to keep them-selves in virtual peonage.

What the Tenant Earns

The average American farm family in 1929 earned $1,240, and this was about a third of the average for non-farm families. The lowest general earnings were in the southern states. The Carolinas, Mississippi, Arkansas, Alabama, Georgia, and Tennessee, the states of the old cotton belt, stood at the bottom of the list. Here, even at the period of national prosperity, a vast farm population barely earned subsistence.

Every study of wages and income in the South makes perfectly clear the low economic position of the rural South. Clarence Heer's exhaustive study of wages and income, covering a period of thirty years, showed that southern agriculture had provided its farmers just about half the per capita income of farmers in other sections. This includes all the "independent farmers, plantation owners, tenants, and share-croppers." When tenants alone are considered, the family earnings slump distressingly below the level of decent subsistence.

The debts are a part of the system and are of two kinds: those accumulating from year to year; and current debts arising from the "furnishing" system. More than a third of the tenants have debts of more than a year's standing. In six widely differing counties included in the field studies of our Committee, 43.4 per cent of the tenants were in debt before they planted their 1934 crop. The average indebtedness, according to the Alabama tenants who were able to keep any record of their accounts, was $80.00.

As to current earnings or deficits, a study of Negro tenant farmers in Macon County, Alabama, in 1932, published in *Shadow of the Plantation*, showed that 61.7 per cent "broke even," 26.0 per cent "went in the hole," and 9.4 per cent made some profit. Of this latter group the total income ranged from about $70 to $90 per year. The special inquiry into tenant farmer earnings by this Committee, which covered some 2,000 families in 1934 and 1935 in Mississippi, Texas, Alabama, and South Carolina, found variations in earnings according to soil fertility and types of management, but universally a sub-standard. Inseparable from the small gross earnings of these farmers was the stern factor of landlord policy, prerogative, alleged supervision charges, and interest rates. It must be remembered that the tenant's actual income is very different from the earnings of his farm as listed in agricultural reports. The landlord's share is taken from the earnings together with the operator's gross expenses.

For the small number of all these 2,000 tenant families who received a cash income in 1933, the average was $105.43. The actual earnings per family, when distributed among five persons, would give a monthly income per person of $1.75. And these incomes, theoretically at least, were benefiting from the federal program of aid to farmers as administered in 1933.

Tenants in general have to consider themselves fortunate if they can farm for subsistence only. One cropper complained dismally: "For 18 years we ain't cleared a thing or made any real money." Another had received his cash in a manner which made it difficult to remember the amounts: "I couldn't possibly go to task and tell you. I got it in dribbles and couldn't keep a record of it, but it wasn't over $75.00." Still another farmer "cleared $45.00 last year; nothing the year before and no settlement; cleared $117.00 the year before that. The most I ever cleared was $260.00—just before the war." Few of the tenants interviewed had cleared cash incomes since 1921, and many had made nothing since the World War.

There could, perhaps, be some compensation for low incomes if the farms were supplying food for the families. But the production of a cash crop rules out the raising of general produce. This much is obvious: if there is any advantage in cotton farming as a profitable business, the tenant does not share it.

How the Tenant Lives

Cotton has always been a cheap-labor crop; its development has rested on keeping this labor cost low. In fact many declare that profit is impossible "if all the labor it requires were paid for." The results appear in the living standards of the millions of families whose men, women, and children produce the crop.

The cultural landscape of the cotton belt has been described as a "miserable panorama of unpainted shacks, rain-gullied fields, straggling fences, rattle-trap Fords, dirt, poverty, disease, drudgery, and monotony that stretches for a thousand miles across the cotton belt." It used to be said that "cotton is and must remain a black man's crop, not a white man's, because the former's standard of living has always been low, and his natural inferiority makes it unnecessary to change it." Now that white families make up nearly two-thirds of the workers, it is clear that meager and pinched living is not a racial trait but a result of the system of cotton tenancy. Submerged beneath the system which he supports, the cotton tenant's standard of living approaches the level of bare animal existence. The traditional status of the slave required only subsistence. The cotton slave—white or colored—has inherited a rôle in which comfort, education, and self-development have no place. For the type of labor he performs, all that is actually required is a stomach indifferently filled, a shack to sleep in, some old jeans to cover his nakedness.

This age-old condition of the cotton worker and the necessity to keep it unchanged, lead to some interesting rationalizing by supporters of the existing order. Serious statements about the happiness of the tenant in his dependent rôle are taking the place of the earlier stories of the contentment of the slaves. Anecdotes of ludicrous spending whenever he gets his hands on money are used to justify the regular condition of poverty. Shiftlessness and laziness are reported as reasons for the dependent state, whereas, in fact, in so far as they exist, they are not necessarily inherent, but are caused by the very conditions of the share-cropping system.

The studies made of tenant families confirm the indignant assertion of a writer in the Dallas, Texas, *News* that "the squalid condition of the cotton raisers of the South is a disgrace to the Southern people. They stay in shacks, thousands of which are unfit to house animals, much less human beings. Their children are born under such conditions of medical treatment, food and clothing, as would make an Eskimo rejoice that he did not live in a cotton-growing country."

The drab ugliness of tenant houses might be condoned if they were comfortable. Many of them are old, some have actually come down from the period of slavery, and all of them, unpainted and weather-beaten, appear ageless. They are crudely constructed, windows and doors are out of alignment, they leak even while still new. Family size and size of house have no relationship. Whatever the number in the family it must occupy the customary three rooms. In fact a family of any size may live in a two-room house; as many as thirteen have been found living in a single bedroom and kitchen.

A Children's Bureau study of the welfare of children in cotton-growing areas of Texas, showed 64 per cent of the white and 77 per cent of the Negro families living under conditions of housing congestion, and this in spite of the common belief that over-crowding is a phenomenon of the city. Another study of white tenant families in Tennessee estimated an average value of all personal belongings of tenants at less than a hundred dollars. In one cotton-growing county of Alabama, reported in *Shadow of the Plantation*, over half of the families lived in one- and two-room cabins, and the comment on the character and inadequacy of these by one of the tenants does not exaggerate the lot of this majority: "My house is so rotten you can jest take up the boards in your hands and cromple 'em up. Everything done swunk about it."

Although living on abundant land in the south temperate zone, tenant families have probably the most meager and ill-balanced diet of any large group in America. Devotion to the single cash crop, and the fact that food crops mature during the same season as cotton, make it virtually impossible under the system to raise subsistence crops. Because the growing of household produce does not fit into the economy of a cash crop, it is not encouraged by landlords, whose prerogative it is to determine the crops grown. As a result the diet is limited largely to imported foods, made available through the commissaries and local stores. This diet can be, and commonly is, strained down to the notorious three M's— meat (fat salt pork), meal, and molasses. Evidence of the slow ravages of this diet are to be found in the widespread incidence of pellagra, which Dr. Joseph Goldberger of the United States Public Health Service bluntly attributes to lack of proper food. This diet is part of the very culture of tenancy, supported by habit, convenience, and cheapness. A dietary survey reported by Rupert B. Vance revealed significantly that the maize kernel constituted 23 per cent of the total food intake of white Tennessee and Georgia mountaineers, 32.5 per cent of that of southern Negroes, chiefly tenant farmers, but only 1.6 per cent of that of northern families in comfortable circumstances. Pork—chiefly fat salt pork—makes up 40 per cent of the food of southern tenant farmers.

Food is the largest item in the tenant's budget, and since almost no food is produced, it must be purchased. In six counties, the average monthly expenditure for food in 1934 was $12.34, or about $3.08 per week for the average family of five. As small as these amounts seem, they consume the major portion of the tenant's income.

FURNISHING

The current credit used by share tenants is commonly known as "furnishing." The landlord furnishes his tenants with food and other necessities during the crop production period and is paid for these advances out of the tenants' share of the crop in the settlement at harvest time. The usual rationing consists of furnishing groceries from the commissary to a tenant and his family. The tenant does not know the money value of what he is receiving or, to be more exact, he does not know what he is being charged for it. Variations of furnishing are the less frequently used "account" from which the tenant makes purchases with some knowledge of what he is being charged, and the "limit," whereby the landlord allows the tenant commodities up to some fixed amount.

Under the "rations" system the tenant receives little, and often suffers rank exploitation. In some instances large plantations allot to each laborer two pecks of meal and four pounds of fat back pork every two weeks. Some of the landlords are even more niggardly, providing tenants only with meal and leaving them to provide meat as best they can. The testimony of tenants, supported by the observation of bare cupboards, points to extreme meagerness.

We can't get any flour, snuff, shoes, sugar, coffee, thread, or anything from the landlord but meat and meal. We have a divil of a time. No soap, soda, or salt. Can't borrow a dime, not a damn cent. If this ain't hell, I'll eat you. We work our damn heads off and git nothing. The harder we work, the deeper in debt we gits.

The restriction of the landlord's advance does not, however, prevent a heavy debt at the close of the year.

Boss said after we's gathered the crop last year, I still owed him $130.00. Sometimes we got less than 15 pounds of meat and two bushels of meal every two weeks.

A Negro woman reported her conversation with her landlord, about furnishing, and his sympathetic response:

Yesterday, Mr. ——, the boss man, come through the field and asked me how I feel. I just stopped my hoeing and said, "Mr. ——, I just don't know how I feel." He says, "What's the trouble, Julia, don't you feel well?" I say, "I'm just hungry, Mr. ——." "Ain't you got nothing to eat at your house, Julia?" "I ain't got nothing but fat back and corn bread, and I done eat that so long that I believe I got the pellagacy, Mr. ——." His face turns red when I say that, and he said, "Well, Saturday I'm gonna give you some flour too. Just come by the office."

The amounts allowed tenants under the several systems of furnishing and the period over which the credit extends are determined by the landlord. The "margin of progress" possible to the tenant is generally so small that he is constantly dependent upon credit at any terms. The amounts croppers receive are not sufficient for a family by any standard of adequacy. The fact that millions live and work under these conditions offers little ground for national pride when death and sickness rates are included in the picture.

No Incentive to Improvement

Since the tenant has no legal claims on any improvements he may make, he has no interest in conserving or improving either the land or the buildings. On the contrary, just as it is to his advantage to rob the soil of its fertility, so he is tempted to burn for firewood rails from any nearby fence or planks from the porch floor or from an outhouse—if the place happens to be distinguished by having any movable materials that have not already succumbed to the ravages of time and tenants. The tenant is not likely to trouble to make any repairs that are not absolutely necessary, and these few will be so made as not to outlast his stay on the place.

Under a system which does not encourage labor and thrift men easily develop habits of improvidence. As matters now stand, the tenant who really works on his place, who labors to restore the soil, who repairs and builds, is merely inviting his landlord to raise his rent. If he should use all his time and energy in improving the place on which he lives, with the hope of ultimately raising his own status, the tenant would have no recourse if his landlord demanded a higher rent or notified him that he would have to leave the next year. It may be argued that landlords generally would not follow any such course; but the absence of any laws on the statute books of the southern states protecting tenants in improvements made by them is a final answer to such arguments. Those who say that legal protection for the tenant is unnecessary, that we have too many laws, will have difficulty in justifying the crop lien laws which protect the immediate interests of the merchants and landlords, but ignore the immediate interests of the tenants and the long-time interests of every one in the region.

Is it any wonder, then, that the soil is exhausted, buildings not fit for habitation, and the tenants themselves thoroughly inured to habits and attitudes that, if undisturbed, will keep them impoverished? There can be no general prosperity among any class for long in such an environment.

WHAT THE STATUS OF TENANCY MEANS

It is a notorious and shameful fact that the stock arguments employed against any serious efforts to improve the lot of the cotton tenant are based upon the very social and cultural conditions which tenancy itself creates. The mobility of the tenant, his dependence, his lack of ambition, shiftlessness, his ignorance and poverty, the lethargy of his pellagra-ridden body, provide a ready excuse for keeping him under a stern paternalistic control. There is not a single trait alleged which, where true, does not owe its source and continuance to the imposed status itself.

The status of tenancy demands complete dependence; it requires no education and demands no initiative, since the landlord assumes the prerogative of direction in the choice of crop, the method by which it shall be cultivated, and how and when and where it shall be sold. He keeps the records and determines the earnings. Through the commissary or credit merchant, even the choice of diet is determined. The landlord can determine the kind and amount of schooling

or the children, the extent to which they may share benefits
ntended for all the people. He may even determine the
relief they receive in the extremity of their distress. He con-
rols the courts, the agencies of law enforcement and, as in
he case of share-croppers in eastern Arkansas, can effectively
hwart any efforts at organization to protect their meager
rights.

The present system is so constructed that the landless remain landless and the propertyless remain propertyless. To
accumulate property, to increase independence, is to oppose
the system itself. In a plantation area it is easier to be a
cropper and conform to the system than to be a small owner
or renter. For a share tenant to rise above his status he must
overcome insuperable obstacles: (1) the agriculture that he
knows fits only the old system, (2) the banks cannot finance
him because they are geared to finance the plantations, (3)
the cost of merchant credit dissipates his accumulated working capital, and (4) the crop lien credit system has destroyed
his independence in the marketing of his crop.

Neither ambition, nor thrift, nor self-respect can thrive in
such a climate. Not only is it impossible to develop a hardy
stock of ambitious farm owners—the persistent American
ideal—but it is impossible to avoid physical and moral de-
cadence.

If the tenant is lazy, this is a result of his mode of life.
As a Mississippian, H. Snyder, writing candidly in the *North
American Review*, observes: "Certainly the common run of
people in the South are poor, and we are told this property
is born of their laziness. But this is upside down, as their
laziness is born of their poverty."

Attempts to justify the existing system of tenure on the
score that it is an adaptation to the latent and innate characteristics and capacities of the southern farm population
are as baseless as they are vicious. All such observable characteristics can be traced directly to the system of tenure and
the mode of livelihood that it promotes. The system, says
Arthur N. Moore of the Georgia Experiment Station, does
not provide ". . . a friendly atmosphere for the development
of latent capacities."

Such in brief detail is the life of the tenant—drear, meager, and changeless. Upon this is reared an agricultural system which custom and a temporary federal subsidy are holding together against the insistent need of complete reorganization.

LAYING THE GROUNDWORK

Preparation for Reading

1. What is the relation between health and a satisfactory diet? between a satisfactory diet and income?
2. What is your idea of the share-cropping system of the South? From what sources did you obtain your information?
3. Can a nation be called progressive if millions of its population, through no fault of theirs, live in poverty?

Vocabulary Building

1. How many of these words can you define and pronounce: *fluctuations, accentuated, computations, thrall, status, subservient, category, commissary, exorbitant, manipulated, exploitation, caste, connives, protagonist, peonage, pellagra, prerogative, panorama, anecdotes, ludicrous, lien, tenure, subsidy?*
2. Distinguish between the meanings of the words in each of the following groups: *destitute, devoid,* and *void; latent, dormant, quiescent,* and *potential; lethargy, torpor,* and *stupor.*

APPRAISING THE RESULTS

1. In what sense is King Cotton a despot whose evil influence affects not only the cotton tenants but the rest of the South as well?
2. In what way is the South still feudal in its organization? How does the system of tenancy resemble the system of Negro slavery?
3. Explain why the center of the cotton-producing area has moved westward.
4. What is the approximate number of cotton tenants? Why is tenancy increasing? Why is the proportion of Negroes decreasing?
5. Analyze the section "What Is a Tenant?" as an example of definition. What information besides the definition is given?

6. What is the economic status of the tenants, and how is their income level reflected in food, housing, clothing, health?
7. Explain the furnishing system.
8. Why do not tenants free themselves from their condition?
9. Try to explain why minority groups (a) foment misunderstanding and hatred between the whites and the Negroes; (b) discourage the formation of unions; (c) limit the franchise to a minority of the adult population; (d) oppose free speech and the extension of education; (e) support lynch law.
10. Do you think the institution of tenancy and the treatment of tenants are in harmony with democratic American ideals?
11. Show how this selection is related to others you may have read, e.g., Overstreet, Cooke, Reisner, Cabot.
12. If you had the power, how would you attack the tenant problem?

SELECTING THE THEME SUBJECT

1. Adapt the procedure of the extended definition exemplified in "What Is a Tenant?" to a definition of one of the following: Dirt Farmers; Marginal Lands; Patriotism; Migratory Workers; Courage; Epic Poetry; Snobs; Captains of Industry; "Ham" Operators; Gambling; Social Tact; A Labor Agitator; Yellow Journalism.
2. Adapt the procedure of this analysis to a problem with which you are familiar: Cosmetic Rackets; Women Workers; Jobless Youth; Industrial Diseases; Child Workers in America; Commercialized Athletics; Reducing Diets; Nutritional Diseases; City Tax Problems; Old Age Pensions; The C.I.O.; Safe Investments.

Problems of Civic Responsibility

THE LIMITATIONS OF THE EXPERT[1]
Harold J. Laski

THE DAY OF THE PLAIN MAN HAS PASSED. NO CRITICISM OF DEMOCRACY IS MORE FASHIONABLE IN OUR TIME THAN THAT which lays emphasis upon his incompetence. This is, we are told, a big and complex world, about which we have to find our way at our peril. The plain man is too ignorant and too uninterested to be able to judge the adequacy of the answers suggested to our problems. As in medicine we go to a doctor, or in bridge-building to an engineer, so in matters of social policy we should go to an expert in social questions. He alone, we are told with increasing emphasis, can find his way about the labyrinthine intricacies of modern life. He alone knows how to find the facts, and determine what they mean. The plain man is simply obsolete in a world he has never been trained to understand. Either we must trust the making of fundamental decisions to experts, or there will be a breakdown in the machinery of government.

Now much of this skepticism is a natural and justifiable reaction from the facile and romantic optimism of the nineteenth century. Jefferson in America, Bentham in England did too easily assume not only an inherent rightness in the opinions of the multitude but also an instinctive wisdom in its choices. They did tend to think that social problems could be easily understood, and that public interest in their solution would be widespread and passionate. From their philosophy was born the dangerous inference that any man, without training in affairs, could hope usefully to control their operation. They did not see that merely to formulate rightly

[1] From *Harper's Magazine*, December, 1930. Reprinted by permission of the author and of the publishers.

the nature of a social problem is far more difficult than to formulate rightly a problem in physics or chemistry. No one assumes that the plain man is entitled to an opinion about the ether or vitamins or the historicity of the Donation of Constantine. Why should it be assumed that he has competence about the rates of taxation, or the validity of tariff-schedules, or the principles of a penal code? Here, as in the fields of pure and applied science, his well-being, it is argued, depends essentially upon accepting the advice of the disinterested expert. The more elbow-room the latter possesses, the more likely we are to arrive at adequate decisions.

No one, I think, could seriously deny to-day that in fact none of our social problems is capable of wise resolution without formulation of its content by an expert mind. A Congressman at Washington, a member of Parliament at Westminster cannot hope to understand the policy necessary to a proper understanding of Soviet Russia merely by the light of nature. The facts must be gathered by men who have been trained to a special knowledge of the new Russia, and the possible inferences from those facts must be set out by them. The plain man cannot plan a town, or devise a drainage system, or decide upon the wisdom of compulsory vaccination without aid and knowledge at every turn from men who have specialized in those themes. He will make grave mistakes about them, possibly even fatal mistakes. He will not know what to look for; he may easily miss the significance of what he is told. That the contours of any subject must be defined by the expert before the plain man can see its full significance will, I believe, be obvious to anyone who has reflected upon the social process in the modern world.

II

But it is one thing to urge the need for expert consultation at every stage in making policy; it is another thing, and a very different thing, to insist that the expert's judgment must be final. For special knowledge and the highly trained mind produce their own limitations which, in the realm of statesmanship, are of decisive importance. *Expertise,* it may be argued, sacrifices the insight of common sense to intensity of experience. It breeds an inability to accept new views from the very depth of its preoccupation with its own conclusions. It too often fails to see round its subject. It sees its results out of perspective by making them the center of relevance to which all other results must be related. Too often, also, it lacks humility; and this breeds in its possessors a failure in proportion which makes them fail to see the obvious which is before their very noses. It has, also, a certain caste-spirit about it, so that experts tend to neglect all evidence which does not come from those who belong to their own ranks. Above all, perhaps, and this most urgently where human problems are concerned, the expert fails to see that every judgment he makes not purely factual in nature brings with it a scheme of values which has no special validity about it. He tends to confuse the importance of his facts with the importance of what he proposes to do about them.

Each one of these views needs illustration, if we are to see the relation of *expertise* to statesmanship in proper perspective. The expert, I suggest, sacrifices the insight of common sense to the intensity of his experience. No one can read the writings of Mr. F. W. Taylor, the efficiency-engineer, without seeing that his concentration upon the problem of reaching the maximum output of pig-iron per man per day made him come to see the laborer simply as a machine for the production of pig-iron. He forgot the complexities of human nature, the fact that the subject of his experiments had a will of his own whose consent was essential to effective success. Business men prophesied the rapid breakdown of the Russian experiment because it had eliminated that profit-making motive which experience had taught them was at the root of Western civilization. But they failed to see that Russia might call into play new motives and new emotions not less powerful, even if different in their operation, from the old. The economic experts of the early nineteenth century were fairly unanimous in insisting that the limitation of the hours of labor must necessarily result in a decrease of prosperity. They lacked the common sense to see that a prohibition upon one avenue of profit would necessarily lead to so intense an exploration of others as to provide a more than adequate compensation for the effort they deplored.

The expert, again, dislikes the appearance of novel views. Here, perhaps, the experience of science is most suggestive since the possibility of proof in this realm avoids the chief difficulties of human material. Everyone knows of the difficulties encountered by Jenner in his effort to convince his medical contemporaries of the importance of vaccination. The Royal Society refused to print one of Joule's most seminal papers. The opposition of men like Sir Richard Owen and Adam Sedgwick to Darwin resembled nothing so much as that of Rome to Galileo. Not even so great a surgeon as Simpson could see merit in Lister's discovery of antiseptic treatment. The opposition to Pasteur among medical men was so vehement that he declared regretfully that he did not know he had so many enemies. Lacroix and Poisson reported to the French Academy of Sciences that Galois' work on the theory of groups, which Cayley later put among the great mathematical achievements of the nineteenth century, was quite unintelligible. Everyone knows how biologists and physicists failed to perceive for long years the significance of Gregor Mendel and Willard Gibbs.

These are instances from realms where, in almost every case, measurable proof of truth was immediately obtainable; and, in each case, novelty of outlook was fatal to a perception of its importance. In social matters, where the problem of measurement is infinitely more difficult, the expert is entitled to far less assurance. He can hardly claim that any of his fundamental questions has been so formulated that he can be sure that the answer is capable of a certainly right interpretation. The student of race, for instance, is wise only if he admits that his knowledge of his subject is mainly a measure of his ignorance of its boundaries. The student of eugenics can do little more than insist that certain hereditary traits, deaf-mutism, for example, or hæmophilia, make breeding from the stocks tainted by them undesirable; he cannot tell us what fitness means nor show us how to breed the qualities upon which racial adequacy depends. It would be folly to say that we are destined never to know the laws which govern life; but, equally certainly, it would be folly to argue that our knowledge is sufficient to justify any expert, in any realm of social importance, claiming finality for his outlook.

He too often, also, fails to see his results in their proper perspective. Anyone who examines the conclusions built, for example, upon the use of intelligence tests will see that this is the case. For until we know exactly how much of the ability to answer the questions used as their foundation is related to differentiated home environments, how effectively, that is, the experiment is really pure, they cannot tell us anything. Yet the psychologists who accept their results have built upon them vast and glittering generalizations as, for instance, about the inferior mental quality of the Italian immigrant in America; as though a little common sense would not make us suspect conclusions indicating mental inferiority in the people which produced Dante and Petrarch, Vico and Machiavelli. Generalizations of this kind are merely arrogant; and their failure to see, as experts, the *a priori* dubiety of their results obviously raises grave issues about their competence to pronounce upon policy.

Vital, too, and dangerous, is the expert's caste-spirit. The inability of doctors to see light from without is notorious; and a reforming lawyer is at least as strange a spectacle as one prepared to welcome criticism of his profession from men who do not practice it. There is, in fact, no expert group which does not tend to deny that truth may possibly be found outside the boundary of its private Pyrenees. Yet, clearly enough, to accept its dicta as final, without examination of their implications, would be to accept grave error as truth in almost every department of social effort. Every expert's conclusion is a philosophy of the second best until it has been examined in terms of a scheme of values not special to the subject matter of which he is an exponent.

Everyone knows, for example, that admirals invariably fail to judge naval policy in adequate terms; and in Great Britain, at any rate, the great military organizers, men like Cardwell and Haldane, have had to pursue their task in face of organized opposition from the professional soldier. The Duke of Wellington was never brought to see the advantage of the breech-loading rifle; and the history of the tank in the last war is largely a history of civilian enterprise the value of which the professional soldier was brought to see only with difficulty.

The expert, in fact, simply by reason of his immersion in a routine, tends to lack flexibility of mind once he approaches the margins of his special theme. He is incapable of rapid adaptation to novel situations. He unduly discounts experience which does not tally with his own. He is hostile to views which are not set out in terms he has been accustomed to handle. No man is so adept at realizing difficulties within the field that he knows; but, also, few are so incapable of meeting situations outside that field. Specialism seems to breed a horror of unwonted experiment, a weakness in achieving adaptability, both of which make the expert of dubious value when he is in supreme command of a situation.

This is, perhaps, above all because the expert rarely understands the plain man. What he knows, he knows so thoroughly that he is impatient with men to whom it has to be explained. Because he practices a mystery, he tends to assume that, within his allotted field, men must accept without question the conclusions at which he has arrived. He too often lacks that emollient quality which makes him see that conclusions to which men assent are far better than conclusions which they are bidden, without persuasion, to decline at their peril. Everyone knows how easily human personality becomes a unit in a statistical table for the bureaucrat; and there must be few who have not sometimes sympathized with the poor man's indignation at the social worker. People like Jane Addams, who can retain, amid their labors, a sense of the permanent humanity of the poor, are rare enough to become notable figures in contemporary life.

The expert, in fact, tends to develop a certain condescension towards the plain man which goes far towards the invalidation of his *expertise*. Men in India who have become accustomed to the exercise of power, cannot believe, without an imaginative effort of which few of them are capable, that the Indian is entitled to his own ideas of how he should be governed. Civil servants tend easily to think that members of Parliament or Congress are an ignorant impediment to their labors. Professional historians, who cultivate some minute fragment of an epoch's history, cannot appreciate the superb incursions of a brilliant amateur like Mr. H. G. Wells. It has taken professional economists more than a generation to realize that the trade unions have a contribution to make to the understanding of industrial phenomena without which their own interpretation is painfully incomplete.

There is, in fact, not less in the expert's mind than in that of the plain man what Mr. Justice Holmes has termed an "inarticulate major premise" quite fundamental to his work. I have known an expert in the British Foreign Office whose advice upon China was built upon the assumption that the Chinese have a different human nature from that of Englishmen; and what was, in fact, an obvious private prejudice was, for him, the equally obvious outcome of a special experience which could not brook contradiction. Judges of the Supreme Court have had no difficulty in making the Fourteenth Amendment the embodiment of the *laissez-faire* philosophy of the nineteenth century; and few of them have realized that they were simply making the law express their unconscious dislike of governmental experiment. The history of trade-union law in England is largely an attempt, of course mainly unconscious, by judicial experts to disguise their dislike of workingmen's organizations in terms of a mythology to which the convenient name of "public policy" could be attached. The attitude of the British High Command to the death-penalty, of lawyers like Lord Eldon to the relaxation of penal severity, of business men to secrecy in finance, of statesmen to proposals for institutional reconstruction are all revelations of the expert's dislike of abandoning premises which, because he has grown accustomed to them, he tends to equate with the inevitable foundations of truth.

The expert tends, that is to say, to make his subject the measure of life, instead of making life the measure of his subject. The result, only too often, is an inability to discriminate, a confusion of learning with wisdom. "The fixed person for the fixed duties," Professor Whitehead has written, "who in older societies was such a godsend, in the future will be a public danger." In a sense, indeed, the more expert such fixed persons are, the more dangerous they are likely to be. For your great chemist, or doctor, or engineer, or mathematician is not an expert about life; he is precisely an expert in chemistry or medicine, engineering or mathematics. And the more highly expert he is, the more profoundly he is immersed in his routine, the less he is likely to know of the life about him. He cannot afford the time or the energy to give to life what his subject demands from him. He restrains his best intellectual effort within the routine about which he is a specialist. He does not co-ordinate his knowledge of a part with an attempt at wisdom about the whole.

This can be seen from many angles. Lord Kelvin was a great physicist, and his discoveries in cable-laying were of supreme importance to its development; but when he sought to act as a director of a cable-laying company, his complete inability to judge men resulted in serious financial loss. Faraday was obviously one of the half-dozen outstanding physicists of modern times; but in the field of theological belief, he retained convictions which no man of common sense could accept. Mr. Henry Ford is obviously a business man of genius; but, equally obviously, his table talk upon themes outside his special sphere reveals a mentality which is mediocre in the extreme. Charles Babbage rendered immense service to the development of statistical science; but when he came to judge one of Tennyson's most famous poems he missed its beauty through an over-vivid sense of its failure to conform to the revelations of the census returns.

The expert, in short, remains expert upon the condition that he does not seek to co-ordinate his specialism with the total sum of human knowledge. The moment that he seeks that co-ordination he ceases to be an expert. A doctor, a lawyer, an engineer who sought to act in terms of his specialism as President or Prime Minister would inevitably fail; to succeed, he must cease to be an expert. The wisdom that is needed for the direction of affairs is not an expert technic but a balanced equilibrium. It is a knowledge of how to use men, a faculty of judgment about the practicability of principles. It consists not in the possession of specialized knowledge, but in a power to utilize its results at the right moment, and in the right direction.

III

My point may perhaps be made by saying that *expertise* consists in such an analytic comprehension of a special realm of facts that the power to see that realm in the perspective of totality is lost. Such analytic comprehension is purchased at the cost of the kind of wisdom essential to the conduct of affairs. The doctor tends to think of men as patients; the teacher sees them as pupils; the statistician as units in a table. Bankers too often fail to realize that there is humanity even in men who have no check-books; Marxian socialists see sinister economic motive in the simplest expressions of the universal appetite for power. To live differently is to think differently; and to live as an expert in a small division of human knowledge is to make its principles commensurate with the ultimate deposit of historic experience. Not in that way does wisdom come.

Because a man is an expert on medieval French history, that does not make him the best judge of the disposition of the Saar Valley in 1919. Because a man is a brilliant prison doctor, that does not make him the person who ought to determine the principles of a penal code. The skill of the great soldier does not entitle him to decide upon the scale of military armament; just as no anthropologist, simply as an anthropologist, would be a fitting governor for a colonial territory peopled by native races. To decide wisely, problems must be looked at from an eminence. Intensity of vision destroys the sense of proportion. There is no illusion quite so fatal to good government as that of the man who makes his expert insight the measure of social need. We do not get progress in naval disarmament when admirals confer. We do not get legal progress from meetings of Bar associations. Congresses of teachers seem rarely to provide the means of educational advance. The knowledge of what can be done with the results obtained in special disciplines seems to require a type of co-ordinating mind to which the expert, as such, is simply irrelevant.

This may be looked at from two points of view. "Political heads of departments are necessary," said Sir William Harcourt, "to tell the civil service what the public will not stand." That is, indeed, an essential picture of the place of the expert in public affairs. He is an invaluable servant and an impossible master. He can explain the consequences of a proposed policy, indicate its wisdom, measure its danger. He can point out possibilities in a proposed line of action. But it is of the essence of public wisdom to take the final initiative out of his hands.

For any political system in which a wide initiative belongs to the experts is bound to develop the vices of bureaucracy. It will lack insight into the movement and temper of the public mind. It will push its private nostrums in disregard of public wants. It will become self-satisfied and self-complacent. It will mistake its technical results for social wisdom, and it will fail to see the limits within which its measures are capable of effective application. For the expert, by definition, lacks contact with the plain man. He not only does not know what the plain man is thinking; he rarely knows how to discover his thoughts. He has dwelt so austerely in his laboratory or his study that the content of the average mind is a closed book to him. He is at a loss how to manipulate the opinions and prejudices which he encounters. He has never learned the art of persuading men into acceptance of a thing they only half understand. He is remote from the substance of their lives. Their interests and hopes and fears have never been the counters with which he has played. He does not realize that, for them, his technical formulæ do not carry conviction because they are, as formulæ, incapable of translation into terms of popular speech. For the plain man, he is remote, abstract, alien. It is only the juxtaposition of the statesman between the expert and the public which makes specialist conclusions capable of application.

That, indeed, is the statesman's basic task. He represents, at his best, supreme common sense in relation to *expertise*. He indicates the limits of the possible. He measures what can be done in terms of the material at his disposal. A man who has been for long years in public affairs learns the art

of handling men so as to utilize their talents without participating in their experience. He discovers how to persuade
antagonistic views. He finds how to make decisions without
giving reasons for them. He can judge almost by intuition the
probable results of giving legislative effect to a principle. He
comes to office able to co-ordinate varied aspects of *expertise*
into something which looks like a coherent program. He
learns to take risks, to trust to subconscious insight instead
of remaining dependent upon reasoned analysis. The expert's
training is, as a rule, fatal to these habits which are essential
to the leadership of a multitude. That is why, for example, the
teacher and the scholar are rarely a success in politics. For
they have little experience of the need for rapid decision;
and their type of mental discipline leads them to consider
truth in general rather than the truth of popular discussion.
They have not been trained to the business of convincing
the plain man; and modern government is impossible to
those who do not possess this art.

Nothing, indeed, is more remarkable in a great public department than to watch a really first-rate public man drive
his team of expert officials. He knows far less than they do of
the affairs of the Department. He has to guess at every stage
the validity of their conclusions. On occasion, he must either
choose between alternatives which seem equally balanced or
decide upon a policy of which his officials disapprove. Not
seldom, he must quicken their doubts into certainties; not
seldom, also, he must persuade them into paths they have
thus far refused to tread. The whole difference between a
great Minister and a poor one lies in his ability to utilize his
officials as instruments. His success depends upon weaving a
policy from the discrete threads of their *expertise*. He must
discover certain large principles of policy and employ them
in finding the conditions of its successful operation. He must
have the power to see things in a big way, to simplify, to
co-ordinate, to generalize. Anyone who knows the work of
Lord Haldane at the British War Office from 1906 to 1911,
or of Mr. Arthur Henderson as Foreign Secretary in the last
eighteen months, can understand the relation between the

statesman and his expert which makes, and which alone can make, for successful administration.

Its essence, as a relation, is that the ultimate decisions are made by the amateur and not by the specialist. It is that fact which gives them coherence and proportion. A cabinet of experts would never devise a great policy. Either their competing specialisms would clash, if their *expertise* was various in kind, or its perspective would be futile because it was similar. The amateur brings to them the relevance of the outer world and the knowledge of men. He disposes of private idiosyncrasy and technical prejudice. In convincing the non-specialist Minister that a policy propounded is either right or wrong, the expert is already halfway to convincing the public of his plans; and if he fails in that effort to convince, the chances are that his plans are, for the environment he seeks to control, inadequate or mistaken. For politics by its nature is not a philosophy of technical ideals, but an art of the immediately practical. And the statesman is pivotal to its organization because he acts as the broker of ideas without whom no bridges can be built between the expert and the multitude. It is no accident, but an inherent quality of his character, that the expert distrusts his fellow-specialist when the latter can reach that multitude. For him the gift of popular explanation is a proof of failure in the grasp of the discipline. His intensity of gaze makes him suspect the man who can state the elements of his mystery in general terms. He knows too much of minutiæ to be comfortable upon the heights of generalization.

Nor must we neglect the other aspect of the matter. "The guest," said Aristotle with his homely wisdom, "will judge better of a feast than the cook." However much we may rely upon the expert in formulating the materials for decision, what ultimately matters is the judgment passed upon the results of policy by those who are to live by them. Things done by government must not only appear right to the expert; their consequences must seem right to the plain and average man. And there is no way known of discovering his judgment save by deliberately seeking it. This, after all, is the really final test of government; for, at least over any considerable period, we cannot maintain a social policy which runs counter to the wishes of the multitude.

It is not the least of our dangers that we tend, from our sense of the complexity of affairs, to underestimate both the relevance and the significance of those wishes. We are so impressed by the plain man's ignorance that we tend to think his views may be put aside as unimportant. Not a little of the literature upon the art of government to-day is built upon the supposition that the plain man has no longer any place in social economy. We know, for example, that he does not understand the technicalities of the gold standard. It is clear that it would be folly to consult him upon matters like the proper area for the generation of electricity supply, or the amount that it is wise for a government to spend in testing the action of pavements under changing temperatures and variations of load. But the inference from a knowledge that the plain man is ignorant of technical detail and, broadly speaking, uninterested in the methods by which its results are attained, is certainly not the conclusion that the expert can be left to make his own decisions.

For the results of the gold standard are written plain in the life of the average man. The consequences of an inefficient electricity supply are apparent to him every day. It is his motor car which uses the roads, and he makes up his mind about the quality of the road-service with which he is provided. Every degree by which he is separated from consultation about decisions is a weakening of the governmental process. Neither goodwill in the expert nor efficiency in the performance of his function ever compensates in a state for failure to elicit the interest of the plain man in what is being done. For the nature of the result is largely unknown save as he reports his judgment upon it; and only as he reports that judgment can the expert determine in what direction his plans must move. Every failure in consultation, moreover, separates the mind of the governors from those who are governed; this is the most fertile source of misunderstanding in the state. It is the real root of the impermanence of autocracies which fail from their inability to plumb the minds of those by whose opinions, ultimately, they must live.

The importance of the plain man's judgment is, in short, the foundation upon which the expert, if he is to be successful, must seek to build. It is out of that judgment, in its massive totality, that every society forms its scheme of values. The limits of possible action in society are always set by that scheme. What can be done is not what the expert thinks ought to be done. What can be done is what the plain man's scheme of values permits him to consider as just. His likes and dislikes, his indifference and his inertia, circumscribe at every stage the possibilities of administration. That is why a great expert like Sir Arthur Salter has always insisted upon the importance of advisory committees in the process of government. He has seen that the more closely the public is related to the work of *expertise*, the more likely is that work to be successful. For the relation of proximity of itself produces conviction. The public learns confidence, on the one hand, and the expert learns proportion, on the other. Confidence in government is the secret of stability, and a sense of proportion in the expert is the safeguard against bureaucracy.

At no time in modern history was it more important than now that we should scrutinize the claims of the expert more critically; at no time, also, was it more important that he himself should be skeptical about his claims. Scientific invention has given us a material power of which the possible malignancy is at least as great as its contingent benefits. The danger which confronts us is the quite fatal one that, by the increase of complexity in civilization, we may come to forget the humanity of men. A mental climate so perverted as this would demonstrate at a stroke the fragility of our social institutions. For it would reveal an abyss between rulers and subjects which no amount of technical ingenuity could bridge. The material power that our experts multiply brings with it no system of values. It can only be given a system related to the lives of ordinary people to the degree that they are associated with its use. To exclude them from a share in its direction is quite certainly to exclude them also from a share in its benefits; for no men have been able in the history of past societies exclusively to exercise its authority without employing it ultimately for their own ends. Government by experts would, however ardent their original zeal for the public welfare, mean after a time government in the interest of experts. Of that the outcome would be either stagnation, on the one hand, or social antagonism, upon the other.

IV

Our business, in the years which lie ahead, is clearly to safeguard ourselves against this prospect. We must ceaselessly remember that no body of experts is wise enough, or good enough, to be charged with the destiny of mankind. Just because they are experts, the whole of life is, for them, in constant danger of being sacrificed to a part; and they are saved from disaster only by the need of deference to the plain man's common sense. It is, I believe, upon the perpetuation of this deference that our safety very largely depends.

But it will be no easy thing to perpetuate it. The expert, today, is accustomed to a veneration not very different from that of the priest in primitive societies; for the plain man he, like the priest, exercises a mystery into which the uninitiated cannot enter. To strike a balance between necessary respect and skeptical attack is a difficult task. The experience of the expert is so different, his approach to life so dissimilar, that expert and plain man are often impatient of each other's values. Until we can somehow harmonize them, our feet will be near to the abyss.

Nor must we forget that to attain such harmony immense changes in our social habits will be necessary. We shall have to revolutionize our educational methods. We shall have to reconstruct the whole fabric of our institutions. For the first time, perhaps, in the history of mankind, we shall have, as a civilization, deliberately to determine what kind of life we desire to live. We must so determine it remembering that the success of our effort will depend upon harnessing to its fortunes the profounder idealism of ordinary men and women. We shall appeal to that idealism only as we give it knowledge and persuade it that the end we seek is one in which it, too, can hope to share.

LAYING THE GROUNDWORK

Preparation for Reading

1. How would you account for the deference we ordinarily pay to the expert? Whom would you rather have govern you: experts in special fields or persons with wide, general experience? Why?
2. Why are politicians frequently looked upon with disrespect? Is this disrespect always, or even usually, justified? If so, why do the critics not seek the offices held by these politicians?
3. Whose opinion would you accept as most valuable on each of the following, and why: the advisability of a cut in W.P.A. funds, the wildness of college youth, the greatness of Shakespeare, the need for a bigger navy, the method of tuning a piano, the comedy rating of Edgar Bergen, the freedom of the press, the beauty of styles?

Vocabulary Building

1. Of the following words, look up those which are not in your active vocabulary: *labyrinthine, intricacies, obsolete, obsolescent, facile, inherent, eugenics, hæmophilia, a priori, dubiety, emollient, inarticulate, commensurate, bureaucracy, nostrum, austerely, manipulate, juxtaposition, discrete, elicit, inertia.*
2. Explain these phrases as they are used in the text: "light of nature," "caste-spirit," "Royal Society," "seminal papers," "private Pyrenees," "major premise," *"laissez-faire."*

APPRAISING THE RESULTS

1. A study of Laski's paragraph technique will teach you much about the requisites of a good paragraph. (a) Find several paragraphs which begin with the topic sentence. Analyze the development of each of these paragraphs. (b) If the first sentence is not the topic sentence, find the sentence which is, or, if you cannot find one which adequately expresses the main idea, write one.
2. Explain the use made of examples as a means of development. Do these examples contribute to clarity? to interest? to the force of the argument? Are they drawn from a narrow or a wide range?

3. What part does the deference shown the expert play in the criticism of democracy, so fashionable today? Is it compatible with the ideals of democracy to believe that the fundamental decisions of governmental and social policy should be made by experts?

4. In what way was the nineteenth century "romantically optimistic" about mankind? How do present conceptions of man and his mental and moral nature limit this view?

5. Study the limitations of the expert summarized in the first paragraph of Section II. Show how these limitations are developed in the succeeding paragraphs. Notice transitional phrases, for they will aid you in tracing this development.

6. Wherein does the expert surpass, and wherein does he fall short of, the man of general training? At what point does he cease to be an expert? Why does he not make a good statesman?

7. In a democracy, who should be the final judge of whether a policy is good or bad: the experts? the press? the professors? the Supreme Court? the mass of the people affected by the policy?

8. What happens when rulers ignore, or are blind to, the interests of their subjects? Illustrate by reference to the Puritan Revolution, which cost King Charles I his head, by the American and French Revolutions, and by the revolutions of this century: Mexican, Chinese, Russian, and German. Do you think the days of revolutions have passed?

9. What is the author's conclusion as to the parts the expert and the amateur must play if our democracy is to thrive? What "immense changes in our social habits will be necessary" to attain this harmony?

SELECTING THE THEME SUBJECT

1. Write a theme answering one of these questions: (a) How could the educational system more satisfactorily prepare youth for citizenship in a democracy? (b) Should college students be encouraged to discuss political, social, and economic problems? (c) How could the channels of information (newspapers, periodicals, radio, screen, theater) play a more effective rôle in developing our democracy?

2. Develop one of these titles: Radio and Education; The Films as a Means of Propaganda; How I Am Educating My Parents; The Library and Education; The Theater as a Painless Means

of Education; War in Fiction; My Opinion of Intelligence Tests; Why Bridge Experts Bore Me; What I Think of Sports "Experts"; How not to Listen to Music; What Makes a Swing Band Good; The Best Way to Fish for Trout; "Not Like Mother Used to Make"; Radio Cooking Experts and Common Sense; What Is the Best Tax?

THE GOVERNMENT HAS ALWAYS PAID[1]

Maurice Neufeld

THE WORD "SUBSIDY" HAS COME TO MEAN "UN-AMERICAN." WITHIN RECENT MONTHS (SINCE STEEL HAS REACHED OVER 70 per cent of pre-depression production and there is a faint touch of prosperity in the air) the important gentlemen who discuss the affairs of the nation at almost every drug-store lunch counter or in the elevators of office buildings in any Eastern city have made it clear that a subsidy was an undesirable and alien device. The farmers of the West were being subsidized by a paternalistic government at the expense of the East which contributed the greatest share of the nation's taxes. Money was being drained from the people of the Atlantic seaboard for the sole purpose of making the most rugged and individualistic of American citizens, the farmer, a permanent ward of the State. These same gentlemen were often heard lamenting the gradual degradation of the American worker through the subsidizing forces of relief which kept him alive. Such methods of solving economic and social problems were foreign to American traditions, they maintained. So confused has the meaning of *subsidy* become with the vocabulary of prejudice and emotion that the Federal Aviation Commission, reporting on January 31, 1935, justified its avoidance of this word by declaring: "We do so because of a desire to be specific in our language, and a genuine uncertainty as to the way in which that much-vexed term should be applied."

Yet it is strange that good Americans should feel ill at ease with a word so thoroughly American in the principle it represents. When the Federal Government created the A.A.A.

[1] From *The American Scholar*, Winter, 1937. Reprinted by permission of the author and of the editors of *The American Scholar*.

as a method of helping the almost bankrupt farmers of the country by subsidizing them on condition that they control their production acreage it followed a tradition older than the D.A.R.

Why then has an old and tried principle aroused such enmity and perturbation? Ever since his inauguration President Roosevelt had insisted that a direct subsidy system be substituted for the old ocean mail contracts provided for in the Jones-White Act of 1920. But one session of Congress after another was unable to force the Post Office Department, the Commerce Department, the Senate Commerce Committee and the steamship owners to agree upon a bill. Finally, in June, 1936, the Ship Subsidy Bill, representing various measures proposed by Senators Copeland, Guffey, and Gibson from time to time, was passed. Again, shortly after Roosevelt assumed office, the scandals of the air mail contracts broke into headlines and since that time the Federal Aviation Committee has reported. It recommended direct subsidies.

Now a subsidy, whether direct or indirect, remains a subsidy. But in this inclination of American politicians and business men to favor the indirect variety, and to frown upon the kind which announces what it is, can be found a distinction which goes to the very basis of American life. It is not enough to dismiss this distinction and to say that, whether direct or indirect, a subsidy is governmental aid. This distinction explains to a large extent why an undisguised subsidy is un-American and why the traditional, indirect subsidy is acceptable as destructive neither of self-reliance nor of moral fiber.

The greatest and most sincere American myth is involved in what seems at first a purely economic problem. Until very recently the guiding principle of American life was a fable—in this land of unexampled opportunity and fertile resources the individual, with mule, cart, cow, and wife could inherit the earth through his efforts alone. The autocracies of the Old World might regulate the life of their people but in America the Government acted best when it governed least. The continuing presence of free land, where under frontier conditions an individual did encounter the forces of nature seemingly single-handed, made the long survival of this fable possible. And although free land disappeared sometime about the year 1890, not until 1932 did the fact receive widespread public recognition when Roosevelt, in a campaign speech in San Francisco, spoke of "looking West on California's shores. . . ." It is worthy of note, too, that Roosevelt's administration marks that time in our national history when a President made a point of demanding emphatically that a subsidy be called a subsidy.

Throughout American history in every crucial period of national development, usually moments of great economic changes, the Federal Government in Washington, either directly or through the States, has aided the stalwart and self-reliant American, whether farmer, manufacturer, railroad promoter, steamship owner, or air-line magnate. Such aid was to be expected in a pioneering country where new and weak communities were a constant phase of successive frontier expansions. Direct subsidies for roads and schools became usual and accepted, but when so-called private interests were involved, like the development of American industry or the creation of a huge transportation system, aid was given indirectly in the first instance and with the implication in the second instance that the railroads were really aiding the Government by enhancing the value of the public lands. Where the consuming ambition of a nation's people was to occupy every inch of arable soil and to exploit every vein of ore and every plank of timber, the belief in the competency and independence of the individual within the field of private enterprise was necessary. It had its roots, moreover, in the best thought of the time and could claim supporters all the way from Rousseau to the classical economists and their disciples. Americans spread over the land, built their factories and their railroads, and acted as though the Government did not aid them, though at every turn it did because they demanded that it should.

Even a swift reading of American history discloses that from the beginning certain classes received aid in the form of tariffs or public lands (in our day in the form of contracts), but while the frontier existed the national myth continued, and it was easier to believe in self-reliance if help were given indirectly than if the President or Congress had announced frankly that a subsidy was a subsidy and not something euphemistically disguised. Those who came to have most influence after the Revolutionary War and shortly before and after the Civil War were precisely those people who wanted aid. Although an occasional free-trader might protest, or a Calhoun might declare that one section of the country, one class in fact, was benefiting at the expense of the entire South, or murmurs might arise that railroads constructed through the gift of national lands would only strengthen the commercial and manufacturing interests at the expense of agriculture, the dominating groups never protested. On the contrary, while holding out their hands, like their 20th century kinsmen, they embraced the national myth and insisted upon its preservation. Indeed when, during the economic crisis following the World War, it became necessary to aid the shipping industry and when within recent years help for the aeronautics interests was urgent, aid was given in a manner which least disturbed the fable—through the indirect subsidy, a substantial contract.

The long lineage of the indirect subsidy—its sturdy branches reach back to the very beginning of the Republic— has made it so acceptable and so much a matter of course in the nation's business that its real character, curiously enough, has been obscured with the passing of the years. When Representative Jones, Chairman of the Agriculture Committee, prepared a resolution in the beginning of April, 1936, directing the Tariff Commission to report to Congress the names of all corporations who had benefited from existing protective tariffs by $100,000 a year or more, he was not only planning a counter-attack upon Republican criticism of the A.A.A. benefit payments but was also uncovering to public view a well-known but often forgotten fact. For the tariff is the greatest of all subsidies. In the early days of the 19th century its subsidizing character was recognized and fought against. But when the industrial interests were victorious after the Civil War only an occasional election triumph of the Democrats kept this feature of the tariff from being forgotten

entirely by the American people. The Republicans had succeeded in obscuring the tariff as subsidy and playing up the
tariff as boon. Whenever the Democrats tampered with tariff
duties a national depression followed. With all this to think
about, who could remember that the Government was paying
the manufacturers to produce?

It was not always so. In his *Report on Manufactures* Hamilton recognized the opposition to the tariff by the Jeffersonian
agriculturalists and devoted a large section of his argument
to an attempt to dispel the amazing notion that duties would
sacrifice the interests of the entire community to those of
particular classes. But free-traders remained unconvinced and
more than fifty years later, in the Treasury Report of 1845,
R. J. Walker estimated that two-thirds of the total tax imposed upon the consuming public by the tariff of that period
was paid to the protected classes in the form of enhanced
prices. He placed that sum at $54,000,000. Henry Clay gave
up the idea of trying to prove what was contrary to everyone's
knowledge. He used another argument. Even if certain sections of the population benefited from the tariff, wasn't this
better than the subservience of America to foreign industry?
The struggle continued, and the opposition of the South to
subsidizing industry at the heavy cost of the plantation owner
and Western farmer brought about the Tariff of 1857 which
reduced the rate to a general level of 24 per cent. But the
Civil War established the Republican tariff, and a permanent, huge subsidy to the industrialists of individualistic
America became an unacclaimed part of the silent American
tradition. After that there was slight mention of the fact that
a tariff was a subsidy. In this way, without weakening the
moral fiber of those who profited most or of those who protest most loudly today, American industry was built and still
continues through governmental aid.

The struggle over the tariff had lasted seventy years. When
the nation faced another economic problem, closely allied to
that of industrial expansion—the building of its continental
transportation system—the method of the subsidy was
adopted. The Land Grant policy in relation to the railroads
was first established in 1850. The good labors of Senator

Douglas had succeeded in getting Congress to transfer 2,500,-
000 acres in Illinois to that State. The State was to reconvey
this land to those who were constructing the Illinois Central.
Estimated at $1.25 an acre, the railroad was subsidized by
$3,125,000. The last of the land grants to railroads was made
to the Texas and Pacific in 1871. The total area of land given
to railroads has been placed at 215,000,000 acres. Riegel, the
historian of the Western railroads, has estimated that the
average price received by the railroads for this land was $5
an acre. This would mean that the American people subsidized the railroads by some $1,075,000,000. But there was
no outcry that the moral fiber of those who participated in
that great venture would be impaired although surely it was,
as the annals of the Grant administration will testify.

Another great branch of the nation's transportation system
has been continued at public expense through the indirect
subsidy. At the end of the World War the Federal Government faced the serious problem of how the huge merchant
marine built up during the War years was to be maintained
in private hands. Its difficulty was solved by the method of
the generous hand. Not only did the Marine Act of 1920 provide an encouraging loan fund for the construction of vessels
but it also provided for ocean contract rates with fine possibilities. The Act of 1928 improved considerably the regulations and conditions of the earlier legislation. At the end of
that year 22 contracts had been let involving an expenditure
of $11,500,000. The National Industrial Conference Board
estimated that on the straight basis of weight this total was
in excess by $8,000,000. In 1935 the ocean mail contracts
totalled $30,000,000. President Roosevelt stated publicly that
they should have amounted to $3,000,000 and that $27,000,000
should have been given as a direct subsidy. The Ship Subsidy
Bill, signed by President Roosevelt on June 30, 1936, au-
thorizes the granting of direct subsidies up to the equivalent
of 50 per cent of the construction cost of the vessels to ship
operators. In the words of *The New York Times*: "The Ship
Subsidy Bill ends a long-standing fictitious situation by dis-
placing with actual subsidies to builders and operators the
ocean mail contracts which have in effect been only subsidies."

The United States Government has been a helpful one. The air mail contracts were cancelled on February 9, 1934. In the ensuing investigation, when Senator Black became curious about the profits of a well-known air transport corporation ($1,488,306 were made in 1930 on an investment of $750), he asked an official of the company: "Derived from a Post Office contract exclusively?" The reply was, "Yes, sir." Somehow or other a Post Office contract sounds less like a gift than a Government check.

The Federal Aviation Commission, reporting on January 31, 1935, showed in definite form that the industry had to be subsidized. Of the routes operating under mail contracts 56 per cent required additional assistance and 25 per cent could keep going without a subsidy only on the most economical basis. Of the route mileage 67 per cent would disappear or suffer lowered standards if assistance were withdrawn. Apparently aid is necessary, but only through the direct subsidy can proper controls be instituted and the public interest be preserved. Those who are concerned about the drain upon the Federal Treasury occasioned by the A.A.A. benefit payments and relief to the unemployed should remember that one air-line official made a cash profit of $1,060,314 on a $40 investment. A government contract boosted the stocks. At the present time there are indications that the Federal Government will subsidize a new dirigible line.

While manufacturing and transportation interests were benefiting through the continuing or past favors of a paternalistic government the principle of the direct subsidy, or aid in the open, was gaining ground in those fields which had not proved attractive to private investment and had then become acceptable as objects of governmental encouragement and backing. Public roads, canals, schools, universities and agricultural colleges were built with public funds. After all, these public works touched neither the citizen's pockets nor his self-reliance since they were far removed both from profits and his main interests. A road or school contract, moreover, was all to the good.

Up to as late as 1912 the United States appropriated only $8,000,000 for the various subsidized projects under its control. But the effects of the World War could not be shaken off. The number of subsidized fields increased steadily and in so normal a year as 1925 these projects were aided to the sum of $147,000,000. This total included aid to agricultural colleges, experiment stations, cooperative agricultural extension work, vocational education, vocational rehabilitation, highways, forest fire prevention, distribution of nursery stock, forest extension work and maternity and infant hygiene. This list increased during the Coolidge and Hoover administration. The R.F.C., created before Roosevelt assumed office, has actually subsidized the banks of the country through loans which many banks are refusing to pay back on the ground that the original loan was unconstitutional. Of course the greatest number of new subsidized ventures arose under Roosevelt. But when the sums expended by the New Dealers begin to oppress the mind it should be recalled that the indirect subsidy has always been with us to our cost and that the direct subsidy has been creeping up on us steadily.

With the misery and want of the depression fast upon it the old American myth could not retain its shining splendor and those who began to receive government money found little to complain of. But those who had long received public funds had much to complain of, and in their trade organizations they started the cry of un-American and disastrous. Now, a glance at the rôle of the subsidy in American history cannot establish whether or not in a particular instance a subsidy is economically sound or whether it will weaken the energies and ambitions of a people or whether it will lead directly to the dangers of bureaucracy—but one thing knowledge of the American past establishes beyond doubt. There is one thing which the subsidy is not: *un-American.*

LAYING THE GROUNDWORK

Preparation for Reading

1. Do you believe the federal government should bear most of the burden of relief? If not, who should?
2. What are the major activities paid for by the government? Who profits most from these activities, or uses them most?

3. When we speak of "the government," what do we mean?
4. What are the common forms of taxation? Which kind of taxes do you consider most fair to the majority of taxpayers?

Vocabulary Building

1. Frequently the same words mean different things to different people because the associated ideas and the emotional colorings influence the interpretation of dictionary definitions. Vague meanings attached to common words play a large part in the looseness and carelessness of our thinking, talking, and writing. Stuart Chase in "The Tyranny of Words," p. 517, discusses this subject of semantics (meanings of words) and its effect on problems of today. A study of this essay will make "The Government Has Always Paid" more interesting, because Neufeld discusses the term *subsidy* and its various meanings under different circumstances. (a) In this connection look up in the dictionary the word *subsidy* and note also what Neufeld says about its use. (b) In the same way study the meaning of *paternalistic* and explain what is meant by *paternalistic government*. (c) Do you think the terms *American* and *un-American* are consistently and carefully used?
2. The study of synonyms reveals careful distinctions in shades of meaning. Explain these differences in *enmity, hostility, animosity; disciple, scholar, student, pupil.*

APPRAISING THE RESULTS

1. What does Neufeld say about the Republican and Democratic interpretation of tariff? Why does he discuss the tariff here?
2. What condition do you suppose prompted Neufeld to write this article?
3. Comment upon his plan of organization. Why do you suppose he approached the problem in this way? What effect has the repetition in the first and last sentences?
4. Is his argument convincing? If not, where do you find your doubts arising?
5. How did the government finance the railroads? Were the profits shared? Was the government reimbursed?
6. Ship subsidies were granted to enable American ships to compete with foreign ships, since competition was supposedly difficult because of our "high standards." Is there any evidence that marine working conditions actually are not very high?

SELECTING THE THEME SUBJECT

1. Discuss at length how a specific subsidy (either hidden or open) has operated, or write a paper showing the effect of different kinds of subsidy on westward expansion.
2. Defend either free trade or a protective tariff.
3. Define what is meant by "rugged individualism."
4. Expand your answer to this question: are monopolies retarding economic progress?
5. Defend or attack federal spending for direct relief, W.P.A., housing, national defense, education, public health, federal buildings, flood control, conservation, old age pensions.

WHAT IS A RACKET?[1]

John Gunther

A RACKET MAY BE DEFINED AS ANY SCHEME OF EXPLOITATION BY
WHICH CRIMINAL CONSPIRATORS LIVE UPON THE INDUSTRY OF
others, maintaining their hold by intimidation, terrorism, or
political favoritism. The word "racket" has come to be loosely
synonymous, on the one hand, with any scheme for making
easy money, whether illegal or not; on the other, as a blanket
definition of organized crime. All gangsters, without discrimination, have come to be called racketeers. Beer and alcohol
running or, for that matter, bank robbery and white slavery,
are rackets from this point of view. . . .

What, in a paragraph, does a racketeer do? How does a
racket work?

Suppose I happen to be a hoodlum, and suppose I want
some easy money. I have friends among crooked labor leaders
and perhaps among politicians. I am in a position to hire
thugs and gunmen. I form an organization and I choose a
field. Suppose I choose pretzels as a field. I then "invite" the
pretzel dealers in Chicago to "join" me. From each of them
I demand, say, one hundred dollars per month. For this sum
my men will "protect" them from competition, since they
must raise their prices to pay my one hundred dollars. If any
pretzel man refuses to join me I bomb him. I slug his drivers.
I cut off his supply. Meantime I delimit the pretzel market
among my dealers, and make anyone who wants to enter the
pretzel business pay me handsomely first. I extend my pretzel

[1] From "The High Cost of Hoodlums," by John Gunther, in *Harper's
Magazine*, October, 1929. Reprinted by permission of the author and of the
publisher.

monopoly in one direction to the big wholesalers (since I control the dealers), and in another direction to the small shopkeepers (since I control the jobbers). And from all of them I exact tribute. The price of pretzels meantime goes up. Simply because I say so, the pretzel people pay a levy to me, and the consumer pays the levy. This is the essence of racketeering—simple extortion based on simple threat.

The word "racket" originated in Chicago six or seven years ago. In the neighborhood of 12th and Halsted Streets, in the district of "alky" peddlers, thugs, and hoodlums, a group of satellites grew up, hanging on the outskirts of the great "mobs"—the O'Banion "mob," the Genna "mob," the Capone "mob." These satellites were not often actual killers. They were parasites. With gangster protection, they went into "business." At first the word describing them was "racketer." In newspaper stories during 1923 and 1924 the word grew to "racketeer." Probably it first referred to the hullabaloo in the "joints" where gangsters assembled. "How's the racket?" became "What's your racket?"

Rackets are, of course, old as the hills. This decade holds no monopoly on extortion. But extortion has rarely reached such a point of development as distinguishes the Chicago rackets today. It would be difficult to trace the exact cause of this efflorescence. Prohibition was certainly one cause. Traffic in beer and whisky enormously increased the amount of easy money in circulation among hoodlums. Gangsters became elaborate spendthrifts. Silver coffins decorated funerals. Politics bought into gangs. Meantime the booze traffic increased the number of professional criminals at large, and their power, ruthlessness, and immunity to law.

So the rackets began, out of criminality begat by alcohol and easy money. The success of racketeering was immense. It existed through contempt of law and, as success increased, contempt increased, to give way to more success. Gangsters saw that there was almost as much money in coats and suits as there was in alcohol; gangsters "muscled in" to various rackets. Politicians saw the enormous sums being made and took their share of this citizens' tribute.

SELECTING THE THEME SUBJECT

Note the structure of this extended definition: a brief dictionary-like definition; a transitional paragraph; an illustration of how a racket works; the origin of the term and examples; a short history of the practice. Apply this method to a theme.

Suggested subjects: A Gerrymander; Panhandling; Sabotage; A Hobo; A Chiseler; Guerilla Warfare; A Playboy; Chauvinism; A Sonnet; Apple Polishing.

Dollars and Cents

THE HIGH COST OF DISTRIBUTION[1]

George Pfeil

STEP BACK TWENTY-FIVE YEARS. WE ARE IN A MAIN STREET CORNER GROCERY STORE. IN THE DIM BACKGROUND, AMID STACKS of brooms and barrels of bulk commodities, a farmer is selling his produce: milk, butter, cheese, potatoes, and eggs. We buy a dollar's worth of each, but do so only through the medium of the merchant. He takes our money to the cash drawer and gives the farmer about 51 cents for each dollar we spend for milk, butter, and cheese; while he allows 60 cents for the potatoes and 64 cents for the eggs.

We want other things, too, such as flour to make biscuits and some loaves of bread already baked. These the merchant has not purchased directly from the farmer, yet the farmer will ultimately benefit from our purchases. From our dollar spent for flour he will get 60 cents; while a dollar spent for bread, due to processing, repetitive handling, and greater waste, will eventually bring him about 23 cents.

Next door, at the Main Street Meat Market, we buy a dollar's worth of chicken, of beef, and of pork. Of each dollar spent for chicken, the farmer will get almost 63 cents; while he also will receive 63 cents from every retail dollar spent for beef and about 81 cents from every retail dollar spent for pork. The rest is margin.

That, however, was in 1912. Twenty years later, in 1932, we stand on the same corner. Where a small gilt emblem once announced Smith's Grocery, a large red glass sign proclaims an A. & P. combination grocery and meat market. Twenty

[1] From *Common Sense,* February, 1937. Reprinted by permission of the author and of the editors.

years later we buy the same commodities we bought in 1912.
The milk is pasteurized, the butter branded, the cheese trade-
marked. Idaho potatoes are cleanly bagged, Brookfield eggs
are neatly boxed, bread comes from the company's own
bakeries, while meats are sold from electrically lighted and
refrigerated show cases.

A farmer no longer stands in the dim background behind
the stacked brooms and the barrelled commodities, but somewhere a farmer has produced all these things, just as in 1912.
In 1932, however, the farmer's share in every retail dollar
was only 34 cents for milk, butter, and cheese, 43 cents for
potatoes, 59 cents for eggs, 29 cents for flour, 9 cents for bread,
52 cents for chickens, 36 cents for beef, and 43 cents for pork.

If all the commodities listed are grouped together, the
farmer receives only 35 cents, in 1932, in contrast to 56
cents, in 1912, for every dollar expended by the consumer.
In other words, the marketing spread had increased by about
half. And low prices reflected the fact that most of the increase had been taken from the American farmer. Are these
examples exceptional? Not at all. In most cases, fruits and
vegetables show an even greater margin for distribution. Including all farm products, the farmers of America
received only 33 cents of every retail dollar spent to purchase
them.

It was not only in the field of agricultural products that
a wide margin became even wider during the twenty years
from 1912 to 1932. This same trend also can be shown in
analyzing the distributive costs of a thousand products of
mine, mill, field, and forest. Thus low-cost minerals and
cheap chemicals have been miraculously transformed into
"amazing new discoveries," such as Climaline to soften water
and lighten housework, Edna Wallace Hopper's Youth Clay
to soften skin and banish wrinkles, and Kruschen Salts for
practically anything that ails you. Ingredients of these magic
preparations cost, at the source, as little as ten dollars a ton,
but in trade-marked packages they may bring more than a
dollar a pound. Such are the wonders of distribution when
assisted by the science of puffology.

DISTRIBUTION'S HIGH COST

To look at any item or group of items alone, however, may easily lead to a false or exaggerated conclusion. Moreover, 1912 and 1932 are not entirely valid dates to contrast the costs of distribution as a whole, if general trends regardless of war and serious depression are to be considered. The period from 1920 to 1929 is more revealing.

In 1920, we had begun to conquer the problem of production, but distribution remained an enormously costly and amazingly inefficient process. Indeed, from 1920 to 1929, while costs of production were being drastically reduced and the man-hour rate of productivity was being multiplied by 300 per cent, the costs of distribution actually continued to rise and the man-unit rate of vending actually declined. In fact, from 1920 to 1929, the proportion of total national income going to pay for distribution increased from less than thirty to more than thirty-three cents of every dollar.

Why was fully one-third of our national income going to pay the costs of distribution, in 1929? Had this not been the period when advertising was credited with building new consumer demands, crushing consumer resistance, and thereby lowering the cost of personal salesmanship? Was this not the period when packaging and branding made possible economical, almost automatic retailing? Was this not the period when the chain system of distribution was coming to maturity and threatening the perpetuation of less efficient independent competitors?

Yes, is the answer to all these questions; but that is not the entire story. Because of, as well as in spite of, these factors distribution costs continued to rise.

ADVERTISING AS A WASTE

Renowned critics of our economic system will, of course, pounce on the suggestion that modern advertising actually reduced total marketing costs by proving that such advertising was highly expensive, ofttimes grossly wasteful, and only the means to a different division of national production. This common argument, however, is not as potent as it frequently has been pictured, for advertising used only from two to three cents of our dollar of national income. Since a moderate share of advertising may have been necessary and some may even have been socially desirable, it is evident that even the abolition of all doubtful kinds of advertising would not have greatly reduced the proportion of national income going to distribution.

Practices made possible through advertising, however, did greatly increase the proportion of national income going to distribution. Packaging and branding, for example, may be directly linked with advertising. It might be supposed that packaging and branding would have reduced marketing costs by facilitating vending; but in actual practice—despite easier handling—both packaging and branding have been fruitful methods of widening the spread between the costs of bulk ingredients and the price of packaged and branded goods.

Reason would indicate that automatic packaging and bottling machinery should reduce marketing costs, especially of goods subject to deterioration when sold in bulk, but analysis indicates that packaging actually increases the price spread almost in inverse proportion to the size of the package. The smaller and more convenient the package the larger the proportion of the consumer's dollar that goes for marketing. In fact, it is sometimes cheaper to ask the grocer to guess at cutting a pound print of butter in half than to buy a half pound already measured and wrapped, though such service necessitates not only extra work, but additional wrapping.

A Million Brands

Similarly, branding is often looked upon as ultimately conducive to narrowing the price spread by the creation of a standard or symbol of quality. Ample evidence exists, however, to prove that this, too, is a false assumption. Branding and labeling, for example, has frequently enabled the unscrupulous to sell cotton-seed oil for the price and under the impression that it is olive oil, due to the use of Italian words, symbols, designs, and pictures. Clever labeling and branding enabled the William S. Merrell Company to sell its Cod Liver Oil Concentrate Tablets in competition with a product with five times as much vitamin D. One of the crassest misuses of branding and labeling was that of another drug store gem: Warm Springs Crystal Compound. Even the president was dragged in to prove that it came from the famous springs in Georgia. As a matter of fact, it contained Glauber's salt, a cheap horse remedy, instead of evaporated salts from the Warm Springs' waters.

Not only does branding make possible the sale of inferior products at high prices, but it has multiplied to such an extent that it is the source of great consumer confusion. When one considers that there are more than a thousand brands each of face powder and toilet cream, that there are fully four thousand brands of canned corn, and that there are at least ten thousand brands of wheat flour it becomes difficult to understand how advocates of branding can argue that the practice greatly simplifies the marketing process. In 1929, the consumer was forced to choose from among more than a million brands, while under the unending bombardment of advertising ballyhoo, as each brand's sponsor zealously sought a great share of the national income. A babble of names buried every effort at logical standardization and reasonable classification. And the consumer paid the price.

The A. & P. and the Corner Grocer

Logically the growth of chain stores should have narrowed the margin of distribution; but independents stirred popular antagonism to oppose the invader. Thus, few independents were driven out by chain competition alone: their own incompetence was their worst enemy. Local independent merchants were temporarily protected against their own weaknesses. Gradually, however, a larger proportion of trade was drawn into chain channels.

Despite a great increase in the number of business failures, between 1923 and 1928, replacements and new entrants actually augmented the number of distributors. The cost of distribution was spread over a greater number of units. Instead of replacing independents, chain stores merely paid toll in rent to proprietor Smith, who moved on down the street or set up shop in the front room of his home. Main street was longer in 1929 than it had been in 1920. Duplication in facilities on Main street could be matched in almost every phase of distribution. And eventually, the consumer paid the bill, except in so far as it was taken from the worker or entrepreneur who lost his wages or investment.

Despite all the efficiencies and economies that were supposed to accrue through advertising, packaging and branding, and the growth of chain systems, the proportion of national production going to distribution costs increased by about 13.6 per cent, between 1920 and 1929. Thus it became apparent that the mass production efficiencies largely credited to the effect of national advertising and the economies widely ascribed to the development of chain systems were being more than off-set by new distributive wastes.

Main street became the apologist for increased costs of distribution. Variety! Specialization! Color! Easy credit! Service! These were the catch-words used to justify increasing costs. Department stores became literally club houses for idle women. Exclusive shops catered to the wealthy and their hopeful imitators. Specialty shops concentrated on the products of a single manufacture. And service stations multiplied in the futile attempt to reduce surplus oil reserves of competing producers. Consumers smiled indulgently and paid the bill.

DISTRIBUTION: OUR NUMBER ONE EXTRAVAGANCE

These embellishments of our distribution system constituted some of the more obvious reasons why distribution took a larger share of the national income in 1929 than in 1920. They represent, however, only a fraction of wastes that ran through the many ramifications of distribution in that year. To gain some idea of where other wastes may be found, consider how the costs of distribution were proportioned in 1929.

CLASSIFICATION OF DISTRIBUTION COSTS, 1929

	Per Cent
Manufacturer's selling costs	13.1
Wholesaling	25.4
Retailing	50.3
Transportation	11.2
	100.0

By far the largest share of national advertising was paid for out of the manufacturer's selling costs. Direct selling and warehousing costs were chiefly paid from the percentage of distribution costs accounted for by manufacturers and wholesalers. Producers as well as consumers absorbed a very large share of the miscellaneous transportation costs, in the form of deductions from gross payments or additions to list prices.

Now as then, through all the divisions of distribution runs the primary waste in unnecessary duplication of activities and facilities. Salesmen of a half dozen wholesale firms attempt to sell the same item, at about the same price, to the same merchants. Parallel railway tracks are maintained in competition with trucking lines, pipe lines, and waterway facilities, though the peak traffic load is often not sufficient to utilize even a single railway track's capacity. Uncoördinated transactions result in unnecessary trans-shipments, the wasteful use of warehouse facilities, and a high rate of loss among perishable commodities.

Over and above all the wasteful distributive practices of manufacturers and wholesalers and the unnecessary costs incurred through excess transportation facilities, however, stand wastes in the field of retailing. It is in that division of distribution—from a utilitarian point of view—that distributive duplication reaches almost the ultimate in stupidity.

Some conception of the cost of distribution may be gleaned from the fact that it far exceeds the combined costs of all crime, gambling, and "illth." The total "value" of all goods and services designated as the opposite of wealth constituted only one-third as much as the cost of distribution, in 1929. Gambling, sometimes designated as our greatest waste, took less than one-fifth as much from the total productive fund as distribution. Amazingly enough, the gross profit margin on gambling was only about twenty per cent, or about fifty-five per cent less than distributive margin on all goods and services.

Gambling and illth, however, are actually detrimental; whereas distribution is generally no more than non-productive. In contrast, therefore, compare the cost of distribution to the value of goods most essential to the country's welfare.

It will be seen from the following table that distribution far outstripped in cost the total value of any important product of American industry in 1929.

Distribution.....................	$27,540,000,000
Gross agricultural income........	11,918,000,000
Value of all construction..........	11,000,000,000
Value of all textiles...............	9,243,000,000
Value of all automobiles...........	5,261,000,000
Value of all steels................	4,137,000,000
Value of all chemicals.............	3,703,000,000

Distribution, in fact, took two and a half times as much from the national productive fund as was paid in factory wages and almost twice as much as the total for all industrial wages and salaries. In the single year, 1929, distribution cost two and a half times as much as the total present value of all the accumulated gold reserves of the United States.

Compared to the cost of fulfilling some of our most vital needs, the cost of distribution is even more striking. It would require, for example, only one-half the 1929 cost of distribution to electrify every farm home in America and to equip every farm with a milk cooler, a feed grinder, an incubator, a cream separator, a portable utility motor, a brooder, a milking machine, a shop motor, and $285 worth of other electrical apparatus, all at current prices.

POVERTY FOR ALL

Had the American people been disposed to eliminate the waste in the distribution system, how they might have raised the American standard of living!

In the decade of the twenties the entire slum problem could have been solved, electrification could have been brought to every American farm and every urban home, railway grade crossings could have been eliminated, the one-room rural school could have been replaced with modern, consolidated structures, the library facilities of the nation could have been doubled, and there would have been some wealth left to be devoted to other needful purposes.

But America preferred to duplicate its distributive facilities, lengthen its Main streets, and raise tall buildings. As a result,

only one in ten farm houses has become a user of electricity,
death still lurks at our grade crossings, more than a million
children attend school in inadequate structures, and the slum
problem has hardly been touched. But we have our Main
streets, ugly and gaudy though they are.

When economists began to add new bottom sections to
their diagnostic charts with the coming of depression in 1929,
few noted one important economic phenomenon: the great
increase in the proportion of national income going to pay
the costs of distribution. From 1920 to 1929, the American
people took 29 to 34 cents of every dollar of their income
and laid them on the altar of the great god Distribution.
That was bad enough; but as the depression deepened—like
superstitious savages fearful of the Thunder god—the American people approached the Main Street Temple of Distribution with an ever-proportionately larger offering until, in
the beginning of 1933, they were leaving on the altars of
Main street 51 per cent of their greatly restricted output of
forest, field, mine, and factory products!

Like a parasite on the body economic, the cost of distribution grew proportionately larger even while the income com-
posing the body economic grew more scarce. In 1933, however,
the body economic received more nourishment and began to
lose its appearance of famishment. In relation to the then increasing size of the national income, the proportion going to
distribution began to decline; but slowly, much more slowly
than it had increased. By 1936, the national income had
increased 50 per cent, but the proportion going to distribution had declined only 14 per cent.

The insatiable appetite of the market is still growing.

LAYING THE GROUNDWORK

Preparation for Reading
1. Approximately what part of the price the consumer pays for a
   quart of milk or a loaf of bread goes into the farmer's pocket?
   What happens to the remainder?
2. To what extent does advertising enter into the cost of commodities? Give evidence to support your answer.

3. What ways can you suggest by which the cost of distribution could be cut? Illustrate by reference to specific problems.

Vocabulary Building

1. Look up these words and use them in sentences: *valid, drastically, perpetuation, facilitating, deterioration, conducive, unscrupulous, zealously, embellishments, insatiable.*
2. Explain "man-hour rate of productivity"; "man-unit rate of vending"; "consumer resistance."
3. Explain the process of pasteurizing. What is the derivation of the word? List other common words which have been derived from proper nouns.

APPRAISING THE RESULTS

1. What was Main Street like in your father's day? How has it changed, and what forces have caused the transformation in producer-seller-buyer relation?
2. Has the trend been up or down in the cost of production? in the man-hour rate of productivity? in the man-unit rate of selling? in the cost of distribution?
3. What three factors should have led to a decrease in distribution costs? Discuss each of these factors as it has actually entered into rising distribution costs.
4. What are some of the wasteful duplications in production and transportation, and what are the "services" which have increased the cost of distribution?
5. Compare the unnecessary distribution costs with the costs of gambling and "illth," with "the value" of goods, and with "the costs of fulfilling our most vital needs."
6. Study the tables. Then summarize in one sentence the meaning of each.
7. With what points made by the author do you agree? disagree? Examine the logical basis of your stand in each instance.
8. Formulate a plan for an intelligent, rational system of distribution which would cut the costs to a minimum, with no loss in quality.
9. Outline the selection.

SELECTING THE THEME SUBJECT

1. Write an analysis of the chain-store system, or defend or attack it.
2. Discuss the overhead, receipts, wage outlay, write-up in costs and service values of the corner grocery store.
3. Write a paper explaining the system of consumer cooperatives.
4. Theme topics: Too Many Gas Stations?; The Door-to-door Salesman; How Packaging and Branding Can Be Improved; Are Brands an Index to Quality?; A Lament for the Village Grocer; Why I Like Chain Stores; "Service"; The Plight of the Farmer.

OPEN YOUR PURSE AND SHUT YOUR EYES[1]

Margaret Dana

I

GIDEON WADE HAD A NOTION OF TRUST THAT SEEMS TO ME BOTH SHREWD AND STRAIGHT. GIDEON USED TO PEDDLE FRUIT AND vegetables to the villagers near his farm, and he also supplied most of the cord-wood for the village stoves. That he had a rather peculiar method of doing business must be admitted; the descendants of his neighbors still tell about it as a bit of American humor. They say that when Mrs. Jones, for instance, wanted a cord of wood, Gideon would appear promptly with a wagonload of good seasoned well-cut wood and pile it neatly in cord formation within Mr. Jones's woodshed. That finished, he would step to her kitchen door and call, "Mis' Jones, I've corded ye up some wood. If ye'd just kindly step out here now and see if it suits . . ."

And Mis' Jones would step out, with Gideon watching her sharply. If she measured his pile roughly by eye and hand length, he was pleased. If she called him to terms for being short a stick or two, or over the cord by a little, he would cheerfully correct the amount and Mis' Jones had gained his respect and unfailing service. If, on the other hand, she casually looked at his woodpile and said carelessly that she guessed it was all right, Gideon would turn without a word and grimly begin to load his wood back on to his old wagon bed again. Mis' Jones might argue as long as she had breath, but she didn't get Gideon's wood. And it would be a long time, perhaps years, before he was willing to give her a second trial as a customer. When his neighbors chided

[1] From *The Atlantic Monthly*, October, 1937. Reprinted by permission of the author and of the publisher.

Gideon for a business policy bound to lose him money, he had one never-varying reply; he might, he'd say, lose some money that way, but certain sure he licked the old devil a-sitting on his shoulder. As a matter of fact, Gideon died a prosperous man.

I should not like to be misunderstood as belittling in any way the quality of real trust between human beings; it is assuredly our most precious medium of exchange. But I do mean to suggest that trust not founded upon information and complete understanding is simply not trust at all. It is, instead, a form of lazy inadequacy, making the seller appear dishonest and the buyer a fool.

We have admittedly become a nation of blindly trusting people. It is our tendency to trust anyone and everyone with something to sell, politically, economically, or over a counter. This tendency appears in an exaggerated form when we buy our consumer goods—and it is one of the most subtly dangerous and subversive factors in our national life.

Consider briefly, from the consumer's angle, the trust which exists between retailer and customer. Its simple origin, of course, must lie at that far point when members of a community found that some of their individuals were better at the job of making pottery, furniture, or clothing than were the others. They knew this because they had seen it done. They had *seen* it. This is a point of enormous importance in understanding this story. And, too, it should be remembered that there was neither secret nor mystery about what went into the product in raw materials, labor, or cost, since every family originally made for itself whatever it needed, and a common knowledge of such homely manufacture was general. The only difference between one man's product and his neighbor's was a matter of skill, ingenuity, or imagination. No consumer need take this difference on trust, since it was easy to watch the work in progress. No farther back than in our own colonial history you will see this gradual transferal of manufacture to those who had the most skill, the greatest aptitude for it.

Imagine if you will the two groups, makers and users, sitting around a conference table, with the users speaking plainly their requirements and the makers demonstrating their compliance. While there were no written agreements, no literal specifications, still such specifications were persistently taken for granted by the consumer group, and for a remarkably long time by the producers. This is the root of the trust which laymen have until recently felt for the professional manufacturer and retailer. Moreover, because the two functions were closely related for so long, we find consumers for generations stubbornly believing that the responsibilities were interchangeable, believing subconsciously that the producer and the seller were one in their service.

Thus experience built up a firm confidence between makers and users, a confidence which lasted for years, as this country has good reason to know. But lately a strange fervor amounting almost to a crusading hysteria has infected many consumer gatherings, causing manufacturers and retailers a good deal of puzzled anxiety. What new form of selling must be evolved to quiet this murmuring consumer unrest, and to prevent the bitterness of rebellion from destroying our traditional trust?

Two points indicate the nature of the solution. One is the fact that consumers no longer *see* their merchandise made, and must arbitrarily take it on trust of some sort. The other is the frequently unrecognized fact that there is no longer any such thing as a "best" in any generic field of production—a "best" at each price level, perhaps, but no dead-centre, static, definable "best" for all.

If this seems unbelievable, consider what is really meant by the term "grades" or "qualities." Everything that is made, from kitchen stoves to baby clothes, is the result of an assembly of many factors in varying proportions. A producer takes these factors—raw materials, labor, style, beauty, wearability, cost—and combines them according to his own particular formula, so much cost in ratio to so much beauty, style, strength, and so on, and produces, let us say, a chair at a certain price to the consumer. Then he or another manufacturer takes the *same* factors but in *different* proportions and also turns out a chair, perhaps at a quite different cost. Now each of these chairs has presumably been designed to offer satisfaction to some consumer. But *which* consumer will be most satisfied with *which* chair is a question that by the immutable laws of human psychology only the ultimate consumer is qualified to decide.

No retailer can select for any consumer the "best" for him, since a purchase only becomes the "best" when it fits squarely the individual consumer's purposes. The buyer who needs a good sturdy commonplace safety pin will be better satisfied with his own choice of a good sturdy safety pin than with the handsomest platinum clip which may be offered as the "best," or a straight pin which in all its insecurity is offered as the "cheapest." There may be an almost infinite variety of grades, each of them satisfactory under certain conditions, but a purchase which fails to fit adequately the individual's purposes and expectations is no better than a pair of shoes two sizes too small.

The consumer of to-day is presented with an amazing number, not only of new products, but of different grades of those products. How, then, do people buy? What are their guides, their bases for decision? The plain fact is that with the exception of a few major purchases of a lifetime—a home, a car, a sable coat, or a diamond tiara (if any)—the average consumer buys according to three things: sight, touch, and price, against a background of *an inherited and unthinking trust of the producer and seller*. This trust may take the form of "going to a good store," or buying "a brand you know," but it is indeed a far deeper, more essential matter than that. It is the projection of a remarkably matter-of-fact trust which has made consumers assume it safe to buy what pleased their eyes, their touch, and their pocketbook, made them assume for long, long years that beneath each purchase —even at a bargain sale—was an *implied guaranteed minimum of worth*. The exploitation of this prime factor in our commercial life goes far to explain that strange abstract often called the American "sucker." But consumers are not "suckers," contrary to Mr. Barnum and all his latter-day disciples; they are victims, sadly enough, of a great trust that has lost its reason for being.

II

There are many people, I am well aware, who resent being told they do not know what they buy—and many who do not believe it. And that brings up the question of the reliability of those three guides, sight, touch, and price. It is fair to ask if these are not, after all, decently reliable, useful, and indicative of value. The answer depends upon what a buyer expects or requires of his purchases. For sight and touch can only inform a consumer as to the outward qualities of a product—style, beauty, fit, comfort, and so on. Price can tell one literally nothing except that the purchase can or cannot be afforded—and then only if first cost be the final consideration! According to every important technician in the country, when it comes to the unseen qualities of a product, the things which ultimately make for performance, the least reliable guides in the world are these familiar three —sight, touch, and price. Just where does that leave the layman buyer who is not blessed with infinite time, means, and patience to sample by the trial-and-error method all the products with which he is daily confronted? It leaves him dependent on one buying guide alone—his blind and inherited trust of the seller.

Let me try to illustrate this insecurity of choice in a random selection of merchandise.

With the approach of winter weather, millions of consumers will again be concerned with the purchase of coats, suits, dresses, blankets, whose chief purpose is to keep the human body warm. Certainly style, beauty, and price will enter into the buying, but warmth is the urgent necessity. And how does one judge warmth? By sight? Many fabrics which *look* warm have virtually no warmth at all. For instance, rayon fiber may be spun and woven to look exactly like wool, and it is common knowledge in the trade that an increasingly vast yardage of fabrics for men's, women's, and children's clothing often sold as "all wool" actually contains from 40 per cent to 80 per cent rayon. Yet how much has rayon of wool's generic warmth properties? By touch, then? But many soft, heavy, and woolly fabrics have little real warmth. By price? But a recent laboratory test of coat linings, for instance, showed that certain linings which had the greatest warmth were also the cheapest, although they were also the heaviest. On the other hand, camel hair in its finest, handsomest, and costliest grade is also the warmest and lightest. Its wearability, however, is below the inferior qualities, which, while heavy, are not warm.

Observe these many factors; remembering what is meant by a "grade," consider whether any consumer actually does know how warm is warmth, and how much of it he receives for his investment in relation to other factors. Yet an efficient testing laboratory can measure every one of these factors in definite understandable terms. Warmth—technically called thermal resistance—can be reduced to a figure, as can the factors of weight and wearability, so that they may be studied in their comparative values by any consumer. But can you remember ever seeing this information given at the point of sale?

Next consider that homely necessity, bath towels. Anyone with half an eye can determine the style, beauty, and color of a towel; the hand may sense its softness, a yardstick will find its size, the label will tell its price. But what about the unseen factors? You buy towels for their faculty of soaking up water freely and rapidly—in other words, absorbency. You want a towel that will wear a reasonable length of time, a color which will stay its best. But here are two towels with their recorded laboratory tests for the hidden factors. One of these towels is widely advertised as the "best buy"; one costs less than the other; one is two inches longer than the other. But neither has been so labeled and described in terms of those hidden qualities that a consumer may decide for herself which is really the best buy for *her*.

Here is the record of a test applied to washable wallpapers by a fine laboratory. Two samples were tested, each made by a "good" company, each called "washable." Under the wet abrasion tests of the laboratory, however, one sample was found to have a breaking point of an average 59, the other of 5000+. No technical knowledge and no involved explanation are needed to convince a layman that one of these wall-

papers is much less deserving of the term "washable" than
the other. Certainly the less washable paper may have compensating qualities in greater style, beauty, or lower price,
but the *unseen* factor, its *washability,* is featured by manufacturer and retailer. Does the consumer, then, truly know
what he is buying, and does he rely safely on his inherited
trust of the seller?

Finally, let me tell you as briefly as possible the story of
shrinkage, which like that other story, fibre identification,
touches all human life, whatever the age, sex, or income.
Perhaps it sounds a very humdrum, inconsequential affair,
but in fact it costs this country every year many millions of
dollars in economic loss, and no one pays that bill but the
plain consumer. To begin with, all woven fabrics are born
to shrink. Every process of their creation holds them under
constant and extreme tension, stretching their fibres nearly
to the limit of their capacity. This tension first really relaxes
when the fabric meets moisture by immersion, steam, or
atmosphere. Part of the finishing process of some fabrics,
notably cotton and linen types, performs some of this relax-
ing function, shrinking the fibres back toward their original
length. But the fibres do not necessarily go *all* the way back
to that normal condition at the first meeting with moisture.
They may shrink more at the second, third, or fourth
immersion.

Now in the trade certain terms are used to indicate that
these fibres have received some degree of relaxation—shrinkage, in short. Consumers are familiar with these terms;
scarcely a woman but will recognize such words as "pre-
shrunk," "shrunk," "shrinkproof," "full-shrunk," and "washable." But what, exactly, do they mean to the average consumer?

A few weeks ago I put that very question to a group of
intelligent, thrifty women, members of a society I had been
asked to address on consumer-buying information. In every
case the answer indicated that these women understood all
of the terms to mean that the fabrics would shrink no further
when washed. The subsequent expressions on their faces as

I explained the real meaning of these words were illuminating.

For actually none of these terms has a commonly accepted and definite meaning. The words "full-shrunk" and "shrink-proof" are usually, to put it most kindly, examples of wishful thinking, for a full-shrunk fabric rarely exists. "Shrunk" and "pre-shrunk" at their best mean only that the fabrics have been shrunk *some* before the consumer purchases them; at their not uncommon worst they mean less than nothing. How much more a fabric will shrink is one of those unseen performance factors we have mentioned. Some manufacturers put a limit of 2 per cent on the further shrinkage to be expected of a fabric marked "pre-shrunk." Others limit it to 3, 4, or 5 per cent, and I have even seen "pre-shrunk" materials that shrank 8 per cent. This perhaps will explain why I say the terms have no real meaning.

As for the term "washable"—this prankish word is the most treacherous of all, for in bitter fact it frequently means only that the fabric can be passed through water without disintegrating like paper. As one eminent technician remarked, "The label adopted by the wash-dress industry furnishes washing instructions incapable of removing honest soil from any wash dress."

Not long since, a greatly irritated gentleman stalked into my office and tossed a freshly laundered but rumpled man's shirt on to my desk. With a look of last-straw exasperation he said, "If that's honesty, then this country's come to a pretty pass. That shirt carries a label that says in plain English 'pre-shrunk.' Yet by actual measurement its collar band shrank more than a quarter of an inch the first time it was laundered. How long has this kind of double-crossing been going on?"

Sympathetic as I was with the gentleman's irritation, I could only reply that "this kind of thing" had been going on for a very long time, and the wonder was not that he had discovered it, but that he had not discovered it before. One can only assume that the wash lady and the commercial laundries have borne the burden of many a complaint not rightfully theirs.

A recent hearing before the Federal Trade Commission on the shrinkage problems for cotton yard goods entered upon the record some remarkable facts presumably only for trade knowledge. Consumers will find some of them interesting if maddening. The New York Board of Trade has had a committee studying the cotton-goods shrinkage situation for four years. The committee eventually proposed to the Commission that all cotton piece goods be marked • with the percentage they might be expected to shrink. Consumers will find this rational, and certainly not asking too much. Nevertheless the converters who are the fabric middlemen, and the finishers who create the surface textures and finishes, sprang to battle. Admittedly it was a fine idea, said their spokesman, and they would gladly co-operate, but the thing was clearly impossible. Too many variables entered into the complicated business to make it fair to ask a finisher to guarantee the percentage a cloth would shrink, and if the finishers could not guarantee it the converters, of course, were helpless, since they depended upon the finishers for *their* guarantee.

Before you feel a little sorry for the finishers and converters, however, let me mention that there is a shrinkage process known as Sanforizing which may be used on cotton, linen, or rayon fabrics and which definitely predetermines the amount of shrinkage of such fabrics—a process which any finisher may be licensed to employ. And this is why various witnesses at the shrinkage hearing asked somewhat dryly how it happens that, if a finisher is asked to do a *Sanforizing* job on goods, he can not only pre-shrink them accurately but also offer a guarantee that no more than three quarters of 1 per cent further shrinkage will occur, and yet virtuously insist that he could not offer a guarantee of 2 per cent, 5 per cent, or whatever was necessary under other shrinkage processes.

But of course cotton goods are not the only fabrics affected by this shrinkage factor. Silk, linen, rayon, and wool also must contend with the condition. I have here a bulletin from the National Better Business Bureau which states that about 50 per cent of the woolen and worsted yarn goods made into women's and children's clothing is not pre-shrunk to any degree at all. This is estimated to represent 13,000,000 garments annually, and dry cleaners say that consumer complaints on woolens and worsteds amount to some six million dollars' worth of claims a year, of which 75 per cent are due to shrinkage. If you add to this the amount of goods returned to dress departments of stores, half of which is because of fabric faults, and 20 per cent of that half because of shrinkage, and if you realize that this comes to many millions of dollars a year, you will perhaps conceive the extent of the waste I have mentioned. That this might be avoided is indicated by the determined drive being made currently by the Texurity Guild, an association of refinishers of woolens and worsteds, in which they undertake to set a maximum of 2 per cent for wool fabric shrinkage—a limit arbitrarily set from experimental testing.

III

With even so slight an excursion into the "no consumer's land" behind the scenes of retailing, it must be plain that there is an utter lack of a concerted attempt on the part of the modern producer-seller combine to replace the general information of the older simple buying period when products were few, materials familiar, techniques limited, and consumer needs and specifications commonly understood. Something is clearly needed to bridge the gap opened by the flood of new things—to bridge the distance between the consumer and the actual manufacture of such goods. What should the "something" be?

Well, when the Federal Government buys, it buys according to specifications which state both the construction and performance to be expected of the product. It buys, in short, on a written statement which tells of *what* the product is made, *how* it is made, and what it will *do* in use. The Federal Bureau of Standards determines by tests what standards shall be the guides for these specifications, and Federal buyers purchase not the handsomest, longest-wearing, or most expensive items, but those which, according to their specifications, give the most of the desired qualities for the money allowed for the purchase. This seems rational and clear. Government standards are not necessarily consumer standards, but the principle is identical. Moreover, scarcely a manufacturer in the country but bases his own buying on the same sort of specifications—construction and performance. This, too, appears to be ordinary common sense. And retailers also buy with at least an understood specification in mind, written or not, so that they have, or may have if they wish, a definite idea as to what they are getting. Only the consumer must apparently buy blind, must open his purse and shut his eyes.

Surely what a consumer wants and needs is no more or less than what the professional buyer demands—specific information in terms mutually understood and authoritative. There are an infinite number of terms open to as infinite a number of interpretations; there are "special pleaders" in industry who have reason to prefer one interpretation, though aware that consumers assume another. Specifications wipe out such Jekyll-and-Hyde words.

Many explanations are proffered as to why such simple practical information is not supplied consumers. Some say it is because manufacturers working in a fluctuating market for raw materials dislike to be pinned down to specifications which will be handed on to the consumer and prevent the substitution of cheaper elements when the market pushes the price of a specified element too high—too high, that is, for the margin of profit a store buyer needs for his department. Again, they say that manufacturers hesitate to set up standards for their products because of the costly burden involved in properly policing all stages of the work to produce accurate results. That the Bureau of Standards and various associations and laboratories have proved repeatedly that standards, once installed, actually cut the cost of production is usually ignored. And indeed there are those who believe with some resignation that inertia, habit, and a worship of the "let well enough alone" policy are responsible for much of the manufacturer's reluctance to set up consumer specifications in a form to carry through the point of sale.

These reasons may very well be accurate; but, just as I

have tried to show in an earlier article[2] that the real main-spring of to-day's retailing mistakes is a fundamentally mistaken public-relations policy, so it seems to me that as direct results of that policy there are other and equally mistaken psychological factors much more responsible for this current plague of "buying blind."

Of these surely the most extraordinary is what I can only call the double standard of ethics which exists among many of those who make or sell consumer goods, particularly evident among retailers, less often discovered among producers considerably removed from the point of sale. It is a curious and shocking kind of rationalization of dishonesty which permits a man of the highest personal integrity to compromise complacently with definitely dishonest merchandising practices under the blanket cover of "good business." This is an unpleasant fact usually never even whispered in public, but often admitted behind closed doors and off the record. That there are conspicuous exceptions to this rule would be silly to deny; there are manufacturers, "middlemen," and retailers who have business ideals as fine as their personal standards, but under the present conditions not only are they apt to be penalized by unfair competition, but also they are so few as to be unable to balance the scales in the consumer mind against the trend toward distrust.

As in the case of the testimony in the shrinkage hearing, trade leaders will offer a thousand and one reasons why consumer information is not practical; these specious reasons run the gamut of assertions from the familiar one that consumers do not want facts to the naïvely egotistical statement that such and such an industry is too technical, too complicated for the layman—much less the laywoman—to understand. There are those who sincerely believe that such information must of its nature be so profound and mystic that consumers could not utilize it. And there are those who make the gesture of providing information by deliberately *making* it so profound and mystic that it cannot be used.

To say that honest, understandable construction and per-

[2] "Fear the Facts and Fool the Women," in the April, 1937, *Atlantic.*—Editor.

formance specifications cannot be given every buyer at the point of sale is to show either an ignorance of or an unwillingness to recognize what has already been accomplished by a few admirable organizations. For instance, although rug makers insist that theirs is a uniquely technical and involved profession, so complicated that to mark any of their products intelligibly for the consumer would require a label the size of a book or terminology so obscure no layman could understand it, one pioneering manufacturer of fine rugs has managed to create a label of remarkably small and handy size which is attached to his rugs—so long as the retailer permits it—and presents all the necessary facts clearly and simply. The hosiery industry, too, is another "highly complicated" business which for long has been utterly chaotic in its own manufacturing standards and its consumer promotion. Nevertheless of its own accord this industry has been putting its house in order, and has developed not only construction standards for its producers to follow, but grade labels which it proposes to stamp on all grades below those which carry brand names and are presumed to be arbitrarily the most nearly flawless.

There are other isolated cases in which manufacturers have boldly broken with current custom and supplied consumer specifications with their products. And certain of the large mail-order houses are admittedly giving their customers a better break than metropolitan retailers have ever attempted. I asked the chief technician of a mail-order laboratory the other day how she explained the fact that local retailers lag so far behind those who sell by mail in giving their customers usable buying data, and her answer was perhaps more illuminating than she realized. "Well, you know," she said, "we mail-order people after all are engaged in interstate commerce, and are necessarily under the direct supervision of the Federal Trade Commission. Local stores aren't, you see."

The thing that awakening consumers do not quite realize is that this discussion is not new. Nothing about it is unique, radical, or startling. For many years conventions of all sorts of trade associations have been lightly tossing about the subject of the consumer and his growing restlessness without ever reaching any agreed conclusion that develops more than word power. Speaking at a recent consumer-retailer session, Miss Ruth O'Brien, chief of the Division of Textiles and Clothing of the United States Bureau of Home Economics, said: "When are we going to get action on standards and labels for consumer goods? For fifteen years I have been coming to these meetings, and for fifteen years we have talked about information for the consumer, but up to now the action that has been taken could be counted on the fingers of my two hands." Even that is a rather generous estimate if one eliminates imitation efforts and gestures to the grand-stand.

It is difficult in a situation where words have for so long taken the place of action, where conferences and commissions bog down by their own weight and pomposity, to gauge accurately the sincerity of any new move toward constructive solution of the problem. So many red herrings are daily dragged across the trail that it is not surprising the target is lost in the confusion. Such ridiculous controversies as the current feverish one concerning whether such terms as "crepe," "print," "taffeta," and "pure dye" belong to the silk industry, or the rayon industry, or any other trade, simply delay the ultimate objective. After all, the simple solvent of all these complexities is just one question, "Does this correctly inform the consumer or not?"

Nevertheless, in spite of the record of futility chalked up against retailing leaders, there seems now to be for the first time in the era real hope of the consumer's eventually receiving the general and specific data he needs. Within the National Retail Dry Goods Association is a group of leaders headed by men who appear both sincere and determined in their effort to alter the situation. Their published programme insists that there must be construction and performance specifications supplied by the producers of goods, and that there must be a dictionary of terms developed to pull to-gether the fantastic jumble now distorting the language of selling. In other words, they admit that the consumer has the right to know, in definite terms of standards and com-

parison, just how fine, how strong, and how absorbent a
"fine, strong, and absorbent" towel may be.

How far this organized retail activity will go, only time
can tell—particularly as two dangers have recently arisen
with the quickening restlessness of consumers and the publicity given the situation. One is the possibility that retailers
and manufacturers, in a desire to utilize facts in their sales
promotion, may hasten the setting of standards before they
have been properly defined and tested. The other and far
graver peril is the possibility that facts may become part of
a new American racket, that the abuse of the words "tested
and approved" may become just one more promotion trick.

Concerning the first danger, all responsible technicians are
seriously anxious. Products to be safely offered consumers on
the competitive ground of construction and performance
should have not only formal laboratory testing, but also the
homely trials of active service under the conditions they
must meet in consumer use. Otherwise trouble is apt to
follow. For instance, there is the story of aluminum foil as
an insulating material. According to laboratory tests, this
product proved to have extraordinary insulating qualities,
and it was hailed and sold as ideal for wall insulation in house
construction. It was advertised and promoted against a background of these laboratory findings, and was received enthusiastically by consumers. After some time, however, the
burden of complaints from consumers became voluminous:
the material appeared to have stopped insulating. An investigation was made, and no one was more sadly shocked than
its makers when it was discovered that some of the aluminum
foil had vanished into space. Only then was it learned that
aluminum foil in the presence of lime, as in wall plaster,
may disintegrate into a gas, leaving the insulation conspicuous
by its absence. But understand, there was here no intent to
deceive the public or withhold information—only the result
of incomplete and inadequate tests.

The second danger I mentioned is sufficiently grave to
warrant the attention of every responsible member of society.
For if there is anything more treacherous than withholding

necessary information, it is exploiting a human being's hunger for information.

There is a steadily growing tendency to make use of the words "tested and approved" or their implication in advertising and promotion, particularly of the retail type. Too often the words are both the beginning and the end of all the testing which has been done. Not only should the consumer be told who did the testing, how it was done, and what the results mean in terms of comparative performance, but there should definitely be some manner of licensing testing laboratories, so that the consumer may know they have official standing and credited efficiency. Nor, it seems to me, should a store be permitted to call its own testing department a "Bureau of Standards"; for there should be but one such in this country, and that in Washington, where it belongs.

There are many organizations these days attempting to evaluate products for consumers. Some are sincere in their desire to be of service, but are so limited in funds that their tests are both inadequate and dangerous. And there are many organizations that see in the demand for information no more than an opportunity to cash in on the well-known credulity of the general public. Let me quote a few sentences from a market letter I received a few weeks ago, written by an organization which does a good deal of manufacturer-retailer merchandising:—

Considerable interest is being shown currently by retailers in movement among consumers for more detailed and more accurate information. Various consumer groups are forming special committees to accelerate trend. National Retail Dry Goods Association is considering formation of group to be known as "Consumer-Retailer Council." No doubt that this apparent demand of consumers for better guidance in buying is claiming more and more of retailers' attention. Formation of such organizations as Consumers' Emergency Council and possibility that Federal Government may establish special division to further trend cannot be ignored. However, we feel that immediate importance of this program to manufacturers may be seriously questioned. No doubt that a vociferous minority is interested. On the other hand, we believe that vast majority of consumers are totally uninterested in so-called merchandise standards and will remain that way for a long time to come. We *see promotional benefits to manufacturers tying up with the movement,* but we feel that in general its significance can be and has already been considerably inflated.

The italics in this remarkable statement are mine. Its implications I leave to your common sense.

Somewhere near the beginning of this story I said that there was a solution to this critical problem so simple and so plain that it was consistently overlooked by both retailers and consumer crusaders.

That solution is nothing more spectacular or original than a return—or an advance—to common honesty. Not lip-service honesty, not a double-standard honesty, not a sleight-of-hand bookkeeping honesty, but the clean and literal honesty once taught us as the bedrock of human decency. That consumers have a vital obligation to meet such honesty with intelligence and appreciation is true, but stubbornly to disregard the signs of consumer rebellion is to invite disaster. Yet, if a renewal of common honesty is to come, it should arrive not through fear of the Federal Trade Commission or any other "goblins that'll get you if you don't watch out." It should come rather in recognition of the profound truth that the greatest insurance of industrial probity and prosperity is an informed and discriminating consumer public.

LAYING THE GROUNDWORK

Preparation for Reading

1. How do you judge the quality of what you buy, or whether you are getting your money's worth?
2. Would it be feasible to describe and grade fabrics and clothing accurately on a label which the consumer could consult?
3. Why has intelligent buying become more difficult? What has caused the increased interest in the problem of the consumer and his education?

Vocabulary Building

1. Check the meanings and pronunciations of these words: *subversive, ingenuity, aptitude, static, immutable, generic, thermal, abrasion, disintegrating, inertia, ethics, integrity, egotistical, arbitrarily, pomposity, vociferous, probity.*
2. Explain the references to Mr. Barnum, "special pleaders in industry," "Jekyll and Hyde words," U. S. Bureau of Standards, "specious reasons," "run the gamut," "red herrings are dragged across the trail," "lip-service honesty," Federal Trade Commission.

APPRAISING THE RESULTS

1. What is the purpose of the introductory story? How is it related to the thesis?
2. Study the beginnings of several essays. Then list various ways of beginning. Why is attention to the beginning necessary?
3. What is the origin, according to Miss Dana, of the trusting attitude of the consumer? Why is this trust often misplaced today?
4. What evidence is there today of consumer unrest?
5. How do the following two points enter into the solution of the rising consumer mistrust: "consumers no longer *see* their merchandise," and "there is no longer any such thing as a 'best' in any generic field of production"?
6. What three criteria govern the buying of the average consumer? What additional factor usually enters? How far are these criteria reliable? What illustrations does Miss Dana use? Are they convincing? well selected?
7. What remedy does Miss Dana suggest? Do you believe her suggestion practicable?
8. How do you account for the slowness of manufacturers and retailers to cooperate in consumer education?
9. What two dangers have arisen in the consumer education movements?
10. Make an outline of the thesis and main points.

SELECTING THE THEME SUBJECT

1. Write a paper analyzing the consumer buying problem as it is related to some product: silk or lisle hose, canned goods,

meats, refrigerators, radios, cosmetics, dentifrices. As far as possible, base your paper on first-hand experience.

2. Write a paper on the consumer education movement in your community.

3. Defend or attack the need for better national food and drug legislation.

4. Write a paper developing one of these titles: "Let the Buyer Beware"; Consumers' Publications; Bargain Sales; Effects of Competition on Quality; Consumer Education on Working Conditions; Your Money's Worth at the Movies; Paying for Style; The High Cost of Hats; Paying for Labels; "I Buy at the Best Stores"; The Girl Behind the Counter; Loss Leaders as Bait for "Suckers"; Men Shoppers; The Folly of Christmas Buying; How to Buy Fresh Fruits and Vegetables; Sales Psychology; Needed: Consumers' Guidance; Fraudulent Merchandise I Have Trustingly Bought; The New Food and Drug Act; The Government's "Consumers Guide" to Cosmetics.

The Outlook for National Health

MEDICAL AID FOR ALL[1]

Hugh Cabot

IT CANNOT REASONABLY BE DOUBTED THAT THE PROVISION OF A SATISFACTORY HEALTH SERVICE FOR THE PEOPLE OF THE United States presents a real problem. This problem has been steadily growing during the last generation for two reasons, first, because of the increasing complication which has come from enormous increase in the application of science to the practice of medicine, and second—really a result of the first—the increase of the cost of satisfactory medical care. A good deal of discussion has taken place as to the whys and wherefores of the very obvious increase in cost, but the reasons are not far to seek. The last quarter of a century has seen an astonishing increase in the possible application of scientific method to the diagnosis and treatment of disease. Today methods which were fairly satisfactory thirty or forty years ago are so make-shift as to be nearly worthless. Scientific method requires expensive apparatus, well-equipped laboratories, hospital accommodations, and an enormous increase in the number of thoroughly trained specialists. Although it is undoubtedly true that the physician of today could offer the brand of medical care which his grandfather supplied at a price as low as or lower than was then possible, such care would today be quite unacceptable.

Very roughly and generally speaking the cost of illness per capita in the United States at about 1930 was $30 per person. This does not sound like a prohibitive sum, but it does not in fact represent the expense which many people bear. The cost of illness is very unevenly distributed, and in

[1] From *The American Scholar*, Winter, 1936. Reprinted by permission of the author and of the editors of *The American Scholar*.

any one year something like 10 per cent of the people will pay 50 per cent of the bill. Such impossible situations as that of a family with an income of $1,200 having medical expenses running to $1,000 in one year are by no means unknown. Under such conditions the burden becomes literally crushing. Furthermore, fairly careful studies at various periods show that in different parts of the country from 15 to 25 per cent of those people with disabling illness removing them from work for two weeks have no medical care. It should also be noted that the amount of medical care received by families of the United States increases directly with income.

It is next important to inquire what proportion of the people of the United States are comfortably able to meet their doctor's bills and what proportion are in more or less serious difficulties. Only a small group, probably about 10 per cent, with a family income of $5,000 or more are regularly able to pay their doctor's bills, as they occur, without serious inconvenience. A large group, something like 40 per cent, with family incomes ranging from $1,400 to $2,500 have sufficient income to pay their doctor's bills on the average but are quite unable to do so regularly on account of the tremendous variation in the load. This load is so uneven and unpredictable as to be practically unbudgetable. As will later be pointed out, it would be possible for this large group to meet their expenses if they could be handled by some method resembling insurance. There is next a considerable group, amounting to something like 15 per cent, with family incomes of $1,000 or less who can meet only a part of their doctor's bills even under the best of conditions. Finally, there is a considerable group properly classified as indigent, amounting to something like 4½ per cent of the population. For these the whole expense of medical care must obviously be provided out of the public purse.

Turning now to the question of the basic requirements for what will be accepted as satisfactory medical care, we find that the situation has changed importantly during the present century. The amount of knowledge necessary to the satisfactory care of illness is now so great that it is quite out of the question for a single physician to keep anywhere near abreast of the times. From this it follows that the relation of the general practitioner, formerly known as the family doctor, has become importantly altered. He cannot today by himself alone furnish what will be regarded as satisfactory care. He must have not only the assistance of laboratories, including x-ray equipment, but hospitals, nursing service, and ready access to a great variety of specialists. Furthermore, we have rather slowly come to realize the importance of dentistry in the general care of the health, and although American dentists have probably led the world in skill and dexterity there remains a tremendous lack of sufficient dental service. It is clear, therefore, that although the general practitioner will continue to be the physician who sees the patients in the first instance he will require a large amount of assistance both technical and from specialists in order to do full justice to many situations. These adjuncts to his practice must be easily available and at prices which are not prohibitive.

Let us next turn to a survey of the present personnel which may be called upon to deliver the service. The number of physicians in the United States is larger in proportion to the population than in any other country in the world. At the present time there is something like one physician to every 780 people. In most European countries the number varies from one per thousand of the population to one to 1,700 or 1,800. With the number we have it should be possible to deliver a good article of service. It is more difficult to estimate the number of people available for nursing service, but it is undoubtedly true that we have considerably more nurses per capita than is the case in other countries, and perhaps enough to fulfill reasonable requirements. The supply of dentists is undoubtedly less than will be sufficient to meet actual needs as they exist today. Of hospitals we have many and they have grown very rapidly in number and capacity during the last twenty years. In total they are perhaps enough, except in certain special fields, but their distribution is faulty. There are more than enough hospital beds in many thickly populated districts and not enough in

many thinly populated areas. Of hospitals for the accommodation of chronic disease, importantly of mental disease,
tuberculosis, cancer, chronic rheumatism, there is a serious
shortage. Of the personnel needed to carry on what is commonly referred to as public health work, that is to say, public
health officers, public health nurses, and their necessary
laboratory assistants—there are not enough at the present
time to do the work properly.

It has already been suggested that we have more physicians
than any other country in the world, and yet it remains true
that there are considerable portions of the country where
there is an actual shortage. This is particularly true of the
rather sparsely settled rural areas where medical service has
never been satisfactory and is not so today. It is further
true that many towns which twenty years ago had one or
more physicians now have none. This arises from the fact
that there are not enough people in these small towns and
villages to support one or more physicians with the equipment for modern medical diagnosis and treatment which
is essential. Obviously physicians will not go to or will not
remain in regions where they cannot support their families.
With the relatively large number of physicians per capita it
has frequently been suggested, chiefly by medical societies
and medical organizations, that there are too many physicians. This question obviously turns upon whether we propose to offer a good grade of medical service to the whole
population or whether we shall continue to offer a good
grade of medical service only to those who can pay in full
or in part. It cannot, I think, be doubted, although it has
frequently been denied, that if we should undertake to offer
full medical care to the whole population of the country
regardless of their economic condition we should find ourselves with no more physicians than were necessary and
probably with not enough. But no such attempt has ever
been made.

The question of the income of physicians in recent years
next becomes important. It is perhaps desirable to take as a
starting point the evidence of the income of physicians before
the recent depression. In 1929 the median income of the

physicians of the country was $3,705. However, 24 per cent had a net income of less than $2,000. Twenty-eight per cent had a net income of less than $4,000, and 75 per cent had a net income of $7,000 or less. Quite clearly these incomes are not high and are probably too low, taking into consideration the long and expensive educational requirements—which run to ten years and not less than $10,000.

The situation is further complicated by the custom, as old as medical practice, under which physicians treat a very large number of patients quite without expectation of reward. It is variously estimated that physicians spend from a quarter to more than half of their time on such charity service. As a result of this there has grown up the "sliding scale" of medical fees under which the more opulent members of society pay very large fees in order that physicians may have time to care for the more or less indigent. This amounts to an unofficial graduated income tax upon which is placed a surtax of amount not stated. Thus it may easily come about that rich people pay an amount several hundred times greater than do their brethren in somewhat straitened circumstances. Periodically there is outcry at the size of medical bills in unusual cases, and it is quite clear that the arrangement is uneconomic and unsatisfactory. On the other hand, as long as organized society continues to expect physicians to treat many patients free of charge they will have difficulty in supporting their objection to this system, which amounts to charging "what the traffic will bear."

Up to this moment we have been considering conditions of medical practice prior to the last five years or during the depression, but it is perhaps this depression which has called attention most sharply to the shortcomings of our present arrangements. Moreover, it seems to me quite clear that the depression has had a serious effect upon the service rendered. It has undoubtedly led to a very considerable increase in the very common, although wholly improper, practice of fee-splitting, under which the general practitioner with patients requiring the services of a specialist distributes his patients, not to the most competent specialist but to the one who will offer him the largest slice of the fee. Another source of less satisfactory service has been the tendency of the general practitioner to undertake, in order to maintain his income, to carry out work which belongs in the field of the qualified specialist. Thus during the depression a very large amount of major surgery both general and special has been done by quite unqualified general practitioners, though the interest of the patient required that it be done by men of special training. On the other hand, during this period many physicians have found themselves in very much straitened circumstances, and a few of them probably actually in the breadline. This has led to the tightening up of medical organizations in the attempt to obtain for their members a larger share of the diminished income of the country. They have discovered, as have other organized groups, the soundness of the slogan "United we eat." This is an altogether human reaction, but I have an uneasy feeling that it is better suited to organizations of labor than to professional associations avowedly dedicated to service. Similar organizations in other countries, such as the French syndicates of physicians, have become frankly and often chiefly concerned with obtaining income for their members quite without regard to the welfare of the patient. Enough has perhaps been said to suggest some of the elements in this complicated problem.

A great variety of remedial methods have been suggested, among them the following.

Compulsory health insurance. In one form or another most of the other great countries of the world have instituted some form of compulsory health insurance. Such a remedy was suggested for this country more than twenty years ago. At that time, and again within the last five years, it met with the bitter opposition of the American Medical Association. Despite the fact, which is apparently true, that in most, if not all, of the countries where it has been instituted, medical service is more widespread than here and that there are fewer people denied service, the opposition of the medical profession in this country has been persistent. On their side they have the undoubted fact that such insurance has nowhere worked entirely satisfactorily. In some countries it has worked better than in others, but it has nowhere succeeded in delivering a really first-class article. Furthermore it stands some chance, particularly where the payments to physicians are taken over either directly by the state or indirectly through insurance companies, of handicapping the development of the practice of medicine and of more or less countenancing slipshod methods.

One of the standing objections regularly voiced by physicians is that the offering of service as the result of compulsory insurance always very much increases the recorded amount of illness. Now it is quite extraordinary that this should be put forward as an objection, since obviously if it means anything it means that the system has at least done a part of what it set out to do, namely bringing to the physician a very large number of people who did not previously consult him because they could not pay for his services. Any system which stands any chance of improving medical service must at the outset enormously increase the apparent incidence of illness, although the increase is obviously apparent and not real. As an objection to compulsory insurance this cannot be regarded as a respectable argument.

On the face of it, it would seem as if the problem for the great middle group, previously referred to as 40 per cent, might be handled by the great existing life insurance companies as a simple insurance problem. In practice, however, this course has not been followed, apparently because the risk does not lend itself to calculation by actuarial methods and consequently the premiums are too high to be attractive. Some progress has been made in what is known as group insurance under which the old-line companies undertake to insure relatively large groups without the requirement of physical examination, the calculation being made on the average sickness rate. As far as the real problem is concerned, however, this has been a mere drop in the bucket. Furthermore I must confess to having grave doubts of the soundness of health insurance carried out for profit. I have an abiding conviction that this is not a proper field for private profit and that the money which accrues in the form of profit belongs in fact to those groups in the population for whom no such provision along the lines of group insurance can be made.

Other forms of voluntary insurance have had some trial and some success.

Insurance by medical groups. In various parts of the country physicians organized into a professional group, often referred to as a clinic, have undertaken to offer complete medical care to considerable groups of people on a prepayment basis. This is perhaps not properly classified as insurance, but under this method, with relatively large groups of patients paying from $22 to $26 or $27 per capita per year, it has been possible to provide very complete medical and surgical service. This seems a promising method but it has been violently attacked by the American Medical Association, and in some cases groups which were offering such service have been required to discontinue it on penalty of being barred from organized medicine. This seems to me distinctly unfortunate since I believe it a valuable method which ought to be encouraged and probably supervised by the medical profession.

Voluntary hospital insurance. Within the last three or four years considerable attempts have been made to insure against an unexpected necessity to find funds to pay large hospital bills. This is of course but one item in the cost of care, but in serious illness it is often a large one, sometimes amounting to more than 50 per cent of the total bill, and one against which it would seem possible to provide on some voluntary prepayment basis. In various parts of the country groups of hospitals, chiefly in the larger cities, have agreed to offer hospital care for reasonably limited periods upon the regular prepayment of moderate sums, generally between $10 and $15 per capita per year. This plan also has been opposed by the American Medical Association, apparently partly because the plan cannot be controlled by physicians and partly because it might tend to interfere with the payments due to physicians. In Great Britain the system has become extensively used as a method of supplementing the care provided under the Compulsory Insurance Act which provides only general practitioner service without laboratory, hospital, or specialist service. Although there are a good many difficult questions involved in working out such a system it would seem a desirable supplement to other methods.

Plans suggested by organized medicine. Particularly during the depression and probably as a result of it a great variety of plans have been made by medical organizations, chiefly on the basis of the county medical societies, whereby the services of interested members of the society are offered to the public on various prepayment plans. It is apparently too early to come to any conclusion in regard to the workings of such plans. They will obviously require time for development and will involve the working out of administrative machinery which is likely to be complicated. If they can be developed upon a sufficiently large scale and include a sufficient number of practitioners, both general and special, they may easily prove a valuable method of voluntary insurance.

There have also developed during the same period various plans by which county medical societies set up what might be called service bureaus to which prospective patients may apply, have their financial condition investigated, and enter into various agreements in regard to charge and deferred payments to make the financing of their illness less difficult. These service bureaus refer patients to a list of physicians who in turn may refer the patient to some charitable organization if he is largely without funds. This type of organization has been of service in increasing the income of physicians, but it is in fact largely a method of collecting fees and does not appear to have increased the amount of service actually offered.

At the outset the fact should be squarely faced that although it is possible at the present time to obtain in this country medical care which is certainly the equal and probably the superior of any service offered in the world, such service is in fact received by a relatively small part of the population. It is no use for us to prate of the excellent service which can be obtained. The fact of the matter is that it is not being obtained and under present methods progress is not being made. It is next important to realize that it is probably not possible to set up for the whole country any system which will work satisfactorily. The size of the country, the relative density of population, the relative income of the population in various states, variations in climate, variations in transportation, all make out of the question for us a single method such as is relatively practicable in small countries like Denmark. On the other hand we have something to learn from experience elsewhere. It has been found expedient and workable in Scotland under the provisions of the so-called "Highlands and Islands Act" to subsidize physicians in outlying or inaccessible communities so that they are guaranteed a reasonable income, part of which is paid by the state and part contributed by patients. It seems almost certain that for isolated communities for whom the proper support of physicians is financially impossible such practices may prove of value here.

It next seems obvious that for a large middle group of the population the distribution of costs of medical care over a term of years by some system of prepayment—often called insurance—is the practicable method. The difficulty arises in obtaining from this group contributions in sufficient numbers. The evidence tends to show that for them some modicum of compulsion will be necessary. Only in this way does it seem probable that sufficiently large sums could be collected to finance proper medical care. Since in the case of this group it will probably be wise to demand contributions from the employer, where there is one, this system will be most easily applicable to the industrial population. This will of course involve another tax on business, and if imposed will have to be adjusted in such a way as not to bear too heavily. Likewise the size of the contribution to be expected from the employee will be difficult to decide. Finally, it will require considerable study to determine the method of obtaining contributions from a large group of people, as for instance the farmer population where there is no employer and where the amount of cash income is relatively small. It will be easy to raise objections. It will be difficult to get agreement. And it will be difficult to decide upon the amounts that must be collected in order to do the job properly.

The next item should be the abandonment of the long-standing custom of expecting physicians to give their services free for the care of the indigent. Although very large amounts of money have been raised for public hospitals through taxes and for voluntary hospitals through charitable contributions, these have never included the sums necessary properly to compensate physicians for their services. Such compensation will require the actual raising of new money, and unless we are prepared to face the increased taxation here involved, there is, I believe, no large probability that the problem of satisfactory medical care will be solved.

Furthermore, whereas before the depression doctors were collecting a large proportion of their income from about 10 per cent of the population—those with an income of $5,000 or more—this source of income has been violently contracted and the medical profession is now trying to make a living out of a group that is smaller and perhaps permanently diminished. This has given rise to the declaration by the American Medical Association that there are too many physicians and that the number should be progressively decreased. This of course, if proceeded with, means that we abandon any idea of offering medical service to the whole population and concern ourselves only with maintaining the incomes of enough physicians to care for the reasonably well-to-do. This is a somewhat brutal method of stating the argument but it is substantially the fact. Now one obvious remedy for this situation is that the public shall make up their minds to pay physicians for their services to the indigent. This would at once importantly increase the income of physicians and might halt the growing demand that we curtail our, in my judgment, already insufficient supply of physicians.

Another very essential prerequisite to a solution will be a less conservative and obstructive attitude on the part of organized medicine. The fact of the matter is that during recent discussions they have become alarmed as to their future status. They have seen visions of what is called "state medicine" under which it is thought that all physicians will be employees of the state. They have seen visions of political control under which their services and their activities will be dictated by the whim of politicians. Now these are not mere ghosts but real dangers which, if they should be realized, would not only injure the physicians but injure everybody concerned, since they would inevitably curtail progress, blight initiative, and probably very much alter the desirable personal relation between physician and patient. If these things should happen our last case would be worse than our first. Driven by these fears organized medicine has too often been obstructive. Its members have adopted a "holier than thou" attitude, they have been intolerant, and even abusive, of the great philanthropic foundations which have made careful, expensive, and valuable studies of the problems at hand. They have adopted much the same attitude in regard to the large groups of social workers, whose contribution to the problem of health service has been very substantial. At times organized medicine has seemed to me to trade a good deal, and in fact more than was wise, upon the reputation which it has achieved and deserved in the past. It has not shown great wisdom or great ability in disciplining its own members. Its efforts to stem the tide of such iniquities as fee-splitting have been futile. It has frequently attempted to discipline its members by expulsion from the society, only to find that the courts are singularly unsympathetic and insist upon reinstatement or damages. Organized medicine has been very insistent upon the doctrine of "freedom of choice" under which the patient is to be guaranteed, under all conditions and under any suggested plans, entire freedom in the choice of his physician, but it overlooks the fact that this much-vaunted freedom of choice is almost a pure illusion. From an economic point of view it resembles nothing so much as the famous tea party in *Alice in Wonderland* which involved Alice, the Mad Hatter, and the March Hare. Freedom of choice involves not only an accurate knowledge on the part of the consumer—hereinafter called the patient—but a very considerable classification of the article to be bought —hereinafter known as medical service. At the present time a patient who is in search of a general medical counselor has no possible method of deciding where such a person may be found. It is notorious that physicians vary in their ability very much as do other people. It is notorious that the reputation of a physician is a very unsatisfactory measure of his knowledge, skill, and capacity. It is notorious that, in this country at least, physicians are licensed as general practitioners of medicine and surgery, and may hold themselves out—and frequently do—as having skill and abilities quite beyond their power to deliver the service. It thus appears to me that before organized medicine is on sound ground in insisting upon freedom of choice, it will be well-advised to set up some accurate guide under which the skill and capacity of physicians is set forth in such a way that the patient may exercise this freedom now offered with one hand and taken away with the other.

Again in many of the pronouncements of organized medicine in relation to various suggested plans for so-called compulsory insurance it has been insisted that physicians should have complete control of the whole performance. This appears to me to endow physicians not only with knowledge and skill in their own fields but with knowledge and skill in the fields of economics, finance, and sociology quite beyond that which they really possess. It seems to me doubtful whether much progress can be made until the medical profession is more willing than it has been in the past to attempt the working out of a solution, the end and object of which is to offer good medical service at all levels and in such a way as to maintain and enhance the progress and dignity of the profession.

It is my best judgment that this will involve very careful discussions among the representatives of three groups, all on an equal footing. Obviously the physicians must be represented, since they are in fact the qualified experts on all the medical questions involved. Next there must be the proper representatives of experts on financial and economic problems, for certainly the methods by which large sums of "new money" are to be come by cannot be satisfactorily settled by medical experts. Finally the largely forgotten man, the consumer, above referred to as the patient, is entitled to full representation. After all, he will appear in two aspects, in one of which he will suffer under the possible lack of skill of the medical experts, and in the other of which he will certainly suffer as to his pocketbook under the arrangements likely to prove possible and to be advised by the financial and economic experts. Obviously the poor old consumer, or patient, must have handsome representation.

Some at least of the difficulties which have so far proved insuperable might be overcome if we started out with the proposition that we turn over to the physicians the job of looking after everybody at every level and providing satisfactory care. The balance of the problem is financial and administrative. There is a group, although I fear a small one, about whom we need have no concern for they can pay their bills. For the next great group, which will probably include considerably more than half the population, some form of compulsory annual contribution seems to me essential. This should be fixed at an amount believed to be sufficient to pay for proper care. It should be collected and administered by the Government, using this word to cover local, state, or national fields. Finally, there is the group classified as indigent for whom payment must be made, and obviously in the long run under the auspices of either state or local governments. There might thus be created a condition under which the profession was responsible for the care of the sick, various commissions were responsible for the collection of prepaid amounts, and local governments were responsible for the collection of those funds necessary to care for the indigent. Physicians would render their bills in three ways: one, directly to the patient, where he was able to pay and not making payments to a commission; two, to a commission which might have the right to pass upon their reasonableness but would have to pay them; finally, to local government units for payment for the care of the indigent. Such a plan would have the advantage of putting the profession on their mettle, of making the community face the care of the indigent, and of requiring of the great middle group of the population that it take heed to the future.

LAYING THE GROUNDWORK

Preparation for Reading

1. Name several discoveries and inventions which have made medicine a more complicated and a more exact science than it was a hundred years ago. Why has medical service become more expensive?

2. How do you explain the fact that the great advance in medical knowledge has not been followed by the widespread utilization of that knowledge to prevent or cure illness? For example, we have learned the cause and cure of tuberculosis and syphilis; why do these diseases still take a terrible annual toll?

3. What changes, if any, in the system of securing medical aid and of paying for it do you think desirable?

4. See the short discussion of the medical profession by H. A. Overstreet in "A Long Train of Abuses," p. 197.

Vocabulary Building

1. What is the meaning of the combining form *chrono*? Explain its use in *chronic, chronicle, chronology,* and *chronometer.*

2. Explain how the following words differ in meaning: *opulent, rich, affluent, wealthy.* What is the noun form of each?

3. Find the derivation and the meaning of the word *auspice.* What is the meaning of the plural, and how do you suppose this meaning arose? What is the adjectival form and its meaning?

4. Look up these words: *indigent, actuarial, accrues, iniquities.*

APPRAISING THE RESULTS

1. This selection exemplifies the procedure of analyzing a problem and then drawing conclusions from the relationship of the parts. Note carefully the following: the central idea of each developing paragraph; the cues given in the transitions, particularly the two transitional paragraphs; the larger units into which the paragraphs can be grouped; and the conclusion reached in the final paragraph. Outline the selection.

2. What two related reasons does Dr. Cabot give for the accentuation of the problem of providing satisfactory medical aid for all?

3. Explain how these factors enter into the problem: the uneven distribution of income; the uneven distribution of need for medical attention; the number and kind of personnel (doctors, nurses, technicians) and of hospitals; the incomes of physicians; the depression.

4. How does compulsory health insurance operate? What objections can be raised to it? What are the arguments in its favor?

5. According to Dr. Cabot, what are the prerequisites to a solution of the problem of providing medical aid to all?

6. State and evaluate the conclusion reached by Dr. Cabot.

7. According to Dr. Cabot, what specific objections to various plans of insurance are raised by the American Medical Association? Explain why you accept or reject each objection.

8. In any discussion of changes in medical practice, certain questions often arise. How would you answer these, for example? (a) To what extent does the average patient have a personal relation to his doctor? (b) If the doctor had security of income, and consequent freedom from pressure, would his initiative in research be encouraged or weakened? (c) Which kind of research is more likely to produce results: that of an individual research worker or that of a group of workers? (d) What were some great medical discoveries which the profession and the public have been slow to accept? (e) What evidence is there that governmental agencies have contributed to medical progress and not interfered with it?

SELECTING THE THEME SUBJECT

1. Write a paper showing how "the application of scientific method to the diagnosis and treatment of disease" has affected the quality and cost of medical care for some human ill.

2. Write a paper based on investigation of medical facilities in your community. Consider such points as the number and kind of hospitals, public health work, and children's clinics.

3. Explain *objectively* how socialized medicine operates: the part of the doctor, of the patient, and of the state, as they enter into training, diagnosis, treatment, costs, research; or prepare an *argument* in favor of, or in opposition to, socialized medicine.

4. Develop one of the following topics: The High Cost of the Common Cold; Medical Practice in Grandfather's Day; The Campaign Against Syphilis; Medical Aid in Rural America;

Radio Advertising and Nostrums; Athletics and Health; Diet
Fads; The Chemist's Part in Medicine; The Doctor in Litera-
ture; The Nurse in Fiction; Women in the Medical Profes-
sion; How to Treat a Cold; Nature's Part in the Fight
Against Disease; The Nurse: An Unappreciated Factor in
Medical Care; The Uses of X-Ray; Medicine in Soviet Russia;
The Patient Looks at the Doctor.

HOW HEALTHY ARE WE?[1]

Mary Ross

ABOUT TWENTY YEARS AGO THE UNITED STATES LEARNED WITH
A START THAT LARGE NUMBERS OF ITS YOUNG MEN WERE NOT
physically fit to go to war. This year, as a by-product of
another kind of warfare—the campaign against hard times—
the nation will be for the first time in a position to see clearly
how large a share of its people are handicapped or wholly
incapacitated for the pursuits of peace.

For more than a year, minds and machines have been at
work classifying and adding up the facts on cards that record
a year's health history of some 865,000 families. Those cards,
in turn, represent months of field work, which at its peak
took 5000 persons. These enumerators trudged from door to
door in 92 cities in 19 states, and in 23 rural counties. In
the middle-sized and smaller places—cities and towns of
100,000 and less—the instructions were to visit *every* family.
In the larger, a given fraction of arbitrary units of census
enumeration districts was taken by rote, every third or fourth
or ninth on the list, or whatever proportion was required to
give a minimum sample of 5000 families; within each unit
every family was visited. The counties and towns and cities
themselves had been carefully picked as representative of
different parts of the country, so that the whole would give
a true sample of modern life in the United States. The
families surveyed entered into the spirit of the undertaking;
less than one percent refused to answer the questions on the
schedule.

The vast National Health Inventory of which this study

[1] From *Survey Graphic*, July, 1937. Reprinted by permission of the author
and of *Survey Graphic*.

is a part has been financed from emergency relief funds. It is sponsored and supervised by the United States Public Health Service, under the direction of George St. J. Perrott, principal statistician. Much credit for the successful outcome of the project is due to Josephine Roche, Assistant Secretary of the Treasury in charge of the Public Health Service, who recognized the value of the undertaking from the beginning and gave it her wholehearted interest and support.

Both in the field work and in the later coding and tabulating, 90 percent of the personnel have been taken from the relief rolls. When able "white-collar" people were in desperate need of work, it was possible to gather a staff of a calibre that could not have been had for this work in ordinary times; in some places, a majority of the field workers were college graduates. If there is a silver lining to depression, one of its brightest spots is in stories such as this, in which the investment of public funds, badly needed by self-respecting men and women, has brought in return a wealth of badly needed information. Even disregarding the fact that those who did practically all of the work would have had to have help in some way in any case, the $3,450,000 allotted for the inventory promises to be a gilt-edged investment.

The eye of a first class researcher will glisten merely at the thought of knowing accurately something which has not been known before. When the tabulations and analyses are completed, the various parts of the Health Inventory will give facts about a substantial slice of the American people that have not been analyzed comprehensively in their interrelationships; facts as to income, housing, employment, occupation and relief, and the bearing of these upon birth and death, health and sickness. It is beside the mark, however, to conclude that an adventure such as this is an excursion into statistics for sweet statistics' sake. The rows of figures which are beginning to emerge from the tabulating machines will be a delight to the technician who rejoices in seeing important work well done, but they also present a ledger of direct interest to the man on the street. They will show, in broad outline, ways in which sickness drains the public purse, and in consequence, the pocket of the private tax-

payer—not to mention the pockets of those who themselves
are sick. They will indicate points at which something can
be done to stop the waste.

The National Health Inventory is divided into four major
parts: surveys of chronic sickness, of communicable disease,
of occupational sickness and deaths, and of health facilities,
this last including hospitals and their outpatient departments
and public and private health agencies. Each of the four parts
includes a range of analysis that has not previously been
attempted on this scale. In addition to alleviation for the
taxpayers, the facts will strengthen the arms of physicians,
health officers, city administrators, social workers, and other
well-disposed citizens. It is to be hoped that the record here
disclosed for the first time on so comprehensive a scale, may
prove a kind of high water mark below which can be measured future success in controlling disease and disability and
their aftermath, poverty and premature death.

Possibly in no field will there be demonstrated greater
rewards for effort than in those shown in the most comprehensive part of the inventory—the field of chronic sickness.
The relative amount of chronic sickness in this country is,
curiously enough, a mark of the progress in public health
and medical science of recent decades. In the Massachusetts
of 1880 and 1900, for example, a group of major chronic
diseases was responsible for about one death in three; in
1930, these same diseases accounted for two deaths in three
in that state.

The explanation is not that Americans are becoming
feebler, but that many of the acute, quickly-killing illnesses
have been brought under control or almost wholly abolished,
important among them diseases of infancy and childhood. A
far larger share of each generation's crop of babies and youngsters live to pass through childhood and youth and to reach
the years when bodies wear out and break down slowly,
sometimes by the inevitable processes of aging, but often by
reason of causes which might have been avoided or post-
poned. Chronic impairment becomes common in middle life
and after. In a series of surveys made in 1929-1931 by the
Massachusetts State Department of Health, it was found

that 29 percent of all persons aged forty and more were suffering from chronic disease. With the rapid drop in recent decades in both birthrates and deathrates, an increasing share of the population has moved into the area of age in which chronic illness or impairment becomes a major risk to health and earning.

It will be some months before findings have been compiled for all the 865,000 families in the Health Inventory's study of chronic sickness so as to permit general conclusions on this evidence. The Public Health Service, however, has recently released findings for one unnamed city, a first report in the series which will outline, section by section, the findings for the various parts of the inventory. This report gives the story of chronic sickness in a northern industrial city which had a population of some 150,000 at the time of the 1930 census. (For the report in detail, see "Chronic Diseases and Gross Impairments in a Northern Industrial Community," by George St. J. Perrott and Dorothy F. Holland, *Journal of the American Medical Association,* May 29, 1937.) While the facts must be marshalled for all the ninety-odd cities before one can say safely what is "typical," perhaps this first city to be reported may be looked on for the time being as a kind of medical Middletown.

Between November 1935, and February 1936, the enumerators visited approximately one in nine of the families in that city, talked with a responsible member, and filled out the schedule for all in the household, getting in all a year's health history for some 18,000 persons. By occupation, most of the workers were skilled or semi-skilled. On the day of the canvass, 71 percent of the family heads were employed; 14 percent were unemployed or were receiving work relief; 11 percent were housewives, and 4 percent were retired. At some time during the survey year, 15 percent of the families had been on relief. Nearly half (45 percent) of the families reported an annual income of $1000 or less; only 5 percent had an income over $3000.

For the purposes of the survey, disease or impairment was defined as chronic when its symptoms had been recognized for at least three months; the condition might or might not be disabling. In the surveyed 18,000 as a whole—old and young, poor, comfortable, and well-to-do—more than one person in five was reported to have a chronic disease, a permanent physical impairment, or a serious defect of sight or hearing. In other words, in this segment of a middle-sized northern city, more than one in five, old and young, was hampered in work, play, or schooling by some gross physical impairment or long standing malfunctioning of his physical organism. A condition was considered disabling when it kept a person from going about his or her usual activities, as a pupil, housewife or worker. On the day of the canvass about two persons out of a hundred were disabled by chronic sickness or impairment. One out of 100 of the whole group had been so disabled continuously throughout the previous year.

For a city or a country, it is important to know not only how much chronic sickness there is, but whose it is. This preliminary report shows two ways of tracing it in the surveyed city.

The more cheerful approach is to look at it in terms of age. Unfortunately chronic physical handicaps exist even among children and young people, but the greatest frequency is in old age, when heaviest responsibilities are—or should be—past. While of the whole group, 22 percent were found to have a chronic disease or gross impairment, the figure for successive age groups rose like a ladder: under fifteen years, 8 percent; ages fifteen to twenty-four, 10 percent; twenty-five to forty-four, 24 percent; forty-five to sixty-four, 36 percent; sixty-five and over, 58 percent. Disability from chronic sickness followed a similar course. Among youngsters of fifteen to twenty-four, for example, the annual rate of disabling chronic sickness was 19 per 1000 persons. In the active middle years, twenty-five to forty-four, the rate rose to 39; by ages forty-five to sixty-four, to 64; and among persons sixty-five and over, it rose to 146. When those figures are translated into graphs showing ages more clearly, one can see a sharp upturn in the fifties and after, both in cases of chronic sickness and in disability from chronic causes. Even in the younger ages, however—in what is hopefully called the prime of life—a substantial share of the surveyed persons in this city knew the burden of chronic physical handicap.

Like the aged, the poor also suffered an undue burden of chronic sickness. The rate of chronic disabling sickness among relief families was 70 percent higher than that of the whole group of families. When certain major chronic diseases were considered, the disadvantage of these poor was even more marked. Their rate of disabling illness from these serious causes was nearly twice that found among non-relief families with incomes under $1000, and more than twice that of families who had $1000 or more. Thus, while the relief families suffered more disability from all forms of chronic illness, their disadvantage was greatest in the more severe and prolonged kinds. About one in ten of the heads of families who were out of work on the day their households were canvassed was unemployed because of disability.

Among these 18,000 persons, during the survey year chronic sickness was responsible for two thirds of all the days of sicknesses disabling for seven days or more, for four fifths of all the days of hospital care, and nearly three fifths of all the deaths. Chronic cases absorbed half of all the services of physicians, and almost three fourths of the time spent in bedside nursing. Chronic sickness, especially in its severe forms, was more prevalent among the persons least able to lose wages or support care. Among unemployed men aged twenty-five to sixty-four, the rate of chronic disabling illness was five times that reported for employed men of the same ages.

The partnership of sickness and poverty has been clear in several earlier surveys. In a notable series of studies on Health and Depression, the United States Public Health Service and the Milbank Memorial Fund had shown earlier the disproportionate extent to which disabling sickness weighed down families with low incomes and families on relief, especially those who had dropped from relative comfort to poverty during the depression. An earlier study made by Jessamine Whitney, statistician of the National Tuberculosis Association, had shown a relationship between death and economic status. Analyzing all the death certificates filed in ten states in 1930 for gainfully occupied boys and men aged fifteen to sixty-five, that study found that the deathrate among unskilled laborers was nearly 90 percent higher than that of the most fortunate social and economic group, professional men. The marked difference between the various occupational classes in the chance for life was true at all ages, even for the boys of fifteen to twenty-four. It was true for nearly all of the important causes of death, including those, such as heart disease, tuberculosis and nephritis, in which death usually is preceded by a long period of more or less incapacitating illness.

In commenting on this study Rollo H. Britten, senior statistician of the United States Public Health Service, pointed out another disturbing fact: that the spread between the deathrates of the most fortunate and the least fortunate occupational groups was 40 percent greater in this country than that shown by similar figures in England. Differences in this country in race and nationality did not serve, in Mr. Britten's opinion, to explain the degree of difference between the American record and the British; factors such as economic status, occupations, and standards of living in this country, he suggested, must be of great importance.

In the light of those figures and of the studies of sickness among the families who suffered the most severe financial reverses during the depression, it seems reasonable to infer that the imbalances and shifts of fortune in the United States have exacted a heavy toll among those who bear the brunt of financial uncertainty and meagerness and change. It makes little difference in effect either to such families themselves or to their communities whether poverty causes sickness or vice versa: the end result is the same, misery and dependency. From the story that is beginning to develop out of the Health Inventory, a comprehensive chapter will be written on what statisticians call noncommittally the association between sickness and insecurity.

The question of that linkage is especially pertinent in 1937. Together, the federal government and the states have shouldered the task of offsetting some of the risks which overhang many or all of the people in childhood, in old age, and in unemployment. In the costs of that social security program, as in the costs of relief and of medical and hospital care, are twined inextricably the financial burdens of sicknesses which have taken savings and prevented earnings. The study of the northern city suggests that among the millions who are without jobs at this time, there are many who can get about to look for work but will not be able to find jobs or to hold them because chronic sickness robs them of their full capacity; that among the dependent aged and dependent children are many whose dependency is the aftermath of their own or their families' disabilities.

In two aspects of chronic sickness the United States has, in general, a considerable and honorable history. These are tuberculosis and mental illness. It is noteworthy that in this surveyed city, cases of chronic sickness of these types were found to be severely disabling but relatively few in number. Even with chance for care, during the survey year the average case of tuberculosis caused more than eight months' disability; nervous diseases caused an average of more than six months' during that year. It is not hard to understand why, in practice, it has been widely accepted that organized effort, public and private, is needed in these fields both for care and prevention. For residents of this particular city both clinics and hospitals were at hand for the care of tuberculosis and mental illness, provided almost wholly by state or local government. Those ailments, however, are only two out of many causes of chronic disablement.

Among the other serious diseases which the survey disclosed were heart and kidney diseases, cancer, diabetes, gastric ulcer, chronic diseases of the gall bladder and rheumatism. A study like the present, made initially by a house-to-house canvass, is not likely to show the part played by syphilis in chronic sickness. That "great imitator" undoubtedly appeared in this list in terms of its results, as heart disease, for example, or nervous ailments.

Fortunately syphilis is coming to be recognized as a field in which public safety demands community action. In some bright spots on the national map, public and private pro-

grams have been undertaken to prevent or alleviate or cure
one or another of the other causes of disability on this formidable list. Acute rheumatic fever, like syphilis, is linked
with needless heart disease; here some communities are
carrying further the job of preventing heart disease already
attacked by health departments generally in their programs
to control communicable diseases of childhood. Programs
for the care of crippled children, now promoted widely under
the social security act, are working in other instances to off-
set the ravages of disease and accident.

In general, however, the slowly killing chronic ailments,
aside from tuberculosis and mental illness, have not been
accepted as an integral part of city or even state public health
programs. The first recognition of public health came in
terms of ailments which obviously menaced the health and
safety of others. Now with the upward shift in age and the
relatively greater part played by chronic ailments, communities may recognize as public enemies not only the bacilli
which cause typhoid and tuberculosis, but also the wider
range of "germs" which spread poverty.

Like cities and states throughout the country, the surveyed
city had no coordinated program of chronic disease control
to combat the whole series of ailments that were so costly
to the community and to individual families. An unusually
effective clinic for medical relief had been organized during
the depression. Probably the poor had more adequate medical care in that emergency period than would prevail under
a system of welfare administration in ordinary times. Even
so, the average case of chronic sickness among relief families
had less care by a physician than was received by cases in
families who were not on relief. To some extent that disparity
was offset—at public expense—by the greater amount of hospital care received by the poor. In fact, the amount of hospital
care they received in chronic illness suggested the need of
central supervision to ensure that only cases which require
hospital care be sent to hospitals and to arrange for others
home care which could be given as effectively and at less
expense.

Fundamentally, however, control of chronic sickness implies community action which cannot limit itself to unrelated efforts to provide care for persons once they are sick. Care is only part of a whole and toward that whole cities generally have exhibited chiefly inertia, doubtless because they have not recognized either its nature, importance or magnitude. The authors of the report, Mr. Perrott, supervisor of the Health Inventory, and Dorothy F. Holland, associate statistician, sketch in outline what a program to control chronic disease might be: in the field of medicine, continued research as to the causes of chronic diseases and the methods of treatment; in the field of public health, prevention of the acute diseases which predispose to chronic ailments, community education to promote early diagnosis, and provision of adequate facilities for the care of chronic sickness in low income groups.

From such a program the surveyed city, and doubtless other cities throughout the length and breadth of the land, stands to gain ground against the forms of illness and impairment which, as a group, were found to account for the majority of deaths, for the greater part of the time lost from disability, and the major share of medical and hospital services. By reason of the vicious circle linking chronic sickness and poverty, progress in preventing or alleviating or curing such illness stands to save not only individual suffering and frustration but also large costs necessarily paid by the public for medical care of the poor and for relief of families whose breadwinners lack the health needed to keep their footing in the labor market. Until further facts are brought to light, one must guess to what extent the "unemployed" are actually the chronic sick. The evidence of this study strongly suggests, however, that here may lie a potent explanation of the plight of many who have not regained a place in paid work even in a time of rising business activity.

Some states, notably Massachusetts, and some cities, among them New York, already have made a start. The outcome of the Health Inventory should turn public and professional attention to this hitherto unmapped province of ill health.

It is not a remote country, but one which is actually or potentially related to the life of every family. Considered in the past almost wholly in terms of personal misfortune, chronic sickness now has a clear claim on professional leadership and public policy. To quote the report: "Its social consequences masked in the larger problems of unemployment and dependency among young and old, chronic disease presses upon the scene today as an essential although undeveloped aspect of the broader program of social security."

LAYING THE GROUNDWORK

Preparation for Reading

1. Are there people in your community who cannot afford medical aid? Is any provision made for them by charity or by some governmental agency? Do they go without medical aid? Or does the doctor bear the burden?
2. Do people of the middle-income group have any difficulty in meeting the costs of medical care?
3. In what sense is it true that a major operation is a major catastrophe for the average family?
4. If you were commissioned to make a health inventory of the United States or of your community, how would you organize the work, and what kind of information would you consider important?
5. Why do you suppose the relative amount of illness increases rapidly as income declines?

Vocabulary Building

1. Look up these words: *incapacitated, arbitrary, calibre* (mental), *chronic, alleviation, nephritis, inextricably, disparity, inertia.*
2. Explain in their context: "by rote," "gilt-edged investment," "a kind of medical Middletown."
3. What is the singular form of *bacilli*? of *bacteria*? What is the difference between bacilli, bacteria, viruses, germs?
4. Explain the difference between the following types of diseases: infectious, contagious, occupational, industrial, organic, and functional.

APPRAISING THE RESULTS

1. What is the purpose of the preliminary discussion (paragraphs 1-5), which precedes the discussion of the actual health inventory?
2. How and why does Miss Ross limit her subject?
3. Explain the increase in the relative amount of chronic illness during the period of rapidly increasing medical knowledge.
4. In terms of age and of income, what general trend in chronic illness was revealed by the study?
5. What two aspects of chronic illness have had "a considerable and honorable history" in this country? Tell what you know of the treatment of these two chronic illnesses in your community.
6. What are some of the chronic illnesses which we have not yet systematically attacked?
7. Do you think it would be possible, and advisable, for the government (local, state, and national) to take the lead in directing and financing a correlated program of health work?
8. How do the following measures aid in the fight against ill health: the minimum wage laws, child labor laws, maximum hours laws, health regulations in industry?

SELECTING THE THEME SUBJECT

1. Discuss the nature of some chronic illness and show how the campaign against it is progressing.
2. Survey the method of combating tuberculosis or mental illness in your community, and decide whether the method is satisfactory.
3. Develop one of these titles: Sanitation and Health; The Work of the Visiting Nurse; Occupational Diseases; Paul de Kruif's Contribution to an Understanding of Our Medical Problem; How Sickness Drains the Public Purse; Children's Clinics; The Profession of Nursing in Fact and Fiction; How My University Conducts Its Medical Service; Tuberculosis and Economics; Radio and Health Education; Aid for the Physically Handicapped; Relief Families and Health; Shacktowns and Health; Health and Decent Housing.

Women Are People

AMERICA'S MEDIEVAL WOMEN[1]

Pearl S. Buck

I AM AN AMERICAN WOMAN BUT I HAD NO OPPORTUNITY UNTIL
A FEW YEARS AGO TO KNOW WOMEN IN AMERICA. LIVING AS I DID
in China, it is true that I saw a few American women; but that
is not the same thing. One was still not able to draw many
conclusions from them about American women. I gathered,
however, that they felt that girls in China had a hard time
of it, because there every family liked sons better than daughters, and, in the average family, did not give them the same
education or treatment. In America, however, they said
people welcomed sons and daughters equally and treated them
the same. This, after years in a country which defines a
woman's limitations very clearly, seemed nothing short of
heaven—if true.

When I came to America to live therefore I was interested
particularly in her women. And during these immediate
past years I have come to know a good many of them—women
in business, artists, housewives in city and country, women
young and old. I have taken pains to know them. More than
that, I have made my own place as a woman in America. And
I find that what I anticipated before I came here is quite
wrong. It seems to me that women are very badly treated in
America. A few of them know it, more of them dimly suspect
it, and most of them, though they know they ought to be glad
they live in a Christian country where women are given an
education, do not feel as happy in their lonely hearts as
they wish they did. The reason for this unhappiness is a
secret sense of failure, and this sense of failure comes from

[1] From *Harper's Magazine*, August, 1938. Reprinted by permission of the
author and of the publishers.

a feeling of inferiority, and the feeling of inferiority comes from a realization that actually women are not much respected in America.

I know quite well that any American man hearing this will laugh his usual tolerant laughter, though tolerant laughter is the cruelest form of contempt. He always laughs tolerantly when the subject of women is broached, for that is the attitude in which he has been bred. And immaturely, he judges the whole world of women by the only woman he knows at all—his wife. Nor does he want the sort of wife at whom he cannot laugh tolerantly. I was once amazed to see a certain American man, intelligent, learned, and cultivated, prepare to marry for his second wife a woman as silly and unfit for him as the first one had been, whom he had just divorced. I had to exclaim before it was too late, "Why do you do the same thing over again? She's merely younger and prettier than the other one—that's all. And even those differences are only temporary." To which he growled, "I do not want a damned intelligent woman in the house when I come home at night. I want my mind to rest."

What he did not see of course—though he found it out later—was that there could be no rest for him of any kind. He was irritated by a thousand stupidities and follies and beaten in the end by his own cowardice. He died a score of years too soon, exhausted not by work but by nervous worry. His two wives go hardily on, headed for a hundred, since he left them what is called "well provided for." Neither of them has ever done an honest day's work in her life, and he literally sacrificed his valuable life to keep them alive.

And yet, going home that day from his funeral and wondering how it could have been helped, I knew it could not have been helped. He was doomed to the unhappiness, or at least to the mediocre happiness, with which many if not most American men must be satisfied in their relationships with their women. For if he had been married to an intelligent superior woman he would have been yet more unhappy, since, with all his brilliance as a scientist, he belonged to that vast majority of American men who still repeat to-day the cry of traditional male pride, "I don't want *my* wife to work."

That is, he wanted a woman who would contain herself docilely within four walls. And he could not have seen that an intelligent, energetic, educated woman cannot be kept in four walls—even satin-lined, diamond-studded walls—without discovering sooner or later that they are still a prison cell. No home offers scope enough to-day for the trained energies of an intelligent modern woman. Even children are not enough. She may want them, need them and have them, love them and enjoy them, but they are not enough for her, even during the short time they preoccupy her. Nor is her husband, however dear and congenial, enough for her. He may supply all her needs for human companionship, but there is still more to life than that. There is the individual life. She must feel herself growing and becoming more and more complete as an individual, as well as a wife and mother, before she can even be a good wife and mother. I heard a smug little gray-haired woman say last week, "No, I don't know anything about politics. It takes all my time to be a good wife and mother. I haven't time to keep up with other things." Unfortunately, her husband, successful doctor that he is, has time to keep up not only with his business and with being what she calls a "wonderful husband and father," but with another woman as well. But that too is one of the things she knows nothing about. . . . Yet who can blame him? He is clever and full of interest in many things, and his wife is dulled with years of living in the four walls he put around her. It is a little unfair that he so encouraged her to stay in the walls that she came to believe in them completely as her place.

But tradition is very strong in this backward country of ours. We Americans are a backward nation in everything except in the making and using of machines. And we are nowhere more backward than we are in our attitude toward our women. We still, morally, shut the door of her home on a woman. We say to her, "Your home ought to be enough for you if you are a nice woman. Your husband ought to be enough—and your children." If she says, "But they aren't enough—what shall I do?" we say, "Go and have a good time, that's a nice girl. Get yourself a new hat or something, or go to the matinée or join a bridge club. Don't worry your pretty head about what is not your business."

If she persists in being interested in things beyond her home we insist that she must be neglecting her home. If she still persists and makes a success through incredible dogged persistence we laugh at her. We even sneer at her and sometimes we treat her with unbelievable rudeness. I do not know the Secretary of Labor in our government, but I have seen her. She looks a quiet, serious, unassuming woman. I have taken pains to inquire of people who know, and it seems her home is not neglected. She has done at least as good a job in Washington as a number of men there in leading positions. But the slurs that have been cast upon her, the rudeness of private and public talk, the injustices that have been done her merely because she is a woman in a place heretofore occupied by a man, have been amazing to a person unaccustomed to the American attitude toward women. It seems nothing short of barbarous.

And yet, vicious circle that it is, I cannot blame Americans for distrusting the ability of their women. For if the intelligent woman obeys the voice of tradition and limits herself to the traditional four walls she joins the vast ranks of the nervous, restless, average American women whose whimsies torture their families, who spoil the good name of all women because they are often flighty, unreliable, without good judgment in affairs, and given to self-pity. In short, she becomes a neurotic, if not all the time, a good deal of the time. Without knowing it or meaning it she falls too often to being a petty dictator in the home, a nag to her husband and children, and a gossip among her women friends. Too often too she takes no interest in any matters of social importance and refuses all responsibility in the community which she can avoid. She may be either a gadabout and extravagant or she may turn into a recluse and pride herself on being a "home woman." Neither of these escapes deceives the discerning. When will American men learn that they cannot expect happiness with a wife who is not her whole self? A restless unfulfilled woman is not going to be a satisfied wife or satisfactory lover. It is not that "women are like that." Anyone

would be "like that" if he were put into such circumstances
—that is, trained and developed for opportunity later denied.

"Plenty of men like that too nowadays," someone may
murmur.

Yes, but the times have done it, and not tradition. There
is a difference. And one man has as good a chance as another
to win or lose, even in hard times. But no woman has a man's
chance in hard times, or in any times.

II

I am not so naïve, however, as to believe that one sex is
responsible for this unfortunate plight of the American
woman. I am not a feminist, but I am an individualist. I do
not believe that there is any important difference between
men and women—certainly not as much as there may be between one woman and another or one man and another.
There are plenty of women—and men, for that matter—who
would be completely fulfilled in being allowed to be as lazy
as possible. If someone will ensconce them in a pleasant home
and pay their bills they ask no more of life. It is quite all
right for these men and women to live thus so long as fools
can be found who will pay so much for nothing much in
return. Gigolos, male and female, are to be found in every
class and in the best of homes. But when a man does not
want to be a gigolo he has the freedom to go out and work
and create as well as he can. But a woman has not. Even if
her individual husband lets her, tradition in society is
against her.

For another thing we Americans cannot seem to believe
or understand is that women—some women, any woman, or
as I believe, most women—are able to be good wives, ardent
lovers, excellent mothers, and yet be themselves too. This
seems strange, for as a nation we have fitted woman to be
an individual as well as a woman by giving her a physical
and mental education and a training superior to that of
women in any other nation. But when she comes eagerly to
life, ready to contribute her share, not only to home, but to
government, sciences, and arts, we raise the old sickening

cry of tradition, "This isn't your business! Woman's place
is in the home—" and we shut the door in her face.

I am aware that at this point American men will be swear-
ing and shouting, "You don't know what you're talking about!
Why, we give our women more than any women on earth
have!" With that I perfectly agree. American women are
the most privileged in the world. They have all the privileges
—far too many. They have so many privileges that a good
many of them are utterly spoiled. They have privileges but
they have no equality. "Nobody keeps them back," the
American man declares. Ah, nobody, but everybody! For
they are kept back by tradition expressed through the prejudices not only of men but of stupid, unthinking, tradition-
bound women. Here is what I heard a few days ago.

A young woman wanted a new book to read and her father
offered to send it to her. "What do you want?" he asked.

"Anything, only not one by a woman," she said carelessly.
"I have a prejudice against books written by women."

Ignoring the rudeness, I asked, "Why?"

"Oh, I dislike women," she said. What she really meant
was she despised women so much that she actually disliked
women who did anything beyond the traditional jobs that
the average women do. There are thousands of women who
uphold medieval tradition in America more heartily than do
men—just as in China it is the ignorant tradition-bound
women who have clung to foot binding for themselves and
their daughters. . . . No, women have many enemies among
women. It goes back of course to the old jealous sense of
general female inferiority. Tradition, if it binds one, should
bind all, they feel.

Sometimes, I confess, I do not see how American men can
endure some of their women—their imperiousness, their
peevishness, their headstrongness, their utter selfishness, their
smallness of mind and outlook, their lack of any sense of
responsibility toward society, even to be pleasant. And their
laziness—look at the motion-picture houses, the theaters, the
lecture halls—crowded all day with women! The average
house, even with no servant, can be no full-time job or they
wouldn't be there in such hordes—they couldn't be there.

But children go to school as soon as they stop being babies, and electricity cleans and washes the house and clothing, and husbands are away all day. So what is there for the restless woman to do? She goes to the show—and comes home, if she has any sense, to wonder what life is for, and to think that marriage isn't so much after all, though if she hadn't been married she would have been ashamed of herself. For tradition is there too, and it would have made her seem, if unmarried, unsuccessful as a female.

"But what are we going to do?" the harassed American man cries. "There aren't enough jobs now to go round. And women are getting into industries more and more."

This is nonsense and a masculine bugaboo, though merely getting a job is not what I mean. The truth is the number of women in industries is increasing at so slow a rate that it is shocking when one considers how long they have had an equal chance with men for education and training. In the past fifty years—that is, half a century, during which education for women has enormously increased—the percentage of women in industry and the professions has increased from fourteen per cent only to twenty-two per cent. That means millions of women have been made ready for work they either had no chance to do or never wanted to do.

As to what men are going to do with women, I do not pretend to know. But I know I have never seen in any country—and I have seen most of the countries of the world—such unsatisfactory personal relationships between men and women as are in America—no, not even in Japan, where women as a class are depressed. For the Japanese are wiser in their treatment of women than we Americans are. They keep them down from the beginning so that they never hope for or expect more than life is to give them. They are not restless or neurotic or despotic, nor are they spoiled children. They have not been trained for equality and they do not expect it. They know they are upper servants, and they fulfill their duties gracefully and ably, and are happier on the whole than women in America. To know what one can have and to do with it, being prepared for no more, is the basis of equilibrium.

III

No, what is wrong in America is this matter of educating women. Life for the American woman is still controlled by old traditions. Men think of women, if at all, in the old simple traditional ways. Then women ought to be prepared for this sort of life and shaped through childhood and girlhood for what is to come. The root of the discontent in American women is that they are too well educated. What is the use of it? They do not need college educations nor even high school educations. What they ought to have is a simple course in reading, writing, and arithmetic—and advanced courses in cosmetics, bridge, sports, how to conduct a club meeting grace-fully, how to be an attractive hostess, with or without servants, and how to deal with very young children in the home. This last course, obviously, should be purely optional.

But all this higher present education is unfortunate. It has led American women into having ideas which they can never realize when they come to maturity. A college educa-tion may, for instance, persuade a girl to become interested in biology, which may lead her into wanting to become a doctor. And yet she will never have the chance to become a first-rate doctor, however gifted she is by birth. People will not allow it—not only men, but women will not allow it. They will look at her tentative little shingle and shrug their shoul-ders and say, "I don't feel I'd *trust* a woman doctor as I would a man." So after a while, since she has to earn something, she takes her shingle down and accepts a secondary position in a hospital or a school or goes into baby-clinic work, supple-mented by magazine articles on child care—or she just mar-ries a doctor. But inside herself she knows she still wants to *be* a doctor, only she cannot. Tradition does not allow it.

Or a college education may lead a girl into wanting to be a banker. It is natural for women to be interested in finance since they own about seventy per cent of America's money. But it is unfortunate if a woman thinks she can be a real banker. I have talked with a good many women who work in our American banking system. Not one is where she hoped to be when she began, and a fair percentage are not where they should be with their high executive ability, or where they would be if they were men. As one of the most brilliant of them said to me bitterly, "I know if I were a man I should now, at the age of fifty, and after thirty years of experience, be a bank president. But I'll never be anything but an assistant to a vice-president. I reached the top—for a woman—years ago. I'll never be allowed to go on."

"Why can't you?" I inquired, being then too innocent.

"They say no one would want to put money in a bank run by a woman," she said.

I pondered this. I had then just come from Shanghai, where one of the best modern banks was run and controlled entirely by modern Chinese women. It was a prosperous bank because most people there thought women were probably more honest than men and more practical in the handling of money. So the Chinese women bankers did very well.

A good deal is said too about the profession of teaching for women. There are a great many women teachers in America—many more in proportion to men than in other countries. Men here, it seems, allow women to teach in lower schools because they themselves do not want to teach in anything less than a college. And even the best men do not like to teach in women's colleges nor in co-educational colleges. The finest teaching in America, I am told, is done by men for men.

As for the arts, I know very well that the odds are strongly against the woman. Granted an equally good product, the man is given the favor always. Women artists in any field are not often taken seriously, however serious they work. It is true that they often achieve high popular success. But this counts against them as artists. American men critics may show respect to a foreign woman artist, feeling that perhaps the foreign women are better than their own. But they cannot believe that the fools they see in department stores, in the subways and buses, or running to the movies and lectures, or even in their own homes, can amount to anything in the arts. Indeed they cannot think of a woman at all, but only of "women." And the pathetic efforts of American women to improve their minds by reading and clubs have

only heightened the ridicule and contempt in which their
men hold them. To educate women, therefore, to think, so
that they need the personal fulfillment of activity and participation in all parts of life is acute cruelty, for they are not
allowed this fulfillment. They should be educated not to
think beyond the demands of simple household affairs or
beyond the small arts and graces of pleasing men who seem
always to want mental rest. The present method is not only
cruel; it is extremely wasteful. Good money is spent teaching
women to do things for which there will be no need. Men
strain themselves to furnish educations for their daughters
which they would be happier without, and not only happier
but better women because they would be more contented
women.

It is not only wasteful but dangerous. To educate women
as we do for our present state of traditionalism is to put new
wine into old bottles. A good deal of ferment is going on.
And if we keep this up more will come of it. No one knows
the effect upon children, for instance, of so many discontented women as mothers. Amiable, ignorant, bovine women
make much better mothers than neurotic college graduates.
And a woman does not need to complain aloud to let her
children know she is unhappy. The atmosphere about her is
gray with her secret discontent and children live deprived of
that essential gayety in which they thrive as in sunshine. So
few American women are really gay. This must have an effect.

IV

So, though I am impressed with the fact that American
women do not, as a group, seem happy, privileged as they
are, I am not surprised. I know that happiness comes to an
individual only as a result of personal fulfillment through
complete functioning of all the energies and capabilities
with which one is born. I do not for a moment mean that all
women must go out and find jobs and "do something" outside the home. That would be as silly and general a mistake
as our present general clinging to a tradition. I simply mean
let us be realistic. Let us face the fact that as a nation we are
in a medieval state of mind about the place of women in

society. Let each man ask himself—he need not answer aloud—where he really wants his woman. The majority, if they are honest, must acknowledge that they would like contented adoring women who want no more than their homes. I do not quarrel with that. What is, is. All I say is, let us realize facts. Tradition rules the relation of the sexes in America. Women are not welcome outside the home except in subsidiary positions, doing, on the whole, things men do not want to do. The great injustice to women is in not recognizing this frankly and in not preparing them for it.

Of course there is the chimeralike possibility that we might change tradition. But I do not see anyone capable of changing it. Men certainly will not. They do not even want to talk about it. They do not want the woman question stirred up, having as they say, "enough on their hands already." To them, of course, women "stirred up" simply means nervous, illogical, clamoring children who must be placated in one way or another. They cannot conceive of woman as a rational being, equal to themselves and not always fundamentally connected with sex. Emotionally, as it has been truly said, many American men are adolescents—kind, delightful, charming adolescents. "He's just like a boy" seems to be considered a compliment to a man in America. It ought to be an insult. This horrible boyishness lingering in persons who should be adult is as dismaying as mental retardation. It is responsible for our childish tendencies to "jazz things up," to make "whoopee," to think of being drunk, of removing "inhibitions," of playing the clown, as the only way to have a good time, to the complete destruction of adult conversation and real wit and subtler humor. It certainly is responsible for wanting women to be nothing but wives, mothers, or leggy relaxations for tired business men. Even a pretty college girl said despairingly not long ago in my presence, "You can't get anywhere with men if you show any brains. I have to make myself a nit-wit if I want dates. Oh, well, that's the way they are!" There are too many nice and rather sad American women who patiently accept even their middle-aged and old men as perennial "boys." "Men are like that," they say, at least as often as men say, "women are like that."

Nothing could show a greater misunderstanding between the sexes than this frequent fatalistic remark. Neither men nor women are like that if "that" means what they now seem to each other. It is a strange fact that in new America, as in old India or China, the real life of each sex is not with each other but away from each other. Men and women in America meet stiffly for social functions, drink together in an earnest effort to feel less inhibited, play the fool guardedly and feel queer about it afterward. Or they meet for physical sex, in the home or out. And they jog along in family life. Of the delight of exploring each other's differing but equally important personalities and points of view, of the pleasures of real mutual comprehension and appreciation and companionship, there is almost none inside the home or out. Tradition decrees that after marriage real companionship between persons of opposite sex must cease except between husband and wife. Tradition decrees that all companionship indeed between men and women is tinged with sex. Such an idea as interest in each other as persons, aside from sex, is almost unknown. Women, talking of this among themselves, say, "Men don't want anything else." I am inclined to think they are right. The average American man demands amazingly little from his women—nothing much except to look as pretty as possible on as little money as possible, to run the home economically with as little trouble as possible to the man when he comes home tired. What educated, intelligent, clever, gifted woman is going to be satisfied with that? What average woman would be satisfied even? Ask the average man if he would change places with a woman—any woman. The idea horrifies him. Yet women are far more like him than he knows or wants to know, and modern times have done everything to make her more so.

No, our men, perennial boys, most of them, will not do anything about changing tradition. They do not know how, absorbed as they are in the game of business, abashed as they are in the presence of sex as anything except simply physical, and afraid as they are of women. They are, naturally, afraid of women or they would not cling so to tradition. They were afraid of their mothers when they were children, their imperious, discontented mothers, and that fear carries over into fear of their wives and fear of all women, in industry as well as at home. It leads to the attitude of petty deception which so many perennially boyish men maintain toward their women.

So, naturally enough, men do not want women "getting too smart." I heard a carpenter working in my home say pontifically to his assistant about to be married, "And why would you want a woman eddicated? Says I, if I want eddication I can go to the public library. A woman should know just so much as when it rains she stands on the sheltered side of the street. It's enough." And after a moment he added solemnly, "You don't want a woman what can talk smart. You want one what can keep quiet smart."

The voice of America's perennial boys, I thought—speaking out in a carpenter, but heard as clearly in the embarrassed reserves of an after-dinner circle in a drawing-room. And yet, I do not blame them. There are so many women who chatter without thought, who stop all attempts at conversation with continual commonplaces uttered with all the petty authority of ignorance. And the fetters of another tradition—that of chivalry—still hang upon American men. Foolish, haughty women, standing in crowded buses, staring at a tired man in a seat, accepting favors as their right; peevish, idle women, wasting their husbands' money; dogmatic women talking ignorantly about practical important matters—men must try to be polite to them all alike. I do not blame American men, except for not seeing that not all women are the same.

We are so clever with machines, we Americans. But we have done a silly thing with our women. We have put modern high-powered engines into old antiquated vehicles. It is no wonder the thing is not working. And there are only two courses to follow if we do want it to work. We must go back to the old simple one-horse-power engine or else we must change the body to suit the engine—one or the other. If the first, then tradition must be held to from the moment a woman is born, not, as it now is, clamped upon her when, after a free and extraordinarily equal childhood and girl-hood with boys, she attempts to enter into a free and equal adult life with men and finds it denied her, to discover then that her education has had nothing to do with her life.

Or else we must be willing to let her go on as she began. This means that American men must cease being "sweet boys" and grow up emotionally as well as physically and face women as adult men. But they, poor things, have not been fitted for that either! Besides of course they are afraid of what women might do. And women, inexperienced and eager, will probably do as many foolish things as men have until they have had as much practice.

Of one thing I am sure, however. There will be no real content among American women unless they are made and kept more ignorant or unless they are given equal opportunity with men to use what they have been taught. And American men will not be really happy until their women are.

LAYING THE GROUNDWORK

Preparation for Reading

1. Would you vote for a woman for the school board? for mayor? for governor? for a judgeship? for President? Would you consult a woman lawyer, or doctor, or architect?
2. What are the characteristics of the ideal wife from the average man's point of view?
3. Are there professions or occupations for which women are not qualified? Give reasons for your answer.

Vocabulary Building

1. Find the meanings of the following adjectives: *docile, neurotic, naïve, imperious, despotic, bovine, dogmatic.* What kind of person do you associate with each? Use the words in sentences.
2. Look up these words: *ensconce, gigolo, tentative, subsidiary, chimera, placated, adolescent, inhibitions, antiquated.*

APPRAISING THE RESULTS

1. When Miss Buck was in China, what was her opinion of the position of American women? How did her opinion change after she came to this country?

2. What explanation does she give of the unhappiness of Amer ican women? of the tolerant laughter of men when the subject of women is broached? Do you think her explanations are sound?

3. What is the traditional attitude toward women in this coun try? Is this the attitude of many women as well as of many men? How is it exemplified in the treatment of a woman who achieves prominence?

4. Is having privileges the same thing as having rights?

5. Summarize Miss Buck's views on the possibility of success for women in medicine, business, teaching, and the arts.

6. What course of study does Miss Buck recommend for women, and why? Comment on her recommendation.

7. Explain what is meant by the "medieval tradition" as it af fects the relationships of men and women.

8. Explain what Miss Buck means by the adolescence of men Are you willing to accept her conclusions?

9. According to Miss Buck, what two courses are open if men and women are to be happy? Does she expect men to do much to change the traditional view? Which course do you intend to pursue?

10. Compare the characteristics of our medieval attitude toward women and the view advanced and supported by the Nazis and the Fascists. (See Dr. Hamilton's article, "The Enslave- ment of Women.")

SELECTING THE THEME SUBJECT

1. Write a paper analyzing the position of women in one of these activities: medicine, law, teaching, politics, arts.

2. Criticize or amplify the following statements made by Miss Buck: (a) "Tolerant laughter is the cruelest form of contempt." (b) "Immaturely, he judges the whole world of women by the only woman he knows at all—his wife." (c) "We Americans are a backward nation in everything except in the making and using of machines." (d) "No woman has a man's chance in hard times, or in any times." (e) "[Women] have privileges but no equality."

3. Titles for themes: Why the Tradition of "Chivalry" Should End; The Characteristics of James Fenimore Cooper's Women; Women in Literature of Chivalry; The Kind of Woman I Shall

WOMEN BREADWINNERS[1]
THEY DON'T WORK FOR PIN MONEY

Beulah Amidon

WHY DO WOMEN WORK? ACCORDING TO THE 1930 CENSUS, THE LAST NATIONAL FIGURES WE HAVE, 10¾ MILLION WOMEN ARE "gainfully employed outside the home." Are these women in factories, on farms, in stores, offices, schoolrooms, studios working "for pin money," "to express themselves," "to earn their own livings,"—or do they work because other people are dependent on them for food, clothing and shelter?

These are questions that have long been debated, usually with more heat than light. The answer, as revealed by a recent study made by the National Federation of Business and Professional Women's Clubs, in which more than 12,000 of its members participated, is that, with median earnings of $1315, one woman in two supports other persons, wholly or in part; and that one sixth of the group are the heads of households of from two to seven persons. Further, it shows that the number of her dependents increases as the worker's income increases—in other words, the more a woman earns, the more responsibilities she assumes.

The differences between what men and women are paid on comparable jobs is not a matter of opinion, but of fact. The U. S. Women's Bureau, in a recent bulletin which brings together information about women workers from a variety of sources, has compiled tables showing wage rates in a wide range of occupations and communities. A sampling of these data shows such comparisons as these:

[1] From *Survey Graphic*, March, 1938. Reprinted by permission of the author and of *Survey Graphic*.

Occupation	Average Full Time Weekly Earnings of Men	Women
Silk Weaving...............................	$28.98	$22.21
Dyeing and Finishing (Cotton)................	17.32	12.46
Paper Box Folding..........................	23.68	14.86
Welt Shoes—Stitching......................	15.15	10.70
Clerical Workers—Ohio, 1935.................	32.75	18.80
Salespersons in Stores (Ohio, 1935)............	19.87	13.54
Beauty Parlor Operators (Four Cities)..........	22.50	14.25

The disparity continues in professional fields. A recent report by the National Education Association, covering salary schedules adopted in 150 cities, revealed that about one fourth provided for differences in the pay of women and men. A report of the U. S. Office of Education gives the salaries of 5822 men and 1068 women in fifty land-grant colleges and universities in 1927-28:

	Median Salaries of Men	Women
Dean........................	$5635	$4375
Professor....................	4139	3581
Associate Professor............	3284	2882
Assistant Professor............	2794	2530
Instructor...................	2087	2016

Back of such figures as these lies not a difference in skill, training or experience. To such factors, many authorities ascribe the fact that men are found in the higher paid occupations in industry, business and the professions in a larger proportion than are women. But the difference in rate of pay for the same job is the expression of the tradition that "women work only for pin money," that "women don't have dependents—men have families to support."

The study made by the National Federation of Business and Professional Women's Clubs covers only its own membership, a fair sampling of the five million women in this country making up four occupational groupings: clerical, professional, trade, transportation and communication; plus some women engaged in domestic and personal service, chiefly beauty parlor operators.

The 12,043 women reporting represent every state in the union except Rhode Island, and Alaska and Hawaii as well;

they represent more than 100 occupations, and all but one
industry grouping (forestry and fishing) of the U. S. Census
general industry categories. By specific occupations, the largest number of women—nearly 27 percent of the total—are
teachers; next in order are secretaries and stenographers; audi-
tors, bookkeepers and cashiers; clerks; executives, managers,
and supervisors. Only one twelfth of the total are independent workers, busy in their own stores, offices or studios.

It is distinctly a middle-aged group, with a medium age of
40.6 years, half the number between the ages 30 and 49.
About 25 percent are 50 and older, less than 20 percent under
30, less than one percent under 20. Out of every ten women
replying, seven are single; three married, widowed, divorced
or separated. Again taking them by tens, four in each ten live
in places of less than 10,000 population, four in places of
10,000 to 100,000, two in places of 100,000 or more.

For the calendar year 1936, the median full time earnings
of the whole group (half more, half less) were $1315. Median
year's earnings of independent workers, $1520, were higher
than those of salaried workers, $1310. Highest median year's
earnings were those of executives, managers and supervisors,
$1715; the lowest those of personal service workers, $610,
with saleswomen only a little higher, $625. In the whole
group, there were 3113 who reported annual earnings under
$1000, 299 of these under $500. Only 487 had earnings in
1936 of $3000 or more; 52 of these above $6000, six above
$10,000.

Contrary to the usual impression, median earnings of the
women participating in this study increase each decade from
$960 for women under 30 to $1615 for women of 50 to 60,
then decrease to $1560 for women over 60.

Almost half the women report no dependents wholly or partially supported out of their earnings. A very small group (3
percent of the total) not only have no dependents, but live in
households to the support of which they do not contribute.
Here may be a genuine "pin money" group—women who are
responsible neither for the support of others nor for their own
maintenance.

The women with dependents are older than their more

carefree fellows, their median age about 44 years, as compared with 40.6 for the group as a whole. Their earnings are somewhat higher than those of the total group, though one sixth of them had less than $1000 in 1936, a few had less than $500.

Everyone knows women of this under $1000 group—the colorless little cashier in the drugstore, who is neither very quick nor very accurate. She lives with a rheumatic old aunt "over beyond the tracks," and "the church ladies" sometimes help out with a Thanksgiving basket, or a cast-off winter coat for "old Mrs. Jones." There is Miss Jackson, who has "kept the library" for so many years, and before and after her day's work, has kept house for her crippled father and her "do-less" brother.

The statistics of relief and health agencies, in their colorless way, tell the story of the malnutrition, bad housing, inadequate clothing, neglected medical and dental needs of this group trying to stretch meager resources to cover the needs of themselves and their dependents.

The women who are the sole support of their households have an average of 1.5 dependents with whom they live, and in addition, they each have 2.1 dependents outside their homes. The women who partially support others have an average of 1.7 dependents in their homes, 1.3 persons whom they help outside.

These trends are sharpened by the facts brought out in a related study made by the National Board of the YWCA, in which 680 younger employed women took part. With a median age of 25, these women had yearly median earnings of $959.92, $415 below those of the older group. Here, too, earnings tend to increase with age. Of the girls under 20, 70 percent earned less than $500 in 1936, while only 4 percent of the women in the 40 to 49 decade earned so little. But even on median weekly wages of eighteen dollars, 450 of these young women (66 percent) had other persons wholly or partly dependent on them, sixty were the sole support of households, with an average of 2.2 dependents apiece.

These figures, with their mathematical absurdities of fractional "persons," take on more meaning if one considers the people behind the statistical tables. Here is a high school teacher in the capital city of a midwestern state. She earns $1800 a year, well above the median for the group. On this she supports not only herself but her husband, permanently crippled by an automobile accident, and their young son, and sends a regular monthly sum to her husband's mother. Another participant in the study is a bank clerk in a Pacific Coast town. It takes a lot of anxious care and ingenuity to make her $1500 salary cover the needs of those dependent on it—her mother and her invalid sister who live with her, an arthritic brother in a desert hospital. And then there is a civil service worker in an eastern city with high living costs. On her exceptionally good salary of $2750 she makes a home for her disappointed and futile father and for her brilliant brother, who is now a college freshman and aspires to medical school; she is paying the debt incurred during her mother's last illness; she sends "what I can spare—something every month" to a widowed sister with several children who lives in another state.

It is worth noting that a woman who is the head of the family usually has more than a budgetary responsibility. Only a small proportion of the women taking part in this study earn enough to have paid household help. Before and after the business day and on their "day of rest" they must themselves do at least part of the actual work of the household.

We are accustomed to think of a home as dependent on two persons, a man who supports it, a woman who maintains it, their common effort centered in the representatives of the next generation born and nurtured there. But when a woman wage earner is the sole support of the household, she heads a different sort of home. Of the women taking part in this study, 55 percent support wholly or in part representatives of the past generation—their parents, grandparents, uncles, aunts; 20 percent carry members of their own generation—brothers, sisters, husbands, cousins; only 25 percent are providing for the oncoming generation, and so earning a stake in the buoyant hopes and plans of youth. The same thing is true of the younger women who took part in the YWCA study: of the 134 persons maintained by the sixty who are "the sole support of the household," 71 (52 percent) represent an older generation.

It is unfortunate that no similar studies have been made of men and their responsibilities. It would be interesting and significant if, beside this picture of women at work, one could place a picture of a comparable group of business and professional men, showing age, occupation, earnings, marital status, number and generation of dependents. But even without such a comparison, these women, in their questionnaire replies, have thrown light on a long disputed question: why do women work? For they have shown that even among the lowest paid members of these large and representative groups, women do not work for "pin money" nor do they have "only themselves to support." Of nearly 13,000 employed women, a relatively small but fair sampling of the millions of American women in business and professional occupations, half work not only to support themselves, but also to support the old, the ill, the handicapped, the children, who depend on them in increasing numbers through the years.

LAYING THE GROUNDWORK

Preparation for Reading
1. Do you think woman's place is in the home? Defend your answer.
2. Why do women work? Base your answers on the working women you know.
3. Do you believe men and women should receive equal pay for the same work done equally well?

Vocabulary Building
1. Look up these words: *disparity, land-grant (colleges), sampling, categories, ingenuity, arthritic, buoyant, budgetary, nurtured.*
2. Explain the difference between a median and an average in statistics.

APPRAISING THE RESULTS

1. On what surveys did the author base her article? Do you believe these sources are reliable? Are the facts sufficient to justify the conclusions?
2. List the major conclusions reached by the author. Evaluate each.

3. How do the home responsibilities of the average working man
   and woman compare? How do their salaries compare?
4. What arguments are used against the employment of women?
   In the light of this article, how sound do you consider them?

SELECTING THE THEME SUBJECT

Titles for themes: State Laws Affecting Women's Rights; Should
Housewives Be Paid Wages?; Should Married Women Work?;
"I Don't Want My Wife to Work"; Working for Board and
Room; Victorian Ideas About Women; Effects of Business Depres-
sions on Women Workers; Why I Don't Want a Woman "Boss";
Working in the "Five and Ten"; Why Men (or Women) Object
to Women's Working; The Woman's Charter and the Equal
Rights Amendment (protective legislation vs. legal equality); Are
Women People?; The Growth of the Woman's Movement; A
Famous Woman and Her Work; The Work College Girls Do.

THE ENSLAVEMENT OF WOMEN[1]

Alice Hamilton

THE "WOMAN'S MOVEMENT" IN GERMANY, THE FAMOUS "FRAUEN-BEWEGUNG," HAS A VERY PROUD HISTORY, A HISTORY OF ENOR-mous courage, persistence, wisdom and of slow but strikingly great achievement in the face of formidable obstacles. It was not characterized by spectacular features as was the British struggle for woman's suffrage and to a much less extent our own, yet it succeeded so well that under the Republic, groups of women sat in the Reichstag at a time when an American Congresswoman was a rare and conspicuous sight. Women were government officials, school councillors, university teach-ers, and judges. The German women I used to meet in Geneva during the years between 1924 and 1930 were unusually able and one could trust them to take a reasoned and practical stand on controversial matters affecting legislation for women which was in strong contrast with that of the women of some national groups.

German women had had a long and hard fight but they had won a fair measure of equality under the Republic. Now all seems to be lost and suddenly they are set back, perhaps as much as a hundred years.

It would be wrong for me to quote any woman by name. I can only say that I talked with some who were leaders in the suffrage movement before Germany had woman's suffrage and whose organization had continued as the General German Women's Union (*Allgemeiner Deutscher Frauen-verein*). I met also officials of the General Federation of Women's Clubs, of the German branch of the International

[1] From *Nazism: An Assault on Civilization*, published by *Opinion*. Reprinted by permission of the author and of the publishers.

Association of University Women, and of Women Physicians, and of the Union of Women Teachers of Germany, an extensive and influential organization. Inside these groups were women who had been members of the Reichstag; others had held office in various universities or municipal governments; others were lawyers, physicians, journalists. These wise, experienced women saw their impending fate—the program of the Nazis against women did not move so rapidly as the one directed against the Jews—and saw no possible way of averting it. They were courageous; they told me that rather than submit, which meant expelling all members with Jewish blood and declaring themselves in sympathy with National Socialism, they would see their organizations dissolved. And it did come to that. For weeks we could not find out what was happening after we left Berlin, only that the *Königin Luise Bund,* which corresponds to our Colonial Dames and D.A.R., had bowed to the command from above and been absorbed in the new organization of Nazi women. The fate of the others was not published, but we saw the announcement that from then on there would be but one association in Germany, composed of Nazi women, Aryans all, with a leader appointed by Hitler. There was no delegation this year [1934] to the International Council of Women, for there was no organization left to send one.

Now at last comes an authoritative statement concerning the women's clubs, which is issued in English by a propaganda society in Berlin *(Wirtschaftspolitische Gesellschaft).* Here we learn that the two large organizations, the German Women's Union and the General Federation of Women's Clubs, together with the teachers' union, voluntarily dissolved early in the year. All the other organizations declared themselves ready to co-operate in the new state and have been combined with the Nazi women's associations into one organization, the *Deutsches Frauenwerk,* or German Women's Work.

So the liberal women's organizations kept their word and did not yield. This is really a proud record. No woman of any prominence in the woman's movement is connected with the Nazi régime. I was told of a spirited young woman who said to her brother, an ardent Nazi, "How can you ask me to join your party when you are turning the finest women in Germany out of the teaching profession?" And he answered, "But what can we do? They will not join us and we cannot let them build up an opposition."

The new Nazi women's association has a man at its head, appointed by the government, State Councillor Krummacher, with a woman as assistant, Dr. Paula Siber, who is also consultant for women's affairs in the Department of the Interior. An irreverent young woman sent me from Germany Dr. Siber's recent pamphlet on the woman question, plentifully adorned with exclamation points, which, however, were not needed to make me see the really appalling silliness of this influential lady. It is a piece of flowery sentimentality such as might have been written in the early part of the last century, without a touch of realism. Woman is a mythical figure, a throbbing heart, while man, equally mythical, is embodied intellect. "To be a woman means to be a mother. . . . All womanly knowledge springs from the deep roots of the woman's soul, while the special mental power of man arises in the colder atmosphere of the absolutely intellectual. The coldness and hardness of the man longs for the softness and warmth of the woman."

This pamphlet cannot be dismissed as merely silly, for it bears the imprimatur of a powerful man, Frick, Minister of the Interior, who, indeed, contributes the preface. We are obliged to treat it as the authoritative expression of the Nazi leaders and so we must delve through the syrupy sentimentality for the hard core that lies inside.

Dr. Siber proclaims at the outset an absolute break with "liberalistic-Marxistic democracy" and all its works, and repudiates the *Frauenbewegung* as a movement among middle-class women for intellectual emancipation and among working women for material comforts, both of them contrary to woman's true nature, and in accordance with Jewish doctrines of sex equality and sex freedom, which render woman rootless. There is much about motherhood and its glories, childbearing and its joys, and we are told that the motives for limiting the number of children in a family are only materialistic, liberalistic, Marxistic, and egotistic. The State is all-important, not the individual child nor the mother; the State needs children, therefore the refusal to bear children is treason to the State. "To awaken and renew the will in men and women for large families is the pressing task of the new woman's movement."

It follows that the education of girls is to be for mother-hood and is to be quite different from that of boys, nor are the two sexes to be allowed to become accustomed to each other—decidedly not, for this leads to the loss of the finest womanli-ness. Girls must have the best of physical training, sports and play, but always with duty in mind, and sacrifice, "yes, with so much joy in their hearts that they will be able to make sacrifices all their lives in the service of duties gladly ac-cepted." Such sacrifices are not required of men and therefore in this, as in all things, the two sexes are different and their training must be different.

The last year of schooling is to be passed in a compulsory labor camp, but the provision for these camps has not yet been made and for the present the voluntary camps must be used. The inference is that the latter are Nazi institutions, but this is far from true. They grew up under the Republic and were founded by Eugen Rosenstock of Breslau, now teaching in this country. The universities are still open to women but the number of women students must not exceed ten per cent of the whole student body and the latter is now limited to 15,000. Formerly it ran from 23,000 to 30,000 and there was no restriction on the number of women students. The schools of law are closed to women but they may study medicine for "who would forbid women to be doctors when the woman's heart is needed at the bedside, as much as is the man's scien- tific knowledge?"

Dr. Siber recognizes the problem of the superfluous women of whom there are said to be 1,900,000; indeed she says that "the large disproportion of women and the bitterness of the lot of the unmarried is at the bottom of women's restlessness and it drove them under the liberalistic régime to strive for equality with men." But she offers no solution for those who under the Nazi régime are being ousted in favor of men ex-cept to say that under National Socialism everything is woman's work that concerns womanhood and motherhood, and goes on to enumerate the wonderful callings open to them, the care of all the helpless, of those sick in mind and body, of the old and the delinquent, and the education of little boys and of all girls. But surely this was true under the Republic and it is hard to see why it should be called "the real liberation of woman from the prison of self and family into the glorious freedom of work for the nation." This is her concluding paragraph:

The woman's movement of National Socialism claims for itself the honor of being the most advanced expression of the movement for the renewal of womanhood. Its foundation and its driving power are in the heart of woman; its determination is to recognize pure womanhood; its aim is the highest development of woman's nature and her incorporation in the service of the National Socialistic Commonwealth.

Nobody would say that the plan to remove women from industrial work and return them to home and family would spell hardship for the majority of German women. It is true that there are women of the educated class who would much rather do professional work than housework and who wish to be self-supporting even if they are married, or at least to supplement their husband's earnings, but I very much doubt if that is true of women of the working class. I believe the vast majority of working women would be thankful to have only their homes to manage, not to do the double task of factory-work and housework. Hitler's program for women would doubtless be hailed with joy and relief by millions of them if it could be carried out, but they know it cannot be, and apparently the leaders are discovering this too.

It is quite evident during the first six months or so of the Nazi régime that the relegation of woman to her position of a century ago was carried on with vigor and with German thoroughness. Not that the newspapers told us much about it, but rumors came of wholesale discharges, first of married women, then of women in families where there were male money-earners. Sometimes we were told that employers were objecting to the substitution of young men for experienced typists and secretaries, and that the telephone exchanges were in a sad way after the girls were turned out. The brochure from Berlin which I mentioned above gives interesting sidelights on this phase of the Nazi régime, not by telling what happened but by assuring foreigners that certain things are not to be permitted any longer. Thus we read that although the Nazi ideal is to place woman in the family it has been found that this ideal cannot always be realized. A woman of mature years who is not yet married probably will not be able to marry and she must not be crowded out of her job, for that simply means that she swells the number of unemployed. So a woman who cannot marry has a right to a job. To be sure it has been laid down as a principle by the Nazis that in case of competition between a man and a woman for a position the man is to have the preference if he is equally suited to it, but women who are better qualified than men are not to be displaced, e.g., saleswomen, stenographers, clerks, and secretaries. Wherever, in the excessive zeal of the first months, women have been dismissed from such posts, failure has resulted and the government has now issued orders that the ousted clerks and stenographers must be reinstated because the men who replaced them were so inexperienced as to considerably affect the smooth conduct of business.

The same thing was true of the dismissal of women welfare workers and teachers, and the Reich Minister of the Interior forbids such dismissals, even of married women, unless there is a qualified man to take the place. He also recognizes the fact that many women work because they must and he decrees that no woman is to be discharged unless her economic future is assured. However, the Nazi government hopes to bring it about that women shall be employed only in womanly work, domestic service—which is to be increased by making it cheaper—and welfare work including nursing, playground and gymnastic work, while young women of course are to be encouraged to marry.

Women doctors, lawyers, teachers, all expressed grave apprehensions at the impending outlook for them in the Germany of today. More than one told me that in a few years not only would they have been driven out of the professions but even excluded from the universities and from all but a rudimentary intellectual training. And anyone who has read Hitler's discussions on the woman question in *Mein Kampf* must admit that their fears are well founded.

It is true that the Nazis promise new professions for women: assistant heads of girls' schools—apparently the head is always to be a man—leaders of the compulsory labor camps for girls, heads of the motherhood schools, mothers' helpers, "spiritual advisers" and so on, but the women who have not been trained under the new system may find it hard to substitute such work for their independent professional life.

Women are entirely excluded from parliament. The National Socialist party has never had a woman on its list of candidates and when Hitler dissolved all the other parties and the question arose as to which of their members were eligible to join the Nazi party, it was decided that no woman and no clergyman was eligible. Still as the propaganda pamphlet naïvely says, since the parliaments of the various states have been dissolved, and in the Reichstag only one party exists, the elimination of women is of no practical importance.

The urge to raise the birthrate, so important a part of Hitler's program, was seen in several measures which were passed in the first three months of his rule. There is a tax on the unmarried, which applies also to the widowed and divorced, but not to those over fifty-five years of age or if they are supporting children or helping support relatives. The government has made it easy for overburdened mothers to employ more domestic servants by abrogating unemployment insurance for those servants and by permitting the head of the family to claim exemption from his income tax for as many as three servants, just as if they were his children.

Young couples are loaned 1,000 marks to buy furniture and cooking utensils, and this can be repaid in monthly instalments of one per cent (no interest is charged) and on the birth of each living child 25 per cent of the debt is written off. Large families are to be encouraged in every way. The new head of the organization of women doctors—the old one was dissolved and all officers were asked to resign—who was of course appointed by the government, urged in her inaugu-

ration speech the necessity for doing everything to increase
the population of the country and condemned all measures
of family limitation as treason.

The attitude of the Nazis toward women is, therefore,
frankly and avowedly a reversion to the past. While all other
countries move on toward a greater degree of equality between sexes, Germany deliberately turns back to the ideals
and standards of a less civilized era.

Two motives seem to be back of this systematic plan to
relegate women to a position of entire subordination to men.
One is frankly economic. As is true of much in the Nazi program, the decisive factor was unemployment and the imperative demand for jobs on the part of adherents who had been
promised work when there was no increase in work and who
must be satisfied at the expense of people who, it was thought,
would submit in silence.

The second motive is far more important. In the Germany
Hitler is planning, women count for nothing except as they
bear children, care for them in childhood, nurse the sick, the
wounded, the aged, and help in the work on the land. For in
the Germany of Hitler's dream, a glorious, conquering Germany, the people who are needed are strong peasants to provide food, so that Germany will never again starve under a
blockade by her enemies, and strong soldiers to restore her
prestige and bring under one Reich all the Germans in Europe. Hitler will therefore have the education and sports of
boys directed toward the production of soldiers who are to
liberate Germany, while the training of girls is to be directed
toward fruitful motherhood so that the supply of Germany's
soldiers shall not fail. If girls are to be trained with healthy
motherhood as the goal, a strong physique comes first in importance, then character-building, last intellectual training.
No more is stress to be laid on the individual, that fatal error
of progressive education. The State is all, the individual
counts only as he serves the State, and the girl is to be taught
that the State requires of her child-bearing and child-rearing,
not work which men can do as well as she or better. Competition between the sexes is to be abolished by the elimination
of women.

That all Nazi women will accept this position of dependence and helplessness may be doubted. We were told that there were some stirrings of revolt among them, that at one of the first meetings of the new Nazi "Women's Work" they were bold enough to announce their adherence to all the Nazi program except that part which deals with women. American journalists reported that there was considerable resentment among the women who came in thousands to the great Nazi rally in Nuremberg last Summer when they found that they were being completely ignored. One of the former leaders of the Woman's Movement (*Frauenbewegung*) told me that the work for sex equality in Germany must be begun all over again, but she did not despair, though she felt that her group could do nothing. The Nazi girls, she said, would not long submit to a system which would mean hopeless drudgery and poverty for the great majority, and there would come a new revolt of women under new leaders.

Just now that seems a dim and far-off hope. Revolt of any kind seems futile and a revolt of women is always especially difficult. But German women can look back on a history of a splendid movement for their own emancipation and surely they may hope for another in the future. It will not be possible for one country, in the center of the civilized world, to turn her back on the march of time and deliberately re-enter the eighteenth century. Yet, it must be admitted, the place assigned to women by Hitler is the place women have always held in a strongly militarized state and the only place they can hope for in such a state. Therefore, until Germany turns from her glorification of physical force and her dream of a great German Reich won by the might of the sword, it is hard to see how there can be any change in the lot of German women.

LAYING THE GROUNDWORK

Preparation for Reading

1. What qualities in women are held in highest esteem in Nazi Germany? Are there men and women in this country who subscribe to the same views?

2. To what extent is the position of women an index to the cultural status of a country?

Vocabulary Building

1. Look up these words: *formidable, Reichstag, conspicuous, imprimatur, emancipation, ousted, régime, relegation, brochure, rudimentary, abrogating, prestige, futile.*
2. How do these synonyms differ in meaning: *repudiate, forswear, renounce, abjure, recant, retract?* Use each in a sentence.

APPRAISING THE RESULTS

1. Why do the Nazis call themselves National Socialists when their objectives have nothing in common with the objectives of socialism, such as equal rights for women, equal rights for all races and nationalities, scientific education?
2. What gains had the woman's movement made in Germany before the advent of Hitler? What is left of these gains?
3. Describe the method used by the Nazis in their attack on the rights of women. Which women's organizations accepted the dictates of the Nazis? Which dissolved rather than accept? Why?
4. What is the Nazi ideal of woman as it is portrayed in the official pamphlet? How has the education of women been adjusted to this view of woman's sphere?
5. What methods were used by the Nazis to relegate woman to the position she held a century ago? How successful have they been?
6. What two motives, according to Dr. Hamilton, are back of this systematic plan to subordinate women entirely to men?
7. Do you believe the German women will be content with their present status? Will it be easy for them to regain their losses? What would you do to carry on the fight if you were in Germany?
8. Compare the American view as it is interpreted in Miss Buck's article "Our Medieval Women," with the view held by the Nazis.

SELECTING THE THEME SUBJECT

1. Write a paper explaining the position of women in Germany, Italy, Mexico, Soviet Russia, Japan, or the Scandinavian countries.

2. Titles for themes: How Much "Equality" Do American Women Actually Have?; Education of Women in Nazi Germany; The Struggle for Equal Rights for Women in America; Evidences of Discrimination Against Women in America; Women in Trade Unions; My Ideal Woman.

War and Threats of War

OUR NATIONAL DEFENSES[1]
George Norlin

IN ADDRESSING YOU AT THIS HONORS CONVOCATION I AM BREAK-
ING THREE PRECEDENTS. FIRST, I ATTEMPT, THOUGH BY REQUEST,
to fill the shoes of a celebrity from abroad. Second, I violate
the proprieties of what is supposed to be an academic occasion, sheltered and aloof from the storms which rage over the
world, on which the lecturer at least should be characterized
by an unruffled, Olympian calm.

"It is sweet," said the ancient philosopher, Lucretius, "to
look upon the mighty contests of war arrayed along the plains
without yourself sharing in the danger; it is sweet to hold the
lofty and serene positions well fortified by the learning of the
wise from which you may look down upon others and see
them wandering all about and going astray in their search for
the path of life . . . their striving night and day with sur-
passing effort to struggle up to the summit of power and be
masters of the world."

I confess at once my inability to rise to such philosophical
aloofness at a time when the very citadels of learning and
wisdom are the least secure from the wild forces which seek
to master the world.

Third, I neglect the fundamental precept to the orator that
he should align himself, or appear to align himself, with the
sentiments, even the prejudices, of his hearers. According to
a recent poll of the Institute of Public Opinion, seventy per

[1] Address delivered at the Honors Convocation, University of Colorado,
April 18, 1938. Reprinted by permission of the author and of the Carnegie
Endowment for International Peace, publishers of *Pamphlet 341*, "Interna-
tional Conciliation," June, 1938.

cent of my fellow countrymen are against what I feel and think and what I shall try to say this afternoon.

Now I am not one of those who think that the minority is always right and the majority always wrong. In fact I believe that by and large and in the long run the majority is most apt to be right, and I feel on the defensive for not being of it. Am I right or wrong? Let me be quite honest and say I do not pretend to know for sure.

But one thing I do know and am sure of and that is that we are all terribly tempted when we are perplexed and perturbed in mind and heart to seek refuge from ourselves in the crowd. There is a great comfort in the escape from personal isolation into a oneness with others, into a keeping of step with a regiment, into a spiritual regimentation.

Anarchy is revolting to our nature. We have an instinct for order, and when we feel unequal to setting our own house in order, we long for some one to order us about, for some one to be captain of our souls. And when he comes, we acclaim him gladly. Heil Hitler, viva Mussolini. That is one main reason why there is such a passion for regimentation in the world today. Men are tired of the anarchy in their own souls and in order to escape from this personal thralldom they are quite willing to lose themselves in the mob and to put on other chains.

That is, I say, a dangerous temptation, which more than any other must be resisted by each and every one of us every day and every hour if we care to live under a democracy and to preserve the democratic way of life. Let this be a warning to you against going with the crowd and at the same time a caution to you not to accept the views which I shall express without examination on your part. You must do what is the most difficult thing in the world to do, namely, set your own house in order.

I appreciate that I am speaking to you partly out of an experience which most of you have not shared, and happily cannot share, though you do, unhappily, share in its consequence. The horrors of the World War and its more terrible aftermath of the devastations which it wrought in the souls of men are to me a present nightmare from which I struggle to awake and cannot. I would not bring that experience to you if I could, and I could not if I would. To you it is an episode in history. You know of it at second hand, from hearsay.

I could wish that that hearsay were more in accord with truth. Certainly it is not in accord with the whole truth. For there has grown up in our country what I call a national myth. I do not know just why or how except that a prolonged debauch of dreams and emotions such as we gave ourselves over to during that war is inevitably followed by a depressing morning after—a period of disillusionment when it is only human to seek some scapegoat for the blasting of our hopes. At any rate there is a general attitude of mind to the effect that we were fooled into participation in the World War, that we were pushed into it by bankers and big business and by foreign propaganda and that we are never, never going to be fooled again.

Well, let us never be fooled again, and let us not be fooled now. In fact we pushed *ourselves* into that war. And why? Because we felt that isolation from that conflict was unworthy of us; because we felt that the issue of that conflict was of profound concern to us; because we felt deeply that though in some respects the motives and aims of the combatants were mixed and confused, yet we had precious and vital interests in common with one side against the other; because we had been moved to indignation by the brutal invasion of a little country by a Great Power in violation of a solemn treaty; because we were more sensitive than we are now to the sinking of American ships by a foreign Power; and, above all, because we were lifted up on the wings of a high hope—the great hope that if we threw into that war our power, our prestige, and our relative detachment from the quarrels of Europe we would be in a strong position to see to it that out of the ashes of that conflict there would grow some parliament of man, some world league, which could prevent such cataclysms in the future. It was, we thought, a war to end all war.

Well, it did not turn out so. We were on the side of the victors, but we won nothing for which we fought. Why? Because of Clemenceau? Because of Lloyd George? Because Woodrow Wilson was a schoolmaster unable to cope with Machiavellians? Or was it that we were unable to follow up our victory and reap its fruits because a minority in the Senate of the United States, hating the President and his initiative, made it impossible for us to join with other nations in a league of peace?

In fact, we fought and won and ran away. We left the League of Nations, the child begotten of American aspirations, a foundling upon the doorstep of Europe; we crawled into our own skins and condemned the nations across the Atlantic, outworn, impoverished, their wounds still raw and bleeding, their hearts torn by rancor and hate, to "stew in their own juice"; and so we made the world safe, not for democracy, but for gangsterism.

It is a marvel that the League of Nations, disowned by us, has lived as long as it has, without our support. Its membership has never given up the hope that we would somehow work with them, whether as members of the League or outside the League, in a collective effort to preserve civilization. And in that hope the League has kept alive, and in the dashing of that hope it has become for a time a ghost to haunt our dreams.

Had we been willing to join with the nations of the League in putting an embargo upon exports without which Italy would have been helpless, we could have prevented the conquest of Ethiopia. The Italian invasion was a motor power invasion. Italy had no oil. But what did we do? We actually contributed to the joy ride of Mussolini by sending him trucks and oil and gasoline in plenty. In effect, we helped in the devastation of Ethiopia. Mussolini himself said as much in his speech to his Cabinet on March 3, 1936, when he expressed his gratitude to the United States for our non-cooperation with the League of Nations.

Again, we "hamstrung" the power of the League in its attempt to prevent the rape of China by Japan. Read, if you will, Mr. Henry L. Stimson's thoughtful book, *The Crisis in the Orient*. (Mr. Stimson, you remember, was the very able Secretary of State in the Hoover administration.) Or read his more recent letter, published in *The New York Times* of the sixth of last November. He points out that the United States and Great Britain are furnishing most of the sinews of war to Japan, that cooperation between these two countries alone in withholding supplies would shortly bring Japan to a standstill, and that by refusing such cooperation, we of the United States, while sympathizing with China, are really aiding and abetting Japan. "China's principal need," he says, "is not that something should be done by outside nations to help her but that outside nations should cease helping her enemy."

Mr. Stimson then asks this question: "Is the condition of our statesmanship so pitifully inadequate that we cannot devise the simple means of international cooperation which would stop our participation in their slaughter?"

These words of Mr. Stimson are not applicable to the present able Secretary of State nor to the President of the United States. Even when Mr. Stimson was writing the letter from which I have quoted, President Roosevelt, in his speech at Chicago on October 5, looking not only to Japan but to the other Great Powers, Italy and Germany, which have made war and violence the foundation of their foreign policy, said in effect in strong and emphatic terms that the people of the United States no less than the other peoples were in great danger of being engulfed in a chaos of violence and brutality and that our safety lay, not in aloofness, not in isolation, not in neutrality, but in active and positive cooperation with other peace-loving countries.

That speech seemed to indicate a sharp departure from our policy of going it alone all these years. In the language of President Butler of Columbia University, "It quickened and heartened the spirit of the whole world." It recalled another occasion when the words of another President of the United States twenty years ago in like manner and matter "quickened and heartened the spirit of the whole world." And last October and November the League of Nations turned with fresh hope to the United States.

But the President of the United States in 1937, like the President of the United States in 1919, had spoken from his heart, without reckoning with Congress. For following the President's speech Congress was deluged with telegrams and letters against any form of international cooperation. The isolationists made a tremendous noise. They almost passed the Ludlow Amendment. Mr. Hull of the Department of State was forced into a public declaration that the policy of the United States was to travel its own road. No company wanted.

Then came the shattering news from abroad. The Prime Minister of Great Britain had scuttled the League of Nations, dismissed Mr. Eden from the Foreign Office, and set out to make terms with the barbarism of Hitler and of Mussolini.

Of course we were and are disappointed in the English Government. It is one thing for us to isolate ourselves from the English, and quite another thing for the English to isolate themselves from us. It is one thing to isolate ourselves and quite another thing to have isolation thrust upon us.

Well, we are reaping the fruits of our isolation, and they are not sweet, but bitter and poisonous. International cooperation—a solid front—seems for the moment out of the question, but only for the moment.

Great Britain will discover, if it has not already been brought home to her by the forcible annexation of Austria by a Power which one day guaranteed the independence of Austria and a few days after marched in triumph into her capital, that no terms can be made with those who make and break treaties without conscience and without honor, and that capitulation to the sworn enemies of democracy means the death of democracy in Europe. And we of the United States will discover (let us hope not too late) that unless we can help actively and positively to turn the course of history in the right direction, for our democracy, too, the pall bearers stand ready at the door.

Our fear of foreign entanglements, even of association with foreigners, seems to me a curious thing. We are afraid that foreign diplomats are too "slick" for us: that they will use us to "pull their chestnuts out of the fire." But that argues an incredible degree of stupidity on our part. If we are as stupid as that, can we be trusted to pull our own chestnuts out of the fire?

But for the moment what? Mr. Hoover, home from European travels and a visit with Hitler, made an eloquent speech the other day, telling us what our course should be. That speech deserves attention because his opinions are entitled to respect and are, furthermore, I believe, the opinions of the majority of our people.

The keynote of that speech, as reported in the press, is "mind our own business." He warns us specifically against joining a democratic front with Britain and France. "We should have none of it," he said; "if the world is to keep the peace then we must keep the peace with dictatorships as well as with popular governments. The form of government which other peoples pass through in working out their destinies is not our business."

But let us pause for a moment and examine into this declaration of policy. (It is, by the way, exactly the policy which we have blamed the Chamberlain Government in London for embarking upon.) If Mr. Hoover means by a democratic front a military alliance with Britain and France to promote democracy where it is not wanted, this is one thing. But if he means that we should not stand by Britain and France in preserving democracy where it is wanted, in checking a Fascist Internazionale from forcing itself upon unwilling countries, this is quite another thing. (I leave the Communist Dictatorship out of this discussion, because Russia is not now a threat to world peace, but the contrary.) Does Mr. Hoover really think that the Spaniards or the Austrians are working out their own destinies, or that even the peoples of Germany and Italy and Japan are working out their own destinies?

We have no quarrel with the domestic policy of a free people. But when the whole policy and philosophy of a ruling Power is to weld the people of the nation by terrorism and propaganda into a monstrous engine of destruction and to glorify war and conquest as the supreme function of the State, when, in other words, the internal policy of the State is built into a foreign policy of ruthless aggression, that is a matter of grave concern to all who want to go about their business in freedom and in peace. Mr. Hoover admits (I quote his own words) that "Fascism is already a raging power, which no longer holds to its original boundaries, but has spread to fourteen European nations with two hundred and forty million people."

What is our own business? A few years ago some sixty nations under the Pact of Paris, better known as the Kellogg Pact, entered into solemn covenants with us to renounce war as an instrument of national policy. Is it none of our business that signatories to that treaty with us have renounced, not war, but the renunciation of war? Again, some years ago we initiated at Washington the Nine-Power Treaty, under which nine World Powers, including ourselves and Japan, pledged themselves to respect the integrity and independence of China. What does that mean? In our Constitution there is a clause which provides that "treaties made, or which shall be made, under the authority of the United States, shall be the supreme law of the land." Are we, then, faithful to the supreme law of our land in keeping peace and friendly diplomatic relations with a signatory to that treaty which is over-running China with fire and sword? Are treaties which we sign the supreme law of our land? Or are they for us, too, scraps of paper?

What is our business? If there should break out tomorrow a war between Germany and Czechoslovakia, should we do what we have done in the case of Italy and Japan—furnish the raw materials of war to aid German aggression as we would do under the operation of our miscalled Neutrality Act? Our neutrality law is our "mind our own business" law; it is what I call our dugout law. But in effect it aligns us with the strong against the weak, with a country which has a navy and a merchant marine against one which is lacking in these advantages, with aggressor nations against those who want to go their own way in peace. Is that minding our own business?

Mr. Hoover is opposed to our having anything to do with collective action. He does, however, urge upon us our duty to join in the force of collective sentiment. If this did not come from an able ex-President of the United States it might sound naïve. We have expressed ourselves morally in company with other nations. We have again and again joined with them in moral astringents. Only last November at the Brussels Conference we joined in saying to Japan in effect, "What

you are doing isn't cricket. Won't you please play the game
according to the rules?" The answer was the wholesale bomb-
ing of Chinese non-combatants—helpless men, women, and
children.

Such moral protests have been as deterrent to the warmongers as the squeal of a rabbit to a wolf. I am reminded of
a speech by John Bright in the House of Commons in which
he told of a man who set out to make a fortune by manufacturing pills for the cure of earthquakes.

Mr. Hoover does couple moral force with military preparedness. Preparedness for what? Does he mean that we
should put teeth in our moral suasion by threat or use of
physical force? Does he mean that we should enforce treaties
and international morals by force of arms?

He doesn't mean that. What does he mean? Is he as confused about this as Congress now seems to be, as the mild and
pacific Senator Norris seems to be, favoring a large navy without quite knowing what it is to be used for?

Senator Norris was one of the eight senators who voted
against our going into the World War. He was then an extreme pacifist. Now he has modified his views. "I feel bound,"
he said the other day, "to keep our country armed to an extent greater than Japan is armed or greater than either Italy
or Germany is armed." "Since," he adds, "it seems almost as if
these nations have gone wild and lost all sense of decency and
honor."

We must, he thinks, be prepared to meet this wildness
somehow, though he does not see why we should indulge in
quite so wild a navy spree.

In that point of view many of us agree. But where are we
to meet this wildness, and when? President Roosevelt in argu-
ing for a mammoth navy has explained that we must defend
ourselves by meeting the enemy, not on or at our borders, but
long before they reach our shores. Where, then, is the line of
our defense?

Except for our distant outposts, like the Philippines, which
our isolationists seem quite ready to throw to the wolves, military invasion of our soil seems as yet a remote possibility.
There is, however, danger of another sort which is not re-

mote. In one sense the enemy has already crashed our gates and is advancing steadily upon us. President Roosevelt in his forthright Chicago speech called down upon himself the wrath of all who would save their own skins by crawling into their own skins, when he used the wicked word "quarantine." Yet it was an appropriate word. He was expressing himself as an isolationist of a different kind. He was speaking of the necessity of an international concert to isolate the madness of fascism and prevent its further spread, not only in the material sense but in the realm of the spirit.

As things are now, or rather as things are going, there is no quarantine against ideas which are the more contagious the more they are diseased. They are not stopped by fortifications; they mock at armies and navies; they overleap the barriers of oceans; and they take possession of any soil where, to use a medical term, there are no antibodies to resist them.

Our spiritual defenses are down. We are divided among ourselves as a nation. There seems to be no clear-cut vigorous national philosophy or faith to bind us together into a spiritual union. In our disunion we cannot but envy the solidarity of fascism, its driving power, its spectacular success; and without strong convictions of our own we permit its fanaticisms to land on our soil, to invade our homes, and to work havoc in our souls.

One of our own students, a graduate of our Medical School, a fine boy with brilliant promise, was invited not long ago to join the staff of an American hospital. When he reported for duty he was told regretfully that fascist prejudice in the governing board refused to approve his appointment.

Does any one suppose that there is no relation between the accentuation of anti-Semitism in this country and the fire which is consuming the Jews in Europe?

Does any one suppose that there is no relation between the spread of crime and the lowering of morals in this country and the fact that whole nations have trampled morals under foot and proclaimed it to be divinely righteous for the State to lie, to steal, and to murder whenever crime seems to advantage the State?

Does any one suppose that there is no relation between the

growing cheapening of human life among us—the dulling of the edge of our concern for human beings—and the wholesale slaughter of innocents, yesterday in Ethiopia, today in China and Spain, tomorrow God knows where?

Does any one suppose that there is no relation between the triumphal march of Nazi brutality in central Europe and the sentiment which one hears on the streets of Boulder or of Denver or of any American town, that "what this country needs is a Hitler"?

That colossal barbarism is debauching us all. There is little danger that you and I may be exiled from our country as others like us have been exiled from Italy or Germany or Austria, but there is danger that we may be exiled from the way of life which many of us regard as more precious than life itself. It is not at all inconceivable that if and when we shall have built up the biggest navy and the strongest armaments on earth, we shall have lost our souls to the enemy and there will be nothing left worth fighting for.

These words may sound like those of an alarmist, and perhaps they are. Forget them if you want to, but I would not have you forget what I now say.

This planet is now a great battle-ground in which two ideas or two sets of ideas—two philosophies—are struggling for supremacy. Not that they face each other for the first time. They have met before on a thousand battlefields—nations against nations, parties against parties, blocs against blocs, man against man, individuals against themselves. But they are now met in a colossal struggle such as the world has never before seen, and the issue of that conflict seems to be in some final sense fateful for mankind.

Two ideas, two sets of ideas, two philosophies—what are they? The one philosophy regards human beings as means to an end, as material for exploitation, though it has seldom been nakedly frank in doing so. Almost always it wears the guise of benevolence. For example, the institution of human slavery not so long ago was preached as a divine ordinance—good for master, good for man. And I have no doubt that the rulers of ancient Egypt thought it good for their subjects to be lashed into the building of the Pyramids.

Fascism, too, grins beneath a mask of patriotism, but fascism is in reality the exploitation of human beings on a national scale. It has no regard whatsoever for human life as such, not even the life of its own subjects. They have no rights, not even the right to live. They are of value only as they contribute to the power of the State. They are just so many cells in a vast organism. If they do not function, or are suspected not to function, healthily and loyally, they are cancerous growths which must be removed by ruthless surgery. They are to all intents and purposes slaves, whipped into step by a leader, alias a driver. The only freedom is the freedom of the State to work its absolute will, and the will of the fascist State is *war*. All the domestic regimentation of the people is for one end—the complete militarization of the State, the welding of every man, woman, and child of the nation into a unified, smooth-running invincible machine of destruction— a machine which is beyond good and evil, which is a law unto itself, which is unmoral and elemental, having no more conscience than an earthquake or a flood. It is, in fact, more cruel than nature in her most savage moods. For nature is merely indifferent to our human kind, whereas this monstrous violence seeks out men, women, and children for destruction. Fascism strives for the triumph of death over life.

These are strong words. One can hardly credit that they are true. It seems beyond belief that such a philosophy even when implemented by a terrorism which is without parallel in its ruthlessness and by a propaganda more thoroughgoing than any which has ever tried to shape or distort the souls of men —it seems, I say, beyond belief that such a philosophy could be rammed down the throats of millions upon millions of supposedly rational beings. Yet it is not altogether incredible to one who has witnessed the triumph of fascism or nazism on the ground.

It is not the whole story to say that fascism has been foisted upon unwilling people. It has, in fact, been welcomed by many people. It has appealed to all whose love of country was measured by hatred of other peoples; it has appealed to the privileged classes, who expected to use the new régime to their own ends; it has appealed to the hungry and destitute, who found in it promise of bread; it has appealed to the down-and-outers, who hoped the revolution would give them a place in the sun; it has appealed to the nobodies who, strutting in uniforms, became swollen with a sense of their own importance; it has appealed to the brutally minded, who under the restraints of civilization had never before been free to express themselves adequately, and to the criminally minded, who now found their lawless instincts sublimated by patriotism; and it has appealed to a large mixed group of the middle-aged and the young, especially the young, who, distraught by the mental and moral disintegration of their lives, and oppressed by a sense of the aloneness and futility of their individual existence, gladly lost themselves in the crowd, merged themselves with the mob, and joined the march towards the dazzling glory of imperial power.

Fascism is, therefore, in a sense, the religion of lost souls, and there is a point to the observation of Heywood Broun that those who have lost their souls feel that they must gain the whole world.

That is one philosophy, one religion. What have we to oppose to the advance of this colossal mob psychology? For the first line of our defenses is not material, but spiritual.

Well, we have no regimented front to present to that spreading frenzy, nor a complete national accord to oppose to it. But we do have an idea, which is more or less our national faith, though it is not exclusively our own. It is a slow and painful birth of ages of human aspiration and struggle; but, transplanted to our new soil, it grew and flourished until it became almost a religion with us and was not so long ago a beacon of hope to the rest of the world.

And what is that idea? It is the simple and revolutionary idea, or set of ideas, that man is not a means to an end, not something to be exploited by class or by State whether for wealth or for war, but an end in himself; that the highest of values on this earth is the preciousness of human life; that the only morality, the only justice, which is built upon a rock is that which respects the sacredness of the human personality; that laws and institutions and States are of his own making, and exist for him, not he for them; and that the first business of men living together, the first business of the State, is not to coerce him under the despotism of the regimented mob for any ulterior purpose but to cherish and promote his individual freedom to grow in peace into the full stature of his being.

That idea, which we name democracy, has never been realized in fact. Democracy is not an accomplished thing, not an established thing. Rather it is a dynamic faith which has always had to do battle. Just now it has its back to the wall abroad, and we ourselves honor it as much in the breach as in the observance.

If we really believe in it, and God help us if we don't, then our first line of defense is to make this principle so vital a thing in our national consciousness and so effective a thing in action that its destructive opposite can find no soil of faithlessness or disaffection in which to root itself. To say that democracy does not work, and that there isn't anything that we can do about it, is simply to say that we are too indifferent, too irresolute, too spiritless to do anything about it. What democracy always needs and what it needs desperately now is a fighting heart. Remember that it is out of the soil of mental and moral disintegration, apathy, and defeatism that the noxious weed of despotism has sprung and spread.

What, then, is our second line of defense? It is to implement our national faith with adequate armaments, so that we will be in a position to say in language that will be heard, that any treaty, such as the Pact of Paris, entered into under the authority of the United States, is the supreme law of our land and that behind it is not only our national honor but our national power.

It is tragic to have to say that it is no time for a peace-seeking nation to disarm when the Nazi Government tells the German people that they must prefer bullets to butter, when the nations that are hell-bent for war are throwing half and more than half their national resources into building of engines of destruction. We must be in a strong position to aid in the quarantine of an international plague and in the prevention of its further spread.

Not that any one in his senses thinks of carrying war into

Germany or Italy or Japan. Nor can any one in his senses imagine that the United States or England or France can accomplish this quarantine by each going it alone in an armament race. That is clearly the way of universal destruction.

But who dares say that it could not be done if these Great Powers, together with the smaller nations which stand for peace, could say with one mighty voice to the gangster nations, "So far you shall go and no further"?

Even the joint withholding of the raw materials of war from criminal aggressors would be sufficient to check their advance, to say nothing of backing up such a measure by collective force.

I am one of those who feel that the League for World Peace, the League of Nations, now lies dead or sleeping because of our absence from it. In every crisis, it has been weak because it lacked our strength. Even at this moment, it could be revived and made an overwhelming force with our support.

But if this be an empty dream, there is still the possibility of cooperation with other like-minded nations through what what Secretary Hull calls parallel action on our part. Such cooperation is, however, impossible under our so-called Neutrality Act. But there is an increasing dissatisfaction with the working of that Act, an awakening to the fact that it operates in favor of strong aggressors and against weaker peoples who want only to be left alone. The first step necessary to international concert of action is the repeal of our neutrality law.

But, it is objected, if we do not rely upon ourselves alone, whom can we rely upon? France is panicky and unstable. But would France be panicky and unstable if France did not stand alone? We are told that the British Government has been shifty and spineless. Shifty and spineless it has been, but would it have been if the English could have felt that they stood shoulder to shoulder with the United States? Did they not feel impelled to make terms with Fascist Powers because they had lost all hope of coming to terms of cooperation with us? When shall we stop this scapegoat business, and begin searching our own hearts?

But our peace-at-any-price isolationists tell us that we must remain aloof from any measure which might give the least offense to war-loving and war-propagating governments lest we risk being involved in war. Good God, is there no risk to us in crawling into our own dugout while civilization crashes about our ears?

There is, as far as I can see, but one hope for world peace and for our own peace, and that is to join to the other like-minded peoples the moral force and the potential power of the strongest nation on this planet today.

LAYING THE GROUNDWORK

Preparation for Reading

1. What do you consider to be the major cause, or causes, of war: the lust for power on the part of evil men, commercial rivalries, munitions makers, overpopulation, the innate pugnacity of mankind, insufficient natural resources, a desire to civilize backward people, racial antagonism, imperialism?
2. What do you understand by fascism? Enumerate the characteristics of this ideology as they are revealed in the actions of countries subscribing to them.
3. Define isolation. If we accept isolation as our policy, does it follow (a) that we cease to trade with all nations at war (declared or undeclared)? (b) that we refrain from using our army and navy to protect our foreign investments? (c) that we refuse financial assistance to a country at war? (d) that we abandon the Monroe Doctrine and allow aggressive powers to seize control in this continent?
4. Could wars be stopped or prevented if an embargo were rigidly enforced by those countries commanding the raw materials necessary for the successful prosecution of war; for example, could the nations controlling oil stop a war by withholding the supply?

Vocabulary Building

1. Look up these words: *proprieties, citadels, align, anarchy, thralldom, debauch, scapegoat, cataclysms, embargo, "hamstrung," scuttled, capitulation, renunciation, astringents, deterrents, warmongers, antibodies, foisted, disintegration, apathy, noxious.*
2. Explain or identify the following: Olympian calm, Lucretius,

the Institute of Public Opinion, Clemenceau, Lloyd George, Machiavellian, Ludlow Amendment, Kellogg Peace Pact, Neutrality Act, John Bright.

APPRAISING THE RESULTS

1. What policy of national defense does Dr. Norlin champion for our democracy as the one most likely to succeed: isolation; armed security; collective action of non-aggressor nations against war-making nations; unconditional pacifism, i.e., "peace at any price"?
2. Enumerate the three precedents which Dr. Norlin states he is breaking. Account for the order in which he states them, and the amount of space he devotes to a discussion of each.
3. What "national myth" has grown up about our reasons for the World War? To what motives does Dr. Norlin ascribe our entrance into the war, at least as far as the rank and file were concerned?
4. Was it a mistake in our foreign policy to participate in the World War? to refuse to participate in the aftermath, the League of Nations? How did our isolation policy assist Italy in her conquest of Ethiopia; Japan in her inroads into China; and Germany in her invasion of Spain, of Austria, and of Czechoslovakia?
5. Summarize the positions taken by former Secretary of State Stimson, by former President Hoover, and by President Roosevelt in his Chicago speech. What is Dr. Norlin's opinion of the wisdom of the course proposed by each?
6. What final conclusion does Dr. Norlin reach? Are you willing to accept this conclusion as sound? If not, give your reasons for rejecting it.
7. Trace the course of international affairs since the time Dr. Norlin gave his speech (spring, 1938) to determine whether his analysis has been verified by the course of events. Give particular attention to such events as the Munich Pact and the dismemberment of Czechoslovakia; the Chamberlain "appeasement" policy; Fascist inroads into the Balkans, the Baltic regions, and South America; the aggression against Spain and China; and the foreign policy of the United States as expressed in the Monroe Doctrine, in the Neutrality Act, and in official and unofficial speeches.

SELECTING THE THEME SUBJECT

1. Answer in full one of the questions given in "Preparation for Reading."
2. Investigate one of these subjects and then write a paper with footnotes: The Neutrality Act, The Munich Pact, The Kellogg Peace Pact, The Peace Policy of the Soviet Union, The English Policy Under Chamberlain, The Rome-Berlin Axis.
3. Develop one of these titles: Why I am (or Am not) a Pacifist; The Church and War; The Blockade as an Instrument of War; Why I Believe in Collective Security; The Technique of Guerrilla Warfare; Making the World Safe for International Gangsters; Non-combatants in Modern War; Chemists and War; Fascist Inroads in South America; The Use of Music in War; The Modern Technique of Undeclared War; World Movements for Peace; Can an "Appeasement" Policy Stop Fascist Aggression?; Scrap Iron for Aggressors?; The Life of a Common Soldier in Times of Peace.

A STUDENT REQUESTS A COURSE ON WAR[1]

Rufus E. Miles, Jr.

WE, WHO OPPOSE THE USE OF WAR AS A MEANS OF SETTLING INTERNATIONAL DISPUTES, URGE THE SUBSTITUTION OF REASON for might in determining the course of our civilization. So, too, do our colleges and universities. If any one ideal could be said to dominate the academic institutions of this country, it is probably the use of reason and its application to all problems, philosophical, social, and personal. There should, then, be a fundamental harmony existing between those who oppose war, and American colleges and universities. Yet this problem of war and peace, one of the greatest facing our civilization, has not been dealt with in any systematic way in these institutions. As such, it has no place in their curricula. It is touched upon in history courses, treated desultorily in international relations, given a third slant by military training courses, but nowhere are the facts brought coherently into a stimulating presentation of the problem. Yet the colleges could make such a presentation without in any way prejudicing their traditions or present policies.

I propose to outline very briefly a few suggestions for a course, called "War and Peace." The aim of the course is to make a thoroughly scientific analysis of the institution of war. It would inquire into the purposes for which war has been fought, investigate the validity of those purposes, and

[1] Second-prize paper in competition offered to students and undergraduates of the colleges and universities of the United States by The New History Society. This essay appeared first in *The New Historian*, July, 1932, organ of The New History Foundation.

From *The American Scholar*, January, 1933. Reprinted by special permission of the author and of the publishers.

attempt to find out in how far they have or have not been accomplished. It would examine cases where both the peaceful and the warlike methods have been used to settle similar disputes, and in so far as the data justify, it would compare the results of the two methods. It would deal with the origin of war, the causes of war, the cost of war in social values, the methods and possibly the future of war. It would look at the problem from all important angles with a view to understanding it and solving it; it would, in short, be a thoroughly unimpassioned and penetrating study of war.

The course would consist, I suggest, of two single semester parts, divided simply into a study of war during the first semester and an analysis of means of coöperating for peace during the second semester. Either could be taken without the other. That is to say: if a student should become convinced of the desirability of war as an instrument of social change, as a result of the first semester course, it would be his privilege to withdraw and devote himself to military training courses. This course on war and peace would probably be optional to all students of sophomore ranking or above, without prerequisite. It would be well in teaching the course to be able to assume more maturity and stability than is possessed by a great many freshmen.

The course might be organized in somewhat the following manner:

I. The Institution of War.
   A. Probable Origin and Pre-history.
   B. History: A before and after analysis of outstanding wars known to history, their avowed purposes and their results.
      1. From a political point of view.
      2. From an economic point of view.
      3. From a biological point of view.
   C. Why We Go to War: An analysis of some of the international complications and difficulties which lead to war.
   D. Modern Warfare: An analytic description of modern war methods.

E. Reason *versus* Might: A sociological and philosophical discussion.
F. The Foundations of Nationalism.
II. Methods of Coöperating for Peace.
   A. Through the Use of Force.
      1. Military Preparedness.
      2. The International Police Force.
      3. The Economic Boycott.
   B. Through Official Inter-governmental Coöperation.
      1. League of Nations and World Court.
      2. Multi-power Pacts and Mutual Non-aggression Pacts.
      3. Disarmament Conferences.
      4. Other Methods.
   C. Through Unofficially Organized Public Opinion.
      1. The Pacifist Movement and the Gandhi Movement.
      2. The Institute of Pacific Relations, etc.

The problem could probably be most effectively presented in a symposium manner. An historian to present the history of war, a political scientist to present the problems of international relations, a militarist to present the methods of modern warfare, and a sociologist or a philosopher to discuss reason *versus* might and the validity of nationalism, could coöperate to present a vivid picture of the existing problem of war. The second semester, devoted to means of coöperating for peace, might again include a militarist, or at least an able advocate of preparedness as a means of securing peace, once more the professor of international relations to present a survey of organizations to promote international coöperation, and again the sociologist to discuss the great non-coöperative protest movements, such as pacifism and the Gandhi movement. Whereas a course somewhat along these lines would possess the added advantage, if conducted by a number of professors, of escaping the possibility of attack on the grounds of its propagandizing, the material can be so organized, as I have attempted to show, that even were it taught by a single broadminded professor, it would not be liable to this criticism.

Considerable emphasis has been laid, it will be noticed, upon the pure study of war. There are, I think, two excellent reasons for this emphasis. In the first place, it is admittedly sensible to be completely acquainted with a problem before attempting to find a solution to it. Many people who wholeheartedly work for world peace make the mistake, however, of failing to understand the problem of war before they advocate a solution. Secondly, a thorough understanding of the problem furnishes an emotional drive toward its solution which can never be obtained in any way other than that of first-hand experience. It has been wisely remarked that unless some concrete method of securing peace is devised before the generation which fought the World War passes on, another and greater world calamity is not unlikely. That statement is based on the well-known principle of human action and inaction, that people are moved to solve only those problems which come close to them in experience. As the World War recedes into history the will to strive toward the solution of the war problem dwindles. Here is where education may show its true mettle. The purpose of education is not only to develop the use of reason, but to give the student a maximum possible amount of experience, vicariously. Unless this is done vigorously and vividly its value is small, but if and when it is done, it may furnish the greatest emotional drive toward the solution of the problems of humanity. It is for these two reasons that so much emphasis is laid on the pure study of war.

The request that is herein made to American colleges and universities is a reasonable one. The board of trustees of every college in the United States should sanction a course of the general type outlined above. If the war problem is impressed in a forceful manner on those who will be the leaders of tomorrow, there may be a real chance of its solution. To what higher ideal could a college be committed?

LAYING THE GROUNDWORK

Preparation for Reading

1. Why do you think all male college students should (or should not) be required to take military training courses?
2. Do you think women students should be required to take courses in first aid and nursing in preparation for war?

Vocabulary Building

1. Explain what these expressions mean to you: *pacifism, militarism, preparedness, collective security, boycott, defensive* and *offensive war, mechanized* and *trench warfare, symposium on war.*
2. Apply what Stuart Chase says of semantics in "The Tyranny of Words," p. 517, to war terminology, such as "peace with honor."

APPRAISING THE RESULTS

1. Do you think the author is correct when he says history as it is usually taught fails to present effectively the problem of war to the student?
2. What is the fundamental aim of the author's proposed course? What are its approaches? its subjects for study? its length?
3. What is your opinion of this proposed course? What changes would you make? Why?

SELECTING THE THEME SUBJECT

Titles for themes: Does the R.O.T.C. Make Soldiers?; The Civilian Population in Modern War; The Student Peace Movement; The Romantic View of Warfare; Child Soldiers; The Church and War; I Would (not) Enlist if War Were Declared; War in Popular Songs; War on the Stage.

PART FOUR

The Arts Today

The Creative Spirit at Work

EYES TO SEE[1]

Helen Gardner

WHAT DO EYES DO? THEY ARE SEEING ALL THE TIME. EVERY WAKING HOUR THEY ARE CARRYING TO THE MIND A PICTURE OF the world in which we live—our homes, our friends, our schools, cities, and the country. But a little reflection or a talk with an artist on the subject reveals the fact that this ordinary daily seeing is quite different from the artist's way of looking at things, though the objects seen are the same and the means of seeing—the human eyes—the same. Has the artist then a capacity of vision not granted average people?

Before answering this question, shall we discuss these two kinds of vision? Let us take, as an illustration, your week-end visit to the country. On your return you talked enthusiastically of your friend's summer home. The family began to ask questions. How near the lake was the house? What kind of trees were there in the yard? What color were the curtains? Your recollection of the visit seemed reduced to a blurred picture and a general feeling of pleasure, with certain impressive details standing out vividly. You say that you really did see everything; it is memory that has failed. Perhaps so. As a simple experiment take a house with which you are familiar. Look at it again and shut your eyes. How many questions can you ask about it that you cannot answer? "Every time I see it, I see something different" is a familiar saying. The more we think about it, the more does everyday seeing, for us average folk, seem a very imperfect sort of thing.

But is it seeing alone that is so makeshift? At the concert last evening you heard pleasurable sounds, sometimes sooth-

[1] From *Understanding the Arts*, by Helen Gardner. Reprinted by permission of the author and of Harcourt, Brace & Company, Inc.

ingly harmonious, sometimes stridently discordant and exciting. Now there was a low tranquil mood, now a thrilling outburst. Was that all? When you listened more closely, did you notice a repetition of a certain melody? Now you heard it in the major, now in the minor; now in one tempo, now in another; played now on the violin, now by the French horn, now by all the instruments in unison. And soon you began to realize that the composition was built up on the various things you could do with that melody.

It is the same with our sense of touch. We handle countless things mechanically. Do we follow with our fingers and palms the rounding surface of the tumbler or the flat surfaces of a square box and the edges where they meet? Do we consciously feel one object as soft or hard, rough or smooth, silky or woolly? What a soothing delight there is in the soft silkiness of velvet! How cool and smooth is polished marble! How rough is the bark of an oak tree! There is an irritating harshness in some kinds of stucco; a quieting pleasure in the pliancy of soft leather; a forbidding sternness in the rigidity of bronze.

Generally speaking, we do not see, hear, or feel more than a fraction of what the mechanism of our eyes, ears, and hands is capable of experiencing. Imperfect, however, as our ordinary seeing, hearing, and tactile sensation may be, still they serve us well for the practical purpose of getting around in the world. This is because the whole process is a much more complex thing than the matter of the actual image, sound, or feeling which the eye, the ear, or the hand sends to the mind. When the picture of a house, for example, travels from the eye to the brain, it does not rest there alone, isolated. It intermingles with countless other impressions of houses and of everything associated with houses, impressions that we have been storing up from earliest babyhood. Another thing that the message from the eye, ear, or hand to the brain does, is to start action somewhere in the body. Touch something hot and you start away. Hear a sudden crackling in the woods, and your muscles tighten in suspense. See a red light flash when you drive a car through a city

and your feet and hands work almost unconsciously to stop
the car.

But what of the unused capacities of the eye, the ear, and
the hand? Can we isolate just seeing as the scientist in his
laboratory isolates a germ, a cell, oxygen, a ray of light?
Let us try, with a tree for our material.

The opening of my porch frames a patch of fairly thick
woods over which towers a fine large oak. How many associations and meanings in the minds of my friends and myself the sight of that oak can arouse because of the thousand
and one impressions of oak trees stored in our minds! My
friend the scientist sees the tree as an example of a certain
kind of oak, and is thinking of its life history. The lumber-
man sees it as so much potential flooring and wonders about
its graining. The builder sees it as an important feature
in landscaping, and broods over the possibilities of its place
in a future garden. As for myself, I am particularly interested
just now in discovering what I can really see. I observe that
sun and shadow fleck the warm gray of its rough trunk, and
glossy green foliage weaves dancing patterns on it. This trunk
is a cylinder, rough and irregular, to be sure. My eyes and
fingers seem to be working together, seeing and feeling the
rough curving surfaces. At the base it spreads outward with a
fine sweep into the wintergreen carpet of the earth. It then
moves upward and sends forth warm-gray gnarled branches
to hold a dome of glossy green foliage which sweeps above
the rest of the woods. Near by is a small pine that shoots
straight up out of the earth. Its horizontal branches are
spaced at regular intervals and its dark spiky foliage masses
itself into a cone. A storm is just retreating and a high wind
from the lake is dappling the sky with swiftly moving patches
of gray, silvery white, and intense blue. I look out to my
oak and pine. What movement and what stability! What
scintillating light and deep rich color! Over the ground
runs the light movement of the bracken and the brush; the
tree trunks are richly dark with wet; the great oak stands
firmly in the wind, while the little pine sways elastically as
if it would pull itself free from the earth and run off with
the wind. The foliage is all aquiver. The oak leaves flash

in the light and a diamond sparkles on the tip of each long pine leaf. Above race the clouds across the blue.

Let us look at another scene, this time at a city thorough-fare. As I emerge from my underground station I meet abruptly a great traffic artery. Huge buildings rear their masses sheer from the sidewalk. This one, not so large, is a warm note with its rough red brick. Next to it is the over-powering cliff of a lofty skyscraper, its gray stone as cold as its sheer, crushing façade. On up the avenue the eye is carried by the wall of buildings whence rise lofty towers which cut sharp angles boldly against the sky or emerge from the mists or recede into them. In rain, snow, or sunshine they create fantastic outlines, whose irregularity is balanced, down at the street level, by the receding line of the black lamp-posts, so sternly regular in spacing and so uniform in design, like an insistent rhythm in poetry or music that forcefully binds all variations into a unity. Along the base of the wall and by the motionless lamp-posts crowds of hurrying people surge backward and forward. Automobiles glide swiftly by, ac-cented and enlivened by the bright yellow of the taxis.

But it is difficult to separate our "just seeing" from the impressions and associations stored in the mind. Shape, color, space, movement, take on meaning; in the case of the city, the meaning of the city, its power and energy, its hurry and restlessness; in the country, the meaning of the forces of nature, as we see them typified in our oak. The cylindrical trunk, we said, spread with an outward curve at the base. Why? Because it thrusts roots downward and outward into the earth, both to give it a firm hold so that it can lift a heavy expanse of foliage without danger of falling over even when storms beat upon it, and also to reach far down for the vital water. The dome of foliage it spreads out to the sun-light to get material for making food. The trunk, with the branches and stems, not only supports this green leafy area, but also contains and protects with wood and bark the chan-nels by which the water and salts are conducted up to the cells of the leaves. Marvelous factories, these leaf cells, where food is made and sent to all parts of the tree. Here then is an orderly organic life that explains the underlying reason

for the two forms,[2] the cylinder and the dome. These forms
are fundamentally the same in all trees, yet they vary in detail, as in the pine and the oak, and give each tree a decided
personality. The forms alone have great capacity for giving
us pleasure with their masses, lines, color, textures, and
movement. But when form is infused with life and meaning,
does it not then give us added delight?

There is another way in which our eyes are working as
they see the tree and the life within it. Have you not observed that the more you see a landscape, the more details
drop away? In the shore of a lake, minor irregularities disappear in the big sweep of line where sand and water meet.
In a tree, twigs are lost in the big masses of trunk and
branches, and single leaves, in the big masses of foliage.
What matters most in seeing the tree is a feeling of strength
in the cylindrical trunk that sends roots down into the earth
to secure a firm hold, not the details of the bark; and a feeling
of reaching out to the sun in the leafy dome, not the exact
shape of each leaf. Trunk and spreading foliage—essentials
of life; cylinder and dome—essentials of form; and both life
and form again in emphasis as tiresome details fade away.

To return, then, to the question asked at the beginning of
the chapter: Has the artist a capacity of vision not granted
every one? If he lacks this capacity, he is not an artist. But
who is the artist? Although we think of him as one who has
built a skyscraper, composed a symphony, painted a picture,
or written a drama, the potential artist exists in every one
who, in his looking about the world, uses his eyes in the artist's
way. He may well be yourself as you hang a picture in your
room, select your clothes, or take your kodak pictures.

[2] Form is used not as a synonym for shape, but in a wider sense, including
shape, proportions, contours, weight, material, texture, color—every element
that enters into the composition of an object which can come to us through
our senses. Everything has form; and this form is not unchangeable. Seen in
the full sunshine, because of light, shadow, and color, it gives an illusion of
depth; seen against the setting sun or in moonlight, it appears to flatten out
into a silhouette; in varying lights its colors vary; at varying distances color,
size, and other elements change.

ART IN EVERYDAY LIFE[1]

Helen Gardner

WE ARE ALL POTENTIAL ARTISTS—ALMOST ALL OF US. THERE ARE BUT FEW WHO SEEM ENTIRELY WANTING IN CAPACITY FOR UNDERstanding or creating; many have considerable ability; a few become great artists. It is a matter of degree. Art and the way of art exist for most of us—not only exist but permeate all life, today as well as yesterday. Today life is most complex and its activities and contacts, however much they differ in number and breadth with the individual, are varied and pressing. With this immediate present we are concerned primarily.

A current opinion, far too common, holds that art is a luxury, a monopoly of wealth, a matter of museums, something to be indulged in only in one's leisure, and quite inessential to and divorced from one's daily activities. How far from the truth! It *is* true that to understand a great painting one must look at it long and contemplatively; that to understand a sonata one must hear it, undistractedly, many times. Few poems reveal all their beauty and meaning in one reading. Real understanding requires concentration of eye or ear, feelings, and intelligence. Granted, however, that great art is relatively rare and requires contemplation and leisure for its true appreciation, still art and a way of art permeate the world in which we live.

But what, you ask, has a *Skyscraper* or a *Navajo Blanket* or Leonardo's *The Last Supper* to do with my everyday life, my humdrum seven days a week? To be sure, our study of some of the arts has been restricted to the work of great

[1] From *Understanding the Arts*, by Helen Gardner. Reprinted by permission of the author and of Harcourt, Brace & Company, Inc.

masters, often of foreign lands, and far-away ages. But in
them all, as we begin "to see what we know how to look
for," we begin to discern certain qualities and characteristics
so constantly recurrent that we conclude that they are the
result of some fundamental universal principles. What words
have we used constantly in our discussion, whether it be of
buildings, or statues or paintings, of books or textiles or
pottery? *Unity, variety, harmony, rhythm, balance, contrast,
proportion, emphasis.* What words do we use in discussing
music, the dance, literature? Are they not the same? Are
there not, then, some guides to point out the way to art
in everyday life?

Let us be specific. The way we look at things may or may
not be an art. Recalling our discussion in the first chapter
of seeing as the artist sees, consider the view framed by your
own window—a yard, a street, a lake bordered by woods, a
group of roofs. Can you apply to it the words we have just
mentioned? Is it lacking in contrasting lines and masses, or
colors? Would you shift the position of some objects, imaginatively, or by shifting your own position can you obtain a
better balance? Everything in the view has a form.[2] When
we look at these forms as artists, we re-form them. Is this not
what we have seen the artist doing in all his works that we
have studied? We have found him nowhere imitating what
he sees, but everywhere taking the forms that he sees as his
raw material and out of them creating new forms that are
more beautiful, more real and significant than the originals.
Sometimes the new form is close to the original; sometimes
far removed. To see everything as form or a group of forms
and with imaginative insight to re-form these forms into
something which has harmony, unity with variety, balance,
rhythm—this is to see the world as an artist. Thus everything
we see, from the small objects about our rooms to skyscrapers and mountains, we see, if we are artists, as forms and
unities of forms which give us a far greater sense of their
reality and significance than any exact copy of their appearance can give. To see significant aspects of commonplace

[2] See p. 387, footnote.

things[3] is to transform what is mediocre, if not ugly, into something that is lovely and worth our while.

She had a sensitivity that was very wide, eager and free . . . it lighted on small things and showed that perhaps they were not small after all. It brought buried things to light and made one wonder what need there had been to bury them.[4]

Do not the same principles hold in what we hear? In our music? As I sit writing on my porch some one on the road below is whistling a melody. He repeats it again and again. The monotony becomes irritating. Ah! He changes the key. This change brings in a pleasing variety. The whistler is the potential artist creating through the medium of tones a form for his melody. I listen for him to create a still more complex form, perhaps by the addition of another melody. In imagination I hear him interweave and contrast these two melodies (each a form) and unite them into a harmonious form which is the entire song. Just as the weaver of the *Navajo Blanket* selected two motifs, the step and the zigzag, which he varied and united into the harmonious form which is the work of art. Thus the whistler and I are two potential artists working together: one an artist in understanding because the ear can hear forms; the other an artist in creating because he can use forms. The eye too, to a limited extent, reinforces the ear in the comprehension of a musical form if one looks at the score.[5] The pattern which a simple folk-melody makes on the printed page contrasts in appearance as well as in sound with that of a theme which consists of a group of melodies in much the same way in which the simple boldness of the *Navajo Blanket* contrasts with the complex richness of the royal *Persian Carpet*.

To see and to hear as an artist is a necessary foundation stone for doing things in an art way—creative activity. For

[3] See Walt Whitman's description of a ride on a Brooklyn ferry and in a Broadway street car, quoted by William James in *Talks to Teachers*, "On a Certain Blindness in Human Beings," Henry Holt & Company, Inc., New York, 1901.

[4] V. Woolf, *A Room of One's Own*, Harcourt, Brace & Company, Inc., New York, 1929, p. 161.

[5] See T. W. Surette and D. G. Mason, *Appreciation of Music*, Gray, New York, 1924, vol. i, p. 32.

this too most of us have some capacity, if it is not left latent. Let us consider a few of our daily activities. Can we be creative artists in their pursuance? Can we make out of them works of art? We might select four, almost at random: writing letters, furnishing our rooms, selecting our clothes, and using our leisure.

Can letter-writing be an art? Are not some letters more pleasing than others? Why? Probably for at least two reasons. First, because the letter presents to the eye a pleasing form. The writing is legible and is thoughtfully spaced with ample margins; and page follows page in a logical, harmonious way. The effect of the form is an enhancement of the content. A pleasing form alone arouses in the recipient an emotional response. But how much greater the response if, in the second place, the content too has a pleasing form! To write a letter, in fact any kind of literature, one starts with an idea, which he expresses through the medium of words. Words are to the writer what stone is to the builder or sculptor, tone to the musician, pigment to the painter, or clay to the potter. By means of words he creates a form for the conveyance of his idea. The better the form, the more forceful the expression, provided the idea is worth expressing. He may elaborate the idea, add other ideas for emphasis or contrast, just as the musician contrasts his melodies (musical ideas) or Leonardo, the figure of Christ (an idea of repose) with those of the disciples (an idea of agitation).

In any kind of literature as well as in the letter, the visual form of the printed words bears a direct relation to the form of the content, just as does the visual score to the audible form of the music. The grouping of words into paragraphs and the separation of paragraphs by space devices is a simple illustration of how the eye assists the mind to grasp a break in the thought.[6] Many poems by Carl Sandburg[7] will afford a more complex illustration in which the grouping of the printed words on the page creates as definite a pattern of

[6] Compare a page of a modern book with a classical manuscript in which all the letters are capitals and follow each other with no punctuation and no paragraphing.

[7] See E. Rickert, *New Methods for the Study of Literature*, University of Chicago Press, Chicago, 1927, chap. vii.

light and dark as do the light and dark colors in the Sienese *Madonna*. In both cases the purpose and result are the same: a form presented to the eye reinforces the idea presented to the mind. Thus we see that the fundamental principles of music and painting (we might carry the comparison further) are the fundamental principles of letter-writing also —in fact of any kind of writing, from the simple memorandum to a complete story or drama.

To turn to our second activity, do we find these principles at work in the furnishing of our rooms? Every one lives in an abode. Does he enjoy it or dislike it? Does it have a feeling of "rightness" about it? Or is he indifferent to it? To which of the two types does your room belong? Is it overloaded with furnishings that are largely useless, and irritating in their demand of time for their care? Or is it reposeful and harmonious, a place in which one really likes to live?

Interior architecture is a complex art with many branches, involving the purpose of the room; its space design by the placement and proportions of walls, ceilings, and openings— the permanent elements; and the furnishings and people— the changeable elements. Its ultimate character is dependent upon not one but all of these elements; working in accord, if harmony results; at cross purposes, if discord results.

For many of us our room is already built. It may be furnished or partly so. If it is ugly to start with, is our objective hopeless? By no means. The room may be small and disproportionately low; a door and windows break three sides and leave the fourth a long monotonous wall surface. Let us consult, imaginatively, our sense of balance. If the room is too small, a quiet, inconspicuous, lightly broken wall treatment of retreating color will add a feeling of spaciousness; while an advancing color and wall paper of strongly contrasted light and dark would make the room appear even smaller. If it is too low, an emphasis upon verticality (as in the hangings and other furnishings) and suppression of horizontality (as in the avoidance of horizontal moldings and borders) will increase the appearance of height. The *Parthenon* is long and low, but the insistent verticals of the fluted columns create a balance and a feeling of "rightness."

Chartres is very vertical, hardly held in restraint by horizontals. Here too is "rightness." Both are "right." Behind the design lie the purpose and the people with their ideas and feelings. Balance for the Greek was different from balance for the Gothic. One must not be dogmatic. Each must determine for himself what constitutes balance in his own room. But balance there must be; without it everything collapses.

What then of the monotonous wall space? It may be needed to balance the broken walls of the other sides. If, on the other hand, the wall still remains monotonous and overbalances with its unbroken space, the furnishings (perhaps a picture or hanging) can be used to break the large area and establish a balance.

In the furnishings, the first question is that of function: what is there in the room that has no use in function or design? What can be eliminated without sacrificing efficient use and pleasing appearance? Having reduced the furnishings to the necessary minimum with a modicum for that which delights by indulging the personal tastes of the owner (for too much impersonality is as bad as none), one may then consider each piece, first as a form and then as related to the other forms and to the form of the room as a unit. A good chair, for instance, *looks* its use. The supporting parts are proportioned to the weight; the back and arms are related to the seat so as to insure comfort. The materials fittingly harmonize and contrast. The upholstery, in pattern, color, and texture, depends upon the material of the frame: massive wood, woven reed, light metal. The construction of a good chair is dependent upon the same guiding principles as the *University Chapel*. In both it is a matter of materials, the way in which they are used, and the purpose for which they are used, subject to the creative sensitivity of the artist who can proportion and balance, contrast and unify. In the *Chapel* the thick stone walls, the great windows, the relative open and solid stone areas of the tower, the relative proportions of all parts—every detail presents itself to our eyes as a contributing element to the unified and harmonious whole; and the visual impression of strength and aspiration dignifies every event which takes place in the building. It is true that the *Chapel* gains in majesty and power through its size. A fine chair, though small in comparison, is as architectural in principle and may appeal to some as strongly as the *Chapel*.

To return to our room, though the chair may be fine of itself, does it belong in the room? Have you not seen a chair look ugly in one place and "just fit" in another? Study that chair, not in itself but in its relation to its surroundings, and you will probably find the explanation. Its form or some details of its form—its materials, their color or texture, its shape, size, proportions—clash too dissonantly or harmonize too mildly with the table, for example, or with the room as a whole. Our objective, the harmony of the whole, is a stern master. Yet by it every piece of furnishing in a good room— furniture, hangings, wall decorations, rugs, pictures, ornaments, lighting fixtures—is measured. Each is a form of a definite material—wood, stucco, tile, metal, textiles, glass— subject to its own guiding principles of material, function, and design, and each is also a contributing element to the whole.

If we can make of our rooms works of art, can we not do the same with ourselves in our personal appearance? Just as we began with what was given us, in making a work of art out of our room, so in the matter of ourselves we begin with what nature has given us. It may or may not be beautiful. We re-formed the ugly room into an attractive one by infusing into it, by means of the furnishings, qualities of balance, proportion, unity, and harmony in accordance with our own personal interpretations of those qualities. In the same way the physical self is re-formed by clothing into something attractive or unattractive in proportion as the garments are selected to secure these qualities. Have you watched people on the street with this observation in mind? How often does a tall gaunt person wear garments that accent verticality! And the stout person, those which emphasize horizontality! A pale type—pale complexion, light eyes and hair—often selects a pale uncontrasted color when it should have a color that in hue and intensity brings in the needed contrasting strength.

Some types need brown; some, blue. Not the prevailing style but suitability to myself. My physical self and my personality (ideas to be expressed) are the basic forms to be re-formed and hence set forth in their essential qualities, not obliterated. Each article of clothing is partly a form in itself and largely a contributing element to the whole. How attractive is a hat in a shop window! How ugly on me!

One more activity we mentioned for discussion—the way in which we use our leisure. Here too can we see the way of art? It depends upon whether we see life itself as an art—a balanced, unified, harmonious whole. If we do, then we know that variety is essential for this harmony.

After all, there is not only variety, but also unity. The diversity of the Many is balanced by the stability of the One. That is why life must always be a dance, for that is what a dance is: perpetual slightly varied movements which are yet always held true to the shape of the whole.[8]

The great wall of the *Egyptian Temple* is more unified when broken by carving and color. The rapid zigzag motif of the *Navajo Blanket* brings in so refreshing a contrast to the more austere step pattern that the unity of the entire design is greater. In Leonardo's *Last Supper* the reposeful room and the poiseful central figure would be uninteresting were they not set over against and united with the restless, moving masses of the disciples. Is there a work of art which does not illustrate this principle of variety in unity? If life, then, is a work of art, may we not see in leisure a vitalizing variety to the main business of life? May we not look upon leisure as a form and ask whether the character of the form is such that it exists partly for itself and partly for the intensification which its contrasts bring to the larger whole? The pattern of life may be like that of the *Navajo Blanket*: simple and forceful; or like that of the royal *Persian Carpet*: complex and rich. It is a difference not of value but of kind. One thing, however, is certain: neither the *Navajo Blanket*,

[8] H. Ellis, *The Dance of Life*, Houghton Mifflin Company, Boston, 1923, p. viii.

nor the *Persian Carpet*, nor any kind of life is a work of art without wisely placed, balanced variety. As for life, the activities of our leisure time form one of the chief sources of this variety.

There is a tendency, in these days of specialization, to pigeonhole our activities—work, play, religion, civics, art— and when engaged in one, to banish all others to their tight compartments. An illustration of the possibility of breaking down these partitions is the late Prof. A. A. Michelson, one of the world's great physicists, who when asked why he persisted in his attempt to measure the velocity of light even more precisely when the present measurement was an acknowledged absolute, said that it "amused" him. A profound scholar, relentless in his demands for accuracy, found "amusement" in his work. Fittingly he has been called the "scientist-artist."

If we conclude that it is possible to look at everything with the artist's vision and to pursue all activities in accordance with art principles, let us restate what is involved. Life is the raw material of the artist, as it is of every one's living. The artist, in the first place, as he looks out upon the world, sees things, people, and incidents as forms and grasps their significance, both outward and inward, and the significant aspects of commonplace things, in proportion as he has within himself the capacity to perceive and feel such significance. In the second place, he creates an appropriate form in appropriate material for a convincing expression of this significance. In the third place, he is a craftsman grounded in the technique of his craft. Some of these activities he pursues consciously, some subconsciously. No one of them is *a priori*, nor are they to be isolated. Each acts on and is inextricably fused with the others. They do not account entirely for the artist. Other forces are at work—social, economic, religious, geographic. But these three are distinguishable and essential wherever we find great art. There is, it is true, a difference in degree between profound, imaginative, universal art and the art of our daily activities—but not in kind. We are all potential artists.

LAYING THE GROUNDWORK

Preparation for Reading

1. Do you think of the artist as an eccentric fellow or as a creative worker in a particular medium? Are you an artist?
2. In America, are the arts regarded as a part of daily life?
3. What kind of pictures or music do you like best—contemporary, classical, exotic? Why? Do you enjoy art galleries or symphonies?
4. Can you think of anything which you do daily with an artist's skill?
5. How do you suppose the various arts originated? To what extent does art express the life and ideals of a people or period?

Vocabulary Building

1. Before you read look up these words: *stridently, tactile, pliancy, scintillating, façade, permeate, mediocre, pursuance, modicum, gaunt, austere, a priori, potential, bracken, graining, contours, dissonantly, obliterated, pigeonhole, velocity.*
2. Explain the meanings of these musical terms or forms: *major, minor, tempo; sonata, symphony, chamber music.* What is a motif in music? in literature?
3. Read Chapter VII in Edith Rickert's *The Study of Literature* to see how such visual devices as punctuation, spelling, capitals, italics, and division into lines, stanzas, and paragraphs influence the stylistic effect of prose and poetry.
4. In Miss Gardner's *Understanding the Arts* or in an encyclopedia look up the characteristics of skyscrapers, Navajo blankets, Persian carpets, Egyptian temples. Check these references in the essay to see whether you understand their use as art symbols.

APPRAISING THE RESULTS

1. According to Miss Gardner, how do we use the different senses to interpret things about us? How do these sense perceptions differ with various people, i.e., artists, scientists, the average man, you?
2. How do associations color what we see, smell, taste, hear, or touch?

3. How are we all "potential artists"? How do you express your love of beauty? Are you an artist as Miss Gardner uses the term?

4. Explain what she means by form. Why does she feel she must define it?

5. Discuss the three essential forces which distinguish great art. According to Miss Gardner, what four other forces are also at work?

6. How do universal art and the art of our daily lives compare? How does the principle of selection enter into the work of the artist? Does he strive for exact representation?

7. How can literature, living, or dressing be an art?

SELECTING THE THEME SUBJECT

1. Study the view from your home or classroom window. Write a description of what you have seen for a child, a blind person, an artist, or an advertisement.

2. Select a musical selection, a sea poem, a description from a novel, or a piece of imaginative writing, and analyze its sense appeal.

3. Go to some art gallery and select a picture or piece of sculpture for study. View it carefully from all angles; study form, arrangement, color, shadow and light, composition. Try to discover what the artist's conception was. Return on successive days to examine it. Then write a paper explaining it.

4. Write a paper based on a consideration of tactile sensations, describing some object or surface by its touch, or the characteristics of tactile sensation. Recall how lines, shapes, quality of surface, and degree of resistance influence one's identification of objects and affect one's emotional response.

5. Write a theme explaining some art or skill you know: weaving, pottery or jewelry-making, bookbinding, photography, printing, music, sculpture, architecture, city planning, needlework, carving, stained glass, etching, wood blocks, painting.

6. Write a theme about the building you consider the most beautiful or the ugliest in your city.

7. Titles for themes: How I Learned to Enjoy Good Music; Folk Music in America; Learning to See; The Principles of Balance (or of color, or of interior design).

FAREWELL TO BOHEMIA[1]

Eduard C. Lindeman

IN EACH RESPECTIVE NATION THE BOHEMIA OF ARTISTS HAS A NAME—THE LEFT BANK, SOHO, GREENWICH VILLAGE—BUT IN reality these are not places; the names are mere localisms. Bohemia is primarily a mechanism of escape designed to liberate artists from the controls of a competitive system which are oblivious, if not antagonistic, to esthetic values. To live in Bohemia is to issue a declaration of independence from a crass society and at the same time to indicate contempt for its standards.

But like all artificial escapes, the Bohemias of the world have failed. In spite of glorification of the artist's garret and the romantic fiction which associated creativeness with poverty, artists turn out to be organisms needing requisites to life which may be had only in exchange for money. And so it comes about that the artist who remains an artist is obliged to compromise with the society from which he thought he had fled; or else become associated with a small maverick group and devote his art to the purposes of complaint and protestation. In either case in exchange for temporary security or for a doubtful liberty in the sphere of personal conduct, the artist sacrifices his natural audience; and allows himself to be detached from the only soil which can permanently nourish true art, namely the people.

The exciting thing is that the American version of this story can begin to be told in the past tense.

Broadway, which is the other side of the shield of which Bohemia became the counterpart, placed its monetary stamp

[1] From *Survey Graphic*, April, 1937. Reprinted by permission of the author and of *Survey Graphic*.

399

upon the drama. The symbol of American music became high priced seats in Carnegie Hall or the Diamond Horseshoe. The arts tended to become so "fine" and so expensive that their products were stored in museums, which were slow to open their doors at hours suitable for the people who do the work of the world. If contemporary examples of valid painting and sculpture broke through their walls, if there were creative links in the speculative sequence of patronage and portraiture, dealers, museums, orchestras, operas and theaters, these may be taken as evidence of the essential strength and character of the esthetic impulse even when it is made subservient to a faulty economy. For the most part the artist was caught in that chain, dissociated from the life and experience of the American folk. In the end the folk developed a thorough-going suspicion with respect to both his products and his purposes, and lent themselves to the exploiters of commercial vulgarity.

The great mass of citizens of the United States who have not yet seen a great work of American art, who can not come to Broadway, who have not yet heard good music save as the radio has brought it to their ears, who live in ugly houses pushed back from the center of communities where stand atrocious public buildings and still more atrocious public monuments, who live in country homes the walls of which are decorated with shiny lithographs advertising life insurance or patent medicines, these have been the major sufferers whose lives were detached from beauty.

But, something has happened!

American artists have come out of the alleys of Bohemia and are now trudging the highways of the American continent. They are shaking hands with farmers, workers, technicians, politicians, teachers; they have seen a "slant ray of quick, American light" leading toward new vistas; they are painting American "stuff" on the walls of American buildings, acting plays before audiences who can pay only 50 cents for a theater seat, furnishing music to farmers and workers in school buildings paid for out of public taxation.

Visitors from foreign lands who sense what has happened seem to apprehend its meaning more accurately than those who have participated in it. Thus Ford Madox Ford used, perhaps, a superlative when on a recent visit he said: "Art in America is being given its chance and there has been nothing like it since before the Reformation."

What, then, has happened? Stated in bald, straightforward and quantitative terms this is the startling and momentous event: *During the past two years well over 150,000 painters, sculptors, designers, actors, musicians, special instructors and writers have received salaries from the Treasury of the United States Government.* Nothing but a crisis could have brought this about. The crisis in turn may be expressed in simple words: In 1933 American artists in increasing numbers applied for unemployment relief. The term "unemployment" does not apply precisely to artists. Most of them have never been employed in a strict sense. Actors and musicians ordinarily work under contracts but even under such circumstances there exists a wide area of uncertainty and speculation. Whatever security actors and musicians have attained may be credited to the fact that they operate under the discipline of organizations of a trade union type. But, most artists have labored on a fee basis, which has meant in the past that art was considered a luxury. In the beginning of the economic crisis school boards sought ways of economizing; they did not hesitate to eliminate first of all courses in the arts—an indication that art had not yet found its place in our national budget. In the midst of this crisis theaters remained closed; concerts were diminished in number; the demand for paintings and works of sculpture dropped sharply. In Greenwich Village artists displayed their wares on the curb.

In short, the American artists were cast adrift upon the sea of economic uncertainty. Their patrons deserted them. Their market collapsed. Hence it came about that many of them received assistance under the Civil Works program of the Federal Relief Administration in 1934. In 1935 when the national administrator, Harry Hopkins, announced that President Roosevelt had agreed definitely to experiment in substituting work for other forms of relief it was already evident that artists as well as other so-called white-collar workers would need to be provided for. Specific projects including drama, music, painting and sculpture, and writing were formulated and became an integral part of the government's program of work under the Works Progress Administration. For the first time in our history, the various arts had become a responsibility of the federal government. In a short time this unique venture will have come to the close of a two-year demonstration.

What is here attempted is, of course, not of the nature of a critical evaluation. The writer is biased; he has been involved in this program and what he says should be partially discounted. Also, he is extremely enthusiastic with respect to this new alliance between government and the arts: in the first place, he believes that our basic frustrations are not economic nor technological in nature but rather cultural, and hence he counts heavily upon the arts as guides to a new sense of value; in the second place, he firmly believes that it is a proper function of government to furnish channels within which all the arts of life may freely flow. This conception does not seem to conform to the notion of government held and projected by most legalists. What is here attempted should be regarded as prolegomena, an introduction to a more thorough-going appraisal which seems definitely called for by reason of the significance of the event.

The principal consequences thus far discernible which have resulted from the government's entrance into the sphere of the arts seem to be:

First: art in general has at last become a topic of public discourse. I do not go so far as the English author already quoted above when he says, "America is a land for artists," but I do say that at last art is becoming democratized and if this process continues, America will soon become a land in which all the arts will thrive. The moment art is seen as a derivative of the people's environment and their experience it ceases to be the possession of the élite: it steps down from the atmosphere of rarefied isolation and identifies itself with the speech of the folk.

Second: artists of many varieties have discovered both the possibility and enjoyableness of collaborating with each other. Art is a form of communication and communication is many-sided. In some instances the highest form of communication results from the inward brooding of the artist isolated from external stimuli; at other times art has something important to say only because the artist has touched life at vital points. But, always true art tends to become a shared experience; its direction of flow is outward. Under government projects artists—painters, designers, musicians, dancers, writers, actors, sculptors, architects—have been obliged to work in concert.

Third: the various arts have entered the life of the people at two new points, namely in education and in recreation. Much of the adult education sponsored by the Works Progress Administration is already colored by the introduction of both elementary and advanced arts and crafts. And the government's recreation program has tended to center about the arts as an appropriate expression for the people's leisure. In this manner a vast new audience for professional artists is being created.

Fourth: the participant, as contrasted with the performance, idea in art is gaining ground. Most artists entertain the dream that their aspirations will have been completed when audiences are induced to come with money in their hands to watch them perform. Now thousands of artists are beginning to learn that another consummation awaits them, namely audiences will also come to participate, not merely to watch.

Fifth: through the government's program, especially through the instrumentality of the Index of American Design, we are at last beginning to learn that art has always had a natural although concealed home in this country. There is an American initiative which has not exhausted itself in material striving. It has been hesitant, true, and its roots have been well-nigh lost, but they are there. The esthetic impulse to create valid design lives in the American tradition and one day we shall know it for what it really is; at that moment we shall also summon the courage to follow it toward a fairer future.

The above effects, although stated in the most generalized terms, seem to me to be patent and readily observable. But there are also deficits and these need not be evaded. There was no experience upon which we could call for an enterprise of this sort and naturally numerous errors have been committed. We learned, for example, that many of the best artists managed somehow to remain off the relief rolls and because of the necessary strictness of government procedures it was not possible to utilize the services of some of them who might have enriched this program. We have also learned that a great many individuals who called themselves artists and insisted upon earning their way as artists had never passed through a rigorous testing process and that surprising numbers of them were definitely incapable. And the alliance between art, politics and relief has proved itself to be a *mis*alliance. These are, however, remediable.

To remove the impediments which stand between the people and the arts, to make room for a valid expression of beauty arising from the people and returning again to nourish the people, and to hold forth promise to the youth of the future whose talents and inclinations urge them toward the arts as occupation—these are the clearly-revealed tasks of this generation. Stated otherwise the need appears to be that of making an honest attempt to give art its place within the democratic process. Certainly, this is not an appropriate undertaking for private philanthropy. To be healthy, the arts must be made integral to democracy. The responsibility must be shared by those whose labors support all other functions of government. But, just as art tends to dissociate itself from the people when it becomes centralized in metropolitan areas—in Bohemias—so it will also suffer if, for example, the federal government should undertake to make art subservient to Washington. We do not want a regimented art, nor do we desire a politicalized art. What the federal government can do is to build the channels and to furnish the initial resources which will permit the growth of a national cultural movement for which the arts will supply tone and depth and quality. Then will arise a new freedom, not founded upon insulation, but a truly democratic freedom which evolves from relatedness.

LAYING THE GROUNDWORK

Preparation for Reading

1. What associations does the title suggest to you?
2. Have you seen any plays or murals or read any writing done by members of the Federal Arts Project? If so, what is your opinion of their quality and success?
3. If you have not yourself seen or read any of the work of the Federal Arts Project, on what have you based your opinions of it?

Vocabulary Building

1. Look up the derivations and meanings of any unfamiliar words: *oblivious, antagonistic, esthetic, crass, valid, subservient, lithographs, dissociated, supplanting, unique, collaborating, instrumentality, misalliance, insulation, maverick.*
2. Explain what these references mean: The Left Bank, Soho, Greenwich Village, Bohemia, Carnegie Hall, Diamond Horseshoe.

APPRAISING THE RESULTS

1. How is Bohemia a "mechanism of escape"? Why is Mr. Lindeman saying farewell to Bohemia?
2. What does he say is the real source of art? What forces in America divorced the artist from this source?
3. Why have artists gone from Bohemia to the highways of America?
4. Discuss the work of the Federal Arts Project under the W.P.A.
5. Summarize the five consequences which Mr. Lindeman sees as a result of federal aid to the arts.
6. What dangers are inherent in "politicalized" art? Do you think the Federal Arts Projects have avoided or succumbed to them? Give specific evidence for your reply.
7. Contrast the present government patronage with the patronage of the Renaissance.
8. What caused the decline of road shows and Chautauquas? Have these been revived recently?
9. Is teaching the arts to all the people irrespective of their artistic skills justifiable?

10. How well are museums, symphonies, and exhibits attended?
11. Will the F.A.P. have any lasting effect on American arts?

SELECTING THE THEME SUBJECT

1. Discuss one aspect of federal art work: murals for government buildings, a state writers' project, the Federal Theater for Children, etc.
2. Make a survey of what your community has done for the arts locally, through federal aid.
3. Write a theme on the experimental theater, modernism in art, surrealism, chamber music.
4. Study the career of an outstanding American in any of the arts and report on his significance.
5. Compare the American theater with the Russian, the French, or the English.
6. How has the Nazi program affected German arts?
7. Additional theme subjects: Puppetry; The Passing of the Road Show; College Theatricals; Workers in Stone or Glass; The Kind of Federal Theater Plays I Have Seen; Shakespeare's Stage; The Max Reinhardt Theater; The Salzburg Festivals; Helen Hayes, or Katharine Cornell, or Lynn Fontanne and the American Stage; The Little Theater Movement; Careers for Interior Decorators; The Return of Victorian Gewgaws; Iconoclasts in the Arts; The Small Town's Growing Interest in Art.

The Printed Word

WHY WE READ[1]
Jay B. Hubbell

Studies serve for delight, for ornament, and for ability. . . . Read not to contradict and confute, nor to believe and take for granted, nor to find talk and discourse, but to weigh and consider.
FRANCIS BACON: Of Studies.

Literature is the effort of man to indemnify himself for the wrongs of his condition.
RALPH WALDO EMERSON.

WHY DO MEN AND WOMEN READ BOOKS? HAVE YOU EVER NO-TICED HOW VARIOUS ARE THE MOTIVES WHICH TURN US TO books? Some of us read merely to pass the time away, or to save ourselves from boredom; some read in order to find something to talk about; others wish to impress somebody, or are afraid of being considered uninformed; some read from habit. One man may read in order to learn more about life, another for ideas, and still another for emotional stimulation. An occasional student reads because he wishes to learn to use the language more correctly and fluently.

These are the more common motives. Which of them move you—the better or the worse? Let us examine a little more carefully four or five of these motives. It is these incentives to reading that literature must satisfy, and we shall understand better the nature of this great art after a brief analysis.

LITERATURE OFFERS A WAY OF ESCAPE

With many readers of a romantic bent—and with all of us in certain moods—literature offers a way of escape from un-pleasant realities. When we are weary of the Here and Now,

[1] From *The Enjoyment of Literature*, by Jay B. Hubbell. Reprinted by permission of The Macmillan Company, publishers.

we like to dream of the far-off in space or in time. In this mood there is no resource like a book, or, as Emily Dickinson has phrased it,

> There is no frigate like a book,
> To take us lands away,
> Nor any coursers like a page
> Of prancing poetry.

In his fascinating narrative, *Revolt in the Desert,* Colonel Thomas E. Lawrence mentions an experience which he had in a winter-bound Arabian Village during the World War: "We were twenty-eight in the two tiny rooms, which reeked with the sour smell of our crowd. In my saddle-bags was a [copy of Malory's] *Morte d'Arthur.* It relieved my disgust. The men had only physical resources; and in the confined misery their tempers roughened." Those who have never discovered the resource of reading go to the movies or turn to idle day-dreaming. The best refuge is a romance. "Fiction," says Robert Louis Stevenson, in "A Gossip on Romance," "is to the grown man what play is to the child." "The great creative writer," he continues, "shows us the realization and the apotheosis of the day-dreams of common men. His stories may be nourished with the realities of life, but their true mark is to satisfy the nameless longings of the reader, and to obey the ideal laws of the day-dream." For men so fortunate as to have preserved something of the eternal boy, there are no romances more satisfying than Stevenson's *Kidnapped, David Balfour,* and *Treasure Island.*

LITERATURE MAY EXTEND ONE'S EXPERIENCE

In an unromantic, or realistic, mood we read not to escape life but to learn more about it and to extend our limited experience of it. A novel by Thackeray or Balzac or a good biography gives one a feeling of reality, of aliveness. We feel that what we are reading, even if it is unpleasant, must nevertheless be true. Paradoxically, art can give us pleasure even when it deals with what is drab and commonplace. Even the ugly and the tragic may become absorbingly interesting. A part of our pleasure comes from our recognizing the truthfulness of the portrait, but much of it is due also to the author's ability to see more in life than we have seen. In Browning's poem the painter, Fra Lippo Lippi, explains why we like to see everyday life mirrored by the artist:

> For, don't you mark? We're made so that we love
> First when we see them painted, things we have passed
> Perhaps a hundred times nor cared to see;
> And so they are better, painted—better to us,
> Which is the same thing. Art was given for that.

Literature, when supplemented by intelligent observation, can teach us much about human nature. The number of interesting people whom most of us know is quite limited. Literature offers us a means of extending our experience almost indefinitely. Biography and history can bring back the great men of the past—Johnson, Napoleon, Lincoln, Franklin. Individuals whom in actual life we should avoid may become extraordinarily interesting in the pages of a novel or upon the stage. In real life few of us have known such men and women as Huckleberry Finn, Uncle Remus, Falstaff, Hamlet, Becky Sharp, Jeanie Deans, Sam Weller, Eustacia Vye, Tartuffe, Jean Valjean, or Silas Lapham.

Not only may literature extend enormously the range of our experience; it can also greatly widen the bounds of our sympathies. One cannot read Tolstoy's *War and Peace* or *Anna Karénina* and still feel that all Russians are half-savage revolutionists, nor Hamlin Garland's *Main Travelled Roads* and think of all farmers as "rubes" and "hicks." Literature can help us to escape the narrowing influences of our own nation, race, religion, social class, profession, our years, our temperament, the age in which we live. If our reading does not make us wiser, more tolerant, and more sympathetic, it has failed in one of its chief aims.

Literature is not a substitute for living; it is a way of living —a means of widening and intensifying one's life. When we have read a play by Shakespeare or a novel by Thackeray, we ought for days afterwards to be able to see the world and its people through the far-seeing eyes of the poet or the novelist. After reading the poems of Burns or Wordsworth, one ought to be able to find unsuspected beauty in a Texas prairie, a Carolina cotton field, or a back street in any town or city. If one knows how to read, the accomplishment places the reader temporarily on a footing of something like equality with the masters. "We are all poets," said Carlyle, "when we *read* a poem well."

LITERATURE AND CONDUCT

If literature is a criticism, or interpretation of life, as Matthew Arnold taught, it should have a definite relation to the problem of how to live rightly. Literature must not be didactic, however, or it will defeat its purpose. Preaching is not a function of literature, especially of poetry. "Literature does not argue," said Cardinal Newman; "it declaims and insinuates; it is multiform and versatile; it persuades instead of convincing; it seduces, it carries captive; it appeals to the sense of honor, or to the imagination, or to the stimulus of curiosity; it makes its way by means of gaiety, satire, romance, the beautiful, the pleasurable."

There is a certain type of fiction which tends to relax the fibers of the will if it is read too exclusively. Plato banished certain types of poetry from his ideal republic because they appealed to the emotions rather than to the will or the reason. "The best romance," said Ruskin, "becomes dangerous, if, by its excitement, it renders the ordinary course of life uninteresting, and increases the morbid thirst for useless acquaintance with scenes in which we shall never be called upon to act." An American novelist, William Dean Howells, has condemned this type of fiction as severely as any moralist:

If a novel flatters the passions, and exalts them above the principles, it is poisonous; it may not kill, but it will certainly injure; and this test will alone exclude an entire class of fiction, of which eminent examples will occur to all. Then the whole spawn of so-called unmoral romances [this is a hit at Stevenson] which imagine a world where the sins of sense are unvisited by the penalties following, swift or slow, but inexorably sure, in the real world, are deadly poison: these do kill. The novels that merely tickle our prejudices and lull our judgment, or that coddle our sensibilities or pamper our gross appetite for the marvellous are not so fatal, but they are innutritious, and clog the soul with unwholesome vapors of all kinds. No doubt they too help to weaken the moral fibre, and make their readers indifferent to "plodding perseverance and plain industry," and to "matter-of-fact poverty and commonplace distress."

No one should limit his reading to a single type, least of all to romantic or sensational fiction. One will do well to read more often the great realistic novels, the tragedies of Shakespeare, and the essays of the ethical stimulators, Marcus Aurelius, Emerson, and Carlyle. The great poets sometimes assume the prophet's mantle. They quicken our sympathy with the right, our scorn for the wrong. Contact with a great and noble personality, like that of Milton or Dante, makes one a better man or woman. And yet the aims of literature are so various that one cannot agree with Emerson that its one aim is "to inspire." The great writer reveals to us life in all its beauty and sadness and complexity as he sees it, but he rarely regards it necessary to attach a moral, which only the stupid would fail to see anyway.

BEAUTY OF FORM

Thus far we have considered only the content, or subject matter, of literature, but a large part of our pleasure in reading a story or a poem is due to its formal, or technical, qualities. Few, to be sure, read a story or a poem purely for its structure or its style; and yet who cares to read a poorly written story, no matter what its content may be? Far more of the reader's pleasure comes from form than he usually suspects. Stevenson goes so far as to say, "There is, indeed, only one merit worth considering in a man of letters—that he should write well; and only one damning fault—that he should write ill." In some writers, like Poe and O. Henry, the content is slight; in others, like Tennyson and Longfellow, it is somewhat commonplace. But there is a pleasure in finding even a platitude well expressed. What is there of originality or freshness about the thoughts expressed in Gray's famous "Elegy"? Practically nothing, and yet we all like it because we find here, in Pope's phrase, "What oft was thought but ne'er so well expressed."

LITERATURE AND COMPOSITION

The study of literature has an incidental but very practical value for the person who wishes to improve his writing or conversation. Any teacher of English composition will tell you that almost invariably his best students have acquired, usually at home, the habit of reading good books. Students who come from homes where there are few books rarely write easily or correctly. Reading gives one a wider vocabulary and cultivates a feeling for the finer shades of meaning in words. To profit fully, however, one must work systematically. Reading, conversation, and writing should all find a place on one's program. There is much wisdom in Francis Bacon's famous sentence, "Reading maketh a full man; conference [speech, discourse] a ready man; and writing an exact man."

In his autobiography Benjamin Franklin tells us how he improved his writing by a systematic imitation of the *Spectator* papers of Steele and Addison. Stevenson, in "A College Magazine," has described his somewhat similar experiences in playing "the sedulous ape" to the authors whom he admired:

Whenever I read a book or a passage that particularly pleased me, in which a thing was said or an effect rendered with propriety, in which there was either some conspicuous force or some happy distinction in the style, I must sit down at once and set myself to ape that quality. I was unsuccessful, and I knew it; and tried again, and was again unsuccessful and always unsuccessful; but at least in these vain bouts, I got some practice in rhythm, in harmony, in construction, and in the co-ordination of parts.

CONCLUSION

These, then, are the chief motives for the reading of books of permanent value. In later chapters we shall recur to all but the last. If your taste is catholic, you will have found that all of these functions of literature appeal to you. Do not ignore any one of them. And do not make the mistake of reading a book in a spirit alien to that in which it was written. To get the best out of any book, one must read it sympathetically.

Finally, do not forget that into the making of a great book go years of thought and of living, sometimes of tragic experience, and months and months of painstaking writing and revision. "For books," as John Milton well said, "are not absolutely dead things, but do contain a potency of life in them to be as active as that soul whose progeny they are; nay, they do preserve as in a vial the purest efficacy and extraction of that living intellect that bred them . . . a good book is the precious life-blood of a master spirit, embalmed and treasured up on purpose to a life beyond life." Of his book, says Ruskin, an author would say: "This is the best of me; for the rest, I ate, and drank, and slept, loved, and hated, like another; my life was as the vapour, and is not; but this I saw and knew: this, if anything of mine, is worth your memory."

LAYING THE GROUNDWORK

Preparation for Reading

1. What kind of reading do you enjoy most? List a few titles or authors you recall with pleasure.
2. What forces conflict with reading as a national habit?
3. Why is reading said to provide vicarious experiences?
4. Have we too great a regard for the printed word? Explain your answer.

Vocabulary Building

1. Look up these words: *paradoxically, didactic, insinuate, multiform, versatile, romance, morbid, sedulous, vapour.*
2. What fossil metaphors are buried in the words *fluent* and *platitude?*
3. Note distinctions in the meanings of these words listed as synonyms: *lampoon, sarcasm, irony, satire, ridicule, burlesque, pasquinade, wit, humor.*
4. If you do not know who these people are and cannot find them listed in the dictionary, look in *Who's Who, The Dictionary of National Biography,* or in other available biographical source books: Francis Bacon, Emily Dickinson, Thomas E. Lawrence, Malory, Robert Louis Stevenson, Franklin, Tolstoy, Hamlin Garland, Thackeray, Balzac, Browning, Samuel Johnson, Burns, Wordsworth, Carlyle, Matthew Arnold, Newman, Ruskin, William Dean Howells, Marcus Aurelius, Milton, Dante, O. Henry, Thomas Gray, Pope, Richard Steele, Addison.

APPRAISING THE RESULTS

1. What motives does Hubbell say prompt people to read?
2. What books would you recommend as excellent avenues of "escape"?
3. Discuss some books which have made you more understanding or sympathetic toward different people.
4. What is meant by "literature must not be didactic," although "it should have a definite relation to the problem of how to live rightly"?
5. Enumerate some of the ways in which beauty of form gives pleasure to the reader.
6. How does reading influence the student of composition?
7. Does the author omit any kind of reading which you consider valuable?
8. If you do not recognize these literary allusions, look them up in the dictionary under *Noted Names in Fiction* or in other source books: Huckleberry Finn, Uncle Remus, Falstaff, Hamlet, Becky Sharp, Jeanie Deans, Sam Weller, Eustacia Vye, Tartuffe, Jean Valjean, Silas Lapham.

SELECTING THE THEME SUBJECT

1. Write a theme discussing the recreational reading you enjoy or explaining why you do not like to read.
2. Study the list of best sellers for the past few seasons and attempt to explain the reasons for their popularity.
3. Make a selection of books you would buy if you had $25 for a library fund with which to purchase your own books. Explain the basis of your selections.
4. Discuss the ideal school library or your own grade, high school, or university library.
5. In a paper explain why you think parents should or should not censor their children's reading; or why there should or should not be a strict censorship of books by some national book committee.
6. Theme topics: Literary Adventurers; The Lure of the Fairy Tale; Literary Friendships; Modern Poetry; The Village School of Literature; The Children's Reading Room in the Library; My Favorite Story; Book Clubs; The Newspaper Room in the Public Library; Sailing the Seven Seas by Proxy; When Reading Is a Vice; How Books Recreate the Past.

PLAY IN POETRY[1]

Louis Untermeyer

THE AVERAGE READER—WHO REGARDS HIMSELF AS A MORE THAN
AVERAGE CRITIC—IS THE PERFECT DOGMATIST. ARMED WITH IM-
patience, predetermination, and six standard adjectives, he
cuts his rapid way through the books of the dead and the
literature of the living. He is particularly dogmatic about
poetry, and that he seldom reads it makes his finalities all the
more final. He has two conclusions about poetry, conclusions
which are as complete as they are inconsistent. Poetry, he
says, in the first place, is merely a tune without music, a
melody without meaning, a set of soothing (and, sometimes,
irritating) sounds without sense. And poetry, he inconsistently
adds, is all too difficult because it is so full of hidden allusions,
so intellectually condensed, so concentrated in meaning.

Actually poetry is neither an attempt to imitate music (except in such isolated cases as Sidney Lanier's) nor (except in
the rhymed essays of Pope) an effort to rival the daily editorial
in compact gravity and density. Poetry is often solemn, even
sombre, but more frequently it expresses the side-spring of
fancy, the leap of the adventurous imagination, the surprising
fantasia of the subconscious. I think it can be maintained that,
on the whole, poetry is as playful as it is profound.

By "playful" I do not mean merely the outburst of high
spirits or the formal lightheartedness of light verse. I mean

[1] This article appeared in *The Saturday Review of Literature*, February 26,
1938. It is a composite of two chapters of Louis Untermeyer's book, *Play in
Poetry*, published in 1938, by Harcourt, Brace & Company, Inc. It contains
a previously unpublished poem by Robert Frost, "Wilful Homing," near the
end of the article. Reprinted by permission of the author and of the publishers.

the essential spirit which unites and intensifies the figures of speech, the hyperboles and similes, all of which represent the poet's varying use of the invariable impulse to play. Poetry begins with metaphor, and the metaphorical power—the ability to see similarity in dissimilar things—is increased or decreased with the playfulness of the poet's mind. It is through metaphor that poetry achieves its rich suggestiveness, and becomes, as Robert Frost wrote half playfully, "the one permissible way of saying one thing and meaning another."

A metaphor is a game in which the wit of the writer and the wit of the reader are matched. The mind of the poet fastens on an object and then rushes halfway across the world to establish a relation between that object and some hitherto unrelated object. Although the objects are not in the least alike, the reader is quick to see the likeness at the point of comparison. My love, says the poet, is like—and, in the spirit of play, he looks about him for something resembling his lady as little as possible—like, he announces triumphantly, a red, red rose. To the solemn scientific eye there is no reasonable resemblance between the figure of a woman and the shape of a rose. But the reader is as little interested in laboratory realism as is the poet. It is an intellectual game, this saying one thing and meaning another, a verbal sportiveness; the poet points the way, and the reader's mind romps along.

No matter how long and deliberately the heart is studied, that variable organ would scarcely seem to be a thrush nesting in the willows, a tree bent down with apples, and a chambered nautilus rowing itself across the ocean—all at the same time. Yet the reader abandons deliberation; he forgets about the auricles and ventricles, the construction, the circulation, the position, even the function of that hollow, muscular organ. For the time being, at least, he is completely convinced when Christina Rossetti tells him:

> My heart is like a singing bird
>   Whose nest is in a watered shoot;
> My heart is like an apple-tree
>   Whose boughs are bent with thick-set fruit;

My heart is like a rainbow shell
  That paddles in a halcyon sea;
My heart is gladder than all these
  Because my love has come to me.

Thus the metaphor is something more than an amusing literary device; it is a continual play of wit, an illuminating
double entendre, a nimble magic in which writer and reader
conspire to escape reality. Perhaps "escape" is the wrong word
—the play of metaphor acts to enrich reality, even to heighten
it. The average reader enjoys its intensification so much that
he cannot help employing it. "My heart leaps," he says, knowing quite well that it contracts and expands quietly within
the pericardium. Or, he declares still more mendaciously but
earnestly, "my heart stood still." Even while he scorns poetry,
the ordinary man helps himself to its properties and symbols;
his daily life is unthinkable without metaphor. Having slept
"like a log," he gets up in the morning "fresh as a daisy" or
"fit as a fiddle"; he "wolfs down" breakfast, "hungry as a
bear," with his wife, who has "a tongue like vinegar," but "a
heart of gold." He gets into his car, which "eats up the miles,"
steps on the gas, and, as it "purrs" along through the "hum"
of traffic, he reaches his office where he is "as busy as a one-
armed paper-hanger with the hives." Life, for the average
man, is not "a bed of roses," his competitor is "sly as a fox"
and his own clerks are "slow as molasses in January." But "the
day's grind" is finally done and, though it is "raining cats and
dogs," he arrives home "happy as a lark."

What the Babbitt says in casual conversation is not so far
removed from what the poet has to say to him. It is only a step
from universal banalities to metaphorical ingenuities, an easy
transition from the average man's colorless stereotypes to the
colorful images of the Elizabethans. "You are a queen," says
the young man breathlessly in the 1937 parked car, "a honey,"
"a knockout," "a riot!" Unconscious of the playfulness, the
novel brilliance, the extravagant humor, of his metaphors, the
hard-boiled youth would snort if you told him he was speaking poetry. Yet Robert Herrick said it not so differently nor
less metaphorically three centuries ago.

You are a tulip seen today,
But, dearest, of so short a stay
That where you grew scarce man can say.

You are a lovely July-flower,
Yet one rude wind or ruffling shower
Will force you hence, and in an hour.

   .   .   .   .   .

You are a full-spread, fair-set vine,
You can with tendrils love entwine,
Yet dried ere you distil your wine.

You are like balm enclosèd well
In amber or some crystal shell,
Yet lost ere you transfuse your smell.

   .   .   .   .   .

No reader can fail to recognize the play of fancy. "A tulip,"
"a July-flower," "a full-spread vine," "balm in a crystal shell"
—the poet has gone somewhat far afield to compare his lady
to these pastoral beauties. But it takes no less imaginative
courage to draw metaphors from the prize-ring and the turbu-
lent streets in order to speak of the beloved as "a knockout"
and "a riot."

Metaphors are so vital a part of our speech, so common and
used so unconsciously, that they become, as William Empson
has indicated, the normal mode of development of a language.
And it is the incalculable reach of the image—the establishment of a kinship between unrelated objects, the combination of exactness and ambiguity—which is its charm and
power. Poetry may rest on the success or failure to establish
that precarious point of relation. The poet balances himself
on this point, just as he vacillates continually between pure
music and pure meaning. Blake cries:

Bring me my bow of burning gold!
Bring me my arrows of desire!
Bring me my spear! O clouds unfold!
Bring me my chariot of fire!

I will not cease from mental fight,
Nor shall my sword sleep in my hand,
Till we have built Jerusalem
In England's green and pleasant land.

To the wholly rational mind this is a statement so illogical
as to be absurd. The logical mind pictures a man overburdened with a bow of burning gold, arrows (of desire!), a
spear, and a sword, all of which he is, somehow, to wield not
in physical combat, but in a "mental fight." And these imple-
ments of war suddenly become architectural tools, for they
are to be used to build Jerusalem on the soil of England—an
undertaking which is as difficult as it is, politically speaking,
undesirable. But we do not read such lines as we read the
report of the British Commission on Palestine. We read them
and are excited by them because of the blend of visual and
sensual effects, of prophecy and muffled heroism, of shifting
images and fixed purpose, of precise statement and vague al-
lusion—in short, because of the shifting play of exactness and
ambiguity which affects us like a spell. A spell, an enchantment, for it was with enchantment, or incantation, that poetry
began. It was an incantation, or invocation, a play of words
and deeds between man and the gods; now it is a play between
man and men.

In Vachel Lindsay, for example, the play was outspoken.
His was a motley America, an America which impartially
acclaimed Daniel Boone and William Jennings Bryan, Johnny
Appleseed and John L. Sullivan, Andrew Jackson and P. T.
Barnum—acclaimed them not as individual, isolated phenomena, but as a galaxy of demi-gods. Lindsay saw these dis-
united States finally united by a congress or a congregation of
pioneers and baseball players, Presidents and movie-queens;
his "golden dream" was to be accomplished by a union of
high idealism and the "higher vaudeville," by heroic endeavor and fantastic vision, by an earnest combination of
beauty and ballyhoo. The humor was unashamed and explicit even when the purpose was most evangelistic; such
poems as the "The Congo," "General William Booth Enters
into Heaven," and "John Brown" are both grandiose and

comic; "The Daniel Jazz" is a grotesque extravaganza, "The Kallyope Yell," that glorification of noise

> —the Gutter Dream
> Born of mobs, born of steam—

is as uproarious as a football cheer, and "The Santa Fe Trail" is frankly labelled "A Humoresque." The conscious exhorter and the not too conscious humorist collaborate in performances where the Gospel is preached through a saxophone.

> Booth led boldly with his big bass drum—
> (Are you washed in the blood of the Lamb?)
> The saints smiled gravely and they said, "He's come."
> (Are you washed in the blood of the Lamb?)

The missionary and the minstrel are similarly combined in the rollicking opening of "The Congo," one of the wildest of contemporary fantasies, which the author gravely subtitled "A Study of the Negro Race":

> Fat black bucks in a wine-barrel room,
> Barrel-house kings, with feet unstable,
> Sagged and reeled and pounded on the table,
> Pounded on the table,
> Beat an empty barrel with the handle of a broom,
> Hard as they were able,
> Boom, boom, BOOM,
> With a silk umbrella and the handle of a broom,
> Boomlay, boomlay, boomlay, BOOM.

In Frost the humor is far more subtle; it is the humor of reservation, of philosophic banter, of understatement—the understatement of the most significant detail. In some of the poems the humor is instinctive and forthright. Even his titles betray his love of double meaning; "Mountain Interval" and "A Further Range" have the nature of puns and "North of Boston" turns a geographical direction into a spiritual suggestion. Humor invades the most serious and tragic of the poems; the very depth and intensity of "The Fear" are emphasized by its climactic anti-climax; "The Self-Seeker" pits the horror of its subject against a broad pungency of tone; "Mending Wall" is an extended piece of persiflage. Even

"The Death of the Hired Man" half conceals its pathos in
asides about self-respect and the way to build a load of hay,
in differences as to the definition of "home" and the sheer
fancy of the passage where the moon falls down the west,
"dragging the whole sky with it to the hills." Perhaps
"Birches" is the best example of this gravely quizzical humor.
"Birches" begins with pure observation, but the angle of observation is a peculiar one; observation soon gives way to
imagination, and the poem develops into a fantasy of trees
arching in the woods

> . . . trailing their leaves on the ground
> Like girls on hands and knees that throw their hair
> Before them over their heads to dry in the sun.

Suddenly the poet interrupts himself in the midst of his
fancies:

> But I was going to say when truth broke in
> With all her matter-of-fact about the ice-storm . . .

This, of course, is sheer play, the play not only of understatement but of contradiction. The poet has been dealing
with anything but matters of "fact," and his truth is true only
in the way that instinct and imagination are the truths of
poetry.

In the lyrics the humor is still more marked. The sharply
turned "Fire and Ice" is a sardonic epigram masking a speculation about that popular topic, the end of the world. Its grim
conclusion etches itself in the mind:

> I think I know enough of hate
> To say that for destruction ice
> Is also great
> And would suffice.

It is revealing to compare Frost's brusque conclusion with
Archibald MacLeish's treatment of the same theme. In Mac-
Leish's sonnet, "The End of the World," the débâcle comes
during a Breughel-like circus; while one set of freaks is performing for another, the top of the tent blows off, and there,
overhead, there hung over

Those thousands of white faces, those dazed eyes,
There in the starless dark, the poise, the hover,
There with vast wings across the cancelled skies,
There in the sudden blackness, the black pall
Of nothing, nothing, nothing—nothing at all.

MacLeish obtains irony with tension by a skilful accumulation of suspense and repetition; Frost achieves it by the concentration of philosophic undertones.

Elsewhere the effect is frankly comic, as in "The Cow in Apple Time," which begins:

Something inspires the only cow of late
To make no more of the wall than an open gate——

The humor is implicit in such a couplet, explicit in such a phrase as the mock-pedantic "of late." It is lightly ironic in "Plowmen," farcical in "Brown's Descent, or The Willy-Nilly Slide," politically Socratic in "Build Soil," critical in "The White-tailed Hornet," deliberately mocking in "Departmental, or The End of My Ant Jerry," bitterly satiric in "The Peaceful Shepherd":

If heaven were to do again,
And on the pasture bars
I learned to line the figures in
Between the dotted stars,

I should be tempted to forget,
I think, the Crown of Rule,
The Scales of Trade, the Cross of Faith,
As hardly worth renewal.

For these have governed in our lives,
And see how men have warred!
The Cross, the Crown, the Scales, may all
As well have been the Sword.

I stress, perhaps unduly, the humorous element, since Frost has been praised for almost everything but this quality. If I maintain that no poet in America has ever so effectively combined play and profundity it is only because it has usually been the critic's habit to appraise the latter and neglect the

former. Frost has been praised for the unity of his thought, for
the intellectual steadfastness which is not deceived by the
schools and slogans of the moment. He has been applauded
for the symmetry of his form and the shapeliness of his technique. He has been acclaimed as one who unearthed a new
kind of poetry from old and stony soil, finding his material in
what was "common in experience, uncommon in writing." It
is not yet ascertainable by what name he will be labelled by
the literary historian of the future. Contemporary theses have
been written proving Frost to be a classicist, a symbolist, a
humanist, a synecdochist (Frost's own half-serious classification), a centrist, and a glorified neighbor. All these designa-
tions are plausible, all have some justification, and none is an
accurate measure of the man. He is actually far more radical
than the extremists. But his is an old radicalism, not dependent on political shibboleths or technical eccentricities; it
is highly personal radicalism, not unlike the individual insur-
gence of Thoreau and the quiet but thoroughgoing rebellion
of Emerson. Frost has always questioned routines of thought,
he has disguised his intransigence in raillery, in offstage whis-
pers, in teasing circumlocutions, but his penetrations have
been none the less thorough. If I were called upon to add to
the categories, I would drop the classicist, the bucolic realist,
and the political humanist. I would call him a revisionist. It is
his power not only to restate, but to revise too easily accepted
conclusions, a power which no contemporary has equalled.

But he is a revisionist who is also a humorist, if the term
can be separated from its vaudeville implications and newspaper columnist connotations. In his introduction to Robinson's posthumous "King Jasper" Frost wrote, "The style is the
man. Rather say the style is the way the man takes himself;
and to be at all charming or even bearable, the way is almost
rigidly prescribed. If it is with outer seriousness, it must be
with inner humor. If it is with outer humor, it must be with
inner seriousness. Neither one alone without the other under
it will do." The sentences were written as a tribute to Robinson; essentially they are an almost perfect description of Frost
himself. His style, so characteristic, so seemingly simple and
yet so elusive, so colloquial and yet so elevated, has a way of

uniting opposites. It combines fantasy with matter-of-fact; or, rather, it is not so much a combination as an alteration, an intellectual legerdemain in which fact becomes fancy and the fancy is more compelling than the fact.

That Frost is both a revisionist and a humorist must be apparent to those who closely examine the alternating play of inner and outer humor in the "Collected Poems," but it is equally discernible in the highly playful "Wilful Homing," which appears here for the first time in print and has more than a little in common with Robinson's "Mr. Flood's Party." There is the same blend of uncertainty and determination, the same flicker of double meanings, the same shifts of mockery and tenderness. But no one can confuse the two inflections; slight though the poem is, its turns of phrase and idea make it indubitably Frost's. Here again is the quiet, careful humor of understatement.

WILFUL HOMING

It is growing late and time he drew to a house,
But the blizzard blinds him to any house ahead.
The snow gets down his neck in a chilly souse
That sucks his breath like a wicked cat in bed.

The snow blows on him and off him, exerting force
Downward to make him sit astride a drift,
Imprint a saddle, and calmly consider his course.
He peers out shrewdly into the thick and swift.

Since he means to come to a door he will come to a door,
Although so compromised of aim and rate;
He may fumble wide of the latch a yard or more,
And to those concerned he may seem a little late.

Such contrasting poetry transcends its material; it makes the reader aware of depths beyond the subject. The reader is grateful not because he has learned something, but because he has experienced something. He has drawn strength and serenity, but, perhaps most of all, he has fed on surprise. "Give us," wrote Frost, "immedicable woes—woes that nothing can be done for—woes flat and final. And then to play. The play's the thing. Play's the thing."

The teachers who tell us there must be a purpose in poetry are unquestionably right; no poet can escape his serious destiny. But, unless he can discard the leaping metaphor, the incalculable music, the free imagination, nothing can be done without play—"play's the thing"—especially when play has a purpose of its own.

LAYING THE GROUNDWORK

Preparation for Reading

1. Do you enjoy reading poetry? Give reasons for your answer.
2. How does poetry differ from prose?
3. How many contemporary poets can you name? Are you familiar with the work of any of them?

Vocabulary Building

1. Define and give an example of each of the following: a figure of speech, hyperbole, a simile, a metaphor, synecdoche.
2. Make a list of unfamiliar words in the selection, and find the meaning and pronunciation of each.

APPRAISING THE RESULTS

1. The author says that the average reader comes to the reading of poetry "armed with impatience, predetermination, and six standard adjectives." Why does this approach doom the reader to failure? What are some of the adjectives which might well be included in the "six standard adjectives"? What two conclusions does this approach lead to?
2. What is the thesis of this selection, and where is it first given?
3. How does the author define "playful"?
4. Show how the use of metaphor is a game of wits. What effects are achieved by this means?
5. Amplify and illustrate this statement: "Metaphors are so vital a part of our speech . . . that they become . . . the normal mode of development of a language."
6. Discuss the "play" spirit as it is exemplified in William Blake, Vachel Lindsay, and Robert Frost.
7. List words and phrases like "persiflage" and "quizzical," which

the author uses to describe humor in his discussion of the
poetry of Frost, and explain the shadings of difference between
the various types of humor.
8. What are the various terms applied to Frost and his work, and
which does Untermeyer accept as most accurate?

SELECTING THE THEME SUBJECT

1. Keeping the content of this selection in mind, read carefully
several poems of one of the following poets: A. E. Housman,
Edna St. Vincent Millay, Edwin Arlington Robinson, W. H.
Auden, Elinor Wylie, Louis Untermeyer, Hart Crane, Robin-
son Jeffers, John Masefield, Carl Sandburg, Emily Dickinson.
Then write a critical appreciation of what you have read.
2. Titles for themes: How I Learned to Like Poetry; The Use
of Poetry in Drama; The Art of Writing Limericks; American
Folk Poetry; War Poetry; Ballads and Ballad-makers; Nature
Poems; Sonnet Sequences; Poetry in the Age of Science;
Regional Poetry in America.

The Screen and the Stage

THEATRE AND FILM[1]

Herbert Biberman

"THE MOTION PICTURE IS A DIRECTOR'S MEDIUM—IT IS NOT AN ACTOR'S OR A WRITER'S MEDIUM."

This pronunciamento, when voiced by actors and writers, has a tone of hurt and frustrations; when voiced by directors, it savors of arrogance. Neither tone is justified although the statement is comparatively true. The truth within the statement, however, is a basic inevitable truth which should be accepted calmly rather than with evidences of wounded pride.

Unlike the theatre, the film impresses with the multiplicity of method, the variety of approach to the realization of subject matter; the limitless physical, psychological and contrapuntal means at one's disposal in the course of creation. Because of the amazing and infinite choices of approach, it is inevitable that the director must be master of the medium.

Since the matter of choice is so vital, let us examine it in relation to one of the complaining groups—the actor. From this group we shall find our way to other aspects of the subject.

Practically the first words I heard upon entering a motion picture studio—very fresh from the theatre—was a director instructing an actor not to be "stagey." Subsequently I heard such other phrases as "The nice thing about her is, she doesn't act," "I don't care whether he can act or not—he has a great personality." Then the ultimate words which resound through every motion picture studio—"Be natural." To such an extent is this effort to negate acting carried, that many directors shoot scenes before the actors are quite sure of their lines in the hope that out of this uncertainty will come a heightened degree of naturalness. For a time the very word

[1] From *New Theatre*, July, 1936. Reprinted by permission of the author.

427

"natural" made my hair stand on end. I had spent too many years in the study and admiration of acting to be party to its destruction. It seemed barbaric and infantile.

Two months later I was urging actors to be "natural" and warning them against becoming "stagey." In so short a time had I overcome my instinctive repulsion and joined the new faith. The explanation is simple and within it lies one of the fundamental distinctions between the theatre and the film. In the theatre the actor has four weeks to attain credible reality and persuasive effectiveness. In motion pictures one hasn't four hours, very often not four minutes. One hasn't half an act to build to a climax, often one hasn't half a second in a given shot. Hence one cannot "act" one's way to naturalness. The conditions attending the making of motion pictures call for the realization of a scene by "non-acting," by summoning up spontaneous reflex activity. In the main we photograph spontaneous personality *per se*, so we do not recreate it. This is a school of improvisation. To such an extent is this true that many actors refuse to look at lines until just before they step before the camera. This is not always sheer laziness. It is often a logically arrived at way of preserving all the spontaneous fluids until just before they are called for. The justification usually offered is that a little rehearsal is worse than none at all.

What is lost in technical brilliance in such performances is compensated for by certain qualities of the medium—qualities which make a neat differentiation between the two mediums under examination. In the theatre one attempts through acting to force an audience to give attention to that part of the whole visual scene which is for the moment the most important. One can never be certain one will completely succeed. An audience, or a part of it, may look at a minor character or a lamp or a fireplace or out of the window while Boy Gets Girl. In the film you can make it impossible for the audience to see anything but the person or thing you wish it to see. The fight necessary for audience attention is minimized. The mere fact that an actor does not have to fight for attention relieves him of the need for half his technical equipment. Not only his problem but the director's problem is rendered more primitive.

The need for sustained performance is totally absent in the film. If an actor speaks but one line effectively in an entire scene and that line is anywhere near a climax, not necessarily the climax itself, the shots can be so juggled that only that particular line will be addressed by that actor to the audience. His other lines may be spoken over close-ups of other actors and still give one the impression that he is being presented in first importance by short flashes of him. Indeed, it is possible to magnify the actor's presence to such a degree that the audience is barely conscious of the words he is speaking. In this connection, it is important to remember that on a strip of film the visual image is three quarters of an inch wide, whereas the sound track is only an eighth of an inch wide. The size of these tracks on the film indicates, in a measure, the relative importance of each. Film, for all its sound, is still primarily a visual medium. To put this broadly and perhaps a mite incorrectly, the theatre is for the ear and the film for the eye. How often have we heard of a play whose scenery swamped the actors? In film it is impossible to swamp the actor, for the scenery can be dissolved in an instant and be a mere haze behind a towering head close-up. Choice in the hands of the director weighs the value, place and importance of people and background, animate and inanimate elements; and he can and must at his own discretion sacrifice actor for scenery or vice versa in his effort impersonally to arrange the manifold elements constantly at his disposal and begging for proper evaluation in the composite mosaic which is film.

These primary distinctions, based upon the choice available to the director, between the two mediums may now be expressed in a more graphic way. The theatre is a telescope, the film is a microscope. This is curiously not the accepted understanding of the two mediums in the lay mind. We hear so much talk concerning the scope of the camera. It is necessary to define the word scope. Actually in any given second the proscenium arch has more effective scope with it than has the lens of a camera. It is, to illustrate, impossible to photograph effectively and without loss of focus or without distortion, a person very near the camera and one twenty feet from it in the same shot. In the theatre this is constantly happening; one sees all there is within the frame of the arch at all times, with almost equal clarity and power. The camera is hitting on only one cylinder when it reveals all of any scene. The camera, however, reaches its great and unique power when it concentrates on the contorted intimacies of one man's back and another man's face, or when it pans down to the signature on a letter. It is when it becomes a microscope that it becomes modern and natural in its own terms. And here one will encounter the heart of the distinction between the two mediums. In the theatre you think of the whole—you have only the whole; vignettes—small sets—spotted areas within blackness—multiple sets—all these cannot break up the whole of the proscenium arch and the set relation of actors to it in size, importance and position. In the theatre there is no smaller unit than the whole—you have it and you must like it. In pictures nothing is fixed in relation to anything else. Your proscenium arch hops around like a bug in a rug—and there is only one limit to your creation—your own imagination. Choice is the lawless law of the film.

In a given shot do you wish to show the people who are talking—the thing they are talking about—the person listening —talker and listener—talker and listener and thing talked about—do you wish a stationary image of the thing selected or a moving image—do you wish to be very near or very far away—do you wish a scene cut into angles—do you wish the camera moving and the people still or the camera still and the people moving—or both still or both moving—do you wish a face here or only the hand fiddling with a match stick —a hand or just a finger—a finger or just a knuckle—a knuckle or just the scar which you suddenly discover on the knuckle—or a man running down three flights of stairs? You can have all of these if you wish, or just one. There is no compulsion except to make your choice.

It seems logical that stage acting must change in taking its place in the film. Not alone must it change its form but even when it does not change, the use made of it changes it almost beyond its control. For in the film the actor is no longer a whole—he is broken up into pieces and the tiny bits of mosaic are then arranged into a pattern which makes the whole.

A scene may run thirty seconds—but its pieces may have been shot through the better part of a week—a shot of the actor's entire body on Monday, his head on Tuesday, his back on Wednesday, his offstage voice on Thursday, his smile on Friday, and his dilated eyes on Saturday. There is a superstition that the best take of every shot is always left in the can—that some mechanical error invariably spoils the best take of any scene and that the shot printed represents a second choice. This is not a source of great worry. For out of almost any shot the chances are that only a tiny portion will be used. What makes a scene, finally, is the general average of all angle takes of the scene plus the arrangement by the director and editor. So we see that the whole is achieved as a result of choice. Out of a thousand possibilities, let us say, of which a hundred have been tried, only ten are selected. Choice grows more imposing as the essential quality of the film. Filmic excellence, not acting alone, is the determinant.

Let us choose a specific example. In a recent picture, a girl told a boy that she was about to have a baby—a scene which is tender, dangerous, commonplace. In the theatre one could use one's talent to make that recitation affecting. This could only be accomplished through the combined acting of the whole—the boy and the girl and the entire expanse of the stage. In the film one never saw the girl at all. One heard her announcement over a close shot of the boy's face. The whole scene was played entirely on the young man's reactions. The girl was an offstage voice. She was the announcer—and she did not act. She did not try to convey an emotion. She was a verbal title. The emotion came to us from what was actually a silent shot of the boy reacting to a title. The scene was effective and fresh. It had been made so by the director. He had used the medium. He had exercised his prerogative—choice. The scene might have been played over a shot of two pairs of hands or over a beer truck rattling along a road. The director chose the close shot of the boy as the one way in a thousand possible ways to play that scene.

Time and space suffer no lesser indignities than the actor at the hands of the film. A second may be turned into ten minutes and an inch into infinity. This will even more fully explain the justification for all that has gone before.

In a recent picture I had a jail break to shoot. My script permitted me eighteen men, a machine gun and a gray wall. Had I been in the theatre I would have had just those elements. In film I had a hundred men, a battery of guns and a prison as immense as the sky is vast. Let us analyze that statement. First we saw these men huddled against a distant wall, puppets, pitiable little crusts, tiny scales on a prison wall daring to dream of liberty. In close-up we had a machine gun pointed at them. The machine gun, actually a half-inch in diameter, was made to appear like a ten inch gun. As the men rushed into blackness the impression was of ants charging infinity. With the firing of the machine gun, each of these crusts grew into ten giants. We see a tiny figure firing a gun, a waist-high figure of a man with a gun at this distance already a person, a close-up of a terrorized desperate man, the sheer boiling humanity within him magnified to defiance, a close-up of the gun in his hands discharging its vehement complaint against the prison as the final symbol of his revolt, the man being hit, shrunk again to the stature of a man, the man falling, the man's face falling, the man's hands falling limp at his side after a reflex tearing at the sky. All of these things each of the men became individually, until finally, in long shot, these dead crusts lay still, scattered about the yard of the prison as a searchlight played slowly over their prostrate bodies, as small and quiet finally as they had been small and terrorized when we first saw them.

The actual length of the scene played from beginning to end was fifteen seconds. The scene we made of it ran for two minutes. In other words, our scene on film played eight times as long as the actual scene. Had we wished, it might have played for ten minutes. The microscope had only begun to analyze, dissect and discover the clues to the complete history of this rebellion. Conversely, had we wished, we could have reduced the fifteen seconds of actual playing time to three seconds and have recorded the entire scene in three shots. A siren, a machine gun exploding, the stiff and open mouth of a man. Time, space, dimension, duration, emotion, these are only points of departure for a writer and a director and an actor in the unlimited exercise of making choices. It must then be clear that one approaches the identical scene very differently depending upon whether one is behind the lens of a telescope or a microscope.

Need I say, this is not an evaluation of the relative values of the film and theatre. That is another question entirely. Certainly the very quality of the telescope was exciting to me in doing such a scene as the final fight between the Chinese and the English in the Theatre Guild production, *Roar China*. There the scene was planned for the telescope—for all the complexity and counterpoint of various movements, all constantly within the compass of each spectator. What I have here is not an evaluation but a differentiation of theatre and film.

When I was working in the theatre many people urged me to work in motion pictures. They said they felt in my work a certain scope and dimension—it was, they said, telescopic and, therefore, eminently suited for the film. I came to pictures very eager to get behind a great telescope, as I thought. It took many weeks for me to get over the shock of discovering that the camera was a microscope and that it did not have nearly the scope within a single frame that the theatre had. Its scope, I discovered, lay in its ability to dissect a second or an inch—its amazing resemblance to the art of mosaics in its ability to make the most complex arrangements of seconds and inches. In the very modernity of its nature lay implicit the opportunity of material analysis of fact and fancy, and the joy of creating not merely sequential thematic development, but of lingering beyond the duration of actual time, of moving faster than actual time, of discovering the immensity of a cell and the smallness of a metropolis, of going beyond the poetry of description into the poetry of fact, factual contiguity, juxtaposition and opposition.

LAYING THE GROUNDWORK

Preparation for Reading

1. In comparison with each other, what are some of the respective advantages and limitations of the theater and of the film? As you read this selection, list the advantages and limitations noted by the author.
2. In your opinion, what characteristics must a great stage star possess? a great screen star?
3. What are your criteria for judging a moving picture?

Vocabulary Building

1. Look up these words: *pronunciamento, frustration, contrapuntal, credible, per se, improvisation, graphic, proscenium, vignettes, prerogative, counterpoint, sequential, contiguity, juxtaposition.*
2. List the expressions belonging primarily to pictures, e.g., "to shoot a picture." Make a similar list of the special diction of some occupation with which you are familiar, such as printing, knitting, flying.

APPRAISING THE RESULTS

1. What characteristics of the films make an "amazing and infinite" choice of approach possible? Hence, who must be preeminent in the production of a film—the writer, the actor, or the director?
2. In the making of a film, what conditions make "acting" practically impossible? How is the attention of the audience held in the theater? in the film? Compare the importance of the spoken lines in the two mediums.
3. Explain: "The theatre is a telescope, the film is a microscope."
4. Illustrate by means of a scene with two people talking, how great a range of choice the director has in directing a scene.
5. In the film, is a scene shot as a unit or in parts? Illustrate. Show how the "essential quality of the film" is the result of the director's choice and not of the actor's skill.
6. Discuss the possibilities of the director's manipulation of time and space. Illustrate.
7. Why is Mr. Biberman well qualified to write on this subject?

What are his conclusions as to the particular opportunities of the film?

8. Study the use of examples. How do they add interest, clarity, and conviction?

SELECTING THE THEME SUBJECT

1. Adapt the method of analysis exemplified in this selection to a study of radio as a medium for the drama.
2. Discuss the technique of the living newspaper form of drama.
3. Analyze and evaluate some moving picture which you have seen.
4. Discuss: "Film, for all its sound, is still primarily a visual medium."
5. Titles for themes: Why I Like the Movies; My Favorite Star; Villains Old and New; The Adaptation of Novels (or Plays) to the Film; Child Actors; Hollywood Types; Russian Films; How the Director Utilizes the Element of Time; How the Director Utilizes the Element of Suggestion; Shakespeare in the Films; How Pictures Are "Shot."

MUCH COULD BE DONE[1]

Ernestine Evans

WE ARE A PICTURE-CRAVING PEOPLE. WE GO ON OUR OWN STEAM
TO SEE THE MOVIES, AS FEW OF US GO TO BOOKS, ONCE SCHOOL
is over. We are Hollywood almost as much as we are Washington, and there are Afghans and even Irish who think Hollywood *is* our capital. The great inclusive audience in America is the crowd that sees the pictures, not the crowd that goes to church. The great listening audience is in the front room, the back room, the bed room, listening to the more than seven hundred privately owned radio stations in the United States, or to the short waves of all the world. It isn't at the New England town meeting—God rest its give and take—or really getting its money's worth about its own interests and its own affairs from the daily press. Should we not, then, use the pictures, still and moving, to build up common knowledge and common feeling, the broad bases of democratic living? Hollywood having got the voters out and assembled, open-minded and starry-eyed at Shirley Temple and Clark Gable, it seems a pity not to let Washington communicate some solid facts about how the ninety per cent do live as addenda to what is going on amongst the stars.

All this I set down because only this morning I had a letter from my Republican friend in Minnesota who is very much upset at the news that the United States government has set up a film unit, to make films for the purpose of recording government work and communicating government policy. I cannot quite make out whether she is galled that a Democratic administration proposes to make good films (I doubt if bad

[1] From *The Virginia Quarterly Review*, Autumn, 1938. Reprinted by permission of the author and of the publishers.

films would trouble her), or whether she is still angry at "The River." For that film, which Pare Lorentz made for the Farm Security Administration as part of the campaign for flood control of the Mississippi, said plainly that we the citizens of the United States had been worse than Esau—that we had sold our birthright of forest for a mess of pottage, and had not even collected the pottage. My friend is the inheriting kin of timber barons, and is loathe to be, as they say, "objective" about the good old days.

We are too accustomed to think of the movies as the great escape diversion, the place to go now that there is no frontier with free land and easy money (was it ever easy?) beyond the blue horizon. I am not ungrateful to Hollywood for these movie houses and palaces where at the end of a farm or factory, an office or kitchen, or even a drawing-room day, the cost is so little to get to Broadway, China, or Paris; and in the dark, to mountains and deserts and battlefields, boudoirs, beaches, and Scotland a hundred years ago. I like machine guns and horses; wisecracks and croonings do less for me.

Of news reels, even in the days when the navy putting out to sea was a safe one-quarter of every program, I am never tired. And until "The March of Time" began to use its immensely dramatic and plastic technique to make films like its recent one on social medicine, which was no better than a fixed fight, with Dr. Fishbein of the American Medical Association warning the audience against government control, and one of those appendicitis operations with a vast display of shiny instruments and a stage doctor, you could get me to give up dinner and go through sleet to see their snatches of the world.

But we have been tardy, I think, in seeing what a means of communication we had, between classes and regions, and finally between the people and the leaders, whether their leaders are dictators or duly elected and conscientious representatives of the masses.

It is a two-way line of communication. Never before has an audience of this size been assembled to look and listen. Never before have leaders been able to send out any instrument or agent comparable with this one, to note conditions, causes, and effects, at home and abroad. The camera, to be sure, can distort, omit, avoid the very point of a matter; it can be obsequious to taboos and it can make fiction; but by and large, it is the great new instrument of record and communication. The Department of Agriculture, for many years the largest manufacturer of "educational" motion pictures in the United States (the use of films was started in a Republican administration), has long been making pictures of country problems, grasshopper plagues, the feeding of pigs, the identification of the Japanese beetle, et cetera; and county agents all over the country have been grateful to have films, as well as eight- and ten-point bulletins from the Government Printing Office, in their effort to get the scientist's information to the layman, the often illiterate owner or cropper. But even Department of Agriculture officials would admit that the films they have made, on the whole, lack zest and talent, any camera art, and emotion. They have little dynamic quality.

At one time or another, several other departments of the government have had a shot at the movies: the Department of Commerce, the National Parks, the Works Progress Administration, and the Tennessee Valley Authority. The War Department (in whose Signal Corps files the Brady stills of the Civil War are one of the priceless possessions) was quick to follow the French military college of St. Cyr in using the camera both for recording all engines of war and for teaching. And the head of the Signal Corps, by special arrangement, always has carte blanche to keep an inspector in Hollywood who examines every new lens and development of technique. The Labor Department, perhaps because Secretary Perkins does not like the movies, is miles behind the Department of Labor in France, which has documented most of the historic handicraft and machine techniques of the past and present, and has put them at the service of the French schools to assist teachers of history and geography, and to be used in vocational guidance.

Hollywood, of course, has kept an eye on government and some of its activities. G-Men, and an Annapolis that left doubt in people's minds whether the navy had time for anything but love, and plenty of aviators, have figured in Hollywood films.

But on the whole, few of the facts of government life, certainly
not in the sense of showing what a united and wilful people
could do to create a commonwealth, have been part of the
Hollywood statement.

Other countries and other governments have made other
uses of films. From the Soviet Union, from Italy, from Nazi
Germany, but most of all from Great Britain, we can learn
what to do and what not to do. All four are concerned with a
broad base of homogeneous common knowledge for their
people; all four have embarked on policies of film reporting
and film exposition of government achievement and apparatus. When the Soviet government built the Turk-Sib railway,
it was as much a part of the plan of its building to have a film
record of the achievement and its relation to the economy of
the whole country, as the very laying of the tracks. In Russia,
films have been of incalculable power in convincing the people that they themselves are making history. T.V.A. and the
Coulee Dam are not less important for us than the Turk-Sib
was for the Russians, but no films of the epic quality of those
contemporary achievements are under way to galvanize the
people to fresh effort. Engineers on both jobs, of course, have
thousands of feet of progress record. But I am talking about
something else—about films that would be works of art, to
make us both feel the achievement and begin to understand
the possibilities of our engineering age. We have plenty of
scientists doing the people's work; and the politicians in their
way were supposed to be the artists who carried the people
with them, but what we need now is the dramatization of the
job. We need a new patriotism that harmonizes and realizes
regional relations and obligations, and gives us again what we
seem to have lost—that continental consciousness that once
made us so cheerful and so envied. The continent is still ours
to husband, though no longer ours to pursue in the old way.
But even that statement is inaccurate. Once we were a people
continually on the move to free land; we are a hundred times
more on the move than ever before, but we understand less
the forces that push us and the dreams that guide us. We need
artists. And we have them.

The two films made by Pare Lorentz have attracted worldwide attention—criticism too—but each has tackled a great social theme; and both of them, by their experimental technique and by their success in telling a story, opened our eyes to national tasks in a way that no speech could do. "The Plough That Broke the Plains" told the story of the Dust Bowl in such a way that even Vermont farmers, hearing and seeing that story in a damp and lush summer, joined in the tragedy of mistaken policy and hideous weather and were in some measure willing, as tax payers, to tide their brothers over. They may not have liked the Resettlement Administration, but they understood that some sort of doctor was needed, and they saw what the sickness of their fellow citizens was. They were drawn out of the circle of too local politics.

"The River" has had even more success, and of course more criticism, too. Where is the school book that could give children such a sense of the waters of that river and the valleys which it drains? I agree with the critics who want a more exact account of what the engineers are going to do about the problem; I would like to know if any domesday book of land titles in that valley will ever be made; I know that the story is told in broad sweeps and not in precise pictures of individual relationships to the big story. But "The River" is memorable not alone for its pictures, but for its poetic narration. A querulous photographer I know scoffed at the verse Lorentz wrote for his picture—"ham singsong," he called it. I laughed, because on that very day I had a letter from Paris from someone who had taken the nearly blind James Joyce to listen to the film, and Joyce had asked to have the film over and over again. "What poetry," he said, "the epic of this century." But he had brought to the film an Irish ear accustomed from aforetime to hear the troubles of a people from the lips of a bard.

From as far West as Idaho—
   Down from the glacier peaks of the Rockies—
From as far East as New York—
   Down from the turkey ridges of the Alleghenies—
Down from Minnesota, twenty-five hundred miles,
   The Mississippi River runs to the Gulf.

Carrying every drop of water that flows down two-thirds the
    continent—
Carrying every brook and rill—
Rivulet and creek—
Carrying all the rivers that run down two-thirds the continent.
    The Mississippi runs to the Gulf of Mexico.

No, I like it. It tells the people, it tells me something. Whitman would have liked it. The hired man can get it, and the
method will last a long time, in spite of the inevitable maudlin imitations that have already begun to whine on other
screens.

The British, too, are beginning to use verse in their documentary films, and a new line of communication is opened.
Poets and narrators on the radio too often, almost always,
are wraiths of the old bards chanting to the people. Too much
modern poetry is written for the eye and not the ear, and
is stopped at the head before it ever reaches the pulse and
heart. Not so the waggish verses of Wystan Auden, jerked
out to the rhythm of the Postal Special hurrying from the
Euston Station, up through Crewe, through the night, to
Aberdeen.

> This is the night mail crossing the border
> Bringing the check and the postal order
> Letters for the rich, letters for the poor
> The shop at the corner and the girl next door;
> Pulling up Beattock, a steady climb—
> The gradient's against her, but she's on time.
>
> Past cotton grass and moorland boulder,
> Shovelling white steam over her shoulder,
> Snorting noisily as she passes
> Silent miles of wind-bent grasses;
> Birds turn their heads as she approaches,
> Stare from the bushes at her blank-faced coaches;
> Sheepdogs cannot turn her course
> They slumber on with paws across,
> In the farm she passes, no one wakes
> But a jug in a bed room gently shakes.

Auden's verses are on the sound track of my favorite British
documentary, made by the film unit of the General Post

Office. "Documentary" is a word that Americans will have to
learn. The British crowd who established the word, and who
have half discarded it in favor of "realist," are a cheerful
group, going new places; they define their field as picturing
"the world of men and women at work and at leisure; their responsibilities and commitments to the world in which they
live." They reproduce cross sections of British life on the
screen.

   As a group, under the leadership of John Grierson, the
British makers of "documentary" films have fought to keep
clear of the British commercial film companies, which are
less talented and just as commercial as Hollywood, and
whose financing has been one of the greatest British rackets.
The group gained its foothold when Sir Stephen Tallents
was head of the government body, the Empire Marketing
Board. American audiences served by the Film Library of
the Museum of Modern Art may have seen one film sponsored
by that agency, Basil Wright's "Song of Ceylon," a lyric film
into which was woven the story of the tea plantations. In
"Drifters" was told the story of the men of the herring fleet.
From the Empire Marketing Board Sir Stephen and John
Grierson moved to a second acre on the public domain, the
General Post Office. They worked within a not too generous
budget. Their business was to make the people aware of the
Post Office—its functions, its services, the character of its devoted personnel. Not a little of the confusion of modern life
is that so many simple services have grown to immense size
and developed complicated relationships. The Post Office is
a great administrative staff running an intricate piece of machinery, touching the lives of men and women in war and
peace, in their personal and working lives. I forget who said
that advertising was of two sorts, the loud reiterant statement of the powers of the article, or the proving of the
pudding. The Post Office film unit set out to convey to the
public what the Post Office did in the public service, and as
they have exhibited, picture by picture, the wonders of the
Post Office technique and dramatized the daily services of its
enormous staff, they have proved that it was worth every
shilling of its budget. Englishmen know vastly more than

they did, not merely about the Post Office, but about the British Isles, about the civil servants who work in all branches of the Postal service, the Savings Banks, and the British Broadcasting Corporation. They know how the telephone book is printed and how the Empire air mail is carried. The Post Office film workers have not always made successful films: good camera work, expert cutting, and the perfect sound track are not always easily come by. But as a group they have held together, and to one end: to build up the use of film to mirror the real world, and to socialize our life by making the public aware, not of cabinet ministers and stars, but of daily work and public policy. They see in the use of film not merely a great technique of reportage, but a dazzling way to propose change, the moving blueprint of possibilities, for a world bogged down in precedent—a world forever moving if we would only let it.

The zest (with a dash, of course, of factional theorizing) of the British documentary group is like that which I recall in the Mexican mural painters in the early days of the Mexican revolution. There has been the same willingness to work at any price, the same anxiety to recruit talent and to build for a team. They were the first in London to shout for the enormous vitality of the technique of "The March of Time," and the first to show their disappointment when its subject matter became shallow. They have influenced British broadcasting, and they know themselves as the fathers of many a regional broadcast and of the fresh use of the people of England on the air. They have played the game of trying to get as much commercial money as possible for their crowd— which they use to make films that are not "commercial." For example, they have made films on nutrition, on crowded schools, and on British slums, backed by the Gas Light and Coke Company, a corporation accepting the principle that to promote a good work is to lay a brick toward an edifice of good name. (Coca Cola, please note. Mr. Ford, why not make a film about fifty million more cows the children need?)

Grierson has now embarked on another job. The empire will be only "the empire," and not a commonwealth of nations, until its parts behold each other at daily living. The

Empire Fair at Glasgow was the occasion for the making of a covey of documentaries, but those who see them do not see merely more travel films, picturesque scenes, but the dramatization of relationships, of trade, of industry. The speech in these films, instead of being ironed out to some synthetic semi-Oxford norm, is kept in all its rich diversity. Words on a page lose much of their cadence. Sound tracks of the people speaking (even in Brooklyn maybe) remind us of infinite variety.

One question interests me. What about the "propaganda" in these films, and of what use in international exchange are films made for internal consumption? To hear people wince at the very word, you would think that propaganda always worked, or that it was illegitimate. It may be true, as Mr. Dooley said when he tried to explain pragmatism, that "if a lie works, it's so." But frank knowledge of the source of any statement and any picture is like vaccination against a polluted message. And then, what *does* capture the heart of the beholder? I remain dazzled but unrecruited by Hitler's pageants and by Mussolini shouting that he has raised Rome from the dead. "Half phoney," I mutter, and accept that part of their message which says that whole peoples can be bamboozled to die for a place in the sun. But envy and irritation often follow on the heels of the other fellow's grandest displays. That is human. Certainly, the Coronation Parade down the Mall last May did not kindle in me the amount of affection for Great Britain that I got from "Night Mail," which left me so beholden to the workers of England who brought my daily letters.

And I think it fair to say that, abroad, "The River" has engendered more affection for and understanding of the United States than any other single circumstance in the last five years. It was, to be sure, a grand album, with the sweep of a continent in it; but it was also a confession of a sorry problem, of neglect, of stupid waywardness with the good earth. And the effect? I have had a dozen letters about it from London, and it was as if the ice had gone out in the spring. It was wonderful to them to hear of our troubles. We

became not the envied lost colony, but a clumsy, strong people, strong enough to take hold of a terrific problem, admitting failure, preparing for something new. Old M.P.'s, men
up from the city, workmen, all sorts of Britishers, loving the
narration for the beauty in it, catching the emotion in the
film, were in communication with their fellow men. They
too have exploited peoples and places. Perhaps that is why
they were moved.

A good film surpasses, in this day, any book's possibility
of building common knowledge and common feeling. The
film-makers must have the books, to carry on to the larger
circle. There is no competition here, but enlargement.

The United States government is going to have a film unit.
It will have a thimbleful of backing compared to the Government Printing Office; but by far more than a thimbleful will
the government print be enhanced by its operation. The
experiment is worth watching; and one wonders which cabinet officer will see in the unit his chance to make plain to the
people what he has never been able to show before. First, the
people must see what is going on; then will come mandates
to act. Suppose the sorry story of the migratory workers who,
homeless or housed like refugees, follow the sun and endure
the rain for the sake of the American standard of living they
do not share, were put upon the screen? Suppose the history
of housing in the past, or the ownership of land as we left
New England and moved across the plains, were really to be
shown to us?

If with four men and their still cameras Dr. Roy Stryker
of the Farm Security Administration has been able to create,
for the public and for students, a vast documentation of the
condition of the people in the South and in the Dust Bowl,
what presentation of facts and revelation of the flow of our
national life, region by region, occupation by occupation,
can we not hope for from a film director who throws his
report on the screen? Hollywood has made us rich in technicians; the audience is organized; why shouldn't the government catch us between Valentino and Hepburn, for an hour
of reality?

LAYING THE GROUNDWORK

Preparation for Reading

1. What kinds of motion picture do you like best? least? why?
2. What are the usual criticisms made of motion pictures? With which do you agree?
3. What are some types of educational and informational films which you have seen? How successful were they? Can you suggest any extension of this kind of film?
4. Have you seen "The River," "The Plow That Broke the Plains," "Song of Ceylon," "The Drifters"? What is your opinion of them, or what have you heard of them?

Vocabulary Building

1. Look up these words: *addenda, plastic, obsequious, taboos, layman, carte blanche, homogeneous, querulous, epic, maudlin, waggish, gradient, covey, cadence, pragmatism.*
2. Identify: Afghans, Pare Lorentz, Esau, Wystan Auden, Farm Security Administration, Tennessee Valley Authority, Dust Bowl, James Joyce, Mr. Dooley.
3. Explain "wraiths of the old bards chanting to the people," "the moving blue print of possibilities," "domesday book," "some synthetic Oxford norm" of speech.

APPRAISING THE RESULTS

1. Refer to Basic Exercise III as a guide to analyzing the devices which give unusual vigor to this selection.
2. Why are motion pictures said to be "the great escape diversion"? Is this a legitimate function?
3. What is Miss Evans' argument for the extension of the informative motion picture?
4. What have been the nature and use of the films made by various of our own governmental agencies? by governments of other countries?
5. Explain how poetry can be adapted to motion pictures. Illustrate.
6. What has been the history of the British documentary films?
7. Is there danger that propaganda will influence documentary films?

8. According to Miss Evans, what was the effect of "The River" upon the opinion held by foreigners about the United States?

SELECTING THE THEME SUBJECT

1. Write a paper about some new technique in the film industry.
2. Discuss in relation to the motion picture the problem of the child, of censorship, or of propaganda.
3. Make a detailed study of the films of a foreign country and report on them in a paper. Give sources.
4. Trace the development of the American film industry. .
5. Defend your own taste in motion pictures, or the salaries of stars, or the naturalization of many foreign actors.
6. Titles for themes: Hollywood Sets the Styles; The Movies and Juvenile Crime; The Movies—Today's Dime Novels; The Western Thriller; The Lure of Hollywood vs. the Lure of Broadway; The College as a Recruiting Ground for Talent; College as Hollywood Portrays It; A Film I Should Like to Make; News in the Films; The Poetry of Wystan Auden.

RADIO: MEDICINE SHOW[1]

John T. Flynn

A POSITIVE, DEFINED, RECOGNIZABLE POLICY ON RADIO BROAD-
CASTING IS ONE OF THOSE THINGS THE NATIONAL GOVERNMENT
has not yet troubled itself to form. But attention to the problem cannot be very much longer deferred. The incredibly
childish approach of the broadcasters to the problem of public discussion, the vague whisperings of plans for government
entry into the business of broadcasting, the scandalous rumors about the Commission set up to represent the public
interest, the vulgarity, banality, sheer ignorance and imma-
turity of the advertisers who sponsor our daily ration of
culture, have so irritated the public conscience that Congress is certain to get around presently to this very serious
matter.

It is impossible to consider radio without discussing the
problem of freedom of speech. It is impossible to conceive
of radio broadcasting without government control. The air
is a series of highways over which messages may be broadcast. The number of these highways is limited—less than
100. There is therefore a sheer traffic problem to be faced.
Unless these radio bands or highways are allocated everybody
would attempt to use the same bands and transmission would
be impossible. These highways are not like public streets
which countless vehicles can use at the same time. In the
air every traveler must be kept off the aerial highway while
the licensed user occupies it. There is, therefore, no escape
from a system of government licenses.

The privilege of granting licenses and of renewing them

[1] From *The American Scholar*, Autumn, 1938. Reprinted by permission of
the author and of *The American Scholar*.

448

comprises the right to refuse them, to cancel them, to deny renewal. Therefore an arbitrary or excessively political government can employ this power as a means of controlling the contents of the broadcast. And thus arises the old ghost of invasions of freedom of speech by the political authority. Everybody will agree that under no circumstances should the government be permitted to influence or dictate the social, economic, religious, political or other intellectual content of broadcast programs, save in so far as the rights of other citizens may be involved. The slander laws and, within properly defined limits, the police power to exclude obscenity cover the government's general sphere of control, so far as content is concerned.

But freedom of speech and of the press may have other enemies than the government. And this makes it necessary for us to be quite clear what we mean by freedom of speech and of the press. The man who owns a newspaper and who is free from every form of government restraint certainly enjoys freedom of speech so far as his newspaper is concerned. But we must distinguish between the individual newspaper and the press as an institution. There is a difference between freedom of the individual owners and freedom of the press as an institution. A group of men who severally own all the newspapers in a society may come together in an agreement to exclude all news and discussion of certain subjects of social concern. They do this in the exercise of their own freedom. But having done it, that society no longer enjoys a free press in so far as the censored subject is concerned. It is entirely possible, therefore, that the individual owners of the press may be free of all government restraint and yet the country be without a free press. It is this view of the matter which remains obscure in most discussions of the subject.

Every newspaper owner is subject to restraints which arise out of his own human weaknesses—fear of offending his community, fear of the hostility of its powerful leaders, fear of religious and social and political groups. These kinds of restraints can never be eliminated. They are in the order of human nature and must be accepted as inevitable. Freedom of the press and of course of the radio means freedom from such restraints as may be controlled. Against these human weaknesses there is but one safeguard—a multitude of journals and a multitude of editors who will not be subject to the same restraints. All will not be trying to please the same people. The very freedom—nay urge—of one man to print becomes a powerful corrective of the restraints upon another to omit the news. Political oppression of the press is so baleful just because it can exercise its influence over every editor, can terrorize and silence any editor who defies its interests.

The restraints upon the press which arise out of these private and social and commercial interests become a grave public problem when the powers which exercise these influences are so great and so united that their pressure may be applied to all editors and to the press as a whole.

Let us suppose that editor Number One publishes his journal at a loss but makes up his loss through a subsidy granted by Mr. X. Editor Number Two also publishes a journal at a loss but meets his deficit by means of sums obtained for some service to Mr. Y. Editor One will feel at liberty to print what he chooses so long as he does not offend Mr. X. Editor Two will feel bound to print what pleases Mr. Y under penalty of losing Y's support. But Editor One will be hampered only by his dependence upon X and will be quite free to print what he chooses about Y. And Editor Two although restrained by Mr. Y will have no compunction about printing anything he wishes about X. But what will happen when Editor One and Editor Two are both dependent on Mr. X? If all the papers in a community are owned by Editors One and Two they constitute the press. In theory both editors are free to defy the powerful Mr. X. But in the nature of things they will not do so because the price of defiance is extinction. And therefore while these editors are legally free and voluntarily relinquish that freedom for a more highly coveted prize, namely solvency, the press is not free.

Something like this has happened to the press in this country. Few if any newspapers can publish their journals at a profit. They must employ those journals in another field than journalism—and that field is advertising, which is in no sense a part of journalism but rather a parasite upon it. It is the advertiser who makes up the editor's deficits.

It is not true, of course, that there is but one advertiser who holds in his hands the power of life and death over the editors. No one can deny, however, that the advertising interests in a community, although they have their special differences on points of religion and social principles and even of commercial policies, are generally a unit upon certain important essential principles. But even where they are not a unit there is a menace to the freedom of the press which arises out of the necessity laid upon the editor to court their favor. The publisher solicitous for the favor of Mr. X and of Mr. Y, even though these gentlemen differ upon a point, will exercise the greatest prudence in seeking to offend neither. The very number of the powerful persons who make up the patron element of the press merely multiplies the number of restraints upon the editor. Altogether it forces on him that conservative timidity which compels him to remain away from certain great areas of news and from the discussion of certain serious subjects which the commercial interests in a community as a whole and separately wish to remain untouched.

Thus it seems clear that before we can have a free press society must find a means not only of protecting the individual editor from the invasions and restraints of government but of protecting the press as an institution from the editors themselves.

Thus far I have discussed this problem in terms of the press alone since that is an instrument with which we are more familiar. But the radio, like the press, is subject to the same observations. It is one of those instruments of public news and discussion which apparently cannot support itself as such and must turn to some other interest to pay its bills. Like the press it has turned to the advertiser. The advertiser is willing to pay the cost of assembling a great orchestra or of forming a troop of entertainers or supplying a dance band because he knows that millions will listen. All he asks is the privilege of interrupting the program at intervals to catch the ears of those millions of listeners. It is an old technique.

The itinerant medicine man of former days carried about
with him his banjo player and minstrel and clog dancer and
magician to attract the crowd to his tent and to put them
in a benevolent mood as a prologue to his own "high pitch"
upon the wonders of his pills and lotions.

Now the radio is hopelessly committed to this form of
operation. The advertiser is and doubtless for some time
will remain the sponsor of the radio program. And because
he pays the piper he is in a position to call the tunes. Thus
the freedom of the radio as an institution of public discussion and news, not the freedom of the individual station, is
threatened. The individual station is a commercial enterprise
in the hands of an enterpriser who wishes to operate it as an
instrument of profit derived from the commercial interests
in the community. He has no wish to offend or battle or defy
them. His only study is to please them to the uttermost,
prove his usefulness to them and advance their interests. He
has no liberty which he is deeply concerned in defending
against them. But the grand result is that the institution of
which he is but a part and which, as an institution, is a public
and not a private function sees its freedom extinguished.
Is it not clear that the freedom of the radio is destroyed if
the government will not grant licenses unless it censors the
programs? Is it not equally clear that that freedom is equally
impaired if the advertising interests will not pay the bills
unless they can impose a practical censorship?

But what then is to be done about it? There is obviously
only one power with sufficient authority to do anything and
that is the government, which is the trustee of the people
for the administration of the air.

But no one will countenance a government-dominated
news agency and forum. Men have not forgotten that the
first struggle for freedom of speech and of the press was waged
against political authority. That battle, certainly in this country, has been won. But a people vigilant for the preservation
of its democratic freedoms will never cease to look with a
certain suspicion upon political authorities, particularly in
a world troubled as ours is today by so many ruling groups
who assail the very existence of these rights. The radio is of

necessity in the hands of the government. We cannot escape its presidency over the administration of the medium through which the radio operates. But every resistance should be offered the establishment of government-owned and -operated radio stations since these are liable to become the instruments not of the government but of the politician who operates the government. But equally we cannot tolerate unregulated private ownership of the air. And there is no regulating authority but the government. How far, therefore, may we trust the government with this function? I offer the following suggestions.

The advertising sponsor presents a twofold problem. First there is the abuse of the advertiser's privileges in the use of the air and secondly the abuse of his power to restrain free discussion over the air. On the first point the abuse arises when the advertiser is permitted to disseminate news and discussions of public questions. The advertiser wishes to advertise his product. He therefore desires to command a large audience. This is a purely practical matter of drumming up a crowd. To do this he uses the most attractive entertainment he can obtain. Having gotten his crowd he should be permitted within decent limits to advertise his product. But he should not be permitted to turn that crowd into a political, religious or economic meeting. He should not be permitted to employ the radio and the crowd to spread religious, social, economic or political propaganda. However bad the newspaper may have become it has not descended to this. It does not, as a rule, rent out its news or its editorial columns to advertisers. It does indeed succumb to the influence of commercial interests but it does not permit the editorial function to pass out of its hands. Its editorials and reports do not have to run the gauntlet of advertising agents, vice-presidents and presidents and managers of commercial corporations, as is the case in broadcasts. The handling of news and views in the newspaper is in the hands of a department separated from the advertiser. And although the advertiser's spirit broods over the editorial room the editorial room resents it, resists it as much as it can. Furthermore, thinking of its function in terms of editorial excellence and obligation, the editorial room does build up an ethical standard which stands as a barricade against the over-insistent business office.

I know too well the bad influence of the commercial spirit upon the press. I know as well as anyone how much better the press could be if it were emancipated from this influence. But I know also how infinitely worse it would be if the advertising agent and the advertiser had moved bodily into the editorial rooms. This is what has happened in the radio broadcasting station. This is what I wish to end.

I would not restrain the radio broadcaster from the dissemination of news or of discussions. But I would compel him to separate this function completely from the programs of the advertisers. To permit the advertiser to become a social and economic propagandist on the air is to give the advertising interest a disproportionate place in the great forum of public discussion. A great manufacturer can pay the immense sum required to support a great symphony orchestra on the air because he gets an advertising return for the expenditure. But having drawn together a vast audience to listen to the symphony orchestra and having subdued the mind by means of the melting music, he may then interrupt the concert for a precious five minutes while he pours into the ears of his guests his economic and political philosophies. There is no public group with sufficient financial resources to meet this kind of propaganda. The advertiser should be permitted to have his crowd and his concert and a brief period to sell his wares but no more. As a citizen with economic and social views to exploit he should have only the same rights, so far as the air is concerned, as any other citizen. Although this would not free the air from the influence of the advertiser it would certainly tend to bring the distribution of the news and views of the broadcasting station under the administration of an editorial group capable of developing a far more civilized ethic with respect to the news.

I would divide the air into its three functions. In one it would be a great medicine show where advertisers, for pay, could put on entertainment and cry their wares, but the ballyhoo would be limited strictly to entertainment. In a second the air would be a great distributor of news and views which would be administered by a separate editorial board at the expense of the broadcaster. In a third I would consider the air as a great public hall which would be open to hire by persons, and by cultural and educational and other public organizations to hold meetings. And a part of this time I would compel the broadcasting station to give freely for educational and public purposes.

I would not permit any newspaper to own or operate a radio station. The newspaper is itself a dispenser of news and views. It tends to become more and more a monopoly in its community. One-paper communities, or communities dominated by a single owner, are growing in number. A multitude of journals and stations, and the inevitable competition between them, is the chief prophylactic against excessive surrender to the sponsoring advertisers in both press and radio. To permit the radio to fall under the dominion of the press as the press itself falls under the dominion of monopoly is to throw away this safeguard.

Regulations covering these points might well be made by the government without infringing the rights of anyone or without setting the government up as a menace to the liberties of the people themselves. No other agency of society can protect it from that usurpation of the instruments of communication by the great, predatory interests of the nation—which is coming to be one of the most sinister problems of the modern democratic state.

LAYING THE GROUNDWORK

Preparation for Reading
1. What do you think is the greatest need in radio today?
2. Why is freedom of speech a special problem of the radio?
3. Should commercial advertising on the radio be controlled?

Vocabulary Building
Look up these words: *deferred, banality, arbitrary, obscenity, compunction, parasite, solicitous, itinerant, disseminate, barricade, prophylactic, predatory, allocated.*

APPRAISING THE RESULTS

1. Why is a system of government licenses inescapable?
2. What is the difference between "freedom of individual owners" and "freedom of the press as an institution"?
3. How are restrictions on the freedom of the press exercised? on that of the radio?
4. Explain the figures of speech, "medicine show" and "itinerant medicine men," as they apply to radio.
5. Compare the problems of radio and newspaper advertisers.
6. What are the three functions Mr. Flynn would separate in broadcasting? Evaluate his proposals. Be specific in your answer.
7. Has the radio raised the level of artistic appreciation?

SELECTING THE THEME SUBJECT

1. Develop your answer to one of these questions: (a) Should radio stations give free time to opposing political candidates? (b) Should advertising rule the radio? (c) Should broadcasters decide who may buy their time? (d) Who should censor the air?
2. Compare a foreign radio system with the American.
3. Additional subjects: The Limitations of Popular Programs; Radio as an Aid to the Police or to Commercial Flying; Children's Programs; Foreign Propaganda on the Air; The Importance of the "Ham" Operator to the Government; The Reasons for the Popularity of a Certain Program or Performer.

Architecture

ARCHITECTURE ASTRAY[1]

Chester Henry Jones

THE SPECTACULAR NATURE OF THE HUGE BUILDINGS NOW RISING
IN THE BIG CITIES OF AMERICA HAS BROUGHT HER ARCHITECTURE
very much to the forefront. Always ready to prize and ap-
plaud any concrete manifestation of her civilization, the
country has marveled at the tremendous height attained by
the skyscraper. Even England, prejudiced and for a long
while skeptical of the good taste of the American, has at last
been willing to accept it within the field of art.

In his own country the American architect has become a
person of prestige unparalleled in Europe. Not only are his
buildings discussed in the popular press, where he himself
is an earnest exponent of the new age, but the name of his
profession is even correctly pronounced by the man in the
street. On the sidewalk, knots of persons gather and gaze up-
wards at the workmen silhouetted against the sky on the
steelwork of the sixtieth floor. In the street car, ordinary folk
dispute the relative heights of the Bank of Manhattan Building and the Chrysler Tower. Cultivated people, who for so
long regarded the skyscraper as a fearful monstrosity, have
come to admire it, and it may be said without contradiction
that in America architecture is now regarded as the foremost
of the arts.

University teachers, perceiving the change in cultivated
taste and pointing to the increasing number of European students in American schools, extol American architecture with
patriotic enthusiasm. Traditionally regarded as conservative,
they thus transcend their predilection for the past as opposed

[1] From *The Atlantic Monthly*, January, 1931. Reprinted by permission of
the publishers.

457

to the present and consider themselves advanced thinkers. The professional press itself, mostly interested in advertising, is loud in its praises; critical correspondence is taboo, and it publishes laudatory articles by architects on the work of their contemporaries and friends. Parallels are found in history which prove that in the greatest ages of culture architecture has invariably been the forerunner of all other arts, and that therefore its prosperity in the United States predicts a bright future in every field.

Yet a careful analysis of American architecture reveals surprisingly little which can really be termed modern. In fact, in the whole evolution of art, as it expresses with inevitable faithfulness the civilization from which it emanates, there is nothing so remarkable as the undue amount of extraneous influence which has been brought to bear on American building and the paucity of genuine, contemporary architecture. In the face of the skyscraper, accepted as the hallmark of the art in America, this must seem a sweeping statement, but a critical examination of the whole field of architecture as it fulfills, or attempts to fulfill, all the varying needs of her twentieth-century civilization shows such an insignificant extent of the truly modern as to be wholly out of proportion to the immense amount of building. In fact, it may be said that American architecture has been modern only as the inevitable outcome of an emphatic twentieth-century need—where utilitarian considerations have unavoidably assumed preëminence over the intellectual predilections of architects.

To the credulous European—and there are many, despite the multitude of voluminous philosopher-critics who flow through New York—this will seem strange, for he accepts everything American as being of necessity "modern." None the less will it surprise the credulous American—and there are many, too—who readily accepts the dictates of his architectural advisers. The European marvels at the sky line of lower Manhattan, the American at the scholastic attainments of the architect. The judgment of both is superficial and irrelevant. It has taken no cognizance of the relationship of art to the age which produces it. Neither novelty nor scholarship is a virtue of art, for architecture, if it is to be alive and vigorous, will express the contemporary need of the day fulfilled with contemporary science. On such a basis alone can the architecture which America is producing to-day be judged. The criterion of the architecture of any age is its "efficiency."

II

We have already gone counter to current opinion in asserting the absence of modern architecture in America. When we assert that American architecture lacks efficiency, popularly regarded as the dominant aspiration of the country, we might seem to add insult to injury. And not only are we raising the hostility of those who assume that efficiency is one with the disordered state to which uncontrolled mechanical evolution has brought our civilization, but in applying the same criterion of efficiency to the past we are antagonizing those who have studied the history of architecture as a spiritual unreality, in the light of which it is popularly represented, and who regard it as the phenomenon of beauty quite divorced from worldly usefulness.

It is the unreal study of the past, fostered by teachers, universities, and schools of architecture, particularly in America, which is chiefly responsible for the popular ignorance which exists to-day. The flow of adjectives and trite and hackneyed expressions, tempered by religious bias, which usually passes for serious criticism of temples and cathedrals has conveyed a very false impression of the why and wherefore. In the constant efforts of the bogus antiquary to find a symbolical interpretation for every feature in a building, however obvious its structural necessity, the columns of temples have been supposed to have originated in the representation of the "pillars of Heaven," and the Gothic nave in the architect's endeavor to reproduce an avenue of trees. Such a warped approach to the masterpieces of the past can only be regarded as provocative of much amusing reading. To imagine that the intricacies of the Gothic vault were a serious attempt to imitate the interlacing of the boughs in an avenue of trees is indeed a poor compliment to the mason. He was concerned with no such fantasy, but with the immense problem of covering a great space with a stone vault—a new type of construction advanced by the greatest mechanical knowledge of the day as a cure for the disastrous fires which had resulted from wooden roofs. His whole interest was in obtaining the maximum area of covered floor space for the worshipers with the greatest economy of materials. To achieve his end he invented the shaft, the vaulting ribs, and the buttress—a form of construction both scientific and economical. The resemblance to trees (if any resemblance exists) was entirely incidental, and only the license of a poetic imagination is justified in associating the nave of the mediæval church with "the arcades of an alley'd walk."

The history of mediæval architecture is one of gradually increasing efficiency in stone construction. An examination of other features of ancient architecture which have been given some romantic meaning will reveal a logical argument for their existence which all the picturesque veneer of the ages cannot obscure when they are rightly studied. Architecture has been, and will be, great only in so far as it satisfies the requirements which give rise to it. The standard by which it must be judged is the degree of success with which it fulfills, with the best workmanship and the most suitable and economical materials available, the demands of the client, whether he be a Pharaoh demanding an everlasting tomb, a priest of Athena Parthenos demanding a temple, a Cæsar demanding an amphitheatre or triumphal arch, a mediæval priest demanding a monastery, a Renaissance potentate demanding a palace, or a modern industrial concern demanding a factory.

If we have studied the past with understanding, we shall have discovered that the Pharaoh received his pyramid, as secure as the age could contrive to build it; that the Cæsar received his ampitheatre, huge and monumental, to unite the citizens of Rome, even in their recreation, in patriotic enthusiasm; that he received, too, his triumphal arch, designed to awe his subject peoples in a distant land; we shall have discovered that the mediæval priest received his monastery brilliantly planned according to his needs. Not until the Renaissance did the dilettante artist presume to exercise his personal preference for styles and become the dictator of fashion to the cultured aristocracy. The client of to-day alone prejudices the purpose of his building by conforming to the fastidious palate of the overeducated architect.

For this the architect and the layman are equally to blame. The client willingly succumbs to the architect and places infinite trust in him. The architect has studied in one of the renowned schools of architecture, he has been abroad, he has aspired to the mysterious École des Beaux Arts,—a certain proof of his genius,—he has passed through the cathedrals of France and England, sketchbook in hand, and has measured and reconstructed some Classic ruin in Italy. Proof of his genius is to be seen in the antiques which adorn the Gothic reception room of his office on the thirtieth floor. How can a man be better equipped than with such a background to design a railway station or a canning plant? So argues the simple client as he waits in the reception room and is duly impressed. He himself was probably raised in the Middle West, and reached his position by hard work and by understanding the men and things with which his business brought him in contact. But now he faces something outside his own sphere, something which smacks of scholarship and European culture. He is conscious of his ignorance of the intellectual snobbery which it represents. To him it is no snobbery, but the manifestation of deep learning. A magnate in railway construction or in cans, he is no magnate in learning. So, in due course, his railway station dons the garb of imperial Rome or his canning plant the armor of mediæval Chartres. In his great philanthropic work of promoting the art of architecture the locomotives and cans are forgotten; yet I believe a future generation, studying the arts of to-day, will recognize the locomotives and the cans as æsthetically the greater.

We may seem to dwell at undue length on the past. But this is because we wish to emphasize that identically the same standards of criticism apply to both past and present. The skyscraper apartment block and the thatched cottage do not differ except in degree. Nor is the phenomenon which we observe to-day without parallel in antiquity. Those who deplore the barbarism of a past in which sound, economical, and ordered building was the necessary accompaniment of good living do so on grounds of twentieth-century "progress," forgetting that "progress" is a new discovery of unproved worth.

III

It would seem, then, that the present state of architecture, which we dare to criticize so severely, is no sudden, postwar development, but that it dates back to the fourteenth century. Since that time architecture and building have become more and more divorced from each other. It has been a time of revivals, Roman, Greek, Gothic, Romanesque, Byzantine, according to the erudition of the historian and the archæologist. It has been a time when art has become a means for expressing culture and class, the monopoly of the wealthy, exemplifying their good taste and their punctuality with fashion. Art has indeed found learning to be a tyrant.

The revival of styles in England made their début with the renaissance of Classic art. But we have only space to consider the Gothic Revival. The Laudian revival of Gothic was too near to the original to be successful, for the original style was not then old enough to have acquired the necessary mystery, nor its civilization sufficiently removed to have received the glamour of age and the popularity and advertisement which it later received in the novels of Sir Walter Scott. But at the end of the eighteenth century, with Horace Walpole and his "Strawberry Hill," the Gothic style had begun to be accepted as sufficiently cultivated for the enjoyment of society. Evelyn, in the early days of the Renaissance, when the imported Italian manner had been the only possible expression of taste, had thoroughly condemned it as barbarous and uncouth, and in derision had labeled it "Gothic," a name which it permanently retained, and which, in a later generation in the mouth of John Ruskin, was to express the very essence of æsthetic beauty in architecture. *Gothick Architecture Improved,* by Batty Langley, published in 1742, is the significant title of a book by one of the first advocates of the Revival. Such are the inconsistencies of dilettantism.

Looking back on the Gothic Revival with that detached and disinterested sympathy which our attitude towards a revival style makes possible, we cannot but regard the earliest works of the Gothic revivalists as their most successful. They had not yet been restricted by the investigations of the archæologists and the limitations imposed by the formation of academic rules. Among the best works of the Gothic Revival may be counted Thomas Rickman's New Court at St. John's College, Cambridge, built as early as the eighteen-twenties. But Rickman himself was one of the first to seek further knowledge, and himself chose to label and standardize the study of the ancient style with a complicated division into "periods." These periods are still the student of architecture's Euclid. So, knowledge of the antique progressed, and modern architecture declined in proportion. Sir Gilbert Scott, renowned Gothicist and restorer of cathedrals, describing himself as "amongst the most scrupulous and conservative of restorers," said that his object had been "to show that Gothic would admit of any degree of modernism." Sir Thomas Jackson, another distinguished Victorian architect, came to the painful conclusion: "We must value Gothic art chiefly because it, rather than any other we know of, is so congenial to our times that it may fairly be expected to live again in modern soil, and to fructify and give birth to a new and living art which we can really call our own." So, the Gothic Revival flourished in England; likewise in America, taking her cue from the mother country. We, to-day, have not yet discarded this outworn philosophy.

If we except the Indian pueblo, which must here be counted with the classics, the whole history of American architecture has fallen within this period of revivals. We must review it briefly in order to appreciate to the full its present position. American architecture originated in the Georgian mansion, transplanted to the colonies as little changed as was possible, and, in fact, so like the original that students of the Colonial period have difficulty in discovering those characteristics peculiar to it which their researches necessitate. Even the porticos of the plantation mansions of the South, so essential in the hot climate, were built, at first, with reluctance. Then

Thomas Jefferson introduced his conception of the Roman manner and promoted it with enthusiasm. Much as we delight in Monticello, we cannot but observe its variance with the characteristics of Roman architecture as he had pictured it. The Greek Revival reached the most remote outposts of the Middle West. It produced a remarkably high standard of scholarship and a consistent adherence to the correct formulæ of the Greek style. In the Greek Revival, America never permitted herself the freedom and originality of a Sir John Soane. The Gothic Revival followed, equally zealous. It is indeed to be regretted that so many admirable examples of these two periods have disappeared in the wake of commercial building, hardly appreciated during the vogue for the Georgian re-revival, and unrecorded by the historian. The Romanesque Revival of H. H. Richardson, the peculiar product of a single individual, but nevertheless of wide influence, illustrates admirably the illogicalities and the wastefulness of a revival style. The World's Fair at Chicago, of 1893, undoubtedly a more finished exhibition from the architectural standpoint than any since, diffused the Classic style with renewed spirit. In the Transportation Building, Louis Sullivan, the barbarian, endeavored in vain to stem the advance of the Roman legions. The importation of French teachers for the schools of architecture, imbued with the training of the École des Beaux Arts, now became a new and powerful influence.

But America, even after such a profound training in the classics as we have outlined, had yet to graduate in the school of McKim, Mead and White, a firm without counterpart in Europe, which can only be described as producing design which was the last word in refined taste and academic correctness. With them the Roman legions advanced into every type and size of building, transcended function and purpose. It might almost be said that what the Roman Empire had not time to accomplish was realized by McKim, Mead and White with expedition.

While ready to condemn the archæological prejudice which colors architecture to-day, we are now in a position to sympathize with it and to understand, to a great extent, the power in America of a background which it is manifestly so difficult to overcome. Again, so much good work has been accomplished in stylistic periods, in spite of them, that even against his good faith the architect is tempted everywhere to fall back on precedent and design in the accepted manner. But however scholarly, however well-read, his design may be, it is impossible to avoid the truth that such work starts from the wrong angle. It differs fundamentally from the original style, as it was once the living expression of a civilization, in that the architect no longer starts from the standpoint of function and material. It is true that he may fulfill the requirements of function, and, at times, of material, with surprising efficiency in spite of the limitations which the style imposes; it is true that the client will believe that culture or advertisement has been satisfied; but the architect is seeking to hide the demands of a new age under an antique veneer absolutely unrelated to it. Whatever his success may be in such counterfeit, his architecture will never be great, for it will never be genuine. In reality it is a cowardly inability to keep pace with the age, and an endeavor to hide it under a mask of erudition.

IV

Among the most absurd results of the archæological prejudice are the Gothic universities of America. Falling back upon Oxford and Cambridge for precedent, the American college has produced some of the most remarkable inconsistencies of our time. It is indeed strange to find modern scientific institutions clothed in architecture which expired more than five hundred years ago on another continent. And in no other class of building have the limitations imposed by an antique style been more acutely felt. Gothic architecture, made of little stones, with little windows of little panes of glass, was built at a time when it took centuries for what can now be accomplished in a few months; when big stones could not be quarried or handled, and when plate glass was unknown, so that little windows were unavoidable. Is it not ridiculous that this inferiority complex of the American university should express learning in such a retrogressive manner? Yet, this is intended to be serious architecture.

The quadrangles of Yale—a *tour de force* in Gothic, and admirable enough had they been erected in a museum— illustrate the limitations of such design, and the manner in which it prejudices efficiency. They are somewhat smaller than the average court at Oxford or Cambridge, but have been built higher to provide more accommodation, without any increase being made in the size of the windows. The rooms are thus unduly dark. At the same time a rough plaster of dull shade has been used in the interiors with the intention of producing an antique effect, though quite contrary to mediæval precedent. And, as if with his tongue in his cheek, the architect, having thus far reproduced the antique antiqued, completes the illusion with scattered repairs in broken panes of glass. It is like the Chinese tailor who, when given a pair of old trousers to copy, reproduced them with the patches in the seat carefully imitated. The only difference is that the Chinaman was concerned with a pair of trousers and the American with a great seat of learning.

It is unnecessary to refer further to the numerous colleges throughout the country which are enshrined in Gothic tracery, with battlemented towers from whose prototypes the warriors of the Middle Ages shot their arrows at the enemy. One only wonders at the inconsistency of the professor of some abstruse branch of science who departs from his mediæval office, through its Norman archway, without donning armor and a helmet and buckling on his sword and shield. At Pittsburgh the new "Cathedral of Learning," a skyscraper university, is rapidly nearing completion. Gothic in its detail, but unavoidably modern in its massing, it is a fine building despite its Gothic veneer, for it has been quite unable to overcome the natural beauty inherent in its size and form. There is no precedent in Gothic times for forty floors. Like the Woolworth Building, however Gothic it may appear in the eyes of the American, it has no counterpart in antiquity, and its modernity is in spite of its architect.

England, lacking the romantic nature of the American, is tiring of the Gothic collegiate style and has sought to try her hand once more at the Renaissance. But she is still unable to divest herself of the Gothic entirely, and in the new buildings for the University of Cambridge ordered planning has been entirely ignored; the various buildings erected for new branches of science, although principally of Classic design, have been scattered about with an indifferent disorder far more fitting to the Gothic, and quite at variance with the exact ideals of the scientist. In England the conservative, stylistic outlook is as much marked as in America, and the English architect has not benefited to the same extent by the saving grace of as sound an academic training. Whether this is not, in the long run, an advantage I do not know, but one cannot but wonder at the continuance of the tame Renaissance mannerism, tempered here and there with Egyptian detail, which still forms the major part of English architecture, despite the propaganda of the modernists and despite a limited amount of advanced Gothic design which the modernists dare not criticize for fear of destroying all inspiration. The Wren tradition—and it has been truly said that English Renaissance architecture should be spelled with a "W"—lasted for a very long time, and it is still dying.

The standard American railway terminal, with its rows of columns, is hardly less remarkable than the college. The criticisms which have recently been directed against the Pennsylvania and the Grand Central terminals can be attributed, to a great extent, to the limitations imposed by Classic design, accepted, quite unwarrantably, for the great majority of American railway stations. One wonders indeed at the strange conservatism which clothes so magnificent a field for design as the modern railway in the architecture of ancient Rome, and studies the possibilities of "Spanish Mission Architecture for Railway Stations." Such is the title of an article in a professional periodical. At the Pennsylvania the taxicabs have to fit into the intercolumniation of columns, and at the Grand Central avoid immense stone piers, when steel and concrete construction could have provided the minimum area for supporting members. Efficiency has been placed second to the interests of Classic design. In London, which has never been renowned for its railway terminals, they consist usually of a track, a platform, an adjacent hotel, and a war memorial. But adequate approach is at least a virtue in which they excel over those in New York. The Greek Gateway at Euston can never be regarded as anything but a white elephant, and, after the Euston Waiting Hall and the great Shed at St. Pancras, it is almost the only piece of railway architecture in London which remains on the memory. The Waiting Hall at Euston, built in 1847, was founded upon Peruzzi's great chamber in the Massimi Palace in Florence, dating from the early sixteenth century. The Pennsylvania Terminal in New York, finished in 1910, goes back as far as the Baths of Caracalla, in Rome, of the third century!

The American capitol building is another incongruity, adopting universally the manner of the French provincial city hall. This is one of the influences of the French Beaux Arts teachers. The State Capitol of Nebraska, alone, is an American capitol building. City halls have followed the same model. Much as one admires the scholarship and the knowledge which lie behind the design of the City Hall of San Francisco, such a building is no genuine product of our age, as anyone must feel who enters its lifeless interior. One only regrets that the dome and cupola were not the product of Mansard in the seventeenth century, for this could then have been counted as one of the three finest Renaissance domes in the world, along with Mansard's dome of the Invalides in Paris and Wren's masterly dome of St. Paul's Cathedral in London. The French Renaissance of Classic architecture has had no competitive style in the buildings for the Government at Washington.

Recent ecclesiastical architecture both in England and in America has been irrevocably Gothic. A leading American architect, with a profound admiration for and technical knowledge of the thirteenth century, which he reproduces with astonishing accuracy and minute attention to detail, even asserts that modern American ecclesiastical architecture is the equal of the mediæval cathedrals and churches of Europe! He has a very large ecclesiastical clientele and his work is the admiration of the romantically-minded. But there are two architects who, though Gothic revivalists, belong to quite a different field. One is an American and the other an Englishman, and their work bears a striking similarity. It would be impossible not to think that they had profoundly influenced each other were it not that their work is of a trend which one would expect at this time as a natural reaction to the intensely accurate revivalism to which we have referred. Bertram Grosvenor Goodhue, whose free interpretation of the Gothic style has been such a healthy influence, became at length the architect of two such radical buildings as the Public Library at Los Angeles and the State Capitol of Nebraska at Lincoln. But an early death terminated a career which might have produced a masterpiece of modern architecture. Sir Giles Gilbert Scott, a grandson of the celebrated Victorian architect, but influenced by the free design of his teacher, Temple Moore, has in his Liverpool Cathedral, won in competition in his early twenties, produced a building as little Gothic as conservative standards would allow. Liverpool Cathedral is the end of the Gothic Revival, and in this fascinating product of our times one may see plainly the revolt against the binding and cramping weight of mediævalism which must ultimately free us from prejudice and fraud.

V

The modern custom of deploring the ugliness and discomfort of our cities is a habit belonging to a new and unhealthy state of civilization. That it is merited is only too apparent, but it comes at a time unequaled in all history for its tremendous opportunities for building, not only, in America, from economic circumstances, but from the magnificent opportunities of new materials, such as glass, steel, and concrete.

Adopting the attitude which sees architecture in relation to the day which produces it, and carrying the term to its logical conclusion as embracing planning and the convenience of the city, an examination of New York will reveal the evils of the skyscraper and of the absence of a wisely preconceived plan. What it is customary to admire in New York is no more than a manifestation of its overdevelopment. New York is probably the supreme example of the inability of human beings to direct their own destiny.

We may accept it as being one of the first stages in the overdevelopment of a city when the business districts become uninhabitable to a degree which necessitates commutation from other more habitable areas, and the consequent waste of time in transit. It is hardly necessary to place New York in this category, for this is a stage in the new concentration of population which all cities of any size have long passed. The position of New York by the sea has so reduced the suburban area that it has become necessary to commute from very considerable distances. In addition to this, traffic congestion in the streets has become so acute that it takes longer to reach the down-town districts by road, or by congested suburban transit, than to travel by train from outlying districts into the centrally located terminals. But it is unnecessary to complain further of the condition of this congestion. It has been enlarged upon often enough by those who have some personal interest to gratify by some minor or irrelevant cure. It is due to no other cause than the fact that the floor area of buildings is quite out of proportion to the facilities for traffic. The fault, without question, can be laid, in a literal sense, at the door of the skyscraper.

It has become too much the custom for architects and others, endeavoring to justify so singular a production of the American civilization as the skyscraper, to commend it without reason. One of the foremost architects of New York, writing recently in a leading newspaper, proclaimed the district about the Grand Central Terminal as illustrative of the value of coördination of various types of buildings in a limited area. He was certainly correct in this, but he described the congestion of the streets as no worse than in certain European cities, and forgot, in what was a very doubtful statement, the fact that the Chrysler and the Lincoln Buildings were not at that time completed. It seems only reasonable to suppose that the congestion of that district is no worse only because it could not possibly become so; and the traffic, realizing the fact more easily than the architect, as it may

well do, circumvents it and enters it only when bound to
do so.

While surface transportation has become a means of recreation for leisured people rather than a serious method of
transit, public transportation by subway and elevated trains
has proved quite inadequate, and it is impossible to believe
that it can ever be otherwise. The building of subways in
New York is of tremendous expense; unlike the tube railways
in London, they can only be built immediately beneath
the surface of the roadway, and even then at the cost of
cutting through rock and providing steel support for roads
and buildings above. Moreover, when all possible subways
have been constructed, they will still be insufficient. These
facts can only be regarded as prohibitive of any real solution
to the problem of congestion, particularly when we take into
consideration the fact that the elevated railways, ruining all
property by which they pass, must eventually be torn down
and their passengers sent into the subway. Added to this
will be the increase in value of the property now fronting
on elevated tracks; mean houses will be replaced by skyscrapers whose occupants must once more multiply the subway crowds. At present every extra train which the subway
companies are able to run, rather than relieving congestion,
only serves to aggravate it by permitting more people to
travel, and consequently the erection of still higher buildings. The public's lowering moral standard of congestion
cannot keep pace indefinitely with congestion's increase, even
though, with the fewer numbers of passengers on Sundays, it
has shown itself willing to accept the same measure of congestion due to the shorter Sunday trains! For increasing
congestion cannot, forever, be as acceptable as the weather.
It may be said with confidence that the part played by town
planning in proportioning buildings to open spaces, to
streets, and to transit, with the intent of the proper functioning of the city, can be counted as negligible.

VI

This town planning, whose absence we deplore, is the backbone of civic architecture. New York will never be a great

city. She can never hope to be more than a collection of great individual buildings, and this does not constitute a city. Uncontrolled development has reached a state where nothing can be done to save her beyond the tickling of the suburbs by some occasional well-meaning body, or some minor legislation to relieve the further encroachments in the city proper of individual interests on public welfare. It has been proposed that, in rebuilding, every block should be forced to adopt a complete architectural treatment. By such means some approach to civic architecture would be obtained, and a certain uniformity created such as is now found in the big apartment houses on Park Avenue, north of the Grand Central Terminal, or on La Salle Street, about Jackson Boulevard, Chicago. In these two instances the single façade to each block produces a rhythmic order in the cross streets which is quite lost with the usual irregular sky line. The endlessness of the streets has made an axial position, even for the chief municipal buildings, almost unknown outside Washington. Such a site—the only one in New York—has not been fortunate in its treatment. The absence of axial positions for buildings is one of the many evils of the gridiron plan. Another is the fact that the gridiron plan gives equal importance to streets in either direction, one of the chief causes of congestion, for it is when one stream of traffic has to cross another at right angles on the same level that congestion occurs, far more so than in the increased volume moving in one direction.

In condemning the uncontrolled height of buildings it would be unjust to ignore the tremendous opportunities which the skyscraper presents for architectural design. Its size, alone, is an attribute of which the old-world architect may well be envious. The skyscraper has passed through a progressive evolution, and the prerequisites of this type of building have, in recent years, been met with surprising success. The skyscraper has no counterpart in antiquity, and, as might be expected in a type of building with such novel requirements, it has escaped the more easily from the clutches of the archæologists.

Nevertheless the skyscraper has had to pass through the

revival period, in which the façade has been covered with a veneer of Gothic shafts and tracery or Classic columns. Its early examples were a veritable catalogue of the orders, from the sturdiest Doric at the base to the most delicate Ionic at the top. This phase has now gone for good, but the second phase is still in progress. In this the columns are confined to the lower and upper floors, binding several floors together on the façade with complete disregard for what is behind them. Only in the newest of the skyscrapers has the absurdity of this type of irrelevant design been fully appreciated and the third phase attained. In this the windows or floors themselves, in either horizontal or vertical treatment, are accepted as the principal motif of architectural expression and as the unit of scale for the whole building. This is now the guiding principle for the design of the best of the recent skyscrapers. Of necessity the architecture of New York is becoming more logical. With the exception of one influential firm in Chicago, New York is the hub of the American architectural world.

Whether the skyscraper has from the owner's standpoint reached its greatest height,—and it has done so long ago from the standpoint of the public,—it has certainly reached it from the practical point of view. The skyscraper cannot be built to a greater height on the area of a single block than that of the highest already built. Engineering ability can certainly build higher, and elevator cables can, no doubt, be constructed sufficiently strong to sustain their own weight, but the point has been reached when the increased number of elevators necessary to feed the increased floor area becomes so great that it leaves no rentable area in the lower part of the building. As it is, at present, spaciousness, so necessary to dignity in architecture, has been sacrificed, and the ground floor of the skyscraper has been almost entirely taken up with vestibule and elevator access, scarcely leaving room for window show space and the stores required for the inhabitants of the building. To obviate this difficulty it has been proposed by a New York architect, whose knowledge of skyscraper construction exceeds his appreciation of public welfare, to build a single building on four city blocks, covering in the streets and lighting them and ventilating them artificially. That it is possible to construct it need not be doubted, but, with conditions as they are, it is inconceivable that traffic facilities could, or would, ever be provided to meet such a building.

The course of true architecture in America may be found in the steel frame of the skyscraper,—evil as such an institution may be from the social standpoint,—in the grain elevators of Chicago, in the steel mills of Pittsburgh, and in the highroads and the great bridges and dams throughout the country—wherever, in fact, the dilettantism of the architect has been unable to exert itself. But the course of true architecture is very limited, and unappreciated as such even where it is found. It happens unavoidably, where art is of no consideration, in big engineering creations and in buildings of purely commercial purpose. It seems unreasonable that, in an age of such opportunity as this, one should question the progress of architecture, but it is most certainly questionable. We have reached a state of overeducation and overdevelopment. The architect has been doing too much "designing" and the lay public has been too much interested in "art." There is no cure but to rid ourselves of prejudice and see our age in perspective. Only by so doing will it be possible for our architecture to become true architecture and great architecture.

LAYING THE GROUNDWORK

Preparation for Reading

1. Study the architectural characteristics of the buildings on your campus: are they "modern," Gothic, Greek, or some other type? Are they satisfactory from the point of view of utility and efficiency? Is the material suitable? Are the buildings aesthetically satisfactory?
2. Find in your dictionary or in some other reference book illustrations of Greek architecture and Gothic architecture. What are some of the characteristics of each?
3. If you were planning a home, to which of the following points would you give most serious consideration: durability, fashion, efficiency, originality, utility? Why?

Vocabulary Building

1. As you read, list unfamiliar words and find the pronunciation and meaning of each.
2. Identify the following: *Pharaoh, Athena Parthenos, École des Beaux Arts, Chartres, Horace Walpole and "Strawberry Hill," John Ruskin, Batty Langley, Monticello, H. H. Richardson.*
3. Make a list of specific architectural terms used in the selection.

APPRAISING THE RESULTS

1. To which of the two views of the "modernness" of American architecture does the author subscribe? Why? Do you agree or disagree with him?
2. What two objections, originating in opposing camps, are made to the assertion that American architecture lacks efficiency?
3. How have schools fostered an inaccurate and artificial approach to the architecture of the past? Illustrate. How does this attitude affect contemporary architectural forms?
4. What point of view toward architecture came in during the period of the Renaissance? How did it differ from the view which had prevailed? Which view prevails today, and why?
5. What is meant by a period of revivals? Show how the whole history of American architecture has fallen within the period of revivals. Why is revival architecture bound to fall short of greatness?
6. Discuss: "Among the most absurd results of the archæological prejudice are the Gothic universities and railway stations of America."
7. In terms of convenience, utility, and the well-being of the inhabitants, what are the deficiencies of the skyscraper and of the planless city? Illustrate by reference to New York City.
8. What final conclusion does the author reach, and how is it related to the title?

SELECTING THE THEME SUBJECT

1. Write a paper on one of the following subjects: (a) the relationship of art to the age which produces it; (b) the criterion of architecture of any age: efficiency; (c) a criticism of the use of Gothic or Greek architectural forms in public buildings in your city; (d) architecture on the campus; (e) community planning.

2. Titles for themes: Building a Skyscraper; The Worship of the Past; America's Planless Cities; Prefabricated Houses and Architectural Problems; The Use of Stone in Building; The Ideal Small Home; The Perfectly Planned Kitchen; Bridges in a Mechanized Age; American Railway Terminals; Frank Lloyd Wright and His Work.

PART FIVE

The Laboratory of Words and Ideas

The Indictment

CAN COLLEGE GRADUATES READ?[1]

Edwin R. Embree

"THE STUDENT AND HIS KNOWLEDGE," A PUBLICATION RECENTLY ISSUED BY THE CARNEGIE FOUNDATION, IS THE MOST DEVAStating report yet to appear on higher education in America. While this survey was centered on the schools and colleges of Pennsylvania, it may be regarded as giving a fair picture of education throughout the nation. The careful and intensive studies, made over a ten-year period, included tests in the many phases of education and were designed to discover not only the amount of useful information acquired by students during the college years but their progress in intelligence and understanding.

The results of the study may well undermine the mystical faith which we in America have had in formal education. We gave expression to that faith by building schools and colleges beyond those of any country in human history and by sending our children not only to school but also to college and university in numbers beyond the dreams—or nightmares—of any other nation. Almost all eligible children are enrolled in elementary schools. And in addition nearly seven million young people are in high schools. This is a high school enrollment of more than two-thirds of all the young people of high school age and is four or five times the percentage of secondary school attendance ever achieved by such enlightened countries as England, France, or Germany. In fact, more children are in high schools in America than in all the rest of the world put together. Another million and a quarter American students are enrolled in those

[1] From *The Saturday Review of Literature*, July 16, 1938. Reprinted by permission of the author and of the publishers.

pleasant custodial halls hopefully referred to as institutions of higher learning. We had fondly dreamed that our children would come out of this great educational mill filled not only with information but with insight and understanding.

The study of Pennsylvania schools and colleges indicates that by and large students are not even getting much information, let alone wisdom. The tests proved, among other things, that there is little relation between the time spent at college and the intelligence or achievement records of students. Though on the average college seniors made higher scores than sophomores, twenty-eight per cent of the seniors did not do as well as second year students and ten per cent had lower scores than the average high school senior. It is distressing to learn of the high percentage of brilliant high school graduates who do not go to college as compared with the average who do, for in the tests more than half of the high school students who were to continue their formal education had lower scores in the intelligence and English tests than twenty-five per cent who were not planning to go to college. Even more distressing is the revelation that those college graduates who plan to become teachers are not only less well equipped for these important posts than most of their classmates, but that seven per cent of them made lower scores than thirty-six per cent of the high school pupils.

But the most appalling item in this Carnegie report is a study of students at a single college. Of some fifty brilliant freshmen followed throughout their course, more than two-thirds knew less at the end of junior year than they did during their first year. They had less accurate information and their insights and understanding had been blunted. Scholasticism, routine, and mediocrity had done their perfect work. Commenting on the progressive degradation of these brilliant entering students, the report says:

The fact that minds of this caliber had been obliged through two years to adjust their stride and intellectual sympathies to colleagues, and probably even to some instructors, who were inferior to themselves cannot have been without its sinister effect.

These students obviously had no intellectual purpose or stimulus appropriate to their ability. Although as freshmen they were already beyond that intellectual level at which the college could serve them effectively, they were obliged to use their wits elsewhere and mark time academically for three more years until the calendar should release them.

This whole report is so damning that it compels educators not only to gasp but to try to do something to correct the present evils. Many ideas will be presented and it will be well to give free play to all reasonable suggestions. No single formula is apt to solve the manifold problems of education. In fact, one of the present evils is that we have supposed that fixed rules and standards and courses could accomplish the very delicate business of education.

My own belief is that a major aspect of sound education is reading. If children learn to read fluently and understandingly, they have acquired the finest of the intellectual tools. If these young people will then proceed to read, they will take care of the greater part of their own education.

Learning to read is an astonishingly delicate and complicated business. It does not consist simply of learning to spell words or to pronounce syllables. It consists chiefly in learning to grasp the quaint symbols of the alphabet in such a way that meaning is conveyed by means of the printed page from the author to the reader. Mechanical skill in reading is a first and essential step, but reading actually takes place only after the initial mechanics is mastered and after the individual begins to get pleasure and understanding from the printed page.

Even in the teaching of the mechanics of reading there must be a close connection between what the child already knows and what is conveyed to him through written words. This is another way of saying that education must have a very close relation to the life of the pupil. Much of the failure both in school and college comes from the fact that we so quickly allow learning to run into scholasticism. Neither the ability to read nor any other kind of learning is an end in itself. Values come only as education tends to enrich the lives of the students and the society of which they are a part. All this seems self-evident, yet waves of argument in behalf of scholastic studies constantly sweep over the country. Schools and colleges are urged from time to time to ignore all current life and to return, for example, to the fragmentary learning of Greece or to the scholastic exercises of the Middle Ages—to "courses," and "credits," and "lessons."

Even the elementary schools easily fall into scholasticism, that is, into rote learning. In work with little rural schools in Southern states I have run on to astonishing examples of this rote learning. In a little school just outside Baton Rouge, Louisiana, the teacher had been hearing a class read a lesson on birds in one of the standard textbooks. To drive home a point from the lesson, she asked a boy, "When do the robins come?"

The pupil promptly answered, "In the fall."

"Now, Jimmie," urged the teacher, "read the lesson carefully again."

After he had droned out the text a second time, she said cheerily, "Now, Jimmie, when do the robins come?"

More hesitantly and sullenly he answered again, "The robins come in the fall."

"James, James," shouted the teacher. "Read that lesson again. Now tell me when do the robins come?"

Almost in tears the boy finally answered, "The robins come in the spring."

And so they do—in Boston where the text was written. But in Louisiana, just in order to avoid the northern winter, they come in the fall, as the boy well knew. Here we had an all too frequent combination of a stupid teacher, who was intent on grinding out a "lesson," and a textbook unadapted to the region. The result must have been either to destroy the boy's confidence in his own common sense, or, more likely, to break down completely his respect for book learning.

In its very earliest stages reading must have something to do with the lives of the children. As the school process continues, the child will become educated in direct ratio not to the amount of rote learning which is crammed into him but to the opportunities offered to him for general reading.

The wider a child's reading the better. There is no need to censor or direct his literary pursuits. The thing is to let him read whatever he finds interesting. He will quickly set his own standards if only he begins to get enjoyment and satisfaction from books. I have seen many cases where children were reading avidly what appeared to their parents to be trash, yet in a few years, making their own selections, these children were reading not only much more than their parents but books which, by anyone's standard, were far above the average of their parents' reading.

The present tendency to provide all schools with at least small collections of supplementary texts and stories is probably the most effective movement in modern education. And the trend toward letting the student educate himself by ample reading and study in well-stocked libraries is a similarly wise movement in higher education. Lessons and lectures do not give a student anything that would compare in value, in understanding, even in information, with the knowledge he can obtain by consulting for himself and on his own initiative the works of the masters. I believe that if children were taught to read properly and if secondary schools and colleges, instead of teaching "courses," encouraged and developed a love of reading, a situation such as that reported in Pennsylvania could not exist.

What I have been saying about reading in the early years applies with even greater force to college education. The difference between good and bad teaching is largely the degree to which the teacher eliminates himself, and inspires the student to do his own study and thus to accomplish his own education. This has been recognized in the laboratory more than in the library. Students of chemistry or biology are expected as a matter of course to work out their own problems, observing growth and reaction from the plants and animals and chemicals they use in their own experiments. Only in this way is the study of science anything more than the rote learning of fixed formulae which in themselves may be as poor intellectual equipment as superstitions and old wives' tales. Good teachers—there are still too few—are seeing similarly that in the subjects other than science the student gains nothing by being stuffed with facts. In this highly complex world there are few fixed and dogmatic answers to any questions. Education, even during the college years themselves, is sterile if it simply pumps information into the none-too-receptive brain of the student. And if college is to be thought of as preparation for life, then the student must be lured into finding things out for himself, using the teacher simply as guide and counselor.

My college days go back to that distant era when William Graham Sumner was teaching at Yale and I had the great good fortune to study with him. His lectures were interesting and inspiring. But the best thing he did for me—and for hundreds of Yale men—was to open up to us the vistas of diverse social systems all over the world. He lured us into balancing the quaint habits of Samoan chiefs and dancing girls against the equally quaint habits of New Haven bankers and debutantes. He sent us scurrying to the libraries to read about the Fijians, the Papuans, and the Hottentots, about British peers, French raconteurs, and German savants. He inspired many of us to get to remote spots of the globe as soon as we could and observe for ourselves the fascinating ways of life which people had built up for themselves about the world.

Old Professor Thomas Seymour did something of the same thing for my generation at Yale by teaching Greek not simply as cross-word puzzles in translation but as a door to the culture and literature of this amazingly creative people. He kept many of us digging in the library for days because he told us—with restrained illustrations—that most of the skits in modern burlesque shows were based on the Comedies of Aristophanes. After prolonged and fascinating research we found that they were.

It has been said that one of the faults of organized education is that the teacher asks the questions, whereas in normal life it is the child and the growing youth who are always doing the asking. And it is the business of the college, the Carnegie report states, to increase rather than to suppress the number of the students' questions. The customary procedure, however, "puts [the student] to bed like a troublesome child by safely tucking him into fixed courses which he can neither hasten nor retard and from which there is no escape. Since he is expected to accept these as they develop, it too often occurs that his curiosity is effectually stilled and his real enthusiasms are gradually diverted to extracurricular concerns in which his own initiative is permitted to count." Certainly true education proceeds as the curiosity of the student is stirred to desire ever greater and greater knowledge and is impelled to reflect and assimilate so that his information may be leavened by understanding.

The Carnegie report, by a systematic survey of the schools and colleges of a whole state, gives damning evidence that there are all too few instances of this kind of education. It makes vehement protest against the rigid course system which gives a student not knowledge and intelligent understanding but disconnected bits of unrelated information. One of the great evils of our system of education, the report states, is the building of the college curriculum around the "average" student when in reality there is no average but a large number of individuals of different grades of intelligence and ability. Each of these students should and must be given the opportunity and the privilege of developing himself unrestricted by what the "average" can or cannot do. The fundamental conclusion of the study, therefore, is that the object of the college or of any other educational institution must be the self-education of the student.

As a basis for aid to this self-education, the report suggests four essentials: (1) The college should have knowledge of the student's mental, physical, and social attainments so that he may be understood and helped. (2) It should prepare, in the light of the student's own goal, a tentative forecast of what he can hope to achieve. (3) It should make provision for the right kind of teaching—if and as the student himself finds it needed—and for libraries and laboratories which he may use at his convenience. (4) It should provide for regular measurement and analysis of his progress in knowledge and of his character and disposition.

I heartily agree to this four-point program, though it is
going to be terribly hard to put it into effect in our large
institutions which are accustomed to mass production by
routine lectures, assignments in texts, and periodic tests as
to the quantity of information acquired. Until the coming
of the millennium when schools and colleges, as advocated
in this report, will be working with the individual needs of
the students, I suggest that a large part of the desired result
may be obtained by concentrating on point three, by throwing
the burden of education from the teacher to the student.
In broad fields of learning the student may well be left to
dig out knowledge for himself from the library and the
laboratory, the faculty being regarded as aides and assistants to the student rather than as task masters to him.
A number of colleges are doing this now. Swarthmore is
increasingly following this plan for her honor students; the
Harvard reading periods and the programs of several experimental colleges are in this direction.

It may be true that many boys and girls now in American
colleges are not sufficiently intelligent or responsible to take
initiative in their own education. If so the sooner that fact
is brought into the open and a divorce effected between
these uncongenial parties the better. For if a person cannot
take a leading part in his own education at the higher levels,
no power on earth can do it for him. A great part of the
congestion and confusion in American colleges is caused by
the attempt to force education into masses of students who
are incapable or unwilling to receive it. The best measure of
the student's capacity to be educated is his ability to read
and study for himself.

Of course reading does not cover the whole of the development of a well-rounded individual. Skill and expression in
many lines are desirable, especially in these days of increasing leisure. But so far as intellectual attainment goes, books
are the great tools. Reading is the greatest of the command-
ments in education: reading for pleasure, reading for information, reading for understanding and insight into personal and social problems. Books and more books in the

schools and in the homes is the surest way to produce an educated nation.

LAYING THE GROUNDWORK

Preparation for Reading

1. Can you read? How do you define reading? What is the relationship between the ability to read and the acquiring of an education?
2. How could our colleges become institutions where students would educate themselves? Under such a system, who would ask the questions—the instructor or the student? What would be the responsibility of the student? of the instructor? What part would libraries and laboratories play in such an education?
3. Survey the reading you have done since you mastered the mechanics of reading. Have your tastes and standards changed? Should parents censor the reading of their children?

Vocabulary Building

1. Explain the following: The Carnegie Foundation, formal education, rote learning, a sterile education.
2. Look up these words: *scholasticism, routine, mediocrity, avidly, dogmatic, raconteurs, savants, assimilate, to leaven, tentative.*

APPRAISING THE RESULTS

1. With what statements in this article do you agree? disagree? Give the reasons for your opinions.
2. Examine your own proficiency in reading in relation to the two steps enumerated by the author: the mastery of the mechanics and the ability to grasp the significance of what you have read. Where do you stand in relation to each?
3. To what extent was your elementary and secondary education marked by the kind of scholasticism evident in the question on the migration of robins? Have you learned to take the major responsibility for your education?
4. Discuss: The child "will quickly set his own standards if only he begins to get enjoyment and satisfaction from books."
5. Discuss: "Education, even during the college years themselves, is sterile if it simply pumps information into the none-too-receptive brain of the student. And if college is to be thought of

as preparation for life, then the student must be lured into finding things out for himself, using the teacher simply as guide and counselor."

6. Evaluate the course system, giving the arguments for and against it.

7. Discuss: "A great part of the congestion and confusion in American colleges is caused by the attempt to force education into masses of students who are incapable or unwilling to receive it."

SELECTING THE THEME SUBJECT

1. Write a paper evaluating your own education in the light of the points raised by this selection.

2. Titles for themes: Education in the Library; Rote Learning in Grade Schools; The Best Teachers I Have Had; Am I Educating Myself?; Books and More Books; Should Everyone Go to College?; The Work of Education in a Democracy; Experimental Schools.

Toward Correction

ON VARIOUS KINDS OF THINKING[1]

James Harvey Robinson

WE DO NOT THINK ENOUGH ABOUT THINKING, AND MUCH OF
OUR CONFUSION IS THE RESULT OF CURRENT ILLUSIONS IN
regard to it. Let us forget for the moment any impressions
we may have derived from the philosophers, and see what
seems to happen in ourselves. The first thing that we notice
is that our thought moves with such incredible rapidity that
it is almost impossible to arrest any specimen of it long
enough to have a look at it. When we are offered a penny for
our thoughts we always find that we have recently had so
many things in mind that we can easily make a selection
which will not compromise us too nakedly. On inspection we
shall find that even if we are not downright ashamed of a
great part of our spontaneous thinking it is far too intimate,
personal, ignoble or trivial to permit us to reveal more than
a small part of it. I believe this must be true of everyone.
We do not, of course, know what goes on in other people's
heads. They tell us very little and we tell them very little.
The spigot of speech, rarely fully opened, could never emit
more than driblets of the ever renewed hogshead of thought
—*noch grösser wie's Heidelberger Fass*. We find it hard to
believe that other people's thoughts are as silly as our own,
but they probably are.

We all appear to ourselves to be thinking all the time
during our waking hours, and most of us are aware that we
go on thinking while we are asleep, even more foolishly
than when awake. When uninterrupted by some practical
issue we are engaged in what is now known as a *reverie*. This

[1] From *The Mind in the Making*, by James Harvey Robinson. Reprinted
by permission of Harper & Brothers, publishers.

is our spontaneous and favorite kind of thinking. We allow our ideas to take their own course and this course is determined by our hopes and fears, our spontaneous desires, their fulfillment or frustration; by our likes and dislikes, our loves and hates and resentments. There is nothing else anything like so interesting to ourselves as ourselves. All thought that is not more or less laboriously controlled and directed will inevitably circle about the beloved Ego. It is amusing and pathetic to observe this tendency in ourselves and in others. We learn politely and generously to overlook this truth, but if we dare to think of it, it blazes forth like the noontide sun.

The reverie or "free association of ideas" has of late become the subject of scientific research. While investigators are not yet agreed on the results, or at least on the proper interpretation to be given to them, there can be no doubt that our reveries form the chief index to our fundamental character. They are a reflection of our nature as modified by often hidden and forgotten experiences. We need not go into the matter further here, for it is only necessary to observe that the reverie is at all times a potent and in many cases an omnipotent rival to every other kind of thinking. It doubtless influences all our speculations in its persistent tendency to self-magnification and self-justification, which are its chief preoccupations, but it is the last thing to make directly or indirectly for honest increase of knowledge.[2] Philosophers usually talk as if such thinking did not exist or were in some way negligible. This is what makes their speculations so unreal and often worthless.

The reverie, as any of us can see for himself, is frequently

---

[2] The poet-clergyman, John Donne, who lived in the time of James I, has given a beautifully honest picture of the doings of a saint's mind: "I throw myself down in my chamber and call in and invite God and His angels thither, and when they are there I neglect God and His angels for the noise of a fly, for the rattling of a coach, for the whining of a door. I talk on in the same posture of praying, eyes lifted up, knees bowed down, as though I prayed to God, and if God or His angels should ask me when I thought last of God in that prayer I cannot tell. Sometimes I find that I had forgot what I was about, but when I began to forget it I cannot tell. A memory of yesterday's pleasures, a fear of to-morrow's dangers, a straw under my knee, a noise in mine ear, a light in mine eye, an anything, a nothing, a fancy, a chimera in my brain troubles me in my prayer."
—Quoted by Robert Lynd, *The Art of Letters*, pp. 46-47.

broken and interrupted by the necessity of a second kind of thinking. We have to make practical decisions. Shall we write a letter or no? Shall we take the subway or a bus? Shall we have dinner at seven or half-past? Shall we buy U. S. Rubber or a Liberty Bond? Decisions are easily distinguishable from the free flow of the reverie. Sometimes they demand a good deal of careful pondering and the recollection of pertinent facts; often, however, they are made impulsively. They are a more difficult and laborious thing than the reverie, and we resent having to "make up our mind" when we are tired, or absorbed in a congenial reverie. Weighing a decision, it should be noted, does not necessarily add anything to our knowledge, although we may, of course, seek further information before making it.

A third kind of thinking is stimulated when anyone questions our belief and opinions. We sometimes find ourselves changing our minds without any resistance or heavy emotion, but if we are told that we are wrong we resent the imputation and harden our hearts. We are incredibly heedless in the formation of our beliefs, but find ourselves filled with an illicit passion for them when anyone proposes to rob us of their companionship. It is obviously not the ideas themselves that are dear to us, but our self-esteem, which is threatened. We are by nature stubbornly pledged to defend our own from attack, whether it be our person, our family, our property, or our opinion. A United States Senator once remarked to a friend of mine that God Almighty could not make him change his mind on our Latin-America policy. We may surrender, but rarely confess ourselves vanquished. In the intellectual world at least peace is without victory.

Few of us take the pains to study the origin of our cherished convictions; indeed, we have a natural repugnance to so doing. We like to continue to believe what we have been accustomed to accept as true, and the resentment aroused when doubt is cast upon any of our assumptions leads us to seek every manner of excuse for clinging to them. *The result is that most of our so-called reasoning consists in finding arguments for going on believing as we already do.*

I remember years ago attending a public dinner to which

the Governor of the state was bidden. The chairman explained that His Excellency could not be present for certain "good" reasons; what the "real" reasons were the presiding officer said he would leave us to conjecture. This distinction between "good" and "real" reasons is one of the most clarifying and essential in the whole realm of thought. We can readily give what seems to us "good" reasons for being a Catholic or a Mason, a Republican or a Democrat, an adherent or opponent of the League of Nations. But the "real" reasons are usually on a quite different plane. Of course the importance of this distinction is popularly, if somewhat obscurely, recognized. The Baptist missionary is ready enough to see that the Buddhist is not such because his doctrines would bear careful inspection, but because he happened to be born in a Buddhist family in Tokio. But it would be treason to his faith to acknowledge that his own partiality for certain doctrines is due to the fact that his mother was a member of the First Baptist church of Oak Ridge. A savage can give all sorts of reasons for his belief that it is dangerous to step on a man's shadow, and a newspaper editor can advance plenty of arguments against the Bolsheviki. But neither of them may realize why he happens to be defending his particular opinion.

The "real" reasons for our beliefs are concealed from ourselves as well as from others. As we grow up we simply adopt the ideas presented to us in regard to such matters as religion, family relations, property, business, our country, and the state. We unconsciously absorb them from our environment. They are persistently whispered in our ear by the group in which we happen to live. Moreover, as Mr. Trotter has pointed out, these judgments, being the product of suggestion and not of reasoning, have the quality of perfect obviousness, so that to question them

. . . is to the believer to carry skepticism to an insane degree, and will be met by contempt, disapproval, or condemnation, according to the nature of the belief in question. When, therefore we find ourselves entertaining an opinion about the basis of which there is a quality of feeling which tells us that to inquire into it would be absurd, obviously unnecessary, unprofitable, undesirable, bad form, or wicked, we may know that that opinion is a nonrational one, and probably, therefore, founded upon inadequate evidence.[3]

Opinions, on the other hand, which are the result of experience or of honest reasoning do not have this quality of "primary certitude." I remember when as a youth I heard a group of business men discussing the question of the immortality of the soul, I was outraged by the sentiment of doubt expressed by one of the party. As I look back now I see that I had at the time no interest in the matter, and certainly no least argument to urge in favor of the belief in which I had been reared. But neither my personal indifference to the issue, nor the fact that I had previously given it no attention, served to prevent an angry resentment when I heard *my* ideas questioned.

This spontaneous and loyal support of our preconceptions —this process of finding "good" reasons to justify our routine beliefs—is known to modern psychologists as "rationalizing" —clearly only a new name for a very ancient thing. Our "good" reasons ordinarily have no value in promoting honest enlightenment, because, no matter how solemnly they may be marshaled, they are at bottom the result of personal preference or prejudice, and not of an honest desire to seek or accept new knowledge.

In our reveries we are frequently engaged in self-justification, for we cannot bear to think ourselves wrong, and yet have constant illustrations of our weaknesses and mistakes. So we spend much time finding fault with circumstances and the conduct of others, and shifting on to them with great ingenuity the onus of our own failures and disappointments. *Rationalizing is the self-exculpation which occurs when we feel ourselves, or our group, accused of misapprehension or error.*

The little word *my* is the most important one in all human affairs, and properly to reckon with it is the beginning of wisdom. It has the same force whether it is *my* dinner, *my* dog, and *my* house, or *my* faith, *my* country, and *my* God. We not only resent the imputation that our watch is wrong,

[3] *Instincts of the Herd*, p. 44.

or our car shabby, but that our conception of the canals of Mars, of the pronunciation of "Epictetus," of the medicinal value of salicine, or the date of Sargon I, are subject to revision.

Philosophers, scholars, and men of science exhibit a common sensitiveness in all decisions in which their *amour propre* is involved. Thousands of argumentative works have been written to vent a grudge. However stately their reasoning, it may be nothing but rationalizing, stimulated by the most commonplace of all motives. A history of philosophy and theology could be written in terms of grouches, wounded pride, and aversions, and it would be far more instructive than the usual treatments of these themes. Sometimes, under Providence, the lowly impulse of resentment leads to great achievements. Milton wrote his treatise on divorce as a result of his troubles with his seventeen-year-old wife, and when he was accused of being the leading spirit in a new sect, the Divorcers, he wrote his noble *Areopagitica* to prove his right to say what he thought fit, and incidentally to establish the advantage of a free press in the promotion of Truth.

All mankind, high and low, thinks in all the ways which have been described. The reverie goes on all the time not only in the mind of the mill hand and the Broadway flapper, but equally in weighty judges and godly bishops. It has gone on in all the philosophers, scientists, poets, and theologians that have ever lived. Aristotle's most abstruse speculations were doubtless tempered by highly irrelevant reflections. He is reported to have had very thin legs and small eyes, for which he doubtless had to find excuses, and he was wont to indulge in very conspicuous dress and rings and was accustomed to arrange his hair carefully.[4] Diogenes the Cynic exhibited the impudence of a touchy soul. His tub was his distinction. Tennyson in beginning his "Maud" could not forget his chagrin over losing his patrimony years before as the result of an unhappy investment in the Patent Decorative Carving Company. These facts are not recalled here as a gratuitous disparagement of the truly great, but to insure a full realization of the tremendous competition which all

[4] Diogenes Lærtius, book v.

really exacting thought has to face, even in the minds of the most highly endowed mortals.

And now the astonishing and perturbing suspicion emerges that perhaps almost all that had passed for social science, political economy, politics, and ethics in the past may be brushed aside by future generations as mainly rationalizing. John Dewey has already reached this conclusion in regard to philosophy.[5] Veblen[6] and other writers have revealed the various unperceived presuppositions of the traditional political economy, and now comes an Italian sociologist, Vilfredo Pareto, who, in his huge treatise on general sociology, devotes hundreds of pages to substantiating a similar thesis affecting all the social sciences.[7] This conclusion may be ranked by students of a hundred years hence as one of the several great discoveries of our age. It is by no means fully worked out, and it is so opposed to nature that it will be very slowly accepted by the great mass of those who consider themselves thoughtful. As a historical student I am personally fully reconciled to this newer view. Indeed, it seems to me inevitable that just as the various sciences of nature were, before the opening of the seventeenth century, largely masses of rationalizations to suit the religious sentiments of the period, so the social sciences have continued even to our own day to be rationalizations of uncritically accepted beliefs and customs.

It will become apparent as we proceed that the fact that an idea is ancient and that it has been widely received is no argument in its favor, but should immediately suggest the necessity of carefully testing it as a probable instance of rationalization.

This brings us to another kind of thought which can fairly easily be distinguished from the three kinds described above. It has not the usual qualities of the reverie, for it

[5] *Reconstruction in Philosophy.*

[6] *The Place of Science in Modern Civilization.*

[7] *Traité de Sociologie Générale, passim.* The author's term *"derivations"* seems to be his precise way of expressing what we have called the "good" reasons, and his *"residus"* correspond to the "real" reasons. He well says, *"L'homme éprouve le besoin de raisonner, et en outre d'étendre un voile sur ses instincts et sur ses sentiments"*—hence, rationalization. (P. 788.) His aim is to reduce sociology to the "real" reasons. (P. 791.)

does not hover about our personal complacencies and humiliations. It is not made up of the homely decisions forced upon us by everyday needs, when we review our little stock of existing information, consult our conventional preferences and obligations, and make a choice of action. It is not the defense of our own cherished beliefs and prejudices just because they are our own—mere plausible excuses for remaining of the same mind. On the contrary, it is that peculiar species of thought which leads us to *change* our mind.

It is this kind of thought that has raised man from his pristine, subsavage ignorance and squalor to the degree of knowledge and comfort which he now possesses. On his capacity to continue and greatly extend this kind of thinking depends his chance of groping his way out of the plight in which the most highly civilized peoples of the world now find themselves. In the past this type of thinking has been called Reason. But so many misapprehensions have grown up around the word that some of us have become suspicious of it. I suggest, therefore, that we substitute a recent name and speak of "creative thought" rather than of Reason. *For this kind of meditation begets knowledge, and knowledge is really creative inasmuch as it makes things look different from what they seemed before and may indeed work for their reconstruction.*

In certain moods some of us realize that we are observing things or making reflections with a seeming disregard of our personal preoccupations. We are not preening or defending ourselves; we are not faced by the necessity of any practical decision, nor are we apologizing for believing this or that. We are just wondering and looking and mayhap seeing what we never perceived before.

Curiosity is as clear and definite as any of our urges. We wonder what is in a sealed telegram or in a letter in which some one else is absorbed, or what is being said in the telephone booth or in low conversation. This inquisitiveness is vastly stimulated by jealousy, suspicion, or any hint that we ourselves are directly or indirectly involved. But there appears to be a fair amount of personal interest in other people's affairs even when they do not concern us except as a mystery to be unraveled or a tale to be told. The reports of a divorce suit will have "news value" for many weeks. They constitute a story, like a novel or play or moving picture. This is not an example of pure curiosity, however, since we readily identify ourselves with others, and their joys and despair then become our own.

We also take note of, or "observe," as Sherlock Holmes says, things which have nothing to do with our personal interests and make no personal appeal either direct or by way of sympathy. This is what Veblen so well calls "idle curiosity." And it is usually idle enough. Some of us when we face the line of people opposite us in a subway train impulsively consider them in detail and engage in rapid inferences and form theories in regard to them. On entering a room there are those who will perceive at a glance the degree of preciousness of the rugs, the character of the pictures, and the personality revealed by the books. But there are many, it would seem, who are so absorbed in their personal reverie or in some definite purpose that they have no bright-eyed energy for idle curiosity. The tendency to miscellaneous observation we come by honestly enough, for we note it in many of our animal relatives.

Veblen, however, uses the term "idle curiosity" somewhat ironically, as is his wont. It is idle only to those who fail to realize that it may be a very rare and indispensable thing from which almost all distinguished human achievement proceeds since it may lead to systematic examination and seeking for things hitherto undiscovered. For research is but diligent search which enjoys the high flavor of primitive hunting. Occasionally and fitfully idle curiosity thus leads to creative thought, which alters and broadens our own views and aspirations and may in turn, under highly favorable circumstances, affect the views and lives of others, even for generations to follow. An example or two will make this unique human process clear.

Galileo was a thoughtful youth and doubtless carried on a rich and varied reverie. He had artistic ability and might have turned out to be a musician or painter. When he had dwelt among the monks at Valambrosa he had been tempted to lead the life of a religious. As a boy he busied himself with toy machines and he inherited a fondness for mathematics. All these facts are of record. We may safely assume also that, along with many other subjects of contemplation, the Pisan maidens found a vivid place in his thoughts.

One day when seventeen years old he wandered into the cathedral of his native town. In the midst of his reverie he looked up at the lamps hanging by long chains from the high ceiling of the church. Then something very difficult to explain occurred. He found himself no longer thinking of the building, worshipers, or the services; of his artistic or religious interests; of his reluctance to become a physician as his father wished. He forgot the question of a career and even the *graziosissime donne*. As he watched the swinging lamps he was suddenly wondering if mayhap their oscillations, whether long or short, did not occupy the same time. Then he tested this hypothesis by counting his pulse, for that was the only timepiece he had with him.

This observation, however remarkable in itself, was not enough to produce a really creative thought. Others may have noticed the same thing and yet nothing came of it. Most of our observations have no assignable results. Galileo may have seen that the warts on a peasant's face formed a perfect isosceles triangle, or he may have noticed with boyish glee that just as the officiating priest was uttering the solemn words, *ecce agnus Dei,* a fly lit on the end of his nose. To be really creative, ideas have to be worked up and then "put over," so that they become a part of man's social heritage. The highly accurate pendulum clock was one of the later results of Galileo's discovery. He himself was led to reconsider and successfully refute the old notions of falling bodies. It remained for Newton to prove that the moon was falling, and presumably all the heavenly bodies. This quite upset all the consecrated views of the heavens as managed by angelic engineers. The universality of the laws of gravitation stimulated the attempt to seek other and equally important natural laws and cast grave doubts on the miracles in which mankind had hitherto believed. In short, those who dared to include in their thought the discoveries of Galileo and his successors found themselves in a new earth surrounded by new heavens.

On the 28th of October, 1831, three hundred and fifty years after Galileo had noticed the isochronous vibrations of the lamps, creative thought and its currency had so far increased that Faraday was wondering what would happen if he mounted a disk of copper between the poles of a horse-shoe magnet. As the disk revolved an electric current was produced. This would doubtless have seemed the idlest kind of experiment to the stanch business men of the time, who, it happened, were just then denouncing the child-labor bills in their anxiety to avail themselves to the full of the results of earlier idle curiosity. But should the dynamos and motors which have come into being as the outcome of Faraday's experiment be stopped this evening, the business man of to-day, agitated over labor troubles, might, as he trudged home past lines of "dead" cars, through dark streets to an unlighted house, engage in a little creative thought of his own and perceive that he and his laborers would have no modern factories and mines to quarrel about if it had not been for the strange practical effects of the idle curiosity of scientists, inventors, and engineers.

The examples of creative intelligence given above belong to the realm of modern scientific achievement, which fur-nishes the most striking instances of the effects of scrupulous, objective thinking. But there are, of course, other great realms in which the recording and embodiment of acute observation and insight have wrought themselves into the higher life of man. The great poets and dramatists and our modern story-tellers have found themselves engaged in pro-ductive reveries, noting and artistically presenting their dis-coveries for the delight and instruction of those who have the ability to appreciate them.

The process by which a fresh and original poem or drama comes into being is doubtless analogous to that which origi-nates and elaborates so-called scientific discoveries; but there is clearly a temperamental difference. The genesis and ad-vance of painting, sculpture, and music offer still other problems. We really as yet know shockingly little about these matters, and indeed very few people have the least curiosity about them.[8] Nevertheless, creative intelligence in its various forms and activities is what makes man. Were it not for its slow, painful, and constantly discouraged operations through the ages man would be no more than a species of primate living on seeds, fruit, roots, and uncooked flesh, and wandering naked through the woods and over the plains like a chimpanzee.

The origin and progress and future promotion of civilization are ill understood and misconceived. These should be made the chief theme of education, but much hard work is necessary before we can reconstruct our ideas of man and his capacities and free ourselves from innumerable persistent misapprehensions. There have been obstructionists in all times, not merely the lethargic masses, but the moralists, the rationalizing theologians, and most of the philosophers, all busily if unconsciously engaged in ratifying existing ignorance and mistakes and discouraging creative thought. Naturally, those who reassure us seem worthy of honor and respect. Equally naturally those who puzzle us with disturbing criticisms and invite us to change our ways are objects of suspicion and readily discredited. Our personal discontent does not ordinarily extend to any critical questioning of the general situation in which we find ourselves. In every age the prevailing conditions of civilization have appeared quite natural and inevitable to those who grew up in them. The cow asks no questions as to how it happens to have a dry stall and a supply of hay. The kitten laps its warm milk from a china saucer, without knowing anything about porcelain; the dog nestles in the corner of a divan with no sense of obligation to the inventors of upholstery and the manufacturers of down pillows. So we humans accept our breakfasts, our trains and telephones and orchestras and movies, our national Constitution, or moral code and standards of manners, with the simplicity and innocence of a pet

[8] Recently a re-examination of creative thought has begun as a result of new knowledge which discredits many of the notions formerly held about "reason." See, for example, *Creative Intelligence,* by a group of American philosophic thinkers; John Dewey, *Essays in Experimental Logic* (both pretty hard books); and Veblen, *The Place of Science in Modern Civilization.* Easier than these and very stimulating are Dewey, *Reconstruction in Philosophy,* and Woodworth, *Dynamic Psychology.*

rabbit. We have absolutely inexhaustible capacities for appro-
priating what others do for us with no thought of a "thank
you." We do not feel called upon to make any least contribution to the merry game ourselves. Indeed, we are usually
quite unaware that a game is being played at all.

We have now examined the various classes of thinking
which we can readily observe in ourselves and which we have
plenty of reasons to believe go on, and always have been
going on, in our fellow-men. We can sometimes get quite
pure and sparkling examples of all four kinds, but commonly
they are so confused and intermingled in our reverie as not
to be readily distinguishable. The reverie is a reflection of
our longings, exultations, and complacencies, our fears, sus-
picions, and disappointments. We are chiefly engaged in
struggling to maintain our self-respect and in asserting that
supremacy which we all crave and which seems to us our
natural prerogative. It is not strange, but rather quite inevitable, that our beliefs about what is true and false, good
and bad, right and wrong, should be mixed up with the
reverie and be influenced by the same considerations which
determine its character and course. We resent criticisms of
our views exactly as we do of anything else connected with
ourselves. Our notions of life and its ideals seem to us to be
our own and as such necessarily true and right, to be de-
fended at all costs.

*We very rarely consider, however, the process by which
we gained our convictions.* If we did so, we could hardly fail
to see that there was usually little ground for our confidence
in them. Here and there, in this department of knowledge or
that, some one of us might make a fair claim to have taken
some trouble to get correct ideas of, let us say, the situation
in Russia, the sources of our food supply, the origin of the
Constitution, the revision of the tariff, the policy of the Holy
Roman Apostolic Church, modern business organization,
trade unions, birth control, socialism, the League of Nations,
the excess-profits tax, preparedness, advertising in its social
bearings; but only a very exceptional person would be entitled to opinions on all of even these few matters. And yet
most of us have opinions on all these, and on many other

questions of equal importance, of which we may know even less. We feel compelled, as self-respecting persons, to take sides when they come up for discussion. We even surprise ourselves by our omniscience. Without taking thought we see in a flash that it is most righteous and expedient to discourage birth control by legislative enactment, or that one who decries intervention in Mexico is clearly wrong, or that big advertising is essential to big business and that big business is the pride of the land. As godlike beings why should we not rejoice in our omniscience?

It is clear, in any case, that our convictions on important matters are not the result of knowledge or critical thought, nor, it may be added, are they often dictated by supposed self-interest. Most of them are *pure prejudices* in the proper sense of that word. We do not form them ourselves. They are the whispering of "the voice of the herd." We have in the last analysis no responsibility for them and need assume none. They are not really our own ideas, but those of others no more well informed or inspired than ourselves, who have got them in the same careless and humiliating manner as we. It should be our pride to revise our ideas and not to adhere to what passes for respectable opinion, for such opinion can frequently be shown to be not respectable at all. We should, in view of the considerations that have been mentioned, resent our supine credulity. As an English writer has remarked:

If we feared the entertaining of an unverifiable opinion with the warmth with which we fear using the wrong implement at the dinner table, if the thought of holding a prejudice disgusted us as does a foul disease, then the dangers of man's suggestibility would be turned into advantages.[9]

LAYING THE GROUNDWORK

Preparation for Reading

1. Read Robinson's "New Conceptions of Man and His Ways," p. 33, and compare the two selections by this author.
2. How do we form our opinions and beliefs? Why are we slow to change them?

[9] Trotter, *op. cit.*, p. 45. The first part of this little volume is excellent.

Vocabulary Building

1. Before you read, look up these words: *philosopher, ignoble, trivial, reverie, frustration, laboriously, omnipotent, negligible, congenial, illicit, preconceptions, rationalization, self-exculpation, abstruse, grouches, patrimony, certitude, chagrin, pristine, begets, oscillations, hypothesis, isochronous, ratifying, omniscience, credulity, lethargic.*

2. Identify: Liberty Bond, Buddhist, Bolsheviki, Epictetus, Sargon I, Aristotle, John Dewey, Pareto, Galileo, Valambrosa, Pisan, Faraday, Veblen.

3. Check the meanings of these words in their context, and their pronunciations: *illusions, specimen, spontaneous, ego, potent, chimera, repugnance, gratuitous, disparagement, ethics, hover, complacencies, ironically, diligent, stanch, genesis, primate, prejudices, supine, susceptibility.*

4. Translate these foreign phrases: *noch grösser wie's Heidelberger Fass, amour propre, graziosissime donne, ecce agnus Dei.*

APPRAISING THE RESULTS

1. What are the four kinds of thinking Mr. Robinson discusses? Give the characteristics of each.

2. Why is he concerned about the way we think?

3. How do we bolster up our convictions? Explain the difference between "good" and "real" reasons.

4. What does Mr. Robinson say may be the judgment of the future about our social sciences?

5. Enumerate some concrete illustrations of creative thought or intelligence. Why is it important?

6. Why is society slow to accept changes in prevailing conditions? Whom does Robinson call "obstructionists"? Why? Do you think he is correct in saying "much hard work is necessary before we can construct our ideas of man and his capacities and free ourselves from innumerable persistent misapprehensions"?

7. Why do college students usually enjoy this selection? Explain your own reaction to it.

SELECTING THE THEME SUBJECT

1. From the questions following the three essays under "Man and the Social Group" (Part One), select a theme topic.

2. Write a paper discussing your own prejudices and how you are influenced by them.

3. In a theme, analyze your habits of thinking.

4. Investigate the work of some psychologist in a specialized field of research, i.e., Pavlov and his work with dogs, Gestalt and the behavioristic theory, Köhler and his work with apes.

5. Titles for themes: What I Have Learned in My College Courses About How to Learn; Why I Like Laboratory Work in Psychology; Mental Fakirs; Popular Delusions About the Mind; What Science Knows About Sleep; Superstitions About Dreams; Everyday Psychology; Controlling One's Thoughts.

ON LEARNING TO READ[1]

Lee Wilson Dodd

FOR THE PAST TWELVE MONTHS OR SO I HAVE BEEN ENGAGED AT TWO SUMMER SCHOOLS AND A JUNIOR COLLEGE, IN "TEACHING literature." What precisely have I been teaching, and what benefits, if any, may my pupils have been deriving from the experiment? Experiment I must call it, for I have had neither the formal and severe training of professional scholarship nor any instruction in the science—if it be a science—of pedagogy. I came to these jobs as a man who had spent much of his life in reading and writing—as a "literary man." To minute, exhaustive knowledge of world literature I could not pretend. Such were and are my disqualifications. What compensating gifts may my employers have hopefully supposed me to be bringing with me?

They must have argued, I presume, that a lifetime devoted to literary pursuits could not, culturally, have been spent wholly in vain. Be it far from me to question this assumption! After all, if a man has written verse, novels, plays, essays, short stories, book reviews, and so forth, for thirty or more years, he is entitled to the benefit of the doubt; he may well have picked up some notions as to the differences between good writing and bad, and if he has put in most of his spare moments in reading he ought at least to have gained a bowing acquaintance with a number of satisfactory authors. It is only fair to add that the one advantage I claimed for myself over many (by no means all) teachers of literature was a really fanatic love for well-written books. This love, I suggested,

[1] From *The Atlantic Monthly*, July, 1932. Reprinted by permission of the publishers.

being white-hot and ineradicable, could hardly fail to com-municate a few sparks of its secret fire to my students.

Has it done so? In this cynical, debunking age, I know perfectly what answer the ungentle reader is expecting, and I am not at all sorry to disappoint him.

Yes, I believe that it has done so. Not, certainly, to all, and perhaps not extravagantly to any who were unmarked from their cradles by the bite of the Bookworm. But a year of teaching, or of teaching at, literature has convinced me, somewhat to my own surprise, that literature can indeed be taught. A desire to read, and to read good books, can at least be stimulated even in more or less obdurate youthful breasts.

Heaven forbid that I should now imagine myself, unaided and untrained, to have discovered some new and revolution-ary technique for "teaching literature"! What little I have accomplished has doubtless been far better accomplished many times before by professional teachers. I have had one or two masters myself in past years who brought to their class-rooms not only scholarship but a winning humor, humanity, and grace. Remembering them, I blush for my present temerity. However, one can do only what one can. What is it that I have at least been trying—and trying very hard—to do?

Briefly, I have been trying to teach my students *how to read*.

The fine art of reading, I quickly and painfully discovered, is in no little danger of being lost. Most of the students, I found, were quite unaware that reading is anything more than a mechanical acquirement. It seldom occurred to them that the great books of the world will not unbosom themselves to slovenly, incurious, inartistic readers. The page of a great book does not differ mechanically from the page of a worth-less book—it is merely a sheet of paper with some black, odd-looking specks on it. It remains that, or is transformed into wisdom, beauty, joy. But this transformation depends finally upon the reader—upon the reader's ability *to read*.

A printed poem, for example, is very like the printed score of a musical composition. The poem itself does not exist for you until you have correctly and artistically performed and interpreted it. With a poem, this performance, this interpretation, is usually a solitary joy, a purely mental re-creation from the printed page. It need not be so. The poem may be performed and interpreted for others, may be read aloud. Comparatively few of us, however, even if we are fond of poetry, can bear to listen to a poem thus recited or read aloud. Why? For a number of reasons, but for one chiefly: the reading aloud, nine times in ten, is wretchedly done. Not many people these days can read prose aloud acceptably; as for verse—! The mere presence of meter before its readers seems to reduce them to a condition of imbecility. They either gabble and stutter through it with no apparent awareness either of its natural movement or of its meaning, or they monotonously chant it in a somnolent singsong, or, worse still, they smother it in all the affected graces and overblown sentiment of professional "elocution." Our poets themselves suffer from this general artistic paralysis, and when they attempt to read out their own compositions they present the horrid spectacle of infanticides publicly butchering their children.

Now, obviously enough, if one cannot read a poem aloud without destroying it, this must partly be due to one's inability to read it to one's self. Partly, I say, because the self-consciousness of unaccustomed public performance, even if the public be only a single suffering friend, tends to exaggerate all one's errors of technique and taste. Nevertheless, if you can read a poem to yourself with pleasure, you should at least be a little better able to read it to others without giving them positive pain; and, if you cannot, the odds are that you have never, in any significant sense of the word, *read* that particular poem.

For what does reading—what I should like to call *re-creative* reading—imply? Many difficult things. A book might well be written—if sensitively written—to enumerate, analyze, discuss them. Such a book would necessarily have much to say of the delicate functions of rhythm (in heightening yet controlling emotion, in regulating emphasis, and so forth), much of the root meanings and sky-branching connotations (suggestive emotional overtones) of words, much of language as logic and of language as representation—of language as architecture, as line and mass, as color, as music. And the lurking presence of an often extremely subtle irony in almost all first-rate writing would have to be pointed out as a quality too frequently missed by the indifferent, unalert reader. We need, in short, a new rhetoric, not to teach good writing, which can hardly be taught, but to teach good reading, which can far more certainly be taught. Why readers go wrong is the underlying question to be dealt with; yet clearly, in a brief paper, I cannot deal with it here. Two widely differing illustrations of the process of going wrong may, however, be given.

A girl student—a lively and lightly sophisticated young modernist—was protesting against my cruelty. "I can't do it!" she almost wailed. "I simply can't read stodgy old-fashioned stories like that! They bore me so. Aren't you ever going to give me something to read that I don't have to begin by hating?"

She had been assigned *The Vicar of Wakefield*, and we had met for a first conference upon it.

I might, fairly enough, have reminded her that since she had herself elected "A Survey of English Literature," she could hardly expect me not to try, at least, to interest her in certain of the established classics. We were at the time supposed to be "surveying" the eighteenth century. But why waste one's breath? I held out the forbidding volume and asked her to read me the opening paragraph. She gave me a single desolated glance, sighed, accepted the book, and hurriedly and indifferently began as follows:

" 'I was ever 'v the opinion that the hones' man ——' "

"Oh, wait, please," I said. "Just read what's there. Don't add or subtract anything."

"I don't understand."

"You put in a word, removed several letters, and subtracted a comma."

Her impatient little wriggle was very expressive.

"Begin again," I suggested. "Take it more slowly."

She began again, with an exaggerated dragging of each syllable:

" 'I was . . . ev-er . . . of . . . the . . . opinion . . . that ——' "

"You've repeated two fatal mistakes in seven words," I interrupted.

"You're just trying to get my goat!" she snapped.

"Yes. I am. And now that I've got it ——"

"You haven't! You can't make me like this book by being angry. It's a stupid, silly book—and just because people used to be dull enough to like it ——"

"Some people are still dull enough to like it. I am, for one."

"I don't believe you really like it. You just think you ought to."

"Oh, no," I said. "There's no 'ought' about it. I'll admit I haven't much respect for the plot of this story. I'll admit the melodramatic coincidences toward the end of it are rather silly. But they're not important. No one ever re-reads *The Vicar of Wakefield* for its plot."

"I can't imagine reading it again!"

"I've read most of it a number of times," I said.

"Oh, you have to—because you're a teacher."

"No, I'm not that kind of teacher—and I've a fairly good memory. I like turning back to it now and then for the pure joy of appreciation."

"What is there to appreciate?"

"A good deal. For one thing, Goldsmith's deceptive simplicity. Whenever he's being particularly deep and subtle, he pretends he is merely being naïve. That's called irony, you know—or perhaps you don't; but it is. Only, Goldsmith's irony has a quite special flavor. There's nothing harsh or ill-tempered about it. He has a secret process by which he blends irony with sympathy and charm—and the secret, worse luck, appears to have died with him."

"I don't see what you mean." She was a little worried, however. "I just thought he was—sort of formal and silly and awfully sentimental."

"Yes. That's because you haven't read the book yet."

"Oh! I did read it. I told you I would, and it nearly killed me—but I honestly did!"

"My dear girl," I said, "suppose I asked you to play a sonata by Mozart for me—and you rattled away at the notes, missing perhaps a third of them, without timing or expression, because you had decided in advance that Mozart's music was silly and old-fashioned and you had no use for it."

"But I love Mozart!"

"Exactly. And I love Goldsmith. So you can imagine how I feel when I ask you to play me some Goldsmith—and you promptly murder him."

"Well—I'm sorry. I didn't know you felt that way. I don't see how you *can*!"

"And I don't see how so bright a girl as you can occasionally be so obtuse. But, of course, girls in general aren't very quick at detecting irony."

"I thought irony was saying one thing and meaning another."

"So, roughly, it is."

"But Goldsmith's so deadly *plain*!"

"Is he? Let me read you this first paragraph—slowly. It shouldn't be read too slowly; the movement is *Adagio ma non troppo*. But Goldsmith is devilish sly. Until you're familiar with him you have to watch him, or you'll miss something delightful every few words." And I reached for the book and began, abominably enough, underlining each lurking point for her.

As I concluded the first page my pupil was actually blushing.

"Please don't go on!" she begged. "I simply didn't realize he was being as cagy as that. I never felt like such an idiot in my life!"

She jumped to her feet and held out her hand. "I'll really *read* it for you this time," she said.

Another student came to me flushed with a great discovery. She had been reading for the first time the lyrics of William Blake.

"They're the loveliest things I ever read!" she exclaimed. "They're poetry—the real thing! I don't see why you've had us poke through all that Pope and Gray and Cowper and stuff. The minute you read Blake you realize all that sort of thing isn't poetry at all."

"Well," I replied, "that's splendid. It's a wonderful gift

to be able to distinguish true poetry from sham poetry at a glance."

"You just *feel* the difference at once," she said.

"Read me one of the lyrics you like best," I suggested.

She opened the book.

"I like all of them! . . . Well, of course, there's 'Tiger, Tiger.' "

"Yes. Read me that."

She did so, with a breathless, happy excitement. "It just thrills me!" she added.

"Why?"

"It's so vivid! It makes you see and understand a tiger as you never have before. It makes you feel that he's the most magnificent thing in the world."

"Rather terrifying, though?"

"That's part of it—that's why it's so exciting. It's so—suggestive!"

"What does the tiger suggest to you?"

"Oh—strength and swiftness and fire and ——"

"Yes ——?"

"But the main thing is—it works you all up so. When I read it the first time I just wanted to jump up and yell!"

"And do you think that's why Blake wrote the poem? Because he'd seen a tiger—or had imagined one so completely that he had to exclaim how magnificent and beautiful and terrifying it was?"

"I . . . yes . . . I suppose so. That's why it's *real* poetry—he was so excited himself."

"I see. It hasn't occurred to you, then, that the poem may mean something more than that—something quite definite that Blake wanted to say to you?"

A shade of disappointment crossed her face.

"You see," I continued relentlessly, "Blake wasn't the sort of man who just got vaguely, however gloriously, excited over tigers and lambs and things. He was a very positive, pugnacious man. He thought he had seized the hidden truth about pretty much everything by direct intuition or inspiration. He thought human reason was of the Devil, but that the poetic imagination was of God. He identified his imagination with Truth, with God himself. In short, he was as pure an example of the seer, of the convinced mystic, as you will find anywhere. His visions to him are reality—the one possible Reality. So you may be certain that through his Tiger he is expressing what he believes to be one aspect of Eternal Truth . . . and you haven't really *read* that poem until you have read it as he intended it."

She looked more disappointed than before, and even a little alarmed.

"But I've read the poem over and over! I know it by heart. And I don't see how you can tell just what he *meant* by it."

"You can't," I explained, "unless you have studied all of Blake's poems and prose writings and designs very closely, in order to discover what he intends by the *symbols* he uses. Like most mystics, Blake was a symbolist, and he had built up a whole system of symbolism. Moreover, he uses these symbols to express as exactly as he can all his ideas about life, death, and eternity. A symbol is nothing but a figure of speech which is used to stand for an idea—and with Blake a given symbol stands invariably for a given idea. Now it happens that the Tiger is one of Blake's fixed symbols; and I repeat that you may know Blake's poem by heart, but you haven't really *read* it until you have discovered what Blake meant by his Tiger— discovered, that is, what he himself was excited about."

"Oh, good Lord," said the girl, "but that takes all the poetry out of it!"

"Which isn't my fault, you see, but Blake's—if it's any- body's. Besides, Blake would violently have disagreed with you. Poetry, to Blake, was the expression of Eternal Truth."

"Oh . . . How can I find out . . . What *did* he mean by the Tiger?"

"He meant the wrath of God," I said. "Just as by the Lamb he meant always the love of God."

"Oh . . . I wish you hadn't spoiled it for me!" she wailed. "It doesn't seem nearly so wonderful any more. It takes the poetry out of it."

"Why? By adding a meaning?"

"Yes—no—oh, I don't know," she said. "I guess I just like to feel things sort of vaguely and get excited about them."

"In other words, my dear girl, you are still a complete romantic. You like one *kind* of poetry, and so proclaim it to be the only kind there is. There are lots of supposed critics, even nowadays, who completely agree with you."

She brightened a little at this.

"Well, anyway," she said, "it's awfully interesting—and I'm going to think it over." And she left me with a little puckered frown between her eyes. I was glad of that frown. It didn't worry me that she should feel, temporarily, that I had spoiled something precious for her. I hoped, indeed, that it might lead her to take one more courageous step in the always difficult re-creative process of learning to read.

These two illustrations of faulty reading—or, preferably, of *non*-reading—have perhaps been given at too great length, for in themselves they are far from exhausting the subject. Yet they do, I think, bring out two very general, opposite, and disastrous tendencies. Both these girls were students of more than average intelligence. Both, in the usual phrase, were "fond of reading." Neither had ever been taught, or had discovered for herself, how to read.

The failure of the first student with *The Vicar of Wakefield* was due to a very common contemporary prejudice. I have discovered that at least a third of my students, if not a good half of them, approach the masterpieces of former generations truculently, with obvious chips on disdainful shoulders; for our young people, it appears, are instinctive and convinced believers in progress. Today, they assume, is necessarily better, more enlightened, than yesterday. At least, I know not how else to interpret the widespread assumption that the best of our new books are necessarily superior to any written, or that could conceivably have been written, in the darker ages of the past.

The argument (seldom precisely formulated) would seem to run as follows: We know more than our ancestors; therefore we write better than our ancestors. So why waste time on inferior productions? The study of literature should rationally be confined to the best, which is clearly contemporary literature. Q.E.D.

That there are possibly a few dropped stitches in the fabric of this argument never seems to occur to them. It is not my purpose for the present to point these out. I am here concerned only with the effect of this attitude upon many promising students—upon their mere ability to *read*.

If you approach a book, any book, with rooted suspicion and bored indifference, the chances of your being able to read that book, re-creatively, are extremely small. To begin with, you will already have abandoned a first principle of good reading—namely, fair-mindedness, a desire to give the author before you a square deal. In other words, you must grant him your complete attention. You must really listen to what he has to say. If, having done so, you find what he has to say false, or dull, or his manner of saying it awkward or meretricious, you may excuse yourself and leave him. But until you have heard him with attention you have not really heard him, and any judgment you may pronounce must necessarily be unfair.

My first student, then, had not been courteously fair-minded to Goldsmith; she had not listened to him; her mind had been elsewhere while her eyes merely fulfilled an appointed task. Now Goldsmith always speaks quietly, politely, with a minimum of emphasis; he is too well bred to solicit attention; he assumes that his readers are equally well bred. This is evidently a dangerous assumption in a period of clamor, public posturing, and impervious ballyhoo.

As for the second student, her inability to read William Blake did not spring (Heaven knows) from lack of attention. She is the type of student, by no means uncommon, for whom reading is always an emotional debauch. If an author thrills her, she asks no more of him; the immediate esthetic thrill is for her the beginning and end of art. To have been made to *feel* something—even if one is hardly aware what it is one has felt or why one has felt it—is enough. Intellectual curiosity, understanding, remain in abeyance. The cheek flushes, the heart beats faster, and the miracle has been accomplished —even if the revolutionary thinker and mystic, Blake, be transformed thereby into a spineless romantic and purveyor of golden gush to schoolgirls.

But the particular error is not the point. Twenty more might as easily have been illustrated and commented upon. The point, in the end, is but this, that a catholic appreciation of the better books of the world depends upon our ability to *read* them, and that reading is an art in itself—an art to be studied as other arts are studied and, within the limits of a given personality, more or less perfectly acquired. Teachers of literature are—if they are anything useful—teachers of reading. Such at least is my present conviction. It is almost the first and last duty of a teacher of literature to master the art of reading himself, and to help, by any means in his power, his students to master it. Our existence as teachers of literature is justified only so far as we are able to teach our pupils how to read.

LAYING THE GROUNDWORK

Preparation for Reading

1. What kind of reading do you enjoy as recreation? Why? If you don't like to read, explain your objections.
2. As you recall your literature courses, what names or books or stories or poems come quickly to your mind? Why do you remember these?
3. Have you any suggestions for making literature and English more enjoyable to the students?
4. Do you dislike certain authors or books? What caused you to form this aversion? Could it have been prevented? How?

Vocabulary Building

1. Look up these words: *pedagogy, fanatic, ineradicable, debunking, obdurate, technique, temerity, slovenly, incurious, cynical, meter, imbecility, somnolent, infanticides, rhythm, truculently, formulated, meretricious, solicit, posturing, impervious, ballyhoo, debauch, abeyance, mystic, purveyor, catholic.*
2. Observe the literary diction of this selection; determine why you like or dislike it.
3. Make a list of figures of speech like "a few sparks from its secret fire," "unmarked from their cradle by the bite of the Bookworm," "overblown sentiment," "artistic paralysis." Discuss their effectiveness.

APPRAISING THE RESULTS

1. What qualifications had Mr. Dodd as a teacher of literature in his opinion? in yours?
2. What is meant by the statement that a printed poem or musical score does not exist until "you have correctly and artistically performed and interpreted it"?
3. What does re-creative reading imply and what does it demand of the reader?
4. Explain Mr. Dodd's choice of the anecdotes he tells.
5. Explain how the ability to read influences one's learning.
6. Do you agree with Mr. Dodd that the teacher of literature must be a teacher of reading? Cite your own experiences.
7. Reread the introduction "To The Student" and Embree's essay on p. 479.

SELECTING THE THEME SUBJECT

1. Write a paper discussing the courses you have had in reading or in literature. Be specific in your comments.
2. Using anecdotes and conversation as Mr. Dodd does, write an essay on your reading in some other course or courses than literature.
3. Make a written report of what is being done to improve the reading habits of school children and college students.
4. Titles for themes: Friends on My Bookshelf; Famous Friends in Fiction; Fairy Tales and Their Influence; My Favorite Author or Character; Substitutes for the Dime Novel of Father's Boyhood; Cheap Editions of Books; Why I Should (or Should Not) Like to Work in a Bookstore or Library; The Books I Haven't Read; Shipwrecked with Five Books; Why the Detective Story Is Popular; Rivals to Reading; Books I Should Like to Own; Silly Readers and Writers I Have Known; The Ideal Teacher of Literature; Literary Figures Who Frequent Our Conversation at Home.

"I Know What I Mean, But . . ."

THE TYRANNY OF WORDS[1]

Stuart Chase

I HAVE WRITTEN SEVERAL BOOKS AND MANY ARTICLES, BUT ONLY LATELY HAVE I BEGUN TO INQUIRE INTO THE NATURE OF THE tools I use. This is a curious oversight when one stops to consider it. Carpenters, masons, and engineers who give no thought to their tools and instruments are not likely to erect very durable structures. Yet I follow a procedure common to most writers, for few of us look to our tools. We sometimes study synonyms, derivations, rhythm, style, but we rarely explore the nature of words themselves. We do not inquire if they are adequate instruments for building a durable structure of human communication. Language, whether English, French, or Chinese, is taken for granted, a basic datum. Writers search their memories for a better word to use in a given context but are no more in the habit of questioning language than of questioning the weather. There it is. We assume that we know exactly what we mean, and that readers who do not understand us should polish their wits.

Years ago I read a little book by Allen Upward called *The New Word*. It was an attempt to get at the meaning of "idealism" as used in the terms of the Nobel Prize award—an award for "the most distinguished work of an idealist tendency." Upward began his quest—which was ultimately to lead him over the living world and back to the dawn of written history —by asking a number of his friends to give their personal interpretation of the term "idealism." He received the following replies:

[1] From *The Tyranny of Words*, copyright, 1938, by Stuart Chase. Reprinted by permission of the author and of Harcourt, Brace & Company, Inc.

517

fanatical	poetical	what cannot be proved
altruistic	intangible	opposite of materialism
not practical	sentimental	something to do with
exact	true	imaginative powers

This gave me pause. I thought I knew what "idealism" meant right enough, and had used it many times with confidence. Obviously, on the basis of Upward's study, what I meant was rarely if at all communicated to the hearer. Indeed, on examining my own mental processes I had some difficulty in determining what I did mean by this lofty word. Thereafter I was unable to escape an uneasy feeling, slight but persistent—like a mouse heard in the wall of a room—that something was wrong. This feeling was strengthened when I stumbled upon a little brochure by H. G. Wells, written I believe for the Fabian Society, which dealt with what he termed "a criticism of the instrument." The forceps of the mind, he said, were clumsy forceps and crushed the truth a little when grasping it. Hum . . . something in that. Even more unsettling was the profound observation of Lao Tse:

> Those who know do not tell;
> Those who tell do not know.

To a writer dealing in ideas this aphorism became presently unendurable. Better to put it away on a dark shelf, duly classified as an ancient Chinese wisecrack.

Another matter which distressed me was that I found it almost impossible to read philosophy. The great words went round and round in my head until I became dizzy. Sometimes they made pleasant music, but I could rarely effect passage between them and the real world of experience. William James I could usually translate, but the great classics had almost literally no meaning to me—just a haughty parade of "truth," "substance," "infinite," "absolute," "oversoul," "the universal," "the nominal," "the eternal." As these works had been acclaimed for centuries as part of the priceless cultural heritage of mankind, it seemed obvious that something in my intellectual equipment was seriously deficient. I strove to understand Plato, Aristotle, Spinoza, Hobbes, Kant, Hegel, Herbert Spencer, Schopenhauer. The harder I wrestled, the more the solemn procession of verbal ghosts circled through my brain, mocking my ignorance. Why was this? Was I alone at fault, or was there something in the structure of language itself which checked communication?

Meanwhile, I had long been aware of the alarming futility of most of the literature dedicated to economic and social reform. As a young reformer I had organized meetings, written pamphlets, prepared lectures, concocted programs, spread publicity with enthusiasm. Those already inclined to my point of view attended the meetings, read the pamphlets, listened to the lectures, adopted the programs, but the apathy of the unconverted was as colossal as it was baffling. As the years went by it became apparent that I was largely wasting my time. The message—and I still believe it was a human and kindly message—had not got through; communication was blocked. What we reformers meant was not what our hearers thought we meant. Too often it was clear that we were not heard at all; noises came through, but no meaning. Few of the seeds I sowed bore out the ancient theory that the seed of truth, once planted, would surely sprout. The damn things would not come up. Why? Why did Mr. Wilson's dubious "war for democracy" go over with a roar, while our carefully reasoned appeals drifted listlessly down empty alleys?

Was there a way to make language a better vehicle for communicating ideas? I read Freud, Trotter, Le Bon, Mac-Dougall, Watson, who gave me some light on motives but little on language. One found in daily life a kind of stereotyped distrust of words, reflected in such phrases as "all generalizations are false, including this one," "campaign oratory," "empty verbalisms," "slogans," "just hot air," "taking the word for the deed." But the distrust was seldom profound; it was usually employed to score off an opponent in a debate or to discredit statements with which one did not agree. Language itself needed to be taken into the laboratory for competent investigation. For a long time I have been puzzled and uneasy about my tools, but only in the past three years have I followed a few hardy pioneers into the laboratory. And as Malisoff has said: "It is a dreadful thing—with no easy escape—to struggle Laocoön-wise with language."

The first pioneer to help me was Count Alfred Korzybski, a Polish mathematician now living in the United States. He had written a book published in 1933 called *Science and Sanity*, and its jacket carried the endorsement of some of the world's most distinguished scientists: such men as C. B. Bridges, C. M. Childs, H. S. Jennings, Raymond Pearl, B. Malinowski, Bertrand Russell, P. W. Bridgman, E. T. Bell, R. S. Lillie. They agreed that Korzybski was working a rich vein, and that the output might be of great importance. He was exploring the possibility of formulating a genuine science of communication. The term which is coming into use to cover such studies is "semantics," matters having to do with signification or meaning. I shall employ the term frequently in the pages that follow. You had best get used to it, for I think we are going to hear it with increasing frequency in the years before us.

Science and Sanity was harder reading than all the philosophers combined, but it connected with my world of experience. The words no longer went round and round. Korzybski had spent ten years on the book, raiding nearly every branch of science, from neurology to the quantum theory, in a stubborn attempt to find how words behave, and why meaning is so often frustrated. As I read it, slowly, painfully, but with growing eagerness, I looked for the first time into the awful depths of language itself—depths into which the grammarian and the lexicographer have seldom peered, for theirs is a different business. Grammar, syntax, dictionary derivations, are to semantics as a history of the coinage is to the operations going on in a large modern bank.

I went on to *The Meaning of Meaning* by C. K. Ogden and I. A. Richards. People said it was hard reading. The title sounded like more philosophy. On the contrary, philosophers were harried from pillar to post: "The ablest logicians are precisely those who are led to evolve the most fantastic systems by the aid of their verbal technique." The book encouraged me to believe that the trouble had lain not so much with me as with the philosophers. With the tools of semantic analysis, the authors laid in ruin the towering edifice of classical philosophy from Aristotle to Hegel. Psychology (pre-

Freudian) emerged in little better repair. Large sections of sociology, economics, the law, politics, even medicine, were as cities after an earthquake.

These three investigators—Korzybski, Ogden, and Richards —agree broadly on the two besetting sins of language. One is identification of *words* with *things*. The other is misuse of abstract words. "This *is* a dog." Is it? The thing that is called "dog" is a nonverbal object. It can be observed by the senses, it can be described, and then, for convenience, the label "dog" can be attached to it, or the label "hund" or "chien" or "perro." *But the label is not the animal.*

We are aware of this when we stop to think about it. The trouble is that we do not stop to think about it. We are continually confusing the label with the nonverbal object, and so giving a spurious validity to the word, as something alive and barking in its own right. When this tendency to identify expands from dogs to higher abstractions such as "liberty," "justice," "the eternal," and imputes living, breathing entity to them, almost nobody knows what anybody else means. If we are *conscious* of abstracting, well and good, we can handle these high terms as an expert tamer handles a lion. If we are not conscious of doing so, we are extremely likely to get into difficulties. Identification of word with thing is well illustrated in the child's remark, "Pigs are rightly named, since they are such dirty animals."

Ogden and Richards contribute a technical term, the "referent," by which they mean the object or situation in the real world to which the word or label refers. A beam of light comes from a moving animal to my optic nerve. The animal, which I recognize through prior experience with similar animals, is the referent. Presently I add the label and say, "That's a nice dog." Like the term "semantics," I shall use the term "referent" frequently in the following pages. Indeed the goal of semantics might be stated as "find the referent." When people can agree on the thing to which their words refer, minds meet. The communication line is cleared.

Labels as names for things may be roughly divided into three classes on an ascending scale:

1. Labels for common objects, such as "dog," "chair," "pencil." Here difficulty is at a minimum.

2. Labels for clusters and collection of things, such as "mankind," "consumers' goods," "Germany," "the white race," "the courts." These are abstractions of a higher order, and confusion in their use is widespread. There is no entity "white race" in the world outside our heads, but only some millions of individuals with skins of an obvious or dubious whiteness.

3. Labels for essences and qualities, such as "the sublime," "freedom," "individualism," "truth." For such terms, there are no discoverable referents in the outside world, and by mistaking them for substantial entities somewhere at large in the environment, we create a fantastic wonderland. This zone is the especial domain of philosophy, politics, and economics.

We normally beg the hard question of finding referents and proceed learnedly to define the term by giving another dictionary abstraction, for example, defining "liberty" by "freedom"—"thus peopling the universe with spurious entities, mistaking symbolic machinery for referents." We seldom come down to earth, but allow our language forms or symbolic machinery to fashion a demonology of absolutes and high-order abstractions, in which we come to believe as firmly as Calvin believed in the Devil.

You doubt this? Let me ask you a question: Does communism threaten the world? Unless you are conscious of the dangers lying in the use of abstract terms, you may take this question seriously. You may personify "communism" as a real thing, advancing physically over the several continents, as a kind of beast or angel, depending on your politics. You give a careful, weighted answer or else an excited, passionate answer, to my question. But you have identified the word with the thing, and furthermore you would be very hard put to it to find lower-order referents for the term. I have been searching for them for years. *The question as it stands is without meaning.* I might about as well ask you: Does omniscience threaten the world? or Does Buzzism threaten the world? If we can agree—if sane men generally can agree—on a series of things in the real world that may properly be summarized by the label "communism," then the question has meaning, and we can proceed intelligently to its discussion. Otherwise not. Can you and I and Jones and Finkelstein come to an agreement about what is meant by "communism"? Try it sometimes with Jones and Finkelstein. In Chapter II you will find the surprising results of trying "fascism" on nearly one hundred people. Yet until agreement is reached, the question can liberate plenty of emotion but little real meaning. Jones will follow his meaning and Finkelstein his, and be damned to you.

I read Bridgman's *The Logic of Modern Physics* and found a similar criticism of language. With four good men in substantial agreement as to the basic difficulty, I seemed to be getting on. "The true meaning of a term is to be found by observing what a man does with it, not what he says about it." Scientists, through observing, measuring, and performing a physical *operation* which another scientist can repeat, reach the solid ground of agreement and of meaning. They find the referents. "If a question has meaning, it must be possible to find an operation by which an answer may be given to it. It will be noted in many cases that the operation cannot exist and the question has no meaning." See them fall, the Great Questions of pre-Einstein science! It is impossible as yet to perform any kind of experiment or operation with which to test them, and so, until such operation be discovered, they remain without meaning.

May time have a beginning and an end?
May space be bounded?
Are there parts of nature forever beyond our detection?
Was there a time when matter did not exist?
May space or time be discontinuous?
Why does negative electricity attract positive?

I breathe a sigh of relief and I trust the reader joins me. One can talk until the cows come home—such talk has already filled many volumes—about these questions, but without operations they are meaningless, and our talk is no more rewarding than a discussion in a lunatic asylum. "Many of the questions asked about social and philosophical subjects will be found to be meaningless when examined from the point of view of operations." Bridgman cites no samples, but we can find plenty on every hand.

Is heredity more important than environment?
What is truth?
What is economic value?
Is the soul more important than the body?
Is there a life after death?
What is national honor?
What is a classless society?
Does labor create all surplus value?
Is the Aryan race superior to the Jewish race?
Is art more important than science?

I read Thurman W. Arnold's *The Symbols of Government* and looked at language from another unsettling but illuminating angle. I read E. T. Bell, Lancelot Hogben, Henshaw Ward, Jeremy Bentham, E. S. Robinson, H. R. Huse, Malinowski, Ludwig Wittgenstein, parts of Pareto, Charles A. Beard's *The Discussion of Human Affairs*, and F. C. S. Schiller's superb destruction of formal logic. I read everything I could get my hands on that dealt with semantics and meaning.

At last I began to know a little about the tools of my craft. Not much, for semantics is still the tenderest of sciences, but something. It proved to be knowledge of the most appalling character. I had hit upon a trail high, steep, and terrible, a trail which profoundly affects and to a degree explains the often tragic failure of men to come to terms with their environment. Most creatures take the world outside as they find it and instinctively become partners with the environment. Man is the one creature who can alter himself and his surroundings, as the geologist John Hodgdon Bradley has wisely observed, yet he is perhaps the most seriously maladjusted of all living creatures. (Some of the fishes, I understand, are badly adapted today.) He is the one creature who is able to accumulate verifiable knowledge about himself and his environment, and yet he is the one who is habitually deluded. No other animal produces verbal monsters in his head and projects them on the world outside his head.

Language is apparently a sword which cuts both ways. With its help man can conquer the unknown; with it he can grievously wound himself.

On the level of simple directions, commands, descriptions, the difficulty is not great. When the words mean "Look out!" "There is your food," "Go to the next white house and turn left," communication is clear. But when we hear words on the level of ideas and generalizations we cheer loudly, we grow angry, we storm the barricades—and often we do not know what the other man is saying. When a Russian speaks to an Englishman unacquainted with Slavic, nothing comes through. The Britisher shrugs his shoulders and both comprehend that communication is nil. When an Englishman speaks to an Englishman about ideas—political, economic, social—the communication is often equally blank, but the hearer thinks he understands, and sometimes proceeds to riotous action.

The trail to which my reading and observation led me was unexpected. I was trying to learn how to write, and found myself, for the first time in my life, learning how to read, how to listen, how to interpret language. I was looking for means to communicate ideas about correcting what seemed to me certain economic disorders, and I found that greater disorders were constantly arising from defective communication. At least this is the conclusion to which the evidence points.

For the individual, as I can testify, a brief grounding in semantics, besides making philosophy unreadable, makes unreadable most political speeches, classical economic theory, after-dinner oratory, diplomatic notes, newspaper editorials, treatises on pedagogics and education, expert financial comment, dissertations on money and credit, accounts of debates, and Great Thoughts from Great Thinkers in general. You would be surprised at the amount of time this saves. But one must know how to apply the tests. A high and mighty disdain for all discussion of abstract ideas is simply another form of mental confusion.

Let us take a brief survey of some effects of bad language in the contemporary scene.

If original sin is an assumption without meaning (and I am afraid Dr. Bridgman would be unable to find an operation to validate it); if people as one meets them—Mr. Brown and Mrs. Smith—are, in overwhelming proportions, kindly and peaceful folk, and so I find them; and if the human brain is an instrument of remarkable power and capacity—as the physiologists assure us—there must be some reason, some untoward crossing of wires, at the bottom of our inability to order our lives more happily and to adapt ourselves and our actions to our environment.

Nobody in his senses wants airplanes dropping bombs and poison gases upon his head; nobody in his senses wants slums, *Tobacco Roads,* and undernourished, ragged schoolchildren in a land of potential economic plenty. But bombs are killing babies in China and Spain today, and more than one-third of the people in America are underfed, badly housed, shoddily clothed. Nobody wants men and women to be unemployed, but in Western civilization from twenty to thirty million are, or have recently been, without work, and many of those who have recovered their jobs are making munitions of war. In brief, with a dreadful irony, we are acting to produce precisely the kinds of things and situations which we do not want. It is as though a hungry farmer, with rich soil, and good wheat seed in his barn, could raise nothing but thistles. The tendency of organisms is strongly toward survival, not against it. Something has perverted human-survival behavior. I assume that it is a temporary perversion. I assume that it is bound up to some extent with an unconscious misuse of man's most human attributes—thinking and its tool, language.

Failure of mental communication is painfully in evidence nearly everywhere we choose to look. Pick up any magazine or newspaper and you will find many of the articles devoted to sound and fury from politicians, editors, leaders of industry, and diplomats. You will find the text of the advertising sections devoted almost solidly to a skillful attempt to make words mean something different to the reader from what the facts warrant. Most of us are aware of the chronic inability of schoolchildren to understand what is taught them; their examination papers are familiar exhibits in communication failure. Let me put a question to my fellow authors in the fields of economics, politics, and sociology: How many book-reviewers show by their reviews that they know what you are talking about? One in ten? That is about my ratio. Yet most of them assert that I am relatively lucid, if ignorant. How many arguments arrive anywhere? "A controversy," says Richards, "is normally an exploitation of a set of misunder-standings for warlike purposes." Have you ever listened to a debate in the Senate? A Case being argued before the Supreme Court? . . . This is not frail humanity strapped upon an eternal rack. This is a reparable defect in the mechanism. When the physicists began to clear up their language, espe-cially after Einstein, one mighty citadel after another was taken in the quest for knowledge. Is slum clearance a more difficult study than counting electrons? Strictly speaking, this may be a meaningless question, but I think you get my point.

It is too late to eliminate the factor of sheer verbalism in the already blazing war between "fascism" and "communism." That war may end Europe as a viable continent for decades. To say that it is a battle of words alone is contrary to the facts, for there are important differences between the so-called fascist and communist states. But the words themselves, and the dialectic which accompanies them, have kindled emo-tional fires which far transcend the differences in fact. Ab-stract terms are personified to become burning, fighting realities. Yet if the knowledge of semantics were general, and men were on guard for communication failure, the con-flagration could hardly start. There would be honest differ-ences of opinion, there might be a sharp political struggle, but not this windy clash of rival metaphysical notions.

If one is attacked and cornered, one fights; the reaction is shared with other animals and is a sound survival mechanism. In modern times, however, this natural action comes *after* the conflict has been set in motion by propaganda. Bad lan-guage is now the mightiest weapon in the arsenal of despots and demagogues. Witness Dr. Goebbels. Indeed, it is doubtful if a people learned in semantics would tolerate any sort of supreme political dictator. Ukases would be met with a flat

"No comprendo" or with roars of laughter. A typical speech by an aspiring Hitler would be translated into its intrinsic meaning, if any. Abstract words and phrases without discoverable referents would register a semantic blank, noises without meaning. For instance:

The Aryan Fatherland, which has nursed the souls of heroes, calls upon you for the supreme sacrifice which you, in whom flows heroic blood, will not fail, and which will echo forever down the corridors of history.

This would be translated:

The blab blab, which has nursed the blabs of blabs, calls upon you for the blab blab which you, in whom flows blab blood, will not fail, and which will echo blab down the blabs of blab.

The "blab" is not an attempt to be funny; it is a semantic blank. Nothing comes through. The hearer, versed in reducing high-order abstractions to either nil or a series of roughly similar events in the real world of experience, and protected from emotive associations with such words, simply hears nothing comprehensible. The demagogue might as well have used Sanskrit.

If, however, a political leader says:

Every adult in the geographical area called Germany will receive not more than two loaves of bread per week for the next six months,

there is little possibility of communication failure. There is not a blab in a carload of such talk. If popular action is taken, it will be on the facts. This statement is susceptible to Dr. Bridgman's operational approach.

Endless political and economic difficulties in America have arisen and thriven on bad language. The Supreme Court crisis of 1937 was due chiefly to the creation by judges and lawyers of verbal monsters in the interpretation of the Constitution. They gave objective, rigid values to vague phrases like "due process" and "interstate commerce." Once these monsters get into the zoo, no one knows how to get them out again, and they proceed to eat us out of house and home.

Judges and lawyers furthermore have granted to a legal

abstraction the rights, privileges, and protection vouchsafed
to a living, breathing human being. It is thus that corporations, as well as you or I, are entitled to life, liberty, and the
pursuit of happiness. It would surely be a rollicking sight to
see the Standard Oil Company of New Jersey in pursuit of
happiness at a dance hall. It would be a sight to see United
States Smelting and Refining being brought back to consciousness by a squad of coastguardmen armed with a respi-
rator, to see the Atlas Corporation enjoying its constitutional
freedom at a nudist camp. This gross animism has permitted
a relatively small number of individuals to throw the economic mechanism seriously out of gear. By economic mechanism, I mean the operation of factories, stores, machines,
whereby men, women, and children are fed, sheltered, and
clothed. If people were armed with semantic understanding,
such fabulous concepts could not arise. Corporations would
not be interpreted as tender persons.

Corporations fill but one cage in a large menagerie. Let
us glance at some of the other queer creatures created by
personifying abstractions in America. Here in the center is a
vast figure called the Nation—majestic and wrapped in the
Flag. When it sternly raises its arm, we are ready to die for it.
Close behind rears a sinister shape, the Government. Following it is one even more sinister, Bureaucracy. Both are fes-
tooned with writhing serpents of Red Tape. High in the
heavens is the Constitution, a kind of chalice like the Holy
Grail, suffused with ethereal light. It must never be joggled.
Below floats the Supreme Court, a black-robed priesthood
tending the eternal fire. The Supreme Court must be addressed with respect or it will neglect the fire and the Constitution will go out. This is synonymous with the end of the
world. Somewhere above the Rocky Mountains are lodged
the vast stone tablets of the Law. We are governed not by
men but by these tablets. Near them, in satin breeches and
silver buckles, pose the stern figures of our Forefathers,
contemplating glumly the Nation they brought to birth.
The onion-shaped demon cowering behind the Constitution
is Private Property. Higher than Court, Flag, or the Law,

close to the sun itself and almost as bright, is Progress, the
ultimate God of America.

Looming along the coasts are two horrid monsters, with
scaly paws outstretched: Fascism and Communism. Confront-
ing them, shield in hand and a little cross-eyed from trying
to watch them both at once, is the colossal figure of Democracy. Will he fend them off? We wring our hands in suppli-
cation, while admonishing the young that governments, especially democratic governments, are incapable of sensible
action. From Atlantic to Pacific a huge, corpulent shape entitled Business pursues a slim, elusive Confidence, with a
singular lack of success. The little trembling ghost down in
the corner of Massachusetts, enclosed in a barrel, is the Tax-
payer. Liberty, in diaphanous draperies, leaps from cloud to
cloud, lovely and unapproachable.

Here are the Masses, thick, black, and squirming. This
demon must be firmly sat upon; if it gets up, terrible things
will happen; the Constitution may be joggled—anything.
In the summer of 1937, Mr. John L. Lewis was held to be
stirring up the Masses; and the fear and horror of our best
people knew no bounds. Capital, her skirts above her knees,
is preparing to leave the country at the drop of a hairpin, but
never departs. Skulking from city to city goes Crime, a red,
loathsome beast, upon which the Law is forever trying to
drop a monolith, but its aim is poor. Crime continues
rhythmically to Rear its Ugly Head. Here is the dual shape
of Labor—for some a vast, dirty, clutching hand, for others
a Galahad in armor. Pacing to and fro with remorseless tread
are the Trusts and the Utilities, bloated, unclean monsters
with enormous biceps. Here is Wall Street, a crouching
dragon ready to spring upon assets not already nailed down
in any other section of the country. The Consumer, a pathetic
figure in a gray shawl, goes wearily to market. Capital and
Labor each give her a kick as she passes, while Commercial
Advertising, a playful sprite, squirts perfume into her eyes.

From the rear, Sex is a foul creature but when she turns,
she becomes wildly alluring. Here is the Home, a bright fireplace in the stratosphere. The Economic Man strolls up
and down, completely without vertebrae. He is followed by

a shambling demon called the Law of Supply and Demand. Production, a giant with lightning in his fist, parades reluctantly with Distribution, a thin, gaunt girl, given to fainting spells. Above the oceans the golden scales of a Favorable Balance of Trade occasionally glitter in the sun. When people see the glitter, they throw their hats into the air. That column of smoke, ten miles high, looping like a hoop snake, is the Business Cycle. That clanking goblin, all gears and switchboards, is Technological Unemployment. The Rich, in full evening regalia, sit at a loaded banquet table, which they may never leave, gorging themselves forever amid the crystal and silver. . . .

Such, gentlemen, is the sort of world which our use of language fashions.

The United States has no monopoly on menageries of this nature. Kingsley Martin, editor of the *New Statesman*, has recently devoted a book to the Crown, the greatest spook in the demonology of the British Empire.[2] It is a careful study in contemporary fetishism, tracing the growth and pointing out the dangers of that totem-and-taboo culture which has been substituted in the British Isles for the rites of the Druids and painting the body blue. Mr. Martin questions whether the labors of the shamans and witch doctors in creating the perfect "father image" have not been a little overdone. It will be hard now to build the new King into a god after the scandalously human behavior of Edward VIII.

Handicraft communities could handle language without too seriously endangering their survival. They tortured and sometimes killed poor old ladies as "witches." They reduced their own efficiency in acquiring the necessities of life by elaborate rituals and superstitions. But while language was a handicap, it was not a major menace. There was not much reading or writing. Plenty of firsthand experience acted as a check on unprovable statements.

Power Age communities have grown far beyond the check of individual experience. They rely increasingly on printed matter, radio, communication at a distance. This has operated to enlarge the field for words, absolutely and relatively, and

[2] *The Magic of Monarchy*, Alfred A. Knopf, Inc., 1937.

has created a paradise for fakirs. A community of semantic illiterates, of persons unable to perceive the meaning of what they read and hear, is one of perilous equilibrium. Advertisers, as well as demagogues, thrive on this illiteracy. The case against the advertising of commercial products has hitherto rested on mendacity. In modern times outright mendacity—such as a cure for cancer—is tempered with spurious identification. The advertiser often creates verbal goods, turning the reader's attention away from the actual product. He sells the package, and especially the doctrinal matter around the package. The plain woman, by using a given cosmetic, is invited to become Cleopatra, vested with all the allure of the East. In brief, consumers often pay their money for the word rather than for the thing.

Without ability to translate words into verifiable meanings, most people are the inevitable victims of both commercial and literary fraud. Their mental life is increasingly corrupted. Unlettered peasants have more sales resistance, and frequently more sense. Foreign traders in Mexico complain bitterly of the "damned wantlessness" of the Indians. The Indians are handicraft people, and take meaning more from doing than from talking.

One wonders if modern methods of mass education promote as much knowledge in children's minds as they do confusion. Certainly in Germany, Italy, and Russia today the attempt is being made to bind the minds of children as once the feet of Chinese gentlewomen were bound. Millions of mental cripples may result. "The outside world," remarks Korzybski, "is full of devasting energies, and an organism may only be called adapted to life when it not only receives stimuli but also has protective means against stimuli." Without knowledge of the correct use of words most of us are defenseless against harmful stimuli. Those who deliberately teach people to fly from reality through cults, mythologies, and dogmas are helping them to be unsane, to deal with phantoms, to create dream states.

Fortunately there is nothing seriously the matter with our natural mental equipment. It might be improved, but the normal human brain, to quote Korzybski, has the possibility of making at least ten (10) with 2,783,000 zeros after it, different connections between nerve cells. There is no name in arithmetic for such a number. It is greater than the number of molecules in the universe, greater than the number of seconds which the sun has existed. With such a switchboard, the human brain ought to suffice for ordinary working purposes.

People are not "dumb" because they lack mental equipment; they are dumb because they lack an adequate method for the use of that equipment. Those intellectuals whose pastime is to sit on high fences and deplore the innate stupidity of the herd are on a very shaky fence. Often, if they but knew it, they are more confused than the man on the street, for they deal in loftier abstractions. When I hear a man say, "We never can get anywhere because the masses are so stupid," I know that I am in the presence of a mythmaker, caught on his high perch behind the bars of a verbal prison.

LAYING THE GROUNDWORK

Preparation for Reading

1. Do all words have exact, clear meanings?
2. Do all words have the same meaning for all people who use them? Illustrate.
3. How does a person's experience color and distort the meanings of words?
4. Without consulting the dictionary, write your definition of each of these words: *liberty, democracy, soul, infinity, beauty, truth, sin, race, honesty.*
5. In class compare your definitions with those of other students.

Vocabulary Building

1. Before you read, look up these words: *brochure, forceps, apathy, neurology, frustrated, lexicographer, entity, demonology, omniscience, validate, perverted, chronic, arsenal, ukase, chalice, harridan, devastating.*
2. As you read, look up these words: *stereotyped, spurious, symbolic, verifiable, reparable, demagogues, animism, sinister, fetishism, shamans.*

APPRAISING THE RESULTS

1. What is meant by "questioning language"?
2. What pioneers in the field of semantics did Mr. Chase consult? What did he learn from them?
3. On what "two besetting sins of language" do Korzybski, Ogden, and Richards agree?
4. What is the "referent" as distinguished from the label? Why may the goal of semantics be stated as "Find the referent"? Into what three classes may referents be placed?
5. Why does our loose use of words handicap us in understanding the various "isms," political speeches, and court decisions? in voting, buying, and reading?
6. From your own knowledge and experience, add other examples of the need for exact terminology.
7. Explain: "A community of semantic illiterates, of persons unable to perceive the meaning of what they read and hear, is one of perilous equilibrium."
8. Explain: "People are not 'dumb' because they lack mental equipment; they are dumb because they lack an adequate method for the use of that equipment."

VOCABULARY AND SUCCESS[1]

Johnson O'Connor

WHAT IS SUCCESS? AND HOW IS IT GAINED? WHETHER ONE THINKS OF SUCCESS AS FINANCIAL REWARD, OR AS ASSURED SOCIAL position, or as satisfaction in able work accomplished and recognized, or as a combination of the three and something more, many factors contribute. Most of them elude our understanding and remain intangibly beyond definition. A vital force drives some individuals over every obstacle. With others that great generalization, character, adds strength of a different sort. Neither may ever be restricted to a hard and fast formula; certainly, at the moment, neither can be measured. But other more concrete constituents of success have been isolated and studied in the laboratory. One of these is a large English vocabulary.

An extensive knowledge of the exact meanings of English words accompanies outstanding success in this country more often than any other single characteristic which the Human Engineering Laboratories have been able to isolate and measure.

What is meant by vocabulary? Just what the word signifies. Does the word *enervating* mean *soothing, exciting, distressing, invigorating,* or *weakening*? For most well-educated persons the choice is between *invigorating* and *weakening*. Fifty-two per cent of the college graduates whom we have measured choose *invigorating* as the synonym; only sixteen per cent choose *weakening,* the dictionary definition. Does

[1] From *The Atlantic Monthly*, February, 1934. Reprinted by special permission of the author and publisher. This article now appears as the introduction to the Johnson O'Connor *English Vocabulary Builder*, published by the Human Engineering Laboratory, Boston.

stilted in the phrase, "his stilted manner," mean *irresolute, improper, cordial, stiffly formal,* or *vicious?* A majority of educated persons mark *stiffly formal,* but more than a third mark *irresolute.* Answers to the meaning of *scurrilous,* in the phrase, "scurrilous rogue," divide themselves more or less evenly between *hurrying, desperate, abusive, frantic,* and *diseased,* with *desperate* the most popular. For *peremptory,* a majority mark *decisive,* but many choose *persuasive, uncertain,* and *angry. Pleasant,* the fifth choice, is not as popular. *Linguist* and *glutton* are equally enticing as synonyms for *polyglot.* For *refulgent,* in "a refulgent smile," *repellent* is most intriguing and *very bright* next, with *mischievous, flattering,* and *sour* all following closely in popularity. For *monograph* forty per cent choose *soliloquy* and less than twenty per cent *treatise* and *epitaph* each.

The word *vocabulary,* as used in this article, signifies a knowledge of the dictionary meaning of just such words as *enervating, stilted, scurrilous, peremptory, polyglot, refulgent,* and *monograph.* Not until one attempts to pick an exact synonym does one realize the difficulty. One may like the sound of a word and use it in a picturesque way without being accurate in its meaning.

I

To measure the vocabulary of an individual, the Laboratory uses a list of one hundred and fifty test words. Each is printed in italics in a short phrase and is followed by five choices, all of which fit the phrase but only one of which is a synonym of the test word. The instructions are: "Underline that one of the five choices which is nearest in meaning to the word in italics." The words to be defined were selected by Alexander Inglis of the Graduate School of Education, Harvard University. His intention was to include words which appear once or twice in 100,000 words of printed matter. It is a general reader's vocabulary from which technical terms have been excluded. The test words vary from some that are quite easy, such as

Thrilling experiences—dangerous, exciting, unusual, disgusting, profitable,

to others that are more difficult, such as

Glabrous heads—bald, over-sized, hairy, square, round,

which only twenty-one per cent of college graduates mark correctly. Since one fifth, or twenty per cent, should guess the correct answer, the meaning of *glabrous* is practically unknown. The test measures knowledge of words one recognizes, not necessarily of those one uses. The words one uses accurately are, no doubt, fewer than those one recognizes, but there is probably a relation between the two.

Three hundred high-school freshmen average 76 errors in the list of 150 words. Seven hundred college freshmen average 42 errors. One thousand college graduates from a wide variety of colleges—most of them, however, in the eastern part of the United States—average 27 errors, and vary from the one person in a thousand who achieves a perfect score to the one who knows less than 50 of the 150 items. The college professors whom we have measured average 8 errors; major executives average 7 errors. Major executives score higher in this English vocabulary test than any other selected group with which we have experimented.

By the term "major executives" is meant all individuals who, for five years or longer, have held the position of president or vice president in a business organization. Such a definition includes both successful and unsuccessful executives, provided only that they have survived five years; it includes alike forceful personalities and figureheads; but it has the great advantage of excluding our personal judgment from the process of selection. Major executives as thus defined average in the top ten per cent of college graduates as a whole.

Although it is impossible to define success rigidly or scientifically, it seems to be true, nevertheless, that a large vocabulary is typical, not exclusively of executives, but of successful individuals. It happens that in the business world successful men and women are designated by this special appellation, "executive." The successful lawyer or doctor is marked by no such name. But if, to the best of one's ability, one selects successful persons in the professions, they also score high in vocabulary.

For one meaning of success the Century dictionary gives "a high degree of worldly prosperity." The measured English vocabulary of an executive correlates with his salary. This does not mean that every high-vocabulary person receives a large salary, but the relation between the two is close enough to show that a large vocabulary is one element, and seemingly an important one.

Furthermore, the executive level which a man or woman reaches is determined to some extent by vocabulary. In many manufacturing organizations the first step in the executive ladder is the leading hand, called sometimes the working foreman. This man is in charge of half a dozen or a dozen others. He works at the bench or at a machine as they do, but is the executive of the group. The next step is the fore-man, who may be in charge of as many as a hundred or more individuals. He does no bench work, he is not a producer, but devotes full time to his executive duties, to the keeping of records and to the handling of the personnel. The next step in many large organizations is the department head or superintendent or manager, who ordinarily does not come in direct contact with the workers, but handles them through his foremen. The final step is the major executive or official, the vice president or president of the organization.

These four executive ranks represent four degrees of suc-cess, in one sense in which that word is used. One is *advanced* from leading hand to foreman, from foreman to manager, from manager to president. As far as we can determine by measurements, the leading hand and the official have much the same inherent aptitudes. They differ primarily in vocab-ulary. Typical non-college-graduate shop foremen average, as a group, about as high as college graduates. Department heads score higher, roughly fifteen errors, and major execu-tives the highest of all, averaging only seven errors. Whether the word "executive" refers only to the major group or is used in the broader sense to mean anyone in charge of other workers, it is still true that the executive scores higher than those under him and higher than other persons of similar age and education.

II

An interesting sidelight on the high vocabulary scores of executives is that they were unforeseen. When a scientist expects a result and finally achieves it there is always the feeling that, regardless of the care he has taken, personal bias may have entered. Six or eight years ago the Human Engineering Laboratories tested forty major executives of the Telephone Company who had offered themselves as victims to be experimented upon in a search for executive characteristics. At the same time the Laboratory was also revising the vocabulary test, not with the notion of using it with executives, but with the hope that it might prove of value in education. One day, with no thought of the consequences, I gave it to an executive, and from then on was asked for it regularly because of the interest it aroused. I paid little heed to the results until one day an executive refused to take the test. He had been obliged by lack of money to leave school at fourteen, and had earned his own living since. With no further formal education, he had worked his way to a major position. He had taken the aptitude tests without hesitation, but vocabulary seemed to him so directly the result of schooling that he knew in advance he would fail. His own words were that he had made his way without being found out and he was not willing to give himself away. But in scientific work one cannot test only those who think they will do well, and we finally persuaded him to try the vocabulary test. He made two errors where the average college graduate makes twenty-seven.

Was it luck? Or was it significant of something which we had not recognized? The Laboratory listed the vocabulary scores of one hundred executives and, parallel with them, the scores of one hundred miscellaneous college graduates. The difference between the two arrays was striking. Only nine per cent of the college graduates scored as high as the average major executive.

Why do large vocabularies characterize executives and possibly outstanding men and women in other fields? The final answer seems to be that words are the instruments by means of which men and women grasp the thoughts of others and with which they do much of their own thinking. They are the tools of thought.

Before accepting so far-reaching a conclusion several more obvious explanations must be examined and excluded. The first and most natural supposition is that successful persons acquire words with age and with the experiences of life. Success does not usually occur early. The successful group were necessarily older in both years and experience than the general run of college graduates with whom they were compared; and their large vocabularies might be the inevitable result of age.

To probe this point a study of the growth of vocabulary with age was undertaken. From twelve, the earliest age for which we have a large number of measurements, to twenty-two or twenty-three vocabulary expands steadily and at a uniform rate. Through this school period the score on the vocabulary test of one hundred and fifty items improves five words a year. From twenty-three to fifty vocabulary continues to increase, but changes no more in these twenty-five years than in two school years—not enough to explain the high scores of executives. Normally, vocabulary is acquired early in life, before most men have made appreciable progress toward a responsible position. The large vocabularies of successful individuals come before success rather than after. Age and the experiences of life may contribute new words, but certainly do not explain in full the high vocabulary scores of business executives.

The next thought is that effective schooling may be the source both of a wide vocabulary and of executive success. It is known, from the work which the American Telephone and Telegraph Company has undertaken, that there is a relationship between school success and business success later in life. Although not everyone who leads his class becomes a brilliant executive, and although not everyone who fails in school fails in life, in general school success preludes executive success. Schooling may be the vital factor of which the large vocabularies which we are measuring are but by-products.

To obtain evidence bearing on this point, we measured the vocabularies of twenty men who had left school at the age of fifteen and who had worked their way into major positions. They also averaged only seven errors. Their scores equaled those of the college-graduate executives. In the case of these twenty men it is their vocabularies which are important rather than their formal school education. Their large vocabularies are not the result of schooling and must, we therefore conclude, be significant for some other reason than as a by-product of an educational background.

Is, then, a college background of no importance? Has the non-college man the same chance of becoming an executive as has the college graduate? This fact seemed worth determining. Of the major executives in a large industrial organization, sixty per cent are college graduates, forty per cent non-college. At first glance, college would seem to have done little, for almost half are not college men. But, to be fair to education, there is another angle from which to view this result. Of the college graduates with this same company, more than three quarters are in executive positions, whereas, of the non-college men, well under a tenth are in similar positions. College graduates, in general, average measurably higher in vocabulary than do non-college persons. Furthermore, of the college group a significantly larger percentage are executives.

One would like to conclude without further preamble that the vocabularies of the college group are large because of directed effort and that these purposefully gained vocabularies have contributed to executive success. Non-college executives, then, are those rare individuals who pick up words so easily that their vocabularies are large without effort. But there is one further possibility which must be investigated.

Although the vocabulary test was designed to measure knowledge which must have come through books or by word of mouth, a high score may reveal an underlying aptitude for language. It may be this flair which is the contributing factor in both vocabulary and success later in life.

It should be possible to isolate and measure diathesis apart from knowledge. We have worked on this approach for a number of years, thus far unproductively. For the time being we must leave the conclusion of this part of the research in abeyance and admit that the vocabularies of successful executives may reveal an aptitude.

III

Vocabularies may always be consciously increased regardless of the presence or absence of any gift. A knowledge of the meaning of each word at one's command must have been obtained by word of mouth or through reading, by some educational process.

Furthermore, with groups of individuals of apparently similar aptitudes, the amount of vocabulary added in a given period varies with different educational techniques. At Stevens Institute of Technology the freshman class is divided alphabetically into four sections. Each of these studies freshman English under a different member of the faculty. Four years ago the entire class took the vocabulary test the first week of freshman year. The four sections averaged about the same in vocabulary, and there was no reason to suppose that, selected as they were, one would score higher than another or have more ability. Yet, when remeasured nine months later, two of the sections had improved more than average academic freshmen, one section had improved only half this amount, and the fourth had retrogressed slightly.

The improvement of one section may have been due to the fact that the instructor was interested in the vocabulary test and its implications. The important fact is that differences in vocabulary improvement were caused by differences in teaching techniques—in other words, that an improvement in vocabulary score can be produced by education.

Those boys and girls whom the Laboratory has measured and urged to better their vocabularies, and then remeasured at the end of two or three years, have shown more than average improvement. Here again vocabulary is induced independent of aptitude. It is for this reason that the Human Engineering Laboratories, in helping a youngster to find himself and start in the right direction, use a vocabulary test in lieu of a general intelligence test.

We come now to the question of whether or not that increment of vocabulary directly due to educational stimulation contributes to success. The four sections of the freshman class at Stevens Institute of Technology to which reference has been made, which took freshman English with different members of the faculty and improved different amounts in vocabulary, were followed to see the effect of these new vocabularies on school work the next year. The four sections averaged nearly the same in school marks freshman year. Sophomore year the two sections which had enlarged their vocabularies the previous year showed general gain in all school subjects—not strikingly, not enough to prove the point once and for all time, but enough to suggest that a vocabulary acquired consciously reflects in general school improvement the next year.

It is always possible that the improvement in school work was due to inspired teaching, to added incentive, but if this were true it would seem as if the improvement in school work should appear immediately freshman year, whereas it did not appear until sophomore year after the vocabulary had been acquired. This seems to indicate that it is the additional words themselves which are the tools used the next year, that words are important in and for themselves.

IV

Granted that diction is important, and many would agree without elaborate proof of the point, how, from the standpoint of the school, can it best be given; and, from that of the individual, how best achieved? Is it a knowledge of Latin and Greek which lays a sound foundation for a real understanding of words? Or is it constant reading? Or the assiduous perusal of the dictionary? Probably all contribute; as yet we have found no straight and easy road.

In the search for a road to vocabulary we have unearthed several facts which throw light on the learning process. One of these, which, if rightly interpreted, may prove to be of far-reaching importance to education, is that vocabulary advances with an almost unbroken front. The words at the command of an individual are not a miscellany gathered from hither and yon. With a very few exceptions they are all of the words in the dictionary up to those of an order of difficulty at which his vocabulary stops abruptly, and almost no words beyond. In the revised form of the test which is now available for school use, the items are arranged in order of difficulty as determined by actual test results. The first fifteen or twenty words of the test are known to the average high-school freshman or sophomore. The next thirty to forty are on the border line of his knowledge. Some he recognizes, others are vaguely familiar, and others he has not yet encountered. The balance are so far beyond him that he marks correctly no more than the one in five which he guesses by pure chance.

For convenience of scoring, the words are divided into ten groups of constantly increasing difficulty. One who knows the words of Group II, second in difficulty, almost invariably marks correctly every word of Group I. Another youngster who may know the words of, let us say, Group VI rarely fails on a single word in any of the first five easier groups. Similarly, one who fails on twelve of the fifteen words in any one group—that is, marks correctly only the one word in five which he guesses—almost never knows a word in any more difficult group. There are not, as we had expected, stray words in the difficult part which one who fails earlier in the test has stumbled upon and remembered. These unusual words, if previously encountered as they must have been in reading and conversation, are too far beyond the point he has reached to make any lasting impression.

The one exception to this rule is the foreign student who may know difficult words because of their similarity to his own language, but miss much easier ones. Thus the Southern European often marks correctly such difficult words as *cephalic, garrulity,* and *piscatorial,* because of knowledge of Italian and French, but fails to know much easier words of Old English origin, such as, for instance, *knack, blotch,* and *cope.*

In the region where learning is taking place, the commonest error is the confusion of the word with its exact opposite. Among seventh- and eighth-grade and first-year high-school pupils, nearly a third mark *found guilty* as the correct meaning of *acquitted. Upright* is the most popular misconception for the meaning of *reclining*; and, strange as it may seem, *neat* is the commonest misconception of *untidy*. The seventh-grade youngster berated for keeping an untidy room quite often evidently receives the impression that he is too orderly. The failing is not limited to the high-school group. For *incontrovertible* the correct answer *indisputable* is usually marked by college men, but of the remaining four choices *unsound* is by far most popular. In the phrase "You *allay* my fears,"—where the five choices are *justify, calm, arouse, increase,* and *conform,*—*calm* is usually answered by the educated group, but *arouse* is next most popular. In the phrase "He *retracts* his criticism," *withdraws* is the correct answer and *repeats* is the most common delusion. In "He *vented* his wrath," *poured forth* is correct and *restrained* is the commonest misapprehension.

One need but turn to words of which one is not quite certain to see how difficult it is to distinguish opposites. One evening at dinner with a delightful Dean of education, we fell to discussing this question. He recognized *cathode* and *anode* instantly as electrical terms designating the two poles, but hesitated a moment before saying which was which. *Port* and *starboard* he admitted he had never straightened out and resorted to some such phrase as "Jack left port." *Gee* and *haw* were beyond him. He surmised that they meant *up* and *down*, but said frankly he did not know the words. When told that they were used in ploughing, he was instantly interested, but did not care at all which was which. He was taking the first step in the learning process, placing them in their correct environment. The fifty-two per cent of college graduates who choose *invigorating* as the meaning of *enervating* are on the verge of knowing the word. The dictum of modern education, never to teach what a thing is not, has perhaps come from a realization of this confusion of opposites. The confusion seems, however, to be a natural step in the learning process.

V

In the study of human beings the factors involved are so numerous and so intertwined with one another that the experimenter, in unraveling the strands, must pause periodically to make certain that he is progressing. What then has been discovered? An exact and extensive vocabulary is an important concomitant of success. So much is known. Furthermore, such a vocabulary can be acquired. It increases as long as an individual remains in school or college, but without conscious effort does not change materially thereafter.

There may be some subtle distinction between a natural vocabulary picked up at home, at meals, and in reading, and one gained by a study of the dictionary. The latter may not be as valuable as the former. But there is nothing to show that it is harmful and the balance of evidence at the moment suggests that such a consciously, even laboriously, achieved vocabulary is an active asset.

LAYING THE GROUNDWORK

Preparation for Reading
1. What is generally meant by success? Is it possible to isolate and measure the qualities that make a man successful?
2. Is there any correlation between vocabulary and success in the professions? in business?

Vocabulary Building
List the words you do not know and look up their meanings, pronunciations, and derivations.

APPRAISING THE RESULTS

1. Explain the methods and results of the vocabulary test given by the Human Engineering Laboratories.
2. What is a word? a vocabulary?
3. Explain the relation between words and thought, between age and the increase of vocabulary, between education and vocabulary, and between grades and vocabulary.
4. Why is the confusion between the meaning of a word and its opposite probably "a natural step in the learning process"?
5. Is the thesis, or general conclusion, of the article stated first

or last; that is, is the plan inductive or deductive? Determine the reason for the plan.

6. State the purpose of each main division and explain the order of arrangement.

7. Note the evidence and examples used. Explain why both are especially important in this article.

THE WORDS THEY DIDN'T KNOW[1]

W. P. Kirkwood

O, the words they did not know,
While the days were going by!

THAT WAS A FOOLISH REFRAIN, THE PARAPHRASE OF LINES IN A HYMNAL, WHICH POPPED INTO BEING IN MY HEAD ONE DAY in 1921, and sang there for days, in the course of an unusually happy association with a group of university students —a happy association in spite of the words they did not know.

The fact is, I was a student myself with the others—two young men and two young women—although I had received my B.A. before any of the others had come to be an I.A.— infant in arms. After something more than a score of years as a newpaper man, I had come to be a member of the faculty of a considerable western university; considerable when it came to scholarship as well as—well, say, football. Then had come my turn for a Sabbatical leave, and I had gone off to another university in pursuit of an advanced—or, should I say, a median?—degree; an M.A.

This brought me into touch with a young man in the school of journalism of the university which was to give me my M.A. on condition that I could "do" the necessary intellectual hurdles, etc. In some of this young man's preliminary studies in journalism a year or two before, he had been sent to me to get a practice interview on the morals of the press, and I had tried to be of such assistance as I could without doing violence to my own morals in expressing my opinions

[1] Adapted from "The Words They Didn't Know," in *School and Society*, June 16, 1932. Reprinted by special permission of the author and of the publishers.

about certain papers and standards in journalism. Through him I met the others.

We soon fell into the habit of meeting around the supper table at the university commons to discuss problems journalistic, and I was struck almost at once with the paucity of the vocabularies of the young folks, their lack of originality both in thought and expression, and their rather frequent sins against the rules of grammar. This moved me to try to devise some means of giving "first aid," and out of this desire sprang the idea of organizing ourselves into an informal club for a round-table study of our English vocabulary, of originality and of grammar. The idea was promptly and emphatically approved. So we called our group the V.O.G.—Vocabulary, Originality, Grammar—Club, and made a start, without any preambles or other formalities.

Each of us was to bring to the table every evening words new to him, which had been met with in the course of the day's lectures or reading. We were also to take each day some well-worn phrase or some common object or experience and try to put it, or tell about it, in phrasing of our own. Then we were to bring up for discussion our grammatical difficulties and to check one another on grammatical lapses.

One of the young men, whom we may call Carter, was a graduate of a college of good standing in his home state. The other, Lake, had been through his home high school and had had two years of work in his state university—one of the best in the middle west. One of the young women, Miss Knight, was a high school graduate who had had a small amount of work in the state university of her home state. The other, Miss French, after completing her high school work, had taken courses in journalism in the university of a neighboring state, a university of high rank. The fathers of all four were, or had been, editors of country newspapers of excellent standing, and the young folks had all done some work in newspaper offices. All four were preparing for newspaper careers. They were in dead earnest about it, and in native mental equipment they all possessed the fundamentals of success. They were bright and alert, and in general very quick to make their own such information or knowledge as came their way from day to day. One could not think of them as having let much escape their attention either in high school or in subsequent studies. They, therefore, entered into our little game with real eagerness.

After our suppers had been disposed of, out would come their notebooks, and in turn each would fire his "new" words at the "head of the table." And the head of the table after the first round felt that he had at least some ideas of what was meant by shell-shock. He was stunned. He went away wondering what had happened to education since he had been put through the mill.

How, for example, could Lake, an omnivorous reader and a frequenter of lectures, in four years at high school and two years of a great university have missed such words as *laceration, pernicious, supinely, avarice?* Yet those were the "new" words which he read from his notebook at the first meeting of the V.O.G. And how could Carter, who had been graduated from a liberal arts college of good standing just the year before—less than four months before, in fact—have escaped acquaintance with *concision* and *the humanities?* He had, indeed, just stepped out of an institution which dealt in the humanities; at least that was the supposition.

But that first meeting held still other surprises. Lake had been reading Joseph P. Tumulty's story of Woodrow Wilson's political career, and had come to the word *miasma*, in such a phrase as, *out of the miasma of politics,* but *miasma* meant nothing to him. *Sardonic*, also, was a word coin as to the value of which he was completely in the dark.

Carter came along with another shock. The head of the table had heard one member of the group use the word *nerve* in the sense of *effrontery* or *audacity*. As a digression into the field of originality, or at least *out of* the field of the trite, he called attention to the use of the word and asked for possible substitutes. *Audacity* was the only one suggested. He then proposed *effrontery* or possibly *temerity*. Carter promptly responded that he had never heard the word *temerity*. Possibly he had never seen it, either. But the chances seem to be that he had both heard and seen it, and had not taken the pains to make it his own by referring to the dictionary. His *alma mater* had not taught him the dictionary habit. Neither of the boys, it was disclosed, had in his room a dictionary. It was only a few days, however, until they reported such a possession, and one evening soon after at the table Carter flashed on the group a pocket edition.

Carter, in making answer to some question from another member of the group one evening, said: "I don't know *if* I have or not." The head of the table, as a word problem and an attack on grammatical lapses, called for comment on such a use of *if*. It was agreed that *whether* was the right word. In subsequent conversations with Carter, the head of the table found that the use of *if* for *whether* was very frequent in Carter's speech. It was doubtless a long-standing habit. Why had not his instructors in college uprooted it? The V.O.G. did ultimately uproot it, but not without a severe struggle.

Both Lake and Carter are good churchmen, regular Bible class students and attendants at church. Yet the first word from Lake's notebook at this session was *shibboleth*. He knew nothing of its history, nothing of its modern usage. He followed this with *adolescence*. Then came *obstreperous, obdurate,* and *introspection*, very appropriately leading up to *crescendo*. Carter continued the crescendo movement with *amenable, stalemate, injudicious, esoteric,* and then *factotum*. That this last word was a complete stranger to him was plain from the fact that he called it *factortum*—had it down that way in his notebook.

At that time the papers were full of news about the conference for the limitation of armaments, and the head of the table, to see whether the members of the group were reading the reports intelligently, called for the meaning and use of the word *agenda*, which the Washington correspondents were daily playing volley ball with. But to the members of the group *agenda* was in and of the occult. The young folks admitted that they had seen the word again and again but had not taken the trouble to look it up; another evidence that in their previous schooling they had not been encouraged sufficiently to develop the dictionary habit. It was suggested, with some attempt at humor on the part of the table's head, that the club must do something to overcome the inertia of its members toward the use of the dictionary, but the humor fell flat because *inertia* itself, instead of having a "place in the sun," was lost in the blind spots of the mental vision of most of the group.

Lake was in the dark as to the meaning of *panacea*, in presenting which he placed the accent on the second syllable. A *cruciform* church conveyed no idea as to church architecture to the boys. In spite of the fact that both of the boys were interested in politics and had heard many a political spell-binder stigmatize some opposing candidate as a knave and a scoundrel, they did not know what *stigmatize* meant when they came on it in a political editorial. Carter also fumbled when it came to handling the word *foible*.

The members of the group, however, were getting keen in their hunt for new words. They wished to bag all they could during the open season of their year in college again, and at the suggestion of their leader, they took to looking up all words before coming to the table, and not only getting definitions but derivations and sentences illustrating word uses.

Let a new word show itself anywhere, and out came a notebook that it might be captured and tamed.

Erudition, when brought up by the head of the table one evening for the consideration of these young folks who had come from schools of higher learning and were then truly eager and industrious students at another, was an enigma. Lake suggested that it had something to do with farming. No one undertook to refute that theory. The head of the table admitted that erudition had something to do with farming as studied in these days, but, of course, the group, not being familiar with the word, failed to get the point until the word was defined. But consider: These young people for several years had been associated with men and women supposed to be more or less erudite. They were supposed to be aiming at the same goal themselves. They did not know whither they were bound—at least not by that name.

Carter, who had taken some courses in economics, was

trying one day to explain to Lake the Malthusian doctrine of the tendency of population to get ahead of the means of subsistence unless checked by war, pestilence or famine. He had the theory rather clearly in mind but he had Malthus, in name at least, mixed up in his mind with that ancient and long-lived patriarch, Methuselah.

However, not to draw this tale out to too great a length, here are some of the other words which the recording angel at the head of the table set down as the members of the group presented them as their discoveries from day to day. It may be said, though, that said recording angel set them down with reservations in favor of the young folks and with certain animadversions directed toward the institutions from which the members of the group had come, for having failed in their educational obligations:

archaism	confrere	vituperation	urbane	irascible
impunity	thorax	euphemistic	rapacity	circuitous
implacable	exigent	rancorous	jeremiad	bedizened
concoction	lucidity	excrescence	dilemma	perspicuity
atrophy	opaque	ludicrous	sophist	pedantry
fustian	coterie	phantasmagoria	gabble	dalliance
inveigle	conjoint	expatiate	solecism	opalescent
ornate	mammon	pantheism	extant	intrepidity
colossal	furtive	utilitarian	mobile	voracious
omnivorous	inimical	immolation	obviate	perennial
lucrative	harangue	multifarious	regale	eccentric
amalgamate	gamut	deflation	efficacy	purveyor
propitiate	expiate	nonchalance	gewgaw	eclectic
voluptuous	ascetic	aesthetics	spurious	transmute
flaccid	contemn	magniloquence	secular	iridescence
delectable	insipid	synchronous	prolix	anthology
palaver	mundane	prototype	ceramics	obeisance
autonomy	incubus	inculcate	obese	inamorata
iconoclast	cortege	predilection	bauble	circumspect
tantamount	bathos	taciturnity	sporadic	connoisseur

Not all of these words were "Greek"—or Latin—to all of the young people. On the other hand, most of them meant nothing very definite to any of them. Indeed, most of the words were "visitors from Mars," just arrived, in so far as the members of the group were concerned. When Lake announced *iconoclast*, for example, Carter immediately revealed his complete lack of acquaintance with the word by asking, "How do you spell it?" When *inimical* was introduced to those present, he came back with the same question.

A study of the list of words brings up that rather threadbare subject: The value of Latin in the high school or college curriculum. A majority of words, it will be noticed, are of Latin origin. If something like 30 per cent of our English words are derived directly or indirectly from the Latin, as the estimates used to say, I am leaning quite strongly toward the belief that Latin has a just claim to "a special and privileged position." But that is to start on an old controversy which there is no need of discussing here. Let the experience of these young folks with whom I have been associated stand for what it is worth in settling the question —if it is ever to be settled.

Certainly, though, if Latin is not to be required, a heavy duty must fall on our English and rhetoric departments. Words, the things most used in this world—and, possibly, in the next—must be taught. Students should not be left merely to absorb such words as become absolutely necessary to meet or to make known their immediate, casual wants. Students must be trained in the business of vocabulary building. Yet are there adequate courses in our schools and colleges and universities to give them even a start in that direction? Words, words, words ought to be drilled—pneumatically drilled, one might say—into the youthful mind if they cannot be lodged there by any other process.

Among the most severe critics of the newspapers are the men in the English and rhetoric departments of our universities. But does not the condition disclosed by the group we have been discussing indicate that a part, and a very considerable part, of the trouble lies at the doors of the very departments which affect to condemn "newspaper English"? The young people in our group were not "slackers" in school—far from it. They were in school with a purpose, and the eagerness with which they entered into the game showed that along the way somewhere they had missed something they were much in need of and that they took to as bees to nectar at the first opportunity.

Incidentally, I should like to suggest that the forming of

little groups like the V.O.G. for an hour of after-supper discussion every evening ought to be encouraged—officially encouraged—in our colleges and universities. They could give direction to thought and study along any line. But I know of no line of study that college and university students, whatever they may be planning to do in life, could take up with greater profit than just that of our little group. The idea is not copyrighted.

LAYING THE GROUNDWORK

Preparation for Reading

1. How often in your daily reading do you encounter words you don't know?
2. Are you in the habit of looking up these unfamiliar words?
3. Is your vocabulary adequate? average? satisfactory? exceptional?

Vocabulary Building

1. Make a list of the words with which you are unfamiliar. Copy their definitions and pronunciations from an unabridged dictionary and add these words to your vocabulary list.
2. What is meant by *journalese, jargon, bromides, triteness, cliché, tautology?*
3. Do any of the words discussed in this essay seem unnecessary to you on the basis of your experience?

APPRAISING THE RESULTS

1. What do you think is the most interesting thing about this essay? Is it the point of view of the author? The characteristics of the four students or the way these are revealed to the reader? Or the words themselves? Or possibly the question raised by the discussion of Latin? Or yet another point?
2. How can you characterize the author's own vocabulary? How do you determine what his vocabulary is like?
3. Comment on the fact that a newspaperman is writing the essay. Why does his criticism of the students' vocabularies surprise you, if it does?
4. Compare the vocabulary range in one issue of your daily newspaper and that in this essay. Comment on your comparison.

WORD STUDIES

1. Give yourself a standard vocabulary test. How large is your vocabulary? How satisfactory? On the basis of this test, what goal in vocabulary building do you think you should set for yourself this year?

2. For three days keep an accurate list of all new words you hear or come across in your reading. After you have looked up all the meanings and pronunciations, study this list, and decide which words you want to add to your speaking vocabulary.

3. The greatest treasury of English words is the *Oxford English Dictionary*, frequently referred to as the O.E.D., a ten-volume work, inspiration for which was given when Dr. Furnivall and Dean Trench delivered a paper before the Philological Society in England in 1857. Thereafter they began accumulating material, until in 1879 Sir James Murray, who had taken over the work of compilation, had one and one-half tons of material, much of which had come from the United States. In 1880 the first section of the dictionary went to press, and in 1928 the publication was finally completed. A supplementary volume was published in 1934. In this comprehensive dictionary English words are traced from their first appearance in print through their successive changes in form and meaning. To become acquainted with this invaluable book, look up these words: *farm, charity, deer, carry, garble, idiot, hodgepodge.*

4. The sources from which you can draw inexhaustible and entertaining information on word study will be opened to you if you examine and compare such books as *Words and Their Ways in English Speech* by James B. Greenough and George L. Kittredge, *The Romance of Words* and *Cruelty to Words* by Ernest Weekley, *The Command of Words* by S. Stephenson Smith, and *Current Usage* by Arthur G. Kennedy. In class discuss these and similar books of which you may know.

5. Equally interesting studies of the development of the English language are books like *The Development of Modern English* by Stuart Robertson, *The American Language* by Henry L. Mencken, and *Growth and Structure of the English Language* by Otto Jespersen. Chapters on the sources of the English

language, the origins of words, and their changing meanings are especially helpful to the student of words. When you have consulted these or similar books, summarize the sources of the English language.

6. The origin of words is made a lively study in books like *Picturesque Word Origins* published by G. and C. Merriam Company. From such a book select a dozen words whose origins you think unusually interesting.

7. The origins of family names and the names of common flowers likewise teach you much about the way in which language grows. For instance, the name *Fletcher* comes from *flèche* meaning "arrow," and was given to those who made arrows; the word *nasturtium* comes from *nasus*, "the nose," and *torquere, tortum,* "to twist," (the odor twists the nose), and applies to any genus of climbing herbs with red and yellow flowers and pungent pods and seed. Ernest Weekley has several books on this subject: *Words and Names, The Romance of Names,* and *Surnames.* A book which will help you pronounce many proper names correctly is *Wild Names I Have Met* by Alfred H. Holt. Try to find the origin of your name and of the names of your favorite flowers.

8. Tracking phrases to their sources becomes fun if one knows *Phrase Origins* by Alfred H. Holt. In a similar way, you may be able to trace picturesque phrases your family uses.

9. An expressive vocabulary should be free from trite expressions. Read some of the following articles and note the overworked words and phrases you use: "Good Set Phrases" by Frank A. Grismer in the college edition of the *English Journal*, Volume XXIII, p. 329; "The Cliché Expert Takes the Stand" in the *Reader's Digest,* November, 1935, pp. 65-66; "The Goon and His Style" by Frederick L. Allen in *Harper's Magazine,* December, 1921; "On Jargon" by Sir Arthur Quiller-Couch from *The Art of Writing.*

10. Acquire the habit of consulting not only the dictionary but also books on synonyms when you find you are overworking certain words. Consult *English Synonyms* by George Crabb, *English Synonyms and Antonyms* by James C. Fernald, *The Roget Dictionary of Synonyms and Antonyms* revised by C. O. S. Mawson, or similar books. List six words with their synonyms and antonyms and use each in a sentence.

11. The study of foreign languages helps develop a rich and varied vocabulary. Translate from some foreign language a

passage you like. Note the shades of meaning you encounter in translating words from one language to another. List three English words taken from Anglo-Saxon, Greek, Latin, French, Spanish, Italian, German, and the Scandinavian languages. Add words from other languages if you can.

12. The King James version of the English Bible is written in sonorous and beautiful prose. Read several chapters or books from it and write a paper on the language or the effect of the Bible on English literature.

Improvement in Writing Technique

BOMBING THE PARAGRAPH[1]

Henry Seidel Canby

SOME ACT OF NATIONAL RECOVERY IS NEEDED IF THE ENGLISH PARAGRAPH IS TO BE SAVED. LET US RECALL TO THE MEMORIES of those who once were accustomed to good English what the paragraph was supposed to be before it ran upon the rocks of mass production and was splintered into incoherent sentences.

The paragraph was a trim little vessel in the days when journalists still wrote for minds trained to hold more than one thought at a time. Rhetoricians spoke of it as one full step in the development of an idea, and might have compared it with a fan which spreads without losing its unity, increasing its usefulness without changing its control. An idea stated in a single sentence (topic, they used to call it) is self-sufficient only for the very wise or the very simple. Emerson and Thoreau, among Americans, wrote self-sufficient sentences for the wise, and the race of columnists (who call themselves paragraphers) have carried on this tradition of apothegm all the way into wisecrack—a sentence paragraph which is a nut that a sharp mind can bite into.

But this is specialists' work. The general utility paragraph led off (in the days of coherence) with a sentence that said simply and definitely what the writer thought. But thought is never so simple as that. It must be qualified, developed, explained, if it is to satisfy the sophisticated. Only the naïve will swallow a generalization without chewing on it. The English paragraph in its prime was raw material made fit for eating by a skilful cook. If the writer began "Democracy

[1] From *The Saturday Review of Literature*, December 30, 1933. Reprinted by permission of the author and of the publishers.

depends upon intelligence," he could not leave it at that. Simple minds might be content, but in those days readers were not that simple. They asked why and were prepared to reserve judgment until, item after item, the explanation or argument unrolled to a Q.E.D. at the end of the paragraph. Macaulay, whose diminishing reputation as a historian still leaves him one of the world's great journalists, could fling out a reverberating paragraph as organized and emphatic and lucid as the simplest sentence, which prepared, held, and satisfied the attentive reader by a structure which had all the advantages of a formula without its dangerous simplicity. The late Frank Cobb of the old *World* could drop his sequent sentences one after another in perfect harmony for a column before the packed theme with which he began had been unpacked and become an organism of thought.

The paragraph, like many other good things, was wrecked by mass production. When newspapers, and then magazines, began to be published for the millions, writers soon found that their readers were short-winded. They would hold their brains together for three or four sentences, not more. News was rewritten for them in short paragraphs, the ramp of the story broken up into little steps, and that was good, especially when the sentences took on the color of contemporary impressionism, for in the reporting of successive incidents, the successive topics are facts which need no logical development. Paragraphs are relatively unimportant in narrative. Not so with editorials and articles. When the writers whose duty it was to exhort or explain discarded the paragraph (the Hearst newspapers began it) and wrote series of short, sharp sentences, each set apart so that it might be easily assimilated by the dumbest readers, they scored at first a great journalistic success. Strong writing, it seemed to be, punches from the shoulder, very persuasive to the man who must have a thought knocked into him, well calculated indeed for a nation of quick readers who seldom read books and lacked the patience (and often the ability) to follow the testing of an idea through a paragraph. And thousands of writers, noting the success with the masses of these portmanteau paragraphs, imitated them, until even when an idea had to be tested, explained, in order to mean anything at all, their paragraphs were still split into groups of pointed sentences, one state-ment at a time, so that even the feeble-minded could read.

That is where we are today in the bulk of English writing outside of books and the better magazines. Unfortunately, however, the immense majority of readers, even among the masses, are not feeble-minded. They are, one suspects, begin-ning to react by not reading at all, or by taking the first punch and dodging all the rest. After all, this method of writing was first devised, not for journalism, but for chil-dren's reading-books, where not only paragraphs but long words were split for immature minds. Our journalists have treated their readers like children and they are getting a child's reactions, violent, brief, and over-simplified. They have violated the natural order of thinking and, as a result, give no training and get no response in thought. Like the advertisers and the politicians, they have been playing upon the unformed mass mind for profits, consistently writing under the normal intelligence in the hope of speedier results. It is a phase of exploitation, and will produce its reactions in both reader and writer, like every other attempt to debase the currency of human intercourse.

For further they cannot go in this direction except into complete anarchy of thinking. They feel it, and when so vigorous a paper as the new *New York Evening Post* adopts the sentence style for its editorials (presumably written for adults) the desperate editors use italics and small caps for their high points in the hope that readers who refuse to bark their shins over disintegrated ideas will carry away at least something from the wreck.

LAYING THE GROUNDWORK

Preparation for Reading
1. How long should a paragraph be? What determines its length?
2. How does the division into paragraphs help one to understand what one reads? How may well-organized paragraphs make the ideas and their relationship clear to the reader?

Vocabulary Building

1. Look up these words: *rhetorician, sophisticated, naïve, reverberating, formula, ramp, exhort, assimilated, calculated, portmanteau, disintegrated.*
2. Explain the meaning of the following words as they relate to writing: *sequent, lucid, coherence, topic, unity, emphatic, theme.*

APPRAISING THE RESULTS

1. How does the modern paragraph compare in length with the paragraph of a few generations ago?
2. What has caused this change in length? What has been gained? What lost?
3. What is the effect of short paragraphs upon the thoughtful response of the reader? upon sentence style?
4. In what way is a carefully written paragraph of some length easier to understand than the same material presented piecemeal in short paragraphs?
5. Make a study of the figures of speech and the concrete diction that contribute to Mr. Canby's emphatic, lucid expression.

EXERCISES

1. Compare the paragraphing of several magazines which you have classified according to the intelligence and education of their average reader. Likewise, compare the paragraphing of textbooks for grade school, high school, and college. To what conclusions do you come regarding the relation between paragraph length and the intellectual maturity of the reader?
2. Compare the paragraph length of serious formal essays and of light, informal essays. What do you conclude about the relation between the purpose of the essay and the length of its paragraphs?
3. Are paragraphs in exposition and narration divided according to the same principle? Explain. How is conversation paragraphed?
4. Run through several essays in the text and estimate the number of words in several long or short paragraphs. Estimate also the length of the average paragraph.

5. Analyze the paragraphs of several of your own themes. Do they meet Mr. Canby's criteria?
6. Distinguish between generalization and detail. What are methods of developing a topic sentence?
7. Using Basic Exercise II as a guide, analyze the paragraph structure of this essay.

PUNCTUATION[1]

Percy Marks

IF STUDENTS OFTEN REGARD PUNCTUATION AS UNIMPORTANT,
THEY RARELY WILL DENY THAT ITS PRINCIPLES, SO FAR AS THEY
are concerned, are esoteric. Since childhood they have been
offered initiation into the mysteries of, say, the semicolon,
but they have failed to learn the ritual. They have taken
their first degree, perhaps, in the comma and the question
mark, but they have never sought the inner shrine. Instead,
they have devised a simpler ritual of their own, which they
are glad to chant whenever requested: "I just put a comma
when I want a pause and a semicolon for a longer pause."
Nothing apparently could be simpler, but some students simplify the completely simple into, "Oh, I just use dashes."

At that, neither method is as bad as it could be. The toss-
and-scatter method is much worse and, sad to say, more
common. Its admirers first write a theme totally devoid of
punctuation; then they fill both hands full of commas,
semicolons, dashes, colons, exclamation and question marks.
Those in the left hand, they toss in the air, trusting that
some of them will land on the theme. Those in the right
hand, they scatter indifferently through the sentences. Sometimes their periods fall at the ends of sentences and sometimes they do not. I may be mistaken about the exact method
employed, but I am sure of the result. I have seen too many
commas curling coyly at the ends of sentences, periods
round and clear at the ends of participial phrases, to have
any doubt. Whatever the method used, it is a rare student,

[1] From *The Craft of Writing*, by Percy Marks. Copyright, 1932, by Harcourt,
Brace & Company, Inc. Reprinted by permission of the author and of the
publishers.

even among those who have learned the rules and punctuate correctly, who recognizes the true purpose of punctuation. To them, it is at best a troublesome duty. They should understand that it is an invaluable help.

In the first place, punctuation is often as essential to the meaning of a sentence as the subject or predicate is. A comma added or a comma deleted may not only alter the meaning; it may even give it wit or subtlety. In *South Wind* by Norman Douglas, there is this simple sentence: "Don Francesco was a fisher of men, and of women." The comma gives the sentence most of its significance; omit the comma and the meaning is not only altered but the significance is lost.

No one understands the construction of a sentence who does not understand punctuation. That statement is undebatable, and its corollary, that no one understands his own thought who does not also understand the construction of his sentence, is equally undebatable. The punctuation indicates the relation of the parts of an idea to each other. If one can punctuate a sentence, he understands the relations of his ideas to each other. If he cannot punctuate the sentence, he does not understand the relation.

Punctuation properly used is an analysis of thought. In effect, the writer says to the reader, "These commas indicate that this matter is parenthetical; this semicolon indicates that the thought in my first clause balances the thought in my second clause; this colon indicates that the clauses preceding it are equal in my mind to whatever may succeed it," and so forth. Only with punctuation can the writer make clear to the reader what one part of his sentence means to another part, and he cannot make the relationship clear unless he understands it absolutely himself.

A student who has learned to punctuate correctly has taken a long stride toward writing clearly and firmly—and clarity and firmness are the basic elements of a good style. The best stylists, it is true, often treat the rules of punctuation as they do the rules of rhetoric; that is, they break the rule to gain a desired effect. I am the last to deny them that right, but I am sure they have little chance of gaining the effect unless they know the rules. If they know the rules, they also know exactly what they are doing when they break them. Otherwise, their chances of spoiling their effect are quite as good as their chances of gaining it.

LAYING THE GROUNDWORK

Preparation for Reading

1. What is the purpose of punctuation? Is its function merely to clarify? Has it stylistic value?
2. How is a standard of punctuation determined in a given age?

Vocabulary Building

Look up these words: *esoteric, devoid, deleted, subtlety, corollary.*

APPRAISING THE RESULTS

1. Why is punctuation essential to the meaning of a sentence?
2. How is it an analysis of thought?
3. What are the basic elements of a good style?
4. When has a writer a right to break the rules of punctuation?

EXERCISES

1. Find out how punctuation developed and how the printing press affected it.
2. Study the effect of punctuation and indention in "Evelyn Hope" and "Love Among the Ruins" by Robert Browning.
3. Make a study of the sentences below: their structure and punctuation.

    a. Homer nods; and the Duke of Bedford may dream; and as dreams (even in his golden dreams) are apt to be ill-pieced, and incongruously put together, his grace preserved his idea of reproach to *me*, but took the subject-matter from the crown grants to *his own family.* (Edmund Burke, *A Letter to a Noble Lord*)

    b. My merits, whatever they are, are original and personal; his are derivative. (Edmund Burke, *A Letter to a Noble Lord*)

    c. But we are all of us made to shun disgrace, as we are made to shrink from pain, and poverty, and disease. It is an instinct; and under the direction of reason, instinct is always in the right. (Edmund Burke, *A Letter to a Noble Lord*)

d. He [a gentleman] has his eyes on all his company; he is tender toward the bashful, gentle toward the distant, and merciful toward the absurd; he can recollect to whom he is speaking; he guards against unseasonable allusions, or topics which may irritate; he is seldom prominent in conversation, and never wearisome. (John Henry Newman, *The Idea of a University*)

e. You would think, in hearing him [Wordsworth] speak on this subject, that you saw Titian's picture of the meeting of *Bacchus and Ariadne*—so classic were his conceptions, so glowing his style. (William Hazlitt, *Mr. Wordsworth*)

f. We behold space sown with rotatory islands, suns and worlds and the shards and wrecks of systems: some, like the sun, still blazing; some rotting, like the earth; others, like the moon, stable in desolation. (Robert Louis Stevenson, *Pulvis et Umbra*)

g. The poorest persons have a bit of pageant going toward the tomb; memorial stones are set up over the least memorable; and, in order to preserve some show of respect for what remains of our old loves and friendships, we must accompany it with much grimly ludicrous ceremonial, and the hired undertaker parades before the door. (Robert Louis Stevenson, *Æs Triplex*)

h. We live the time that a match flickers; we pop the cork of a ginger-beer bottle, and the earthquake swallows us on the instant. (Robert Louis Stevenson, *Æs Triplex*)

i. And the entire object of true education is to make people not merely *do* the right things, but *enjoy* the right things:—not merely industrious, but to love industry—not merely learned, but to love knowledge—not merely pure, but to love purity—not merely just, but to hunger and thirst after justice. (John Ruskin, *Traffic*)

j. Their palaces were houses not made with hands; their diadems, crowns of glory which should never fade away. On the rich and the eloquent, on nobles and priests, they [the Puritans] looked down with contempt: for they esteemed themselves rich in a more precious treasure, and eloquent in a more sublime language, nobles by the right of an earlier creation, and priests by the imposition of a mightier hand. (Thomas Babington Macaulay, *Milton*)

k. Thus the Puritan was made up of two different men, the one all self-abasement, penitence, gratitude, passion; the

other proud, calm, inflexible, sagacious. He prostrated him
self in the dust before his Maker; but he set his foot on the
neck of his king. (Thomas Babington Macaulay, *Milton*)

l. A sovereign almost invisible; a crown of dignitaries
minutely distinguished by badges and titles; rhetoricians
who said nothing but what had been said ten thousand times;
schools in which nothing was taught but what had been
known for ages: such was the machinery provided for the
government and instruction of the most enlightened part
of the human race. (Thomas Babington Macaulay, *The
Philosophy of History*)

m. The charm of Addison's companionship and conversation has passed to us by fond tradition—but Swift? (William Makepeace Thackeray, *Jonathan Swift*)

n. I should like to have been Shakespeare's shoeblack—
just to have lived in his house, just to have worshipped him
—to have run on his errands, and seen that sweet serene face.
(William Makepeace Thackeray, *Jonathan Swift*)

A SENTENCE OUTLINE

of Embree's "Can College Graduates Read?"

Thesis Sentence: Teaching the student to read in such a way that he may educate himself is in a large measure a cure for the evils revealed by the report of the Carnegie Foundation.

I. The report on higher education by the Carnegie Foundation gives devastating evidence of evils which educators must correct if faith in education is to be saved. (¶¶1-6.)

  A. The report probably gives a fair picture of education throughout the nation even though the survey was centered in one state. (¶1.)

    1. The survey was centered on the schools and colleges of Pennsylvania.

    2. The report consists of studies made over a period of ten years.

      a. These studies included tests in the many phases of education.

      b. These studies were designed to discover the amount of useful knowledge acquired in college and the progress in intelligence and understanding.

  B. The report may well undermine the faith we Americans have had in formal education. (¶¶2-4.)

    1. We have expressed faith in education in two ways. (¶2.)

      a. We have built an unprecedented number of schools and colleges.

      b. We have educated an ever-increasing number of children.

(1) Almost all eligible children now attend elementary schools.

(2) Seven million young people now attend high school.

(3) A million and a quarter young people now are enrolled in institutions of higher learning.

2. The report indicates that, by and large, students are getting little information or wisdom. (¶3.)

   a. The tests showed little relation between the time spent in college and the intelligence and achievement records of students.

   b. The tests showed that many of the better students do not go to college.

   c. The tests showed that many of those planning to teach are even less prepared than are other students.

3. The most appalling item in the report is the study of a single college in Pennsylvania. (¶4.)

   a. This study, based on the careers of fifty brilliant freshmen, followed them throughout their courses.

   b. This study revealed that two-thirds of them knew less at graduation than when they were juniors.

   c. This study placed the responsibility upon scholasticism, routine, and mediocrity.

C. The report is so damning that educators must try to correct the present evils to save our faith in education. (¶5.)

1. All of the reasonable suggestions should be given full play.

2. No single formula should be relied on, for to do so will merely preserve one of the present evils.

II. The ability to read with fluency, understanding, and enjoyment is the foundation of real self-education. (¶¶6-23.)

A. Children will have acquired the finest of the intellectual tools if they have learned to read fluently and with understanding. (¶¶6-16.)

1. Learning to read, an astonishingly delicate and complicated business, consists of two interrelated parts. (¶7.)
   a. The preliminary step consists of acquiring mechanical skill.
   b. The actual reading consists of acquiring meaning and pleasure from the printed page.
2. Even teaching the mechanics of reading requires a close connection between what the child already knows and what is conveyed to him through written words. (¶¶8-16.)
   a. Education must have a close relation to life.
   b. Education which runs into scholasticism is a failure.
      (1) Learning must enrich the life of the student, not be an end in itself.
      (2) This self-evident fact is ignored by the advocates of scholasticism.
   c. Education even in the elementary schools often falls easily into scholasticism such as that found in a rural school in the South.
      (1) A child was forced by his teacher to accept a printed statement which ran counter to his observation.
      (2) He was probably affected in one of two ways by this combination of stupid teacher and faulty text: loss of confidence in himself or in books.
B. Children will become educated in direct ratio to the amount of reading they do, not to the amount of rote-learning crammed into them. (¶¶17-19.)
   1. Encouragement should be given children to read as widely as possible. (¶18.)
      a. Children should not be directed in their reading.
      b. Children will set their own standards by wide reading.
   2. Some encouragement is now given by two trends in present-day educational procedure. (¶19.)
      a. The most effective movement is the tendency to

provide all schools with at least small collections of supplementary texts and stories.

   b. Another effective movement is the trend in higher education toward letting students educate themselves through reading.

     (1) Lessons and lectures cannot give students anything that can compare with what they can get for themselves by reading.

     (2) The ability to read gives students means of self-education.

C. College students, to an even greater degree, will become educated in direct ratio to the reading they do. (¶¶20-23.)

  1. The good teacher should eliminate himself except as a guide and counselor. (¶¶20-22.)

    a. Teachers of sciences have recognized this need. (¶20.)

    b. Teachers of subjects other than sciences are also seeing that the student gains nothing by being stuffed with facts. (¶20.)

    c. A few teachers were pioneers in good teaching of this type. (¶¶21-22.)

     (1) William Graham Sumner inspired his students to self-education in social studies. (¶21.)

     (2) Professor Thomas Seymour inspired his students to self-education in Greek. (¶22.)

  2. The good teacher should inspire students to educate themselves. (¶23.)

    a. Organized education, instead of stimulating the normal curiosity of youth, stills it.

     (1) The procedure in normal life is for the child to ask the questions.

     (2) The procedure in college is to suppress this natural tendency by putting him into fixed courses.

      (a) The student's curiosity in his courses is stilled.

        (b) The student's real enthusiasms are diverted to extra-curricular activities.

      (3) The procedure in college should encourage this natural tendency.

    b. True education stimulates the student to desire more and more knowledge and impels him to reflect.

III. The ideal of true education is self-education, which can be achieved by reading. (¶¶24-28.)

  A. The report gives damning evidence of too little true education in the schools at the present. (¶24.)

    1. It protests against the rigid course system.

    2. It protests against building a college curriculum around "the average student."

      a. Each student is an individual with his own intelligence and ability.

      b. Each student must be given the opportunity of developing himself.

    3. It concludes that the objective of education must be the self-education of the student.

  B. The report suggests four essentials as a basis for aid to self-education. (¶25.)

    1. The college should have knowledge of the student's mental, physical, and social attainments in order to understand and help him.

    2. The college should prepare, in the light of the student's goal, a tentative forecast of what he can hope to achieve.

    3. The college should make provision for the right kind of teaching and for the laboratories and libraries the student needs.

    4. The college should provide for regular measurements and analysis of the student's progress in knowledge and of his character and disposition.

  C. The entire four-point program suggested by the report is not at present feasible. (¶26.)

    1. Large institutions will be slow to change their methods of mass production by routine lectures,

        assignments in texts, and periodic tests on the quantity of information acquired.

    2. Schools and colleges will be slow to work in recognition of the individual needs of students.

D. The right kind of teaching and equipment, Point Three of the report, will bring about a large measure of self-education.

    1. Self-education means shifting the burden from the teacher to the student.

        a. The student may well be left to dig out knowledge for himself from the library and the laboratory.

        b. The faculty should be assistants rather than taskmasters.

        c. Some colleges already follow this plan.

            (1) Swarthmore is increasingly following it with her honor students.

            (2) Harvard has several experimental colleges and reading periods.

    2. Self-education requires that the student be capable of directing his own education. (¶27.)

        a. The college should exclude the irresponsible and unintelligent student.

            (1) No power on earth can educate a person who cannot take a leading part in his own education.

            (2) The cause of a great part of the congestion and confusion in college is the attempt to force education into masses of such students.

        b. The college can determine the students capable of self-education by their ability to read and study for themselves.

    3. Self-education must have reading as its greatest commandment. (¶28.)

        a. Reading does not cover the whole development of a well-rounded person.

        b. Books are, however, the great tools of intellectual attainment.

    c. The surest way to produce an educated nation is to have books and more books in the homes and schools.

GUIDES FOR MAKING A SENTENCE OUTLINE

The outline can serve two purposes: to summarize an article already written, or to present a blue print for an article to be written. Fundamentally, the aim is the same, since in an outline the purpose is first to state the main idea, or thesis, and then to indicate the relationships between this main idea and the ideas or details which elaborate on, or substantiate, it.

The outline which precedes the writing of the theme aids the student in planning his paper just as a blue print aids the builder in constructing a building. By making such a preliminary plan of his material before he writes, the student achieves unity, coherence, and emphasis in his theme. Outlining an article already written helps him to isolate the thesis sentence, or main idea, and to see the plan which the writer followed. This analysis leads the student to a clear understanding of the meaning of the article and helps him to remember its content. Thus an outline is a valuable tool both in reading and in writing.

The most common kinds of outlines are sentence, topic, and paragraph. Each of these has a form peculiar to itself. The paragraph outline states the idea of each paragraph in a sentence, as though each paragraph were coordinate. The topic outline distinguishes between coordinate and subordinate ideas, indicates their relationship by major and subheadings, and states each idea in a word or phrase. The sentence outline likewise distinguishes between coordinate and subordinate ideas, but states each in a sentence.

The sentence outline, because it requires the student to express all the ideas in complete statements, has certain advantages over the other two forms. First, it helps him as a reader to understand more fully the article he is reading and, at some later date, to recall more exactly what he has read; and, second, it forces him as a writer to think through his ideas before he writes. Hence he should make his outline before he writes his theme, not after: by planning his theme first he saves time because much of the purposeless rewriting he would otherwise do is unnecessary.

To assist the student to see the relation between an outline and a finished piece of writing, Embree's "Can College Graduates Read?" has been outlined. This outline includes much more of the essay than is common in order that the student may see how details in an article can be accounted for in an outline. It is rarely necessary, however, for the student to make so detailed an outline as this one.

Certain conventions which should be observed in making the sentence outline are summarized below.

1. *The thesis sentence should state, as concisely as possible, the central idea which binds all the parts.* It should be a simple or complex sentence.

2. *The conventional symbols should be used:* Roman numerals for the main headings, capital letters for first-degree sub-headings, Arabic numerals for second-degree subdivisions, and small letters for third-degree subdivisions.

3. *Subordination should be indicated not only by a change in symbols, but also by indention.* Therefore subordinate headings should be indented farther than the headings to which they are subordinate, and all subheadings of equal rank should be indented an equal distance.

4. *The symbols should stand out conspicuously.* Therefore there should be no writing under them.

5. *The first word of every statement should begin with a capital letter.*

6. *A period should be used after each symbol and after each statement of both the main divisions and the subdivisions.*

7. *An outline should not be developed partly by phrases and partly by sentences.* In a sentence outline all divisions should be expressed in complete sentences.

8. *Coordinate divisions should be mutually exclusive.* One division should not contain the whole or a part of another.

9. *Headings which are not logically coordinate should not be coordinated.*

10. *A heading which is logically coordinate with another heading should not be subordinated to it.*

11. *The divisions should be arranged in logical order;* they should lead naturally one to the other.

12. *Headings of the same rank should be expressed in as nearly parallel forms as possible.*

13. *The inclusion of a single division under a heading should be avoided.* Such a subdivision should be (a) omitted if it merely amplifies, (b) supplemented by other statements if it fails to analyze the major heading, or (c) incorporated into the major heading if it logically belongs there.

BIOGRAPHICAL NOTES

WILL WINTON ALEXANDER (1884-), formerly a minister in the Methodist Church, has been administrator of the Resettlement Administration and Farm Security Administration since 1937. He is also a director of the Julius Rosenwald Fund. He is the co-author of *The Collapse of Cotton Tenancy*.

BEULAH AMIDON is an associate editor of the *Survey Graphic* and a contributor of articles to other magazines. She has written and edited articles on various subjects, specializing in labor and industry.

HERBERT BIBERMAN (1900-), a motion picture director, was a product of Baker's Workshop 47 at Yale and then worked abroad in the theaters of Russia and Czechoslovakia. He was a director for the Theatre Guild of New York before he became associated with the motion pictures. He directed *Red Rust, Roar China, Green Grow the Lilacs, Miracle at Verdun,* and *Valley Forge*.

CURTIS BILLINGS, formerly a newspaper reporter and later a member of the National Safety Council, is now Director of Publications and Publicity for the Northwestern University Traffic Institute and Director of the Safety Division of the International Association of Chiefs of Police. He has written numerous articles on traffic problems.

MALCOLM H. BISSELL (1889-), who was educated in the United States, France, and Germany, has done special studies in economic geography, climatology, and geology. He is now a professor of geography at the University of Southern California.

FRANZ BOAS (1858-), professor emeritus in residence at Columbia University, is an eminent anthropologist who has received many professional honors in recognition of his authoritative position in his profession. He is the author of *The Growth of Children, Changes in Form of Body of Descendants of Immi-*

grants, Kultur und Rasse, Primitive Art, and *Anthropology and Modern Life.*

JOHN HODGDON BRADLEY, JR. (1898-   ), geologist and author, has been a professor since 1929 at the University of Southern California. His books include *The Earth and Its History, Parade of the Living, Autobiography of Earth, Farewell Thou Busy World,* and *Patterns of Survival.*

PEARL S. BUCK (1892-   ) was awarded the Nobel Prize for literature in 1938 in recognition of her novel *The Good Earth,* which had already received the Pulitzer Prize. Others of her books are *Sons, A House Divided, The Mother, The Exile,* and *Fighting Angel.*

HUGH CABOT (1872-   ) is a surgeon at the Mayo Clinic and a Fellow of the American College of Surgeons. He has been a member of the faculty at the Harvard Medical School and at the University of Michigan, and is now professor of surgery at the Graduate School of the University of Michigan. He has contributed numerous articles to medical journals since 1900, and has written *Surgical Nursing* and *The Doctor's Bill.*

HENRY SEIDEL CANBY (1878-   ), well-known writer and literary critic, taught at Yale for a number of years. He has been associated in an editorial capacity with *The Yale Review* and the *Saturday Review of Literature.* Since 1926 he has been chairman of the board of judges of the Book-of-the-Month Club. Among his own books are *Definitions, Better Writing, American Estimates, Classic Americans, The Age of Confidence, Alma Mater—The Gothic Age of the American College.*

RACHEL L. CARSON, who is an aquatic biologist in the United States Bureau of Fisheries, is also a writer in her leisure time.

STUART CHASE (1886-   ) was educated at the Massachusetts Institute of Technology and at Harvard. For a time he was a partner in a firm of certified public accountants, and later an investigator for the Federal Trade Commission. He is now with the Labor Bureau of New York. A well-known writer on social and economic subjects, he is the author of numerous books, including *The Nemesis of American Business, A New Deal, The Economy of Abundance, Mexico, Rich Land—Poor Land,* and *The Tyranny of Words.*

Morris Llewellyn Cooke (1872-), a consulting engineer, has been active in many water- and power-conservation movements. He was chairman of the Mississippi Valley Commission of Public Works in 1933, chairman of the Great Plains Commission in 1936, and is now Administrator, Rural Electrification Administration.

Margaret Dana is primarily a merchandising counselor, whose career has included teaching; designing, manufacturing, and retailing children's clothes, furniture, toys, and nursery equipment in her own shops; newspaper promotion; and writing. In the past four years she has written hundreds of special shopping columns, and published thirty-five articles on consumer information. She has also written a book on the subject, *Behind the Label*.

Lee Wilson Dodd (1879-1933), lawyer, teacher, and writer, was well known as a poet, playwright, and novelist. His books include *Speed, The Changelings, Pals First,* and *The Book of Susan*.

Sir Arthur Stanley Eddington (1882-) is professor of astronomy at Cambridge University and director of the observatory there. Widely known as an eminent scientist, he has written many books and articles, among them popular interpretations of new concepts in astronomy and physics. They include *The Nature of the Physical World, Science and the Unseen World, The Expanding Universe, New Pathways in Science,* and *Relativity Theory of Protons and Electrons*.

Edwin Rogers Embree (1883-) has specialized in studies of races, especially the Negro, and of education in primitive cultures. He was vice-president of the Rockefeller Foundation, and since 1928 he has been president of the Julius Rosenwald Fund. He is the author of *Brown America, Prospecting for Heaven,* and many magazine articles on education and on questions of race and culture. He is co-author of *The Collapse of Cotton Tenancy, Island India Goes to School,* and *Human Biology*.

Ernestine Evans (1889-), free-lance writer and newspaper correspondent, is well known for her many articles; she is also an authority on children's books. In 1915 she was Balkan correspondent for the London *Times*. She has been feature editor of the *Christian Science Monitor* and is the author of *The Story of the Harbour* and *The Frescoes of Diego Rivera*.

JOHN FLYNN (1882-   ) is an author, journalist, and lecturer on economic subjects. He served as an adviser of the Senate Committee on Banking and Currency in the investigation of the Stock Exchange in 1933-1934, and with the Senate Committee investigating munitions in 1934. He has been a columnist for the *New Republic* since 1931. He has written a biography of John D. Rockefeller, *God's Gold; Graft in Business; Investments Gone Wrong;* and *Security Speculation—Its Economic Effects.*

HELEN GARDNER has taught at the University of Chicago and the University of California at Los Angeles. She is now professor of the history of art in the School of the Art Institute of Chicago. Her books, *Art Through the Ages* and *Understanding the Arts,* are widely used as texts.

GEORGE W. GRAY, a free-lance writer, writes with authority on scientific research. His articles are the result of consultation with many scientists. In addition to articles for magazines, hc has written *The Advancing Front of Science* and *New World Picture.*

JOHN GUNTHER (1901-   ) is a newspaperman who, as foreign correspondent of the Chicago *Daily News* from 1924-1935, covered most of the major European events. He has written many articles, mostly on European topics. His books include *The Red Pavilion, Eden for One, The Golden Fleece, The Bright Nemesis,* and *Inside Europe.*

ALICE HAMILTON (1869-   ) is a physician who supplemented her American education by work in the University of Leipzig and the University of Munich. She has the distinction of having been at one time the only woman on the medical faculty of Harvard University. For nineteen years she investigated industrial poisons. A frequent contributor to magazines, she has also written *Industrial Poisons in the United States* and *Industrial Toxicology.*

JAY BROADUS HUBBELL (1885-   ), a professor of English at Duke University, is an editor and writer. He edited *American Life in Literature,* and is the author of *The Enjoyment of Literature,* and co-author with John Owen Beatty of *An Introduction to Poetry* and *An Introduction to Drama.*

CHARLES SPURGEON JOHNSON (1893-), an authority on Negro life, is director of the Department of Social Science, Fisk University, and a member of the Board of Trustees of the Julius Rosenwald Fund. Some of his books are *Economic Status of Negroes, A Preface to Racial Understanding,* and *The Negro College Graduate.* He is co-author with W. D. Weatherford of *Race Relations,* and with E. R. Embree and W. W. Alexander of *The Collapse of Cotton Tenancy.*

CHESTER HENRY JONES (1906-1933) was an English architect. He was graduated from Cambridge University and studied architecture in the United States on a fellowship maintained by the Commonwealth Fund.

WILLIAM P. KIRKWOOD (1867-), now professor emeritus, was professor of journalism at the University of Minnesota for more than twenty years. Previously he had been on the editorial staff of the Minneapolis *Journal,* part of the time as literary critic. He has also been a free-lance writer.

HAROLD J. LASKI (1893-), a distinguished political scientist, has been professor of political science at the University of London since 1926. Over a period of several years he has taught or held lectureships at various universities and colleges in the United States, among them Harvard University, Yale University, Amherst College, the New School of Social Research, and the University of Washington. He has written many articles and books of liberal political thought. Among his best-known books are *Liberty in the Modern State, Democracy in Crisis, A Grammar of Politics, The State in Theory and Practice, The Rise of Liberalism, Parliamentary Government in England.*

EDUARD C. LINDEMAN (1886-), teacher and author, has been adviser to the National Housing Association since 1933, and director of the Department of Community Organization for Leisure, Works Progress Administration, since 1935. He has written many articles and books, including *Dynamic Social Research, Social Education,* and *Wealth and Culture.*

PERCY MARKS (1891-) for several years was a member of the staff of the English department at the Massachusetts Institute of Technology, Dartmouth College, and Brown University. His experience as both author and teacher makes his *Craft of Writing* valuable. He is the author also of *The Plastic Age* (a novel dealing with college life), *Which Way Parnassus, Lord of Himself, Better Themes, Tree Grown Straight,* and *And Points Beyond.*

RUFUS E. MILES, JR. (1910-   ), was graduated from Antioch College with a major in political science. He took special courses in economics at the University of Berlin and the graduate school of the Ohio State University. Since 1936 he has been Administrative Assistant in the Office of CCC Selection, Department of Labor.

MAURICE F. NEUFELD was a student at the famous Experimental College at the University of Wisconsin, directed by Dr. Alexander Meiklejohn. The Experimental College Press published his metrical translation of Sophocles' *Antigone* in 1930. An essay in the *American Scholar* for Autumn, 1936, "The Crisis in Prospect: Henry Adams and the White City," summarizes his dissertation for his doctor's degree. He is now acting secretary of the New Jersey State Planning Board.

GEORGE NORLIN (1871-   ) has been president of the University of Colorado since 1919. He is an Elector to the Hall of Fame and a trustee of the Carnegie Foundation for the Advancement of Teaching. As Theodore Roosevelt Professor of American Life and Institutions at the University of Berlin in 1932-1933, he saw the growth, advance, and triumph of Hitlerism in Germany. Since then he has spoken and written much on the international situation. Best known among his publications on the subject are a pamphlet, *Hitlerism—Why and Whither,* and a book, *Fascism and Citizenship.* He is also the author of *Integrity in Education and Other Papers,* and *Nationalism in Education,* and has edited and translated into English the works of Isocrates.

JOHNSON O'CONNOR (1891-   ) is director of the Human Engineering Laboratory at Stevens Institute of Technology in Boston. He is the author of magazine articles and brochures describing measurable occupational characteristics; of such technical reports as *The Study of Vocabulary Scores of 75 Executives*; and of the books, *Born That Way, Psychometrics,* and the *Johnson O'Connor English Vocabulary Builder.*

HARRY ALLEN OVERSTREET (1875-   ) is head of the department of philosophy at the College of the City of New York and lecturer at the New School for Social Research. His books are especially notable for a simple presentation of difficult material: *Influencing Human Behaviour, About Ourselves—Psychology for Normal People, The Enduring Quest, We Move in New Directions, A Guide to Civilized Leisure,* and *A Declaration of Interdependence.*

DONALD CULROSS PEATTIE (1898-   ), author and botanist, has specialized in the flora of Indiana and is popular as a sensitive writer about nature. Among his many books are *Almanac for Moderns, Green Laurels, Book of Hours, Singing in the Wilderness, Prairie Grove.*

GEORGE PFEIL (1908-   ) is associated with the Milwaukee *Journal* and the School for Workers in Industry of the University of Wisconsin.

EDWARD HARTMAN REISNER (1885-   ) is professor of education at Teachers College, Columbia University. He has written *Historical Foundations of Western Education, The Evolution of the Common School,* and *Faith in an Age of Fact.*

JAMES HARVEY ROBINSON (1863-1936), noted historian and editor, was for many years professor of history at Columbia University. He was also one of the organizers of the New School for Social Research. In addition to many textbooks of history, he wrote such books of general interest as *The Mind in the Making, The Humanizing of Knowledge, The Ordeal of Civilization,* and *The Human Comedy.*

JAMES DELMAGE ROSS (1871-   ), a nationally recognized pioneer and authority on electric power development, has been superintendent of the municipal power system of Seattle, Washington, since 1903. He was advisory engineer for the Public Works Administration from 1933 to 1935, and a member of the Securities and Exchange Commission from 1935 to 1937. At present he is Administrator of the Bonneville Project, Columbia River, Department of the Interior.

MARY ROSS, after graduation from Vassar and the Columbia School of Journalism, was a reporter for a year on the old New York *World.* As associate editor for the *Survey,* and in doing field studies, writing, and editing for the Julius Rosenwald Fund in Chicago, she specialized in medical health and medical economics. Since September, 1936, she has been with the Bureau of Research and Statistics of the Social Security Board, as chief of the Reference and Review Section.

MAXWELL HICKS SAVELLE, formerly of Columbia University, is now a member of the history department of Stanford University. He has specialized in early American history. His essay on liberal education, however, was the outgrowth of his work as director of the course in the History of Western Civilization required of all freshmen at Stanford. He is the author of numerous articles; a biography, *George Morgan, Colony Builder;* and of *Diplomatic History of the Canadian Boundary, 1749-1763.*

PAUL BIGELOW SEARS (1891-   ) is a professor of botany at Oberlin College. He was formerly at the University of Oklahoma, and has served as collaborator in the soil conservation service of the United States Department of Agriculture. He has written *Deserts on the March* and *This Is Our World.*

THOMAS HALL SHASTID (1886-   ), an ophthalmologist, and the inventor of numerous eye, ear, nose, and throat instruments, is the author of medical treatises, including *Outline of History of Ophthalmology,* and numerous articles in the *American Encyclopedia of Ophthalmology.* He has also written several novels.

ARTHUR TRAIN, JR., at present a free-lance writer, has been a newspaper reporter, has written for the moving pictures, and has acted in summer stock. He lived for some years in Europe, where he was at different times assistant conductor of the Pavley-Oukrainsky Ballet, a successful farmer, and assistant naval attaché at the United States Embassy at Brussels.

REXFORD GUY TUGWELL (1891-   ), economist, formerly Assistant Secretary of the United States Department of Agriculture and Under-Secretary of Agriculture, is now chairman and head of the Planning Department of the New York City Planning Commission. He is the author of several books, among which are *The Industrial Discipline* and *Battle for Democracy.* He is co-author with Leon H. Keyserling of *Redirecting Education,* a collection of essays on the social sciences, based on a course, Contemporary Civilization, at Columbia University, with which he has long been associated.

Louis Untermeyer (1885-   ) was at one time a successful business man, but in 1923 he decided to devote his entire time to study and writing. He is well known in literary circles as editor, poet, and contributor to magazines. His anthologies of poetry, excellent collections, include *Modern British Poetry, Modern American Poetry, Yesterday and Today, The Book of Living Verse,* and *Rainbow in the Sky.* Among his books are *Heinrich Heine: Paradox and Poet* and *Play in Poetry.*